THE RISE AND FALL OF THE SOVIET EMPIRE

DMITRI VOLKOGONOV joined the Soviet Army in 1945, entered the Lenin Military Academy in Moscow in 1961, and transferred in 1971 to the army's propaganda department, rising to the rank of Colonel-General. A philosopher and historian by training, he began research on his biography of Stalin in 1978; seven years later, his views were regarded as unacceptable by the army's Political Administration and he was compelled to leave the political branch. He became Director of the Institute of Military History, a post he held until June 1991, when his editorship of a new history of the Second World War was attacked as 'Un-Soviet'. Following the failed coup of August 1991, he became Defence Adviser to President Yeltsin. His biography of Lenin was published in the UK in 1994 and of Trotsky in 1996. He died in December 1995, shortly after completing this book.

HAROLD SHUKMAN is an Emeritus Fellow of St Antony's College, Oxford, where he was also Director of the Russian Centre from 1981–91 and 1997–8. He has edited and translated the memoirs of Andrei Gromyko, Dmitri Volkogonov's biographies of Stalin, Lenin and Trotsky, the novels of Anatoly Rybakov (*Heavy Sand* and *Children of the Arbat*), and the plays of Isaac Babel and Yevgeni Shvarts. He is general editor of Longman's multi-volume *History of Russia*, a member of the editorial board of the journal *Istoricheskii arkhiv*, published by the Russian State Archive Commission, and author of *Lenin and the Russian Revolution*, *The Blackwell Encyclopedia of the Russian Revolution* and *Rasputin*.

Further reviews for *The Rise and Fall of the Soviet Empire*:

'Volkogonov, as a three-star general, was well-placed to examine documents which had been inaccessible for more than half a century. This confers on his seven short biog⋯⋯ ⋯y ... It makes compelling readin⋯⋯ ⋯is of the post-war era through the⋯⋯ ⋯le is grippingly told. The writing⋯⋯ ⋯s, to the editor and translator Ha⋯⋯ ⋯v himself. I should not be surpr⋯⋯ ⋯d students of modern history, not least because it brings to life the less celebrated of the leaders.' MICHAEL BIRKETT, *Observer*

'Dmitri Volkogonov was the outstanding revisionist historian to come out of the Soviet Establishment ... admirably translated and edited by Harold Shukman ... Let us hope that the post-Soviet political generation learns something from the depressing story of the seven leaders so graphically recounted in this fascinating book.'

ALEX PRAVDA, *The Times*

'[A] brilliant biographic history of the Soviet Union ... as we move from one engrossing canvas to the next, Volkogonov expertly directs our eye to the telling details and the dark textures until we discern the underlying pattern ... Volkogonov is the perfect guide ... his research is exhaustive and authoritative. Even more appealing, his prose is fluent, a sterling tribute to Shukman, his friend and translator at Oxford.'

RAYMOND SEITZ, *Sunday Times*

'Seven political portraits, which singly or together make for compelling reading in their own right.'

JOHN ERICKSON, *Times Higher Education Supplement*

'It is to be welcomed that publishers are translating books by Russians about the history of the Soviet Union. The story undoubtedly comes well from a Russian, who can say things with the authority of personal experience ... Volkogonov has picked up some juicy morsels in the archives. They are the best things in the book. For example, he gives a sharp sense of the way Lenin barracked his comrades into using vicious terror techniques. And as the book passes beyond the 1950s, Volkogonov's touch gets surer since he was acquainted with the leaders in question.'

ROBERT SERVICE, *Guardian*

'Volkogonov makes use of his special access to documents – he is one of the few people to have seen the tightly controlled Presidential archives – to throw in new information, weaving it all into his main argument ... His book should be read not only for its historical revelations, but also as a document reflecting the mood of contemporary Russia as well.'

ANNE APPLEBAUM, *Sunday Telegraph*

THE RISE AND FALL
OF THE
SOVIET EMPIRE

*Political Leaders
from Lenin to Gorbachev*

DMITRI VOLKOGONOV

Edited and translated by Harold Shukman

HarperCollins*Publishers*

HarperCollins*Publishers*
77–85 Fulham Palace Road,
Hammersmith, London w6 8jb

This paperback edition 1999

1 3 5 7 9 8 6 4

First published in Great Britain by
HarperCollins*Publishers* 1998

Copyright © The Estate of Dmitri Volkogonov 1998
Translation copyright © Harold Shukman 1998

The Author asserts the moral right to
be identified as the author of this work

ISBN 0 00 638818 3

Set in PostScript Janson by
Rowland Phototypesetting Ltd,
Bury St Edmunds, Suffolk

Printed and bound in Great Britain by
Caledonian International Book Manufacturing Ltd, Glasgow

All rights reserved. No part of this publication may be
reproduced, stored in a retrieval system, or transmitted,
in any form or by any means, electronic, mechanical,
photocopying, recording or otherwise, without the prior
permission of the publishers.

This book is sold subject to the condition that it shall not,
by way of trade or otherwise, be lent, re-sold, hired out or
otherwise circulated without the publisher's prior consent
in any form of binding or cover other than that in which it
is published and without a similar condition including this
condition being imposed on the subsequent purchaser.

Contents

Illustrations

(*Photographs courtesy of ITAR-TASS, Novosti News Agency and Publishers, L. Sherstennikov and the personal collections of I.Yu. Andropov, S.N. Khrushchev and M.S. Gorbachev.*)

Editor's Preface

The disintegration of the Soviet Union was preceded by a relatively brief period of some five or six years during which cautious economic reforms were quickly overtaken by an information revolution. Almost overnight the face of the regime changed from the familiar mask of concealment, mendacity and deception to an increasingly open expression of honesty, truth and self-exposure. Like Siamese twins, *perestroika* (reconstruction) and *glasnost* (openness) seemed to be inextricably linked, as the effort to raise living standards was mirrored by an outburst of free expression on a breathtaking scale. The first target was Stalinism, and the role Stalin had played in Soviet history.

Dmitri Volkogonov was an improbable candidate for launching the first full-scale, documented Soviet assault on the Stalinist system. A three-star general, a former head of the Army's Political Adminis-tration and from 1985 Director of the Institute of Military History, he was, however, well placed to examine the Party's secret archives. He began writing his biography of Stalin in 1978, and it was almost complete by 1985 when Gorbachev came to power. By the time the book was published in the Soviet Union in 1990, virtually every hal-lowed principle of the previous seventy years had been challenged and rejected, and most taboos of Soviet history broken. Volkogonov followed his biography of Stalin with an even more iconoclastic study of Trotsky, published in Russia in 1992. But by the spring of 1990 he had begun research for a root and branch demolition of Lenin, as the founding father of a system that had brought the Soviet people to the crisis they found themselves in at the beginning of the 1990s. *Lenin: Life and Legacy* was published in 1994, and its completion left

Volkogonov free to tackle the present book, which was his last. It is noteworthy that he wrote his studies of Trotsky and Lenin and his last book at a time when he was fighting the cancer from which he died in December 1995, and indeed this book frequently reflects his mental struggle to come to terms with his imminent death, when he felt he still had so much to contribute to public life and so much left to write. In the early 1990s he underwent a Christian baptism, from which, he told me, he derived much of the spiritual strength he displayed in his last years.

Each of the seven chronological chapters of this book is a self-contained political study, but they are all linked by a common thread of ideology, outlook and, in some sense, practice. Throughout the Soviet period, with one important exception, the leadership remained committed to Marxist orthodoxy, to a greater or lesser extent a militantly command economy, the unitary constitutional state of the USSR, the dream of world revolution, and the holiest of holies, namely the political monopoly of the Communist Party of the Soviet Union. Even in what might have seemed the slackest, most corrupt period, under Brezhnev, these commitments remained intact.

The great exception was, of course, Gorbachev. Yet even here, as Volkogonov shows, the leader's resistance to diluting, let alone jettisoning, Leninism, or to introducing a mixed economy or loosening the Party's hold on many social institutions, remained stubborn until relatively late. Gorbachev's greatest strides were in bringing about radical change in international relations, ending the Cold War and fundamentally altering the outside world's view of his country. *Glasnost* meanwhile was eroding the foundations of belief in the system, undermining and disorienting the political establishment, and generally softening up the regime and making it amenable to the new conditions. As Volkogonov shows, the regime was not in fact amenable to such extreme change without inflicting terminal damage on itself. Like an absolute monarch, a Communist regime either is, or it is not. Both are brittle forms of government that cannot bend or adapt beyond a certain point without breaking. The monarch departs, one way or another, and the system is altered. In the Soviet case, the system and the leader both succumbed.

While the portraits of the last five leaders contained in this book represent entirely new work, it is legitimate to ask in what ways Volkogonov's studies of Lenin and Stalin differ from or add to what he wrote in his major books on them.

As far as Lenin is concerned, Volkogonov has rewritten rather than recapitulated his earlier work, sharpening his focus on the malign effect of Lenin and Leninism on the history of Russia. New documents and analysis highlight aspects of Lenin's policies which were of long-term significance and which foreshadow policies more commonly associated with Stalin.

For example, immediately following the October Revolution, Lenin ordered the destruction of all legal documents showing property ownership. This was to be done in secret, without formal instruction from the government, in order to make it impossible for former owners to prove title. It was in effect the first offensive in the civil war.

New material shows Lenin ordering the virtual starving of the Red Army prior to demobilization, at the same time that he was telling his officials to conceal special privileges for the Party elite. The para-noia about foreigners in the Soviet Union, which characterized the darkest days of Stalin's rule, was first expressed by Lenin.

As for Stalin, by the time Volkogonov's earlier book was ready for publication in the West, he was ready to revise it drastically. He was, however, too impatient to get on with his studies of Trotsky and Lenin, and a dozen other projects, to do so. He wished, above all, to show that the Lenin portrayed in *Stalin* was now obsolete, and he wanted to show a seamless connection between the first and second leaders. Thus, the Stalin we see here is not a distortion of Leninism, but its continuation. For that reason, the burden of the chapter on the second leader focuses on the criminal and violent aspects of the regime.

At the time this book was being written, Soviet historians were arguing over whether Stalin was wholly committed to a defensive posture on the eve of Hitler's invasion of the USSR, as Volkogonov claimed in his book on Stalin, or whether in fact he was planning an offensive but was beaten to the draw by Hitler, as had been claimed in a book called *Icebreaker* by Viktor Suvorov. That argument has now been generally resolved in Volkogonov's favour, and new material reproduced here consolidates his findings.

Soviet–Chinese relations provide an excellent basis for the study of Stalin's foreign relations and his decision-making style, and here Volkogonov has broken new ground, especially in relation to the end-game of the Chinese civil war. Of extraordinary interest and historical value are the materials reproduced here on the part played by Stalin in his relations with Mao Tse-tung and Kim Il-sung in the origins and conduct of the Korean War.

Born on 22 March 1928 in Chita, Eastern Siberia, Dmitri Antonovich Volkogonov was the son of a collective-farm-manager father and a schoolteacher mother. In 1937 his father was arrested and shot for being found in possession of a pamphlet by the disgraced Bolshevik Bukharin, as the son later learned from his own archival research. The family were then exiled to Krasnoyarsk in Western Siberia: Volkogonov joked that as they were already in the Far East, and Stalin was not in the habit of sending his political prisoners to Hawaii, they had to be sent west.

Volkogonov's mother died during the Second World War, and he joined the army in 1945. He showed a talent for military theory and organization, and entered the Lenin Military Academy in Moscow in 1961, transferring in 1970 to the propaganda department of the army, where he wrote numerous books on military themes, ranging from Cold War propaganda tracts to manuals on psychological warfare. In the process he gained a well deserved reputation as a hardliner.

It was, he told me, when he was a young officer in the mid-1950s, with access to the Party journals of the 1920s, that he first began to see how stifled and sterile political debate in the Soviet Union had become by comparison with the early days. Khrushchev's 'secret speech' to the Twentieth Congress in 1956 pushed him further in this direction, and it was from about this time that he began collecting material for his book on Stalin. In it he intended to show how the dictator and his minions had actually operated, concentrating in particular on the central role of terror as an instrument of political control. By the time he was writing the latter part of the book, in the early 1980s, however, he had arrived at the view that Soviet history had been a lethal combination of Lenin's authoritarian Communism, Stalin's ruthless drive for personal omnipotence and manipulation of internal Party rivalries, inertia, the passive character of the Russians and their love of a strong leader, and their ignorance of democracy and personal autonomy.

Volkogonov admitted publicly that, like many senior Soviet officials, he had lived two mental lives, rising higher and higher in his career while burrowing deeper in the archives, as if symbolically undermining the system that nurtured him. Such a high degree of disaffection could not continue for long without consequences. In 1985 he was ordered to give up either his historical research or his job in the Main Political Administration. He chose to become Director of the Institute of Military History, where he completed his book on Stalin.

In June 1991 the draft of a new history of the Second World War, prepared under Volkogonov's editorship at the Institute, came under savage attack from the military top brass, and he was forced to resign. He was now effectively a free agent, and already an open supporter of the new Russian President, Boris Yeltsin.

I first met Dmitri Volkogonov in Oxford in February 1989. He had been invited to address a seminar on his research, having already agreed that his book on Stalin would be published in English by Weidenfeld & Nicolson. Lord Weidenfeld had mentioned the book to me several months earlier, so when we met he and I were already known to each other. I found him utterly unlike my idea of a Soviet general. He did not strut or swagger, or drink or smoke, and in the many different situations in which I was to see him – in other countries, in Russia, with academics, military men, students, his personal staff, his doctors, his family or among ordinary people – he was invariably easy-going and relaxed, and plainly popular.

He was also exceptionally easy to work with. The Russian editions of the three biographies he wrote in the last phase of his life, on Stalin, Trotsky and Lenin, were each around a thousand pages long, and he accepted without demur that his English-language publishers, giving me total editorial discretion, wanted them reduced in length by as much as 40 to 50 per cent. It was also necessary for me to insert explanatory material of my own where I felt Dmitri had left Western readers uninformed. I visited him in Moscow when I had completed translating and editing *Stalin*, and explained the principles I had applied. All my cuts and additions were readily accepted, and we proceeded on the same basis with his subsequent books.

I was about to leave Moscow at the end of June 1991 when Dmitri's wife Galina told me that a routine medical check-up had found that he was suffering from cancer of the colon. Having just been ousted from the Institute of Military History, his political position was precarious, and the thought of undergoing extensive surgery in a military hospital was most unappealing. Immediately on my return to Oxford, I arranged for him to be admitted to the John Radcliffe Hospital, and two days later he underwent a successful operation. Regrettably, a small tumor was found in the liver, and that meant more extensive surgery only two weeks later. During the six weeks he spent in Oxford – nearly four of them in hospital – I saw the extraordinary reserves of physical and mental strength he could draw on to sustain him, in a foreign country, during the most testing experience imaginable.

It was on 19 August 1991, as I was driving him to the hospital for the second operation, that I told him the news from Moscow that a coup was under way. 'So, they've done it,' he murmured. He had heard a lot of talk among senior military figures in the past few months, and Marshal Yazov, the Defence Minister who had sacked him from the Institute three months earlier, had virtually admitted that 'something will happen to get rid of the likes of you'. From his hospital bed, as he was waiting to be taken down for surgery, he took an enormous risk in broadcasting through the BBC an appeal to the Soviet Army not to obey the illegal orders of the conspirators. He also dictated a fax to the Speaker of the Russian Parliament, expressing his opposition to the coup.

Returning to Moscow in early September, after the defeat of the coup, and taking up his appointment as President Yeltsin's special adviser on defence, Volkogonov earned a reputation as one of the most approachable, humane and considerate senior figures in the new establishment. He rarely refused an interview, and received countless petitioners, whether from the provinces or the army. His military functions were now mostly confined to stripping down the Political Section to a minimum: political indoctrination was no longer required, and he was advising political officers to seek employment as psychological consultants.

From summer 1991 to late 1993 Dmitri was also head of the commission for the declassification of state and Party papers, and was unjustly castigated by Russian historians for allegedly monopolizing the archives for his own advantage. In fact, during his tenure seventy-eight million files were released into the public domain. He was also to come under attack from the democrats when Yeltsin brought his confrontation with parliament to a violent and bloody close in October 1993. In December of that year, as Deputy Chairman of the commission charged with putting down the insurrection, Volkogonov was unapologetic about the government's use of force. He claimed to have spoken many times by telephone to the insurgents, guaranteeing their safety if they would lay down their arms. 'The choice was simple,' he argued. 'We either had to suppress the rebellion or have the start of a new civil war.' While lamenting the use of force, he believed that a victory for the anti-reformers would have led Russia back to the Gulag. It was an acute moral dilemma for a historian who had recently denounced the Soviet system precisely because it had been founded on the use of physical violence.

An even more difficult phase opened with the decision by the Yeltsin administration at the end of 1994 to invade Chechnia in the Caucasus in an effort to end its self-proclaimed independence and restore Russian rule. As a member of the President's advisory council, Volkogonov issued public warnings against the use of force to settle ethnic conflicts, although he accepted Yeltsin's argument that the regime in Chechnia was criminal and must be removed.

Volkogonov was sometimes accused of political trimming, of publishing books to suit the current leadership and changing course to remain in favour. It was a false accusation. He was quickly out of favour with the Gorbachev regime and its military leadership, and he was far from an obedient servant of the Yeltsin administration. In the bloodbath that followed the decision to invade Chechnia, he criticized the Russian leader in the Russian and Western media for having taken the advice of wrong-headed counsellors.

In addition to the books mentioned above, Volkogonov collected a wealth of miscellaneous material on various related topics. As Director of the Institute of Military History he produced an unpublished two-volume collection of data on the forty-five thousand Red Army officers arrested during the purges of the 1930s, of whom fifteen thousand were shot; he began to collect material for a book we were to have written on the Battle of Stalingrad; and he wrote a large number of brief studies of political figures he had met in his life as an army officer and civilian. His daughter is currently preparing a volume of these for publication.

As his editor and translator, I dedicate my work on this book to his memory.

Harold Shukman
Oxford, March 1997

INTRODUCTION

The Path Of Leaders

For seven decades of the twentieth century, the Soviet Union followed the path mapped out by Lenin. It became a military superpower feared by the rest of the world, and it built a mighty technological, industrial, military and scientific economy. But it failed to make its people either happy or free. It was the first country to send a man into space, but it did nothing to improve human rights for its citizens. The people who carried out the 'Great October Socialist Revolution', who won the 'Great Patriotic War' and who advanced towards the 'Great Constructions of Communism' gained neither liberty nor prosperity for their efforts. 'Shoulder to shoulder' they marched along the Leninist path which had room for the masses only, elbowing the individual out of the way.

After centuries of living under a succession of tsars, in 1917 Russia turned to a new form of absolutism, namely Bolshevik leadership, 'leaderism', the way of the *vozhd*, or leader. In Italy, Mussolini would soon emerge as *Il Duce*, while in Germany Hitler would later be called *Der Führer*. As it happened, for the seven decades of its existence the Soviet Union was governed by seven leaders, one of them ruling for more than thirty years, two of them for little more than one year.

This book is about those seven leaders. It is in a sense seven short books in one, although each section, while it has its own story to tell, is nonetheless connected to the others: my aim is to describe the history of supreme Soviet power in the persons of these individuals. Naturally, a portrait of any leader of the only political party in the country – which in practice in the USSR also meant the head of state – can in no way substitute for the vast range of subjects that go to make up the history of a people. Such portraits can, however, reveal something essential about the country, the regime and the system.

For instance, not one of the seven leaders was ever elected to office by the population. They were all, in today's parlance, illegitimate. Power was simply passed from hand to hand, often following a fierce but unseen struggle at the top, within the small clan of 'professional revolutionaries'. Supreme power remained in the hands of the leaders of the party that staged the *coup d'état* of October 1917. Throughout the Soviet period, the country was governed by people who had no legal right to rule.

All seven leaders considered themselves Marxists, and always strove to appear as orthodox 'Leninists'. Each was confined in the same Procrustean bed of Bolshevik tenets: the leading role of the Communist Party, the primacy of the class approach, the supremacy of state ownership and Leninist ideology, the dominion of state power over the law, and the Comintern mentality, or an expansionist view of the world. All seven put morality very low on their list of priorities. They extolled the mass, the class, the collective, all to the detriment of the individual. The harshness of these Bolshevik tenets predetermined the dogmatic mentality of the seven Soviet leaders, with the possible exception of the last of them. Marxism-Leninism for the leaders, as for the people, was virtually a secular religion in which they had to believe above all else, and about which there could be no doubt.

All seven leaders came from the provinces. None of them was raised in the Party organizations of either Moscow or St Petersburg. Provincialism tends to be conservative and orthodox. None of them was of 'pure' proletarian origin, even though they all recognized and never ceased to swear by the leading role of the working class. It was not the working class that governed, however, but a rapidly formed bureaucratic 'partocracy'. The leaders were extremely remote from the workers, the peasants and the intelligentsia precisely because they emerged from deep within the group of 'professional partocrats'. Apart from the last of them, the intellectual, educational and cultural level of the leaders was low. Even Lenin, who undoubtedly had a powerful mind, was strictly one-dimensional intellectually; his was a purely political mind, which greatly impoverished him as a man. He had little feeling for Russian culture or its exponents.

All seven leaders saw the country they governed in their own way, and this shaped both their achievements and their significant mistakes.

The first leader, Vladimir Lenin, saw Russia through the eyes of a partisan political émigré, a reader of books and newspapers. An enemy of tsarism and bourgeois democracy, he possessed a political vision which condemned him to a strictly 'revolutionary' view, first of the empire and then of the Russian Soviet republic. Lenin never worked, in the normally accepted sense of the word, and this was of enormous importance to his understanding of reality. Eighteen months' experience as assistant to a provincial lawyer, with no practical knowledge of industry or agriculture (though he was the co-owner of an estate for a brief spell), provided only the most superficial idea of the deep processes of Russian life. From this stemmed Lenin's assurance that Communism could be 'introduced' at once, as did his lack of understanding of the integrating role of the Russian provinces in a multi-national state and his policy of gradually abolishing them, his hostile attitude to the peasantry, and his certainty that the destruction of entire social groups, such as the Church, would bring 'sovietization' nearer.

The Menshevik Rafail Abramovich described Lenin's activities in early 1918 as 'the history of a violent attack of Utopianism in the form of War Communism'. 'In early 1918,' Abramovich wrote, 'at practically every session of the Sovnarkom [the Council of People's Commissars], Lenin insisted that socialism could be realized in Russia in six months ... Six months, not six decades, not six years, at least? No, Lenin insisted on six months. And in March 1918 the plan for moving straight to Communist production and distribution was put into effect.'[1] Mercilessly, Lenin experimented on the gigantic state and its people, as he created the system of Bolshevik absolutism. His greatest error was believing that it was possible to make the entire planet Communist.

The second leader, Joseph Stalin, was one of the small number of people in Russia who belonged to the world of the classless, the *déclassés*. Lacking any profession, and never having done a day's work, he knew the country as a conqueror of power, a merciless dictator, a Bolshevik clan chief. His knowledge of Russia was strictly functional: how and what to make use of in order to strengthen his personal hold on power, or what was called the 'dictatorship of the proletariat'. He inherited Lenin's aptitude for social experimentation – the bloody collectivization, the hideous purges, the alliance with Nazism. Rather than the cult of personality, which the Party tried to use to depict the external expression of its totalitarian tyranny, Stalinism was characterized by the complete denial of the people's right to decide how to live their own lives and to make independent choices. In extreme and crude form, Stalin expressed the essence of the Bolshevik regime, which expunged the last vestiges of liberty in Russia: 'The dictatorship of the proletariat consists of the Party's main instructions, plus the implementation of those instructions by the mass organizations of the proletariat, plus the bringing into life of those instructions by the population.'[2] Stalin believed that this arrangement could be applied everywhere and at all times. His fatal miscalculation lay in his fanatical, profoundly mistaken belief, especially after the victory in the Second World War, that history had confirmed his strategy and methods in developing the Soviet state and its vassal states.

Nikita Khrushchev, the third leader, knew the country better than either of his predecessors. But his was empirical knowledge, largely lacking in comprehension of the deep trends and norms of social development. It is impossible not to respect Khrushchev's efforts to understand and reform the country, but they were in constant conflict with his arbitrary behaviour as a Bolshevik leader. His fatal error was in believing – as so many Russians did – that, if only the scab of the cult of personality could be removed, the Leninist system would not fade away. Khrushchev was a prisoner of the Great Utopia. He seriously thought that the bright future of Communism could be brought closer by sheer willpower. It could be achieved in two decades! The third leader was no mere dreamer: he believed that his plans could be realized.

Leonid Brezhnev, the fourth leader, saw society through traditional Party spectacles. He was probably the most accurate embodiment of the system. For him, the Soviet Union was above all the Leninist fruit of Communism, which had to be preserved and protected at any price. He knew the country through Party reports. He was content with the stagnation that he genuinely saw as stability. His chief mistake was to imagine that he could achieve everything without changing anything.

The fifth leader, Yuri Andropov, was cleverer than most Soviet leaders. He knew what was happening in the country, and he knew what was coming. But his knowledge was that of a KGB man, a policeman. For him, the Lubyanka Prison was the peak from which it was possible to view the state and increase its might, above all its military might. He certainly wanted positive changes, but he believed they could be achieved by administrative methods. Perhaps he had too little time to declare his real intentions, but he certainly wanted to strengthen and 'improve' the Bolshevik system without touching its Leninist foundations.

The sixth leader, Konstantin Chernenko, knew the country as a top Party official. He genuinely believed that by means of commissions of inquiry, reports, resolutions and instructions, it was possible to change Soviet society – within the framework of 'Leninist norms' and traditions, of course. Appointed to the supreme post by the logic of the system, this ridiculous leader saw ruling the country largely as a clerical job. On the whole, Chernenko did not try to do anything except to remain the titular head of the Party and the state. The penultimate General Secretary glimmered for a moment in the firmament of Soviet history, leaving no trace behind him.

The seventh and last leader of the Party and the Soviet state, Mikhail Gorbachev, had had a classic Party career. In the early years of his administration, it seemed that he understood the country in the way a provincial Party leader would. But quite soon he came to realize something very important: it would be difficult to solve the vast country's problems in isolation from the global context and unless a broad reformation took place.

Although Gorbachev's knowledge of the array of problems facing the country was inadequate, it was combined with vision and a strong will to govern. His chief failing was to imagine that it was possible to make reforms and still preserve the Communist system. However, the great effort he made to eliminate the threat of nuclear war, his opening of the floodgates of *glasnost*, and his expectation of democratic change in society made Gorbachev an epoch-making historical figure, whose true importance will only be fully realized in the next century.

Each leader, then, surrounded as he was by the Party élite, knew the Soviet Union and its people in his own way, but each was dominated by a confrontational, class-based way of thinking. Communist ideology was entirely suffused with the idea of struggle, whether with internal or external enemies, with nature or other systems and ideologies. The Soviet leaders could not see that the dominant trends in world development had become integrative processes, that a shift had taken place from confrontation to co-operation, to social unification and to the search for harmonious forms of co-existence. Their minds remained in eternal conflict with everything that did not correspond with the Marxist plan and Bolshevik sensibilities. This meant preserving the system created by Lenin, it meant freezing the public mind, it meant hostility towards and distrust of any alternative social experience. Ultimately, this led to the loss of a great nation's capacity for civilized, evolutionary social change. The drive to raze the old world to its foundations created in the Soviet character a stubborn tendency to accept radical policies, upheavals and convulsions.

Gorbachev was the only one of the seven leaders to attempt to make the Soviet people reflect on the fundamental questions of the Soviet system. But to reflect is not the same as to rethink.

The history of the Russian state in its various forms will continue to exert an influence on its people's lives. It should not be forgotten that, although seventy years of Bolshevik absolutism hangs over the country, there is also a backdrop of several centuries of autocracy. If the Russian political tradition was mostly negative, and the idea of civil society and democratic politics was stifled by the Bolshevik regime, there was nonetheless a certain amount of constructive social policy under the Soviet regime, including free education, a national health service and social security. This suggests that it is the social democratic path, the synthesis, as far as is practicable, of the desire for social justice and the free market, that offers the best way out of the country's present crisis.

Secondly, Russia is located between Asia and Europe: she is neither Asian nor European. This is both a curse and a blessing. For centuries Russia lagged behind other countries in gaining the social experience of development. The underlying motive of Lenin and his successors was to overtake other civilizations. They failed, but that does not mean that Russia is doomed to follow the models and ways of thinking of others. Both Gorbachev's exhortation to get 'back to Lenin' and the tendency of today's Russian democrats to measure themselves only by Western values, are old-fashioned metaphysics. The debate about building socialism or capitalism is long out of date. The twenty-first century will see further liberation from totalitarian and authoritarian traditions. Russia does not lie between two continents, but between two civilizations. She should take the best from each, but not blindly follow either. The Russian people were given a painful historical lesson when Marxism was 'borrowed' and transferred to Russian soil.

Thirdly, it should not be overlooked that the Soviet regime was to a large extent assisted by its clear – if Utopian – goals of social development. For most Russians, that clarity has disappeared, and this has done much to devalue and weaken the course of the post-Communist reformation. At least the Bolshevik leaders knew what they wanted, even if their methods left much to be desired. What is needed now are a unifying idea, renewed values and ideals for the advancement of all the peoples of Russia, an idea based not on negating, but on creating. This is one of the most difficult aspects of the changes taking place in Russia. Such ideas do not emerge from the mind of some new messiah, or at a congress or conference. A new way of thinking and acting is required, so that people will understand that the country will not be saved by class struggle, or by looking for new enemies and new saviours. It is democracy, founded on respect for liberty and the harmony of human rights and civil society, that will help the people out of their spiritual distress.

The first two Soviet leaders, Lenin and Stalin, not only possessed the power of dictators, but were recognized as such by the people. There was something mystical, irrational, classically revolutionary about them. They were 'real' leaders in the eyes of the masses.

The succeeding five did not carry the same imprint. Under the impact of outside circumstances, their style of governing gradually, imperceptibly, absorbed an element of reformism, even a degree of outward liberalism. It is difficult to refer to Khrushchev and Brezhnev, Andropov and Chernenko, to say nothing of Gorbachev, as 'leaders' without quotation marks. Their powers were far greater than those of the Russian emperors, but they were living and acting in the second half of the twentieth century. Historical changes could not but affect the style and methods of these powerful men.

The history of government in the USSR reveals two opposing and conflicting tendencies. The first, initiated by Lenin and Stalin and carried on by Brezhnev, Andropov and Chernenko, was baldly orthodox Bolshevik and deeply conservative. None of their 'transformations' touched the foundations or supports of the system created after the October revolution. This conservative tradition owed much of its viability to a philosophy based on absolute loyalty to the past and unadulterated faith in the unitary ideology of the state.

The second, reformist, tendency found its expression in the third and seventh leaders, Khrushchev and Gorbachev. If Khrushchev's reforms were essentially aimed at purging and repudiating the cult of personality (though not Stalinism itself), then the last leader was the initiator of the most major reform of the twentieth century.

This book deals with the seven supreme leaders of the USSR. This is not the only possible approach to historical analysis, but it is often easier to become acquainted with the history of a period if it is seen through the lives of individuals. These seven leaders were the men who decided, among many other things, whether the Red Army should invade Poland in 1920; whether or not to preserve the provinces as administrative units; whether to make a 'friend' of Hitler; whether to shoot twenty-one thousand Polish officers in 1940; attack Finland; send nuclear missiles to Cuba; deploy SS-20s in Eastern Europe; send Soviet troops to Afghanistan; 'pardon' the dissident scientist Andrei Sakharov. These men had colossal power, but it was precisely the excess of such power and the absence of any means of controlling it that led to its irreversible erosion and destruction.

The underlying causes of the crisis of the Soviet system are numerous. The collapse of Leninist Bolshevism was predetermined, first, by genetic causes: Marxism claimed the role of a universal theory. The Soviet people believed that 'Marx's teachings are omnipotent because they are true,' as Lenin declared in March 1913.[3] With great intellectual self-assurance, Marxism declared the real possibility of building a just society in which there would be neither rich nor poor. The founders of the Marxist movement qualified the goal of creating Communist society, as defined in Marx's *The Communist Manifesto*, with the important proviso that it could be achieved 'only by means of the violent overthrow of the entire existing order'. The *violent* overthrow.

Transplanted to Russian soil, Marxism took on its Leninist form, an uglier variety of the 'Communist restructuring of the world'. The Party and its seven leaders followed both the logic and the letter of Leninism. Gorbachev, although undoubtedly the best of the seven, told the Politburo on 15 October 1987 that they must 'build a bridge from Leninism, connect Leninist ideas and the Leninist approach to the events of [Lenin's] day to the affairs of our own present day. After all, the dialectics which Lenin applied in solving problems is the key to the solution of today's tasks.'[4] The door which the Leninist key would open did not, however, lead to the truth.

The political causes of the collapse of the Leninist system lay in class intolerance, or aggression towards those who did not hold Marxist views. This deep conflict of social practice in time fostered the monstrous Stalinist regime, which embodied all the chief sins of Marxism-Leninism. The Bolsheviks justified the civil war that followed the revolution as a means of liquidating all social groups which did not accept their views. And they wanted to transfer their methods to other countries as the primary way to ignite world revolution. Nikolai Bukharin, whose image is otherwise that of a reasonable and civilized intellectual, could write: 'civil war in the more "cultured" countries must be even more harsh and merciless and must exclude any grounds for "peaceful" and "judicial" methods.'[5]

The spiritual causes of the demise of the system lie in the Marxist claim that the real history of mankind begins only with proletarian revolution. Leninism is essentially the concept of 'history interrupted'. Discarding much of world and Russian culture of the last thousand years, Bolshevism, itself an impoverished, one-dimensional doctrine, tried in effect to make the political myths of Marxism the chief content of the Soviet people's spiritual life. The persecution and repression of poets and writers like Esenin, Mandelstam, Pasternak, Zoshchenko, Akhmatova, Platonov, Babel, Meyerhold and hundreds of other 'creators of the spirit' bears witness to the vulnerability of a system that was not capable of co-existing with honesty and truth. Ideologized public and private mentality served as the soil for double-thought, for profound scepticism about the efforts of the gigantic propaganda machine and for apathy. Ideology in a totalitarian state is a kind of uniform which, in the end, cannot conceal spiritual poverty.

This book is based on sources of many kinds. First, I myself, like millions of other Russians, was a participant in and witness to many of the events described. I found much useful material in the memoirs of Alexander Yakovlev, Georgy Shakhnazarov, Alexander Alexandrov-Agentov, Anatoly Chernyayev, Andrei Grachev, Roy Medvedev, Mikhail Geller, V. Soloviev, E. Klepikova, Andrei Gromyko and others.

My work has been immeasurably helped by the directors and staff of various archives: GARF (State Archives of the Russian Federation), APRF (Russian Presidential Archives); the two parts of the archives of the former Communist Party Central Committee, RTsKhIDNI (Russian Centre for the Preservation and Study of Documents of Recent History) and TsKhSD (Centre for the Preservation of Contemporary Documentation); TsAMO (Central Archives of the Ministry of Defence); Arkhiv MB RF (Archives of the Security Ministry of the Russian Federation, i.e. former KGB); and several others. I have been able over the last few years to see many documents of the Communist Party Central Committee and the Politburo. They became accessible after being processed by the Parliamentary Commission which I chaired in 1992 and 1993. During that time the Commission declassified no fewer than seventy-eight million files that had lain for decades in the Party's most secret vaults.

I should say something here about my personal views. For many years I was an orthodox Marxist, and it was only late in my life, after long and tortuous inner struggle, that I was able to free myself of the chimera of Bolshevik ideology. I felt enormous relief, and at the same time a sense of deep regret that I had wasted so many years in Utopian captivity.

Perhaps the only thing I achieved in this life was to break with the faith I had held for so long. I have spoken about this openly wherever I have had the opportunity: from the platform at congresses, at high-level meetings, in my books and in conversation with many people in Russia and abroad. I bear my share of guilt for the past. By my modest efforts to conciliate our disordered society, I have tried to express my atonement.

Disillusionment first came to me as an idea, rather like the melancholy of a spiritual hangover. Then, it came as intellectual confusion. Finally, as the determination to confront the truth and understand it.

During the reigns of six of the seven leaders, I was in the Soviet Army. As a colonel-general, I had direct working contact with the last four leaders. Much that I saw then has helped me write this book. I do not think I hold any serious prejudices about my subjects – even about Stalin, who was responsible for my father being shot, for my mother dying in exile and for the deaths of other relatives. It is senseless to try to avenge history, just as it is senseless to mock it. One must understand it. The past is irretrievable. The present is incomplete. The future has already begun.

THE RISE AND FALL
OF THE SOVIET EMPIRE

1

The First Leader: Vladimir Lenin

Vladimir Ilyich Ulyanov-Lenin was the founder of the Communist Party, the Soviet state and the Bolshevik system in Russia. Not only like-minded revolutionaries, but also his countless enemies saw in him the leader of a movement which threatened in time to swathe the world in the red flag.

It is surely indisputable that no single leader in the twentieth century exerted as great an influence on the course of world history as Lenin. And he managed to make his mark in a little over six years, from the moment of the October coup in 1917 to his premature death in 1924, at the age of fifty-three. Given that for nearly two of those six years he was seriously ill, and took an increasingly limited and eventually purely symbolic part in the political life of the country, his achievement seems monumental.

The historical role of this unattractive, bald, stocky man, with piercing eyes and the look of an intelligent craftsman, was enormous, if only because the entire world, except Russia herself, benefited from his experiment. Having seen the appalling methods Lenin's government was applying to make the Russian people 'happy', many leaders, thinkers and public figures in other countries recoiled in horror from what they saw.

The movement for a just and classless society in Russia began with unbridled violence, denying millions of people all rights except the right to support Bolshevik policy. Even those who at first sympathized with the revolution soon saw that it would culminate in a monopoly of political power, domination of the public mind by Bolshevik-inspired myths, guaranteed poverty, physical and psychological violence and compulsory atheism, and recoiled from such a prospect. Most of the countries of the world, although not all, managed to avoid their own 'October'.

The role of accident in history is great. A rare combination of military, political, social and personal factors in the Russia of autumn 1917 had created a situation in which it was necessary only to determine the time at which to seize the power that was, in Trotsky's words, lying on the streets of Petrograd. And Lenin fixed the time precisely. Had it not been for his perceptiveness, the coup might never have taken place. This view was advanced by 'the second man of the revolution' himself, Leon Trotsky. After he had been deported from the Soviet Union in 1929, he wrote that if Lenin had not been in Petrograd in October 1917, there would have been no seizure of power. In those pre-October days, Lenin expended superhuman energy and exerted maximum pressure, demanding, inspiring, exhorting, threatening and insisting that his organization take the initiative and seize power. And he got his way.

As Trotsky wrote, things could have gone very differently without Lenin. A new and more capable general than the government's commander-in-chief, Kornilov, might have emerged; Kerensky's Provisional Government might somehow have managed to survive; and if Pavel Malyantovich, Kerensky's Minister of Justice, had succeeded in carrying out the order to arrest Lenin for staging an armed uprising in Petrograd on 3–5 July,[1] the picture would have been very different. According to his son Vladimir, the wretched Malyantovich lamented in the 1930s: 'If I had carried out the Provisional Government's order to arrest Lenin, none of these horrors would have happened.'[2] Instead, in his seventies he was transported and shot.

But the triumphant coup did take place, and its brain, mainspring and guiding force was Ulyanov-Lenin. As a result he became the most powerful politician and revolutionary of the twentieth century. The scar he left on the face of civilization is deep. Even now, after it has become painfully clear that the seventy-year experiment launched by him was a failure, millions still admire him and his teaching. Most Russians today, however, are indifferent to the man who, perhaps motivated by the best of intentions, convinced the people to take his false path.

Lenin was a man of one dimension. He seems to have loved only one thing: power. He hated the autocracy, the bourgeoisie, landowners,

Mensheviks, Socialist Revolutionaries, kulaks, the clergy, religion, liberals, the lower middle class, parliaments, reformism, compromise, social democracy, the Russian intelligentsia, the hesitant and confused – all those who were not on his side. He hated the entire old world, and therefore once the Bolsheviks were in power, it had to be swept away into the dustbin of history, as Trotsky put it. The Leninists proceeded to destroy entire classes and groups of the population, and thousands of churches. They were responsible for the loss of thirteen million lives in the civil war and for two million Russian citizens leaving the country, and, of course, for the extermination of the entire Russian royal family.

Moscow had already given the order for the murder of the Tsar and his family, and the order was being carried out, when Lenin was asked by the Copenhagen newspaper *National Tidende* on 17 July 1918 to comment on reports that the Tsar was dead. He replied: 'The rumours are not true, the former Tsar is well, all these rumours are lies put out by the capitalist press.'[3] In fact, on the following day the Soviet government debated and fully approved the murders.

Lenin resorted to the assassination of his political enemies on other occasions. Early in 1920, hearing of the arrest of the White leader Admiral Kolchak, he ordered a coded telegram to be sent to the Bolshevik chief in Irkutsk, Smirnov: '. . . don't publish anything at all, but after we have occupied Irkutsk send a strictly official telegram, explaining that, before our arrival, the local authorities [consisting of Socialist Revolutionaries and Mensheviks] had done such and such under the influence of the . . . danger of White plots in Irkutsk.'[4]

The Bolsheviks took Irkutsk, and Kolchak, on 21 January, and Lenin's instructions were carried out to the letter. The Military Revolutionary Committee sentenced Kolchak and the Chairman of the Omsk Government Council of Ministers V.N. Pepelyaev to be shot, and the sentence was carried out within a few hours. Smirnov duly sent a telegram to *Pravda*:

> The Irkutsk revolutionary committee, knowing of plans by officers to launch a counter-revolutionary attack with the aim of overthrowing the authorities and liberating Kolchak, who had been arrested by the Czechs [the Czech Legion then roaming Siberia] and handed over to the revolutionary authorities, and not being able to communicate with

the Siberian Revolutionary Committee, thanks to the telegraph lines at Irkutsk being damaged, at its session of 7 February the Revolutionary Committee, intent on averting a clash, ordered the execution of Admiral Kolchak ... The sentence was carried out the same day.[5]

The 'leader of the world proletariat' was a good mentor to his bloodstained successor.

Despite his illness, Lenin managed to do a great deal in the last few years of his life. He destroyed the old empire and created a new one, eradicated the old social structure and laid the foundations for a completely different order. Having promised the Russian people peace and land, he took away the liberty they had gained in February 1917, without which land and peace were worthless. In any case, he nationalized the land, and quickly turned the First World World into a civil war which cost the country terrible losses.

Speaking at the Bolshoi Theatre on 20 November 1922, at a plenary meeting of the Moscow Soviet – his last public appearance, as it turned out – Lenin remarked that, having decided to build a new order, '[there] is a small, minuscule group of people, calling themselves a party, who have set their hands to this task. These Party-people are an insignificant kernel in the entire mass of the workers of Russia. This insignificant kernel set itself the task of actually changing everything and it has done so.'[6]

Lenin had begun building the new society within days of the October coup. He signed nearly sixty decrees in order to dispossess the landowners. As if he was afraid everything would one day go into reverse, he wrote to People's Commissar for Justice D. Kursky: 'Is it not time to deal with the question of *destroying* the title documents of private property: notarized deeds of land-ownership, factories, buildings, and so on and so forth. Prepare for this *in secret*, without publicity. Seize [the property] first ... In my view, the documents should be turned into *pulp* (you should *first* find out how to do this technically).'

The expeditious Kursky replied at once: 'This is an appropriate measure and can be carried out quickly as the notary archives are in our hands.'

Lenin was satisfied, and settled the matter with another note to Kursky: 'So, you'll get on with this *without* waiting for a special instruction from the Sovnarkom (and you'll arrange a meeting with the

Commissariat of the Interior and others. But *in secret*.)'[7] Lenin had seized the private property of the country, and was now concerned to ensure that no trace remained of documented ownership. He knew that, whatever else, it was not possible to build a new society on the foundations of the old.

In his eighteen-month career as a lawyer, Lenin had defended only four or five cases of petty thieving, and he lost virtually all of them. But in 1909, when a vicomte knocked him off his bicycle in Paris, he immediately sued, put up a vigorous case and won his action. Lenin regarded himself as a winner, whether in a petty lawsuit or in the great game of world revolution. At the Eighth Party Congress in March 1919 he announced in his greeting to the workers of Budapest: 'Our congress is convinced that the time is not far off when Communism will conquer the entire world.'[8]

Such was Lenin: self-confident and cynical, strong-willed and pitiless, and unique in his single-mindedness. The Socialist Revolutionary leader Victor Chernov wrote of him: 'Lenin does not have a broad mind, but he does have an intensive one, not creative, but versatile and in that sense inventive. Lenin had no respect for the convictions of others, nor was he touched by zeal for liberty.'[9] This was the man who would bring about the most profound social upheavals of the twentieth century.

'The Evil Genius'

What did Alexander Potresov, a Menshevik who had known him well in the early days, see in Lenin that led him to describe him in 1927 as an 'evil genius'?[10] 'Neither Plekhanov, nor Martov, nor anyone else,' Potresov wrote elsewhere, 'possessed the mysterious hypnotic effect on people that emanated from Lenin, what I might call his domination over them. People respected Plekhanov and they loved Martov, but only Lenin did they follow unquestioningly as their sole and indisputable leader. For only Lenin presented himself, especially in Russia, as the rare phenomenon of a man with an iron will and indomitable energy, and who blended fanatical faith in the movement and the cause with a no lesser faith in himself . . . Behind these virtues, however, lurk equally great defects, negative features which might be more appropriate in some medieval or Asiatic conqueror.'[11]

For his part, Lenin, in the laconic style appropriate to geniuses, wrote to the writer Maxim Gorky: 'What a swine that Potresov is!'[12] Potresov was not alone in describing Lenin as an evil genius. Mark Aldanov, an émigré novelist, wrote that 'in one case Lenin has the character of a genius, and in a hundred others the character of a barbarian.'[13]

In January 1919 Lenin received a letter from an old Social Democrat acquaintance, Nikolai Rozhkov, an economist and publicist. He wrote, among other things: 'Vladimir Ilyich, I am writing you this letter not because I expect to be heard and understood by you, but simply because I cannot remain silent . . . I have to make even this hopeless effort.' He went on to say that the food situation in Petrograd was desperate, that half the city was dying of starvation. 'Your entire food policy is based on a false foundation . . . Without the collaboration of private trade, neither you nor anyone else can deal with the inevitable disaster.' He urged Lenin to adopt what would later be called the New Economic Policy, NEP. 'You and I have moved too far apart. Perhaps it is truer to say we wouldn't understand each other . . . Even this letter of mine seems to me like a bit of silly Don Quixotism. Well, in that case, let it be the first and last.'[14]

Lenin replied: 'Nikolai Alexandrovich, I was very glad to receive your letter, not because of its content, but because I hope for a rapprochement on the generally common ground of Soviet work . . . As for freedom of trade, an economist should especially see that we cannot go back to free trade, and that we must go forward to socialism by *improving* the state monopoly.' Later in his letter Lenin took up Rozhkov's lament for the demise of parliamentarism in Russia, meaning the Constituent Assembly which the Bolsheviks had dispersed by force in January 1918. He mounted his hobby-horse: 'history has shown that this was the universal collapse of bourgeois democracy and bourgeois parliamentarism and that we will get nowhere without civil war.'[15]

Rozhkov had seen the complete futility of Lenin's policy of War Communism as early as January 1919, and had in effect proposed the New (i.e. old-capitalist) Economic Policy. Lenin, the 'prophet', had not seen this. He did not forget about Rozhkov, and he was unforgiving. At the end of the summer of 1922, at his initiative, the question of expelling abroad a large number of members of the Russian intelligentsia was debated. Lenin wrote a disjointed and vicious directive to Stalin, which said in part:

> On the matter of deporting Mensheviks, Popular Socialists, Kadets and so on from Russia, I'd like to raise several questions, seeing that this operation, which was started before I went on leave, hasn't been completed even now. Has the decision been taken to 'uproot' all the [Popular Socialists]? Peshekhonov, Myakotin, Gorenfeld, Petrishchev and the others? In my opinion, they should all be expelled. They're worse than any [Socialist Revolutionary], as they're more cunning. Also A.N. Potresov, Izgoev and all the staff at the *Ekonomist* (Ozerov and many, many others). The Mensheviks Rozanov (he's an enemy, a cunning one), Vigdorchik, Migulo and anyone else of that ilk, Lyubov Nikolaevna Radchenko and her younger daughter (I hear they're sworn enemies of Bolshevism); N.A. Rozhkov (he has to be expelled, he's stubborn); S.L. Frank (the author of *Methodology*). Mantsev and Messing's commission must draw up lists and several hundred of such gentlemen must be expelled abroad without mercy. We're going to cleanse Russia for a long time to come.[16]

When Lenin heard that Rozhkov was ill, he modified his orders: 'Postpone expelling Rozhkov. Send Rozhkov to Pskov. At the first sign of any hostile activity from him, expel him from the country.'[17] But he did not lose track of the one-time acquaintance who had shown such perspicacity about the economy. Six weeks later he wrote to Zinoviev, the Petrograd Party chief: 'Is Rozhkov in [Petrograd]? He has to be deported.'[18] Lenin's assault on the intelligentsia was directed not against their ideas, but against them personally.

Certainly, there were many good reasons for calling Lenin a genius. He had a powerful and tough intellect, vast willpower, the ability to make sharp changes of policy, and an infinite capacity to focus on the achievement of his goal. After he returned to Russia from Switzerland in April 1917, these qualities quickly put him ahead of all the other politicians. By sheer force of will he could convince his opponents, and crush them if need be. No one was able to beat him in face-to-face argument. But if he sensed that he might be wrong, or that his position was shaky, he would withdraw from the spoken word and resort to print. It is a clear sign of Lenin's leadership that although he was Chairman of the Council of People's Commissars, Sovnarkom, he held no office in the Bolshevik Party; yet in the Politburo, which was effectively the supreme political body, he was implicitly regarded as chief. He was recognized as *leader*, and as a rule he chaired its meetings.

The Politburo was in session on 7 December 1922. Only a few members were present, dealing as usual with a host of problems. Lenin was business-like and to the point. He spoke rarely, but what he said usually counted as the 'collective decision' of the entire body, even when there were serious doubts about it. A.D. Tsyurupa, the People's Commissar for Food Production, was reporting on the export of grain. The country had not yet recovered from the famine that had carried off millions of people, yet Tsyurupa claimed that that year 'we'll come out of it', NEP would help. There was no real debate. Lenin declared that up to fifty million *puds*, about a million tonnes, of grain must be exported, and he put Tsyurupa in overall control of its sale.

If a powerful and unfettered mind are signs of genius, it is difficult to reconcile them with such arbitrary and wayward decisions as those to expel Rozhkov and to export grain from a starving country, and to limit the number of copies of Mayakovsky to be printed. When Polit-buro member Anatoly Lunacharsky suggested that five thousand copies be printed of Mayakovsky's poem '150,000', Lenin remon-strated: 'Rubbish, stupid, utter stupidity and affectation,' and issued the unequivocal instruction that 'only one in ten of such things should be printed at all and no more than 1500 copies for libraries and cranks.'[19] Lenin thought it proper for him alone to decide what should be written, what should be read and what published. For him power was absolute, and he exercised it to issue verdicts purely on the basis of his own convictions and impressions.

As co-architect with Trotsky of the repugnant policy of hostage-taking during the civil war, Lenin never tired of urging the application of this inhuman principle in everyday revolutionary practice. In a note to Nikolai Sklyansky dictated in the dead of night on 8 June 1919, Lenin demanded that 'bearing in mind the increasing pace of change, the taking of hostages from the bourgeoisie and officers' families should be stepped up. Talk to Dzerzhinsky [head of the Cheka].'[20]

Politics, to be sure, tends to be immoral, but in Lenin immorality was exacerbated by cynicism. Almost every one of his decisions, even when they were guided by level-headed pragmatism and careful calculation, suggests that for him morality was totally subordinated to political realities.

It is commonly argued that Lenin was constrained to act as he did because of the circumstances: having to carry out the revolutionary breakthrough, creating new institutions, bringing new values into play – 'You can't make a revolution wearing white gloves!' But the fact is that his political cynicism was no less evident before the revolution than it became after it. That was his essence: the achievement of the political goal justified all necessary means and methods.

For instance, in order to protect his favourite, the Bolshevik Roman Malinovsky, later exposed as a police agent, Lenin heaped insults on those who suspected him: 'Martov and Dan are filthy slanderers'; 'We have to teach our own people (who are naive, inexperienced and don't know) how to fight against shits like Martov'; 'Martov and Co. are still making a stink. Go on, stir the shit!!! Let them choke on their own muck, it's the best thing for them'; 'slime and filth'.[21]

The significant point about the Malinovsky case is not Lenin's error of judgement, but his stubborn persistence in it. Malinovsky himself was not of particular interest to Lenin; more important was his value as a means of destroying his political opponents. Malinovsky was not only a favoured member of Lenin's Central Committee, he was also a Bolshevik deputy in the Russian State Duma, and Lenin gave him his unconditional support, without making much effort to investigate the accusations against him. Even in December 1915, over a year after Malinovsky had been substantially exposed, Lenin was prepared to maintain contact with the former police spy, writing to him: 'My dear friend, Roman Vatslavovich, I received your letter and passed your request on to the local committee for some things to be sent to you ... I hope you are well and in good spirits. Write about yourself and pass on greetings to all the friends you must have made, even in your new surroundings. Nadezhda Konstantinovna sends warm greetings. Yours, V. Ulyanov.'[22] The letter, like many others, was sent to Alten-Grabow, a camp for Russian prisoners of war and interned civilians where Malinovsky was active in spreading Bolshevik defeatist propaganda, and exhibiting precisely the sort of personal loyalty Lenin most valued.

It emerged later that Malinovsky had been one of the most effective *agents provocateurs* in the Okhrana, the tsarist secret service. On police instructions, he had taken a hard line in the Bolshevik Central Committee and the Duma in order to sabotage any attempts by his colleagues at reconciliation with the Mensheviks. He liked to talk about the need for 'the most decisive actions' by Lenin's party. This pleased its leader, and the pair spent more than one evening in long conversation when Malinovsky visited Lenin in Cracow on the eve of the First World War. In 1914 they travelled together to Brussels and Paris, where Malinovsky made a speech described by Lenin as 'a great success'. When the Okhrana archives were opened after the February revolution, the truth finally came out: Malinovsky had been a well-paid agent.

Lenin had to give extended depositions in Malinovsky's trial, which was heard on 26 May 1917. He did not, of course, mention the passion and conviction with which he had formerly defended Malinovsky. But even after everything had come out, he was extremely reserved in his judgement:

> Malinovsky was in my opinion outstanding as an active [party] worker ... Malinovsky came to us in all six or seven times, at any rate more often than all the other [Bolshevik] deputies. He wanted to play a leading part among the Central Committee members in Russia, and was evidently unhappy when someone else was given a responsible job by us ... [He] would have liked to be given more audacious illegal work to do and we had frequent conversations about this in Cracow ... Without doubt a commission of clever people stood behind him and guided his every political step.[23]

Lenin had no regrets about his intimacy with Malinovsky, and expressed no chagrin over his prolonged, and at times frenzied, defence of the agent. In 1918, when the Bolsheviks were in power, Malinovsky unexpectedly arrived in Petrograd from Europe, where he had been living comfortably on his police earnings. Being vain and audacious, he must have thought the authorities would respond to his repentance and that, above all, Lenin would intercede for him. The documents relating to this episode have not been found, but it is possible, on the basis of circumstantial evidence, to draw certain conclusions. Malinovsky sought Lenin's help, but he was of no further use to him. His trial was short, as was the sentence: he was to be shot. In a letter to Gorky, Lenin would remark: 'I couldn't get to the bottom of that swine Malinovsky. He was very shady.'[24]

What importance did Lenin place on democratic values? According to him, only what corresponded with his own views on the essence and content of proletarian revolution could be considered democratic. He was capable of calling the dictatorship of the proletariat 'democratic'.[25] Democracy for him was above all a form of violence, and it is precisely here that the combination of 'genius' and 'evil' was rooted. As for the power of the people, Lenin (and his successors) firmly appropriated the right to speak in their name. In conversation with the German Communist Clara Zetkin, he once said: 'Art belongs to the people ... It must be understood and loved by them.' Of course, he never asked 'the people' what they understood when, for instance, he took the decision practically to ban Futurism and other modernist trends. His thinking was simple: if he could not understand such things, how could the masses? Zetkin replied perceptively: 'Comrade Lenin, do not complain so bitterly about illiteracy. To a certain extent it probably made it easier to make the revolution.'[26]

It is impossible to understand Lenin without considering the meaning of Bolshevism. Thanks to the efforts of Lenin's followers in the Party, Bolshevism became synonymous with revolutionary-mindedness, class superiority and an obsession with the proletariat. Bolsheviks believed that to express doubt or hesitation and lack of self-assurance could only be a sign of bourgeois liberalism, conciliation, reformism and intelligentsia-style vacillation. It is appalling to think that, almost by sleight of hand, Lenin managed to make the very word 'intellectual' [intelligent, in Russian] come to mean the opposite of revolutionary-mindedness and radicalism. In February 1908 he wrote in a letter to Gorky, as if of some great achievement: 'The importance of the intelligentsia in our party is declining: we are getting news from everywhere that the intelligentsia is *running* away from the party. Good riddance to bad rubbish ... This is all wonderful.'[27]

This attitude suggests that Lenin's 'Bolshevism of the soul' in effect amounted to little more than social racism. Only the proletariat, he intimated, were the real revolutionary force. In his most Utopian, and least impressive, book, The State and Revolution – once regarded by all good Leninists as a jewel of theoretical wisdom – Lenin gave in concentrated form his views on the classes, the state, and the role of the proletariat in world history. He was indignant that so many socialists dared to see the state as 'an organ for reconciling the classes'. That was monstrous, in his view. How could they forget, he asked, that 'all social civilization is divided into hostile and therefore irreconcilable classes'? *That* was the point! One had to do everything possible to ensure that the proletariat was not oppressed by the bourgeoisie, only the opposite. Then the dictatorship of the proletariat would arise, the salvation of mankind.[28]

The essence of Bolshevism was radical thinking and radical action. In its classic form, it found its expression in Lenin's own life. He believed what he wrote. And he wrote some dreadful things:

> Accounting and control, that is the *main* thing that is needed to 'get things going', for the proper functioning of the *first phase* of the Communist society ... When the majority of the people begin to produce independently ... the monitoring of capitalists (converted into office-workers) and gentlemen intellectuals who haven't lost their capitalist ways, will become genuinely universal, general, nationwide, and it will be impossible to escape from it in any way, there will be nowhere to hide ... The entire society will be one office and one factory with equality of labour and equality of pay.

The point of this approach was that to avoid accounting and control 'will inevitably become so incredibly hard and such a rare occurrence, and will no doubt also be accompanied by such swift and serious punishment (for armed workers are people from practical life, not sentimental little intellectuals, and they're not likely to let anyone mess with them), that *the need* to observe the simple, basic rules of any human community will very quickly become *a habit*'.[29]

The image was of a barracks rather than of 'one office and one factory'. Everyone would be watching everyone else to see how much they worked and how much they consumed, and hanging over all of them would be the threat of 'swift and serious punishment', with the 'little intellectuals' most at risk.

Never mind that we Russians believed in all this – we actually saw with our own eyes how in Stalin's time a peasant would be sent away to the camps for ten years, if not shot, for nothing more than stealing a handful of wheat from the collective farm where he worked; how a worker might be sent straight to prison for arriving at his factory fifteen minutes late; how for failing to fulfil the required number of 'work days' a person could be sent to a 'special settlement'. The control system was perfected, developed and so universalized that the Russian people accepted as normal the ubiquitous presence of norm-setters, stock-takers, inspectors, instructors, 'social controllers', and many other similar Leninist categories.

The development and perfection of 'accounting' was continued by Lenin's loyal pupil, Stalin. In his notorious article 'Dizzy with Success' of 2 March 1930, Stalin wrote: 'On 20 February this year, 50 per cent of peasant households were collectivized throughout the USSR. This means that by 20 February 1930 we had more than twice overfulfilled the five-year plan for collectivization.'

Even Gorbachev, barely having come to power, began with 'control', or perhaps more precisely verification. I attended a meeting of the Central Committee Secretariat at which he made a passionate speech calling for the introduction of a new system of quality-control in factories that would deny managers their bonuses if the number of their products passing new state-imposed standards did not reach a certain threshold. Thousands of new inspectors had to be installed, although, of course, nothing improved. The system, introduced by Lenin, exercised control not only over weights and measures, but also over the conversations and thoughts of the citizens. Bolshevik absolutism was the result.

In the first phase of the Bolshevik regime, Lenin and his supporters attempted to create at least the appearance of an alliance with the Left Socialist Revolutionaries, who had influence among the peasant population. The Bolsheviks themselves had no clear agricultural programme, and in effect borrowed one from the Socialist Revolutionaries. Fearing that the Bolsheviks might not be able to hold on to power on their own, Lenin, with some trepidation, opted for the alliance, though it would not last for long. The Sovnarkom met three times, on 7, 8 and 9 December 1917, under Lenin's chairmanship, to discuss broadening the political base of the new regime by including some Left Socialist Revolutionaries (Left SRs), and finally agreed to include seven of them, five as People's Commissars and two as ministers without portfolio. It was made clear to them that they must perform their duties in accordance with the policies laid down by the Bolsheviks, who would brook no attempts to dilute or alter the absolute power the new regime represented.[30]

The notion that this might have been a step towards political pluralism, or that it might have led to the inclusion of Mensheviks in the
government, and that a more social democratic course might have
ensued, is, of course, illusory. It was not in the Bolsheviks' nature to
want to share power. The monopoly of dictatorship was in their blood.

What made Lenin what he was? Why should this member of the
Russian gentry, supported, like his siblings, by his mother's generous
government pension, turn out to be such an irreconcilable revolutionary? How did it come about that he could think and talk of nothing
but revolution?

Lenin's family background was well ordered, and was influenced
by several different cultures: Russian, German, Jewish, Kalmyk and
some Swedish. A product of the great Eurasian state, Lenin was a blend
of many of the features of his origins: Russian radicalism, European
civilization, Jewish intelligence, and Asiatic audacity and cruelty.

Of enormous importance to the life-choices Lenin made was the
death of his older brother Alexander, who was hanged in 1887, when
Lenin was seventeen, for an attempt on the life of the Tsar. A university student at the time, Alexander's life could have been spared by
his intended victim, but as a committed terrorist, he thought it dis-
honourable to beg for mercy. His brother's execution was devastating
for the young Vladimir. It led to a degree of social ostracism for his
family, and soon brought him, too, to the attention of the Okhrana.

Lenin was shaken by his brother's death, but also by his courage.
He drew the lesson, and was reputed to have said: 'We shall not go
by that path.' The testimony for this declaration is dubious – his then
nine-year-old sister. He had no concept at that time of any path of
his own, though he was drawn towards radicalism and uncompromising views, and, certainly, in the future he would go by a different
route. No one would ever see him as a bomb-maker, or the organizer
of direct action on the barricades or of frontal attack. He would
become a back-room revolutionary, refining and polishing the ideas
of his harsh philosophy.

The thirst for knowledge, cultivated in his family, and redoubled
by his growing radicalism, prompted the young Ulyanov to imbibe
enormous quantities of literature. But it was literature of a peculiar
sort. As well as the standard works to be found on the desk of any
educated young Russian of his generation – Nekrasov, Turgenev,

Saltykov-Shchedrin, Uspensky – Lenin also read Darwin, Buckle, Ricardo, Dobrolyubov and, especially, the radical philosopher Nikolai Chernyshevsky. He read Marx's *Capital* while he was still at home on the estate at Kokushkino, in the province of Kazan. His outlook on life began to include social and political ideas very early.

At the turn of the century, the Russian intelligentsia was experiencing a great cultural uplift that came to be known as the 'Silver Age' in prose-writing, and in the work of thinkers, historians and political writers. Already nourished by the works of Tolstoy, Dostoevsky and Chekhov, the reading public eagerly consumed the poetry of Fet and Nadson, Balmont, Severyanin and Gippius, and debated the latest philosophical and historical treatises of the Solovyevs, father and son, of Trubetskoy, Berdyaev, Bulgakov, Rozanov, Lossky, Frank, Karsavin and Fedorov. Even a century later, one is still astonished at the bounty of providence and nature that gave Russia such a priceless intellectual heritage at that time. It was perhaps only thanks to this that Soviet Russia, which pitilessly trampled on this unique gift for seventy years, did not become a barren archaeological specimen in the excavations of Slavonic culture. Russian intellectual achievement without doubt reached its highest peak at the turn of the century.

And yet Lenin somehow skirted this peak, and did not attempt to scale even its lower slopes. The ethical maxims of Solovyev, or Berdyaev's reflections on liberty, remained as closed to him as the secrets of the spiritual world explored by Dostoevsky. The cultural poverty of his powerful intellect was expressed in his obsessive single-mindedness, his unequivocal political approach, and his dismissal of universal moral principles. It is enough to recall that he found a substitute for the broad palette of Russian philosophy in the works of Chernyshevsky. For Lenin, Chernyshevsky was 'the only really great Russian writer', simply because he wrote in terms of 'undiluted philosophical materialism'. It was not, however, Chernyshevsky the philosopher that Lenin admired, so much as Chernyshevsky the radical, who could say: 'whoever is afraid to dirty his hands, should not get involved in politics'.[31]

Significantly, Lenin thought Dostoevsky was 'the foulest of writers'.[32] Tolstoy, on whom he wrote several strictly political articles, was useful only because Lenin could describe him as a 'fiery protester' and denouncer of the tsarist order, though even Tolstoy exhibited 'a lack of understanding of the causes of the crisis and the means to get out of it, as might be found in some patriarchal, naive peasant, rather than a writer with a European education'. The Russian liberal view of Tolstoy as the 'great conscience' of the people Lenin called 'an empty phrase' and 'a lie'. He managed to persuade himself that Tolstoy had 'said nothing that had not already been said long before him in both European and Russian literature'.[33]

It was hardly surprising, therefore, that he should find what he called 'various Berdyaevs' capable only of 'philosophic' obscurities, political banalities and 'literary critical yelping and whining'. Or that the Party editors of Lenin's collected works should officially dub Berdyaev 'an apologist of feudalism and medieval scholasticism'.[34]

Many writers idolized by student youth as luminaries of the progressive intelligentsia would forever remain unknown to Lenin, or at best not understood. Berdyaev described Lenin as 'a poor man' in the field of philosophy, and Lenin's book *Materialism and Empiriocriticism* (1908), defined in the official literature as 'a work of genius' and 'the main philosophical work of the twentieth century', completely ignores the greatest Russian achievements in this sphere. Not a single major Russian thinker – except for Chernyshevsky, of course – is even mentioned in Lenin's 'work of genius'.

As the head of the caste of 'professional revolutionaries' he had himself created, Lenin despised the Russian intelligentsia because they were the bearers of liberalism. With his caste in power, he would have no need of liberty. 'He distrusted intellectuals,' his biographer the American journalist Louis Fischer wrote. 'They doubt. They think. They rebel against orthodoxy. Sovietism, however, is a new orthodoxy.'[35] For their own part, émigré writers gave as good as they got. Speaking in Paris on 16 February 1924 on 'The Mission of the Russian Emigration', Ivan Bunin declared with great bitterness:

> Once there was Russia, a house bursting with all kinds of goods and chattels, inhabited by a mighty family, created by the blessed labours of many, many generations, illuminated by worship for God, a memory of the past and by everything that is called religion and culture. What has been done to this house? The overthrow of the head of the house has been paid for by the destruction of literally the entire house and by unprecedented fratricide, by the whole bloody nightmare farce whose monstrous consequences are countless ... This global villain, bearing

a banner with the mocking slogan of liberty, fraternity, equality, has climbed onto the neck of the Russian 'savage' and is calling for conscience, shame, love and mercy to be trampled in the mud ... That degenerate, that congenital moral imbecile, Lenin, has revealed to the world in the very heat of his activity something monstrous and devastating: he has ravaged the greatest country in the world and murdered millions of people, yet in broad daylight people are debating the question of whether he is a benefactor of mankind or not.[36]

Lenin would never hear or read those words.

The Bolshevik seeds produced such poisonous shoots that it is hard to say when they will be brought under control. The interruption of Russia's long intellectual tradition by Lenin and Leninism was one of the chief causes of the countless miseries heaped on the people. 'That which saves,' the nineteenth-century Russian philosopher Vladimir Solovyov wrote, 'saves itself. That is the secret of progress, there is no other nor will there be.' The Bolsheviks did not save Russia and, as history has now shown, they did not save themselves.

The Sin of October

It was the third year of the First World War. Millions of soldiers were dying in the trenches, bombarded and gassed, hanging in grey tatters on the barbed wire. The war had crossed its 'equator'. Few doubted that Germany and its allies would be defeated in the end, especially now that the United States had entered the war on the Allied side. Russia's position was bad, but not desperate. The front had been stabilized. However, socialist agitation was having a serious effect on army morale. Reinforcements were frequently arriving at only half strength. Mass desertion had begun. The last President of the Russian State Duma, Mikhail Rodzyanko, later recalled that in 1917 'desertion from the front amounted to one and a half million. About two million soldiers had been captured by the Germans ... The Bolshevik agitators were working on the natural reluctance of the peasants to fight.'[37]

Lenin, meanwhile, in peaceful Switzerland, was engaged in philosophical self-education, writing articles, going for walks in the company of his wife and his friend Inessa Armand, eagerly following the news from the front. He himself had never worn military uniform or squatted in a blood-soaked trench. He had never looked into the dreadful face of war. He realized that the combatants themselves were incapable of ending this ugly, savage war, and he also knew that the war held the key to his own future.

The desire to end the bloodshed was felt by some people in a position to exercise influence. As early as February 1915, King Gustav V of Sweden wrote to Tsar Nicholas II: 'You understand, dear Nicky, how much the horrors of this frightful war upset me. And therefore it is quite natural that my thoughts are preoccupied in seeking the means that could put an end to the dreadful slaughter ... I am prompted by my conscience to tell you that at any moment, sooner or later, whenever you find it convenient, I am willing to serve you in any way in this matter ... What do you think of my offer to help?'[38] Nothing came of this initiative.

Two years later, on 4 February 1917, the Bulgarian envoy to Berlin, Rizov, visited the Russian envoy to Norway, Gulkevich, and requested that a telegram be sent to Petrograd reporting 'Germany's desire to conclude a separate peace with Russia on highly favourable terms'. Petrograd replied to Gulkevich: 'Listen [to the proposal] and be sure to obtain a precise formulation of the terms.'[39] It was all too late. February was pregnant with irreversible events.

From the beginning of the slaughter, Lenin was not, as might have been expected, in favour of its termination, but instead called for its 'socialization'. Writing to one of his agents, Alexander Shlyapnikov, on 7 October 1914, two months after the outbreak of fighting, he roundly condemned the campaign for peace. 'The "peace" slogan is not the right one. The proper slogan must be to turn national war into civil war.'[40] Lenin had already created another plank of the Bolshevik platform on the conflict when Germany declared war on Russia on 1 August 1914. He immediately sat down to write his 'Theses on the War', later published in collected form under the title *War and Russian Social Democracy*. In it there appear lines that only a rigidly orthodox thinker like Lenin could have written. He described the attempt 'to slaughter the proletarians of all lands by setting the hired slaves of one nation against the hired slaves of another for the benefit for the bourgeoisie' as being 'the *only real* content and meaning of this war' (emphasis added).

The absurdity of this proposition is obvious, but the foundation stone of socialist propaganda had been laid. He went on to state that: 'From the point of view of the working class and the labouring masses of all the peoples of Russia, the lesser evil would be the defeat of the tsarist monarchy and its forces.'[41] Lenin was calling for nothing less than the defeat of his own government, of his country (which was incidentally not an instigator of the war), and better still for turning the war into a revolution and a civil war. For all their professed internationalism, the position taken by Lenin and the Leninists did nothing to bring the ending of the slaughter any nearer. On the contrary, theirs was a policy of throwing still more fuel on the flames of war.

At the same time, Lenin's line on the war represented a blatant national betrayal derived from profound contempt for both Russia's state interests and those of her allies. He could not have made this clearer than when he stated that 'tsarism is a hundred times worse than kaiserism.'[42] It was possibly this sentiment that led Lenin in time to the idea of a coincidence of interests between the Bolsheviks and Berlin. The Tsar, his government and his armies were an obstacle to Germany's far-reaching plans for expansion, and also to Lenin's for seizing power in Russia. From the moment the war broke out, Germany and the Bolsheviks had a common enemy in tsarist Russia, and from this Lenin drew the conclusion that the Russian army must be made to disintegrate. 'Even where the war is being waged,' he declared, 'we must remain revolutionaries. Even in wartime we must preach class struggle.'[43]

At the end of September 1914 the Russian newspaper *Russkoe Slovo* (Russian Word) published an appeal from writers, artists and actors condemning German aggression. Among the many illustrious signatories was Maxim Gorky, who for years had been an active supporter of Lenin's organization. Lenin wrote an open letter addressed to Gorky in which he condemned his 'chauvinistical sermonizing'. He remarked in passing that the world-famous operatic bass Fedor Chaliapin, who had also signed the appeal, 'should not be judged too harshly ... He knows nothing about the proletarian cause: today he's a friend of the workers and tomorrow – the Black Hundreds.'[44] For Lenin, everyone was divided strictly into those who adopted a class (Leninist) position and were therefore allies, and those in the 'chauvinistical' camp who were therefore sworn enemies. Even in his article 'On the National Pride of the Great Russians', which every Soviet citizen was supposed to have read as a profoundly 'patriotic' piece of writing, Lenin asserted that 'the Great Russians should not "defend the father-land" other than by wishing for the defeat of tsarism in any war, as the lesser evil for nine-tenths of Great Russia.'[45] The slogans of pacificism and the idea of 'paralysing the war' were mocked by Lenin as 'ways of making fools of the working class', and he thought the notion of a 'democratic peace' without revolution 'profoundly wrong'.[46]

It was typical of Lenin that, while calling for 'decisive action' against the militarists and for 'unleashing class struggle in the army', it did not occur to him to set an example himself. During the 1916 socialist conference in Zimmerwald, Switzerland, he loudly insisted that the delegates return to their native countries and personally organize strike movements against their belligerent governments. The German Social Democrat Karl Ledebour responded: 'But they'll just put me on trial in a court martial.' Lenin persisted, however, at which Ledebour retorted: 'And will you be going back to Russia to organize strikes against the war? Or are you going to stay in Switzerland?' Lenin did not dignify such a 'provocative' question with a reply.[47]

In February 1915 five Bolshevik Duma deputies, along with a number of other Social Democrats, had been sentenced by a special session of the Petrograd court for being in possession of the manifesto of the Central Committee of the RSDLP, written by Lenin and entitled *War and Russian Social Democracy*. In it, as we have seen, he called for the defeat of his own country and the conversion of the imperialist war into civil war. All five Bolshevik deputies were exiled for life to Turukhansk in Western Siberia, while the author of the manifesto continued to enjoy a quiet life in Switzerland. Ironically, and more appropriately, on 28 September 1914, during discussion of Plekhanov's paper 'The Socialists' Attitude to the War', Lenin frankly advised the socialist ministers of belligerent governments to 'go to a neutral country and tell the truth from there'.[48] He regarded it as legitimate revolutionary tactics to utter bold criticism of tsarism, the autocracy and chauvinism – from a safe distance.

Lenin always avoided physical risks to himself. When on the crowded streets of St Petersburg in 1906 the cry went up, 'Cossacks!'

and everyone scattered in all directions, Lenin ran off clumsily, fell into the gutter and lost his bowler hat. The cry turned out to be a false alarm.[49]

Lenin lived abroad not because he was being pursued by the authorities, but because he feared the possibility of being pursued. In fact, nobody was looking for him or breathing down his neck. He could abuse any aspect of Russia he liked without risk to himself. 'Trembling with excitement', he wrote about the revolutionary events of 1905 in the wildest, most savage terms: 'We will give the order to units of our [sic] army to arrest the Black Hundredists ... who are rallying and bribing the ignorant masses' and hand them over to 'an open, all-people's revolutionary court'. More precisely, a lynch mob. As early as the spring of 1906 Lenin was saying that 'there will be no trace left of the institutions of the tsarist regime.' For him, 'whoever is not a revolutionary is a Black Hundredist.'[50]

These fragments of 'revolutionary' delirium were written at the end of 1905, at a time when it was already clear that the Tsar's October Manifesto had lowered the public temperature and given the country a unique opportunity to take the path of constitutional monarchy. But Lenin had at once called for 'the tyrants' to be 'finished off', leaving no room for compromise.

In the People's House in Zurich on 22 January 1917, Lenin gave a long and boring speech to young workers on the anniversary of the 1905 revolution. When I visited the hall in the early 1990s, I found it to be quite small. It was not hard to imagine Lenin's guttural voice: 'Up to 22 January 1905, the revolutionary party of Russia consisted of a small handful of people mockingly called a sect by the reformists ... Feudal, patriarchal, pious and obedient Russia awoke from her bear-like slumber and threw off the old Adam ...' The audience in the half-empty hall listened politely to the stocky, bald gentleman with burning eyes as he lamented that 'unfortunately the peasants then destroyed only one-fifteenth of all gentry estates, only one-fifteenth of what they *ought* to have destroyed.' The speaker was a member of the gentry, whose family had sold their estate and were now living on the interest from their capital. His audience was drifting away when he injected new life into his speech by describing the forcible Russification, as he put it, of 'precisely 57 per cent' of the population. 'In December 1905, in hundreds of schools, Polish children burned all the Russian books and pictures and portraits of the tsars, beat up and chased out their Russian teachers and Russian comrades with cries of "Get the hell out back to Russia!" ' Finally, as more and more seats emptied, he declared: 'My time is nearly up and I do not wish to abuse the patience of my audience.' He then spoke for another fifteen minutes on his favourite subject, revolution, and ended by saying: 'We old folk might not live to see the decisive battles of the coming revolution . . .'[51]

The Russian government's failings in the war and its weakness at home led to the self-destruction of the autocracy on a wave of discontent. A historical mutation began in 1917 which would lead in a few years to the creation of a new civilization, a new culture, and new political and social institutions which had little in common with Russia's history. Had the democratic February revolution managed to hold, most likely Russia today would be a great democratic state, rather than one that has disintegrated.

Stuck in Zurich, Lenin became increasingly agitated by the thought that the train of the Russian revolution might depart for the future without him. He was saved from that eventuality by secret and unofficial contacts that had been established between certain Leninists and individuals who had the trust of the German authorities. Among these were Alexander Helphand, known as Parvus, an émigré from Russia, German social democrat and successful businessman in Scandinavia and Germany. Parvus was the author of an audacious plan according to which Germany, in order to win the war, would assist the outbreak of revolution in Russia. In declaring that tsarism's defeat 'here and now' would be the best way out of the war,[52] Lenin was publicly, repeatedly and precisely stating his position as a virtual ally of Germany in its fight against his own country and its people.

General Erich von Ludendorff, 'the military brain of the German nation' and First Quartermaster of the army, described the role played by Lenin in Berlin's plans with frankness and extreme cynicism: 'In helping Lenin travel to Russia our government accepted a special responsibility. The enterprise was justified from a military point of view. We had to bring Russia down.'[53] This was also Lenin's aim.

Research into these matters was strictly forbidden in the Soviet Union, but in the West much direct and indirect evidence has been discovered which established beyond doubt that a firm link existed between the Bolsheviks and Berlin. In recent years, documents from Russian archives that had previously been inaccessible have revealed the financial connections between Lenin's agents and Germany. Despite repeated 'purges', the archives preserved 'book-keeping' telegrams, accounts and statements of the amounts made available to the Bolsheviks by a generous German government.

After a meeting between Lenin and Parvus in May 1915, a close association was formed between a small circle of Lenin's most trusted agents, of whom the most important was Jacob Stanislavovich Ganetsky (Fuerstenberg), and the German side, with Parvus as the link. Ganetsky and Parvus were the mainspring of an ingenious mechanism. With money made available to him by Count Ulrich von und zu Brockdorff-Rantzau, the German ambassador in Copenhagen, and other sources, Parvus established a so-called Institute for the Study of the Social Consequences of the War, where he employed a number of Russian social democrats. Meanwhile, using German funds, Ganetsky established a firm in Stockholm for purchasing pharmaceutical products, such as medicines and contraceptives, for shipment to Petrograd, where they were in great demand. The proceeds from these sales enabled Ganetsky's assistant, Kozlovsky, to transmit large sums of money to accounts in different banks, usually to a woman called Yevgeniya Sumenson. Hundreds of thousands of roubles were thus made available to the Bolsheviks for purposes such as the printing and distribution of newspapers and leaflets, the purchase of arms, and salaries for a large number of 'professional revolutionaries'. Dozens of telegrams testify to the constant flow of funds between Berlin and the Bolsheviks via Ganetsky and Parvus, aided by several intermediaries who knew nothing of this covert support for Lenin's party. Lenin, the consummate conspirator, did not mark these documents with his own instructions or give direct financial orders himself. He stood in the wings, watching the machine work for him and exercising only verbal authority.

Despite some remaining gaps in the evidence, there is no doubt that the October coup was supported by German money. And it continued to flow after the Bolshevik seizure of power, as the Germans tried in every way to prevent the accession of an anti-Bolshevik regime that would make common cause with the Western Allies and revive Russia's war against Germany. Count Wilhelm Mirbach, the German ambassador in Moscow, sent a cipher telegram to Berlin on 3 June 1918, one month before he was assassinated: 'Due to strong Entente competition, 3,000,000 marks per month necessary. In event of early need for change in our political line, a higher sum must be reckoned with.' Two days later, the German Foreign Ministry informed the Treasury that Mirbach had spent large sums to counter Allied efforts in Russia to persuade the Bolsheviks to change their line and accept Allied demands. Since it was the German view that the new regime was hanging by a thread, Mirbach's efforts were regarded as of cardinal importance, and in order to sustain them a fund of 'at least 40 million marks' was required.[54]

In 1921 the leading German Social Democrat Eduard Berstein published a sensational article in the socialist newspaper *Vorwärts* in which he wrote: 'Lenin and his comrades received vast sums of money from the Kaiser's government for their destructive agitation . . . From absolutely reliable sources I have now ascertained that the sum was very large, an almost unbelievable amount, certainly more than fifty million gold marks, a sum about the source of which Lenin and his comrades could be in no doubt. One result of all this was the Brest-Litovsk Treaty.'[55]

In effect, the Bolshevik leadership had been bought by the Germans, and it was therefore not surprising that Lenin should compel the Russian delegation to the peace talks in March 1918 to accept the harsh terms dictated by Germany. The 'indecent peace' was the price Lenin had to pay to acquire and retain power. Having not long before declared that the Bolsheviks would never agree to a separate peace, Lenin in fact accepted a defeat – after preaching defeatism for three years – that never was. He accepted defeat from an enemy who was already on his knees before the Allies. He not only accepted defeat, he also agreed to give the Germans a million square kilometres of Russian territory and 245.5 tonnes of gold. In the autumn of 1918, with Germany facing imminent defeat, the curator of the Russian gold reserve, Novitsky, reported to Lenin that another ninety-five tonnes of gold was ready for shipment to Germany.[56]

Having utterly rejected all social democratic principles, soon after returning from exile to Petrograd in April 1917 Lenin embarked on a course of violent seizure of power. He refused to meet the socialist Prime Minister Alexander Kerensky. His slogans, primitive and rabble-rousing, worked without fail. The Bolsheviks promised the war-weary, land-starved and hungry people peace, land and bread, and told them that to achieve this they must first stick their bayonets into the ground, abandon the trenches and go home, where they should seize their allotments. Promised by Lenin's agitators that they would never be sent to the front, the troops of the vast Petrograd garrison threw their support behind the Bolsheviks. The power of Kerensky's Provisional Government melted like ice in the spring thaw. Meanwhile the Bolshevik demagogues promised the gullible and ignorant peasants-in-uniform prosperity, peace, land, bread, hospitals, liberty. At the First All-Russian Congress of Peasants' Deputies in May 1917, Lenin described the idyllic life they would lead: 'This will be a Russia in which free labour will work on free land.'[57] His listeners would not have to wait long to discover whether his predictions were accurate.

In the capital, meanwhile, the political manoeuvring continued. Kerensky, the Don Quixote of the February revolution, tried to rise above the nation, to rally and unite it, and to hang on until the Allies won the war. Russia had little possibility of making a significant contribution to the war effort, but could certainly survive another eight or nine months. But Lenin and the Bolsheviks were rapidly increasing their following in the factories and in army units. The gulf between liberal democracy and the radical wing of the ragged-trousered masses was widening. As always in Russia, there was no influential political middle ground. The Bolsheviks decided to attempt an assault on the amorphous, flabby centre of power and, should it succeed against the background of a huge demonstration – armed if necessary – take power themselves.

Lenin naturally distanced himself somewhat from the epicentre of events. Accompanied by his sister Maria and two bodyguards, he left for the border village of Neivola, near Mustamiaki, and stayed in the house of Vladimir Bonch-Bruevich, one of his Bolshevik associates. In the event of the failure of the demonstration, Finnish refuge was near at hand, and Sweden was little more than a stone's throw further. Lenin realized, however, that real control was in the hands of neither the government nor the soviets (councils of workers', soldiers' and peasants' deputies that had sprung up following the collapse of the tsarist state). Indeed, he described Russia at this time as 'the freest country in the world', clearly meaning that power was there for the taking, if one had the courage and audacity to make the attempt.

In the middle of July the Bolsheviks decided to test their strength. Tens of thousands of demonstrators took to the streets of Petrograd, with army units and sailors among them. Early in the morning of 17 July, Lenin was summoned back to the capital by his comrades. Now he waited. The soldiers and sailors had been well primed by Bolshevik agitators. They had been told that, after their unsuccessful demonstration in June, the Provisional Government was preparing to send garrison troops to fill the breaches at the front. The troops, appalled by the thought of the blood and mud of the flea-ridden trenches, were enraged. The liberal leader Paul Milyukov wrote later: 'On [17 July] Lenin was in place on his famous balcony at the house of Kshesinskaya, greeting the soldiers and giving them their orders. All the military intelligence of the Bolshevik Central Committee was there; military units were coming and going. In a word, here was the military headquarters of the uprising.'[58] Lenin had already stated in public that 'peaceful demonstrations are a thing of the past.'[59]

From his balcony Lenin called for 'All Power to the Soviets!' The original text of his speech has not been found. It was considered too dangerous to publish, since Lenin was inciting the crowds to overthrow the government, as the testimonies of numerous witnesses confirm. On the other hand, the most detailed chronicler of the revolution, the Menshevik Nikolai Sukhanov, recalled that Lenin's speech was rather cautious, and that although he agitated forcefully against the government, he also called for the defence of the revolution and loyalty to the Bolsheviks.[60] The attempt failed, and thereafter the Bolsheviks always presented it as a 'peaceful demonstration'.

The Bolsheviks had hoped that by force of numbers the government would be pressured into capitulating, especially as it seemed they would receive virtually no support from the army. Yet the hundreds of thousands of people who came out onto the streets met growing resistance from forces loyal to Kerensky. Shooting, rioting and unorganized clashes took place. Blood flowed. The outcome looked uncertain. Disquieting reports were coming into the Kshesinskaya palace that the telegraph offices were being well defended, that Cossack reinforcements were arriving, that loyal troops had closed off yet another strategic street.

Finding himself perhaps for the first time in his life within range of danger, Lenin decided that for the sake of the future he should terminate the demonstration. To save face, and to put the government on the defensive, he began accusing the authorities of 'bloody atrocities', and then went into hiding.

Trotsky recalled that when he met him after the failure of the July rising, Lenin was frightened: 'Now they can shoot us down. It's the best time for them to do it.'[61] Once he had settled in a safe haven, however, he could focus all his energy on writing articles and sending orders and messages designed to inflame the masses still further. By whipping up hatred for the still fragile institutions of the bourgeois democracy, he was making sure that national and social peace should not prevail.

Knowing that the government had issued a warrant for his arrest as the instigator of the July uprising, Lenin changed his hiding place frequently, while maintaining constant contact with his Central Committee. Money was no object, since the Bolsheviks were receiving funds transmitted from abroad by Ganetsky and his associates.

Lenin saw that Russia was facing a choice. Kerensky's Provisional Government represented a painful transition from centuries of autocracy to parliamentarism. Kerensky, however, was morally prevented from seeking a separate peace with Germany: it would be a betrayal of Russia's allies. The government's military commander, General Kornilov, or any other politically minded general, would drown Russia in blood and install an order more harsh than that of Nicholas II had been. Either would continue the war 'to a victorious conclusion'.

Only Lenin had something different to offer the exhausted nation: in exchange for power, he promised them peace, and for the peasants also land. The price was national betrayal, the disintegration of the army, and reneging on Russia's promises to the Allies. Only Lenin realized that the nation would accept the option of betrayal and suffer the shame of it later. He did not appeal to the higher instincts, to patriotism and civic-mindedness, but rather to hatred, fatigue and unfulfilled expectations. He knew how to manipulate the influences of the moment in the public mind, and he knew exactly what he wanted. He was capable of launching a rabble-rousing slogan in the knowledge that he could recant at any time.

Three months earlier, he had declared categorically that he would never seek a separate peace. Now, as he scurried from one hiding place to the next, he asserted that 'there are ninety-nine chances in a hundred that the Germans will at least give us an armistice. And to get an armistice now would mean winning the entire peace.'[62] In September he was even more precise: 'Victory in an uprising is now *guaranteed* for the Bolsheviks: we can (if we don't "wait for the Soviet congress") strike *suddenly* from three points: from [Petrograd], from Moscow and from the Baltic Fleet ... it is 99 per cent sure that we will win with fewer losses than we had on [16–18] July, because the soldiers *will not go* against a government of peace.'[63]

Aware of the Central Committee's hesitation and vacillation, and after taking proper security measures, Lenin returned to the capital on 23 October. He would wait no longer.

Kerensky made desperate last-ditch attempts to alter the course of events: he held meetings with members of the Duma, sent despatches to the front with the aim of preventing its collapse, and enquired whether Lenin had been apprehended. On 1 September he had proclaimed Russia a republic and declared the chief task of the Provisional Government to be the restoration of state order and the fighting ability of the army.[64] Desertions, however, had mounted under the impact of Bolshevik propaganda, while in the rear Lenin's exhortations reached a frenzied pitch. 'After the seizure of the cadet schools, the telegraphs, telephones and so on,' the Bolsheviks' slogan, he wrote, must be: 'We shall all die before we let the enemy pass.' Strategic points must be taken 'at whatever cost'.[65]

At two crucially important meetings of the Bolshevik Central Committee on 23 and 29 October, Lenin insisted a decision be taken to stage an armed uprising. Only twelve of the twenty-one members of the Committee were present on 23 October, and only two of them – Zinoviev and Kamenev – stood up to Lenin and voted against the proposal. Showing enviable caution and perceptiveness, they urged the Party to wait for the elections to a Constituent Assembly that the Provisional Government had already set in train, and that would better reflect the political mood of the huge Russian population. Kamenev declared: 'The Party has not been consulted. Such matters are not settled by ten people.' His remark exposed the full extent of Lenin's political cynicism.

Two weeks later, on the night of 6 November,* the Bolshevik Red Guards seized a number of key locations in Petrograd, including the main post office and telephone exchange, stormed the Winter Palace and arrested Provisional Government Ministers. Next day, Trotsky informed the Second Congress of Soviets that the Bolsheviks had seized power in the name of the Soviets of Workers' and Soldiers' Deputies, thus ushering in the new era of Soviet rule in Russia. In fact, it was the Bolshevik Party under Lenin and his successors that would govern the country for the next seventy years, even if they continued to uphold the fiction that they were doing so in the name of the Soviets. The clan of professional revolutionaries would henceforth simply pass the sceptre of power from one pair of hands to the next.

For seven decades much would be written about 'Lenin's theory of socialist revolution'. In fact, it was not a consistent, synthesized body of theory. Its salient features were: the maximum manipulation of public opinion; the frenzied cultivation of the image of the class enemy, whether the Tsar, the bourgeoisie, the Mensheviks or the liberals; the disintegration of the army and state machine by means of outright rabble-rousing; pushing the state and the regime towards chaos and dislocation; staging a coup at the precise moment when the government was most weakened and compromised; establishing a harsh dictatorship which took away 'bourgeois liberties and rights'; using terror as a means of keeping millions of people in check; unleashing civil war.

These are only some of the features of Lenin's technique. They were implemented by a disciplined, organized party led by professional revolutionaries like Lenin himself, people capable of issuing an order to reduce rations for those not working on transport and to increase it for those who were: 'Let thousands die, but the country will be saved.'[66] Lenin's logic was that some should be killed so that others should live.

Lenin was able to determine the precise moment at which the government was totally paralysed and defenceless, when if the Bolsheviks did not seize the moment, others would. The American

* Until 1 February 1918 the Russian calendar was thirteen days behind the Western calendar in the twentieth century. All the dates cited here are in Western, or New Style. It is for this reason only that the events which took place on 6 and 7 November 1917 were always known as the 'October Revolution', even though they were commemorated on 7 November.

journalist John Reed, who became a hero of the revolution, recorded Lenin saying on 3 November: '6 November will be too soon to act; the eighth too late. We have to act on the seventh, the day the [Second] Congress [of Soviets] opens.'[67]

Yet, until the last minute, Lenin did not believe deep down in the success of the operation. As Richard Pipes has written: 'Lenin did not dare to show himself in public until the cabinet (presumably including Kerensky, of whose escape he was unaware) fell into Bolshevik hands. He spent most of [7 November] bandaged, wigged, and bespectacled. After Dan and Skobelev, passing by, saw through his disguise, he retired to his hideaway, where he took catnaps on the floor, while Trotsky came and went to report the latest news.'[68]

The dying regime managed to issue a distress signal on the radio and in *Rabochaya gazeta* (Labour Gazette) on 11 November 1917:

> To All, To All, To All! The Provisional Council of the Russian Repub-lic, yielding to the force of bayonets, was compelled on [7 November] to disperse and to interrupt its work for the time being. With the words 'liberty and socialism' on their lips, the usurpers are committing violence and mayhem. They have arrested and imprisoned in tsarist casemates members of the Provisional Government, including the socialist ministers ... Blood and anarchy threaten to overwhelm the revolution, to drown liberty and the republic ... [69]

The Russian Revolution preserved the traditional popular link between mystique and practice. Lenin's dogmas became the mystique, and destruction became the practice. 'Everything was destroyed except the tradition, except the plan, the blueprint of hatred and the leader's indomitable will,' wrote E. Bogdanov, an émigré philosopher. 'The people's instincts did the rest; a spicy broth which would with micro-biological speed multiply the bacteria of Bolshevism in Russia ... The people spat on the liberty and democracy they were offered [in February 1917] and were content only with their new and harsher slavery.'[70]

Lenin's Comrades-in-Arms

Before he became a national figure in Russia, which in effect did not happen until the attempt on his life on 30 August 1918, Lenin's comrades were able to engage him in heated discussion and severely criticize his positions. He was not yet the earthly god he would become. His wife Nadezhda Krupskaya recalled that he was 'very tactful towards those he had trained', but that none of his comrades received any quarter from him. In 1903 in Brussels at the opening of the Second Congress of the RSDLP, Krupskaya wrote, 'after a clash with Plekhanov, he sat down at once to write venomous replies to Plekhanov's venomous remarks'.[71]

Late in the evening of 6 March 1918, the Seventh Party Congress opened in the Tauride Palace in Petrograd. It was conducted in virtual secrecy. Lenin nonetheless prefaced his speech by ordering that 'the secretaries and stenographers shouldn't even think of writing this down'.[72] The question being debated was the Brest-Litovsk peace talks, which, as Lenin proudly boasted to the delegates, had 'turned the imperialist war into civil war'.[73] The Bolshevik government suited Germany's purpose as no other could.

Some of those present at the congress recognized the true cost of the terms being offered. V.V. Obolensky (Osinsky) declared: 'This deal between Russia and German imperialism, that Comrade Lenin wants to make at the cost of submitting to German capital, will not save the remaining [part of Russia].'[74] Others were even more outspoken. Bukharin especially had no qualms about calling Lenin's assertions 'speculations', and stating that he was living 'on illusions', and that 'the prospect offered by Comrade Lenin is not acceptable.' He sharply attacked Lenin's rabble-rousing: 'When Comrade Lenin constantly resorts to the argument, "Look, every soldier will understand it," "Any peasant can understand it," and imagines that he can "kill" us with such an argument, he is seriously mistaken.'[75]

The fact that many Bolsheviks were prepared to oppose Lenin openly showed that while he was the first among them, he was not the only leader. As Krupskaya recalled, Lenin was considerate and attentive towards his closest followers, but none of them could consider himself a friend. All were of course professional revolutionaries, as cut off from ordinary people as they were from ordinary working life, and none had thought to ask themselves what right they had to take power, or why a civil war would bring happiness to the population, or why it was a 'revolutionary necessity' to destroy entire social groups. Yet Karl Radek could write: 'Lenin was our Moses who brought the slaves out of captivity and went with them into the promised land.'[76]

Among the comrades-in-arms who accompanied this new Moses while he was in exile abroad were Zinoviev and Kamenev, for whom Lenin had particularly warm feelings – before their opposition to the armed uprising, of course. He regarded them as 'writer-Bolsheviks, as well as organizers'.[77]

Grigory Yevseyevich Zinoviev, whose real name was Radomyslsky, joined the Bolsheviks after the Second Congress in 1903, and met Lenin in the same year. He spent long years in exile abroad, obediently carrying out the orders of his leader, and writing colourless articles on 'liquidationism', 'recallism' and 'Kautskianism', always in tune with the line being taken by Lenin. He was in a sense Lenin's shadow, following the leader when he returned to Russia in 1905 and, like him, making no impression on the revolution then going on. When that revolution failed and Lenin packed his bags and returned with Krupskaya to their cosy life in emigration, Zinoviev and his wife, Zinaïda Lilina, went along too. In December 1908 Lenin and his wife moved to Paris, where sure enough the Zinovievs soon turned up. Lenin went to Capri to give lectures at the Party school, and was joined by Zinoviev, who also accompanied him when he spent time at the Party's other school at Longjumeau, outside Paris. When Lenin took up residence in Cracow in 1912, Zinoviev shared the house with him; Lenin moved to Switzerland, and Zinoviev, as if attached by a cord, followed behind. When they were not together, Lenin kept in touch with his disciple by letter and telegram, of which there are more than two hundred in the archives.

When with German assistance Lenin returned to Russia in April 1917, he was not alone. With him was Zinoviev. Together they published an account – more of a justification – of their return in *Pravda* and *Izvestiya*.[78] Their attempt to explain why they had accepted Berlin's help did not produce the desired effect on public opinion. Finally, when Lenin had to go into hiding after the events of July 1917, Zinoviev accompanied him.

The main deviation Zinoviev made from Lenin's line was in October 1917, over the question of the armed uprising, when he and Kamenev published their dissent in the newspaper *Novaya Zhizn* (New Life). Whether they were acting out of a premonitory sense of the disaster to come, elementary caution or plain cowardice, it is impossible now to be sure. Lenin's response was unequivocal: 'I no longer count them as comrades.'[79] Once the coup had succeeded, the two returned to Lenin's favour, but the intimacy of the exile years was no longer there. Where Lenin's letters to Zinoviev had earlier been addressed to 'My dear friend' or 'Dear Grigori', they now acquired the more official form, 'Comrade Zinoviev'.

As a member of the Politburo and chief of the Petrograd Soviet, Zinoviev mostly carried out Lenin's will. He deviated from his leader's line on the question of war and peace at the Central Committee session of 24 January 1918, when he said: 'we are facing a difficult surgical operation, as this treaty will strengthen chauvinism in Germany and for a time weaken the [socialist] movement everywhere in the West. And there is another prospect beyond this, namely, the demise of the socialist republic.'[80] Soon, however, Zinoviev was back in line and supporting the 'indecent peace'.

Zinoviev was the obedient subordinate in this relationship, and although Lenin generally adopted a comradely tone in their correspondence, when the occasion called for it he issued orders in a peremptory tone.[81] On 7 January 1919, for example, he wrote: 'According to Lunacharsky, the Chekists Afanasiev, Kormilitsyn and others at the Detskoe Selo Cheka are guilty of drunkenness, rape and a range of other crimes; I demand that all the accused be arrested, that none of them be released, that the names of the special investigators be sent to me, because if the accused in such a case are not exposed and shot, then unprecedented disgrace will descend on the Petrograd Soviet of Commissars. Arrest Afanasiev.'[82]

Lenin went on 'training' his comrades, to use Krupskaya's expression, after the revolution. In the critical civil war days of October 1919, Zinoviev requested reinforcements for an assault on General Yudenich's White forces. Lenin sent a note to Trotsky with instructions for Zinoviev in Petrograd: 'It is *diabolically* important for us to finish with Yudenich (precisely to finish with him, finish him off). If the offensive has begun, couldn't you mobilize another 20,000 or so

Petrograd workers plus 10,000 or so bourgeois, put machine-guns at their backs, shoot a few hundred and put real pressure on Yudenich?'[83] (The reference to ten thousand bourgeois was cut by the editors of Lenin's collected works.) Zinoviev received many similar orders from Lenin, such as: 'Send the reliable ones to the Don, the unreliable ones to the concentration camps, the indeterminate to Oryol and similar ... provinces.'[84] As the rebellious poet Zinaïda Gippius wrote of the Lenin years: 'No revolution is redder than ours:/It's go to the front or to the wall, take your choice.'[85]

The archives contain two volumes of notes written by Zinoviev to Lenin and others during Politburo meetings. Most of it is insignificant, superficial and posturing. Nevertheless, his assistant, R. Pikel, and other staff members of his presidency of the Executive Committee of Comintern (ECCI) laboured between 1923 and 1929 to bring out sixteen volumes of his collected works. After Lenin's death, Stalin, having cunningly used Zinoviev and Kamenev in his fight against Trotsky, gradually shunted them further away from the pinnacle of power. Zinoviev continued to glorify Lenin and the Party, but his voice became more and more muffled.

In his book *Leninism* (1925) Zinoviev dwelt particularly on Lenin's position on the dictatorship of the Party: 'According to the teachings of Lenin, the dictatorship of the proletariat is realized through the dictatorship of the *avant garde*, through the dictatorship of the proletarian party ... In that sense we have a dictatorship of the Party.'[86]

Zinoviev was the first to attempt a biography of Lenin. In it he wrote that during the chaos of 1918, when everything was hanging by a thread, it was Lenin who saved the situation: 'One has to recall those anxious, crucial moments in order to understand that, had Comrade Lenin not been there, one cannot say what would have become of our revolution.'[87] With Lenin's departure from the scene the careers of Zinoviev, Kamenev and others quickly began to go into decline. Stalin gave Zinoviev minor posts – and also took them away: he was made a member of the Presidium of Gosplan (the State Planning Agency) for the Russian Federation, then a member of the council of the Lenin Institute, and a member of the board of the People's Commissariat of Education. His last post, as a member of the editorial board of the journal *Bolshevik*, lasted only four months. In November

1927, then again in October 1932 and finally in December 1934, he was expelled from the Party he had helped to create.

Having been as close as he had to Lenin, and knowing as much as he did about Stalin and what went on at the centre of power, Zinoviev was a doomed man. It is an unwritten law of dictatorships that only the supreme chief can possess such knowledge. The ten-year prison sentence that Zinoviev received at a secret trial in 1934 was duly altered after the show trial of August 1936 to the death penalty by shooting.

One wonders whether, as he waited for his end, Zinoviev mused on the triumphs he had so recently enjoyed at Lenin's side. What is certain is that in his last hours this professional revolutionary was praying only for the mercy of Stalin, whom he had so underestimated. As he left the court with fourteen other similarly condemned defendants, including Kamenev, Zinoviev still retained a flicker of hope. After all, Stalin had once before commuted his death sentence to ten years. At 4.30 a.m. on 25 August 1936, in solitary confinement in the NKVD prison, his hands shaking with terror, his stub of a pencil constantly breaking, Zinoviev struggled to write a declaration: 'I have said everything to the proletarian court about the crimes committed by me against the Party and the Soviet regime. They are known to the [government]. I ask to be believed that I am no longer an enemy and that I earnestly wish to dedicate my remaining strength to the socialist motherland. I hereby request that the [government] grant me a pardon.'[88]

Zinoviev, Kamenev and their co-defendants in fact had only a few hours left to live. Even before they had taken up their prison pencils to write their pleas for mercy, Kalinin, the nominal head of state, and Unshlikht, on behalf of the government, had signed a decree rejecting any further written petitions. Most of Lenin's comrades-in-arms would suffer the same fate.

Leo Borisovich Kamenev was almost as close to Lenin as was Zinoviev. He may have lacked Zinoviev's qualities as an orator and theorist, but he had more solidity and apparently more backbone. Also, he was one of the first to notice Stalin's dictatorial tendencies and to try to curtail them during Lenin's lifetime. At a meeting of the Politburo on 15 May 1920, Kamenev wrote Lenin no fewer than four notes, and received three in reply. The question under discussion was the reorganization of the People's Commissariat for Nationalities and government policy towards the Bashkir republic.[89] In one of his notes, Kamenev wrote that questions on national relations 'will not be properly prepared as long as there is no one at the centre who is constantly and systematically keeping track of this issue. Stalin is just an expert. If it is not offensive to Stalin, I put myself forward for the post.'[90]

Lenin did not want to offend Stalin, however, and replied: 'The job is not for you; shouldn't we form a commission? Or put you on the board of the C[ommissariat for] N[ationalities]?'[91] Kamenev would not give in so easily. He suggested to Lenin that in addition to the Commissariat, a Council should be formed with representatives of all the nationalities, adding, 'I am willing to be its chairman.'[92] Lenin appeared to agree, but in the decree on reorganizing the Commissariat, Stalin remained People's Commissar, with the new function of 'Chairman of the Council of Nationalities'.[93]

While Lenin was not as personally close to Kamenev as he was to Zinoviev, he nonetheless valued him highly. Among the more than 250 letters, notes and telegrams he sent to Kamenev, Lenin frequently entrusted him with delicate commissions. He often asked him to deal with family matters, such as arranging trips, organizing a monument for Inessa Armand after her death in September 1920, settling accommodation problems, and so on.[94] It was to Kamenev that he gave the task of 'bringing in Germans as teachers' to show the Russians how to manage things.[95] When Lenin resolved to make his separate peace with the Germans, he tried to mitigate this betrayal of the Allies by sending Kamenev to London in January 1918. The British, having only just released the Bolshevik exile Georgy Chicherin from Brixton Prison for his anti-war activities among London factory workers and future conscripts, not only rejected Kamenev's pseudo-diplomatic status, but arrested and deported him. He was interned on his way home through Finland, and it was not until August 1918 that he managed to get back to Moscow.

Kamenev edited the first edition of Lenin's collected works in twenty volumes, which began to appear during the leader's lifetime. Lenin moreover handed over his entire personal archives to Kamenev, who, as it happened, had tried as early as 1907 to publish Lenin's three-volume *For Twelve Years*, of which only one volume saw the light of day, and which sold so badly that the other two were never brought out.

Lenin took care of Zinoviev and Kamenev's material welfare in emigration, and when they were underground he dished out more money to them from Party coffers than to anyone else. On one occasion in 1913, he suggested that *Pravda* pay Kamenev, as a regular author, a monthly salary of seventy-five roubles. Any disagreements between Lenin and his two lieutenants were temporary, for they tried zealously to follow Lenin's policies, and it is hard to imagine Lenin as leader without them.[96]

Lenin had constantly to manoeuvre in the Politburo to ensure that the natural frictions that arose among the other Bolsheviks did not flare up into something worse. He was particularly exercised by the virtually open hostility between Trotsky and Stalin. The cause of this enmity was to some extent Trotsky's justified feeling that his role in the revolution was second only to Lenin's, and he did not hide his condescending attitude to his peers. They in turn tolerated him, but did not like him. Intellectual superiority is rarely forgiven. Lenin was also partly responsible, to the extent that he frequently extolled Trotsky for his part in the revolution and civil war. At the end of August 1918, for instance, he sent Trotsky a telegram, co-signed by the Chairman of the Central Committee Yakov Sverdlov: 'The treachery on the Saratov front, even though it was curtailed in time, has still caused extremely dangerous hesitation. We consider your immediate visit there absolutely essential, as your presence at the front has an effect on the soldiers and on the entire army.'[97] Despite news from Saratov that this particular plot had been smashed and the conspirators shot, Lenin felt it important to send Trotsky to the trouble spot. Trotsky's special armoured train ran from one front to the next throughout the civil war, Trotsky and his flying squad of leather-clad troops bringing new zeal to the forces. Lenin greatly valued Trotsky's ability to rally the men and inspire them with new vigour. He himself never went to the front, nor had he any intention of doing so. He preferred operating from afar, had little or no conception of military matters, and no desire to endanger his own life.

Another source of friction among members of the Politburo was caused by another of Lenin's closest followers, Anatoly Lunacharsky, over the attitude shown by Zinoviev and Kamenev, as well as by Lenin himself, towards cultural issues, notably the administration of theatres. In the summer of 1919, Lunacharsky protested against Kamenev's draconian measures. The conflict intensified when, on Kamenev's instructions, the Moscow Soviet ordered the closure of a number of the capital's theatres, ostensibly because of a fuel shortage.[98] When Lunacharsky protested to Lenin, Kamenev accused him of intrigue, and in turn appealed to Lenin and Trotsky jointly: 'I am shocked to the core by Lunacharsky's letter. Never before in any clash has anyone accused me of being a schemer. This is the second time Lunacharsky has done this behind my back, while maintaining the friendliest of relations. It really is intolerable. I shall henceforth be merciless towards him. He plays dirty.' Lenin tried to smooth things over by adding to Kamenev's note, 'There's no trace of any accusation of scheming,'[99] and thus terminated a squabble that had threatened to turn into a major quarrel. He was perfectly happy to set his enemies against each other, but his plans had no room for enmity among his comrades.

Lenin was always tactful and correct in his relations with his comrades-in-arms, but he maintained a certain distance from them all. He valued zeal and commitment in them, and so had high regard for Georgy Chicherin and Jacob Ganetsky, although they were perhaps aides and accomplices rather than comrades-in-arms. He was, however, very open with them, and gave them the most delicate tasks. Chicherin, especially, could sense what Lenin wanted from a mere hint. A former employee of the tsarist Foreign Ministry, an aristocrat by birth, homosexual, in poor health and overweight, Chicherin was interested only in foreign policy and music. He left no memoirs about the formation of Soviet foreign policy, but he did write a book on Mozart, whom he described as 'the ideal of beauty and the embodiment of the cosmic sense of present-day, universal, flaming life, of the human spirit and the unbounded'.

According to Louis Fischer, who knew Chicherin well, Chicherin 'had an anti-West European, notably anti-British, bias which resembled tsarist Russia's and sprang from Anglo–Russian rivalry in Central Asia and the Near East. British intervention in Soviet Russia strengthened the bias. Europe interested Chicherin because of its power, Asia because of its possibilities. British strength curtailed the possibilities.'[100] This did not prevent him, when the Red Army was marching on Warsaw, from ludicrously suggesting to Lenin that they should try to form 'volunteer units' from among the English workers to help the Red Army. Lenin agreed, but the idea went no further than their exchange of notes.[101]

Chicherin fully supported Lenin's German policy as a weapon against both the Allied intervention and the White movement. As Lenin wrote in August 1918: 'No one asked the Germans for "help", but we did agree *when* and *how* they, the Germans, would carry out their offensive against Murmansk and [the White General] Alexeev. It was a coincidence of interests. We would have been idiots not to have taken advantage of it.'[102]

Just as in the October coup Lenin relied on German financial help, so in the civil war, for which he had been so keen, he exploited the German factor. Fortuitously, Chicherin was a close friend of Count Brockdorff-Rantzau, the German ambassador in Moscow who succeeded Count Wilhelm Mirbach when he was assassinated by a Left SR in July 1918. Brockdorff-Rantzau was an avid supporter of Germany's 'active Eastern policy', which suited Lenin's interests. Lenin always believed that if revolution occurred in Germany, it would be impossible to prevent the ensuing world conflagration.

Until he became incapacitated by his last illness, Lenin probably had more telephone conversations with Chicherin than with anyone else, discussing diplomatic initiatives as if they belonged naturally in the revolutionary context. On 27 January 1922 a special session of the government agreed the composition of the Soviet delegation to the forthcoming Genoa Conference, which was expected to settle the question of the war debts incurred by the Tsar, and to normalize relations between the former belligerents and Soviet Russia. Lenin was to head the delegation. A telegram to Chicherin from Leonid Krasin and Jan Berzin, his emissaries in London, however, warned that it would be 'inadvisable' for Lenin to go to Italy, owing to the presence there of numerous Russian terrorist groups, including 'Savinkovites, Wrangelites and Fascists'. Lenin agreed at once, writing to the Politburo: 'The reason given by Krasin, among other reasons, excludes the possibility of a trip to any country, by me, as well as by Trotsky and Zinoviev.'[103]

Chicherin proposed that Russia accept some of the terms offered by the Allies, while putting forward counter-claims of its own over the debts. Then, having reduced 'our counter-claims *lower* than their demands', the Soviets would be able to obtain a new loan.[104] Lenin wanted to go further. He wrote 'arch-secretly' to Chicherin: 'It would suit us if Genoa broke down, though *not through our doing*, of course. Talk this over with Litvinov and Ioffe and drop me a line. Of course, this must not be written down *even in secret documents. Return this to me and I'll burn it.* We'll get a *better* loan without Genoa if Genoa is wrecked not by us. For instance, the fool Henderson and Co. can be very helpful to us if we give them the right nudge.'[105] Arthur Henderson, the leader of the British Labour Party, represented moderation. Lenin's idea was to help the Labour Party win power, and then mobilize the Communist Party of Great Britain to undermine them.

Chicherin cautiously objected: 'We desperately, ultra-insistently, need the West's help: a loan, concessions, economic agreements . . . And, as this is the case, we shouldn't turn our backs on them, we should come to an understanding . . . You are undoubtedly wrong if you think we can get a loan without Genoa, if we fall out with England . . . If we start smashing glass at Genoa, they'll just shy way from us.'[106]

Lenin wanted a lot: he wanted both to 'smash glass' and to get a loan. Chicherin, though he was more civilized and more liberal than Lenin, was not offended by his leader's harshness. When the famous Norwegian explorer Fridtjof Nansen, now the League of Nations representative on prisoners of war and refugees, wanted to visit Soviet Russia, Chicherin supported the request, but Lenin had other ideas: 'I don't think it's time to let him in. We have no one to watch him. He'll *catch us napping*. If other members of the Politburo are in favour of letting him in, I'll table an amendment to the effect that absolutely no one should accompany him.'[107] Lenin was a better Chekist even than Dzerzhinsky.

As a rule, however, Chicherin followed Lenin's line. When an American journalist called Beatty wanted to come to Russia in July 1921, Chicherin wrote to Lenin: 'Beatty's visit will bring nothing but trouble. The main point is that it will mean letting in many Americans. At the present time, it would be better not to allow unsupervised observation of our activities.'[108] Lenin agreed.

Adolf Ioffe, another diplomat who was highly regarded by Lenin, despite his frequent differences with Chicherin, left unpublished fragments of his highly informative memoirs. In the early years, he wrote, Lenin's foreign policy was entirely 'staked on world revolution'. Before sending Ioffe as ambassador to Berlin, Lenin told him that the embassy there must prepare and distribute agitational material on how to create a revolutionary situation, that he must use money for these purposes, and that he should 'throw a fat slice to the local Russian intelligentsia who agree to work for us'.[109]

Ioffe, who was to shoot himself in 1927, was not one of Lenin's inner circle, although they met quite often and engaged in correspondence. His memoirs reveal Lenin as a cynical but pragmatic politician, for whom nothing was sacred apart from power and the revolution. As the Menshevik Fedor Stepun put it: 'What is essential about Lenin's psychology is that he did not see the goals of the revolution, but only the *revolution as a goal*.'[110]

Among Lenin's aides, both pre- and post-revolutionary, an important back-room part was played by Jacob Stanislavovich Ganetsky, known also as Hanecki, Fuerstenberg, Borel, Hendricek, Frantiszek, Nikolai, Marian Keller and Kuba. Issues involving Ganetsky were discussed by the Politburo more than two dozen times. They included his new posts, trips to Western capitals for financial purposes, reviews of his remuneration and financing, journeys abroad for medical treatment and to recover documents that had belonged to Lenin. Despite the fact that he was not a front-rank politician, his reputation and influence were considerable. In money matters he was almost certainly Lenin's most intimate and trusted agent. With Parvus, Ganetsky had been responsible for transmitting German money into Bolshevik coffers for 'peace propaganda', and he conducted negotiations on financial matters with foreign delegations, as well as handling personal financial tasks for Lenin. On more than one occasion he was accused of machinations by his colleagues on the Politburo and his personal dossier was reviewed, but Lenin always stood up for him. As Lenin wrote to Ioffe in Berlin in the summer of 1918: 'Krasin and Ganetsky, being businesslike people, will help you and the whole affair will be put right.'[111]

Lenin's 'cashier' carried out the most delicate missions abroad, as well as buying food and goods for Lenin and Krupskaya.[112] Ganetsky knew the state of Bolshevik funds both before and after the revolution, and it is amazing that he survived as long as he did after Lenin's death. Having handled millions, when he was finally arrested in July 1937 he was found to be in possession of all of two dollars and a collection of antique revolvers, which had been a hobby. The accusation against him was the standard one of being 'an agent of German and Polish intelligence'. But once he started revealing the facts of his close association with Lenin and of Lenin's attitude to him, 'German' was dropped from the charge-sheet, as it was felt to be too dangerous to raise this connection when Lenin's name was mentioned.

Ganetsky, his wife and his son were all shot during Stalin's terror. His daughter Anna was arrested and, still wearing her light summer dress, sent straight to a concentration camp in the north, where she endured many long years. NKVD Lieutenant Shavelev left a brief note in the case file: 'The sentence of death on Jacob Stanislavovich Ganetsky (also known as Fuerstenberg) was carried out in Moscow on 26 November 1937. Notice of execution is filed in the Special Archive of the 1st Special Section of the NKVD of the USSR, vol. 2, page 395.'[113] Most of the Lenin cohort of 1917 would go the way of Ganetsky.

As a rule, the roles of Lenin's comrades-in-arms, whether in the epicentre of internal Party disputes or in the revolution and civil war, were as part of the evolution, the completion and the drama of the Bolshevik experiment. Lenin was such a grandiose historical figure, however, that his followers could never be more than a complementary appendage to him. Without Lenin, only Trotsky and Stalin had independent historical significance. The portrait gallery of Lenin's closest followers, as they disappear into the gloom of the past, is a long row of the shadows of men who believed in the delusions of the Bolshevik leader.

World Revolution

Lenin was not, like Thomas More, Robert Owen or Campanelli, a Utopian philosopher in the direct sense, but he was nevertheless the progenitor of a Utopia which survived for much of the twentieth century. And it did not merely inhabit people's minds: in its name Lenin launched unprecedented efforts, and for a time the mirage of a world revolutionary conflagration assumed solid contours – Russia, Germany, Hungary, Italy, Persia, China, Spain.

Lenin referred incessantly to this desired effect. Speaking on 17 July 1921 at the Executive Committee of Comintern, he declared: 'Only stupidities can impede the victory of Communism in France, England and Germany.'[114] His speech remained unpublished in the archives, whether for tactical reasons or because his comrades thought it was nonsense is not clear.

Lenin arrived in Petrograd in March 1919 for the funeral of Mark Yelizarov, his sister Anna's husband, and on the evening of 13 March spoke in the Iron Hall of the People's House, where he gave his ideas more solid content. He declared that the Versailles Treaty would lead to the sharpening of contradictions between the victors:

> France is ready to invade Italy, and they did not share their spoils; Japan is arming herself against America ... The working masses of Paris, London and New York have translated the Soviet's words into their own languages ... We are guaranteed full victory because the imperialists of other countries are bent double, the workers have already woken up from their euphoria and deception. The Soviet regime has already won the battle for the minds of the workers of the world. Once more we tell ourselves and we tell you that our victory is guaranteed on a world scale ... We shall soon see the birth of a worldwide federative Soviet republic.[115]

Apart from a contemporary newspaper report in *Severnaya Kommuna* [Northern Commune], this nonsensical speech never saw the light of day.

Lenin was not, of course, the author of the idea of world revolution. The slogan 'Proletarians of all lands unite' was formulated by the founders of 'scientific socialism' in the *Communist Manifesto*. It was only towards the end of his wartime exile in Switzerland that Lenin became preoccupied with the idea of world revolution. He was cut off from Russia, dealing with the trivial cares of life in a neutral country, troubled as always by squabbles and rows, and engaged in endless correspondence with Inessa Armand, Ganetsky and others, and only a few months away from his sensational departure from Berne, via Germany to Stockholm.

Whether from lack of action, some aberration of political vision or his isolation from reality, Lenin turned his attention to Swiss social democracy. In letters, theses and addresses to Swiss social democratic leaders, aimed at raising support for defeatism among the belligerent governments, he called on them to agitate for 'an immediate socialist revolution in Switzerland'.[116] Realizing the impracticality of this idea, he then argued: 'But of course the great powers will not tolerate a socialist Switzerland and the first shoots of a socialist revolution in Switzerland will be smothered by the colossal overwhelming force of these powers.' On the other hand, he went on: if the great powers interfered in the affairs of a small country, then 'that would just be a prologue to revolution breaking out all over Europe'.[117]

Even at the beginning of 1917, when Lenin publicly announced in Zurich that, like other old men – he was forty-six – he would not live to see it, he continued to insist on his theory of the coming revolution. In a long letter to his Swiss opponent H. Greulich in mid-January 1917, Lenin asserted that the Swiss proletariat faced two paths. The first was to remain under threat of being drawn into the war, 'to register 100,000 dead, and to put yet more billions of war profits into the pockets of the Swiss bourgeoisie'. The second path was 'to call forth the socialist revolution'.[118] It is not surprising that such pseudo-revolutionary exercises, which embarrassed his comrades, were not published during his lifetime.

There were not many people who would promote Switzerland as the detonator of world revolution. Lenin, however, genuinely believed that he was expressing the view of the overwhelming majority, not just of his handful of followers, but of the 'toilers' of the entire planet. In December 1916 he had written that one must make 'the greatest sacrifices for socialism. For the interests of nine-tenths of all mankind.'[119] How this civilian émigré could know that 90 per cent of the world's population was thirsting for his particular brand of socialism, and ready to make great sacrifices for it, is hard to fathom.

Lenin was a man of extremes: he could see a mortal threat in the least triviality, and *vice versa*. In a first, faint sign he would discern the beginnings of the greatest event. He was frequently wrong, but continued to prophesy constantly. After the seizure of power, he accompanied practically all his speeches with the assertion that the world proletariat was 'coming to the aid of the Bolsheviks', that class solidarity would 'guarantee victory over the bourgeoisie'. But generalizations such as these were producing no concrete results. What was needed was an international Communist organization, of which he first spoke in Switzerland in the autumn of 1914 and in whose creation after 1917 he was himself active. But who was to constitute such an organization? The Bolshevik Party was established only in Russia, although it had affinities with the Spartakus Bund in Germany. Lenin, having undertaken to form this 'worldwide party of the dictatorship of the proletariat', was at times despondent: whom to unite? The revolutionary Angelica Balabanova recalled Lenin, having dreamed up the idea of such a party, suddenly announcing: 'Most likely nothing will come of it.'[120] He recruited the effervescent Zinoviev to bring the idea to life.

Thus it was that in February 1919 several invitations were broadcast over the radio from Moscow to 'all those who share the views of the Russian socialists now in power' to attend an international Communist conference. This revolutionary call, scarcely more audible than the whine of a mosquito, was heard by no one – not that there were many to whom it was addressed. Eugen Leviné and Hugo Eberlein of the German Communist Party left Berlin for Russia, but only the latter arrived in Moscow. Zinoviev meanwhile had established the Communist Parties of Austria and Hungary out of sympathizers among prisoners of war. Delegations were also 'formed' from Russia, Ukraine, Belorussia, Latvia, Poland, Finland, Armenia, the Volga Germans, the vaguely named 'Peoples of Eastern Russia' and, even more nebulous, various 'international groups'. Fifty-two delegates were scraped together – only thirty-four of them mandated to sign anything.

Apart from Lenin, the only well known figures from the international socialist movement were Eberlein (Germany), Kuusinen (Finland), Platten (Switzerland), Skrypnik (Ukraine) and Sadoul (France). The meeting, which opened on 2 March 1919, was chaired by Lenin, Vorovsky, Chicherin, the Chekist Unshlikht, and the Tsar's murderer Mikhail Yurovsky. There could be no doubt that this 'international' body was going to be dominated and indeed run by the Russian Communists. It was a Bolshevik proposal – acclaimed by the other 'parties' – to constitute the meeting as the Third Communist International. Henceforth, the Bolshevik Party and its Central Committee had an international tributary.

Opening the Congress, Lenin declared that 'our meeting is of enormous world-historical significance. It demonstrates the collapse of all the illusions of bourgeois democracy ... In Germany, for instance, civil war is a fact.'[121] The proletariat, he went on, must 'realize its supremacy' by means of 'the Soviet system with the dictatorship of the proletariat'. The Soviet system, he declared, had 'conquered not only in backward Russia, but also in the most developed country of Europe, Germany, and also in the oldest capitalist country, England'.[122] Signs that councils of workers' deputies in several countries were attempting to function as economic organizations were interpreted by Lenin as a 'victory for the Soviet system'.

Zinoviev was appointed President of the new organization, with Balabalova as Secretary. If Zinoviev's regular utterances were to be believed, it seemed the planet was already consumed by the flames of world revolution. 'The victory of Communism in the whole of Europe is totally inevitable. The movement is progressing with such dizzy speed,' he shrilled, 'that it can be said with assurance that in a year we'll start to forget that there ever was a struggle for Communism in Europe, for in a year the whole of Europe will be Communist. The pressure on the stronghold of capitalism has begun. The revolution has come!'[123] It seemed to the fanatics that they had only to shout the idea into space for it to become reality.

In his hour-long opening address on 4 March, Lenin was savage in his attacks on what he called 'pure democracy', with its freedom of assembly, speech and the press, all of which he dismissed as meaningless. He was as good as his word in this regard: from October 1917, Russians would no longer have to endure the 'empty slogans of pure democracy'. For Lenin, however, that was only the start: the same order must be established throughout the world. When he closed the Congress on 6 March he repeated that the victory of the proletarian revolution was secure, and that the foundation of the international Soviet republic was at hand.[124]

Lenin believed that the first country, following Russia, in which revolution was imminent was Germany, where military defeat would lead to the rapid radicalization of the war-weary proletariat. One year after the coup in Russia, on 9 November 1918, Karl Liebknecht proclaimed the German Soviet Republic. Sailors rose in Kiel, thousands of workers came out on the streets of Berlin. It looked as if Liebknecht was about to do in Germany what Lenin had done in

Russia. However, the cooler heads of the social democrats Friedrich Ebert and Philipp Scheidemann prevailed, and the 'revolutionary current' was redirected into a more peaceful channel. Instead of lynching generals, as had been done in Russia, the German Communists sought their support in preserving time-honoured German 'order'. An alliance was established. The government was called, Moscow-fashion, a Council of People's Commissars. Socialist influence, however, soon declined, and although in January 1919 Berlin experienced a few days of armed clashes, Lenin's German disciples were unable to turn the imperialist war into a civil war.

Russian historians have been silent on the fact that the Soviet embassy in Berlin, headed by Adolf Ioffe, was, in Ioffe's own words, 'the headquarters of the German revolution'. Ioffe recalled, in private conversation with Louis Fischer, that he had a hundred thousand marks at his disposal to buy weapons for the revolutionaries. 'Tons of anti-monarchist and anti-war literature were printed and distributed at my embassy's expense ... Almost every day after dark, Independent Socialists slipped into the embassy to consult me.'[125] But it was all in vain. The German people did not surrender to the rabble-rousing – on this occasion. The brutal murder of Rosa Luxemburg and Karl Liebknecht in prison in 1919 marked the defeat of the radical, 'Russian' variant of the revolution. Moscow's financial help, its arms purchases for the workers and the Bolshevik 'instructors' it sent, did not help.

Moscow naturally accused the social democrats of treachery, but the fault lay elsewhere: neither the German workers nor the intelligentsia found the Leninist model appropriate, while the army, the bureaucracy and the peasantry were downright hostile to the idea of revolution. The defeated German army did not, unlike the Russian army, fall to pieces. The level-headed Germans began to defend the Weimar Republic of Friedrich Ebert and Philipp Scheidemann far more effectively than the liberals and the army in Russia had defended Kerensky. The internal situation in Germany, moreover, was fundamentally different from that in Russia. The 'objective conditions' for the transfer from capitalism to socialism, trumpeted by Communist ideologues long after Lenin, were extremely superficial in Germany. 'Eleven months of Bolshevik dictatorship in Russia,' Louis Fischer rightly pointed out, 'killed what taste the SPD, and [their leader Karl]

Kautsky, had for revolution. Bolshevism needed a Communist Germany and helped make it impossible.'[126] It was not 'the renegade Kautsky', as Lenin called him, who was responsible for the defeat of the German revolution.

Yet, even when the Bolshevik regime was at its most desperate, Lenin continued to look to Germany, where, he believed, if it were only possible to smash the 'traitorous' social democrats, the revolution would catch fire. It was thus in the context of the 'German idea' that one of Lenin's most audacious adventures was undertaken. In 1920, sensing that he was going to win the civil war in Russia, he insisted on shifting his aim to world revolution. As Trotsky recalled, 'we took a risk – this time at Lenin's prompting – in feeling out the Polish bourgeoisie with the bayonet.'[127] The documents clearly show that Lenin was indeed the chief architect of the 'Warsaw Campaign', which had as its aim the 'sovietization of Poland' and the 'revolutionization of Germany'. At Politburo meetings he behaved like a gambler who has made a big win and wants to double his money. On balance, the rest of the Politburo only put up token resistance. Lenin, who had little understanding of strategy, was running the campaign himself, and it ended in ignominious defeat.

On 17 March 1920 he signalled Stalin, then in the south: 'Don't drag out the Crimean operation . . . We've just heard from Germany that a battle is in progress in Berlin and that the Spartakists have occupied part of the city. We don't know who will win, but we must speed up occupation of the Crimea so that our hands are free, as a civil war in Germany may compel us to move west to help the Communists.'[128] This message was inspired by the so-called Kapp putsch of 10–17 March. It was suppressed, and its organizer, Wolfgang Kapp, escaped to Sweden.

Among the many orders and notes Lenin issued as he excitedly prepared to 'feel out the Polish bourgeoisie with the bayonet', was a set of proposals to Unshlikht, his representative on Polish affairs, then on the Western front:

> Let me have your assessment, and that of other Polish comrades, on the following tactics:
> 1. We declare with great ceremony that we shall guarantee to the Polish workers and peasants a frontier further to the east than the one offered by Curzon and the Entente;

2. We will harness all possible force to finish off Pilsudski;

3. We shall enter Poland proper only for the shortest possible time to arm the workers and leave immediately;

4. How likely and how soon do you think a soviet revolution will take place in Poland?[129]

This document is as frank as it is cynical. Lenin was prepared to make more territorial concessions at Russia's expense in order to win the support of the Polish 'workers and peasants'. The Red Army would invade Poland only to arm 'the workers', yet he could still ask when the soviet revolution would take place. The onward advance to Germany was not stressed at this point.

Lenin sent his insistent, if sometimes incoherent, instructions to military councils and headquarters. He ordered Trotsky's deputy Nikolai Sklyansky to tell Smilga, a Political Commissar in the Red Army, 'that (after the grain harvest) he has to recruit each and every adult man into the forces. He has to ... Each and every Belorussian peasant must be mobilized. Then they will thrash the Poles even without Budyonny [and the Red Cavalry].'[130]

With Warsaw now so close, it seemed that triumph was at hand. Lenin went on sending his instructions over the heads of the Military Revolutionary Committee and chiefs of staff, sometimes without bothering to have them encoded, and mostly to Sklyansky. On the question of transferring divisions from the Petrograd area to Brest, Lenin urged: 'If it is possible from the military point of view (we'll smash Wrangel anyway), then from the *political* point of view it is arch-important to crush Poland.' But Sklyansky already sensed impending disaster outside Warsaw: the commander-in-chief Mikhail Tukhachevsky was moving fresh troops on Warsaw 'not so much to crush the Poles as to prevent them from exploiting their success and pushing us back'. Lenin refused to hear this, remaining convinced that it was possible to 'thrash' the Poles. He ordered Sklyansky to 'pile on the pressure: we must at all costs take Warsaw in three to five days'.[131] As never before, Lenin studied the operational map he had installed in his Kremlin office, and saw that the Red Cavalry was approaching the German frontier. On 17 August 1920 he cabled Sklyansky: 'The Germans are writing that the Red Army is close to Graudenz. Couldn't we pile on the pressure and cut Poland off from Danzig altogether?'[132]

Thousands more Communists were sent to the front on Lenin's orders. On 19 August 1920 the Kremlin cabled the Petrograd Party Committee: 'The Poland–Wrangel front demands the highest pressure of force. [We] suggest you concentrate all forces and means for a front that will determine the fate of the international revolution for a long time to come ... Thousands of Communist men and women are needed ... Do not waste an hour. Set a fresh example to the Party organizations of the entire country.' The cable was signed by Lenin, Krestinsky, Trotsky, Stalin and Bukharin.[133]

Warsaw was a stepping-stone to Germany, as far as Lenin was concerned. The adventure cost the Red Army more than 120,000 peasant lives. The divisions that were despatched to the Polish and Prussian frontiers were virtually without ammunition, or any reconnaissance, engineering or transport services. In what the Poles described as 'the miracle at Warsaw', many Russians died, tens of thousands were taken prisoner, and the fate of them is not known to this day.

Lenin was never troubled or repentant over this episode. Nor did he ever refer to the Red Army men who perished in Polish captivity. 'Sentimentality,' he wrote, 'is as much a crime as looking after number one in a war.'[134] The SR leader Viktor Chernov, who knew Lenin well, confirmed that, 'For Lenin, nothing could be worse than sentimentality.' Lenin was overjoyed, with Trotsky, when he succeeded in turning the world war into a civil war. The fact that it cost Russia thirteen million lives and drove two million of his countrymen abroad was of no matter. The harsh philosophy of Bolshevism freed him from the torments of conscience. He had, in Chernov's words, 'permitted himself to go beyond conscience'.[135]

Nor did Lenin feel shame for having humiliated Russia by losing a war against a former province and having to pay reparations of tens of millions of gold roubles. He merely initialled the routine advice-slips of cash consignments to Warsaw, such as, for instance, one which reported that another 5,010,900 gold roubles had been sent.[136]

After the 1920 Treaty of Riga, Poland gained fifteen entire districts and a further eleven in part from Russia. The population of this area was 6.75 million, of whom some 400,000 were Poles.[137] Thus had Lenin 'felt out' the Poles with his bayonet. In the name of world revolution he had sacrificed many thousands of lives, thrown to the wind vast sums of the nation's wealth, and brought unprecedented humiliation.

Money for Lenin was less an element of the market, which the Bolsheviks had utterly destroyed, than a political weapon, a means for attaining the goals of Comintern. Soon after the formation of that body, Lenin conceived the idea of using the gold and money reserves left by the tsarist state to create new Communist parties, to undermine the social democrats in Western Europe, and to provoke revolutionary activity by the proletariat and colonial peoples against their oppressors. Cash and precious stones became virtually the chief instrument for revolutionizing countries, even entire continents. The gold confiscated in vast quantities from the old regime, the bourgeoisie and the Church went straight to Comintern, often sticking to the fingers of enterprising businessmen who buzzed in large numbers around the Russian honeypot. Many millionaires and billionaires outside Russia received their start-up capital from Lenin.

Lenin often questioned the State Depository, the People's Commissariat for Foreign Trade and the Main Board of the Gold, Platinum and Diamond Industry about the availability, movement and sale of valuables, a great part of which was destined for Comintern's needs. He was told, for instance, in June 1920 about some of the quantities that had been sent abroad 'for revolutionary purposes': 'gold coins – 383,448,144; supplementary – 101,000,000; diamonds – 140,006,036 carats'. Unclear as to the meaning of these figures, he wrote to Deputy Foreign Commissar Maxim Litvinov: 'Write your opinion on this document, please, and send it back to me as top secret.' In his reply, Litvinov suggested that, in addition to trading in precious objects abroad, the government should also sell stocks and shares, and added that more control was needed over the gold-mining operations at Bodaibo in the Irkutsk fields.[138] There are numerous documents showing the extent of the Bolsheviks' dealings in state treasure. In one period of ten days, for instance, the State Depository reported to Lenin that it had prepared for use, shipment, reserve and transfer for Polish reparations, support for Communist parties, 'the purchase of agents' and so on: diamonds worth 55,887,000 gold roubles; 160,000 gems; 91,827 puds (3,305 tonnes) of gold-scrap; 1,362,087 gold objects; 309,224 puds (11,132 tonnes) of silver. The list goes on.[139]

When the Bolsheviks seized power, they found that the State Bank contained 1.0643 billion gold roubles in ingot and coin, not including 117 million in gold belonging to the Romanian government[140] or the large quantity of valuables held outside the Bank, or the platinum, gold and gems which they began to squander with such extravagance. It was with such wealth at his disposal that Lenin could sign the Brest-Litovsk agreement according to which Russia – which, let us recall, had not lost the war against Germany – was made to pay Germany six billion marks, in the form of 245.5 tonnes of gold.

Seven months after the seizure of power, on 20 May 1918, the Sovnarkom ordered the removal of significant gold reserves from Moscow, Tambov, Nizhni Novgorod and Samara to Kazan on the Volga. Fearing that the Germans might seize the gold in the capital, they scattered it to the periphery with little concern for its safety. 1,440 tonnes of gold and platinum ingots and 1,080 tonnes of silver soon fell into the hands of Czech former prisoners of war and White forces.[141] In February 1920, when the White leader Admiral Kolchak was finally crushed, Soviet forces ostensibly returned to 'the revolutionary people' eighteen railway-wagonloads of valuables, but a third of the original haul had vanished without trace.[142]

In a very brief period the Bolsheviks squandered an almost incredible amount of the nation's wealth. It is not easy to trace the ways in which all this money was used for Comintern, especially as much of it was dispensed on the authority of a simple note, or even a word, from Lenin to one or other of the Central Committee's many commissions. For instance, on 16 October 1919 Lenin wrote to S. Yelyava, the chairman of the Turkestan Commission, advising him to establish a base in Turkestan to supply 'the peoples of the East' with arms: 'We must help them in their struggle with imperialism.' He added that it was 'essential, of course, to conduct this business under conditions of arch-secrecy (as we used to do in the days of the Tsar)', and remarked that 'money is no object, we'll send enough gold and foreign gold currency.' He concluded: 'Let me know about anything important that happens and about your needs.'[143]

Lenin stressed the importance of providing financial support for spreading propaganda throughout Europe. Writing to Jan Berzin, the Soviet ambassador to Switzerland, in October 1918 (before Comintern even came into being), he urged that Berzin 'should not mind spending millions on illegal links with France and on agitation among the

French and English'.[144] A few days later he insisted that Berzin devote three-quarters of his time to 'organizing agitation', using Germans, Italians and Frenchmen for the purpose: 'As for the Russian idiots, dish out the work for them: send newspaper cuttings here, but not from odd numbers as these fools have been doing up to now.' He recommended that leftists be invited from various countries: 'Appoint agents from among them, pay them extremely generously for their trips and their work. To hell with your official work: give it minimum attention. Give your maximum attention to publishing and to illegal trips.'[145]

The Secretary of Comintern, Angelica Balabanova, recalled in memoirs published after she had left the USSR that when she was in Sweden as a Comintern emissary Lenin had demanded that she and the other Soviet representatives abroad 'spare no money. Spend millions, many millions.' She was told to use the money to support left-wing organizations, to undermine oppositional groups, to discredit certain individuals and so on.[146] Balabanova took him at his word. On 18 December 1919 Lenin was informed that Balabanova had 'given half a million in objects and fifty thousand in foreign currency to Grunzberg', a Comintern agent.[147]

From the moment Comintern – a wholly Moscow-run operation – was brought into being, it came under the direct influence of Lenin's special services, and in due course the State Political Administration (GPU) and NKVD would control the central administrative body of this 'worldwide Communist party'. Some national Communist parties, or more properly their leaders, went straight onto the payroll of the Russian Central Committee as soon as they were founded, although this was not made public. In a telegram to Stalin, Litvinov warned that 'the serial numbers of the banknotes we took out of the bank have been recorded. We can't use this money for Comintern purposes. Nonetheless, when Bordiga [an Italian Communist leader] was arrested, they found pounds from London on him.'[148] One of the Finnish Communists in Helsinki, E. Rakhia, informed Lenin that he needed ten million Finnish marks to pay the 'wages' of his functionaries. Lenin wrote 'Agreed' on the request.

Many parties were wholly dependent on Moscow in other ways. On holiday in the Black Sea resort of Sukhumi in January 1923, Zinoviev wrote to Moscow that it was time to 'start work on writing the programmes for the parties that don't yet have one'.[149] Such parties were virtually created as puppets by Moscow. Even the most routine and inoffensive decisions had to be referred to the Kremlin. In August 1921 the 'little bureau', or organizing group, of ECCI, chaired by Mátyás Rákosi, a refugee from the Hungarian Soviet Republic, decided that the national sections should hold a 'party week' in early October, and asked the Politburo if such an event could also be held in Russia. On behalf of the Central Committee, Zinoviev replied that 'the "week" should be postponed to 7–15 November, and limited only to propaganda.'[150]

Even the rations allocated to Comintern functionaries in Moscow were more meagre than those given to Central Committee workers. Several times, Comintern officials asked Lenin and his inner circle to consider increasing their ration of flour, meat, fish, butter and so on.[151] ECCI rubber-stamped whatever instructions came from the Bolshevik leadership: on stepping up the attack on the Mensheviks, on social democrats in parliament and on revolutionary tactics to be applied east and west. The Bolshevik Central Committee was in complete control of the so-called 'worldwide Communist organization'. For instance, it was the Politburo, chaired by Lenin, that determined the date, place, agenda, list of speakers and appointment of functionaries before the Second Congress of Comintern convened in the summer of 1920.[152] From its very inception, the puppet body was no more than an international sect of Bolshevik agents, agitators and special operatives inside the 'fraternal' parties and trade unions.

Lenin especially favoured agitation. He believed that it was necessary only to explain Comintern's goals to the 'oppressed masses', recount the lessons of the Soviets in Russia, point out the universal nature of the dictatorship of the proletariat, and thousands and then millions of toilers would take the path leading to world revolution. The most varied plans were drawn up with these aims. On Lenin's initiative, Lev Karakhan, a senior official of the Foreign Commissariat, prepared a proposal that the Central Committee should regularly allocate large sums for Bolshevik agitators sent to countries in the East. The fee – to be paid, prudently, on their return – for a trip to Korea and China was ten thousand gold roubles, and for southern China, twenty thousand. Persia, India and other Asian countries had their own rates of pay.[153]

At the Second Comintern Congress, Lenin urged that it was important to begin organizing 'the Soviet movement in the non-capitalist
countries. Soviets are a possibility there; they will not be workers'
soviets, they will be peasants' soviets or soviets of toilers.'[154] The
ultimate aim was the same: the creation of a worldwide Soviet republic.
Lenin's unquestioning belief in agitation almost led him on one
occasion to be hoodwinked. A Comintern agent in the Balkans, known
only as 'E', reported to Moscow: 'We can seize Constantinople using
the Wrangel forces we have propagandized, in whose eyes Soviet
Russia's prestige is very high. We could then hand it over to the
Kemalists. The Wrangelites could easily take Andrianopol and Sal-
onika, our commissars will get there, and the tottering Balkan governments will be overthrown, which will have a huge effect elsewhere in
the Balkans.' 'E' asked for more money. Lenin was hesitant; suppose
the world revolution was indeed started from this unexpected quarter?
He conferred with Chicherin and Trotsky. Trotsky, though a revolutionary through and through, cautioned that the proposal was an
unacceptable risk. Lenin reluctantly agreed.[155]

Why was Lenin so committed to the idea of world revolution? Why
in the early years of the Soviet regime was he literally obsessed with
it, and why not long before his death did he go cold on it? The fact
is that for a long time he did not believe his regime would survive.
He saw world revolution as an aid to the Russian revolution, as its
defence, and in time this became written into the future goals of the
Russian Communists. Lenin sincerely believed, as he said in Petrograd
in March 1919, that Soviet Russia would 'win a feeling of support
and the attention of the whole world', which meant that 'our complete
victory is secure.'[156]

In the years 1919 to 1921 Lenin again behaved like a gambler,
throwing the dice of class conflict, money, gold, agitators, and his
own authority in order to ignite the flames of an international conflagration. The Polish campaign had a sobering effect on him, but the
ideas behind it survived for many decades after his death, changing
from frontal assault on capitalism to long-drawn-out siege tactics.
When Lenin was already seriously ill, he read with satisfaction the
draft of a speech Chicherin was to read at the Genoa Conference
in March 1922, and underlined the following passages: 'We Communists regard violent overthrow and the use of bloody struggle as

inevitable ... ; We, for whom the historical concept includes the use of force ... ; We, for whom the historical concept presupposes the inevitability of new world wars ...'[157]

In fact the 'world Communist movement' was a fiction. Nowhere was there any success in building mass parties, apart from in China, Italy and France. Otherwise, there were several dozen more that resembled small, dying sects. As a rule, the leaders of these parties lived on money sent from Moscow, and were prepared to utter speeches that had been written for them in the offices of the Central Committee on Staraya Square in Moscow. The appearance of a mass movement was important to the Soviet leadership for many reasons: to create an illusion of support for the USSR, to show that the old system was doomed, and to demonstrate that Leninism was inexhaustible. The Soviet special services retained their close involvement in many of the foreign Communist parties right up until the collapse of the system.

Behind the Scenes

Lenin's personal life holds no great enigmas. Until 1909 his wife, Nadezhda Konstantinovna Krupskaya, was both the woman he loved and his closest Party comrade. In practice, his fanatical devotion to the Party and political affairs left him little time to engage in the subtle sphere of human relations, including love and the attractions of women. Until his marriage to Nadezhda in July 1898 in Shushenskoe, Siberia, he is known to have courted only one other woman, Nadezhda's friend, like her a socialist and teacher, Apolinaria Yakubova. Already not so young – at twenty-six – Ulyanov wooed Yakubova, and received a polite but firm refusal. The evidence suggests that this was not a major event in his life. Later, when they were both abroad, Lenin and Yakubova, then married to the social democrat K. Tekhterev, carried on correspondence, though on strictly Party matters.

It is also known that Lenin met a young Frenchwoman, a writer, in Paris, although she has not yet been identified. In the 1930s, when Stalin was keen to bring all of Lenin's manuscripts under his own control, the former Bolshevik émigré Grigory Aleksinsky arranged for Stalin's emissaries to read several letters that Lenin had written to this woman. They were of an extremely personal and intimate nature. The woman would not, however, sell the letters to Moscow as long as Krupskaya was still alive.

When Krupskaya joined Lenin in Shushenskoe at the turn of the century, she had her mother with her, and the formidable Yelizaveta Vasilievna insisted the couple get married at once, and in accordance with 'full Orthodox custom' at that. Ulyanov, then twenty-eight, and Nadezhda, one year older, bore the rituals patiently and started their peaceful, settled married life together. Alexander Potresov, who knew the couple well in the early days, recalled that Lenin 'in his domestic life was a modest, unpretentious, virtuous, family man, good-naturedly carrying on a daily struggle with his mother-in-law that was not without its comic element. She was the only person in his immediate circle who stood up to him and gave as good as she got.'[158]

The Ulyanovs did not indulge in noisy squabbles or lengthy tiffs. To outside appearances, the couple were Party comrades serving the cause, while Nadezhda conscientiously dealt with the household chores wherever they settled in their nomadic life as revolutionaries. Never did either of them discuss with anyone the painful fact of Nadezhda's inability to have children, suffering as she did from Basedow's Disease, among other health problems. In 1900 Lenin wrote to his mother: 'Nadya must rest: the doctor has said (as she wrote a week ago), that her (woman's) illness requires intensive treatment and that she must rest for 2–6 weeks. I have sent her some more money (100 roubles from Vodovozova), as the treatment is going to be expensive.'[159]

In time, though, the sadness Nadezhda felt about her childlessness came through in her letters and memoirs. Speaking of the early revolutionary Vera Zasulich, she remarked: 'She had an enormous need for a family. One just had to see how lovingly she handled [a friend]'s sweet little baby boy.'[160]

Krupskaya wrote very sparingly about her domestic life, preferring instead to talk about friends and acquaintances, the cause, the foreign cities they were living in, and the Party affairs to which both she and Lenin devoted their entire existence. She was somewhat more forthcoming about the last years of Lenin's life, his illness and his death in Gorki. In her frank memoirs, *The Last Six Months of Vladimir Ilyich's Life*, she recounted the course of his decline. After his third stroke in 1923 only she could decipher his gestures, sounds and mutterings. 'It was possible to guess,' she wrote, 'only because when one has spent a lifetime living together, one knows the associations that are evoked. I would say, for instance, something about Kalmykova and know that, if he said "what?", he was asking about Potresov and his present political position.'[161] (Alexandra Kalmykova and Alexander Potresov had been close associates during Lenin's early years as a revolutionary.)

At the end of December 1909, after much hesitation, the Ulyanovs moved to Paris, where Lenin was to meet Inessa Armand, a lively young Russian-Frenchwoman. Krupskaya could not but see that her forty-year-old husband had been stirred by feelings that were not unrequited. According to Alexandra Kollontai, Krupskaya was prepared to leave and to give her husband his freedom, but Lenin persuaded her to stay.[162] It may be assumed that this affair was in Krupskaya's mind when she recalled the Paris years of emigration as the hardest. To her credit, she did not stage emotional scenes, and maintained outwardly friendly relations with the beautiful Inessa. She even recalled that her mother became very attached to Inessa and that it was 'nicer, more lively, when Inessa came by'.[163]

But Bolshevik morality could not allow the biography of its sainted leader to contain any dubious features. Lenin's letters to Inessa, and those of the unnamed Frenchwoman to him, were only published in his collected works with extensive cuts. Much of the correspondence was never published, even though it is precisely these letters that show Lenin to have been a man of passion and intimate suffering. Lenin was of course extremely cautious himself, and no doubt destroyed many of Inessa's letters to him. In July 1914 he wrote to her: 'When you come, please bring (I mean bring with you) all our letters (it's not a good idea to send them by registered post: registered mail can be opened very easily by friends. And so on . . .) Please bring all the letters, come yourself and we'll talk about this.'[164] He wanted the letters not to re-read them, but to make sure no one else should learn of the liaison.

The intensity of feeling between Lenin and Inessa is best documented in a long letter she wrote to him from Paris in December 1913, when he and Krupskaya were in Cracow:

Saturday morning.

My dear,

Here I am in Ville Lumière and my first impression is one of disgust. Everything about the place grates – the grey of the streets, the overdressed women, the accidentally overheard conversations, even the French language ... It was sad that Arosa was so close to Cracow, while Paris is, well, so final. We have parted, parted, you and I, my dear! And it is so painful. I know, I just feel that you won't be coming here. As I gazed at the familiar places, I realized all too clearly, as never before, what a large place you occupied in my life here in Paris, so that all our activity here is tied by a thousand threads to the thought of you. I wasn't at all in love with you then, though even then I did love you very much. Even now I would manage without the kisses, if only I could see you, to talk with you occasionally would be such joy – and it couldn't cause pain to anyone. Why did I have to give that up? You asked me if I'm angry that it was you who 'carried out' the separation. No, I don't think you did it for yourself.

There was much that was good in Paris in my relations with N.K. In one of our last chats she told me I had become dear and close to her only recently ... Only at Longjumeau and then last autumn over the translations and so on. I have become rather accustomed to you. I so loved not just listening to you, but looking at you as you spoke. First of all, your face is so animated, and secondly it was easy for me to look at you because you didn't notice ...

Well, my dear, that's enough for today. I want to send this off. There was no letter from you yesterday! I'm rather afraid my letters are not reaching you – I sent you three letters (this is the fourth) and a telegram. Is it possible you haven't received them? I get the most unlikely ideas thinking about it. I've also written to N.K., to your brother, and to Zina [Zinaïda Lilina, the wife of Zinoviev]. Has nobody received anything? I send you a big kiss. Your Inessa.[165]

This letter eloquently testifies to the character of the relationship between Inessa, a mother of five children, and Lenin, the 'Bolshevik moralist'. Lenin faced a difficult choice between his feelings and what he perceived as his duty. He managed to find a compromise, as he would in his political life on more than one occasion. He preserved his family and he kept Inessa.

It was in the spring of 1912 that the Ulyanovs moved to Cracow. Inessa joined them the following year. Krupskaya recalled that in

Cracow Inessa told her a lot about herself, and the Ulyanovs and their inseparable friend went for long walks together.[166] Lenin's Complete Works contain a letter from him to Inessa with a large cut in the last paragraph which is preserved in the archives: 'Never, never have I written that I respect only three women! Never!! I wrote to you that my experience of the most complete friendship and absolute trust was limited to only two or three women. These are completely mutual, completely mutual business relations . . .'[167] It is plain that Krupskaya and Inessa were two of these women.

When Inessa was not near Lenin, he wrote to her, sometimes very long letters. In July 1914 he wrote at length about a number of topics: a lecture she was about to give, the Belgian socialist minister Emile Vandervelde, Rosa Luxemburg, Kautsky and other social democrats. Intermingled with these 'business' affairs, the text is sprinkled with very intimate passages. After a discussion, for instance, of trade unions and insurance funds, he writes, in French: 'Oh, how I want to kiss you a thousand times, to see you and wish you luck: I'm absolutely sure you're going to triumph.' He goes on: 'My dear, most dear friend, I forgot to mention money. We will pay for the letters and telegrams (please send telegrams more often) and your rail fare, hotel expenses and so on. Remember this.'[168] The 'kisses' are deleted in the published version.

If Inessa had become a part of his life in emigration, once they were back in Russia, after the famous journey in the 'sealed train' – she was of course in the group – she saw less of Lenin, who was swept up in the vortex of events.

When the question of getting out of Switzerland and back to Russia came up, Lenin wrote to Inessa on 19 March 1917: 'You say that perhaps the Germans won't give us a railcar. Let's bet on it, I say they will!'[169] He knew that Berlin shared with him and his Party the aim of, in Ludendorff's words, 'bringing down Russia' and opening the road to revolution. The revolution, however, soon began to sap Lenin's strength, and Inessa's too. Ardently, she took on any job she was given by the Party, but she did not have the energy needed in those fevered times. Within three years she was drained. In the diary which she kept in the last months of her life, she wrote:

Now I'm indifferent to everyone. The main thing is I'm bored with almost everyone. I only have warm feelings left for the children and V.I. In all other respects it's as if my heart has died. As if, having given up all my strength, all my passion to V.I. and the work, all the springs of love have dried up in me, all my sympathy for people, which I used to have so much of. I have none left, except for V.I. and my children, and a few personal relations, but only in work. And people can feel this deadness in me, and they pay me back in the same coin of indifference and even antipathy (and people used to love me) . . . I'm a living corpse, and it's dreadful![170]

In Petrograd and then Moscow Lenin had seen less and less of Inessa. He no longer owned himself, but belonged to his deity, the revolution. But he often sent her notes, enquiring about her health and that of her children, getting her telephone repaired, having food and galoshes delivered to her, and sending his personal physician when she was ill. In the autumn of 1920, Inessa was close to total collapse. On 9 September she confided to her diary:

It seems to me that as I move among people I'm trying not to reveal my secret to them that I am a dead person among the living, a living corpse . . . My heart remains dead, my soul is silent, and I can't completely hide my sad secret . . . As I have no warmth anymore, as I no longer radiate warmth, I can't give happiness to anyone any more.[171]

She wanted to go back to her native France, to remove herself briefly from the embrace of the revolution and restore her strength. She telephoned Lenin, who was busy and sent her a note:

Dear friend, I was very sad to learn that you are overtired and not happy with your work and the people around you (or your colleagues at work). Can't I do something for you, get you into a sanatorium? I'll do anything with great pleasure. If you go to France, I will of course help with that, too. I'm a bit concerned, in fact I'm afraid, I'm really afraid you could get into trouble . . . They'll arrest you and keep you there a long time . . . You must be careful. Wouldn't it be better to go to Norway (where many of them speak English), or Holland? . . . Best not go to France where they could put you inside for a long time and are not even likely to exchange you for anyone. Better not go to France . . . If you don't fancy a sanatorium, why not go to the South? To Sergo

[Ordzhonikidze] in the Caucasus? Sergo will arrange rest, sunshine, interesting work, he can fix it all up. He's the real power there. Think about it.[172]

Inessa made up her mind quickly. She completely trusted the man she loved, and on 17 August 1920 she telephoned him to say she would go to the South. Lenin at once dictated an official request to the authorities 'that you help in every way possible to arrange the best accommodation and treatment for the writer, Comrade Inessa Fedorovna Armand, and her elder son. I request that you give complete trust and all possible assistance to these Party comrades with whom I am personally acquainted.'[173]

A month later, only two days after Ordzhonikidze had reported that Inessa was fine and well, Lenin received a telegram: 'Top priority. Moscow. To Central Committee RKP, Sovnarkom, Lenin. Unable to save Comrade Inessa Armand sick with cholera STOP She died 24 September [1920] STOP Sending body to Moscow signed Nazarov.'[174]

Lenin was profoundly shaken by Inessa's death. Her friend Alexandra Kollontai told a friend: 'He could not survive Inessa Armand. The death of Inessa precipitated the illness which was fatal.'[175]

It took nearly three weeks to bring Inessa's body to Moscow, where she was buried at the Kremlin Wall. Alexandra Kollontai recalled that on 12 October 1920, as 'we marched in the funeral cortège, Lenin was unrecognizable. He walked with his eyes closed and every moment we thought he might fall to the ground.'[176] Inessa was buried near the spot where, in a little over three years, Lenin would also be laid to rest, if less conventionally; it was her fate to lie forever in his shadow.

The habit of secrecy, understandable when the Party was an illegal underground organization, was embedded in Soviet practice by Lenin himself. Most government business is conducted confidentially, until it is thought proper and prudent to make it public. In Lenin's case, the constant references to secrecy and the need for it, even in routine matters, betrays what can only be described as a phobia.

Following Lenin, successive Soviet leaders made entire areas of Soviet life into secret domains: the salaries of Politburo members, the quantity of grain purchased abroad or of gold mined in the USSR, the number of prisoners, the results of the census, the number of people expelled from the Party, the amount of money sent to friendly organizations abroad, the crime rate, and much else. This constant drive for secrecy was a product of the totalitarian impulse which required the sort of overall control that is impossible without the rule of secrecy.

An example of Lenin's obsessive secrecy occurs in a note to Stalin in May 1918 in which he asks whether it wouldn't be a good idea to establish 'one or two model rest-homes no nearer Moscow than 400 miles. We'll spend gold on this; we'll also use gold and we'll do so for a long time to come on necessary trips to Germany. But the rest-homes will only be model ones if we can show that they have the best doctors and administrators, and not the usual Soviet bunglers and oafs.' He goes on: 'In Zubalovo, where dachas have been built for you, Kamenev and Dzerzhinsky, and one is going to be built for me nearby, we must organize the repair of the railway branch-line by the autumn and the regular running of the self-driven trolley. Then we'll have a rapid and secret connection the year round.'[177]

The practice of creating secret privileges for the Party élite began with the declaration of 'war on the palaces', and by the spring of 1918 Lenin and his entourage had converted the Kremlin into their living accommodation. Simultaneously, they commandeered fabulous country houses, acquired their own sanatoria, their own sources of supply, special medical facilities and other 'despised' trappings of capitalist life. All this could be known only to those initiated into the Party's secrets.

In February 1921 Lenin received news from Viktor Kopp, the Soviet envoy in Berlin, that the Germans, in breach of the Versailles agreements, were proposing military collaboration with Soviet Russia to benefit both countries. Kopp reported that 'in conditions of the utmost secrecy the firms Blohm and Voss (submarines) and Albatross Werke (aircraft) and Krupp (ordinary weapons) have been engaged.' Lenin wrote to Sklyansky: 'Drop a line to say how you have replied to this. I think the answer is yes. Return this to me. Lenin. Secret.'[178]

It was as if Lenin had forgotten that, as a condition of the Versailles accords, Germany had had to give back to their former owners the million square kilometres he had so dutifully handed over to her at Brest-Litovsk. Now he was once again prepared to enter a secret game with Berlin that would ultimately lead to the Molotov–Ribbentrop Pact in 1939, with its secret protocols and 'friendship' with Nazi Germany.

Even in the humanitarian field, Lenin's conspiratorial tic was activated. The dreadful famine of 1921–22 compelled the Bolsheviks to compromise their 'ideological purity' and accept help from the capitalists. Aid from the US was particularly substantial. Millions of Russians were saved from starvation by the American Relief Administration. But Lenin smelt danger. He wrote to Central Committee Secretary Molotov on 23 August 1921: 'Secret: In view of the agreement with the American, Hoover, there is going to be an influx of a mass of Americans. We should think about surveillance and keeping ourselves informed. I propose the Politburo order a commission to be created to prepare, work out and operate intensified surveillance and information on the foreigners, through the Cheka and other organs.'[179] Back in June 1919, he had ordered that 'any member of the bourgeoisie, between the ages of 17 and 55, who is the subject of any foreign country conducting hostile and military actions against us, is to be imprisoned in concentration camps.' The only exceptions were 'individuals who have proved their loyalty to the Soviet regime'.[180]

It was a typically Bolshevik approach: watch even your guests and friends, and see all foreigners as spies – 'class alertness' must come first. Soon suspicion, informing and secret collaboration with the 'organs' became a hallmark of the Leninist system. In the year of Stalin's death, 1953, the number of unofficial, i.e. secret, collaborators, the *seksots*, would amount to no fewer than eleven million, virtually a state within a state. At its source stood Lenin, who regarded the Cheka as 'the mind, honour and conscience of the epoch'.

Lenin did not speak often at the Politburo, but when he did his word was law, and his ideas were generally radical. On the eve of a Politburo meeting on 27 August 1921, hearing that White General Baron von Ungern-Sternberg had been captured in Mongolia, he proposed: 'We should aim for a solid accusation, and if there's plenty of evidence, about which there can be no doubt, we should organize a public trial, carry it out at maximum speed and shoot him.'[181] After a two-minute discussion, a telegram was sent to Novonikolaevsk in Siberia, and at noon on 15 September, before a vast crowd in a local theatre, the trial began. The tall, slim, thirty-five-year-old general – whose record as a White military chieftain in Mongolia was bloody enough – was asked: 'How have the clan of Ungern-Sternbergs distinguished themselves in service for Russia?' He replied tersely: 'Seventy-two members of the family have died in wars for Russia's interests.' But, as Lenin had demanded, evidence for a 'solid accusation' was accumulated, the trial was conducted at speed – three hours – and the sentence, prepared in Moscow three weeks earlier, was greeted by the masses in court with 'a storm of applause'. Thus, even though the trial was 'public', its outcome had been prearranged behind the scenes.

Financial affairs were also dealt with, in true Leninist style, behind the scenes. Lenin's signature is on countless orders for millions of gold roubles to establish new Communist parties and support them, and to carry out undercover operations abroad. On 15 October 1921, on his initiative, the Politburo decided that 'no single expenditure from the gold reserve may be undertaken without a special resolution of the Politburo.'[182] In the summer of 1921 Lenin approved a proposal to shift into the Kremlin 1,878 trunks containing the basic gold reserve, to which were added valuables assessed at 458.7 million gold roubles that had belonged to the Romanov family.[183] In November 1921 Chicherin suggested to Lenin that 1.1 million gold roubles be given to the Turks. Lenin wrote to Stalin: 'Secret: In my view, we should give it.'[184] Karakhan suggested that well-paid Bolshevik agitators be sent to China, India and Persia to spread Communism.[185]

Sometimes Lenin did not discuss such initiatives with the Politburo, but approved the expenditures himself. For instance, he wrote to Karakhan in 1918: 'I think 500,000 roubles should be given to Comrade Roth [probably a German Communist working for Moscow]. Handle it with extreme care, and talk to Sverdlov first.'[186] Equally, the Politburo often merely rubber-stamped a previous decision, as when on 1 September 1920 it formally approved a request 'to sell 200 puds [7,200 pounds] of gold abroad'.[187]

The account of the squandering of Russia's wealth could go on and on. A significant part of that wealth ended up in the safes of enterprising dealers who had no interest whatever in Lenin's adventures. And the money that did find its way to foreign Communist parties did nothing to bring Lenin's goal nearer.

Lenin's last year was also spent behind the scenes. Overburdened by the mountain of work as leader of the Party and head of government, his health deteriorated rapidly. Numerous symptoms of serious illness appeared as early as 1921, and then a series of strokes reduced him to the condition of a helpless child. The terminal stage began in late 1922. As the attending neuropathologist, Professor V. Kramer, noted in his records:

> transient paralysis of the extremities, noted at the end of 1922, and broken speech became more pronounced and prolonged from day to day and led on 6 March 1923, with no other visible causes, to a two-hour attack, manifesting as total loss of speech and complete paralysis of the right limbs. A similar attack took place on 10 March and led, as is known, to the changes becoming stable, both in his speech and the right limbs ... In the period between 10 and 21 March ... he suffered another stroke ... producing symptoms of so-called sensory aphasia, i.e. difficulty in understanding what is being said to him.[188]

The regular bulletins on Lenin's health made it impossible to guess the real state of affairs. On 17 March 1923, for instance, Bulletin No. 6, signed by Professor Kramer, Dr A. Kozhevnikov and the Commissar for Health, Nikolai Semashko, stated: 'Together with an improvement in speech and the movement of his right arm, there is a noticeable improvement in the movement of his right leg. His general state of health continues to be good.'[189] The rumours, though, spoke of a different situation. Regional leaders questioned the Central Committee about Lenin's true condition. Telegrams arrived from abroad. When Bulletin No. 6 was published, the Soviet envoy in London sent a cipher to Moscow: 'Anyone here who feels like it is issuing bulletins on Lenin's health. For instance, today it has been reported that, having lost the power of speech, Lenin has been put in a madhouse and replaced by a *troika* consisting of the liberal Kamenev, Rykov, the father of NEP, and the Turk Stalin. In the absence of information, we are unable to say anything. I request that you keep us informed on the state of Lenin's health.'[190]

On 17 March, the day Semashko and the doctors signed the bulletin, ratified by the Central Committee and describing Lenin's condition as 'good', Stalin, as General Secretary, wrote a note to the Politburo in which he reported that Lenin was urgently requesting a lethal dose of potassium cyanide. Krupskaya was 'stubbornly insisting that Ilyich's request should not be refused'. She had even 'tried to give it to him herself, but had lost her nerve', and that was why she had asked for Stalin's help. Stalin concluded by saying that although he believed giving Lenin cyanide would be 'a humane mission', he himself would be unable to carry it out.[191]

The facts of Lenin's last illness, which employed more than twenty Russian and foreign physicians, were locked up for decades in the Central Committee archives. The climate of secrecy around the treatment even led some of the doctors to remark on the special nature of the illness. For instance, after Lenin died, Kramer noted in his diary: 'It is a deeply embedded belief that everything associated with outstanding people is unusual: their lives and their illnesses proceed differently from the way they do with ordinary mortals.'[192] It was therefore not surprising that after Lenin's death, the Politburo decided that his brain should be examined to find 'material evidence of the leader's genius'. Before any experiments were carried out, Professors A. Demin, V. Bunak, B. Veisbrod, L. Minor, A. Abrikosov, V. Kramer and O. Focht had given a positive opinion,[193] knowing perfectly well what result the almighty Politburo wished to obtain.

Krupskaya's 'top secret' memories of Lenin's last days are not clouded by such official considerations.

> On Monday [21 January 1924] the end came. At eleven he drank black coffee and slept again. I lost track of time somewhat. When he woke up again, he could not speak at all; he was given bouillon and again coffee, which he drank thirstily, and felt slightly better, but then he started having gurgling in the chest. His gaze became unconscious, [the male attendant and head of security] were practically lifting him bodily, he occasionally moaned quietly, a tremor ran through his body, at first I held his hot, damp hand, but then just watched as the towel turned red with blood, and the stamp of death settled on his deathly pallid face. Professor Foerster and Doctor Yelistratov sprayed camphor and tried to give him artificial respiration, but in vain; it was not possible to save him.[194]

Like the events surrounding Lenin's death, the Politburo would continue forever to make its decisions in secret. The people were given the right only 'to show initiative and Soviet patriotism'. Lenin was the founder of a closed society, where public opinion, if it could be called that, was totally formed and guided by the Party. The conspiratorial Party of 1917 transferred its anti-democratic methods to running a state which consisted of two levels: the upper level, where the leaders carried out their 'wise, Leninist, correct' policies; and the lower level, where the masses laboured. This arrangement could survive only as long as dictatorial methods prevailed. When it came to world competition, economic comparisons, or the achievement of real human rights, the structure turned out to be profoundly flawed and unviable. When the lies came under pressure after 1985, it was clear that Lenin's creation could not survive.

The Creator of the System

On 18 or 19 October 1923, Lenin unexpectedly arrived in Moscow from Gorki, where he had been convalescing. The trip had been unplanned, and was not authorized by his physicians. Leaning on his attendant's neck, Lenin had somehow indicated that he wanted to be put into his automobile. Once settled in the back seat, he demanded, as his staff guessed, to be driven to Moscow, and would not be dissuaded. The journey took two hours and ended at the Kremlin, where Lenin was pushed in his wheelchair through all the empty rooms of his apartment. He incoherently muttered *vot*, *vot*, or yes, yes, with evident pleasure. His doctors and the others guessed that he had either come to say his farewell to the capital, or to show the other leaders that he was still alive, or to see what Moscow looked like after the whirlwind of revolution.

Next day, after rising at eleven, he asked to be taken to the library, where he selected a dozen or so books. Then he was driven around the Kremlin and the city streets in the rain. From the car Lenin stared at the gloomy pedestrians and the placards naming the institutions that they passed.

What had prompted him to make this trip to the capital of the new empire he had created on the ruins of the old? His diseased brain could hardly have provided an answer. Not one of his comrades-in-arms came to see him, though they must have been told that their leader was suddenly in town. They all knew it was no longer possible to have a normal conversation with him, and none of them thought he would ever return to political life. In their eyes Lenin was already dead.

The visit to Moscow was highly symbolic. Moscow was the capital of the 'revolutionary' state with the Bolshevik system he had created. It was a system that embodied Lenin's own personality. The Party was his creation and the state it governed was an expression of his mind and his will. It is impossible to separate the history of one from the biography of the other.

Adhering to Marxist precepts on nationality, among Lenin's first acts was the abolition of the old provinces which were the basis of the Russian Empire. This move was to prove fateful. When they first seized power, the Bolsheviks could not resist the break-up of the empire. In March 1917 the Provisional Government had proclaimed the independence of Poland, and Russia itself was declared a Democratic Republic in September 1917. In overthrowing the Provisional Government in October 1917, the Bolsheviks also overthrew the new republic.

In December 1917 the Sovnarkom recognized the Ukrainian People's Republic and the independence of the Finnish Republic, which was ratified on 4 January 1918. On the eve of the war, in Cracow, Lenin had maintained contact with the Union for the Liberation of Ukraine, behind which stood Austria. It was not love of Ukraine that moved him: he would make common cause with anyone who opposed the tsarist regime, including Germany.

In December 1918 Moscow recognized the independence of Estland (Estonia), Latvia and Lithuania, in 1920 the Soviet Republics of Belorussia, Azerbaijan and Armenia, and in February 1921 that of Georgia. Recognition came easy, when the Bolsheviks were simultaneously urging their supporters to 'sovietize' these countries, to establish governments of workers and peasants and to rely on 'the proletarian centre' in Moscow. Having destroyed the ancient state, Lenin set about rebuilding it on a new, Bolshevik foundation. Reading Ioffe's letter to the Soviet Ambassador to Germany Nikolai Krestinsky, Lenin underlined the words: 'What is really necessary is the factual subjugation of Ukraine while retaining its formal independence.'[195] Soon the Russian Soviet Republic was making bilateral treaties with these newly 'independent' states, until the Declaration on the formation of the Union of Soviet Socialist Republics was signed on 30 December 1922.

It had been a strange policy: first the destruction of the Russian province-based empire, and then its recreation on a Soviet, 'international' basis. From separation to reunification. The new 'national structure' soon caused friction, however. On 30–31 December 1922, Lenin, from his sickbed, dictated an article 'On the Nationalities or on "Autonomization" ', in which he attempted to exclude manifestations of great-power chauvinism and regional nationalism from the process of reunification. The article first appeared in Berlin in *Sotsialisticheskii vestnik*, published by émigré Mensheviks who had acquired it through their contacts in Soviet Russia. It was not, however, published in the Soviet Union until 1956, when it appeared in the journal *Kommunist*.[196]

Defending the creation and consolidation of the Union of Soviet Socialist Republics, Lenin argued that the way to reduce friction was 'to make concessions to other nationalities', and to reduce 'the distrust, suspiciousness and insults that were inflicted on them in the past by the "great-power" nation'. This apparently reasonable approach, however, was devoid of meaning. His request to Trotsky to 'take on the defence of the Georgian affair',[197] his efforts to write 'notes and a speech' in defence of the Georgian Bolsheviks who had become victims of Stalin's heavy-handed methods,[198] and a skirmish between Trotsky and Stalin over the article,[199] changed nothing. The abolition of the old provinces had been decided, and the process of creating national entities was shifting the problem onto an entirely new plane. Under the guise of 'internationalism', the destruction of the provinces, the only units capable of reducing national differences to a minimum, went ahead. The example of the immensely multi-national United States of America has shown that it was precisely the states that facilitated the emergence of an American people. Contrary to all the much-vaunted 'new historical community', no Soviet people ever emerged, as the events following August 1991 showed. As soon as conditions allowed the centrifugal forces of nationalism to come into play, the union created by Lenin fell apart. The intra-national links formed between republics proved to be much weaker than had been the case under the provincial system. The Leninist structure was deeply flawed.

Lenin destroyed the Russian state system and pursued his Marxist programme, although when it came to purely national issues he sometimes had other ideas. On 18 November 1920, for instance, he replied to a telegram from Stalin about 'the need to occupy Georgia' by saying: 'We have to think very carefully about whether it's worth fighting Georgia, if we just have to feed her afterwards.'[200] In the last analysis, however, he succeeded in replacing the old order with a new, Soviet one. As long as the USSR was a unitary state, which it undoubtedly was, its national form was meaningless: the bonds holding the union together depended on the totalitarian power of the Communist Party of the Soviet Union.

Lenin had destroyed any possible allies when he got rid of the Mensheviks and SRs. His papers are full of instructions on ways to 'root out' all Russian socialists who did not accept Bolshevik authority. In June 1921, for instance, on Lenin's orders Unshlikht reported to the Politburo that 'the Cheka proposes to continue the systematic work of destroying the SR and Menshevik organizations, picking off individual underground operatives and leaders, alike. Mass operations have to be conducted against these bodies on a state-wide scale.'[201] Soon the Politburo was ordering the deportation of Mensheviks to the provinces, or expelling them abroad.[202]

Lenin had chosen to rely on his 'iron party', and he had won the political battle. On 20 November 1922, the last time he addressed his followers in public, he delivered a frank speech to the Moscow Soviet in the Bolshoi Theatre – a speech that has been mentioned only in a contemporary newspaper report, while the text remained unpublished.[203] Socialism, he said, 'is the task we have set ourselves. There is a small, minuscule handful of people, calling themselves a party, who have set about doing this. They are a negligible kernel within the entire number of working masses of Russia. This negligible kernel has set itself a job, namely to change everything, and it has done just that.'[204] He had achieved his goal; his party alone was responsible for turning everything upside down. Aware perhaps that he would not be making any more speeches to such large gatherings, he was categorical: 'We have created this state structure in three years of work in order to prove and to show that we would change the old course of international life at any cost, and we have done that. In our present circumstances we have never had time to choose whether we are smashing too much, never had time to determine whether there have been too many victims, because there have been plenty of victims.'[205]

On that dank evening, speaking for the last time at a Bolshevik meeting, Lenin could claim that the new state order had indeed been created. Henceforth, his successors would only have to reinforce it, develop and 'defend' his initiatives. Above all, he had established the Bolshevik Party's supremacy. The Politburo and the Central Committee embodied a new form of ideological and political absolutism which controlled every aspect of state and public activity. When Lenin left his posts on 14 June 1923, the Party confirmed the Politburo as the supreme organ of power.

Soon the notorious *nomenklaturas* were established, with control of all important posts throughout the administration, from the economic ministries and Gosplan to the diplomatic service, the Supreme Court, the army and the security organs.[206] Throughout the Soviet period, from Lenin to Gorbachev, all state and Party officials would be appointed by a small group at the top, and power would simply be handed on from one to the other within the 'clan'. This self-contained and self-promoting arrangement was one of the chief causes of the ultimate collapse of the system.

Another element of the Leninist system was what Stalin delicately termed 'the punitive organs'. Over the years they grew to vast proportions, so that by the time of Stalin's death there were eleven million people employed in one way or another on the task of watching the rest of the population. There had never been anything like it in history, and Lenin himself had set an example by showing his concern for the welfare of the Chekists. In a note to Unshlikht on 21 September 1921 he wrote: 'I saw Radek today, just back from [Petrograd]. He says the city is bubbling. It's a port. Foreigners are bribing everyone, including starving and threadbare Chekists. The danger is enormous. Create a Party commission (All-Russian Cheka + Petrograd Cheka + Petrograd Party organization + Central Committee), get some money (we'll have to give some gold) and feed and clothe the Chekists in [Petrograd], Odessa, Moscow and so on. This must be done and quickly.'[207] Unshlikht acted quickly. He requested from Lenin 4,356,690 gold roubles 'to make uniforms for 105,000 Chekists'.[208] Lenin released the funds and later added a further 1,132,000 gold roubles for the other needs of this most reliable arm of the Party.[209]

Everywhere, and in the front line of the most unpopular actions of the Party, the Cheka could be relied on. To the loud applause of trade union leaders on 12 January 1920, Lenin said, referring to the tough measures used during the requisitioning of grain: 'We did not hesitate to shoot thousands of people, and we shall not hesitate, and we shall save the country.'[210]

The Politburo gave the Cheka a free hand by authorizing it to employ 'extra-judicial executions', as well as 'exile and concentration camps'.[211] All in the name of 'revolutionary legality'. It is difficult to reconcile these views with the notion that less than twenty years earlier Lenin had been a social democrat. Worse, the people grew accustomed to violence being perpetrated by the state in the name of a bright future.

True, the Bolsheviks made several attempts to abolish the death penalty. Speaking on 1 February 1920 to chairmen of provincial and district Soviets, Lenin assured them that the Sovnarkom would do everything it could 'to make the use of the death penalty in Russia impossible'.[212] Yet, after crushing the anti-Bolshevik uprising of soldiers and sailors at Kronstadt a year later he would ensure that anyone found inside the fortress or on a ship would be executed. On 20 March 1921 a special commission sentenced 167 Marines from the battleship *Petropavlovsk* to death, next day another thirty-two were shot, and on 24 March a further twenty-seven. The Petrograd Cheka alone sentenced 2,103 men to be shot.[213] The Commander of 7th Army, Tukhachevsky, ordered an attack on the battleships *Petropavlovsk* and *Sevastopol* with the use of 'asphyxiating gas and poison shells'[214] (the poison shells did not arrive in time). In addition to the executions at the time, 6,459 were imprisoned or exiled, only to be shot later by Stalin.

In December 1919 there was a fuel crisis in the country. Lenin appointed A. Eiduk to deal with the problem, and all manner of 'bourgeois' were mobilized to gather and load wood onto trains: clerks, intellectuals, tsarist officers – any 'ex-person' whom the new order had impoverished and as a rule denied a ration card. It was a common sight to see frail people, wrapped in what remained of a once-fine coat, clumsily loading frozen logs under the watchful eye of some 'authorized' comrade. Later harried by a rule of 20 April 1921 under which their apartments could be packed out with poor and homeless people, or taken over altogether, these desolate individuals sought any excuse to avoid the drudgery of manual labour. Religious holidays were one such excuse. On 25 December 1919 Lenin told Eiduk: 'it is stupid to tolerate "Nikola" [i.e. St Nicholas' Day]; all Chekists have to be on alert to shoot anyone who doesn't turn up to work because of "Nikola". Special measures are needed at once: 1) to increase loadings, 2) to warn against absenteeism on Christmas and New Year. Report to me today what special measures you are taking.'[215]

In the zealous pursuit of his goal, Lenin regarded not only 'bourgeois' lives as disposable, but those of Bolsheviks too. In a speech on 12 January 1920, he said: 'We have laid down the lives of tens of thousands of the best Communists for ten thousand White Guard officers, and this has saved the country.'[216] These methods, Lenin advised, should not be forgotten; they should be applied. And applied they were. In November 1920 Dzerzhinsky reported to Lenin that 'the republic has to organize the internment in camps of about 100,000 prisoners from the Southern front and vast masses of people expelled from the rebellious [Cossack] settlements of the Terek, the Kuban and the Don. Today 403 Cossack men and women aged between 14 and 17 arrived in Oryol for internment in concentration camp. They cannot be accepted as Oryol is already overloaded.'[217] Almost a third of the Cossack population was exterminated on Lenin's orders.

In February 1920, Lenin cabled Ivan Smilga and Grigory Ordzhonikidze on the North Caucasus front: 'As we are in desperate need of oil, draw up a notice to the population that we'll slaughter every one of them if the oil and the oil installations are set on fire and that, on the contrary, we'll spare everyone's life if Maikop, and especially Grozny, are handed over intact.' At the same time, he wanted Saak Ter-Gabrielyan, a member of the Main Oil Committee, to be told 'to make all the preparations to burn Baku down completely if there is an invasion, and to announce this in the Baku press'.[218]

The savagery of the civil war somehow instilled in the Russian people a sense that death, arrest and coercion were normal conditions of life. In order to achieve this state of mind, the Bolsheviks had to abandon the slogans of freedom with which they had come to power. Lenin's first steps after October 1917 were to close down the non-Bolshevik press. In due course the idea of a free press, like the rights of the individual, came to be seen as deeply heretical and counter-revolutionary. In a letter of August 1921 to Gabriel Myasnikov, a Bolshevik critic of his suppression of democracy, Lenin called freedom of the press 'a weapon in the hands of the world bourgeoisie'.[219] It was therefore natural that when in April 1919 the 'Red printworkers' had struck for better conditions, Lenin and Kamenev had rapidly drafted a decree for the Moscow Party Committee to pass calling for the Moscow Cheka to 'carry out arrests of strikers and their delegates mercilessly and without regard for past considerations'.[220]

Myasnikov had written two articles in which he stood up for basic democratic freedoms for the workers, above all freedom of speech and freedom of the press. Lenin had at once smelt danger and responded in a long letter, which was published in book form under the title *Discussion Materials*. As usual, he was emphatic: ' "Pure democracy" is a joke.' He was right to assert that 'there is no other country in the world that has done and is doing so much to emancipate the masses from the influence of the priests and landowners, as the RSFSR [i.e. the Russian Socialist Federation of Soviet Republics, as Russia was now called]. We have carried out the task of "press freedom" and are doing so better than anywhere else in the world.'[221] But the ease with which Lenin was able to abandon even the cosmetic use of the old democratic slogans is amazing. Myasnikov was of course expelled from the Party. He fled abroad, but in 1945, like many former Soviet citizens, he returned to the USSR on a promise of immunity, and died in a concentration camp the following year.

Leninism was the theory and practice of the total control of all aspects of Russian life. It is doubtful that any other regime in history has had the population so completely in its grip. In one of Lenin's articles he wrote: 'Rich men and crooks are two sides of the same coin, two of the main elements nourished by capitalism, two of the chief enemies of socialism. These enemies must be kept under special observation by the entire population, they must be dealt with mercilessly for the least transgression of the rules and laws of socialist society.'

How did Lenin suggest that such control be exercised? 'In one place a dozen rich men, a dozen crooks, and half a dozen workers who have shirked their work should be put in prison. In another place they should be put on cleaning the latrines. In a third place they should be given a yellow card, when they have done their time in prison, so that until they have improved their ways all the people should keep an eye on them as harmful individuals. In a fourth place one in ten accused of parasitism should be executed on the spot.'[222] These proposals were put into practice by a Politburo decree of 14

May 1921, which widened the powers of the Cheka in its use of the death penalty.[223] And all in the name of 'revolutionary legality'.

Like the word 'freedom', the words and idea of 'private property' also fell victim to the Leninist test of counter-revolutionary intent. Lenin wanted to expunge them as soon as possible, and as early as October 1918 he ordered People's Commissar for Justice Dmitri Kursky to destroy all documents relating to private property that he could find in the archives. It must be done 'secretly and with no publicity'. Speaking as a former landowner himself, Lenin advised Kursky to begin with 'deeds of landholdings, factories and real property, and so on and so forth'.[224]

The system, however, could not manage without private property at first. Reckless nationalization, constant requisitioning and confiscation proved unable to feed starving Russia. With gritted teeth, therefore, Lenin recognized the disastrous consequences of Bolshevik practice, heeded the advice of more sober heads in his entourage and softened the policy towards private ownership. He made it perfectly plain, however, that the New Economic Policy was 'a definite gesture, a definite movement. We are now withdrawing, as if retreating backwards, but we are doing it in order to retreat and then take a run and leap forward more strongly. Only under these circumstances have we retreated by introducing our new economic policy . . . NEP is becoming the main, next almighty slogan of the day.'[225] Lenin's view of NEP was purely tactical. He wrote to Kamenev on 3 March 1922: 'It would be the biggest mistake to think that NEP put an end to terror. We shall return to terror and to economic terror.'[226] NEP saved the Leninist system. But to give him his due, when he faced the total collapse of his War Communism policy, Lenin was able to display an astonishing tactical ability by rejecting – temporarily – what he had held sacred.

Another idea Lenin was prepared to throw over was that of workers' self-management, which he had always advocated as preferable to the bureaucratic management of production. War Communism itself, however, had been a form of ruthless dictatorship. The soviets, commissions and boards that had sprouted abundantly after October soon gave way to harsh authoritarianism and state bureaucracy. In his speech of 12 January 1920, Lenin mocked Georgy Lomov, Alexei Rykov and Mikhail Larin for their defence of collegiality in industry and decentralization of management. 'All this "chatter" about centralization and decentralization,' he said, 'is nonsensical, pitiful rubbish, and it's shameful and disgraceful to waste time talking about it.' He concluded on a more conciliatory note: 'We will sometimes use self-management, and sometimes one-man management. We shall leave self-management to those who are weaker, worse, backward and undeveloped; let them talk, they'll get bored and will stop talking.'[227] He knew that the Bolsheviks had won the civil war because they had concentrated all their ruthless power in one pair of hands which had not been afraid to use terror and the most savage means of governing.

The same system remained long after Lenin had gone. There would still be soviets, commissions and boards, and many other ephemeral kinds of administrative unit, but the whole conglomeration was ruled by the Party with the leader at its head. In such circumstances, concepts like people's power, freedom and human rights became simply 'unnecessary'.

Lenin genuinely believed that his system would prove contagious throughout the world. He told the Ninth All-Russian Congress of Soviets: 'capitalism will perish, and its demise may cause tens and hundreds of millions of people unimaginable suffering, but there is no force that can prevent its downfall.'[228] In espousing such a distant goal, Lenin postponed further and further the interests of ordinary people. He may have shown concern for an individual petitioner, writing a note giving some visitor a pass to the cafeteria, ensuring that the railcar carrying his relatives was connected to a military locomotive in good time, but the ordinary needs of ordinary people were not on his agenda.

In 1921 the Red Army was reduced by half a million men. It was realized that if they were sent home all at once, the railways would not cope, while if the demobilization was carried out gradually, they would have to be housed, fed and clothed while they waited. Lenin wrote to Zinoviev on 5 April: 'The policy needs to be altered fundamentally: stop giving them anything at all. Neither bread, nor clothes, nor boots. Tell the Red Army man: either leave right now on foot "with nothing". Or wait a year on one-eighth of a pound of bread and no clothing or boots. He'll leave on his own and on foot.'[229] Next day, the Politburo issued a decree: 'The rate of demobilization must be radically altered. To this end, demobilized men are not to be

carried by railway, but allowed to disperse on foot.'[230] As if the Bolshevik victory had owed nothing to them, the Red 'heroes' straggled
their way back to the villages.

Dealing with the peasant masses, Lenin used applied psychology.
When grain requisitioning was replaced by a tax in kind under NEP,
he was concerned that the same commissars, with pistols in their belts,
should not go to the villages to collect the grain. He told the People's
Commissar for Food Production, A.D. Tsyurupa, that it was 'politically essential to reshuffle the personnel of the food committees before
the start of the new campaign. The peasants must see new faces. The
new policy must be carried out not by the old food committee officials,
who are hated by the peasants, but by other ones. Think about how
to do this and drop me a line soon.'[231]

Reshuffling personnel made little difference. The bureaucracy
would multiply according to laws of its own. Though he railed constantly against 'red tape, sabotage and bureaucracy', Lenin did not
realize that the system he had created was organically permeated with
these evils. In vain he threatened foot-dragging officials with public
trials, arrest and execution. He came to detest what he called
'Communist arrogance', which he blamed on Soviet Russian tendencies. He wrote to Zinoviev in December 1919 to ask for proofs of his
writing to be sent to him for correction, and demanded that harsh
measures be taken against anyone causing delay: 'Unless you do this
these Soviet swine will do nothing!'[232] In February 1922 he expressed
his exasperation with Russian ineptitude: 'In my view, we shouldn't
just preach, "Learn from the Germans, you lousy Russian Communist
sluggards!", we should bring Germans here as teachers. Otherwise,
it's all just words.'[233]

In a few short years Lenin was able to do so much that it is hard
to believe one man capable of it. The Party had become a state within
a state, its dictatorship a fact. Religion had been replaced by the harsh
Bolshevik ideology of Leninism. Party absolutism had replaced tsarist
autocracy. Coercion became a permanent feature. Democracy and
civil rights became 'bourgeois manifestations', human life a soulless
statistical unit. Even some of Lenin's own entourage were worried by
the growth of offices and bureaucratic appendages. In a letter to Trotsky, who showed it to Lenin, Foreign Commissar Chicherin complained: 'The "Board of Affairs" is a state within a state. Karakhan

and I have been elbowed out of the management. There used to be "lack of system", now we have "the system", i.e. every little detail has to go up and down five or six levels of the hierarchy, a mountain of paper is generated, and meanwhile visiting missions have nowhere to sleep and all the journalists are escaping abroad from hunger, I cannot escape abroad myself and so I am now extremely weak and am gradually conking out to the greater glory of "the system".'[234]

Chicherin was indispensable to Lenin, with whom he shared a strong belief that Germany had a special part to play in Russia's interest. His letter to Trotsky came as a surprise to Lenin, who wrote at once to the Chief of Affairs, Nikolai Gorbunov: 'I am sending this to you secretly and personally. Return it to me when you've read it. And tell me: 1) Can we not get better food for Chicherin? Doesn't he get his allocation from abroad? How did you fix this allocation and couldn't Chicherin, as an exception, be given it in full, as a high-calorie diet?'[235] Gorbunov replied that he was to blame as he had put some leaders on a 'slightly reduced diplomatic-foreign ration'. He reassured Lenin that Chicherin would 'today receive a delivery of ordinary produce, but from tomorrow he will be regularly sent milk, eggs, chocolate, fruit and so on'.[236]

More striking than the 'allocation from abroad' is Chicherin's remark about the tight control of the hierarchy. Soon everyone in Soviet Russia would become its prisoner. The system would take care of supplies, medical treatment, accommodation and security for the large number of senior Party officials. Their privileges were so considerable that the Central Committee would come to protect them as state secrets of the highest importance. Up until the collapse of the system, all documents on such matters were kept in 'Special Files' in the Party archives. The free ticket a minor Party instructor in the provinces was given for a stint in a sanatorium, the extra money and various other perks – it was all shelved in 'Special Files'. The Party apparatus held the system together, and it had to be properly looked after.

Lenin himself initiated this privileged treatment for top officials, and the secrecy surrounding it. When he heard in May 1921, for instance, that yet another sanatorium had been established for the Sovnarkom, he wrote to Molotov: 'I fear this may provoke reproaches. I would ask the Orgburo to look at this question carefully. It may be more rational just to give this home a number: "Sanatorium No. 9". Otherwise I'm afraid there will be reproaches.'[237] Future Central Committee officials would learn how best to hide their sanatoria, hospitals, clinics, studios, restaurants and special shops from the public gaze.

Lenin's system could not have survived without the state of extreme tension it created, without constant campaigns and 'new revolutions' – in industry, agriculture, culture, social life and ideology. Class dogmas justified violence and coercion, and therefore the system was doomed from the start. The fact that it survived for seventy years owed more to its harsh authoritarianism and manipulation of the public mind than to any inherent virtues. In wartime, the system exhibited a certain efficiency, but this did not mask the growing rift between itself and the people.

The Fate of Leninism

In addition to millions of copies of Lenin's Collected Works, in five separate editions – a sixth was promised, but was mercifully aborted by the failed coup of August 1991 – the country was inundated by monuments, museums, factories, collective farms, libraries and educational insitutions bearing his name. Lenin medals, prizes, scholarships and decorations proliferated. Every scholarly book opened and closed with reference to him as an authority, every scientific meeting, Party and other congress would begin with the ritual incantation of an oath of loyalty to his 'teachings'. Lenin and Leninism became a state religion for atheists.

Myths about him were manufactured, and his canonization was not merely a Party duty, it was state policy. Yet the public became so familiar with his image and his name as fixtures of their environment that a certain contempt was also bred. A joke was told of collective farm-workers being given rewards: 'For work in the field, Comrade Ivanova gets a sack of grain. For work on the farm, Comrade Petrova gets a sack of potatoes. And for outstanding social work, Comrade Sidorova is awarded Lenin's Collected Works.' The crowd laughs, and someone calls out: 'Bastards! That's all she needs, the poor cow!'[238]

Lenin changed considerably after seizing power. His political character became impulsive, harsh, immoral. With no pang of conscience he could, for instance, order 'the execution of ringleaders among the clergy' in 1922,[239] and not long afterwards pass a decree that 'the death penalty should be used on priests'.[240] Mocking the efforts of self-management, he ensured that democracy and workers' autonomy – however inefficient they may have been under War Communism – were uprooted and destroyed in Soviet Russia.

The Party's control reached everywhere, extending to the most trivial arrangements. For instance, on 15 October 1920 the Politburo determined that meetings of the Trade Unions Directorate should be held on Wednesdays at 11 a.m., and that its agenda should be circulated to all members of the Politburo.[241] Profintern, the Moscow-controlled international organization of trade unions, was treated similarly. Its chairman, Jan Rudzutak, was appointed not by its members, but by the Politburo.[242] Social organizations were strictly curbed by the Party, and any official who did not toe the line was simply removed.

War Communism, Lenin said, was intended to effect the immediate transition to Communist production and distribution: 'We decided that the peasants would supply sufficient grain through requisitioning and we would distribute it to the factories and enterprises, and thus we'd have Communist production and distribution.'[243] The result was in fact the total collapse of the economy. Pressed to the wall by this self-inflicted disaster, Lenin was compelled to introduce NEP, a *volte face* presented to successive generations of Soviet history students as a brilliant example of revolutionary dialectics in action.

The separate peace with Germany, half a year after declaiming that it must not happen; the dispersal by force of the Constituent Assembly, only weeks after lambasting Kerensky for delaying its opening; the short-lived coalition with the SRs; freedom of the press; relations with Russia's allies – the significant shifts made by Lenin were not the great 'dialectic' at work, nor even the force of 'new circumstances', so much as the Bolshevik manipulation of principles.

Trotsky wrote: 'Marx was all in the *Communist Manifesto*, in the preface to his *Critique* and in *Capital*. Lenin, on the contrary, was all in revolutionary action. If he had never published a single book, he would still have gone down in history as he does now, as the leader of the proletarian revolution and founder of the Third International.'[244] Trotsky was right. It was not his writings, but his ability to convert

Marx's concept of class struggle into a tool for the achievement of his main goal, the seizure of power, that made Lenin a giant in history. The world changed in the twentieth century in large measure because of Lenin's intervention. While one part of mankind began to 'live according to Lenin', the other recoiled in horror and fear of repeating the experiment themselves. To avoid it, many countries sought acceptable reform and social change, and concentrated their efforts on economic growth and the rights of their citizens. It was not armed force and barbed wire that saved the people of capitalist countries from the temptations of revolution. It was their incomparably higher standard of living and the guarantee of their civil rights.

2

The Second Leader: Joseph Stalin

On 25 November 1936, the General Secretary of the CPSU, or second leader of the USSR, Iosif (Joseph) Vissarionovich Stalin, addressed the Extraordinary Eighth All-Union Congress of Soviets. As he paced slowly to the rostrum, the auditorium erupted in an ovation. Standing and clapping, the delegates shouted: 'Hurrah for Comrade Stalin!', 'Long live Comrade Stalin!', 'Long live the great Stalin!', 'Hurrah for the great genius of Comrade Stalin!', 'Vivat!', 'The Red Front!', 'Glory to Comrade Stalin!'[1]

Stalin surveyed the excited audience, glanced at the platform, waited a minute or two, and with a minimal, magisterial gesture, silenced the assembly. His speech was, as usual, divided into numbered sections, the third part being devoted to 'the basic features of the constitution'. In soft tones he declared that 'the new Constitution is not restricted to fixing the formal rights of the citizen, but shifts the centre of gravity to the question of guaranteeing those rights.' Calmly he responded to 'the bourgeois critics' of the Soviet Constitution: 'I have to admit that it indeed leaves the dictatorship of the working class in force, just as it preserves without alteration the present leading position of the Communist Party of the USSR [a storm of applause]. There are no grounds in the USSR for the existence of several parties, nor therefore for the freedom for such parties. Only one party can exist in the USSR, and that is the party of Communists ... And that is why I think the Constitution of the USSR is the only thoroughly democratic constitution in the world.'[2]

He did not of course draw his audience's attention to the fact that, against this background, Nikolai Yezhov and Lavrenti Beria were giving him regular reports on the NKVD's Special Boards, which were handling hundreds of thousands of men and women condemned without any kind of trial. To relieve the 'centre' of this murderous work, in May 1935 Stalin had extended the rights of the Special Boards to the infamous NKVD *troikas* in the regions and republics. Initially these bodies were empowered to sentence citizens to no more than five years in a correctional labour camp or exile, but they were soon given extra powers. By the late 1940s, for instance, weekly reports such as this one from Minister of the Interior S. Kruglov to Stalin were typical: 'On 2 September the MVD [Interior Ministry] Special Board examined 197 cases. Sentences given were: 10 persons to 25 years, two persons to ten years, 30 persons to 25 years hard labour.'[3]

Stalin occasionally underlined the figures in blue pencil. He noted that the MVD had despatched fifty-two people to hard labour on 10 September 1949, thirty-one on 16 September, and seventy-six on 24 September.[4] The lists go on and on, right up to 1 September 1953, when the Special Board was liquidated as an institution, following Stalin's death earlier in the year.

The system designed by Lenin was built by Stalin and the Party. The dictatorship of the proletariat had, long before the adoption of Stalin's 'most democratic' Constitution, become the dictatorship of a single party, which had in turn become the dictatorship of a single leader. By the end of his life, Stalin personified the regime and symbolized a way of thinking and acting. The Russian people believed everything the Bolshevik authorities told them. They submitted to enormous deprivation, endured unprecedented suffering and accepted monstrous sacrifices in the name of a nebulous future. They believed in Stalin, or at least very many of them did.

Uniformity of thought, the rule of a single political force and a system of obligatory ideological myths gradually shaped the population. Stalinism, as the materialization of Lenin's ideas, arose not only from the peculiarities of Russian history – the specifics of Marxism planted in Russian soil, the traditions of tsarism, populism and Jacobinism – it was also to a great extent the manifestation of ideological faith. Russia has always been a country of faith, the USSR no less, if only of the faith of anti-Christianity. Stalin was the embodiment of the system's drive for ideological faith.

The struggle for the 'purity' of Lenin's teachings led to an absolute lack of choice in the form of Russia's development. Even the term 'social evolution' came to be seen by the Bolsheviks as heresy. The one-dimensional approach laid down by Lenin doomed Stalinism historically. Created as the theory and practice of 'Lenin's precepts', Stalinism from its inception was hidebound by ossified dogmatism. By welding the Party organization to that of the state, Stalinism gradually reshaped the legions of 'revolutionaries' into an army of bureaucrats. By adopting revolutionary methods to speed up the natural course of events, Stalinism ultimately brought the country to real backwardness.

Totalitarian demagogy, constant fear, social pressure and a newborn political pseudo-culture created a kind of irrational faith for millions of people. They believed in the Party, they believed in Leninism, and they believed in Stalin. He knew it, and he cynically made full use of it.

Little is known of Stalin's childhood, and he was not one to impart much information about himself. He was born on 21 December 1879 (New Style), his parents, Yekaterina and Vissarion Dzhugashvili, being poor Georgian peasants who later became poor town-dwellers in Gori. Two of their sons died in infancy, and only Iosif – or Soso – survived, although he too almost died at the age of five from the smallpox whose distinguishing marks would figure in his police dossiers and biographies.

In old Russia, cobblers were typically dubbed 'drunken shoemakers' and Vissarion evidently deserved the sobriquet. He would beat his wife and son before falling into drunken sleep, and he left Soso's education and upbringing entirely in the hands of his long-suffering wife. She it was who fought to get a place for him in a theological school and later a seminary, hopeful that he would escape the poverty and degradation of their family life and find a respected place in society as an Orthodox priest. In due course Stalin's parents separated. His father moved to the Georgian capital Tiflis, where he died alone in a cheap lodging house and was buried at the state's expense.

The young Dzhugashvili did well at school in Gori and at the seminary in Tiflis, which he entered in 1894. He displayed a phenomenal talent for memorizing religious texts, as well as a deep interest in the Old and New Testaments. Like many other students at the time, he became interested in the idea of socialist revolution, and as the study of theology began to pall he became more involved in illegal activities. He was expelled from the seminary in 1899, and became a 'professional revolutionary'. Two years later he was elected a member of the Tiflis Social Democratic Committee. He was arrested for the first time in 1902, and in the following year married Yekaterina Svanidze – said to be his one true love – before being transported to Eastern Siberia.

Escaping from exile in 1904, Dzhugashvili returned to Tiflis, where he became a Bolshevik and adopted the alias 'Koba', the name of the hero of *The Patricide*, a novel by the Georgian writer Alexander Kazbegi. His first son, Yakov, was born in the same year.

In 1905 Dzhugashvili attended a Bolshevik conference in Tammerfors, Finland, where he met Lenin for the first time, and in the following year he took part in the Fourth Social Democratic Party Congress in Stockholm. During this time he was engaged in organizing bank robberies – the so-called 'expropriations' – in Georgia on behalf of Lenin and his secret Bolshevik Centre. In 1907 he went abroad again, this time to the Party Congress in London, and in the same year his wife died of tuberculosis, a blow from which he is said never to have recovered. From 1907 to 1909 he was a member of the Bolshevik Committee in Baku, operating among the ethnically mixed labour force of the oil industry.

Arrested again in 1909 and exiled to Solvychegodsk in the north of the province of Vologda, he escaped after four months and got back to Baku. In 1912 he was arrested again, this time in St Petersburg, and deported to Western Siberia, escaping yet again and returning to the capital. That year he met Lenin again in Cracow, went on to Vienna, where he met Bukharin and Trotsky, and wrote an essay on the national question. It was in 1912 that he adopted the alias 'Stalin' – man of steel – and apart from the code-names he used in correspondence during the Second World War, Stalin was the name to which he adhered for the rest of his life. At the Twelfth Bolshevik Party Conference in Prague in 1912 he was elected *in absentia* onto the Central Committee.

In 1913 he was arrested again in St Petersburg and exiled for four years to Turukhansk in Western Siberia, which he was able to leave only after the fall of the Tsar in March 1917. Ten years of theological training and as many in prison and exile, as well as his criminal activities on Lenin's behalf, combined to give Stalin a dogmatic turn of mind, a tough, self-protective personality, and a strong sense that he had earned a place in the Party leadership. When he returned to Petrograd in March 1917 he did not hesitate to reopen the Bolshevik newspaper *Pravda* with Lev Kamenev, and to promote a policy of supporting the Provisional Government as long as it pursued revolutionary aims, while backing a war policy that defended the revolution from defeat by German militarism.

It was a policy that drove Lenin, still in Swiss exile, to distraction: there must be no conciliatory gestures towards the new liberal regime, and no alliances with other parties. Once Lenin succeeded, with German help, in getting back to Petrograd himself on 13 April, within a matter of four weeks he managed to persuade the Party that it must remain aloof and stick to its own policy.

Between the March revolution and the seizure of power in November, Stalin was not much seen. His was a behind-the-scenes role. Indeed, in John Reed's popular account of the Bolshevik coup, *Ten Days that Shook the World*, Stalin's name does not appear even once – an omission which ensured that the book suffered a long period of suppression when the history of 1917 was being rewritten. But when, after the failure of the attempted rising of July, Lenin decided to go into hiding, it was Stalin who shaved off the leader's beard and escorted him through the night to the railway station. With Lenin temporarily out of the picture, it was Stalin who, despite his apparent anonymity, gave the political report to the Party's Sixth Congress in August, was elected to the new Central Committee and made responsible for the political line to be followed by *Pravda*.

Following the Bolshevik seizure of power, Stalin became People's Commissar for Nationalities, with the main task of preventing the old empire from coming apart at its ethnic seams. The policy, which Stalin helped to formulate, was to promise the right of national self-determination, but only to those countries deemed by the Bolshevik regime to be proletarian. Since, in Stalin's view, a truly proletarian state would not voluntarily opt to secede from the new workers' republic, any country that attempted to do so would by definition be anti-proletarian and anti-Soviet. The Soviet constitution of July 1918, which Stalin helped to draft, reflected this approach by defining the new state as federal.

During the civil war, Stalin was most active as a Political Commissar on a number of different fronts. In this capacity he was frequently in conflict with Trotsky, the chief architect of the Red Army and, as War Commissar, the most prominent military commander of all the leaders.

Stalin was elected to the Politburo and Orgburo in March 1919, and by the end of the civil war he had the widest range of experience of all the leaders, possibly including even Lenin. By April 1922 he was well placed to fill the new post of General Secretary, a post which in effect gave him the keys to the strategically most important top Party jobs, and which thus set him on course to become virtually omnipotent.

On 11 December 1937 the vast auditorium of the Bolshoi Theatre was packed with voters and candidates for election to the local soviets. Stalin, like the rest of the leadership, was standing for election in an electoral system that was democratic and representative in name only. No candidates were opposed, and all of them had to be approved by the Party. The soviets, moreover, had been drained of their power within months of the Revolution. Outside, a vast banner proclaimed 'Stalin is the Lenin of Today'. One in ten of all these 'electors' was an employee – covert or overt – of the NKVD. Suddenly Stalin appeared, unexpectedly. The audience rose as one as he took the rostrum. The storm of applause lasted for several minutes. Hesitantly, as if trying to find the right words, and with enormous theatrical effect, Stalin began to speak:

> Comrades, I must admit I had no intention of speaking. But our respected Nikita Sergeevich [Khrushchev, the Moscow Party chief] dragged me here, I might say, by force: give us a good speech, he said . . .
> Of course, I could have said something light about anything and everything [laughter] . . . I understand there are masters of that sort of thing not just in the capitalist countries, but here, too, in our Soviet country [laughter, applause] . . . But still, as I'm out here now, I really should say something [loud applause]. I have been put forward as a candidate for Deputy, and the Electoral Commission of the Stalin District of the Soviet capital has registered me as a candidate for Deputy . . . Well, it's not done for us Bolsheviks to decline responsibility. I accept it willingly [stormy, prolonged applause]. For myself, comrades,

I want to assure you that you can count on Comrade Stalin [a stormy, prolonged ovation].

Never before in the world have there been such genuinely free and genuinely democratic elections, never! History knows no other example [applause] ... our elections are the only genuinely free and genuinely democratic elections in the whole world [loud applause] ... [5]

Electors, the people expect their Deputies to be as clear and precise as activists as Lenin was [applause], that they be as fearless in battle and merciless to enemies of the people as Lenin was [applause], as free of any sort of panic as Lenin [applause], as wise and unhurried in deciding difficult issues requiring an all-round view and multi-faceted reckoning of all the pluses and minuses, as Lenin [applause], that they should be as upright and honest as Lenin [applause], and that they should love the people as Lenin loved them [applause].[6]

Stalin knew perfectly well that the candidates had already been appointed to their posts: he had himself signed the lists of the future 'servants of the people'. But a political spectacle was required to demonstrate just how 'democratic and free' the elections were. Cheated by Bolshevik brainwashing of the justice and equality they might have gained from the February revolution of 1917, the people were now putty in Stalin's hands, as he demonstrated brilliantly in his speech in the Bolshoi.

After Stalin's death, many Russians made the error of believing that the country's troubles came from having 'forgotten Lenin', whose message they believed had been distorted by the despot Stalin. Mikhail Gorbachev, when he launched *perestroika*, said: 'When you re-read Ilyich, and you really have to, you come to the conclusion that you must begin with him and also go [back] to him.'[7]

At the beginning of the 1980s I decided to write a book about Stalin. Everyone, except my wife, tried to talk me out of it. When I asked Central Committee Secretary M. Zimyanin to help me gain access to Stalin's archives, he was silent for a moment, and then started to lecture me: 'It's not a job for one man. The time will come when the Central Committee itself will decide which institute should do it. Your venture isn't necessary.'

Nevertheless, I finished the book by the middle of the 1980s. What I wrote about Lenin and the October Revolution was in the traditional form, yet even so, extracts from the book did not begin to appear in

Russia until 1988. Not everything in that book is out of date, and for me it is evidence of our gradual awakening from the Bolshevik delusions that held us for so long. Marshal D. Yazov, when he had read it, said to me: 'You're not just bashing Stalin, you're bashing the system Lenin created. I can't agree with that.' In fact, I was still a 'Leninist', though I now regard my emancipation from Leninist dogmas as the chief accomplishment of my life. We were all deceived. Lenin was, after all, Stalin's spiritual father. It seemed easier to live when someone else made all your decisions for you: whom to love and whom to hate, what to read and what to say, what to know and what not to know.

In fairness, it must be said that there always were tiny islands of free thinking, dignity and historical perspective. Sometimes this was expressed in absurd ways, for instance in political jokes, which proliferated in the worst times and which it was dangerous to repeat. A typical example made the rounds in the 1930s: 'It's the October anniversary march. Old-age pensioner Rabinovich [such jokes were usually of Jewish origin] comes out with a placard saying: "We thank Comrade Stalin for our happy childhood." A Chekist and a Party organizer rush up to him and say, "Have you gone mad? What childhood, old man? When you were a kid, Comrade Stalin wasn't even born!" "That's exactly what I want to thank him for."' [8]

Such small, weak protests, like those also of the poets and writers in emigration, had no effect on the supremacy of the system for seventy years, but at least they underlined the fact that, if conscience survives, there is a chance.

Lenin's Outstanding Pupil

In 1939, to celebrate his sixtieth birthday, a short – seventh – biography of Stalin was published in an edition of eighteen million copies. Stalin himself edited the second edition scrupulously with his customary blue pencil. On page 93 we read: 'The banner of Lenin, the banner of the Party was raised high and carried further by Stalin, Lenin's outstanding pupil, the best son of the Bolshevik Party, the worthy successor and great continuer of Lenin's cause.' The words 'Lenin's outstanding pupil' were inserted in Stalin's hand. Many similar self-generated panegyrics can be found throughout the book. At the end, Stalin wrote in the margin of page 240: 'Stalin is the worthy continuer of Lenin's cause or, as we say in the Party, Stalin is the Lenin of today.'[9]

This was undoubtedly true. Stalin was indeed the Lenin of his day. With diabolical inventiveness he applied and developed Lenin's ideas on the dictatorship of the proletariat, class war, total control, homogenized, sterilized culture, world revolution and so on.

To understand Stalin's role in Soviet history, it is important to understand the evolution and character of the relationship between him and Lenin. Why was it Stalin who inherited the sceptre? What made him victorious in the internal Party struggle for power? Had there been a close relationship between him and Lenin?

Until October 1917, as far as Lenin was concerned, Dzhugashvili-Stalin was just one of many Bolsheviks. In 1915 Lenin wrote to Zinoviev: 'Can you remember Koba's name?' Zinoviev could not. Lenin then asked Vyacheslav Karpinsky: 'I have a great favour to ask: find out for me (either from Stepko or Mikha etc.) "Koba's" name – (Josef Dzh . . . ? We've forgotten).'[10] Clearly, no great friendship existed between them at that time. There had been a few meetings and sporadic correspondence before October 1917. In November 1912 Dzhugashvili visited the Ulyanovs in Cracow, where he told Lenin he was working on an article on 'The National Question and Social Democracy'. Judging by the letter Lenin wrote to Maxim Gorky at the beginning of 1913, Dzhugashvili made a very good impression: 'About nationalism, I agree with you entirely that it has to be studied more seriously. We have a wonderful Georgian who has settled down to write a long article for *Prosveshchenie* [Enlightenment].'[11]

After Lenin returned to Russia in April 1917, he met Stalin fairly often, and after the seizure of power and especially during the civil war he became one of Lenin's closest comrades-in-arms. In all, Lenin sent him some 180 telegrams, letters, notes and similar documents. In April 1922 Lenin concurred with a proposal from Zinoviev and Kamenev, and Stalin became the first General Secretary of the Party Central Committee. Henceforth, he would, in Lenin's words, concentrate enormous power in his hands.

Lenin's choice fell upon the unprepossessing Stalin, who had done little during the October coup but had dutifully carried out the orders of the leadership in the civil war, because he needed someone who would organize the work of the Central Committee and serve as a willing instrument of his own wishes. And it seems that that is what he got, except that Stalin was not satisfied with the job of an executive, and on more than one occasion he had differences with Lenin which led to sharp exchanges. Once it was clear that Lenin was seriously ill, Stalin became even more independent in his actions.

Stalin did not provoke confrontation with Lenin, but repeatedly and by degrees he acted on his own and expressed his own opinions, for example over the formation of the Soviet Union, which Stalin saw as a large unified state. Through Kamenev, Lenin, then ill, sent a note to the Politburo setting out the principles of federal state structure. Stalin dismissed the proposals in a highly disrespectful manner: 'In my opinion, Comrade Lenin has jumped the gun by demanding the merging of the people's commissariats into federal commissariats ... His haste will provide ammunition for the "independentists" ... Lenin's amendment to paragraph 5 is, in my view, unnecessary ...'[12]

Lenin rejected the charge of being too hasty, and flung it back at his accuser. His letter 'On the Nationalities or on "Autonomization"', dictated on 30–31 December 1922, expressed his concern over the 'Georgian incident', in which Stalin and other emissaries from Moscow had resorted to physical force to compel the local Bolsheviks to toe Moscow's line: 'A fatal part was played here by Stalin's tendency to rush in and play the administrator against infamous "social nationalism". Animosity in politics usually makes things worse.'[13]

The problem was not, however, Lenin's or Stalin's "haste" over the nationalities issue, but rather the fact that it was being decided by the Party centre, who destroyed the old and tested administrative system of provinces and then started experimenting recklessly, handing down instructions from above and ignoring the deep national and social needs of the local population. At one of the many leadership meetings in the Kremlin, when strengthening the Union was under discussion, the trade union leader Mikhail Tomsky scribbled down a poem which he sent to Stalin and which encapsulated his understanding of the Union, the individual republics and the role of the Central Committee:

'No one alone
can teach the kids, judge and cure them,
we fight together – that's a must!
We have the right to rule them!'[14]

Stalin evidently liked Tomsky's doggerel, and kept it with his papers. Tomsky, a close ally of Bukharin's and a believer in workers' rights, was one of those who escaped Stalin's guillotine in the 1930s by committing suicide.

The friction between Lenin and Stalin extended to their personal relationship. Stalin in his early career was extremely boorish, coarse and unreserved. The émigré writer Mark Aldanov wrote of him: 'What is it that Stalin lacks? Culture. But, then, what do these people need culture for? Their rubber-stamp mentality works by itself – it's the same with practically all of them.'[15] In his relations with colleagues Stalin was often capricious, touchy and uncompromising, though he was generally constant in his hostility. He took a dislike to Krupskaya and thought that Lenin was too indulgent towards her work in education and cultural affairs. After Lenin had dictated his notorious postscript of 4 January 1923 to his 'Letter to Congress' of 24 December 1922, his so-called 'Testament', in which he said of Stalin: 'We should find someone who is more patient, more loyal, more respectful and more attentive to his comrades, less capricious and so on,'[16] Stalin assaulted Krupskaya with a torrent of abuse on the telephone, demanding to know why she had allowed the sick leader to write this.

A year earlier, Stalin had written to Lenin concerning an approach Krupskaya, as head of political propaganda, had made to the Politburo to separate the responsibilities of her organization more clearly from the Central Committee's own agitation and propaganda department. He irritably accused Krupskaya of being too hasty, and added: 'This is either a case of misunderstanding or flippancy. I understand your note of today to mean you want me to leave agitprop. You recall that the work in agitprop was put on me and that I didn't ask for it. It follows from this that I ought not to object to leaving it. But if you raise this precisely now, in connection with the abovementioned misunderstandings, then you'll be putting yourself in an awkward situation, as well as me. Trotsky and the others will think you're doing it "because of Krupskaya", that you're demanding a "sacrifice".[17]

Ten years after Lenin's death, V. Adoratsky, the head of the Marx-Engels-Lenin Institute, asked Stalin for permission to publish his speech honouring Lenin's fiftieth birthday in 1920, in which he had spoken of Lenin's ability 'to correct his own errors'. Stalin's note on Adoratsky's letters is eloquent: 'The speech was in general correct, though it needs some editing. But I wouldn't want it published: it's unpleasant to speak about Ilyich's mistakes.'[18]

Had Lenin had a few more years of good health, it is doubtful that Stalin would have succeeded him, though the nature of the system itself would not have changed, and it would still have found its 'Stalin'. But even the short time Stalin spent at Lenin's side taught him a lot and enabled him to do much. Lenin had been a model of how to struggle for power, and Stalin had learnt pragmatism and cunning from him. He had seen how at the crucial moment Lenin would stop at nothing, whether it was mass terror, pushing his own country into defeat or making peace with the enemy. Lenin had shown that it was possible to change political slogans overnight, organize monstrous actions such as the murder of the Romanovs while leaving no trace of his own complicity, or do away with his 'revolutionary allies', the SRs, decisively. Stalin was a diligent pupil.

Recognizing Lenin's huge authority in the Party, Stalin sensed that the key to his own fortunes lay in attaching himself as closely as possible to the ailing leader. He saw that Lenin's days were numbered and that the Party was already preparing to canonize his teachings, his 'precepts' and his style of operation. Dutifully, he would appear in Moscow from Gorki with greetings to the Politburo from a Lenin who was still just capable of understanding the situation and of giving instructions. Gradually an impression was created that the dying Lenin had put particular trust in his 'wonderful Georgian'. With the assistance of his then allies Kamenev and Zinoviev, Stalin was able to weaken, block and in effect neutralize the effect of Lenin's 'Testament'. The other senior figures were made aware that Stalin had donned the mantle of 'Lenin's protector'. That mantle would serve as an ideological suit of armour, making him impregnable in the fierce struggle for power to come.

Stalin's first major victory came when he misinformed Trotsky of the date of Lenin's funeral, causing him to miss it and thus to weaken his standing. This was not to be the last occasion on which jockeying for position at the funeral of the late Party leader assumed enormous significance; indeed, it would become a key indicator in a system that lacked any other overt, let alone constitutional, means of settling the succession.

It was in effect at Lenin's funeral on 26 January 1924 that Stalin took the crucial step towards becoming his successor. He had taken great care in preparing his speech to the Second All-Union Congress of Soviets that day, rewriting and polishing it until it acquired the precise semi-catechistic, semi-religious form he desired. He recited it to a stilled auditorium as a sacred oath to the dead leader: 'Leaving us, Comrade Lenin bequeathed to us the task of holding high and keeping pure the great calling of member of the Party. We swear to you, Comrade Lenin, that we will carry out your commandment with honour!' Seven times he repeated the words 'We swear.' He had not been empowered to speak in the name of the Party, yet his oaths gave precisely that impression: 'We shall preserve and strengthen the unity of our Party . . . preserve and strengthen the dictatorship of the proletariat . . . strengthen with all our force the union of workers and peasants . . . strengthen and broaden the union of the republics . . . strengthen our Red Army, our Red Fleet . . . strengthen and broaden the Communist International.'[19] The speech established the precedent for the ritual obsequies to the deceased leader whose 'precepts' everyone must follow. Largely as a result of Stalin's efforts, Lenin and Leninism were made into a pseudo-religion, a canon of revolutionary dogmas, the violation of which would be punished by death in the 1930s.

The foundations of the edifice of idolatry were laid with Lenin's death and the construction of the temple that was to hold his mummified remains, followed by thousands of monuments and millions of books. All of this was calculated to cloud the Russian public's mind with dogma. Stalin monopolized the exploitation of this heritage, labouring at his task not because he had loved Lenin – in the 1930s he made extremely disparaging remarks about him, which he alone could utter safely – but because the posthumous cult of the leader was useful to him as a weapon of power. A quotation from Lenin's burgeoning heritage would suffice to support an argument about sharpening the class war, the need for collectivization, or any other position.

While Lenin was alive, Stalin knew how to manipulate such terms as 'revolutionary expediency', 'revolutionary conscience' and 'revolutionary legality'. In July 1922 he sent a telegram to Gusev, the head of the Central Committee's Central Asian Bureau in Tashkent, and Sokolov, its representative in Bukhara: 'We have received your report of the arrest of the conspirators and leaders of the bandit gangs. The Central Committee suggests you do not let them go, but hand them over for trial to the Revolutionary tribunal for the supreme penalty, if evidence is found. The Central Committee is sure that this kind of punishment in present circumstances is the only way to teach the enemies of the people of Bukhara, and to clear the ground for Soviet statehood and revolutionary legality in Bukhara.'[20]

Stalin realized that, as its chief 'interpreter', he must develop Leninism. What sort of leader would he be if he were not also a theorist? It was an attitude that became a tradition. Every General Secretary, however uneducated, thought it his duty to publish bulky volumes of his 'works', even though they themselves often could not find the time to read them before publication. They had of course been written by numerous scribes. Stalin became a theorist by writing commentaries and exegeses of Lenin. The two most characteristic of these are *The Foundations of Leninism* and *Questions of Leninism*.

I remember as a cadet in tank school reading from cover to cover the six hundred pages of Stalin's speeches and articles, collected under the title of his central work, *Questions of Leninism*, with all the supplementary material it included. We had to write synopses of these works, to which our instructors paid particular attention. The more extensive the synopsis, and the more key passages were underlined in coloured pencil, the better our grade. This was the ideological fodder that fed millions of people: revolution – counter-revolution; socialism – imperialism; friend – enemy; white – black. Although after Stalin's death it was no longer necessary to copy his thoughts into thick exercise books, the spiritual nourishment changed little. We 'returned' to Lenin.

It was not only political knowledge that the people imbibed, it was also Bolshevik pseudo-culture, intolerance towards anything regarded as un-socialist, un-materialist, un-Soviet. Millions genuinely believed that the USSR was 'the most advanced state in the world in all respects', that 'the victory of Communism worldwide is inevitable', and that 'the higher the USSR's successes, the more insidious the enemies of the people will become'. The Leninist system created people who blindly believed such dogmas of the pseudo-religion as 'Marx's teaching is almighty because it is true', 'Politics is the concentrated expression of economics', 'Leninism is the Marxism of the era of imperialism'. It was possible to tell people that genetics and cybernetics were false sciences, that war was inevitable, capitalism doomed, and that there was no exploitation of man by man in the USSR.

Until the Twentieth Party Congress of 1956, the Russian people believed that Lenin and Stalin were indissoluble in their Bolshevik unity; and, strange though it seems, we were right. Even Nikolai Bukharin, as he sat in solitary confinement hoping in vain for Stalin's mercy, could write on the twentieth anniversary of the October coup:

> The epoch of the transition to socialism fell to the genius of Lenin and he embodied that stormy epoch in its mighty movements ... But an epoch produces the people it needs, and new steps by history have put Stalin in his place, whose centre of gravity of thought and action constitute the next passage of history, when socialism has conquered forever under his leadership. All active functions have been synthesized in the victorious achievement of the great Stalinist Five-Year Plans and theory unites with practice on a gigantic social scale.[21]

Not long before his arrest Bukharin had been in Paris, carrying out Stalin's orders to find and retrieve the archives of Marx, Engels and others. After much hesitation, he decided to visit the family of the Menshevik leader Fedor Dan. Dan's wife, Lydia Tsederbaum, recalled the visit. They touched on Stalin. Bukharin became excited and said: 'You say you don't know much about him, but we certainly do. He is even unfortunate in not being able to convince everyone, including himself, that he is bigger than everyone. If someone can speak better than he can, that person is doomed, as he won't let him remain alive, because that man is a constant reminder to him that he is not the first, not the very best. If someone writes better than he writes, that person is in trouble ... No, no, Fedor Ilyich [Dan], this is a little, evil man, no, not a man, a devil.'[22] Thus spoke Bukharin, one of the martyrs to the false idea, when for an instant he was free of the personal fear that is the inevitable psychological product of any despotism.

It should be noted that many Soviet citizens had, even at that time, a sort of 'lower storey' of awareness where they kept a secret refuge for their political scepticism, a silent protest against their lack of personal freedom. Often political conscience would withdraw to the subconscious, held there by fear. After Stalin's death this fear began to recede, and an entire genre of jokes emerged that it would have been fatal to voice during his lifetime: Kozlovsky, hearing that Stalin liked to hear him sing, asked a favour: 'I've never been abroad. I'd like to take a trip there.' 'Will you escape?' 'Comrade Stalin, how could you? My native village is dearer to me than anywhere abroad.' 'Good! Well spoken! Go and take a trip to your native village, then.'[23]

Stalin's main works on Leninism are not long. *The Foundations of Leninism* runs to around eighty pages, while *Questions of Leninism* amounts to no more than fifty. Yet Stalin managed to compress the whole of Lenin into this space: the historical roots of Leninism, class war, the dictatorship of the proletariat, the peasant question, the national question, strategy and tactics in revolution, the idea of socialism in one country, the world socialist revolution, Lenin's teaching on the Party and more, all in 130 pages. He at least deserves credit for his ability to simplify and abridge the most complex issues into short, telegraphic phrases. But he did so not to make them more accessible, but because that was the way he thought: in schematic, binary terms.

The entire 'theory of proletarian revolution' was encapsulated in 'first proposition', 'second proposition' and 'third proposition'. The concept of the Party was defined in a few characteristics: 'the party as the leading formation of the working class', 'the party as an organized unit', 'the party as the highest form of class organization', 'the party as a weapon of the dictatorship of the proletariat', 'the party as a unity of will'. He naturally relished Lenin's definition of the dictatorship of the proletariat as 'the supremacy of the proletariat over the bourgeoisie based on force and unrestricted by law', but he also preserved Lenin's – and Marx's – Utopian idea that the dictatorship of the proletariat 'is capable of preparing for the withering away of the state' under Communism. The peasants were, using Lenin's formulation, merely 'reserve proletarians', while the national question was 'no more than part of the question of the proletarian revolution, part of the question of the dictatorship of the proletariat'.

Stalin's thinking on the strategy and tactics of the Party in class war is noteworthy. Up to February 1917, he wrote, the basic attack had been 'to isolate the liberal-monarchical bourgeoisie'; from March to October 1917, 'the direction of the main attack was the isolation of petty bourgeois democracy' (the Mensheviks and SRs); and after October 'the main attack was to isolate the parties of the Second International'. It thus appears that only the liberals and other supporters of liberty in Russia were targets of the Bolsheviks.

As for reform, both Stalin and his mentor taught that 'the revolutionary accepts reform in order to use it as a hook for combining legal work with illegal work, in order to use it as a cover for intensifying illegal work.' Stalin wrote in his notebook before seeing the Italian Communist leader Palmiro Togliatti: 'Reformism consigns to oblivion the final goal and the basic means for achieving the final goal, i.e. the dictatorship of the proletariat.'[24]

Stalin made good use of Lenin's definition of the Party as 'a weapon of the dictatorship of the proletariat'. When in the late 1920s large numbers of Soviet citizens were fleeing abroad, and Soviet representatives were increasingly refusing to return home for fear of arrest, Stalin proposed: 'Individuals who refuse to return to the USSR place themselves outside the law. Placing oneself outside the law brings with it a) confiscation of all the convicted person's property; b) execution of the convicted person twenty-four hours after confirmation of his identity. This law has retrospective force.' On 21 November 1927 the Soviet government introduced the new law in virtually Stalin's original wording, and it was invoked to carry out the secret assassination abroad of anyone regarded as harmful to the regime. The NKVD used well-planned suicides, automobile accidents and mysterious disappearances.

It is rare to find in Stalin's works any imaginative writing. One example is in a section on 'Style in Work' in his *Questions of Leninism*, where he suddenly asserts that a 'particular type of Leninist worker has two qualities: Russian revolutionary audaciousness and American efficiency. American efficiency,' he informed the reader, 'is the kind of indefatigable strength that knows no limitations, that by efficient persistence sweeps before it all and every obstacle, that cannot leave unfinished any job it has started, even the smallest, and without it serious constructive work is unthinkable.'[25] The eleventh edition of

Stalin's 'work of genius' came out in 1945, at a time when pro-Allied sentiments were permissible, but only if uttered by the General Secretary himself, and when efficiency was much needed at home.

Stalin developed and 'enriched' Lenin's ideas in other ways. Speaking at the February–March 1937 Plenum of the Central Committee on 'Inadequacies in Party Work and Methods for Liquidating Trotskyist and Other Double-Dealers', he made a theoretical argument that would cost millions their lives. Point 7 of 'Our Tasks' in his report stated: 'The more we move forward, the more successes we have, the more embittered the remnants of the destroyed exploiting classes will become, the sooner they will resort to sharper forms of struggle, the worse dirty tricks they will play on the Soviet state, the more they will seize on the most desperate means of struggle, as the last resort of the doomed.' He concluded: 'These gentlemen will have to be smashed and rooted out mercilessly. That is what history teaches us. That is what Leninism teaches us.'[26]

As one of Stalin's longest-serving comrades-in-arms, Anastas Mikoyan, wrote in an article entitled 'Stalin is the Lenin of Today': 'Comrade Stalin, as an orthodox pupil of Lenin, has shown by all his thoughts and actions that he stands on the ground of creative Marxism, and also that he has enriched and raised to unprecedented heights the theoretical science of Marxism-Leninism.'[27] As an 'orthodox Leninist', Stalin was especially talented in the use of propaganda, as one neglected event in his life shows. In September 1927 a six-man American labour delegation arrived in Moscow. They were welcomed and well treated, as it was thought that through such delegations it would be possible for Comintern to exert influence on the labour movement in the USA. The visit was reported in *Pravda* and *Izvestiya* and on the radio. Stalin himself received the delegation in the Kremlin on 9 September. During the four-hour conversation, Stalin persistently asked why there was 'no special [i.e. Leninist] mass workers' party' in the USA. For their part, the Americans asked questions which Stalin could not answer satisfactorily without resorting to classic Leninist cant.

Asked whether the Communist Party controlled the Soviet government, Stalin replied that in the USSR there were 'no financial bigshots' or 'money-bags', and their control 'over the government is unthinkable'. But, he added, the Party did control the government. This kind of control, he went on, worked because the Party enjoyed the confidence of the majority of workers and toilers, and had the right to control the organs of government in the name of that majority. The Americans at once asked: 'How do you know the masses are sympathetic to Communism?'

Stalin then gave his visitors a half-hour lecture, claiming that during the October coup and civil war, and in the present peaceful period, the Communists had gained the upper hand and held the leading positions in all state governing bodies. 'Could that be accidental?' he asked. The Communists ruled in the trade unions and youth organizations. 'Could that be an accident? Can it be accidental that the influence of the Communist Party is so great at conferences and meetings? That's how I know that the broad masses of workers and peasants are sympathetic to the Communist Party.' He could not of course tell his guests that under an unrestricted dictatorship it made no difference whether or not the workers and peasants really did support the Party, or that thousands had been shot or exiled to concentration camps for showing a lack of such support.

The Americans asked Stalin what in the Soviet system replaced the incentive of profit that motivated production in the US. Stalin replied, without batting an eye: 'Knowing that the workers are not working for a capitalist, but for their own state.' He was then asked whether the Party was sending money to support the American Communist Party and its newspaper the *Daily Worker*. His reply was quite categorical: 'I have to state that I know of no occasion when representatives of the American Communist Party have asked for help from the Communist Party of the USSR. You may think it strange, but it is a fact that speaks of the excessive scrupulousness of the American Communists.'[28]

He could hardly have forgotten that since 1919 the Politburo had been sending large sums of gold roubles, and subsequently dollars, to America through various individuals: in 1919–20 alone one Kotlyarov received 209,000 roubles, Khavkin 500,000 roubles, Anderson 1,011,000 roubles and the journalist John Reed 1,008,000 roubles. Dozens of groups in other countries received similar cash injections over the years to start revolutionary movements and found parties, and the practice continued until 1991. Stalin answered a dozen more questions in the same mendacious vein.

Lies and force were the two main weapons of totalitarianism. Speaking at the Eighteenth Party Congress on 10 March 1939, Stalin said: 'In 1937 Tukhachevsky, Yakir, Uborevich and other monsters were sentenced to be shot. Following that, elections to the Supreme Soviet of the USSR took place. Those elections gave the Soviet regime 98.6 per cent of all the votes. At the beginning of 1938 Rozengolts, Rykov, Bukharin and other monsters were sentenced to be shot. Following that, elections to the Supreme Soviets of the Union Republics took place. The elections gave the Soviet regime 99.4 per cent of all the votes cast.' This showed, he claimed, that 'purging Soviet organizations of spies, murderers and saboteurs' would lead to the strengthening of the Soviet state.[29] What it really showed was that without lies and force the Soviet regime could not exist. Elections with no choice of candidate and against a background of massive blood-letting created a permanent climate of fear in which votes of nearly 100 per cent were the natural outcome in Soviet 'elections'.

Terror was not dreamt up by Stalin. It had been Lenin's first resort after seizing power in 1917. Lenin had wanted to 'turn the state into an institution that will force the doing of the will of the people. We want to organize coercion in the name of the toilers' interests.'[30] Stalin had not forgotten Lenin's words to the representatives of the food commissions at the Petrograd Soviet on 27 January 1918: '[As] long as we do not apply terror to speculators – shooting on the spot – we'll achieve nothing ... We have to deal with thieves just as decisively – shooting on the spot.'[31] 'The dictatorship – and take this into account once and for all –' Lenin had made emphatically clear, 'means unrestricted power based on force, not on law.'[32]

As we have seen, when editing his own biography Stalin described himself as 'Lenin's outstanding pupil' and the great continuer of his work.[33] After his death, the Party was compelled to make some corrections to the relationship between the first leader and his successor. In a report to a closed session of the Twentieth Congress on 25 February 1956, Khrushchev mercilessly dethroned the 'pupil' and attributed all his evil doings to the 'cult of personality'. The 'teacher', Lenin, meanwhile, was extolled to even greater heights.

For the next thirty years, all the General Secretaries carried on the Sisyphean task of 'resurrecting Lenin's principles',[34] of 'going back to Lenin'. The teacher, however, was worthy of his pupil, and vice versa.

Lenin and Stalin were consistent in applying the harshest orthodox Bolshevik line, that deified the higher aim and the leader. The Party was the instrument, and human beings merely a means of social movement. Thanks to Lenin, mankind has learnt that Communism is a road to nowhere. Nevertheless, without Lenin's false Utopia it is impossible to conceive of the twentieth century. The system he and Stalin created proved to be both inhuman and unreformable.

The Stalinist System

As a Secretary of the Central Committee, and from 1922 its General Secretary, as well as holding the office of People's Commissar for Nationalities and wielding executive control of all senior Party posts, Stalin had enormous power, just as Lenin had said. In the struggle for succession, no other Bolshevik could call on so many supporters in the hierarchy to secure the necessary majority or the acclaim that was needed to stay on top. By 1930 Stalin had eliminated Trotsky as a rival, and emasculated all other possible contenders. That did not mean that he did not face opposition, but it did mean that as supreme leader he was virtually invulnerable.

Like his predecessor, Stalin thought in terms of classes and masses. While terms like 'rank and file Communist', 'worker' and 'poor peasant' all figure prominently enough in his speeches and writings, they are no more than the building blocks for the edifice of Communism in the minds of the leaders. Individuals, apart from the Communist leadership, cultural figures, military commanders and 'enemies of the people', were of interest to Stalin only as objects of his demagoguery, his propaganda or 'demonstrations' of love for his fellow man.

At a passing-out ceremony of military academy graduates in the Kremlin on 4 May 1935, Stalin opened his speech by saying: 'we have not yet learned to appreciate people, appreciate personnel, and appreciate the cadres.' He recalled an incident from his days in exile in Siberia. During the spring floods, the peasants collected the wood carried down by the rivers. 'They returned to the village one evening minus one of their number. Asked where the thirtieth man was, they replied casually, "He's still out there," "Maybe he drowned," and one man left in a hurry, saying, "I have to go and feed the mare." When

I reproached them for caring more about livestock than people, one of them replied, to the general approval of the rest, "Why should we care about people? We can always make more. But a mare? Just try."' Stalin then declared: 'Of all the valuable assets in the world, people are the most valuable and the most decisive capital.'[35] In the previous five years the mindless collectivization of agriculture over which he had presided had cost 9.5 million lives. More than a third of these had been shot or tortured, perished on long death marches into exile, or died in the frozen wastes of Siberia and the far north. The rest had died of famine.

Stalin shaped a system founded on an infallible, universal ideology, a party consisting of legions of bureaucrats, a single and almighty leader who was virtually an earthly god, a vast military machine, and total political surveillance by 'punitive organs'. The amorphous, anonymous crowd was wrapped in a blanket of ideology and used as an obedient tool. As for the Party, it was, as Stalin put it in a speech of July 1921, 'a kind of order of sword-bearers within the Soviet state',[36] and with the aid of the 'transmission belts and levers' provided by the trade unions and other organizations, the Party held the masses in its grip. As Stalin said: 'No important political or organizational issue is decided by our Soviet or other mass organizations without directional instruction of the Party.'[37] The individual, in other words, was no more than a tiny cog in the machine that executed the dictator's will.

Stalin's wishes were carried out by a huge Party apparatus of local secretaries, whom he liked to think of in military terms. In a long speech he gave at the February–March 1937 Plenum on ways to liquidate the Party's enemies, he declared: 'In our Party, if we look at the leading strata, there are some three to four thousand top leaders. That's what I would call the high command of the Party. Then there are about thirty to forty thousand middle leaders. That's our officer corps. Then there are about 100–150,000 lower ranks. They are, so to speak, the Party's NCOs.'[38] The tendency to clothe bureaucrats in army uniform is a well-established principle of totalitarian systems. Slogans initiated by the dictatorship and promulgated by the bureaucracy were translated into 'direct orders'[39] for the masses. Between the hands holding the reins and the society they guided was the intervening pyramid of the Party structure. At every level of this structure the ever-alert eye of the omnipotent NKVD kept watch on the reliability of the 'cogs', their loyalty to the idea and to the leader.

Like the state organs, industrial and agricultural institutions also became instruments of coercion. At a combined session of the Central Committee and Central Control Commission, Stalin declared on 11 January 1933: 'From the Leninist point of view, and seen as a form of organization, the *kolkhozes* [collective farms], like the Soviets, are a weapon, and only a weapon.'[40] Henceforth, coercion was a permanent feature of village life.

In addition to the 'absolutely true' Idea of Communism, the system also had the Plan. Approved by the leader, the Plan was law for everyone, from People's Commissars and members of the Politburo down to political prisoners. The most important was the Five-Year Plan – the *pyatiletka*. Even if it was not met, every newspaper, radio station and meeting would declare that the Five-Year Plan had been 'over-fulfilled'. In January 1933, for instance, Stalin announced that the first *pyatiletka* had been 'completed in four years and three months'. The Plan was everything. The planning of the economy, and of the whole of socialist life, was considered the top priority of the system.

Nevertheless, the leader had the right to introduce changes to even the most audacious plans. On 10 March 1939, at the Eighteenth Party Congress, Stalin declared:

> We have overtaken the main capitalist countries in terms of production technology and the rate of industrial development. That is very good. But it is not enough. We also have to overtake them in economic terms (i.e. in the production of goods which the population wants). We can do it and we must do it . . . we shall have an abundance of goods and be in a position to move from the first phase of Communism to the second phase. To do this, there must be an indomitable desire to go forward and a readiness to make sacrifices.[41]

The 'great purge' was barely over. More than five million people had been arrested, and nearly a million shot, yet Stalin was talking about sacrifices. Economic realities were completely disregarded, as precedence was given to the 'general line', which of course only he could define. To ensure that the masses could comprehend it, Stalin paid particular attention to the brainwashing function of the Party's work. At the Eighteenth Congress he said: 'Had we been able to prepare our cadres ideologically, we have every reason to assume that nine-tenths of our problems would have been solved by now.'[42] In fact, there was a widespread belief that things were not going well at all. Alexander Solzhenitsyn has recalled conversations with close friends in concentration camp who were convinced that Bolshevism would ultimately collapse. The archives confirm that the authorities were receiving letters from all over the country and from all kinds of people expressing rejection and condemnation of Party policy. It therefore came as no surprise when at the end of the Second World War more than a million Soviet citizens made every effort to avoid returning to their native land, many of them no doubt afraid of punishment, but most of them simply seeking freedom from Stalin's 'paradise'. In May 1946 intelligence chief F.I. Golikov reported that 300,000 Soviet citizens were under US or British administration in camps in western Europe.[43] By 1952 there were 452,000 Soviet citizens in western Europe.

The Stalinist system arose as a kind of pseudo-culture which rendered the fate of the individual unimportant and the power of the state overwhelming. It had for years fed off ideas of social justice and protecting the poor and the proletariat, resorting to Utopian treatises of the past that promised a golden age. Leninism and Stalinism took from Marxism one of its less emphasized aspects, namely the idea of dictatorial power.

For all the monstrously inhuman and secretive nature of Stalinist society, it nevertheless held a certain fascination for many intellectuals and ordinary people in the West. The propaganda about the 'workers' and peasants' state' which Moscow-dependent Communist parties pumped out sustained trust in the USSR among various Western groups. During the Stalin years, the regime simultaneously alarmed and attracted outsiders. Foreign writers promulgated the false myth of Stalin the genius. The French novelist Henri Barbusse, for example, wrote: 'Whoever you may be, the best thing in your life is in the hands of a man who is vigilant and who works for everyone, a man with the head of a scientist, the face of a worker and the clothes of a simple soldier.'[44]

In 1935 Stalin initiated a new constitution to replace the one that had been adopted in 1924, the year of Lenin's death. Stalin explained that the new constitution would reflect the new industrial base of the state, the destruction of the kulaks and the victory of the collective farm system, and the complete liquidation of private property.[45] Having eliminated the 'antagonistic' elements of society, the government now proposed a democratic electoral system of universal, direct and secret voting to replace the class-based system of the old constitution. All the civil liberties were now included, and a citizen could only be arrested with the sanction of a court. Most important – since it vitiated all these rights – the role of the Communist Party as the 'leading core of all organizations and of the working people, both public and state', and as the body that judged and determined the political correctness of every aspect of public and private activity, was enshrined in the new constitution as Article 126.

Stalin failed to mention two things. First, he wanted international recognition of his strength. His meetings and long conversations with foreign writers like Emil Ludwig and H.G. Wells were aimed at creating an attractive world image of the Soviet leader. Ludwig had said: 'For more than twenty years I have been studying the lives and activities of great historical figures,'[46] while Wells announced that he had 'just had a long talk with President Roosevelt . . . Now I've come to you to ask you what you are doing to change the world.'[47] Like any dictator, Stalin wanted worldwide popularity, but he also wanted the Soviet system to have an appeal and to inspire the workers of the world. The new constitution, his constitution, was intended to help achieve this. Addressing the Eighth Congress of Soviets in December 1936, he declared: 'This will be a document testifying to the fact that what millions of honest people in capitalist countries have dreamt, and still dream of, has already been accomplished in the USSR. It will be a document testifying to the fact that what has already been accomplished in the USSR can also be fully accomplished in other countries.'[48] The new constitution was duly approved.

The second thing Stalin failed to tell his listeners was that while he had been preparing the new constitution, he had also been preparing a vast and bloody purge. Why he felt it necessary is still a matter of controversy. His power was unshakeable, all open opposition had been crushed, and the intimidated population gazed in fear and ecstasy at the ubiquitous portraits of their pockmarked leader. To understand why Stalin launched the great purge, it is important to understand that he was driven by a powerful need to win. He was obsessed by the idea of 'overtaking' everyone, of 'racing forward' a hundred years in ten. He told the Party in February 1931: 'Either we do this, or they [the capitalists] will crush us.' He was trying to outrun the natural course of events. People, however, change slowly. Soviet society, Stalin maintained, still harboured countless members of the old middle classes, former officers, unreconstructed members of the pre-1917 political parties, covert saboteurs and spies, and 'the sharpening of the class struggle' was at hand.[49] The system needed a general purge, from which it would emerge stronger and more homogeneous, and hence able to speed up 'the transition to the second phase of Communism'. The creation of a new constitution and the act of 'clearing' the social field for its operation were thus closely connected.

It is a mistake to assume that the 'great terror' took place only in the years 1937–38. For the Stalinist system to function on all levels, for it to achieve its economic, social and political goals, permanent purge was a necessity. The entire period of Stalin's rule was a bloody one, though the 1930s saw the worst excesses, as Stalin sought to secure a greater 'moral and political unity of society'. The population, silent except when told to shout the slogan of the day, was made to expose and 'uproot' a seemingly endless succession of hostile groups.

In 1932–33 the OGPU took action against the so-called 'Union of Marxist-Leninists', headed by M. Ryutin, V. Kayurov and A. Slepkov. These 'romantic' Marxists had said that the crisis in the Party could be overcome if it 'returned to Lenin' and removed Stalin as General Secretary. Arrest, torture and imprisonment ensued. An exceptional man in many respects, Ryutin displayed remarkable courage. He wrote in his last letter to the government that he was 'not afraid of death', even though he was 'utterly defenceless, without rights, tied hand and foot, tightly cooped up from the outside world'. His resistance, like that of his comrades, was finally broken by a bullet in the back of the neck on 10 January 1937. When Stalin was informed that the 'case was closed', he snapped: 'It should have been done long ago.'[50]

Under Lenin, and to a greater degree under Stalin, cases were brought against so-called 'national deviationists'. Georgian, Belorussian, Kazakh, Bashkir, Ukrainian, Bukharan and other republican leaders were shot for nothing more than attempting to preserve the national culture and consciousness of their peoples. They were executed because their loyalty to Stalin's policy of the 'fusion of the nations' was under question. The system levelled everyone down and made them into uniform citizens, but this was much harder to accomplish in the sphere of ethnic relations.

The 'punitive organs' began with industrial, agricultural and 'ideological' cases. The military were largely untouched until, in the summer of 1937, Stalin not only initiated a case, but conducted it himself. Playing with his victim like a cat with a mouse, he invited Marshal of the Soviet Union Mikhail Tukhachevsky to see him in the Kremlin on the afternoon of 13 May. He saw him for forty minutes, with Molotov, Yezhov, Voroshilov and Kaganovich in attendance. Tukhachevsky was silent when he left, his face dead white. On 22 May Stalin ordered his arrest, and that of many other senior military men. Within a week, the youngest marshal in the army had been broken. He confessed to spying, meeting Trotsky's son Lev in London, selling himself to the Fascists, and various other charges. A special judicial hearing of the Supreme Court was held, Stalin himself instructing the prosecutors, Vyshinsky and Ulrikh, several times. The court opened on 11 June 1937. Before sentence was passed, Ulrikh was summoned by Stalin.[51] The exchange was brief: 'He has confessed to everything, just like the others.' Stalin approved the sentence which Ulrikh announced at 11.35 that night. All the defendants were shot. A week after Tukhachevsky and his seven 'accomplices' were executed, twenty-one corps commanders, thirty-seven divisional commanders, twenty-nine brigade commanders and dozens of regimental commanders and army commissars were arrested. In the next two years, more than forty-five thousand officers and political army personnel would be arrested, and fifteen thousand of them would be shot. Of the eighty-five members of the Military Army Council, only nine escaped arrest, while sixty-eight were shot. Stalin had decapitated the army on the eve of a world war.

The war slowed down the terror machine, although in the autumn of 1941 the Soviet Germans were deported to Siberia and Kazakhstan, and the suspicion of disloyalty among certain other small nationalities, including the Chechens, Ingushes and Crimean Tatars, led to their wholesale deportation.

There is evidence to suggest that shortly before his death Stalin was planning a major new purge. On his personal initiative, in May–June 1952 the Military Board of the Supreme Court of the USSR reviewed the case of the Jewish Anti-Fascist Committee, which had been established in the spring of 1942 to rally support among the world's Jews – especially in the USA – for the Soviet war effort. As always, the charge was espionage, and all considerations of the great work the committee had done for the country were consigned to oblivion. The trial was conducted without counsels for the prosecution or the defence, and Stalin had already settled that all the defendants would be shot, with the sole exception of Academician Lina Shtern, the only woman.

Like the notorious 'Doctors' Plot' that was to follow shortly, in which a number of leading physicians who treated the Kremlin leaders, including Stalin, were accused of plotting to murder their illustrious patients, the case of the Anti-Fascist Jewish Committee both launched a new wave of terror and stirred up the traditional anti-Semitism of the Soviet regime. Following the trial, many Jews were arrested and shot or exiled to the Gulag for periods of fifteen to twenty-five years.

Although the system strove to maintain itself by every means at its disposal, the archives show that not all the regime's efforts to ensure uniformity of thought succeeded. The new constitution was received with acclaim, yet the Secret Political Section of the NKVD security branch reported hundreds of negative responses to the Politburo. A report on the region of Ivanovo is typical. Collective farmer Ya. Loginov said: 'What does your constitution give us? What Stalin has written, so be it, but it's not what we want . . . just look, we've got to the point where we've absolutely nothing to live on . . . We've nothing to eat, but they still tell us to give it all to the state.' At the M. Gorky Weaving Plant a meeting was called to discuss the draft constitution: 'To keep the workers in, the doors were locked. Apprentice Skurikhin and a group of others managed to trick the guard, open the doors with a shout and let forty people out of the meeting . . . Those who didn't manage to get out slept until the meeting was over.'[52] In all such instances, the reaction of the regime was the same: 'Step up the battle with hostile elements.'

In these circumstances the line between lies and truth, force and authority, was obliterated. In December 1936 a Plenum took place to discuss Trotskyist and right anti-Soviet organizations,[53] and another in March 1937 debated 'inadequacies in Party work and measures to liquidate Trotskyists and other double-dealers'.[54] The record of these proceedings creates the appalling picture of an irrational world where common abuse served as a substitute for anything remotely approaching political debate. It was as if these were not the leaders of a great state assembled in convocation, but a mob of criminals with no sense of civilized values or the basic norms of human relations, even those they themselves proclaimed in their 'most democratic constitution'.

The Generalissimo's Baton

Some six weeks before the German invasion of the USSR, on 4 May 1941, Hitler addressed the Reichstag, repeating triumphantly that Poland had been crushed, France, Norway, Belgium and Holland occupied, and that German forces were succeeding in Greece. As usual, he aimed his threats at 'Jewish capitalism', 'the English and American instigators of the war', and Winston Churchill.

He uttered not a single word about the USSR. He could have pointed out that in August 1939, having intervened in talks between the Soviets and the Western powers, he had 'picked off' Stalin, who had not only signed a non-aggression pact almost at once, but within a month also a treaty on friendship and borders. On 20 August 1939 Hitler had sent a sharply worded six-point ultimatum to Stalin, ending: 'I believe that should both governments intend to enter new relations with each other, it would be wise not to lose time. Therefore I suggest once again that you receive my Foreign Minister on Tuesday 22 August, and at the latest on Wednesday 23 August.'[55] Late in the evening of 23 August an excited Ribbentrop telephoned his Führer from Molotov's office to say 'It's in the bag.' He had signed a treaty 'on demarcating the spheres of mutual interest in Eastern Europe', meaning in effect the division of Poland between Germany and the USSR. In January 1941, for declining to take a piece of Lithuania, Germany received Moscow's written assurance of compensation in the sum of 31,500,000 German gold marks.

Why had the two dictators come to terms so quickly? Stalin had been talking to the British and French for many months and not even agreed on the terms of their talks, yet with Hitler it was all over in two or three days. Both leaders had world plans, both detested democracy and were committed to super-rearmament, and both were used to manipulating the weapons of totalitarianism: lies and force. Stalin was a social racist, Hitler an ethnic racist.

In his speech on 4 May 1941, Hitler said nothing about Stalin or their treaty of friendship, except in the form of a veiled threat when he pointed out: 'The German armed forces will constantly intervene whenever and wherever it is necessary ... for the German soldier, nothing is impossible.'

Next day, 5 May, Stalin was scheduled to address military academy graduates in the Kremlin. Half an hour before the banquet was due to start, he was handed a telegram from Berlin with a brief summary of Hitler's speech.

'Why,' Stalin asked in his speech to the graduates, 'is Germany winning?' He remarked on the high level of German organization and combat technology, and referred significantly to the fact that Germany had allies. But, he added in direct response to Hitler's speech, as a result of its victories the German army was 'displaying arrogance, self-satisfaction and conceit. Their military thinking is not progressing, their military technology is lagging behind ours.'

Many toasts and congratulations were raised at the banquet. Stalin proposed three himself. When a vodka-flushed tank general proposed a toast to 'our peaceful Stalinist foreign policy', Stalin rose slowly and interrupted with: 'Allow me to make an amendment.' Carefully choosing his words, he declared: 'A peaceful policy is a good thing. For the time being, and for as long as our army was not rearmed, we have been following a policy of defence ... But now that we have reconstructed our army, built up sufficient technology for contemporary warfare, become strong – now is the time to move from the defensive to the offensive. To carry out the defence of our country, we are obliged to act in an offensive way. [We have] to move from defence to a military policy of attack. We must restructure our training, our propaganda and agitation, and our press in an offensive spirit. The Red Army is a modern army, and a modern army is an offensive army.'[56]

It would appear that this speech supports the thesis (advanced by Viktor Suvorov in his book *Icebreaker*) that Stalin was preparing to invade Germany. It was never a secret that Stalin and the Bolsheviks were always preparing for an offensive war – this was implicit and explicit in the Leninist idea of world revolution. Of course Stalin was preparing for a war with Germany. It is possible that he was even warning Hitler, though of course he would not give any clue as to a timetable. No document, however, has yet been produced that proves this. But we can surmise the possibility from the fact that on 14 May 1941 Defence Commissar Timoshenko and Chief of the General Staff Zhukov sent orders 'of special importance' to the commanders of Western, Baltic and Kiev military districts. Their task was defined thus: 'By 20 May 1941, you personally, with your headquarters chief of staff and district headquarters chief of operations, must work out: a detailed plan of defence of the state frontier.' Nothing was said about preparing an attack on the Germans, or about a pre-emptive Soviet invasion of Germany. It was, moreover, impossible to contemplate a large-scale offensive against Germany without a detailed and documented operational analysis, without creating the necessary army groupings, and many other undertakings. It would be possible to send a unit into battle on verbal orders only, but never a multi-million-man army. If Stalin was preparing to attack Hitler first, the possibility of which certainly cannot be excluded, he must have been planning to do it later.

Suvorov's assertion that Stalin was planning to attack Germany on 6 July 1941 is not sustained by any known documentation. Perhaps aware of accusations that might be levelled against him of his real intentions, Stalin declared in a radio address on 3 July: 'Our peace-loving country, not wishing to take the initiative in breaking the pact, could not choose the path of perfidy.'[57] Even Hitler, in a frank letter to Mussolini on 21 June 1941, says nothing about his invasion being 'pre-emptive'. 'Collaboration with the Soviet Union,' he wrote, 'was extremely appealing to me. For it meant a break with my entire past, my world-view and my previous circumstances.'

Early in the morning of 22 June 1941, troops of the German Wehrmacht and their allies carried out an offensive against the Soviet Union, in defiance of the non-aggression pact between the two countries. Had Stalin undertaken a number of essential measures, as he was urged to do by his generals, his intelligence sources and Winston Churchill,[58] the terrible war that followed might have been shorter and less costly in lives. Had the forces at Stalin's disposal been deployed in full war-alert in their planned defensive positions even a week before the invasion, the blow from Hitler's war machine would have been absorbed to a significant degree. Perhaps the Red Army would have fallen back 150 kilometres into Soviet territory, but the invaders would never have reached Moscow, still less the Volga. Stalin's miscalculation was of such vast, catastrophic proportions that it is hard to find anything comparable in history. On a message sent by Comintern agent Richard Sorge from Tokyo on 15 June 1941, to the effect that Hitler would attack on 22 June, Stalin scrawled 'German disinformation.' On 16 June a report came from the chief of the First Section of the Commissariat of State Security, Fitin, who wrote: 'Preparations for an armed invasion of the USSR are fully complete and the attack may be expected at any time.'[59] Stalin responded with a note to Commissar for State Security Merkulov: 'You can tell your "source" in German air force headquarters to go fuck himself. He's not a "source", he's a disinformer.'[60]

Immersed as he was in an atmosphere of spy-mania of his own making, Stalin was clearly unable to evaluate the various kinds of information arriving in the Kremlin on the eve of the war. Nor was there the possibility of sober collective judgement while he was the subject of such total adulation. He believed that his judgements and wishes coincided with the real needs of the Party and the country which he ruled like an absolute monarch.

The appalling suffering inflicted on the Soviet people in the war was no less the result of German force and treachery than of major mistakes by the Soviet leadership. Apart from the damage caused by dismissing vital and, as it transpired, accurate intelligence, flawed strategic thinking compounded the disaster. The General Staff were committed to defending the country from an attack either on its western approaches or from the east. On the grounds that all of Hitler's successful campaigns had been won by going straight for the capital of the country under attack, Soviet strategists advised that the main thrust would come in the Minsk-Smolensk direction. This is precisely what happened. Stalin, however, regarded the south-west as the area most likely to attract Hitler's main strike. He was still thinking in terms of the civil war period, when coal from the Donbass, grain from Ukraine, and 'a direct line to the oil' had dominated strategy. The military leadership, well trained not to dispute Stalin's views, agreed at once, and it was decided to strengthen the south-west by transferring twenty-five divisions from the Western front.

It was envisaged that the first strategic echelon would be deployed in depth, with fifty-seven divisions for cover, fifty-two in the second line, and sixty-two in reserve. This allowed the Germans an easy breakthrough, as the Soviet strongpoints were not invested with high concentrations of forces, and the Germans could therefore pick off Soviet formations unit by unit. Stalin would later blame the military for these failures. Ten years after the war, Colonel-General Leonid Sandalov wrote: 'The defeat of our troops in the western districts took place as the result of our weaker technical equipment and the feebler training of Red Army troops and headquarters staffs by comparison with the army of Nazi Germany.'[61] Sandalov was not ready to speak his mind on the role of the leadership in Moscow.

The catastrophic start of the war required scapegoats, and many of them. Dozens of generals were arrested. Typical of their fate was the tragedy of forty-four-year-old commander of the Western front General Dmitri Pavlov, a Hero of the Soviet Union once much-favoured by Stalin. In his last words at a hastily arranged trial just one month after the invasion on 22 July 1941, Pavlov said: 'We are here in the dock not because we have committed crimes in time of war, but because we prepared for this war inadequately in peacetime.' Pavlov behaved with dignity, resolutely rejecting the standard charges of malicious intent and treason. Persistent efforts were made to force him to admit that he had taken part in an 'army plot' to 'open the front to the enemy'. Investigators Pavlovsky and Komarov succeeded in getting him to 'confess' on 7 July that 'hostile activity' had been present in his actions, but during the trial he defiantly repudiated the testimony that had been beaten out of him. A few hours after the proceedings, along with the other 'conspirators', Generals V. Klimov-skikh, A. Grigoriev and A. Korobkov, Pavlov was shot.

The same fate befell Marshal of the Soviet Union G. Kulik, who had been known to Stalin since the civil war. In the first months of the war, however, Stalin became disillusioned with Kulik, who had been unable to carry out a single order from the Supreme Commander properly. Kulik's downfall came when he was sent on Stalin's orders to hold Kerch in the Crimea. On 11 November 1941 he had arrived at the besieged city, where the 271st, 276th and 156th Rifle Divisions amounted to little more than their identification numbers, as they had no more than two or three hundred troops at their disposal. Naturally, these demoralized remnants of the Red Army could not withstand the might of 42nd German Army Corps.[62] Nor could Pavlov, with his distinctly limited martial skills, do anything either, and Kerch fell on 15 November.

On 16 February 1942, on Stalin's orders a special hearing of the Supreme Court stripped Kulik of his marshal's rank and all his decorations. Like Pavlov, he faced execution, but at the last moment, and quite out of character, Stalin showed 'clemency'. His working diary for that day reads: 'Today. Question of Kulik – to Siberia?'[63] In the event Kulik avoided Siberia as well. He was made a major-general and given second-rate postings. During his last years in the service, in Volga Military District, he complained about his fate to the similarly disgraced Colonel-General V. Gordov, whose deputy he was. This was enough to get them both, and a third unfortunate, district headquarters chief General F. Rybakchenko, arrested and shot on 24 August 1950.[64]

Thanks to the 'punitive organs', which were not idle for a moment, every serving officer at the front was in mortal danger, not just from the enemy, but also from the unsleeping eye of the 'special sections'. The climate of the time is graphically described in a report to Stalin by commander of 43rd Army Major-General K. Golubev: 'The army has stopped running away and for about twenty days has been smashing the enemy in the teeth. In the thick of the battle, thirty men had to be shot, while those who should have been were treated kindly. I request that the policy of the knout not be applied any more to me, as commanding officer, and as took place in the first five days. The day after I arrived they promised to shoot me, the next day to put me on trial, and on the fourth day they threatened to shoot me in front of the ranks.'[65]

Stalin himself was among the first to collapse in confusion and shock. By the end of June 1941 he was devastated, and did not appear in the Kremlin for some days. This has been disputed, the assertion being made that not for one hour did Stalin taken his hands off the levers of government. In fact it is now possible to prove by documentary evidence that this was not the case.

Stalin arrived at the Kremlin before lunchtime on 28 June. Between then and 12.50 on the morning of 29 June he received twenty-one people, the overwhelming majority of them military. Timoshenko and

Zhukov were with him from 9.30 to 11.10 p.m., Golikov, chief of the Main Intelligence Directorate, having left half an hour earlier. The military chiefs reported that German tanks had been seen to the east of Minsk. Stalin could not believe this. 'Surely not Minsk? You must have got it wrong.' Air chiefs Zhigarev and Suprun confirmed the facts. Stalin then received Politburo member A. Mikoyan and People's Commissar for State Security V. Merkulov.

At around 1 a.m he left for his dacha at Kuntsevo, and did not return to the Kremlin until 1 July.[66] Earlier that morning, Molotov, Beria, Malenkov, Kaganovich and Mikoyan had arrived at Kuntsevo. Stalin had recoiled from them with a look of fear on his face. He evidently thought they had come to arrest him. Instead, they made a number of proposals for organizing resistance to the aggressor. Stalin gradually regained his composure and recovered from the state of psychological shock he had been in. For three days he had been prostrate and in no condition to run the nation's affairs.

Stalin exacerbated the already extreme violence of the war by pursuing his customary methods of ruling. He was extricated from his disastrous miscalculations not only by the unprecedented self-sacrifice of the Soviet people, but also by the mass terror applied to those who wavered, lost heart or displayed temporary confusion, which occurred most frequently when they lost control of their troops. The Main Political Directorate of the Red Army received daily reports of the execution of order No. 227, which Stalin had dictated, edited and signed on 28 July 1942. In accordance with this order, penal battalions were rapidly formed consisting of senior and middle-ranking officers who had 'shown panic', and penal companies of other ranks and junior officers. Having experienced German encirclement, officers were sent to special camps at Lyubertsy, Podolsk, Ryazan, Kalach, Kotluban, Stalingrad, Belokalitva, Georgiev, Ugol, Khonlar and elsewhere. Rifle regiments formed of officers who had escaped from encirclement were 929 men strong.[67]

Stalin waited impatiently for reports that his order, dubbed at the front the 'not one step back' order, was being implemented. He bawled out commanding officers in crude terms, demanded merciless treatment for 'panic-mongers', and urged more active use of 'blocking units', whereby soldiers who were under threat of punishment were placed behind advancing infantry with orders to stop, by any means, troops who tried to retreat. Commanders would take his calls on the direct link to Moscow with a heavy heart, knowing in advance the kind of instructions and demands he was about to issue. No one could be sure that the call would not end badly for himself. The telegraph tapes of these calls show that often the same question was put: 'Why aren't you carrying out my order No. 227? What have you personally done in this regard?'

Every political administration, at headquarters and at army level, prepared daily reports for Moscow. The following is typical of many: 'Between 1 and 10 August, 2,099 men were seized by blocking units, of whom 378 were trying to run from the field of battle, 713 had escaped from encirclement, 94 were cases of self-mutilation, and the remaining 914 were absent from their units. Of those seized, 517 have been sent to penal companies, 111 to special camps, 82 to despatch points, 104 were arrested, and 83 have been shot in front of the ranks for cowardice, panic-mongering and self-mutilation.'[68]

During this period, on the Stalingrad front alone 140 men were shot by the blocking units, while for the whole of 1941 and 1942, for 'panic-mongering, cowardice and unauthorized abandonment of the field of battle', no fewer than 157,593 men – a full sixteen divisions – were sentenced to death by HQ or army tribunals.[69] Stalin personally drew the attention of the security organs at the front to officers who, in his view, needed looking at. One entry in his notebook for the period has: 'Dubious: Skulsky, Pinchuk, Germuni, Matveishin, Kamynin, Kochetkov.'[70] It is now possible to say that the majority of those who were thus executed had been in a position of disorderly retreat because of the loss of command structures at various levels, and that their sacrifice served to 'correct' the mistakes made by Stalin himself.

Cases of 'cowardice, etc.' in the rear were dealt with no less harshly. In the autumn of 1941, many people in Moscow lost faith in the regime, and tried to leave their factories and get out of the capital. The military administration reported that in October and November 6,678 people, mostly servicemen or men liable for military service, had been arrested, 32,599 had been sent to reinforcement companies, 357 had been sentenced by military tribunals and shot, and fifteen had been executed on the spot.[71]

The effect of Stalin's savagery in the early months of the war was to make the people dig their heels in, summon up all their courage, and overcome their faint-heartedness through fear of the mortal punishment they knew he would mete out. Stalin's order in effect expressed the idea Trotsky had voiced in 1918 when he created blocking units: 'They provide the chance of dying with honour at the front or with shame in the rear.' This does not diminish the fact that the arrests of military personnel, in particular, were a terroristic means of compensation by Stalin for his own major and unforgivable strategic errors.

The work of the blocking units was sharply reduced as soon as the enemy's advance had been stopped and the counter-offensive launched. Inevitably, success in the field raised the troops' morale and resolve. This was precisely what Stalin had counted on. Not only did he summon up the ghosts of Russia's distinguished past, the glorious traditions of the Slavs and the service of the Church, he began handing out rewards, and taking other unusual steps. For instance, on his initiative, on 12 November 1942 the State Defence Committee resolved to issue one hundred grams of vodka to all men engaged in battle, and fifty grams to reserves. Nor was the Party leadership forgotten. When Leningrad was under siege, secret instructions were issued by the Kremlin, and executed by Zhdanov, concerning 'the special supply of foodstuffs to the leading Party and Soviet staff' of the unhappy, heroic city.[72]

Under the Soviet system, a very great deal depended on decisions taken by the man at the top. Stalin, though he made himself a Marshal of the Soviet Union and, in June 1945, Generalissimo, was not in the true sense a military leader. He was a political leader who had to deal with military matters. The war taught him much, and the lessons were fearfully bloody; but by trial and error he gradually, by the third or fourth year of the war, grasped quite a lot about the preparation and execution of major strategic operations by several army groups. It sometimes took him a long time to understand or accept an original idea, as happened with the plan to encircle the German forces at Stalingrad. Zhukov and Vasilevsky had to explain it to him three times before he understood their original and audacious plan for a counter-offensive at the crucial moment, when yet another heavy defeat looked like a real possibility.

Soon after the start of the war, Stalin devised a style of behaviour that best suited his abilities. He rarely took a decision without consulting his war chiefs, and he generally agreed with their proposals, though he would often add a touch of his own, such as 'making more effective use of aviation and artillery'. If a decision he had approved was carried out successfully, he would receive the acclaim. If it failed, he would inevitably find the 'guilty' parties, charging those in command with poor use of aviation and artillery, or weakness of will. Either way, his reputation as a war leader was left intact.

Stalin was especially inspired by the Russian counter-attack outside Moscow at the end of 1941. At a meeting of GHQ in early January 1942 the strategic tasks for the coming year were being discussed. The war chiefs agreed that the Moscow performance must be sustained and developed, and a number of consecutive operations were proposed in order to wrest the strategic initiative from the enemy. A 'directive letter' was read out, based on discussions by a narrow circle consisting of Vasilevsky, Molotov, Malenkov and a few others. Everyone waited in silence for Stalin's approval or disapproval. As was his wont, he paced softly back and forth across the carpet, deep in thought. The silence became oppressive. Suddenly he stopped and, pointing with his unlit pipe at the text, declared: 'Write this: "Our task is not to allow the Germans a breathing space, to pursue them westwards without pause, to force them to use up their reserves before the spring, when we will have large new reserves and they will have no reserves left, and this way to secure the complete rout of the Nazi forces in 1942." '[73]

This clumsy, repetitive text overturned all previously agreed plans. No one could contradict Stalin, and who could object to the distinctly appealing goal of destroying the aggressor within the year? Stalin's lack of realism laid the foundations for the appalling losses the Red Army would suffer in the spring and summer of 1942. Following his instructions, it was decided in essence to go onto a general offensive, on a broad front from the Black Sea to Lake Ladoga, without a pause in operations after the Moscow counter-attack. Between 7 January and 30 April twelve fronts attempted decisive offensive operations. As A. Volkov has established, all twelve 'remained incomplete'.[74] Some of these incomplete offensives were impressive in themselves: breaking through the Leningrad blockade; retaking the Crimea; liberating Kursk, Stara Russa, Oryol, Kharkov, Rzhev; and many more. But the chief object, to smash the enemy's main Army Group 'Centre' and other formations, was not accomplished. The Red Army lost over 2,350,000 men,[75] including over half a million on the Western front alone.[76] German losses were less than a quarter of Soviet losses.

The cost in human lives was of no concern to Stalin, as a note he added to a telegram to Stalingrad in 1942 illustrates: 'The Supreme Command orders both Colonel-General Yeremenko and Lt-General Gordov not to spare their forces and not to stop, whatever the losses.'[77] This was the way of thinking and fighting that Stalin instilled into his commanders. He did not reprimand them for major losses or unnecessary sacrifice, but he never forgave operational blunders and unfulfilled orders.

Shortly before the remarkable offensive at Stalingrad in November 1942, Soviet foreign intelligence reported to Beria, as head of the NKVD, on a matter of the utmost importance. On 6 November Beria informed Stalin: 'Research has begun in the capitalist countries on the use of atomic power for military purposes.' He described the stage this research had reached in Britain and the United States, and proposed, having consulted Soviet physicists, that: 'We should discuss setting up a scientific advisory body, under the State Defence Committee and consisting of authoritative people, to co-ordinate, study and direct the work on the issue of atomic energy. Through the NKVD we must acquaint distinguished specialists with the object of evaluating and making appropriate use of these materials.' On the recommendations of his scientific advisers, Beria proposed bringing in Skobeltsin, Kapitsa and Slutsky, and 'some others'. Of these 'others', M.P. Bronshtein and A.A. Vit had already perished in the Gulag, while Academicians I.V. Obremov, L.D. Landau, V.A. Fok and others were still languishing there.

Stalin was highly excited by the possibilities of this new weapon, as they were described to him: 'Can't we speed it all up to use in the war with the fascists?' His ardour was somewhat cooled by a memorandum from I. Kurchatov to the Defence Committee: 'Soviet research on the problems of uranium is considerably behind the English and Americans. We do not have sufficient materials to calculate the practical possibility or impossibility of producing uranium bombs. Abroad, they have made such definitive judgements. The possibility of introducing such a fearful weapon as the uranium bomb into the war is not excluded. But it is essential to develop on a wide scale the work needed to study the problem of uranium.' Kurchatov suggested that a large group of physicists be brought in to work on the project.

Stalin issued an order to step up the intelligence investigations, and soon the project assumed full state proportions. When Stalin asked how much such a bomb would cost, he was informed that, according to English figures, each one would cost £236,000. The Germans were at the Volga, but Stalin, mightily impressed by the devastating possibilities of what atomic energy might accomplish in the war, ordered the construction of a special laboratory with the job of producing a hundred tonnes of uranium in 1944–45.

Far from leading to the 'complete rout' of the German armies, Stalin's improvised strategy for 1942 led to huge Soviet losses in the summer and autumn of that year. This did not prevent the message being trumpeted after Germany's final defeat that Stalin was 'the greatest military leader of all time'. The official theoretical Party journal *Bolshevik*, in an article entitled 'The Great Leader and Teacher of the Communist Party and Soviet People', wrote in December 1949:

> With a force unseen in history, the military genius of Stalin emerged in good time during the Great Patriotic War. A military commander's talent is demonstrated by the importance of the battles he wins, by the scale and nature of the tasks he had to decide, by the magnitude of the difficulties he had to overcome, by his ability to find and use all available possibilities to organize the victory. In these respects Comrade Stalin, the military commander of the Soviet state, has no equal in history.[78]

It was as if Stalin had shown that he could manage perfectly well without the Military Council he had eliminated at the end of the 1930s, and that had included the flower of the Soviet military élite. A new generation of officers replaced the forty-four thousand who had been arrested or shot on the eve of the war. It is impossible to calculate the number of additional casualties this cost. More than half the 26,452 million Soviet people who died in the war were civilians. Stalin and the military leadership were responsible not only for the catastrophic beginning of the war, the loss of many major operations and the drive to achieve the goal 'without regard to losses', but also for yielding vast tracts of territory to the enemy, thus ensuring that many millions of defenceless people would perish. For decades the inhabitants of the Soviet Union's western regions were reminded of this shameful fact by a routine question in most application forms that seemed to imply guilt on the respondent's part: 'Have you lived in occupied territory?'

Secret Dialogues

Shortly before midnight on an icy night in February 1938, Stalin, his Prime Minister Molotov and Defence Minister Kliment Voroshilov received Chiang Kai-shek's special envoy Sung Fo in Molotov's office. Through an interpreter Stalin made the customary enquiries: Had his guest had a pleasant journey to Moscow? How was Chiang Kai-shek? Was Sung Fo ready for discussion? They arranged themselves along one side of the long conference table that was obligatory in the office of every high Soviet official.

After a brief formal introduction, Stalin came to the point, and asked Sung Fo what was worrying Chiang Kai-shek, and how the Kremlin could help. Sung Fo replied that he had brought a special message from his leader, and the interpreter began to read out a long text that had already been translated into Russian. Chiang was asking for advisers and weapons – many weapons – but above all that the USSR should declare war on Japan, which was occupying large areas of China. This would help both China and the USSR, he added.

Stalin interrupted: 'It would not be expedient for us to declare war on Japan. Above all, from the political point of view. It should not be done now,' he said with emphasis. 'As for weapons, this is a fundamental issue. We will give what we can. But you have to build one or two aircraft factories and one or two artillery-weapons factories of your own. We shall help.'

The conversation continued in this vein for a long time. Sung Fo asked questions and Stalin answered. Occasionally, Molotov or Voroshilov backed Stalin up with facts and figures. At 3 a.m. Molotov announced: 'There is a suggestion that we take supper at my house. My wife has been waiting for some time . . .' Everything had of course been rehearsed beforehand, including the late-night supper. The party rose and set off for Molotov's house, where Foreign Trade Minister Mikoyan and NKVD chief Yezhov soon joined them. The meal lasted until 5.15 a.m., and many toasts were drunk – 'To Comrade Stalin', 'To the leader of the Chinese people, Chiang Kai-shek', 'To the friendship of our two great states', to name only a few. Yezhov soon became drunk, and muttered something about 'the importance of strengthening the punitive organs'. Stalin and Voroshilov praised Chiang as a war leader, though Stalin also stressed in a reference to his leadership of the conflict with the Chinese Communists in the 1920s that he had caused many unnecessary deaths.

The interpreter, who was the only sober person in the room, managed to make sense of Stalin's farewell toast: 'History likes to make jokes. Sometimes she chooses a fool to use as a stick to force historical progress. The Japanese war party are such a fool. Japan will not conquer China. I drink to a strong China that will include Sinkiang and Outer Mongolia!'[79]

When Stalin met Sung Fo three months later, on 23 May 1938, he was ready to give Chiang weapons, arms production equipment and a loan of many millions of dollars. This was the Bolsheviks' preferred way of conducting international policy: not through international congresses or the League of Nations, but by way of secret talks, closed deals and mutual obligations made with countries the Kremlin thought might be useful to its global plans.

The question of China is important in any assessment of Stalin as a leader. He regarded himself as something of an expert on the subject, and gave speeches at the Comintern Executive Committee 'On the Perspectives for Revolution in China', and on 'Revolution in China and Comintern's Tasks' in the 1920s. In the following decades Stalin constantly had to manoeuvre between Kuomintang and the Communist Party of China, using the 'China question' to the maximum advantage in crushing Trotsky, Zinoviev, Kamenev and Bukharin. A decade after Sung Fo's nocturnal visit, *Pravda* would write: 'With the penetrating gaze of a strategic genius', Stalin had shown 'that the reactionary circles of Kuomintang have long made a deal with the sworn enemies of the Chinese people, the American and English capitalists'. Chiang was by then in the counter-revolutionary camp.[80]

From a frontal attack on the citadel of imperialism, with the aim of igniting world revolution, the Bolsheviks switched to the strategy of prolonged siege. Stalin believed that 'world revolution will develop by means of the revolutionary exit of several new countries from the system of imperialist states.' In these circumstances the Soviet Union would 'become a base for the further development of the world revolution, a lever for the further dislocation of imperialism'.[81] He arrived at this formulation in December 1924, and remained faithful to it until the end of his life. However, when on 1 March 1936 he was asked by the American publisher Roy Howard, of Scripps-Howard Newspapers, if the Soviet Union had any plans or intentions to carry out a world revolution, he replied without batting an eyelid: 'We have never had any such plans or intentions.'[82]

For two decades Stalin tried to make maximum use of Comintern, which virtually from its inception was an instrument of the Kremlin leadership and the NKVD. Resistance by the 'fraternal parties' to such exploitation was feeble and short-lived. Those which tried to protest were at first unceremoniously expelled, and in the 1930s physically destroyed. In December 1928 Bukharin's supporters in ECCI, the Swiss Jules Humbert-Droz and the Italian Serra (A. Tasca), protested against the effects of Stalin's influence in Comintern and were ostracized and removed from their posts at the Institute of Red Professors. After he had left the USSR, Tasca wrote to the secretariat of the Italian Communist Party: 'Stalin is the flag-bearer of counter-revolution ... For him it is not principles that are important, but the monopoly of power.'[83] In intensifying the fight against fascism, Stalin launched a bloody crusade against both his own people and the functionaries of the long-subdued Communist International. The NKVD ruled over ECCI as if it were some provincial Party committee. The bloody purges of 1936–37 swept through all the structures of Comintern.[84] In October 1937 Dimitrov, the Secretary-General of Comintern, and Manuilsky, the Secretary of ECCI, approached the Party Central Committee for help: the executive committee had been paralysed because the NKVD had 'uncovered a number of enemies of the people and exposed an espionage organization in the apparatus of Comintern'.[85] They needed more personnel.

Having irrevocably broken with the European social democratic movement – 'the social fascists', as he called them – and emasculated Comintern, Stalin resorted to strictly totalitarian methods in international and Communist affairs. Secret deals, toughening the NKVD's agencies at home and abroad, and initiating procedures by which anti-imperialist tendencies could be identified became his preferred style of 'revolutionary activity', especially after the formal dissolution of Comintern in June 1943.

Stalin and his special services attempted to acquire a more civilized image in the 1930s, and it became increasingly unlikely that official memoranda such as this one from the 1920s, discussing the motivation and disposition of Soviet diplomats, would circulate again:

> A diplomatic mission, like a military fortress, must be externally so arranged and internally organized in such a way that no single unreliable, suspicious or foreign person can be constantly inside the building, while strangers may gain access only under precise conditions which secure the mission against espionage from the outside or betrayal from within ... Every permanent member of the mission must be regarded as a potential traitor, and every 'guest', a potential spy. A Soviet diplomat, like any honest Soviet representative abroad, is the implacable and ruthless foe of all official authorities and all private individuals who own land or the means of production. He is their enemy, even when he signs some treaty or other or concludes a deal that is of clear advantage to the other side at the time. Then, more than at any other time, the hand that signs the treaty or the deal must be clenched in readiness for the moment when it will seize 'the other side' by the throat and strangle him, strangle him to death, like a freak, a perversion of the laws of nature and truth.[86]

Stalin may well have thought in this way to the end of his life, but he could hardly approve the publication of such a document. His diplomats gave every appearance of behaving as diplomats should, but in essence the service was motivated by the attitudes expressed in the memorandum.

Stalin's preferred form of democracy was through secret dealings, especially with like-minded countries or organizations. He had long forgotten the romanticism of 1917, when the Bolsheviks had shrilled against the 'secret diplomacy' of tsarism and the Provisional Government and called for the publication of secret treaties. Now he was an absolute dictator, taking decisions on domestic and foreign policy, and he loved the whole business of weaving the fabric of treaties, agreements and deals himself. He developed an entire ritual of closed, usually secret talks, and received numerous requests for audiences, from Mao Tse-tung to Tito, from Kim Il Sung to Dolores Ibarruri. Usually he agreed.

The visitor would arrive in Moscow, and would usually then have to wait a few days or a week, giving time to 'ripen' him for the great event. He would be installed in a luxurious dacha, meet his bodyguards from the special services and various officials from the Central Committee apparatus, and wait, and wait. Then, with only a few hours' notice, he would be told: 'Comrade Stalin will receive you today.' The audience would usually take place at 11 p.m., midnight, or even later. The visitor would go to see the earthly god in the dead of night, amid great secrecy. He would be charmed by Stalin's simple manners and hospitality, and as a rule the great leader would get what he wanted.

The Albanian leader Enver Hoxha wrote in his memoirs that he did not have to wait at all long for his first meeting with Stalin. Hoxha was flown to Moscow by special Soviet plane on 14 July 1947, and was received at midnight on the sixteenth. He was impressed by everything he saw, from the great size of Stalin's office and the Generalissimo's delicate courtesy, to the certainty of his judgement, the toasts he proclaimed, and not least his comments on the film *The Tractor-Drivers*, which he showed his guests in his private cinema. Stalin used the meeting to issue instructions on, for instance, how to deal with internal enemies, how to establish Party control of agriculture, how to secure the Albanian coastline and how to make use of Soviet advisers. Hoxha was especially pleased by Stalin's decision to deliver the weapons he had requested, free of charge.[87]

Stalin always gave his foreign visitors something: personal gifts such as gold sabres, automobiles, vases, weapons (often), money (sometimes), as well as Soviet experts and manufacturing equipment. And he got something in exchange, usually his guests' independence. The meetings almost invariably took the same form. Stalin's aides would ask in advance for a note of the questions the guest intended raising, and Molotov, sometimes Malenkov or a senior military man, would usually be present. Little is known about what took place at most of these secret encounters. The newspapers occasionally carried a line or two saying that a meeting had taken place, usually without specifying the date, but that was all.

Some Communist parties attracted Stalin's interest more than others. He was always very attentive, for instance, to Palmiro Togliatti and the Italian party. He was equally interested, though less favourably, in the Poles, especially during the 1920s and 1930s. It may be that the heavy defeat inflicted by the Poles on the Red Army at Warsaw in 1920 left its effect on him, especially as he himself had been among the beaten Soviet leaders at the front. There is much evidence of Stalin's persistent distaste for the Poles and their Party, and at the same time of his reluctant admiration for their resilience and bravery. For instance, when after the civil war Soviet Russia wanted to break out of its international isolation, it conducted complicated diplomatic manoeuvres with its western neighbours. At a Politburo meeting of 18 October 1923 Stalin wrote in a note, probably to Chicherin: 'I think it would be best to refrain from sounding out the Poles and rather sound out the Latvians. You can scare the Latvians, push them up against the wall and so on. You can't do that with the Poles. The Poles have to be isolated, with them you have to fight. We won't find out a damn thing from them and we'll just show our own cards ... The Poles have to be isolated. You can buy the Latvians (and frighten them). And you can buy Romania. But with the Poles you have to sit it out.'[88]

This note eloquently illustrates Stalin's extreme cynicism, and suggests that the humiliation inflicted in 1920 still rankled. In the 1930s he launched a savage persecution of the Polish functionaries in Comintern. The Secretary of ECCI, M. Moskvin, a senior NKVD figure, supported accusations fabricated by Yezhov that the Communist Party of Poland was 'riddled with spies and saboteurs', and thus gave Dimitrov grounds for stating that 'a ramified espionage organization' existed within Comintern.[89] When ECCI took its shameful decision to disperse the Polish Party in December 1937, Stalin noted on the decree: 'The dissolution is two years late. It has to be done, but I don't think it should be publicized in the press.'[90]

There were some occasions which Stalin made use of for public consumption and propaganda purposes. For instance, on 5 November 1927 he met representatives of the Danish, French, German, British, Chinese, Belgian, Czechoslovak and other Communist parties. On that occasion the talks were anything but secret, and the frankness of the foreign representatives' questions is a sharp reminder that in 1927 Communist thinking was far from monolithic:

QUESTION: Why does the Soviet Union ban social democratic parties?

STALIN: They are banned because counter-revolutionaries are banned. They are the parties of open counter-revolution.

QUESTION: Why is there no freedom of the press in the USSR?

STALIN: There is no press freedom only for the bourgeoisie.

QUESTION: Who holds the power in the USSR?

STALIN: Our power is the power of a single class, the power of the proletariat.

QUESTION: Why have the Mensheviks not been released from prison?

STALIN: Only active Mensheviks are affected.

QUESTION: How do you propose to carry out collectivization in the peasant question?

STALIN: Gradually; using methods of an economic, financial and cultural-educational kind.[91]

The meeting went on for almost six hours, during which Stalin subjected the foreign Communists to this propaganda barrage.

No less surprising than his mendacious replies is the fact that his audience was prepared to swallow them. He was, however, a past-master at lying. A few months before his death he declared: 'The bourgeoisie used to like to act the liberal. Now there isn't a trace of liberalism left. There's no more so-called "freedom of the individual": rights of the individual are recognized only for those with capital, and all other citizens are so much human raw material.'[92] He could speak of the absence of the rights of the individual in the capitalist countries at a time when 4.5 million Soviet citizens, who had committed no crimes, were languishing in his concentration camps.

In private, Stalin did not waste time on the sort of lies he peddled to Party Congresses or the press. In private, he laid down the law, lectured and hectored, and told his vassals how to act and how to lie. His conversations with foreign Communists after the war, mostly held in secret, became an important part of his strategy for spreading Marxism-Leninism-Stalinism throughout the world.

Several times he addressed the Politburo on the question of the Communist movement. Apart from China, there were, he said, only two strong foreign parties in the capitalist world after the war: the Italian and the French. On 30 November 1947 he sent a cipher to Togliatti through the Soviet Ambassador in Rome. It was signed 'Fillipov', one of the pseudonyms he used in such communications:

A meeting recently took place in Moscow at the request of Nenni [head of the Italian Socialist Party and a government minister]. Nenni described the present position in Italy and asked a number of questions to which he was given answers. We report the content of the meeting for your information. Unity with the Communists: this would be strengthened. Both parties will enter elections as a unified bloc and with a single list. But Nenni thinks the establishment of a united labour party in Italy is premature, as it might repel the middle elements which traditionally support the socialists. The Communists and socialists missed an opportunity after the occupation forces left. The Communists are more to blame, because they did not want to create a Greek situation. We will help Nenni, as he wishes, with a low-cost paper loan. In the event of a left-bloc seizure of power in Italy, the USSR can guarantee grain supplies to Italy. Coal is more difficult. Poland can help.[93]

Stalin saw a Communist takeover in Italy – with the socialists playing the part of Menshevik-style fellow-travellers – as a serious possibility, and he was reproaching Togliatti, through Nenni, for missing the chance soon after the war. He could, moreover, promise to feed the Italians while his own people were surviving on beggarly rations.

Two weeks later, on 14 December 1947, Stalin received Italian Communist leader Secchi at one of his midnight sessions. He strongly advised his visitor to establish intelligence resources in Italy which would help 'penetrate the headquarters and agencies of the enemy'. Secchi must bear in mind, Stalin continued, 'that there are always spies in the party', and the central committee should 'have its own security guards, a small guard of experienced people'. Asking after the health of Togliatti, he offered advice in the form of a banal homily: 'The heart is an engine. It needs oiling, you have to take care of it. After all, can a plane fly without an engine? Lenin used to say that it takes ten to fifteen years to train a good worker, and that you can lose him in an hour. Surely we mustn't treat human material in such a way?'

There was, however, more to this secret talk than homespun philosophy. With no obvious connection, Stalin suddenly announced: 'We can give you $600,000. Secchi can take it himself.'

Secchi, somewhat nonplussed, though pleased, thanked Stalin and then, as if thinking aloud, asked: 'But how will I get it into Italy?'

Stalin replied that the money would fit into two bags weighing no more than forty or fifty kilogrammes. Secchi suggested the money be sent via the Soviet embassy, and requested that it be in the form of large notes. He was still expressing his thanks when Stalin cut him off with: 'No need to thank me. It's our working class that is helping you.'[94]

The working class, of course, had no idea that their leader was handing out state funds to foreign Communist parties, and that he was doing it rather frequently. On 5 August 1948, at one of his midnight meetings, he received Dolores Ibarruri, Francisco Anton and Santiago Carillo, leaders of the Spanish Communist Party who had lived in Moscow since the defeat of their cause in the Spanish civil war. Seated alongside Stalin were Molotov and the fast-rising Party ideologist Mikhail Suslov. When the Spaniards complained about the parlous state of their finances, Stalin broke in with: 'We can help. How much and in what currency?'

Ibarruri replied, 'Best in US dollars.'

Stalin said, 'Will $US600,000 be enough?'

The Spanish Communists thanked him profusely and asked for the money to be sent to Czechoslovakia, where they held their accounts.[95]

At the same meeting Stalin instructed the Spanish Communists on how to unite the forces of anti-fascism and how 'to get in everywhere'. He urged them to form an anti-government partisan movement, just as he had in January 1937 when he wrote to the head of the Republican government in Spain, Largo Caballero, whom he had advised to 'form peasant partisan units in the rear of the fascist army'.[96] Perhaps a new attempt would succeed. His guests diligently recorded his words in their notepads.

Despite the fact that the world had entered the nuclear age, and Comintern had formally been dissolved in 1943, Stalin was unwilling to relinquish his Comintern way of thinking, although he modified it to some extent. He did not seek a direct confrontation with the capitalist world, but tried instead to create the maximum difficulty by manufacturing shocks and upheavals, and by organizing partisan attacks. At the end of his life he spoke of the Party as a 'shock brigade', and predicted that similar formations would emerge 'from China and

Korea to Czechoslovakia and Hungary'.[97] He believed that 'Red Brigades' would spring up with Moscow's help in the West and in countries with unpopular regimes.

His conversations in March 1951 with a delegation of Indian Communists are illuminating in this regard. They had asked him, in prepared questions, to comment on partisan warfare, and he replied emphatically that it was a form of 'revolutionary action' that must be used. 'Communists,' he said, 'must be in favour of terrorist activities by the masses, but against terrorist activities by revolutionary individuals acting outside the mass movement.'[98] The discussion on terrorism continued at the following meeting. Molotov, Malenkov and Suslov murmured agreement with every word uttered by their master, and although the minutes describe the meeting as 'a conversation between Comrade Stalin and Comrades Rao, Dange, Ghosh and Punnaya', in fact it was a long monologue by Stalin. Sitting at the long table and turning their heads in unison as Stalin padded around the huge room, pipe in hand, the Indians absorbed his words of wisdom: 'Individual terror achieves nothing ... Partisan warfare can be started wherever the people want it. Don't try to be too clever, just take the land away from the landlords, and if you take too much, you can always sort things out later. As the Russians say: when you chop wood, chips fly ... You can make a fine regime in your country ... The important thing is to be able to renounce your personal interest.'[99]

From all over the 'socialist camp' and the 'People's Democracies', leaders came to Stalin as if to Mecca. They had little choice. Apart from his one and only flight to the Allied conference in Tehran in the winter of 1943, and his elaborately choreographed journey by train to Potsdam in 1945, Stalin had no intention of ever crossing the border of the USSR.

Yugoslavia occupied a special place in his thinking. It was a large country, with wide access to the Mediterranean, and well placed to build on a successful uprising led by the Greek Communists, and hence to create a powerful socialist federation in the Balkans. If the Balkans 'went red', then almost half of Europe would come into the Soviet orbit, and without the help of a 'world revolution'. It was time to talk to the Yugoslav leader Marshal Tito, who had long been waiting for a meeting. The two had met in September 1944 and April 1945, but now, on 27 May 1946, Tito came as a statesman, and with a large delegation. He stayed for two weeks, enjoying the lavish hospitality showered on him by his generous host.

Contrary to custom, Stalin received Tito and his delegation in the Kremlin at 11 p.m. on the day he arrived in Moscow. The two sides vied to find adequate expressions of their mutual admiration and praise. They discussed ways of improving their economic relations and broadening their military cooperation, and Yugoslav–Albanian relations. As usual, when he saw an opportunity, even indirectly, to strengthen the Soviet position, Stalin was generous with offers of money, tools, grain and guns. Tito, who had an army of some 400,000 men, had already received weapons and equipment enough for thirty-two full divisions.[100] Now Stalin agreed with practically every request the Yugoslavs made, both on deliveries of weapons and for establishing an arms industry of their own.

The conversation turned to the question of including Bulgaria and Albania in the Yugoslav Federation. Tito agreed that Albania could be brought in, but added that 'nothing will happen as far as Bulgaria is concerned.'

Stalin replied sharply: 'It must be done. The first stage can be limited to a pact on friendship and mutual aid, but more must be done in reality.'[101] He saw the possibility of creating a powerful satellite that would facilitate the sovietization of the Balkans.

The talks were over quite soon, and Stalin invited his guests to his dacha at Kuntsevo 'for a bite'.[102] Twenty minutes later they were deposited by black limousines at the famous residence. The meal, which lasted several hours, consisted mainly of Georgian dishes, washed down with wine from silver goblets. Tito presented platinum and gold watches, diamond rings and other gifts to be passed on to Stalin's daughter, Molotov's wife and daughter, and the wives of Mikoyan, Zhdanov, Beria, Bulganin, Vyshinsky and Dekanozov. He also had decorations for a number of Soviet military commanders, from which the Soviet side insisted Zhukov must be removed.[103] (Stalin had made sure that Zhukov's great popularity at the end of the war was not translated into the political power of a potential rival.)

Stalin played gramophone records of Russian ballads and sang along, tapping his foot. There was a great deal of back-slapping and constant toasts. He advised his guests to plant eucalyptus trees in Yugoslavia, questioned them about Enver Hoxha, and teased

Ranković, the security chief, by asking him who would recruit whom first, he Beria or Beria him? When he asked Tito about a new Comintern, Tito replied that it was 'out of the question', but that they should rather think about creating some other sort of coordinating organ for the Communist parties. It was finally decided between toasts not to force the issue of Albania joining the Yugoslav Federation, as it 'might complicate the international situation of Yugoslavia and Albania'.[104]

As dawn approached, Stalin suddenly began expatiating on the leaders of the various Communist parties. In avuncular, concerned tones, he spoke of Palmiro Togliatti, Maurice Thorez, Jose Diaz, Dolores Ibarruri, Wilhelm Pieck, Klement Gottwald, Georgy Dimitrov, Jacques Duclos and Harry Pollit, noting a common flaw in all of them: they were all too soft, they were incapable of 'gathering people into a fist'. He remarked of the French leader Thorez, for instance: 'Even a dog that doesn't bite, when it wants to scare someone, bares its teeth. Thorez can't even do that.'[105] He then turned to Tito with a smile and said: 'Take care of yourself ... I won't live for much longer ... it's nature's way ... but you'll be there for Europe.'[106]

Stalin met Tito several more times before the Yugoslav leader's departure on 10 June 1946. They continued to discuss mostly Balkan affairs – on one occasion with Dimitrov, who had come to attend the funeral of the nominal Head of the Soviet State, Mikhail Kalinin – and they also talked about creating Cominform, as Tito's idea for an informational centre came to be called. It seemed inconceivable that by the second half of 1947 the two leaders and their parties would be at daggers drawn. Belgrade would be peppered with accusations of 'haste' in establishing a federative structure, of 'belittling' the Soviet experience, of Trotskyism among its leaders, of 'wilfulness', 'degeneracy' and much more. Long before the Informburo of Cominform met in the old royal palace in Bucharest at the end of June 1948 to debate a resolution on the situation in the Communist Party of Yugoslavia, the final outcome was obvious. Zhdanov declared: 'We have facts at our disposal showing that Tito is a foreign spy.'[107]

Tito was an independent-minded dictator in his own right, and his split with Stalin was therefore inevitable. After it came, Stalin at first decided to sit and wait for while, as his telegram to the Czechoslovak leader Gottwald, with a copy to Togliatti, shows:

I have received Silin's report of his discussion with you on the Yugoslav question. I have the impression that you are counting on the defeat of Tito and his group at the Yugoslav Party Congress. You are suggesting publication of compromising material on the Yugoslav leaders. We Muscovites were not and are not counting on such an early defeat of Tito's group. The Congress has been carefully chosen ... Tito will have a majority. We have achieved the isolation of the Yugoslav Communist Party. Henceforth, Marxist groups will gradually fall away from Tito. This will take time and the ability to wait. It seems you do not have the patience for this ... The victory of Marxism-Leninism in Yugoslavia after a certain time is not open to doubt.[108]

But Stalin lacked the patience to sit it out. Angered and surprised that Tito remained in power, he ordered Beria to 'get rid of' him. Several assassination attempts were mounted, but none succeeded. Stalin was not as omnipotent as he had thought. It was his first post-war defeat.

Still with his global goals in mind, Stalin turned his attention to China. He had counted on the success of the Kuomintang, then strove for cooperation between Chiang Kai-shek and Mao Tse-tung. Whatever the outcome, he was determined that the government in Peking should be anti-imperialist and friendly to Moscow. Stalin needed China as a strategic ally, and who ruled the country was of secondary importance. In December 1941, after the Japanese attack on Pearl Harbor, he had cabled Chiang: 'I would very much ask you not to insist that the USSR declare war on Japan at once. The Soviet Union will have to fight Japan, as Japan will undoubtedly break the treaty on neutrality and we have to be prepared for that. But preparation takes time, and we must first finish with Germany. So I ask you once again not to insist that the USSR declare war on Japan at once.'[109] In fact, the USSR did not declare war on Japan until 8 August 1945.

In 1946 Stalin was still counting on Chiang Kai-shek. In a conversation at the beginning of the year with Chiang's emissary, Chiang Ching-kuo, he announced that the Soviet government had recalled its representatives from Mao's headquarters at Yannan because it did not agree with Chinese Communist policy. The Soviet government recognized the government of Chiang Kai-shek as the legitimate government of China: 'There must not be two governments and two armies in the country.'[110] Chiang Ching-kuo remarked that the

Chinese were worried in case Japan should rise again, to which Stalin gave the reassuring answer: 'The Soviet Union will make sure that Japan is deprived of the possibility of being reborn as an aggressive power. To achieve this Japan must be deprived of its military force by imprisoning 500–600,000 officers and arresting about twelve thousand Japanese generals.' At their farewell meeting, Chiang Ching-kuo remarked that Chiang Kai-shek and Mao did not trust each other, to which Stalin responded in a placatory tone: 'Coexistence between the Kuomintang and the Communist Party can last for many years.'[111]

He was wrong. At the close of 1949 he had to receive Mao as a conqueror. The Chinese leader sent a cipher to Moscow pointing out that recent Communist victories had reduced Chiang Kai-shek's forces to 170 divisions, and noting that 1.2 million Red Chinese were presently surrounding General Tu Yu-ming's troops. It is tempting to think that Mao's closing remark was ironic: 'Please report this telegram to the comrade chief boss and the Central Committee.'[112]

At Mao's request Stalin sent a plane to collect Mao's wife Jiang Qing and his daughter Li La, both of whom wanted to have medical treatment in Moscow.

On the night of 16 December 1949 the meeting between Stalin and Mao duly took place. With Molotov, Malenkov, Bulganin and Vyshinsky alongside him, Stalin rose to greet the Chinese leader, and for twenty minutes they talked generalities, exchanged pleasantries and took a good look at each other. Mao's opening move was unexpected: 'China needs a breathing-space of about three to five years of peace . . . The Central Committee of the Communist Party of China has instructed me to ask you how and to what extent international peace is guaranteed.'

Stalin replied that there were no direct threats to China at present: 'Japan hasn't yet got back on its feet. America shouts about war but is afraid of it . . . in Europe they're scared of war . . . No one wants to fight China.' He added with a laugh: 'Surely Kim Il Sung isn't going to invade China?'

They talked about a treaty of friendship, alliance and mutual aid, the Sino–Soviet controlled Port Arthur, a large loan to Peking, Soviet assistance in building the Chinese Navy, its arms industry, its communications. Stalin promised generous help.

Mao then turned the conversation to the difficulty faced by the

People's Liberation Army in taking the island of Formosa (Taiwan). Would it not be possible, he wondered, 'to use Soviet volunteer pilots or secret army units to speed up the seizure of Formosa?' Stalin edged away from this awkward topic by reminding Mao that 'this might give the Americans an excuse to interfere.' His preferred solution, he said, would be 'to put together a company of commandos, land them on Formosa and through them organize an uprising on the island'.[113]

He then abruptly offered Mao the opportunity to publish his works in Russian, to which Mao agreed at once, requesting only that an experienced Marxist be given the job of editing them. In April 1950 the Kremlin sent the sociologist Pavel Yudin to Peking. Stalin had read some of Mao's writings in translation, notably the article 'Stalin, Friend of the Chinese People', written on the occasion of Stalin's sixtieth birthday in 1939. The 'comrade chief boss' had marked in blue pencil the lines: 'To celebrate Stalin means to stand for him, to stand for his cause, for the victory of Communism, for the path that he is pointing out for mankind ... The overwhelming majority of mankind is still living in torment, and only the path pointed out by Stalin, only Stalin's help, can deliver mankind from distress.'[114] Mao quickly returned the compliment by sending Stalin an official offer from the Chinese Central Committee to publish Stalin's works in Chinese, an offer Stalin accepted with alacrity.[115]

Mao presented Stalin with the difficult problem of trying to understand someone from a completely different civilization, culture and way of thinking. The philosophical dialogues conducted by the Chinese were enigmatic, obscure and unfamiliar to Stalin. He noted Mao's tendency to speak in aphorisms and to allude to ancient philosophers, while Stalin was generally content to quote himself as the only required authority on any subject. Mao's language was literary, vivid and, while more convoluted, much richer than Stalin's. Mao referred to the four books of Confucius, and a host of early Chinese poets, while Stalin tried to fathom the meaning of the allegories and historical excursions made by this man, who so patently had already grown accustomed to the role of 'great leader'.

Mao remained in Moscow until mid-February 1950, and the two leaders met several times. Their agreements were given concrete detail by China's prime minister Chou En-lai, who made a number of trips to Moscow for the purpose. For instance, in August 1952 Stalin and

Chou agreed to build 151 major projects in China. On 3 September of that year Stalin told Chou: 'It would be good if there were a pro-Chinese government in Burma. There are quite a few crooks in the Burmese government trying to make themselves into statesmen.' When he heard that the Chinese had suppressed a rebellion in Tibet, Stalin advised: 'You should build a road to Tibet. Without a road it will be hard to maintain the necessary order. The Tibetan lamas will sell themselves to anyone – the Americans, the English, the Indians, whoever pays the highest price.'[116] On 22 January 1950, when Mao expressed his fear that their agreements would 'clash with the [understandings of the] Yalta Conference', Stalin replied: 'Certainly they will, but the hell with it! Once we have decided to alter treaties, we have to go the whole hog.'[117]

Stalin was prepared to break any agreement or treaty if he thought it would serve his own interest and strengthen the position of the USSR. At one of his nocturnal conversations with the East German leaders Wilhelm Pieck, Walter Ulbricht and Otto Grotewohl, the talk turned to the question of 'whether we should take measures to create an army for the GDR'. Stalin broke in: 'Not measures, just create an army. What do you mean, "measures"?' The German leaders had come mainly to ask for grain, ores, cast iron, sheet iron, brass, lead, cotton and credit, but Stalin's lecturing focused on the need to build collective farms, have a good police force and stage public trials of saboteurs from the West. At the end of the conversation, Pieck thanked Stalin for sending an orchestra to Berlin. Stalin, rising from his seat, replied with a grin that music was fine, 'but it's more interesting to have an army'.[118]

Stalin's approach to foreign policy was based on the twin pillars of Communist internationalism and Soviet great-power status, with the emphasis on the former. He dedicated his last important public speech, at the Nineteenth Party Congress on 14 October 1952, to the issue of world revolution in a new form, even though he did not utter those precise words. In his last major written work, *The Economic Problems of Socialism in the USSR*, he advanced the thesis that the struggle for peace would become the struggle 'for socialism', for 'the overthrow of capitalism ... To eliminate the inevitability of wars, imperialism must be destroyed.'[119] The struggle for peace, he told the Congress, was a struggle for 'emancipation', and he concluded with the slogan

'Down with the warmongers!'[120] In other words, the struggle against the warmongers was the struggle for socialism. The midnight conversations in the Kremlin were aimed at creating more and more 'shock brigades' to carry the struggle into the enemy camp.

As for the second pillar of his thinking, Stalin had no intention of accepting the situation as it stood after his territorial gains of 1939. The Balkan Federation he had dreamed of was meant in time to become part of the USSR. Indeed, Tito's critic over the conflict with Moscow, S. Fujović, declared to the Yugoslav Party central committee in April 1948: 'I believe our aim to be that our country will become part of the USSR.'[121] Fujović did not recant until the end of 1950.

The Stalin Papers

The marks left by Stalin on the face of the earth cannot easily be wiped away. Whether the thousands of buildings in the 'Stalinist' style of architecture, the canals, highways, blast furnaces, mines and factories – built to a large extent by the slave labour of millions of anonymous inmates of his Gulag – or nuclear weapons, his traces are steeped in blood. Between 1929 and 1953 the state created by Lenin and set in motion by Stalin deprived 21.5 million Soviet citizens of their lives. No one in history has ever waged such war on his own people.

Much of what is known of Stalin's doings has come from people who spent years in his camps, and from the stories of their families. But there is also the vast evidence of his own writings, obligatory reading for millions of people. As well as articles and reports, the thirteen volumes of his 'Works' contain replies to letters and personal and official messages. For instance, replying to the flood of greetings on his fiftieth birthday in 1929, he wrote in the press: 'Your greetings and congratulations I attribute to the great party of the working class that gave birth to me and raised me in its own image and likeness. Never doubt, Comrades, that I am still willing to give the cause of the working class, the cause of the proletarian revolution and world Communism, all my strength, all my capabilities and, if need be, all my blood, drop by drop.'[122] Spoken ten years later, these words would have sounded even more hollow to Soviet ears. The publication of two further volumes of 'Works' was curtailed by Stalin's death.[123] Volume 14, covering the period 1934 to 1940, was ready for printing in 1946, but Stalin, for reasons known only to himself, issued instructions that it should not be published 'yet'. Could he have been concerned about the repressive and punitive tone of its contents?

Numerous collections and miscellanies of Stalin's writings and speeches were published, but it was his *Short Course* of the history of the Party and his brief biography that were in virtually every Russian home. I remember receiving the biography as a school prize in 1943. It includes the lines: 'The *Short Course* ... contains an exposition of genius, in the clearest and most compact form, of the foundations of dialectical and historical materialism, and is a genuine peak of Marxist-Leninist philosophical thought.'[124]

Stalin regarded himself as an expert on the national question, and wrote a number of articles on the subject. He could not avoid the issue of Jewish assimilation, which was a major topic of debate at the time, especially in the pre-war Russian Social Democratic Labour Party, in which many revolutionaries were of Jewish origin. He wrote in 1913 that the 'question of national autonomy for the Russian Jews is of a curious nature: autonomy is proposed for a nation whose future is being repudiated and whose very existence has yet even to be established!' As for 'cultural-national autonomy', which was then the platform of certain Jewish political groups, it was 'even more harmful when linked to a "nation" whose existence and future are open to doubt'.[125] In due course he would put flesh on these notions by encouraging every kind of covert anti-Semitism. He could claim, moreover, that his way of dealing with anti-Semitism was highly effective. When in January 1931 the Jewish Telegraph Agency asked for his views, his reply was clear and unequivocal: 'Active anti-Semites are punished according to the laws of the USSR by the death penalty.'[126]

During Stalin's rule, and especially after his death, the huge quantity of his writings were subjected to repeated 'weeding'. He himself frequently ordered the destruction of pieces he had written, and a great number of documents disappeared after his death.[127] When Beria was arrested in 1953, Khrushchev also ordered 'the arrest' of his personal papers, which contained a mass of Stalin's notes to the NKVD. The commission that was created to deal with this matter thought fit, without even reading them, to burn eleven sacks of documents. The members of the commission, high Party officials all, were no doubt afraid that Stalin's papers contained compromising material on them.

A.N. Shelepin, the former head of the KGB, told me that a big purge of Stalin's archives was carried out by the then head of the KGB, Army General I. Serov, on Khrushchev's personal order. The order was issued in Shelepin's presence: 'Look through all the papers with "death sentence" lists, where there is more than just Stalin's signature,' Khrushchev instructed Serov. 'Find them and report to me.' Serov's own record would not have withstood a moment's scrutiny, but Khrushchev was concerned about his own responsibility for the horrors of the 1930s; horrors in which practically every other leading Party figure was implicated.

According to Shelepin, two or three months later Serov delivered a number of fat files to Khrushchev. I asked him where they were now. 'I think they don't exist any more,' he replied.

Stalin himself frequently ordered documents, manuscripts or other written material to be brought to him from the NKVD. Soon after the German invasion in 1941 he had the most important of the Central Committee's papers, numbering some five million files, evacuated from Moscow to Chkalov (formerly and now again Orenburg) and Saratov, an operation requiring two hundred railway wagons.[128] After the war, when he was told that a huge Russian émigré archive had been found in Prague, he ordered that the whole collection be shipped to Moscow. At the beginning of January 1946 the NKVD duly supervised the transport of nine wagonloads of priceless documents, and its chief archives department was charged with their 'sorting and use'.[129] Much of the material evaporated into thin air in the course of this process.

The members of Stalin's Politburo behaved in various ways during sessions. Molotov was always concentrated, only making occasional notes. Voroshilov appeared apathetic, coming to life only when Stalin spoke. Beria rarely took part in the discussion other than to answer Stalin's questions, and remained inert, except occasionally when he would suddenly seize his briefcase and search for papers. Malenkov was all ears, always ready with facts and figures. Voznesensky, Bulganin and Zhdanov took part when the discussion touched on their own area of responsibility. Kalinin almost always remained totally silent, as did Andreyev and Shvernik. Always ready with opinions of their own were Kaganovich, Khrushchev and Mikoyan.

Stalin would sit at the head of the long table, his blue pencil always at the ready, jotting down names, numbers and – to the innocent eye – seemingly meaningless phrases. At a meeting of the OGPU organizing bureau on 3 May 1933, for instance, he noted: '1) Who can make arrests? 2) What should we do with former White military men in our economic agencies? 3) The prisons need emptying ... 4) What should be done with various groups that have been arrested?' The meeting dealt with the question of kulaks who had been deported to the north and Siberia, and with 'supplementary deport-ation'. Stalin noted: 'Ukr[aine] – 145,000; N[orthern] Cau[casus] – 71,000; Mosc[ow] Reg[ion] – 58,000; Leningr[ad] Reg[ion] – 44,000; West[ern] Reg[ion] – 23,000; Urals – 50,000; [Central Black Earth Region] – 34,000; Transcaucasus – 23,000; Gorky Region – 29,000; Crimea – 5,000; Bashk[iria] – 11,000; Tat[ar] Rep[ublic] – 12,000; Iv[anovo]-Vozn[esensk] – 21,000.'[130] The lives of more than half a million innocent people were reduced to a few scribbled notes during discussion of one item at one session.

It was probably in the mid-1930s that Stalin made the following notes on the law restricting the migration of labour: 'To be agreed today: 1) A law on workers who have left the factory, and on taking away their apartments as a result of their leaving the factory. Combine this with a law on depriving such workers of their ration cards. 2) Relieving Moscow and Leningrad and the passport system.'[131] The author of these draconian laws against the workers was Stalin himself. It was he who thought of making the permit to reside in towns an instrument of NKVD control, and it was his idea to deprive the peasants of their internal passports, thus making them once and for all a caste of serfs without rights.

The security and punitive organs figure in virtually every one of Stalin's notepads, alongside evidence of his concern that the right people be appointed to top jobs in the cultural field, or that military production was on target. He evidently enjoyed meeting the heads of arms factories, and inventors and designers of new military technol-ogy. He knew by heart the identification numbers of almost all the defence industry plants and the names of the chief weapons developers. Notes he made at a meeting with Nikolai Polikarpov, who had designed a number of training aircraft and the I-16, one of the Soviet Union's principal fighter planes at the beginning of the war, indicate that he paid close attention to technical matters, whether or not he understood precisely what was being described: '1) Turbo-compressor; 2) propellers not good; 1) aircraft radiator; 2) twin-speed supercharger; 3) Turbo-compressor; 4) central draught.' The list was followed by notes on American and Soviet engines, on who should be 'leaned on', how delivery times of new products should be reduced, on the need to 'raise responsibility', and so on.[132]

Sometimes an entry has a distinctly personal flavour: 'It's a good idea to set up fights more often; it makes you feel suddenly better (after a fight), makes you feel respectable, better than anything else.'[133] Theoretical thoughts are also scattered through his notes, such as: 'Reformism is the suppression of the final goal and basic means for reaching the goal, i.e. the dictatorship of the proletariat.' 'Compromise, i.e. opportunism, belongs to the sphere of "tactics".'

These notes were clearly not idle jottings, as underlining in different colours shows that Stalin referred to them subsequently, as for instance in the case of a list headed 'Strategic leadership': '1) Don't lose the course; 2) Don't lose tempo; 3) fix the moment carefully for going over from one tactical plan to another; 4) It is sensible to manoeuvre.'[134]

Entries headed 'For the Bureau meeting' suggest the outline of some future agenda. One for a meeting in late 1935 includes: 'Set up a competition for a good play; Awards for Vishnevsky [possibly David Vishnevsky, a weapons designer] and [film director] Dzigan; A textbook on the history of the [Party]; Discuss the historians (Yaroslavsky) [the Party's semi-official chief historian]; Send 50–60 artillery officers (for the time being) to France (what about Savchenko [senior officer in military intelligence]? Tukhachevsky?; The Volga–Moscow Canal (Yezhov, Berman, Zhuk).'[135]

It is noticeable that Stalin almost never records what his colleagues said, or even mentions them. During a discussion on the delivery of tanks to the army, he noted that Voroshilov asked a question, but one searches in vain for what it was. Stalin was not interested in what was said by his entourage. He had long realized that, except for Molotov, they simply tried to read his thoughts and anticipate his decisions. They were there to grasp his intentions and then to see that they were implemented expeditiously.

When necessary, Stalin gave his comrades-in-arms concrete instructions, some of them in written form. In notes filed under 'Molotov' and headed 'Some directives for the Berlin trip', dated 9 November 1940, he told his Foreign Commissar to clarify the aims and intentions of the Tripartite Pact between Germany, Italy and Japan, and to assess the possibility of the USSR's joining it. The fact that the Tripartite Pact was also known as the 'Anti-Comintern Pact' reveals an astonishing degree of cynicism on Stalin's part, mitigated perhaps only by the knowledge that he was already engaged in his 1939 Pact with Hitler. It seems he discussed global strategy of this kind only with Molotov, but as the war brought Russia to the brink of disaster, he began listening with greater attention to his military leaders, such as Shaposhnikov, Zhukov, Vasilevsky and Antonov, and usually agreeing with them.

The notepads would provide interesting material for the psychological analysis of their owner. Sitting at sessions of the Politburo, which became increasingly rare in his later years, Stalin would doodle combinations of triangles and circles, linked by strange ovals. He also sketched weird, shapeless animals with angular features, some of them resembling wolves, coloured red. These movements of pencil on paper may have helped him concentrate or maintain focus, or they may suggest an effort to hold onto a failing imagination.

Stalin showed an abiding concern for state funds, state gold and state valuables. As soon as he was informed of an infringement at a gold refinery, Stalin made a note to ask the NKVD chief Yezhov or his deputy about the case, adding that 'a commissar must be appointed at the refinery without whose signature the assay mark should not be given, nor the gold released.'[136] His notes frequently refer to the need for greater gold reserves to cover the costs of the Communist movement, and after 1940 he personally fixed the sums any particular party should be given. When the 'People's Democracies' came into being in the post-war period, they were expected to do their part. In a letter to Mao Tse-tung in February 1953, less than a month before his death, Stalin wrote: 'The work of the West European Communist parties, such as the French, Italian and English, has become difficult. They are demanding more help than before. The Communist Party of the Soviet Union has decided to increase its contribution to the fund and thinks it necessary to raise it from 800,000 to 1.3 million dollars a year. If the CPC [Communist Party of China] would contribute 1.1 million dollars in 1953, we could satisfy the demands of the above-mentioned parties. We await your reply.' Mao agreed at once: 'We'll transfer the cash to Panyushkin [Soviet Ambassador to China].'[137]

Every year Stalin carefully studied the report on the country's gold reserves submitted by the Ministry of Finance, and he became convinced that the ministry was not doing its job at all well. In November 1946 he transferred responsibility for the gold and platinum industry to the MGB, or Ministry for State Security (as the NKVD became that year, when ministries replaced People's Commissariats). Large numbers of unfortunates were put to work mining gold in the most inaccessible locations and inhuman conditions, and production began to rise steeply.[138] As long as Stalin was alive, millions were enslaved and starved to build up the gold reserves. In the year of his death, the state repository was holding more precious metal than at any other time in Soviet history, including 2049.8 tonnes of gold and 3261 tonnes of silver. Within a year of his death the reserves began inexorably to fall, and when in the early 1960s gold started to be traded for grain, they evaporated at catastrophic speed.

The reports Beria sent the Politburo on hunger in the country were not read by its members, apart from Stalin. The conditions in the Tatar Republic, Khabarovsk, Amur and the Jewish Autonomous Regions in the east were appalling. In one village, a twelve-year-old girl called Natasha Maximova stole food from her neighbours. She was savagely beaten, trussed up and dragged through the village. A rock was tied round her neck and she was about to be thrown into the river, when it was decided instead to tie her to a cart and leave her out in the rain, and finally to lock her in a cold cellar.[139] Another report that came to the Central Committee on 21 December 1949, Stalin's seventieth birthday, concerned the discovery of the corpses of three murdered children at the Sun Yat-sen Collective Farm in the Maritime Province. The children had been killed by their mother, a worker at the farm. She testified that she had been driven to desperation by the harshness of the conditions she had endured since her husband had been sentenced in 1946, under the 1932 law on passports, and since losing her job as a schoolteacher and being thrown out of her apartment.[140] Still the gold reserves went on growing.

It came to light in 1995 that Molotov had held onto eighty-five letters written to him by Stalin between 1925 and 1936. He had removed them from the Party archives when he fell from grace in 1957, and clearly destroyed the most incriminating evidence against himself, as there is practically nothing from the 1930s. He handed them back in 1969, after Khrushchev had departed the scene and the Party was again in 'safe' hands.[141] These letters apart, although the Stalin archives do contain files of correspondence on internal affairs, they are not 'correspondence' in its common meaning. Countless papers were brought to him every day by Poskrebyshev – reports, notes from Politburo members, ministers, department chiefs and old Bolsheviks – but he would write a comment on only some of them. Usually he would snap out a verbal order to his assistant, marking the relevant document only with a minimal 'Agreed', 'They should report again', 'What are they wasting their time on this for?', 'We'll discuss this at the Politburo', 'This should have been here months ago.' Poskrebyshev would scribble his notes and pass the decisions to the proper quarters.

Stalin carried on a real correspondence only with foreign Communists such as Mao Tse-tung, Kim Il-sung, Togliatti, Thorez, Dimitrov, Pieck, Gomulka and Tito. His most interesting correspondence is with Mao. It shows the clash and contact of two styles of thought, two styles of action – the partisan and the state imperialist. In May 1951 Mao sent instructions to Peng Du-hue, the commander-in-chief of Chinese and Korean forces in Korea, with a copy to Stalin, stating: 'At the present time we have eight corps in forward positions. If each corps destroys one battalion, the enemy will lose eight regular battalions in all. This alone will deal a heavy blow to the enemy. If each battalion destroys two battalions, that will make sixteen battalions. Each operation must be given the task of destroying one battalion. In the course of three or four operations, four regular battalions will be destroyed each time, and that will cause a drop in the enemy's morale and shake his self-confidence.' Stalin must have regarded this 'arithmetical strategy' with some scepticism, but his reply was scarcely less simplistic: 'This plan looks risky to me. It might work once or twice. But the Anglo-Americans will soon see through it. You are not dealing with Chiang Kai-shek's forces.'[142]

As with his subordinates at home, so in his relations with his allies and satellites Stalin's natural inclination was to give advice almost in the form of orders. In early 1952 he sent a telegram to Mao urging that, in order to put an end to dependence on the imperialists for such a basic commodity as rubber, the Chinese 'should plant rubber trees in China in sufficient quantity to secure at least 200,000 tonnes of natural rubber a year. The island of Hainan should be the centre for rubber. We'll help with the technology.'[143]

Something like a real correspondence existed between Stalin and Roosevelt and Churchill during the war. All previous abuse forgotten, or at least temporarily buried, Stalin's approach now was mostly in the form of requests, whether for the widest imaginable range of essential supplies or, more insistently, the opening of a second front in Europe. Early in 1942 he wrote to Churchill that '1942 will be the decisive turning-point in events at the front,' and in the summer of the same year, when the Red Army was in a critical situation on the Southern front, he adopted a frankly demanding tone: a second front could be put off no longer, and Churchill, he claimed, had promised that it would be opened in 1942. Unruffled, Churchill replied: 'Neither Great Britain nor the United States has broken any promise,' and indeed in all the talks between the sides, in Moscow, London and Washington, it had been repeatedly urged on the Russians that the Western powers could give no firm date for opening a second front, only that every effort would be made to do so. After the Soviet victory at Stalingrad, Stalin toned down his demands, telling his Western counterparts that 'our success at Stalingrad was also helped by the snowfalls and fogs which prevented German aviation from deploying its forces.'[144]

In the spring of 1943, an episode erupted with potentially dangerous consequences for the tenuous good relations between the Allies. The bodies of large numbers of Polish officers and other Polish citizens were discovered buried in eastern Poland. General Sikorski, head of the Polish government-in-exile in London, had already on 3 December 1941 asked Stalin about the fate of four thousand Polish officers taken prisoner when the Red Army occupied eastern Poland late in October 1939, and now being held in Soviet camps. He even produced a list then and there. Stalin replied that it was impossible: 'They have run away.' 'Where could they have run away to?' queried Sikorski's companion, General Anders. Stalin: 'Well, to Manchuria.'[145]

The fact that they had in reality been trussed and shot in the back of the head in their own homeland, and buried in great secrecy, needed explanation. While the Germans claimed the NKVD had committed the atrocities, and the Russians flung the accusation back at the Nazis, the Poles in London believed Stalin was responsible. Stalin argued that the Nazis were using the story to inflame Polish feeling and undermine Allied goodwill towards the USSR.[146] He stuck consistently to this line, knowing full well that in fact the Poles had been shot on his own personal orders. Politburo Minute no. 13 (P13/14) of 5 March 1940 recorded that 14,700 Polish officers, civil servants, landowners and others, and also eleven thousand Poles held in prisons in the western districts of Ukraine and Belorussia, were to be shot. The victims were not to be arraigned, nor were they to be informed of any charges against them. The act was to be supervised by NKVD officers Merkulov, Kabulov and Bashtakov.[147] Stalin was a master at simulating indignation, and his anger at the Polish 'anti-Soviet campaign' appeared genuine. The Poles would have to wait almost fifty years for proof of their suspicions.

Stalin was acutely conscious of his image as a war leader. After visiting a front sector in the summer of 1943, he hastened to inform the Allied leaders of the event, writing to President Roosevelt: 'Only now, on returning from the front, can I reply to your last message . . . I am having to make more personal visits to various sectors of the front and to subordinate everything else to the needs of the front . . . In the circumstances, you will completely understand that at this moment I cannot depart on any journey . . . to fulfil my promise [to meet Roosevelt in the region of the Bering Straits].'[148]

He could hardly admit to the US President that he was terrified of flying. The only flight he ever made, to Tehran, had taken every ounce of his psychological strength. He had not forgotten an air crash of March 1925 in the Northern Caucasus, when three personal acquaintances had been killed. He was convinced it was no accident, and that two of those who died, 'the Chekists Mogilevsky and Atarbegov, were targeted out of revenge for executions they had carried out,' and the third, Myasnikov, 'because he's an Armenian'. He had proposed that 'the strictest prohibition on flying be placed on senior officials'.[149] This was quite impracticable even then, and it became virtually impossible in due course.

Stalin was perpetually afraid of attempts on his life, and took extreme measures for his personal safety. In 1944 one P.I. Tavrin and his wife, L.I. Shilo, were charged with plotting to assassinate him. They had come nowhere near achieving their aim, but to the end of his life Stalin lived in fear of a real attempt. The Soviet accommodation at the Potsdam Conference in the summer of 1945 was guarded by no fewer than seven NKVD regiments and 1,500 operatives.[150] When Stalin went on vacation, his route, the Crimean coastline and his villa were guarded by literally thousands of troops and agents. Before leaving for Sochi in the autumn of 1945, he was informed that action had been taken against local anti-Soviet elements and that 'arrests are taking their usual course'.[151]

By the end of the war relations between the USSR and the Western Allies were cooling, and after the war they worsened drastically. Stalin would not even agree to Roosevelt's proposal for a joint portrait of the 'Big Three' for the Capitol, and he responded to a request from Roosevelt's successor Harry S. Truman to sit for Douglas Shandor, an American artist with: 'Unfortunately, it would be difficult for me to find the time for Mr Shandor. Naturally, I am willing to send him my portrait if you think it useful for the purpose.'[152]

At the Potsdam Conference of July–August 1945, during a discussion of amendments to the documents on reparations and frontiers, many of Stalin's comments were negative: 'This is a misunderstanding'; 'I don't see the relevance here'; 'We cannot agree with this'; 'I cannot possibly agree with that interpretation'; 'That is quite wrong.' He nonetheless described the conference as 'successful', and when Truman, as chairman, closed it with the words, 'To our next meeting, which will I hope be soon,' Stalin muttered, 'Please God.'[153] He knew that the profound antagonism between the USSR and the Allies, which had been submerged by their common interest in wartime, would resurface after it in a sharpened form. As it became clear that victory was at hand, Stalin, who had displayed an ability to collaborate and compromise, gradually changed his tone. His territorial ambition, class approach and Communist ideology had all been set quietly aside for a time, but the war, which began disastrously because of his gross miscalculation, finally convinced him of his 'historical correctness'.

After the war, as before, it was the security organs and the armed forces that served as his chief instruments of policy, both inside the country and abroad. As usual, thick files from Beria's various agencies were deposited on his desk every day, and he would study them carefully and mark each one in the top left-hand corner with either 'I.St' or 'I', for Iosif.

One such file contained a report from Minister of the Interior Kruglov that the whole of western Ukraine was engulfed by a nationalist movement. In March 1946 alone, '8,360 bandits were liquidated (killed, captured or surrendered)'. Reports were coming in of victories over the nationalist underground in Lithuania, Latvia and Estonia, and even in Belorussia, where more than a hundred people were liquidated, and some thirty Soviet servicemen killed. Stalin for some personal reason underlined the numbers of 'kulaks and their families, bandits, nationalists and others' deported from the Baltic republics: 'From the Lithuanian SSR – 31,917; Latvian SSR – 42,149; Estonian SSR – 20,713.'[154] The World War was over, but another war went on. Stalin ordered Poskrebyshev to allocate additional troops to get rid of the 'bandits' as soon as possible.

A year later, in March 1947, Kruglov reported that in the corrective-labour camps and colonies alone, not counting prisons, there were 2,188,355 prisoners, and that twenty-seven new camps had been built.[155] Another report showed that at the end of the 1940s in Siberia, the Urals, Kazakhstan and elsewhere there were 2,572,829 'resettled and specially resettled' people, including ethnic Germans, Chechens, Ingushes, Crimean Tatars, [Black Sea] Greeks, Armenians, Turks, Kurds. An order of the Presidium of the Supreme Soviet of the USSR of 26 October 1948 stipulated that all these people had been deported forever.[156]

No doubt with these deported peoples in mind, Stalin introduced a law imposing twenty years' hard labour for anyone attempting to escape from exile. In December 1934 he had insisted on an amendment to the criminal code, by which investigations should not continue for more than ten days, and cases should be heard without prosecution or defence. He had himself added: 'Appeals against sentence and the submission of petitions for clemency are not allowed.' And although Kalinin and Yenukidze signed it, Stalin was responsible for a further amendment: 'The death penalty must be carried out immediately after the sentence has been given.' He signed the document with the pencilled remark: 'For publication, I.St.' A little further down, Molotov also signed it, and the new law was duly published in the main newspapers on 4 December 1934.

It appears from Stalin's papers that there were not enough special camps. On 5 March 1950 he approved an MGB application to expand their capacity from 180,000 to 250,000.[157] With a minimum sentence of twenty years, no inmate was expected ever to return to the outside world. The sentence of hard labour was established in the USSR by Stalin in 1943. It seemed at first that it was a special category for spies and traitors, but soon it was being applied to anyone suspected of the least political unreliability. Nearly two hundred people were sentenced to twenty years' hard labour in September 1949 alone.[158] The conveyor belt kept on moving, carrying its victims into oblivion. Under Stalin there were more than five million camp inmates and exiles at any one time. The space allocated to a camp prisoner, according to Kruglov, should not exceed 1.8 square metres, that is, about the size of a grave. And all that was required to establish a camp was tarpaulin for tents, barbed wire to define the 'zone', and the prisoners. No other agency could build housing, mines, factories and roads as quickly and efficiently as the Ministry for State Security. And it worked economically, too. A high-rise apartment block on Kotelnicheskaya Embankment in Moscow was commissioned dead on time in 1951 at a cost of 154 million roubles, against a budget of 162.9 million.

Korean Blind Alley

In the last years of his life Stalin suffered political defeat at the hands of Tito, and in another venture he managed only a draw where he had expected victory. In the moral sense, he suffered a defeat. This was the Korean War of 1950–53. The cost of a war conceived in the minds of a handful of politicians was enormous: more than a million lives.

Stalin was very satisfied with his puppets in Mongolia and North Korea. Kim Il-sung, brought from the USSR to North Korea by the Soviet army in 1945 and assiduously nurtured by Soviet advisers, was visibly growing and acquiring experience as a statesman of the Communist type. Kim was reporting on the successes of 'socialist construction' in his country and in 1949 he asked Stalin if he might visit Moscow. Stalin was keen to see his protégé at closer quarters, and six weeks later, on 5 March, Soviet Foreign Minister Vyshinsky and his aide Terenti Shtykov, the Soviet Ambassador to North Korea, ushered the Korean delegation into Stalin's presence. Kim was accompanied by his Foreign Minister Pak Heon Young, and several senior officials.

Vyshinsky is notorious as the chief prosecutor in the shameful purge trials of the 1930s, but Shtykov is less well known. Born a peasant in Lyubko, in the province of Vitebsk, he became a commissar in the 1930s and rose quickly through the hierarchy. He was a member of the military council of 7th Army in the inglorious Finnish War, and of the Leningrad, Volkhov and Karelian fronts during World War II. He was in charge of political affairs at the 1st Far Eastern Front in the brief war with Japan, and was one of the very few political officers to be raised to the rank of Colonel-General by Stalin. In 1946–47 he headed the Soviet side in the joint US–Soviet commission on Korea, which no doubt led to his appointment as ambassador to Pyongyang in 1948. He was in practice Kim Il-sung's chief adviser.

The conversation in the Kremlin lasted an hour and fifty minutes, and was conducted between Stalin and Kim almost entirely, Pak and Shtykov providing information only when asked. Stalin came quickly to the point, and asked what assistance North Korea required.

KIM: We have ratified a two-year plan for the recovery and development of the economy. We need machines, equipment and spares for industry, communications and transport, and other branches of the economy. We need Soviet specialists to plan new factories and plants and carry out geological surveys.

STALIN: We'll give you this help, and specialists, too.

KIM: Korean exports do not cover our imports, so the country needs credit from the Soviet government.

STALIN: How much credit do you need?

KIM: Between $40 and $50 million.

STALIN: We'll give you 200 million roubles credit, that is, $40 million.

The discussion continued in this vein, with Kim asking, and Stalin for the most part granting, favours. He demurred once, when Kim asked for fifty-eight kilometres of branch railway to be built from Kraskino in the USSR to Aouji in North Korea, saying 'We must think about it.' Kim moved on to military issues.

KIM: There are still American troops in the south of Korea and they are increasing their intrigues against North Korea, which has a land army but no naval defences. We need the help of the Soviet Union.

STALIN: How many American troops are there in South Korea?

KIM: About twenty thousand.

SHTYKOV: Between fifteen and twenty thousand.

STALIN: Is there a national army in South Korea?

KIM: Yes, it has about sixty thousand men.

STALIN(laughing): And you're afraid of them?

KIM: No, we're not afraid of them, but we'd like to have some naval units.

STALIN: Whose army is stronger, the North's or the South's?

PAK: The North's army is stronger.

STALIN: We will give you help in all military questions. Korea must have military aircraft.

Stalin then wanted to know if the North had managed to infiltrate the South's army.

PAK: Our people have penetrated there, but they have not yet shown themselves.

STALIN: Quite right, nor should they. It would be wrong to reveal themselves at this time. But the South presumably also sends its people north, so caution and awareness are essential.

The discussion then turned to military assistance, the training of Korean officers in the USSR, the development of economic relations and other matters.[159] No mention was made of the possible reunification of the two Koreas, although Stalin knew from Shtykov that the government of North Korea lived for nothing else.

Throughout 1949 the Soviet Union delivered weapons and other military equipment to North Korea at an intense pace, each consignment personally approved by Stalin. The North probed the South to test the strength of its defences. They crossed the border and conducted 'reconnaissance in force'. Following one such sortie, Shtykov received a threatening telegram from Stalin, dated 27 October 1949: 'You were forbidden to advise the government of North Korea to undertake active operations against the South Koreans without permission of the Centre ... You failed to report the preparation of major offensive actions by two police brigades and in practice you allowed our military advisers to take part in these actions ... We require an explanation.'[160]

A key document is a special report from Shtykov to Stalin dated 19 January 1950:

On the evening of 17 January Foreign Minister Pak Heon Young arranged a reception for the departure of the Korean ambassador to Peking. During the reception, Kim Il-sung said to me: 'Now that the liberation of Korea is nearing completion, the question arises of liberating Korea in the south of the country ... The partisans will not settle the issue. I cannot sleep at night, thinking of how to deal with the question of unifying the whole country.' Kim then declared that when he had been in Moscow, Comrade Stalin had told him he should not invade South Korea; if the army of Syngman Rhee were to invade the North, then it would be right to make a counteroffensive against the South. But since up to this time Syngman Rhee has not started an offensive, it means that the liberation of the people of the southern part of the country continues to be delayed. He, Kim Il-sung, needs to see Stalin to ask for permission to invade the South in order to liberate it. Kim Il-sung said that he could not begin an offensive himself because he is a Communist, a man of discipline, and Comrade Stalin's instructions are for him the law. Mao Tse-tung had promised to help, and he will be meeting him, too. Kim Il-sung insisted on a personal report to Stalin about permission to attack the South from the North. Kim Il-sung was slightly drunk and in a state of excitement.[161]

Stalin pondered Shtykov's report for more than a week. Mao was in Moscow for medical treatment and rest, and Stalin saw him. It seems no account of their meeting exists. Both leaders were cautious. Judging by their later actions, they appear to have agreed to reply to Kim after a further meeting and after their military experts had studied the matter. On 30 January 1950, Stalin finally replied to Kim in a telegram to Shtykov: 'We received your message of 19 January. Such a big affair requires preparation. It has to be organized so that there is no big risk. We would like to receive 25,000 tonnes of lead a year. We are prepared to give technical assistance.'[162]

In Pyongyang, Shtykov's report itself was taken to mean practical approval of the operation, as long as the North could guarantee success. On 4 February Shtykov sent another telegram to Moscow with a request from Kim to speed up payment of the loan and for additional credit for arms purchases. He also asked for permission to increase the size of his infantry from seven to ten divisions.[163]

Following further consultation with Peking, on 9 February Stalin authorized the start of wide-scale preparations, thus approving Pyongyang's intention to 'unify' the peninsula by military means. Soviet deliveries of tanks, artillery, rifles, military and medical supplies and fuel were stepped up. In exchange Stalin wanted lead, silver and gold. Kim readily agreed.[164]

It seems certain from the evidence that at the beginning of April 1950 Kim visited Stalin again, this time in secret. No documentary evidence of their meeting has been found, but two months before, on 30 January, Stalin agreed to a visit by Kim, and in several telegrams after April there are references to agreements made in personal conversation 'at the beginning of 1950'.[165]

With preparations in top gear, Stalin decided to consult Peking again. In his correspondence with Mao, as he had in the war and with some other Communist leaders, he signed himself 'Fillipov'. On 14 May 1950 he dictated a telegram to Mao:

> In conversation with the Korean comrades, Fillipov and his friends expressed the opinion that, in view of the changing international situation, they agree with the Koreans' proposal to move towards unification. We qualified this by saying that the issue must be settled in the end by the Chinese and Korean comrades jointly, and that if the Korean comrades do not agree, then the issue should be postponed until further discussion. The Korean comrades can give you the details of our conversation.[166]

Peking agreed.

On 30 May Shtykov informed Moscow:

> Kim Il-sung reports that (with his Soviet adviser Vasiliev) the Chief of General Staff has finished working out the operational decision for an offensive. He, Kim Il-sung, has approved it. Organizational preparation will be completed by 1 June. Out of ten divisions, seven are ready for offensive action. The rains will begin in July. Generals Vasiliev and Postnikov have reported that it will then take more time to concentrate. The General Staff advise starting at the end of June. The North Koreans intend to use camouflage by offering the South peaceful unification of the country 'in the name of the Patriotic Front' ... My opinion: As Kim Il-sung wants to start the operation at the end of June,

and the troops can be ready by then, we can agree with this timetable. The Koreans are asking for gasoline and medical supplies. I urgently request your orders.[167]

Stalin wrote on the telegram: 'The Instance [i.e. the Central Committee, i.e. Stalin] approves your proposals. Delivery of medical and fuel supplies will be speeded up.' It was not uncommon for Stalin to sign communications not only with pseudonyms, but with the names of his subordinates, to enhance their secrecy. On this occasion he signed himself 'Gromyko', then scrawled: 'Reported to Comrade Gromyko for transmission to Comrade Shtykov.'[168] Gromyko was Vyshinsky's deputy at the time.

Stalin was anxious not to let the Americans know of his complicity in starting the war. His task was made harder when on 20 June 1950, on the eve of hostilities, he received an urgent telegram from Shtykov, addressed to him personally: 'Kim Il-sung has requested this transmission: ships are needed for invasion and landings. Two ships have arrived but there was no time to train their crews. He is asking for ten Soviet advisers to be deployed on the ships. I think the request should be met.'[169]

A reply was sent on 22 June, signed 'Gromyko': 'Your request is declined. It offers an excuse for interference.' Stalin directed the unfolding events himself. Apart from telegrams from Shtykov, he received several reports on the progress of the 'unification' from the chief of staff of the Soviet Army.

On 25 June Radio Pyongyang broadcast a report that had been prepared long in advance: 'Early today troops of the puppet government of South Korea launched a sudden attack on North Korean territory along the entire line of the 38th parallel. The enemy penetrated up to a depth of two kilometres.' Stalin's earlier instructions had been that Kim should invade only if the South were to attack first. The United Nations Security Council, however, meeting on the same day, concluded that 'North Korean troops have staged an armed invasion of the Korean Republic.'

With the start of hostilities, Kim asked for Soviet advisers to be attached directly to units at the front. Shtykov promised he would persuade the Kremlin to agree. Instead, he got a sharp rebuke from Stalin, signing himself this time 'Fyn Si': 'You are plainly acting improperly in promising to give the Koreans advisers without even asking us. Don't forget that you are representing the USSR, not Korea. Our advisers may, in the required numbers, join front and army group headquarters in civilian clothes as *Pravda* correspondents. You are personally answerable to the Soviet government to ensure that they are not taken prisoner.'[170]

After the North Koreans had taken the South Korean capital Seoul in the first days of the war, Stalin would not allow General Vasiliev to enter the captured city to assist in commanding the forces on the nearby front. He was still wary of being seen as being directly implicated in the war, even though there was little doubt about it. He wanted to preserve the myth of the 'defensive' nature of the war, and the Soviet Union's purely 'technical' role.

According to the official Soviet and North Korean version, as contained in the *Soviet Military Encyclopedia*:

> The Korean War was launched by the South Korean military and US ruling circles with the aim of liquidating the Korean People's Republic and turning Korea into a bridgehead from which to attack the Chinese People's Republic and the USSR. The plan of attack was developed by the American military mission and the South Korean army command in May 1949 ... By the beginning of the summer of 1950 the puppet regime of Syngman Rhee succeeded with the help of the USA in preparing an army of more 100,000 men, armed with American weapons and military equipment.[171]

The *Encyclopedia* continues: 'on 25 June South Korean troops went on the offensive. They succeeded in overcoming the security units and penetrating one or two kilometres into North Korean territory.'[172] This does not answer the question: if the South Koreans had planned and started the 'aggression', how was it that after only three days they had lost their capital city?

Kim was inspired by his opening success to create 'people's committees' in the 'liberated' areas. His advisers urged him to press on quickly, to mobilize all his forces for a complete military victory. They had after all assured Stalin of a guaranteed success. More and more was needed from the USSR. On 30 June Shtykov sent an 'extremely urgent' telegram to Stalin with a long list of military requirements, including fifteen million rifle bullets, 21.5 million pistol rounds, forty-three thousand revolver rounds, anti-aircraft guns and shells of various calibre, mortars, tank ammunition and hand-grenades, all in very large quantities, communications equipment, aircraft spares, fuel and lubricating oils. Shtykov ended his message with: 'I support Kim Il-sung's request. I request your instructions regarding the delivery of at least 50 per cent of the amounts indicated by 10 July 1950.'[173]

Stalin approved the list without further consultation. So soon after the Second World War, the USSR had more than enough military hardware to keep the North Koreans supplied. He did what he could to shift some of the burden onto the Chinese, ordering, for instance, the shipment of equipment for two air force divisions to China, so as to provide cover for Soviet transports into Korea.[174]

The war swung back and forth, from one side to the other. In the first phase, up to the middle of September, the North, with the element of surprise on their side, enjoyed major success. They captured Seoul and many other cities, and it looked as if total victory was a foregone conclusion. On 28 August 1950 Stalin wrote to Shtykov: 'Pass on the following verbally to Kim Il-sung. If he wants it in writing, give it to him in writing, but without my signature. The Central Committee of the [CPSU] congratulates Comrade Kim Il-sung and his friends on the great liberation struggle of the Korean people, which Comrade Kim Il-sung is conducting with brilliant success. The Central Committee of the [CPSU] has no doubt that the interventionists will soon be thrown out of Korea with ignominy.'[175] Three days later Kim replied: 'We are deeply touched by your concern. We offer you our gratitude, our dear teacher, for your warm participation and advice ... We are firmly resolved to fight to a victorious conclusion in the struggle against the American interventionists who have been trying to enslave Korea again ... We wish you many years of life and good health. Your devoted Kim Il-sung (on the instructions of the Political Council of the Central Committee of the Labour Party of Korea).'[176]

Despite the euphoria of Kim's message, on 16 September the South, with American backing, launched a powerful counter-attack. The operation involved a naval landing by the US 10th Army Corps in the region of Inchon, while an advance from the Pusan bridgehead got under way. The US–South Korean offensive swept north. Kim's forces suffered heavy defeat, with many killed or taken prisoner, and a large part of their artillery and tanks destroyed. The Americans had air supremacy, and destroyed everything that moved on the ground. It was soon obvious that without the direct involvement of Chinese or Soviet troops, the North would not survive.

Stalin did not fully grasp the seriousness of the situation. He dictated a telegram to Peking: 'Liquidation of the new danger can be accomplished by moving significant forces from the main front into the region of Seoul, and by creating a firm front to the north and east of Seoul.'[177] Faced with a catastrophic position, Stalin's orders were totally unrealistic.

On 1 October the North Korean Foreign Minister handed Shtykov a long letter from Kim for Stalin. Written with the help of Soviet advisers, it outlined the development of the battle:

> Suffering defeat after defeat, the enemy was chased into a small area in the extreme southern tip of South Korea and we had a good chance of gaining victory in the last decisive battles. But the USA, mobilizing nearly all the infantry, naval and air forces located in the Pacific Ocean, carried out a landing in the region of Inchon on 16 September 1950. Having taken Inchon, the enemy is carrying out street fighting in Seoul ... Enemy aviation, finding no resistance from our side, has complete command of the air ... Part of our forces are encircled by the enemy ...
>
> Dear Comrade Stalin! If the enemy is able to force offensive operations into North Korea, we will be unable to resist on our own. Therefore, dear Joseph Vissarionovich, we cannot but request your special help. In other words, from the moment enemy troops cross the 38th parallel we shall be in urgent need of direct military help from the Soviet Union. If for any reason this is not possible, then help us in establishing international volunteer units in China and other people's democracies to give us military assistance in our struggle.[178]

Stalin was informed of Kim's panic-stricken telegram at 2 a.m. on 1 October while he was on holiday at one of his numerous villas on the Black Sea. He replied, as 'Fillipov', within an hour: 'For Mao Tse-tung or Chou En-lai. I am far from Moscow on holiday and somewhat cut off from events in Korea. However, from information sent to me today from Moscow, I understand the Korean comrades are in a desperate situation. At least five or six divisions should be moved up to the 38th parallel. Chinese divisions could figure as volunteers.'[179]

In telegrams sent later that day to the Soviet representatives in Pyongyang, Stalin criticized their 'major mistakes' in managing the forces, and dictated an entire page of instructions on how to act as a vanguard and where to deploy tanks, always reminding his representatives 'not to allow a single military adviser to be taken prisoner'.

The war now moved north, and along with Kim's prestige as a war leader and liberator, that of Stalin and Mao was also thrown into the balance. Stalin composed a strong letter to Mao, speaking, in effect, of the possibility of a third world war:

> For the sake of its prestige, the USA might become involved in a big war; China will be drawn in and with it the USSR, which is tied by a pact of mutual assistance with China. Should we be afraid of this? I don't think so, because together we are stronger than the USA and England, while the other capitalist countries without Germany, which cannot at this moment give the USA any form of assistance, do not represent a serious military force. If war is inevitable, then let it happen now, and not in several years' time when Japanese militarism will have been restored as an ally of the USA.[180]

Mao's response was immediate: 'I am very glad that in your reply you speak of the joint struggle of China and the USSR against the Americans ... Without question, if we are to fight, we should fight now ... It would be sensible to send not five or six divisions, but at least ten.'[181]

This telegram was followed by new information to the effect that Peking was now considering the possibility of military intervention. Stalin was seriously concerned, and all the more so when another telegram arrived from Peking which referred to the risk of 'open conflict with the USA'. Mao allowed the possibility that 'even if North Korea is defeated, it will turn the struggle into a partisan war.' He was sending Chou En-lai and Marshal Lin Piao to Moscow to discuss the situation.[182] Peking was weighing up the pros and cons of the direct use of its own forces, while Stalin waited anxiously to hear more from Mao. The Chinese were in a position to save the situation. Stalin would throw his own forces into the balance only at the last moment and only if there was no alternative, although he had committed himself to consider flying Soviet aircraft from Chinese airfields.

Finally the long-awaited telegram arrived. Mao had agreed to give open support to the North Koreans. At once, on 13 October, Stalin dictated his reply through Shtykov: 'I have just received Mao Tse-tung's telegram in which he states that the [Chinese Central Commit-tee] has discussed the situation again and decided after all to give military support to the North Korean comrades, despite the inad-equate armed strength of the Korean forces. I await details from Mao Tse-tung. I wish you success.'[183]

Endless columns of Chinese troops crossed the Korean frontier and moved up to the front. According to information from Peking, there were twelve divisions in the first echelon, with another twelve being prepared in China, and a further echelon available. Stalin's allies could count on the support of nine armies, or some thirty divisions. When Chou En-lai requested ten thousand tonnes of fuel, Stalin replied that 'Seventeen thousand tonnes will be supplied.'[184]

Stalin must have sighed with relief at the Chinese involvement. It was not going to be an easy war, and he could see that no one was going to emerge as the victor, but he also saw that defeat would be avoided. The main burden of the war would now rest on the Chinese, whom he would supply with air cover, weapons, equipment and fuel – everything but personnel. He was not, of course, concerned that Soviet lives might be lost, but that the Americans would be able to accuse him of direct complicity and involvement. Despite Stalin's expressed willingness to engage in a major war, Russia had only just begun to produce atomic weapons, and he knew that he lacked the means to drop them on the USA. He was also experiencing increas-ingly frequent spells of weakness and dizziness, and he was tired of fighting.

When on 25 October 1950 the Chinese launched a powerful counter-offensive along the entire front, Stalin knew that a respectable draw was in the offing. The mass offensive by troops described in the socialist press as 'volunteers' was long and hard, opposing American air supremacy with trench and tunnel warfare, in which entire companies, battalions and regiments became so well dug-in that neither bombs nor napalm were as effective as they had been in the first phase of the war. The fighting began to shift southwards, but then the Southern forces counter-attacked and the front more or less stabilized at the 38th parallel again.

With the experience of the Second World War behind him, Stalin realized that not even the vast numerical superiority of the Chinese 'volunteers' would bring success if there was no reliable air cover. On 14 November 1950, following consultation with his military advisers, he therefore ordered the formation of a special air corps to provide such cover. It was to be called the 64th Fighter Air Corps, and it consisted, unusually, of two fighter divisions, two anti-aircraft divisions and one aircraft technology division. The 64th Corps was constantly replenished; the divisions were in combat for periods of eight to ten months, some of them for as much as a year, with only a short break. Over the three years of the Korean War, some fifteen Soviet air divisions and several anti-aircraft divisions gained battle experience.

The Corps was based at airfields in northern China. When the fighter squadrons received a signal that US bombers had been sighted, they were able to attack suddenly and swiftly. Often the US aircraft followed the Soviet fighters into Chinese airspace, using up valuable fuel. The Soviet pilots for their part were ordered not to approach too close to the front, certainly not to cross it, and not to fly over the sea. Stalin had issued the strictest order that no Soviet adviser or pilot was to fall into enemy hands and thus give the game away. Identification marks on the MiG-15b planes were in Chinese, and the pilots wore Chinese or Korean uniform, and even carried little Mao badges. Amazingly, not one Soviet serviceman seems to have been captured by the Americans, while several US aircraft that had had to force-land in China were sent to the USSR for examination by Soviet aircraft designers.

The 64th was made up almost entirely of air crew with experience of the Second World War, and their quality as fighter-pilots was thus very high. The corps commander, Colonel E.G. Pepelyaev, shot down nineteen US aircraft, and other Soviet pilots achieved similar success. From the end of 1950 until the cessation of hostilities in July 1953, the 64th shot down 1,309 US aircraft, of which about 18 per cent were downed by the Corps' anti-aircraft batteries. Over the same period, the Corps lost 319 planes.

The Corps was commanded in turn by Generals I.V. Belov, G.A. Lobov and S.V. Slyusarev. Its number fluctuated between ten and fifteen thousand men, all of them convinced they were fighting an 'aggressor'. It was only after the war that Stalin allowed decorations to be awarded, as he feared that the news would be leaked in the

Soviet Union. Several thousand men eventually received medals, a number of pilots being made Heroes of the Soviet Union.

After the setbacks of autumn 1950, Stalin expanded the Soviet role. With the agreement of Mao and Kim, general command of land forces was transferred to the Chinese – 'the Koreans don't follow orders,' Stalin remarked in a telegram. General Vasiliev was removed as military adviser, several Korean generals lost their posts and some were put on trial. Until the middle of 1951, when the unstable balance was established at the front, Stalin personally saw to it that his orders were carried out. The telegrams he exchanged with Mao, Chou and Kim are most revealing, showing as they do that while discussing military issues with his allies, Stalin did not miss the opportunity to settle some of his own affairs along the way.

Thus, in October 1950, when the war in Korea hung by a thread, Stalin reminded Chou En-lai of the Chinese promise to transfer US$10 million to Moscow 'for the support of left-wing organizations in Europe and America'.[185] It appears that even the special fund operated by Stalin, who was able to donate $600,000 at a time to his 'devoted colleagues', required topping up from time to time. In another telegram, informing the Chinese of a supplementary supply of gasoline, he asked for a consignment of fifty thousand tonnes of natural rubber in exchange. He received rubber and US dollars from the Chinese, and gold and silver from North Korea.

Stalin gradually lost interest in the Korean War, as it became less likely that there would be an outright winner. He still advised Kim on several occasions 'to use aircraft and artillery on a massive scale', 'to smash the reaction with merciless and immediate measures and restore order in the rear', and to 'keep a strong and reliable military fist at the government's disposal',[186] but he was acting from inertia. He told Vyshinsky not to oppose peace offers, though he was not to force them, either: 'The Americans need peace more than we do,' he said.

At a meeting with Chou En-lai on 19 December 1952, Stalin discussed the question of preserving China's and North Korea's position in the war, and also the exchange of prisoners. He warned Chou that 'the Americans would try to recruit some of the prisoners to use as spies ... That's what happened with our prisoners-of-war in the last war, and now every day we capture a number that the Americans sent over to our side.'[187] He also confirmed his readiness to supply weapons for sixty Chinese infantry divisions. Peace talks were going on in Korea, but Stalin did not exclude the possibility of the war continuing. Closing the conversation, Stalin presented new Zim limousines to the Chinese delegation, together with his respects to the leadership in Peking.

At an earlier meeting with Chou in Moscow, on 20 August 1952, Stalin had asked him whether they should try for peace or continue the war. Chou had replied that, according to Mao, 'the continuation of the war is good for us.' China was prepared to let the war go on for another two or three years. Stalin agreed that 'the war was putting the Americans out', adding: 'The North Koreans have lost nothing but lives in this war. They need patience and endurance. It has to be explained to them that this cause is big. We will do everything for Korea.' (In a telegram to Kim Il-sung in April 1952, he had said: 'I have heard that the Korean people are short of grain. We have fifty thousand tonnes of milled wheat flour. We can send it as a gift to the Korean people.' Kim was beside himself with gratitude, and wished Stalin 'many years of life and health for the happiness of mankind'.[188])

The dialogue with Chou continued in an interesting vein:

CHOU: If the Americans don't want peace, then we must be ready to continue the war for at least another year . . .
STALIN: Correct. The Americans are not able to carry on a big war. All their strength is in air raids, the atom bomb. The Americans are merchants. It took the Germans twenty days to conquer France; the USA haven't been able to deal with little Korea for two years. What kind of force is that? You cannot win a war with the atom bomb . . .

Perhaps this was the source of Mao's view that the atom bomb was a 'paper tiger'.

The Chinese informed Stalin that South Korea had 116,000 prisoners-of-war, including twenty thousand Chinese. The peace negotiators in Korea were not especially concerned with this issue, and Stalin merely asked how many Americans had been captured. Chou consulted his notes and replied that out of twelve thousand 'southerners' in North Korean captivity, 7,400 were Koreans, and the rest either Americans or other United Nations servicemen.

Looking to the future, Chou said that after the war China intended to maintain 102 divisions, or an army of 3.2 million men. Stalin frowned: 'But that's the minimum. You want 150 air regiments. That's not much. You need two hundred air regiments.'[189]

The warm words of friendship and mutual regard that had been exchanged between Stalin and his Western counterparts in the Second World War were by now of course completely forgotten. Only a few short years before, on 7 April 1945, Stalin had written to Roosevelt: 'I never doubted your honesty and reliability, nor the honesty and reliability of Mr Churchill.'[190] Similar words were addressed to President Truman, who reciprocated in kind.

Stalin had cause to recall Truman's toughness, however, as well as his kind words. After the defeat of Japan, on 16 August 1945 Stalin sent Truman a telegram in which he suggested 'including the northern half of the island of Hokkaido in the region yielded by the Japanese armed forces to Soviet forces ... This proposal has particular importance for Russian public opinion. Russian public opinion would be seriously offended if Russian forces did not have a particular piece of specifically Japanese territory in their area of occupation. I would hope very much that my modest desire, described above, will not meet any objection.' Two days later Stalin received a sharp refusal from Truman with no word of explanation. At the same time, the US President announced that 'the US government wishes to have the right to use air bases for land and seaborne aircraft on one of the Kurile Islands, preferably in the central group.'

Stalin replied indignantly: 'I have to say that I and my colleagues were not expecting such a response ... Demands of that kind are usually made either to a defeated state or to the sort of allied state that is not capable of defending one part of its territory or another ... I do not think the Soviet Union can be included among such states ... Neither I nor my colleagues can understand the circumstances that have given rise to such a demand being made on the Soviet Union.'[191] Stalin had kept his dignity, despite abandoning the idea of an assault on Hokkaido, and even though the troops had already been partly embarked.

The war in Korea illuminated Stalin from some new angles: it revealed an ability to exploit dependent allies, it showed that he was prepared to risk a major war without burning his bridges at the same time, and it demonstrated his ability to turn political cynicism into state principles. The war nevertheless foreshadowed Stalin's approaching historical defeat, even as he reached the peak of his power.

Is Stalinism Dead?

Shortly before he died, Stalin wanted to know how the translation of Mao's works into Russian was going. The next day, V.N. Malin, who at Beria's instigation had replaced the long-serving Alexander Poskrebyshev as Stalin's personal assistant, laid a number of translated articles on his master's desk. Stalin riffled through them in a desultory way, then pushed them aside. Only one passage seems to have attracted his attention sufficiently for him to mark it: 'The Chinese people are facing two paths, the path of light and the path of darkness. China has two destinies – a bright one and a dark one.'[192] Mao's phrase echoed Stalin's own thinking. He had long believed in a bright Communist future for the Soviet Union, and that the impulse he had given would be lasting. Nothing in the notes, remarks and resolutions of his last years suggests anything but unfailing confidence that his life's work was eternal.

He thought he had brought Soviet society right up to the threshold beyond which the people would enter the radiant world of Communism. His last theoretical work, *The Economic Problems of Socialism in the USSR*, was devoted to the question of what was to come. He evidently believed that after his conditions for the shift to Communism had been fulfilled, that for which millions of people had perished would come to pass.

Having proposed that his own 'modest' variant of Leninism be named 'Stalinism', he declared that 'the shift from socialism to Communism and the Communist principle of distribution according to need preclude any goods exchange, and consequently also preclude the conversion of products into goods and their conversion into value.'[193] What he envisaged was a huge barracks, a vast commune, a single-dimensional distributive society, where it would be impossible to distinguish the individual from the crowd, the so-called 'masses'. Stalin believed in the coming of this paradise on earth. The Soviet people also believed it, with varying degrees of conviction. Communism was especially associated, on an everyday level, with the idea of abundance and sufficiency, as living conditions in the Soviet Union were so poor.

As Churchill reminded Stalin in a message of 22 November 1941, concerning the post-war organization of the world, the common struggle against Nazism did not alter the fact that 'Russia is a Communist state and Britain and the USA are not such states nor do they intend to become such.'[194] It was this truth that led to the rapid cooling of relations between the Allies by the end of the war. The coalition had been a hard-headed calculation by all the parties. The viability of the Stalinist system depended to a great extent on keeping the Soviet people isolated from Western values and the democratic institutions of the free world, whose attractions Communist propaganda did its best to destroy.

On 15 November 1944 Stalin received a delegation from Warsaw headed by M. Spychalski. During the lavish entertainment Stalin said: 'the Soviet Union, we Leninist people, have always been renowned for the honesty and sincerity of our politics. You see, I received Churchill here. He thought that if an ally was inexperienced he could be fooled. Whereas I believe that it is wrong.'[195] At this time Stalin's correspondence with Churchill was at its most intense, each leader trying to out-do the other with compliments and eloquent epithets. Yet when front commanders began sending in reports to Stalin of the warmth of meetings between Soviet and US and British troops in Germany, Stalin at once dictated an order: 'The senior troop commander, in the sector where such a meeting has taken place, must first of all make contact with the senior commander of the American or English forces and establish with them a dividing line agreed by General Headquarters. No information on the plans and battle tasks of our forces must be given to anyone. Undertake no initiatives yourself to organize friendly meetings.'[196]

Though it could not be admitted at the time, Stalin feared the 'corrupting influence of the West'. The strength of his system depended on the Leninist-Stalinist idea remaining unadulterated, on unwavering faith in himself and in the infallibility and absolute truth of the path on which he was leading his people. This helps to explain not only the need to 'filter out' traitors and spies, but also the fact that soon after the triumphal days of May 1945, Stalin signed an order which read: 'Front army councils are [ordered] to form camps in rear areas for accommodating former prisoners of war and repatriated Soviet citizens, 10,000 in each camp. In all, 2nd Belorussian Front is to form fifteen camps, 1st Belorussian, thirty, 1st Ukrainian, thirty, 4th Ukrainian, five, 2nd Ukrainian, ten, 3rd Ukrainian, ten. Former Red Army service personnel are to be screened by counter-intelligence organs of "Smersh" [Death to Spies], civilians by NKVD and NKGB commissions, and "Smersh".[197]

These hundred new 'prophylactic' camps sifted through tens of thousands of people who had been released from Nazi camps only to be put straight into Stalin's. Out of 1.9 million who went through the checking process, 900,000 ended up in the camps or so-called labour battalions of the NKVD scattered throughout the Gulag system.

After the war, Stalin was quick to terminate contact with Western leaders. They were, for him, what they always been: implacable class enemies. He did not yet start the name-calling that would come later, such as at the Nineteenth Party Congress in October 1952, where he described them as 'the chief enemies of the liberation movement' and 'war-mongers'.[198] For now, he merely began to distance himself. He set about preserving the system. Perhaps for the moment only he understood that its stability depended on the immutability of the Bolshevik postulates of power: one-party rule, the special status of a single class, a single 'correct' ideology, absolute hostility to everything un-Communist, and fanatical belief in the 'precepts of Lenin' and himself by millions of people.

In the last two or three years of his life, Stalin lost his former energy. Certainly he exerted himself over Tito, the Korean War, meetings with foreign Communist leaders, rare meetings of the Polit-buro (or Presidium, as he renamed it in 1946). He continued to read reports, to receive military men and scientists engaged on the nuclear programme, and he still attended the Bolshoi Theatre. But his strength was abandoning him. Life had taken its toll. He could still gain per-sonal satisfaction from launching such monumental schemes as the Volga hydroelectric dam system, or the construction of a railway from the northern Urals to the Yenisei. And still, with a small gesture of one finger, he could cause millions of people to be moved from one place to another. While orders and directives might emanate from the Central Committee and the government, he was still the mainspring of the machine. But he was undoubtedly weakening. The fifty-minute speech he gave at the Nineteenth Congress was almost beyond his strength.

He began more often to deal with important papers at the Kuntsevo dacha. When members of his close entourage were summoned, they were likely to find him sitting in an armchair, immobile, his face to the window. He could remain thus for an hour or more. For some time he had been spending three winter months at a stretch in the south. He might occasionally emerge from the villa and wander slowly in the grounds, or sit on the veranda and watch the sea.

His papers and the reminiscences of people who had close contact with him at this time, as well as his last theoretical writings, suggest that his mind kept returning to certain ideas. He thought often about his childhood, his mother, Georgia. On a number of letters sent to him by Georgian political prisoners he wrote: 'Beria – Look into this. If they're telling the truth, let them go.' Also, he began to seek out some of his Georgian childhood friends, and sent them money. After his seventieth birthday a small photograph of his wife, Nadezhda Alliluyeva, who had committed suicide in 1932, appeared on his desk, and he brought his daughter Svetlana Alliluyeva to be close to him, spending the summer of 1951 with her at Borzhomi; he also made a vain attempt to save his son, Vasili, from alcoholism. These may be signs that he was trying, if only in his thoughts and occasionally by a weak effort, to restore the scattered family that he had sacrificed for the cause.

Hardly a man to be accused of sentimentality, he nevertheless on one occasion re-read some fifteen letters or notes his wife had written him from the south. Perhaps he was taken by her imagery: 'Moscow looks better, but in places it looks like a woman who has powdered over her shortcomings, especially in the rain when the colours streak.'[199] Perhaps he was intrigued by passages such as: 'I'll send you in the next post, if you're not back by then, a book by Dmitrievsky (a non-returnee) called *On Stalin and Lenin*, I can't send it at the moment because Dvinsky hasn't got it yet, I just read about it in the White press, where they say there is the most interesting material on you. Curious?'[200]

Khrushchev, like several other political figures, recalled in his memoirs that at the end of his life Stalin began to wonder what would happen to all his work after he had gone. At the midnight dinner table he often asked his cronies how they would get on without him, and just as often would say: 'They'll crush you like kittens.'

It emerges indirectly from his marginal notes that he sought analogies of himself in history. His sympathies lay with Ivan the Terrible, in whom he saw a clever and powerful despot, his unbridled cruelty a state virtue. The conquest of the Tatar khanate of Kazan, the attainment of a way out to the Baltic and the creation of a ruthless cohort, the so-called *oprichniks*, made Ivan even more appealing in Stalin's eyes.

Stalin could see no worthy successor, and this plainly irked him, although had there been one it is certain he would not have survived for long. The system, however, called for a leader. His doubts about his fawning entourage did not, though, shake his absolute certainty that the regime's ideological goals would be reached.

For many years Stalin had favoured Molotov, seeing him more often than others, and taking counsel on the most important decisions only from him. Molotov was probably the only member of the Politburo prepared to stand up to Stalin and to express his own opinion. In 1949, however, Stalin had done nothing to save Molotov's Jewish wife from arrest as an alleged Zionist, or from torture in January 1953. Demoted from the post of Foreign Minister in 1949, Molotov had remained Deputy Prime Minister and a member of the Presidium, but by 1952 Stalin had cooled towards him, and at the Central Committee Plenum after the Nineteenth Congress he subjected him – and Mikoyan – to sharp, if meaningless, criticism. Khrushchev was sure that 'had Stalin lived much longer, the lives of Molotov and Mikoyan would have ended tragically.'[201]

Stalin did not take Khrushchev seriously, seeing in him a 'peasant-leader', forthright and practical, but not a candidate for the top job. He became guarded towards his fellow Georgian Beria in his last years, and it is possible that he was waiting for the right time and occasion to blame him for all the suffering inflicted on the Party organization in the post-war period.

As for Voroshilov and Kaganovich, Stalin had long ago had enough of them, while Mikoyan, Shvernik, Bulganin, Pervukhin and the rest had never rated as potential leaders in his eyes. There remained Malenkov, quick-witted, efficient and obsequious, and an organization man to the core. When Poskrebyshev was let go, Malenkov took over all of Stalin's personal affairs, sorting and sifting his correspondence. He was, however, accused by Stalin of spinelessness and unforgivable 'softness' at more than one of the midnight feasts. Stalin could not have seen this pallid, podgy-faced functionary as his successor. He felt the end approaching and sensed he would be followed by a vacuum, as indeed he was.

At the end of 1952 Stalin suffered a number of fainting spells, twice falling down in his study. His blood pressure rose to an alarming level. He had given up smoking, but still enjoyed wine and Russian steam-baths, which could not have been good for his condition. Khrushchev recalled that from time to time Stalin 'had a mental blackout or lapses of memory ... I remember him once starting to say something to Bulganin, but he could not recall his name. He stared hard at him and said, "Look, what's your name?" "Bulganin." "Right, yes, Bulganin. That's what I meant to say." '[202] He was deteriorating, just as Lenin had done, and had his stroke been less severe, there might have been a repeat of Lenin's Gorki scenario, this time at Kuntsevo. Despite its monolithic appearance, a totalitarian system, in which all power is concentrated in the hands of one man, is as vulnerable as he is himself. And all dictators are mortal.

After the war, Stalin began to devote more attention to his health. He relied less on doctors, many of whom would end up in prison, and more on the herbal infusions prepared for him by Poskrebyshev, until he too was set aside. Stalin had counted on living the long life of a Caucasian, who commonly reach a hundred and more. He had often said in private that the Caucasus always renewed his energy, and every year in August he would spend long periods relaxing by the Black Sea. Between 1950 and 1952 he spent three to four months there each year. Still, on his return to Moscow he would complain to Beria and Molotov of dizziness, nausea and not feeling well. Somehow the fact that he had been seen to fall down was leaked to diplomatic circles, and rumours of his death were reported in January 1948 in Stockholm and London. But as he was still turning up at the Bolshoi to watch the ballet, they quickly subsided.

On 1 March 1953 Stalin's closest comrades left his dacha at 4 a.m. after the usual late-night feast. They had drunk, talked and drunk again. Stalin himself was drinking very little by now, though

Khrushchev claims that he was 'quite drunk' that night.[203] At first Stalin had been in a good mood, but then he became irritated, reprimanding everyone, especially Molotov and Beria. He was angry with all of them, telling them that if it were not for the Gulag, neither industry, nor timber and mining, nor transport and the power stations would ever meet their targets. What were the members of the Presidium up to? People in the leadership seemed to think they could sit on their laurels. They were wrong, dead wrong!

A graveyard silence descended on the heavily-laden table. Stalin never issued empty threats.

They didn't manage to keep Yugoslavia in the camp, he continued angrily, they missed the opportunity and with it the possibility of victory in Korea, and now there were widespread signs in the country of renewed sabotage. There was the Doctors' Plot, another clear sign. Why did he have to think of everything?

During breaks in this tirade, Beria, Malenkov and Bulganin attempted to reassure their leader: 'We'll take measures ... Your orders will be fulfilled, Comrade Stalin ... We'll sort the situation out ...' Stalin swept those present with a slow, heavy look, threw down his napkin and left the room without another word. The others also got up and left in silence.

It was common for Stalin to sleep until midday, but when there was still no sign of him after noon on the following day, 1 March, the domestic staff became concerned. Beria, though, had given instructions that no one could enter Stalin's rooms without being called. Towards evening the lights went on in Stalin's study, then in his dining-room, and the staff sighed with relief. In fact Stalin had his fatal stroke at 8 or 9 p.m., when he had gone into the dining-room for a glass of mineral water.

During the previous night's dinner Stalin had talked about Comintern, about how the Party had thrown huge sums into the effort of establishing Communist parties, yet still hadn't managed to ignite the world revolution. In 1922, when they had thought Japan was on the verge of revolution, they ordered the construction of a radio station near Vladivostok for broadcasting propaganda in the region. In May 1923 Adolf Ioffe, who was in talks with the Japanese, was instructed by the Politburo not to object to the sale of the Pacific island of Sakhalin for $US1 billion, 90 per cent of it in cash. Nothing came of this initiative. The question of Sakhalin had come up again on 12 April 1941, in talks with Japanese Foreign Minister Matsuoka, who suddenly offered northern Sakhalin for sale. Stalin promptly reacted with: 'But then you'll be able to coop us up and smother us. What do we want cold Sakhalin for?' 'For your peace of mind,' Matsuoka replied.

Without permission, at about 11 p.m. on 1 March, Stalin's guards and his housekeeper, Matryona Petrovna, went into his rooms and found him on the floor, unconscious and wheezing. Beria, who had been located with difficulty, arrived and whispered to the staff, 'Can't you see, Comrade Stalin is sleeping soundly! All of you get out of here and don't wake him up.' It was not until early on the morning of 2 March that a sobered-up Beria arrived in the company of a group of physicians. Perplexed members of the Politburo were standing in the next room. Beria showed his agitation by pacing back and forth. The frightened doctors examined Stalin, and reported their diagnosis:

During the examination, which took place at 7 a.m., the patient was lying on a divan on his back, his head turned to the left, his eyes closed, with moderate hyperaemia of the face; there had been involuntary urination (his clothes were soaked in urine). While his pulse was being felt in the left radial artery, motor disturbances were seen in the left arm and left leg. The breathing was not irregular. The pulse was 78 with rare prolapses. The heart tones were dull. Blood pressure was 190 over 110. There was no wheezing in the lungs from the front. There were signs of contusion in the area of the right ulna (excoriation and a small swelling). The patient is in an unconscious state. The right nasal-labial fold is slightly fallen. The eyeballs move to right and left when the lids are lifted. The pupils are of average size, with reduced response to light. There is no movement in the right extremities and occasional disturbance in the left.

Diagnosis: hypertonic disease, generalized atherosclerosis with predominant damage of the cerebral blood vessels, right-handed hemiplegia as a result of middle left cerebral arterial haemorrhaging; atherosclerotic cardiosclerosis, nephrosclerosis. The patient's condition is extremely serious.

Treatment: absolute quiet, leave the patient on the divan; leeches behind the ears (eight now in place); cold compress on the head, hypertonic microclism (one glass of 10 per cent solution of magnesium

sulphate). Remove dental prostheses. No food today. A neuropathologist, therapist and nurse should be on duty round the clock. A teaspoon
may be used with care to give liquid when there is no choking.

The report was signed by chief Kremlin physician I. Kuperin, and
Professors P. Lukomsky, I. Glazunov, P. Tkachev and V. Ivanov-
Neznamov.[204]

Kuperin handed the typewritten report to Beria and Malenkov, who
were in whispered conversation. There and then, in the next room at
midday a meeting of the Presidium was convened under Malenkov's
chairmanship. Kuperin delivered his report, with Tkachev providing
the documents. Kuperin was terribly nervous. Apart from having to
address this particular group of individuals, he could hardly have forgotten that two months earlier Stalin had signed a note to the Health
Minister, E. Smirnov, 'on removing serious shortcomings in the work
of the administration of the Kremlin clinical services', connected with
the 'Doctors' Plot'. More arrests were expected.

The Presidium heard the report and waited in silence. No one was
prepared to begin a discussion on what to do next, or what was to
happen when the inevitable occurred. Then Beria turned to Kuperin
and said: 'You are responsible for Comrade Stalin's life. Do you understand? You must do everything possible and impossible to save Comrade Stalin!' Kuperin, already pale, turned white.

Malenkov then read a prepared draft decree, approving the
measures taken by the medical team, establishing constant surveillance
of the leader by members of the Presidium, and fixing the next meeting
for eight o'clock that evening.[205] As with Lenin, it was in effect the
Party leadership that handled the leader's treatment, hiring and firing
the physicians and deciding the regimen. A totalitarian hierarchy of
power, that controlled every other aspect of society, could not imagine
handling even this crisis in any other way than by secrecy and threats.

That evening, Kuperin reported that Stalin's condition had
worsened. He was still unconscious, his breathing was uneven, his
pulse rate faster, his heartbeat irregular and his blood pressure now
210 over 120. He must be kept in bed. Six to eight leeches would be
applied as before, magnesium sulphate would be administered by
enema and intra-muscular injection, cold compresses should continue
and sweet tea be given if possible. The Presidium approved these

measures, and ordered that four more specialists be added to the team: A. Myasnikov, E. Tareyev, N. Konovalov and I. Filimonov.[206]

From 7 a.m. on 2 March, the duty physicians began keeping a log of the progress of Stalin's illness. With a note of his condition every twenty or thirty minutes, it runs to dozens of pages. Khrushchev claimed in his memoirs that at a certain moment Stalin recognized the Presidium members and even squeezed a few hands, but the doctors' notes make no mention of this. They recorded that at 12.35 he was still unconscious, his breathing was deep and even and his pulse and blood pressure were satisfactory. An hour and a quarter later his condition was unchanged, except that the twitching in his left leg was more frequent. None of the doctors was prepared to speak his mind and say that Stalin's position was hopeless.

The members of the Presidium sat around in armchairs in the next room, exhausted by waiting and uncertainty. They would occasionally get up to stretch their legs or exchange a few words with each other, or leave the room to make a phone call. Someone had sandwiches brought in. Only Beria left the villa altogether, to spend two or three hours at the Kremlin. He returned in an excited state.

The medical team was ethnically 'impeccable', that is, it included no Jews, even though new faces were constantly being brought in. They whispered to each other, applied more leeches, and went on giving injections and enemas. At 4 p.m. they noted that the patient's condition had worsened. A second report was formally received during the night, and it was agreed that the patient's head and upper torso should be raised slightly with a small pillow, that he should only be given glucose and lemon juice by mouth, that hot-water bottles should be placed at his legs, mainly the left one, for one or two hours, and that penicillin in a novocaine solution should be given three times a day. Five other measures were listed.

Although by now the leader's comrades-in-arms were all thinking about it, no one would actually ask who was going take over. It was too terrible even to imagine that Beria, the monster in glittering pince-nez, might occupy Stalin's seat, but as Stalin's daughter Svetlana recalled, he was bursting with excitement.[207]

It is quite possible that Beria was to blame for Stalin's condition. Since his Siberian exile, Stalin had become accustomed to taking a weekly Russian steam-bath. When his blood pressure began to rise dangerously, however, Academician Vinogradov persuaded him to give it up, and for nearly two years Stalin had heeded his doctor's orders. Then, two weeks before he had the stroke, Beria told Stalin he shouldn't believe everything the doctors said, as there were many saboteurs among them. Stalin started going to the baths again.

At 10.15 on the morning of 3 March the physicians again met the Presidium, and reported a worsening in Stalin's condition. His pupils responded lazily to light, his right cheek puffed out as he breathed, there was no movement in the right arm or leg, and the left extremities showed disturbance at times.

Stalin's son Vasili appeared several times, drunk and shouting 'The bastards have killed father.' Khrushchev put his arms around his shoulders and led him into the next room, where he gradually quietened down.

The medical reports continued. From 2.30 p.m. on 4 March Stalin's breathing began faltering more frequently, and he was given oxygen. The Politburo members agreed to meet at eight the next evening, and issued a decree declaring that, 'in Stalin's absence it is crucially important for the Party and government to secure the uninterrupted and proper governance of the country, which requires the closest possible collective effort of the leadership and the avoidance of any disorder or panic.'

At 11.30 p.m. the doctors noted that Stalin had showed signs of wanting to vomit. His face and upper torso had become deathly pale, his breathing extremely shallow and with longer pauses. His pulse was rapid and weak, there were frequent tics in the left side of his face and jerking in his left leg. Kuperin quietly informed the assembled leaders that the position was critical. They were all silent except Beria, who had loudly declared once again, 'Take all measures to save Comrade Stalin!'

On 5 March, despite the hopelessness of the situation, the doctors continued with the use of camphor, caffeine and chest massage, in an attempt to halt Stalin's decline. It was to no avail. At 3.35 in the afternoon they recorded that his breathing was stopping for four to five seconds every two or three minutes. The twitching in his left hand and leg came and went.

Beria left again for the Kremlin, where he searched Stalin's personal safes, now secure in the knowledge that he would not be disturbed by the leader's sudden recovery. He, Malenkov and Khrushchev had been instructed to see that all of Stalin's 'documents and papers, both current and archival, are put in proper order',[208] but he had left Malenkov and Khrushchev behind at the dacha. He had reason to suspect that Stalin had made a will, as he had once said he 'ought to write something down for the future', and since the leader had cooled towards him lately, he had no great expectations. It will probably never be known whether or not Stalin left a will, as Beria got to his safe before anyone else.

Thousands of telegrams and letters were flooding into Moscow with warm wishes for Stalin's speedy recovery. Another consultation took place, at which the doctors reported that Stalin had vomited blood in the night and suffered what they called a serious collapse. His lips and hands were blue and his head shook. Malenkov and Beria moved apart and engaged in a whispered conversation, joined at times by Khrushchev. There was the forthcoming joint meeting of the Presidium, Council of Ministers and Presidium of the Supreme Soviet to consider.

They all dispersed to the Kremlin in the evening, leaving Bulganin at Stalin's side, and believing that Stalin had only a short time to live. The joint conference began at 8.40 p.m., delayed by forty minutes while Malenkov, Beria and Khrushchev waited for Bulganin to call to announce Stalin's death. The call did not come.

At 9.30 p.m. the physicians recorded that Stalin began sweating. His pulse was minimal, he was turning bluer, his heartbeat was duller, his breathing shallower. Ten minutes later his pulse was barely perceptible. Camphor and adrenaline were injected, and he was given artificial respiration, but at 9.50 the doctors recorded that Stalin was dead. The leaders rushed back from the Kremlin. Beria was the first to bend and kiss the still-warm corpse, and the others followed suit. Their long and agonizing wait over, most of them felt sadness and relief, and deep anxiety. The future was uncertain as they returned to the Kremlin. The domestic staff they left behind were equally unsure of what lay in store, blinking back their tears as Stalin's housekeeper Valentina Istomina wailed openly.

It is noteworthy that in the unfinished meeting in the Kremlin, lasting only an hour and ten minutes, the leadership had managed, even before hearing that he was dead, to agree to remove Stalin from the post of Chairman of the Council of Ministers and to appoint Malenkov in his place. They also reduced the size of the Presidium from twenty-five to eleven, curiously leaving Stalin as a member. Khrushchev was instructed to 'concentrate on the work of the Central Committee', in effect making him the Party First (formerly General) Secretary. The ministries of State Security and the Interior were merged into a single ministry – the Ministry of the Interior – headed by Beria, and all the most important posts were defined in seventeen points of a decree.[209] The meeting also formed a funeral commission, consisting of Khrushchev as chairman, Kaganovich, Shvernik, A. Vasilevsky, N. Pegov, P. Artemiev and M. Yasnov.

In the Central Committee propaganda section on Staraya Square, meanwhile, a huge team was labouring over the text of an 'Address to All Toilers'. Secret telegrams were sent out to the localities, and the 'organs' were put on extra alert in case the enemy chose this moment for his dark purposes. It was not yet daybreak on 6 March when the funeral commission met. Khrushchev read out the draft decree: 'The commission considers it expedient for the autopsy and embalming of Comrade STALIN's body to be carried out in the special laboratory of the mausoleum of V.I. Lenin.'

Various other tasks were also defined: security, preparation of the Hall of Columns for the lying-in-state, a death-mask to be made by the sculptor Manizer. It was decided that Stalin should be laid to rest in his generalissimo's uniform. There would be a military guard of honour.[210] Two further decisions, however, required another meeting of the Presidium, which took place on the morning of 6 March. First, that 'the sarcophagus containing the body of I.V. Stalin be placed in the mausoleum on Red Square alongside the sarcophagus of V.I. Lenin'. And secondly, that 'a Pantheon be built as a monument to the eternal glory of the great personages of the Soviet land.' After the funeral, the Presidium set more precise terms for this project: 'The Pantheon will be built in Moscow, 3.5 kilometres south of the new building of Moscow State University on the site of the Vorontsov Vitamin Institute.'[211] This decree would be amended before a competition was announced for a project that was never realized.

The commission struggled to think of new ways of immortalizing the late leader. On his seventieth birthday in 1949, Stalin himself had cautiously mentioned that he would very much like a Stalin Prize to be created after his death. He had selected a design, similar to the Order of Lenin, from nine submitted by the artists N. Moskalev, A. Kuznetsov and I. Dubasov, but no one on the commission could remember what Stalin had wanted the prize to be given for.

The autopsy, which took place on 6 March, lasted seven hours. It was carried out by nine specialists, all of them with Russian names, as no one was yet aware that the anti-Semitic 'Doctors' Plot' had died with Stalin. The eleven-page autopsy report was left to gather dust, and only a simplified version of a page or so was published.

The entire country was plunged into mourning. The workers grieved out of traditional 'proletarian consciousness', the peasants from their serf-like dependency, the intelligentsia for their plundered liberty, and the military for their costly victories. Only the millions of inmates of the Gulag did not mourn, but were instead buoyed up by the thought of an immediate amnesty, especially the political prisoners. Their hopes were vain. For the time being, at any rate, there was no thought of releasing 'enemies of the people' into the community at large.

Some time after the funeral, State Counsellor of Justice R. Rudenko reported to Malenkov: 'In Rechny (special) camp, which contains special state criminals, mass disorder has broken out, prisoners have refused to go to work. They are actively resisting the camp administration. On 1 August a group of five hundred prisoners tried to break out into the camp zone. They demanded a review of their cases and an amnesty following Stalin's death. Weapons were used. Forty-two prisoners were killed and 138 were wounded.' Order was restored using typical Stalinist methods.

A four-day period of mourning was announced, and an artillery salute was fixed for noon on 9 March, when everything in the land stopped for five minutes and factory sirens were sounded for three minutes. All of the leaders from the socialist world came to Moscow, and lesser ones from elsewhere.

Four figures dominated the Presidium's funeral meeting: Khrushchev, Malenkov, Beria and Molotov. They all swore allegiance to 'the cause of Stalin'. As if he were not already immortalized in countless ways, Stalin's name was given to yet more streets, villages and collective farms, in Russia and throughout the socialist world. As early as 7 March Warsaw decreed that the town of Katowice be renamed

Stalinogrud, while the Palace of Science and Culture should bear the name of Stalin, with a monument raised to him outside. The Kremlin leadership decided to establish a Stalin Museum at the Kuntsevo dacha. A director was appointed, salaries were fixed, and large sums of money allocated before they changed their minds, realizing that there were already enough museums, institutes and monuments in Stalin's name, let alone that of his predecessor.

The death of Stalin closed a gloomy chapter in the history of the USSR. But history never stands still. Within a short time, the Stalinist Khrushchev would deal his former idol a devastating and fatal blow.

3

The Third Leader: Nikita Khrushchev

With the two giants of Bolshevism gone, it at once became apparent that their successors were political pygmies by comparison. Unlike Lenin, Stalin left no 'Testament'. Instead, he left a mighty and enigmatic empire.

Dictators never like to appoint a successor, if only because they think they are going to live forever. The absence of a democratic mechanism for the transfer of power invariably leads to a struggle among those remaining. Despite their assurances of 'unity', 'the monolithic Leninist leadership', 'loyalty to the cause of Lenin-Stalin', this was what took place following the death of Stalin.

Given the absence of an obvious successor, and even though the population was traditionally without a voice, Stalin's heirs nevertheless realized that in order to maintain the Leninist course, as well as their total control of the vast country, they needed to enhance the prestige and role of the Party. For two decades it had been the magical incantation of Stalin's name that had moved the levers of power. Now he was gone. 'Collective leadership', as they all knew, was a fiction. Whoever ran the Party would now run the country. Khrushchev had been made chairman of the funeral commission – a position of enormous significance – and charged with 'concentrating on the work of the Central Committee', but had not yet been made head of the Party.

Nikita Sergeevich Khrushchev was completely unlike the average dictator. He was outwardly affable, with a peasant-like bluntness, an open face, snub nose and big ears, unfeigned humour and boundless energy. The members of the Presidium had for so long been gripped by fear that it was natural for them to want the Party to be run by someone more yielding, more obliging than Stalin. From March to

September 1953 Khrushchev was merely one of the Central Committee secretaries, though with the special task of handling its organizational affairs. On 8 September, following the arrest of Beria, in which Khrushchev played the main part, he became First Secretary. It was the Beria Affair that lifted him above the other members of the Presidium, and from which his later fearlessness would derive.

Khrushchev was fifty-nine when he ascended the Party throne. He belonged to the generation of Bolsheviks that arose after the 1917 revolution, notably in the 1920s and early 1930s. He had stepped into the shoes of men who had been executed, but had no moral qualms on that score. He was one of the lucky ones whose career was meteorically advanced by the savagery of Stalin's dictatorship and the purges.

Bolsheviks of the post-1917 generation like Khrushchev were generally speaking not very well educated, many of them having passed through only a brief spell in the so-called 'workers' faculties', in effect adult education day or evening classes that were meant to prepare workers and peasants for higher education. In Khrushchev's case it was the Yuzovka Mining Workers' Faculty in Ukraine. True, he also did a spell in the Moscow Industrial Academy in the mid-1920s, but this barely enhanced his academic abilities, and according to Shepilov, who was a close associate, he never learned even to compose a literate resolution.

Many of the middle-ranking regional leaders were from this second generation of Bolsheviks, but by the end of the thirties their number had been reduced to a handful, as most were consigned to oblivion in Stalin's purges. Khrushchev, however, was never threatened with this fate. Not even the most rabid Chekist could have accused him of anything. He personified a particular type of 'peasant' leader, a man from the very midst of the people, and this helped to create an atmosphere of trust around him in the eyes of simple folk. He was a typical leader of the Stalinist type: uneducated – 'two winters of schooling' – energetic, expeditious, never doubting the correctness of a Party instruction. He was also one of the most zealous executives of Stalin's will.

Khrushchev was a member of the Central Committee from 1934 until he was removed from all his posts in 1964 – thirty years in the 'Leninist headquarters of the Party'. He became a candidate (i.e.

non-voting) member of the Politburo in 1938, and a full member the following year. He was briefly Chairman of the Council of Ministers of Ukraine, and between 1958 and 1964 occupied the same post for the USSR. It was customary for the top Party boss also to be Supreme Commander-in-Chief of the Soviet Armed Forces, and in April 1957 Khrushchev was confirmed in this post as well. This does not exhaust the list of his jobs. Suffice it to say that in becoming First Party Secretary, he held enormous power.

In his time as First Secretary of the Moscow Party committee in 1935–38 and as First Secretary of the Ukrainian Central Committee from 1938, Khrushchev made his own contribution to the evil of the Stalinist inquisition. Speaking at a Party meeting in Moscow on 22 August 1936, he said: 'Just as Comrade Stalin, with his sharp Leninist eye, has always accurately pointed out the path for our Party, as for the whole of the construction, so he has pointed out the corners where vermin can crawl out. We have to shoot not only this scum, but Trotsky should also be shot.' Pausing for the applause to die down, he went on, whipping up the hysteria: 'At one Moscow factory . . . there was a young Bakaev snake [the son of I. Bakaev, who had been purged] working under his own name. Yet the Party organization didn't even know about such odious names . . . With a name like Bakaev he ought to have been put under a magnifying glass . . . Do you call that vigilance? They've got to learn to organize their work, how to target someone, make a rapid study of him and bring the case to a conclusion.'[1]

Khrushchev's work in Moscow was not restricted to the political field. He was also involved in the 'reconstruction' of the city, though he had a distinctly Bolshevik understanding of the task. Speaking on 5 November 1936 at a Party meeting in the Kirov district of Moscow, he said: 'I would tell anyone who hasn't been on the Garden Ring for the last three months to go and take a look; you won't recognize it. We are cutting [the boulevards] at night, so people won't notice. We'll be working through the winter, too, so the people won't know whether we're cutting down dead trees or green ones (*laughter*). And when it's all done, the people will come and say: the street looks good. We've demolished the Triumphal Arch. The street is wonderful without the arch. We tore down the Sukharev Tower and the Kitaigorod Wall, even though the architects told us it was a historic monument. We're sharpening our axes for next year, too, and we'll continue with our work.'[2]

Such zeal was duly noted. Khrushchev was sent to Kiev, the capital of Ukraine, where he was able to apply what he had learnt in Moscow. Speaking as First Secretary of the Ukrainian Communist Party at its Fourteenth Congress on 13 June 1938, he declared: 'Here in Ukraine, almost the entire membership of the Politburo of the Ukrainian Party, with few exceptions, turned out to be hostile. Yezhov arrived and did a real demolition job. I think we are finishing off the enemies in Ukraine right now.'[3]

This was the sort of speech that was being made by every right-thinking Stalinist, and like the vast army of Party organization men, Khrushchev believed every word of it. In the use of terror, Khrushchev was an ardent exponent of Stalin's will, and for that reason he survived, although it would have been difficult to portray this outwardly good-natured and comic figure as a Polish spy or Trotskyite saboteur.

As a graduate of the Stalinist school, Khrushchev had been taught to believe in Bolshevik tenets, to hate anyone defined as an enemy, and not to spare himself in carrying out the Party's orders. This elementary, harsh political thinking and ideological primitivism, combined with native peasant wit, inexhaustible energy and simple optimism, secured for Khrushchev a firm place in the top rank of the leadership, as far as that was possible under Stalin.

Despite the purges of the 1930s and its huge losses in the Second World War, the Communist Party was still led by men of the old 'Leninist-Stalinist' school. After Stalin's death, the Presidium consisted of Bulganin, Beria, Voroshilov, Kaganovich, Malenkov, Mikoyan, Molotov and Khrushchev, plus Pervukhin and Saburov, who had latterly been advanced by Stalin. It was clear that of these, Beria, Malenkov and Khrushchev would lay claim to the top job. As Shelepin put it a dozen years later: 'After Stalin came Khrushchev. He was also a leader. So the leadership psychology continued.' Khrushchev, like the others, saw that it was the feared Beria, as head of the almighty Interior Ministry, who held all the important cards. He decided to take bold action.

Khrushchev was at first motivated by a desire to save himself, as well as the other members of the Presidium: it is impossible to find in his words or deeds any hint of protest against the Stalinist system as such. The political struggle in the Kremlin, however, acquired a logic of its own. The Khrushchev who took up arms against Beria was not the one who has gone down in history as the first Soviet leader to challenge Stalin's memory. But the 'plot' against Beria provided the original platform from which it became possible to strike the first, devastating blows against Stalinist totalitarianism.

Encounter with a Monster

Stalin's embalmed body was installed in the Mausoleum very slightly raised above that of Lenin, beside which it was to remain until 1961. Oaths of loyalty to 'the great continuer of Lenin's cause' were echoed around the whole country. The Kremlin leadership understood that the system was still sustained by three main supports: the Party, Bolshevik ideology and the vast repressive apparatus. There was no dominant leader, yet the Leninist system could not exist without one, and one must emerge. But who was it to be?

Given the virtual equality prevailing in the Presidium, Malenkov, as Chairman of the Council of Ministers, looked increasingly authoritative. It seemed he must become Stalin's successor, but he lacked the necessary leadership qualities. As Roy Medvedev has rightly observed, Malenkov was 'a man without a biography. His was a life of special departments and privy councils. He had no image of his own, not even his own style.'[4] Malenkov was not capable of clinging to the pinnacle of power: he had been created by Stalin as a leader of the second rank, in effect a high-level Party functionary. Indeed, the fact that he had been Stalin's favourite worked against him.

Stalin's heirs were as yet untroubled by the fact that there were still more than four million people in the camps, that entire nations had been deported, and that the 'punitive organs' were still keeping a close eye on everyone. Also still active was the infamous NKVD Special Board, which had condemned 442,531 people to death and long terms of imprisonment.[5] Stalin's heirs were more concerned with their own fate – how to preserve their exalted positions, how to protect their future careers, and above all their personal security.

The possibility that Beria might become the new leader caused profound disquiet. In his personal notes on Khrushchev, Fedor

Burlatsky, who had served as one of his advisers, recalled his chief telling him: 'We stood alongside the dead body [at Stalin's funeral], practically without a word, each man thinking of himself. Then we left. We travelled two to a car. The first to go were Malenkov and Beria, then Molotov and Kaganovich. Then and there Mikoyan says to me: "Beria's gone to Moscow to take power." I say to him: "As long as that bastard's alive, none of us can feel safe." And the idea took a firm hold in my mind that the first thing to do was to get rid of Beria.'[6]

The many accounts of what took place next all agree that Khrushchev's part in the affair was crucial. He exhibited extraordinary courage by undertaking to organize a compact with the other members of the Presidium, all of whom were primarily motivated by fear and a sense of self-preservation. It was not that they saw in Beria the odious personification of the system and the most repellent features of Stalinism; they saw in him a threat to themselves. At Khrushchev's secret meetings with the other members of the Presidium – including Malenkov, who was closest to Beria – they all agreed that Beria must go, but were terrified that the plot might go wrong. The plotters secured the assistance of a dozen or so senior army men, including Zhukov, Moskalenko, Batitsky, Zub and Yuferov.

Khrushchev would recount the tale of Beria's arrest on numerous subsequent occasions, each time adding new details and flourishes, and always emphasizing his own role. In the revealing reminiscences dictated by him and published in the West as *Khrushchev Remembers*, he recounts what took place at a joint meeting of the Presidium of the Council of Ministers and Party Presidium. 'As soon as Malenkov opened the session he said, "Let us discuss Party questions. There are some matters which we must deal with right away." As had been arranged in advance, I requested the floor from Comrade Malenkov and proposed that we discuss the matter of Beria. Beria was sitting on my right. He gave a start, grabbed me by the hand, looked at me with a startled expression on his face and said, "What's going on, Nikita? What's this you're mumbling about?" I said, "Just pay attention. You'll find out soon enough." '

Khrushchev then made a brief, confused speech, ludicrously accusing Beria, among other things, of spying for the Caucasian Muslim opposition, collaborating with British intelligence and intriguing with

Tito, being negative about the prospects of socialism in East Germany, and, more realistically, interfering in the Party affairs of the national republics, and seeking to undermine the unity of the Soviet people. He concluded, equally ludicrously, by declaring that 'Beria is no Communist.'

Everyone else then voiced their agreement. Malenkov, according to Khrushchev, was in a state of panic. Khrushchev proposed that Beria be relieved of all of his posts. Without putting this to a vote, the terrified Malenkov pressed a button, whereupon Zhukov and the other generals marched into the room. 'Malenkov,' Khrushchev continues, 'said in a faint voice to Comrade Zhukov, "As Chairman of the Council of Ministers of the USSR, I request that you take Beria into custody pending investigation of charges made against him." "Hands up!" Zhukov commanded Beria.'[7]

By the afternoon Beria was being held in the Kremlin. In the evening he was moved to a military post in the capital, and then finally to the underground command headquarters of Moscow military district. The other leaders were still so afraid of him, even when he was under arrest, that more than once they had to give the 'all-clear' to local forces that had been put on alert.

When Beria had more or less come to his senses, he began banging his fists on the door. At once the guard commander, a full colonel no less, and several other armed officers poked their heads in. 'What's going on? Why all the noise?' Beria replied: 'I demand an immediate meeting with Malenkov, or at least pen and paper.' Within a few minutes, after permission had been obtained from the Kremlin, a sheaf of paper and a pen and ink were brought. Before the start of the investigation, Beria wrote ceaselessly. Malenkov, Khrushchev, Bulganin and collectively all the other members of the Presidium received letters. On 28 June 1953 Beria wrote to Malenkov:

> I was convinced that I would draw all the necessary conclusions from the Presidium's serious criticism, and that I would be of use to the collective. But the Central Committee has decided otherwise, and I think it has acted correctly. I think it is necessary to say that I have always been infinitely loyal to the Party of Lenin-Stalin and to my motherland, and always active in my work ... I tried to select cadres according to their business-like qualities ... That applies to the Special Committee and the First and Second main boards, which dealt with

atomic affairs and guided missiles ... I ask Comrades Georgy Malenkov, Vyacheslav Molotov, Klementi Voroshilov, Nikita Khrushchev,
Lazar Kaganovich, Nikolai Bulganin, Anastas Mikoyan and the others
to forgive me. Dear Comrades, I wish you all great success in the cause
of Lenin-Stalin ... Georgy, I ask you, if you think it possible, not to
neglect my family (my wife and my old mother), and my son Sergei
whom you know.

Signed Lavrenti Beria.[8]

For two weeks, Beria wrote to his former comrades every day, until
Khrushchev ordered the removal of writing paper.

The members of the Presidium decided that Beria must be tried,
even though their ardent wish was to exterminate him with all due
despatch. They seemed to fear that, even incarcerated in a prison cell,
he still mysteriously retained some of the authority he had wielded
as head of the Gulag and the entire system of punishment and control.
It was decided to proceed by resorting to the practice of 1937–38,
handing the case over to a *troika* which would deal with it in half an
hour. Many, however, feared that such a procedure could unleash a
repeat of the great terror, the thought of which made their blood run
cold. Khrushchev objected that on 29 June 1953 the Presidium had
passed his resolution calling for an investigation of the 'criminal, anti-
Party and anti-state actions of Beria'. It had further agreed that the
case would be handled by the General Prosecutor, that the investigation team should be formed within twenty-four hours, and its composition reported to the Presidium.[9]

The investigation was also to deal with the actions of Beria's deputies and assistants B. Kobulov, A. Kobulov, P. Meshik, R. Sarkisov,
S. Goglidze, P. Sharia and others.

It was decided that the case should be debated by a special plenary
meeting of the Central Committee. The session lasted five days, and
the case was presented by Malenkov. Khrushchev took a less conspicu-
ous part, opening the Plenum and chairing the sessions.

Malenkov's speech was detailed, but contradictory. He stressed the
fact that Beria had tried to put the Ministry of the Interior above the
Party – which had in fact been the practice since Lenin's time –
and had carried out surveillance on the activities, conversations and
correspondence of every member of the Presidium. He described how
Beria had attempted to normalize relations with Yugoslavia over the

Party's head, as if trying to set up a meeting between Yugoslav and Soviet officials after Stalin's death had been the work of a common criminal. In fact, at the time both states had been moving tentatively towards improving relations, but the Presidium was determined to use any possible weapon, and this seemed like a powerful one.

The charge that Beria had opposed forcing the construction of socialism in East Germany was equally biased. Malenkov defined Beria's position on this as that of a 'bourgeois degenerate'. Illogically, he was accused, as he sat in his underground cell, of having caused the explosion of the Soviet hydrogen bomb: 'It was his personal decision.' Equally, the amnesty following the death of Stalin had, it was claimed, been 'too broad'.[10]

Following Malenkov's introductory speech, Khrushchev spoke for an hour. Frequently departing from his text, which was not unusual for him, the speech was disjointed and confused, though it drew the applause and laughter of the audience. Like other speakers, Khrushchev gave not the slightest hint that a phenomenon like Beria, whose hallmark was terror and complete disregard of the law, was a classic example of the Bolshevik system at work. Beria's close association with Stalin was plain for the Plenum to see, but Khrushchev set out to deflect any suspicions from the former leader: 'While Comrade Stalin was still alive we saw that Beria was a big schemer. He is a crafty, cunning careerist. He got his claws deep into Comrade Stalin's soul and was able to impose his opinions on Comrade Stalin.' Explaining why Stalin had allowed this to happen, he went on: 'We all respect Comrade Stalin. But time takes its toll. In recent years, Comrade Stalin did not read his papers or see people, as he was in poor health. And it was these circumstances that the scoundrel Beria exploited, very cunningly.'[11] Khrushchev thus in effect reduced the criminal nature of the regime to a matter of Stalin's poor health.

It was Khrushchev who for the first time raised the question of the exaggerated power of the Interior Ministry and its fabrication of fake charges, and who first cast doubt on the legality of the Ministry's so-called Special Boards. They had been established by a Party and government order of 5 November 1934 as extra-judicial organs with broad penal powers.[12] Angrily, he recalled that he had seen a tsarist gendarme for the first time in his life at the age of twenty-four, but now Interior Ministry officials were thick on the ground, and they were paid the highest salaries, more than a district Party secretary. Having raised the curtain to some extent on the secret services, Khrushchev could not, however, restrain himself from uttering the ritual Bolshevik formula: 'We must further strengthen the intelligence and counter-intelligence organs. We must put good, honest Bolsheviks onto this work.'

Like Malenkov and the rest of the Presidium, Khrushchev was blind to the fatal flaws in the Leninist system, which relied on repression and the Party's unlimited monopoly of power. Nor could they see that, like all 'good, honest Bolsheviks', they had themselves lived in a world of lies and coercion.

With the earthy humour that made him what he was, even at this grim Party meeting Khrushchev could make the delegates laugh. Describing Beria's reaction when he was arrested, he remarked, 'He dropped a load in his pants.' The official report modified this to: 'He turned to jelly, and possibly more than that.' The meeting was convulsed in mirth. Khrushchev recalled the last time he had seen Beria on the eve of his arrest: 'I shook him "warmly" by the hand, thinking to myself, well, you swine, this is your last handshake, tomorrow at 2 o'clock we'll really shake you!' This too got a good laugh.

Khrushchev did not remind his audience that he himself had given vocal support to Beria. Speaking to Ukrainian NKVD officials on 13 December 1938 he had declared: 'The new head is now Lavrenti Pavlovich Beria. He has spent his whole life working in the Party. He has shown himself as a Bolshevik-Stalinist who has defended the Party organization and Georgia in general from hostile elements. He has united Georgia in love for the Soviet people and love for Comrade Stalin (*stormy applause*). You have to unite and with Comrade Beria in command smash our enemies.'[13]

Others added their own details to the list of charges against Beria. Although everyone knew that Malenkov had been closest to Beria, as he was now Chairman of the Council of Ministers such a charge could not be uttered; not that this prevented Malenkov himself from noting sadistically, when the Secretary of the Azerbaijan Party Central Committee rose to speak: 'Comrade Bagirov, you were close to Beria, but that issue is not under discussion at present.'[14] A. Andreyev's tone matched that of Beria himself when he said, 'We must put this swine on the rack and get the whole picture of his relations with foreigners, just who and how he served them.'[15] To any suggestion that there had been a cult of personality, Andreyev objected: 'Why has the issue of a cult of personality arisen? It's Beria's dirty tricks. We must not undermine Comrade Stalin's teachings. Comrade Stalin's teachings are eternal and immutable.'[16] The other delegates muttered, 'Quite right.'

Stalin's former aide A. Poskrebyshev had been groomed to make a speech at the Plenum, but when the members of Presidium read what he had written, they found that he had gone beyond merely unmasking Beria, and had set himself up as an interpreter of many hitherto unknown sayings and declarations of his old master. It was agreed to drop him from the agenda and merely to attach the draft of his speech to the evidence for the Special Judicial Hearing.[17] As for Poskrebyshev himself, at least he was rehabilitated after having lived during the last months of Stalin's life under a cloud.

The Plenum itself was not of particular significance. It served chiefly as a prop for the leadership in the emerging struggle for power, a means of dissociating itself from the universally hated hangman. No one saw the need to examine the roots of the system that had produced and nurtured Beria: all that was required was to replace this 'bad' Bolshevik with a 'good' one, and everything would be fine.

Unexpectedly, Malenkov's closing speech turned out to have some importance. He did not criticize the system or the genesis of Stalinism as such, but he did condemn attempts by such delegates as Andreyev and Tevosyan to 'defend' Stalin. Malenkov was probably the first person to state that there was a Stalin personality cult. He declared, 'nothing justifies the fact that we did not hold a Party congress for thirteen years, or a Central Committee for years, and that the Politburo did not function normally and was substituted by the *troikas* and *pyaterkas* [committees of three and five] and so on, working on Comrade Stalin's orders in an uncoordinated way on different issues and various tasks.' Anticipating to some extent what Khrushchev would say three years later at the Twentieth Party Congress, Malenkov added: 'We do not have the right to hide from you the fact that such a deformed personality cult led to arbitrary individual decisions and that in recent years this began to cause serious harm to the business of leading the Party and country.' The solution was, characteristically, 'to raise the revolutionary vigilance of the Communists and toilers all round'.[18]

Towards the end of 1953 Beria's trial took place *in camera* in the office of a member of the Military Council of the Defence Ministry. The Special Judicial Hearing was chaired by Marshal Konev, assisted, among others, by former head of state and now chairman of the trade unions N. Shvernik, E. Zaidin, M. Kuchava (a Mingrelian, like Beria), Marshal K. Moskalenko and Moscow Party boss N. Mikhailov. It 'proved' that Beria and his aides had established contacts with bourgeois intelligence services for the purpose of 'destroying the Soviet worker-peasant regime, restoring capitalism and resurrecting the rule of the bourgeoisie'.[19]

For days the members of the hearing examined in meticulous detail the intimate contact Beria had had with a multitude of women in Moscow and elsewhere. They made a close study of the deposition extracted from Beria's chief bodyguard, Colonel R. Sarkisov, which included his admission that he had delivered dozens of underage girls, as well as older girls and women, to his boss. Long lists were submitted containing the names of women Beria had raped, indecently assaulted or forced into performing sexual acts. Among them were some well-known names, including the wife of a Hero of the Soviet Union, actresses and others.

The daughter of the writer Maxim Gorky, N. Peshkova, pleaded with Khrushchev over her own daughter, Marfa Peshkova, who had married Beria's son Sergei in 1946. After Beria was arrested, Marfa, her husband and their two small children had in best Bolshevik tradition also been arrested and spirited away,[20] and her mother now wanted to know what had happened to them. Khrushchev saw that they were released. Sergei Beria was given a new name and the family was sent to Sverdlovsk, where Sergei got work in a factory. Marfa left Sergei at the end of the 1950s and returned to Moscow, where she still lives.[21]

The trial dragged on. In December Khrushchev told Konev and Rudenko to 'get on with it'. For the summing-up by the prosecution and pronouncement of the sentence, the Presidium again crowded into a room in the Kremlin. Beria admitted everything, and begged only for his life to be spared.

Konev read out the charges, and then the verdict: 'Beria, L.P.,

Merkulov, V.N., Dekanozov, V.G., Kobulov, B.Z., Goglidze, S.A., Meshik, P. Ya., Vladzimirsky, L.E. are sentenced to the supreme capital penalty, death by shooting.' According to Marshal Moskalenko, Beria fell off the bench onto the floor and, whining quietly, crawled on all fours to the desk where Konev and the others were sitting, and begged incoherently for mercy. Konev brusquely gave the order: 'Take him out.' The Kremlin had already issued their orders: the sentence must be carried out immediately.

At the end of a staircase leading down to a bunker a large board had already been fixed to the wall, to which Beria was to be tied before being shot. There are numerous accounts of what happened next. A general who was a member of the team said in 1961: 'When they brought Beria down, a large group of generals and other officers were following behind. I don't know if there had been an order or whether the senior guards simply lost their nerve, but when they were a few steps before the threshold of the bunker, a shot rang out, then more shots. Beria was hit in the back. It was all over in seconds.'

One of the long, confused letters Beria wrote to the Presidium from his cell ends:

> I am a true son of our motherland, a true son of the Party of Lenin and Stalin and a true friend and comrade to you. Send me wherever you like, to do any work you choose, find the smallest job for me, I can still give ten good years of work with all my heart and all my energy . . . You will see that in two or three years I'll have straightened out fine and will still be useful to you. To my last breath I am faithful to our beloved Party and our Soviet Government. I ask the comrades to forgive me for writing somewhat disjointedly and badly because of my condition, and also because of the poor lighting and not having my pince-nez.[22]

It was not in the nature of Bolsheviks of the Leninist school to forgive, especially as the members of the Presidium knew full well the extent of the lawlessness, terror and savagery that Beria's agencies had carried out, in effect in their name as the supreme Party institution. It is more surprising that they took so long to execute him after his arrest.

Khrushchev could breathe freely at last: the personal danger to himself and the others had been dealt with. His position was finally secure. On 7 September 1953 he had been appointed First Secretary of the Central Committee, making him Party chief and, effectively, the top man in the country, the third leader.

He was above all indebted to the military leadership, especially to the decisive role played by Marshal of the Soviet Union Zhukov. On 7 July 1953 Khrushchev had proposed that Zhukov be promoted from non-voting status to full membership of the Central Committee. Army General I. Serov also became one of Khrushchev's favourites. He was an unsavoury character who had been made a Hero of the Soviet Union for organizing the deportation of nations from the Northern Caucasus, the Crimea and elsewhere, and similar atrocities. He had sat on 150 of the infamous *troikas* that had sent thousands of people to their deaths. He was also responsible for destroying Beria's archives, on Khrushchev's orders, in July 1954. He reported that they included 'documents containing provocative and libellous facts'.[23]

The Party leadership simply removed the evidence of Serov's involvement in the terror. Khrushchev gave him his protection for a very long time (he was deprived of his decorations in December 1963 when some of his criminal activities as Beria's assistant were exposed), while nearly all the generals who had taken part in Beria's arrest and execution were decorated and promoted. Moskalenko said that after Beria had been 'liquidated', Bulganin, a member of the Politburo, arranged on Khrushchev's orders for all the 'basic' generals who had taken part in the affair to be made Heroes of the Soviet Union. When Batitsky and Moskalenko heard about this, they pleaded indignantly with Khrushchev not to shame them with an award for such work. They nevertheless accepted the decoration when Khrushchev ignored their pleas.

The physical extermination of Beria was a highly significant step, but it did not address the main problem, the de-Stalinization of the country. Laudatory references to Stalin no longer appeared in the press, but whatever issue the Presidium turned its attention to, whether agriculture, defence, or raising the material well-being of the population which had been reduced to poverty, it still felt gripped by the leaden shackles of the system.

In this respect, Khrushchev was helped by the torrent of letters that came from the camps in Siberia and elsewhere, and which expressed the hope that their writers' cases would now be reviewed. Khrushchev knew that inmates in special camps were not allowed visits by relatives, that they worked in harsh conditions for ten hours a day, and that only the strongest could expect to survive the twenty-five-year sentences most of them were serving. He also knew that the least infringement meant solitary confinement for twenty days, and no doubt that, as Abakumov had informed Stalin in July 1947, 'apart from a stool, bolted to the floor, and a cot with no bedding, a cell has no other fittings; the cot (which comes down from the wall) may only be used for sleeping six hours a day. A prisoner in solitary gets only 300 grammes of bread a day and boiling water. Once every three days he gets hot food. Smoking is forbidden in the cells.'

There was a good deal of unrest in the camps, as demands for review rose in number. Hundreds of thousands of people were due for release in 1955 in any case, as the categories that had been given ten-year sentences at the end of the war came to the end of their terms. These included Vlasovites (i.e. Red Army men who had joined the German Army), former prisoners of war, Baltic citizens and the like. Some decisions had to be taken. Malenkov, Molotov, Kaganovich and Serov suggested leaving the entire problem with the MGB: when prisoners finished their sentences, they would just have to stay put. There were about four million people in camps and prisons when Stalin died, as well as 2,572,829 'deportees' or 'special deportees'[24] who had been condemned to deportation 'in perpetuity' in Siberia and Kazakhstan by an order of the Presidium of the Supreme Soviet dated 26 November 1948.[25]

Khrushchev had come to realize that he was no longer capable of signing such a document. The time had passed when, as a young secretary, he could declare to a cheering audience of Party members: 'A Bolshevik is someone who feels himself to be a Bolshevik even when he's sleeping!' and added: 'The blow must be merciless, but the blow must also be well-aimed!'[26]

The 'blow' he delivered to Beria and his gang was the last one Khrushchev would land, as it would have meant continuing the Stalinist line of terror. The Twentieth Party Congress was at the top of the agenda; not the liberation of millions of prisoners, nor the freedom of the Soviet people. The Stalinist system had reached the apogee of totalitarianism and, for the system to survive, changes were needed. It was the task that Communism was least capable of achieving.

Crimea – A Gift from Khrushchev

It is clear enough today that Beria was no more guilty than the rest of Stalin's Central Committee. He had simply been chosen to act as its professional inquisitor, and for that reason was feared by everyone, including his so-called comrades. He knew everything about all of them, and could cook up a case against any one. If Beria had not been given the job, any of the others could have done it. But if before Stalin's death their lives had been in the hands of Stalin and his hangman, after it only Beria sat in judgement, or so they felt.

In recent years Beria has been written about almost as if he was a frustrated reformer, a forerunner of things to come. Some of his acts, such as his attempts after Stalin's death to limit the terror, to break up the Gulag by shifting some of its structural elements into agriculture, to improve relations with Yugoslavia and not compel East Germany to adopt socialism were those of a sober politician. Beria had grounds for thinking that after Stalin had gone he might succeed him. He already had ideas for changes in the system, but none of them would have been fundamental. He simply wanted to 'improve' it. Any idea that he was a genuine reformer is simply wrong-headed.

It is, however, equally clear that Khrushchev regarded Beria not as the curse of the system, but as the sword that hung over his own head and those of his comrades. Khrushchev could not accept that Beria had been a mere tool of the Party leadership. With Beria gone, the country was for a time ruled by a dual-power arrangement based on the Party and state, represented respectively by Khrushchev and Malenkov.

For two or three years before Stalin died, Malenkov had been the second-most important figure in the Party and state apparatus. It had been no secret that he was not only Stalin's favourite but also his most likely successor, and it had come as no surprise when he was appointed Chairman of the Council of Ministers after Stalin's death, or that he continued chairing meetings of the Presidium and was the first to speak at Stalin's funeral. Furthermore, it was also well known that he was a close confidant of Beria. Thus, Khruschchev's success in removing Beria also signified a sharp decline in Malenkov's position. By the end of 1953, all important decisions required not only Malenkov's approval, but that of Khrushchev as well. Malenkov had few friends in the Presidium. Behind his back, Molotov and Kaganovich derisively nicknamed him 'Malanya' (Melanie), poking fun at his feminine appearance.

Khrushchev sensed that Malenkov was surrounded by a vacuum, and he exploited this to strengthen his own position. He no longer concealed his claim to supreme leadership, which he couched in terms of 'the need to strengthen the role of the Party' in all spheres of state and social life. He was already taking unilateral decisions on a wide range of issues. One such was the transfer of the Crimea from the Russian Federation to the Ukrainian Soviet Republic. Ostensibly, Khrushchev came to this decision suddenly. He spoke about it to Malenkov in December 1953 and, encountering no objection to the idea, added, virtually in the form of an order: 'Let's not delay on this. We'll discuss it at an early session of the Presidium.' Malenkov, to whom it was all too clear that Khrushchev had eased him into second or third place, agreed at once.

Just why, so soon after the death of Stalin, Khrushchev should have wanted to alter the administrative map of the country is impossible to answer definitively. As a district and then city Party Secretary, he had always felt a close physical proximity to the leadership. He had never overstepped the line, and had been an obedient and exacting executive of the Kremlin's orders. Despatched as First Party Secretary to Ukraine in 1938, he had soon become aware of the differences between the capital and the provinces. While Moscow's authority seemed to Communists in Kiev absolute and autocratic, in fact there were greater opportunities for the top man in Ukraine than there were in Moscow for someone lower down the hierarchy.

Back in Moscow in 1939, Khrushchev was still mentally in Ukraine, as it were, and he never lost an opportunity to refer to his Ukrainian experience and success. In his memoirs he remembered his time there with special warmth: 'I myself am a Russian and wouldn't want to slight the Russian people, but I must attribute our success in the restoration of Ukrainian agriculture and the reconstruction of Ukrainian industry to the Ukrainian people themselves.'[27]

At the beginning of 1954 the three hundredth anniversary of Ukraine's reunification with Russia was to be celebrated. On the eve of these events Khrushchev had a number of meetings with Ukrainian leaders. They discussed in particular how to observe the anniversary with due gravity, and it was in this small circle and in this context that the idea of transferring the Crimea to Ukraine arose, although who initiated it is unknown. Khrushchev saw nothing offensive to the dignity of the Russians in such a move, since the whole Soviet state was a single political entity, even if it was called a 'union'.

Having become the pre-eminent leader by the end of 1953, Khrushchev began persistently raising the question of the Crimea with his colleagues. He advanced no cogent reasons or motives, and none were asked for. He had decided, and that was that. He might even have already promised the Crimea to Kiev. Rational arguments were not required of the supreme leader, and in any case, what difference could it make?

Khrushchev also loved the Crimea, the 'All-Union health resort', as it was known. At the Yalta Conference of February 1945 the Soviet, American and British delegations had been housed in the Yusupov, Livadia and Vorontsov palaces respectively. Reinforced air-raid shelters had been specially built for the occasion, and several hundred anti-aircraft guns had been moved into the area, along with a large number of fighter aircraft. The palaces were guarded by four special NKVD regiments and many other units and special detachments. Stalin had turned the place into an impregnable zone.

At the end of February 1945, after the conference was over, Stalin approved the transfer of all the palaces, with domestic staff drawn from neighbouring collective farms, into the hands of the Ministry of State Security. Now Khrushchev insisted that these gems of Crimea's past be handed over to the Health Resorts Board of the Trade Unions.[28] Having removed the palaces from the clutches of the security ministries, Khrushchev went further and handed over the Crimea itself to a new owner, Ukraine.

It was normal procedure for major issues to be settled first by the Presidium and then rubber-stamped by the appropriate agencies. Thus it was that 'the transfer of the Crimea from the RSFSR to the Ukrainian SSR' became item 11 on the agenda of a routine Presidium meeting under Malenkov's chairmanship on 25 January 1954. There was no discussion. The Presidium's draft resolution consisted of two points, which were duly read out: 'To confirm the draft decree of the Presidium of the Supreme Soviet of the USSR on the transfer of Crimea *Oblast* from the RSFSR to the UkrSSR.'[29] The meeting of the Presidium of the Supreme Soviet that had supposedly passed this decree had in fact not yet taken place, and was only convened later that day. The decree also called for a 'special session of the Presidium of the Supreme Soviet to review the joint representation of the Presidiums of the Supreme Soviets of the RSFSR and the UkrSSR on the transfer of Crimea *Oblast*'.[30] The whole question was covered in fifteen minutes. The decree was signed by Khrushchev. The rest was a matter of Party 'mechanics'. Needless to say, no one thought even to ask what the population of the Crimea, the majority of them Russians, might want. The entire territory of the Soviet Union was at the disposal of the leaders of the CPSU to do with as they wished.

Khrushchev had embarked on this project in ignorance of Crimea's history. He did not know that, in the process of creating the centralized Russian state, Moscow had conducted a fierce and prolonged struggle with the Crimean Tatar khans in the eighteenth century. The military expropriation of this fragment of the Golden Horde's territory had been a major preoccupation and a constant source of threat to the south of Russia. In the course of the Russo–Turkish wars of 1771–91, when the Crimean khanate was a vassal of the Ottoman Empire, Crimea, Taurida and the territory between the Bug and the Dniester were conquered by Russia. It was during this time that Russia built the Black Sea Fleet and established the port-cities of Sevastopol, Odessa, Kherson and Nikolaev. The Crimea, and particularly Sevastopol, were symbols of the empire's might and glory. The fleet's victories were a matter of Russian national pride, as were the names of its great admirals. Khrushchev knew none of this. Nor could he be expected to foresee that one day Ukraine would become a sovereign power and would make use of his generous gift. Ignorance was to be responsible more than once for Khrushchev's making a fool of himself. His relations with China, the Suez crisis and the Cuban missile crisis come to mind, and his decision on Ukraine fits the same mould.

Following the Presidium meeting of 25 January, events moved

rapidly. Meetings were held by the two governments, which decided that 'in view of the territorial attraction of Crimea *Oblast* towards the Ukrainian SSR', and 'taking into account the community of their economies and their close economic and cultural ties', the Crimea should become part of Ukraine.[31] There was of course no 'decision' made by the obedient functionaries who signed the decree: they were simply doing what Khrushchev had told them to do.

On 19 February the Presidium of the Supreme Soviet of the USSR met in the Kremlin, in less than full complement, chaired by Voroshilov. Khrushchev was there as one of its members, watching as the scenario concocted by Suslov and Pegov was acted out. The speeches for all the participants had been scripted by the propaganda department of the Central Committee. The Supreme Soviet Deputy for the *oblast* of Ufa, Mikhail Tarasov, declared that the Crimea was 'as it were an extension of the southern steppes of Ukraine', and thus its transfer would 'serve to strengthen friendship of the peoples of the great Soviet Union'. As Ukrainian head of state, Demian Korotchenko expressed his 'heartfelt thanks to the great Russian people for this uniquely remarkable act of fraternal assistance'.

Two speakers inadvertently let the cat out of the bag. Nikolai Shvernik declared that 'the transfer of such a major *oblast*, rich in mineral resources, with a developed industry and valuable natural therapeutic assets, could only be done in the conditions of our socialist country.' Otto Kuusinen developed this theme: 'Only in our country is it possible for such a great people as the Russian people without any hesitation magnanimously to hand over one of their richest *oblasts* to another fraternal people. Only in our country are such highly important questions as the territorial attachment of a particular *oblast* to another republic decided without the slightest difficulty.'[32]

Voroshilov wound up the 'debate' by declaring: 'Only in the conditions of the Union of Soviet Socialist Republics is such a just resolution of all territorial questions possible. In the distant and not so distant past, our enemies tried repeatedly to take the Crimean peninsula away from Russia, to use it for the plunder and ruination of the Russian and Ukrainian lands, to create there a military base from which to attack Russia and Ukraine.' He added that the 'donation' of the peninsula was very important as 'the Soviet peoples celebrate the splendid historical date of the three hundredth anniversary of the reunification of Russia with Ukraine'.[33]

The news of the reunification, when it was published a week after the meeting, was greeted with indifference even in Ukraine itself. The population was used to decisions being made in the Kremlin without prior notice, let alone public consultation. Like his predecessors, Khrushchev acted decisively and without standing on ceremony. Like Stalin, and like his own successors, he used the words of Lenin to support his actions, deploying such ritualistic incantations as 'We must remember what Lenin taught us', 'The Leninist norms of Party life must be regenerated', 'That's how it was under Lenin'. Also like most of the top Soviet leadership, Khrushchev's knowledge of Lenin's writings was extremely limited. They all had Lenin's Collected Works on their shelves, but rarely if ever consulted them. Worship of Lenin was a common feature of all the General Secretaries. Indeed, without him they could hardly have clung to their positions at the summit of power.

De-Stalinization

Khrushchev's attack on the so-called 'personality cult' was in many respects mendacious and superficial, and did not touch the foundations of the Leninist system. Yet, in all the seventy years of Soviet history, it would be difficult to find another political act of such importance for the future of the country, and not only that. Khrushchev's courageous assault on this particular aspect of Bolshevism had far-reaching consequences. He concentrated on demolishing Stalin's role, genuinely believing that he had only to uproot the cult, restore 'Leninist principles' to the internal life of the Party and repair the damage done to 'revolutionary legality' for the country to get back on the rails of 'Soviet socialist democracy'. It was a bold, but naïve dream.

Once he began to feel secure in his own position, Khrushchev undertook a number of bold initiatives, such as inaugurating the 'virgin lands' project in Central Asia, and instituting some effective changes in agriculture, while beginning the process of rehabilitating hundreds of thousands of people from the camps. In so doing, he also reinforced his own place as the new leader. In foreign policy, he gained the friendship of several Arab countries by his decision to give aid to President Nasser of Egypt. It proved to be a popular move with the Russian people.

Yet, even though he had reached the pinnacle of power, he had a permanent feeling that Stalin's shadow was hanging over him. The penal system was still working, if with greater circumspection than before; it was still impossible to tell the truth about the political trials of the pre-war and post-war period; and the Stalinist taboo still operated on many questions of domestic and foreign policy. Khrushchev knew a lot about the Soviet past, having been a primary participant, and now it haunted him. He could either reveal the truth, or leave things alone.

The Twentieth Party Congress, set for February 1956, was approaching. It would be the first nationwide Communist forum to take place since the death of Stalin. Khrushchev set up a number of working parties to prepare for it, and met no opposition. When he proposed, however, that there ought also to be a commission 'to investigate Stalin's activities', his former supporters in the Presidium, Molotov, Kaganovich and Voroshilov, raised a vociferous protest. Molotov was especially incensed. 'To investigate Stalin's activities,' he stormed, 'would mean revising the results of the entire great path of the CPSU! Who would benefit from it? What purpose would it serve? Why stir up the past?' Kaganovich seconded him: 'Stalin personifies a host of the Soviet people's victories. To re-examine the possible errors of Lenin's successor would put the correctness of our entire course under question. Also, the people will simply say: "And where were you? Who gave you the right to judge a dead man?" '

The argument was heated, and was not cooled by Khrushchev's promise that only 'violations of socialist legality' for which Beria had been chiefly responsible would be considered, and only in conditions of the greatest secrecy. He urged that the commission be allowed to do its work, and that the Presidium make up its mind about how to proceed only after it had seen the results. This was agreed on 31 December 1955.

The commission was composed of a very small group, consisting of Academician and Central Committee member P. Pospelov, Central Committee Secretary A. Aristov, chairman of the trade unions N. Shvernik, and P. Komarov, an official of the Central Committee Party

Control Commission. The chairman was Pospelov, who was particularly knowledgeable about Stalin, having co-authored the second edition of the unctuously hagiographic *Short Biography* of the former leader that appeared in 1951 in a print run of nearly seven million.

Khrushchev summoned the members of the investigative commission on the mass arrests, and raised the cases of a host of senior Party figures who had been shot, but not including the chief defendants in the great show trials such as Kamenev, Zinoviev, Bukharin, Radek and the like. Nor did he touch on the question of Trotsky's assassination in Mexico. The intention was to create a picture of Stalin's arbitrary and lawless rule.

The commission sat practically day and night, sifting files and trying to find the appropriate quotation from Lenin to condemn the personality cult and Stalin's violations of 'socialist legality'. The plan outlined by Academician Pospelov was primitive but comprehensible: everything boiled down to Lenin's wisdom, modesty, humanity and norms of behaviour on the one hand, and Stalin's violation of those norms on the other. The report stated that absolutely everything Lenin had ever done had been truly Marxist: 'Vladimir Ilyich demanded harsh treatment of enemies of the revolution and the working class, and when the need arose he employed such methods mercilessly . . . But Lenin had used those methods against genuine class enemies, not against those who had made mistakes.'[34] Just who had been genuine class enemies and who not, Pospelov and his commission did not venture to suggest. The entire object of the report was to show that the system, created by Lenin, had nothing in common with arbitrary terror, which was the result of Stalin's personality cult.

The report was fully approved by Khrushchev, and when it was presented to the Presidium many of the members were satisfied. Others, however, found it highly objectionable. First, they did not like the assertion that it was Stalin who had introduced the idea of 'enemies of the people'. They were quite right: Lenin had used the term, having borrowed it from the lexicon of the French Revolution. The report stated: 'This term obviated the need to prove that someone you were arguing with was ideologically incorrect: it provided the opportunity for anyone who disagreed with Stalin over anything, or who was suspected of hostile intent, or anyone who was simply slandered, to be subjected to harsh repression, and for all norms of revolutionary legality to be violated.'[35]

The opponents of the report argued vehemently over the facts of the purges, for the obvious reason that they themselves had been deeply implicated in them, and had no stomach for publishing the truth and accepting responsibility. The report, moreover, included documents addressed by Stalin to Kaganovich, Molotov and others. On 25 September 1938, for instance, while resting in Sochi, Stalin had sent a telegram to the Politburo – of which Khrushchev was not then a member – that read: 'We regard it as absolutely essential and urgent to appoint Comrade Yezhov as People's Commissar for the Interior. Yagoda is plainly not on top of the job, as far as unmasking the Trotskyite–Zinovievite bloc is concerned. The OGPU is four years late with this case . . .'

Kaganovich reminded the others that they had all approved Stalin's circular to Party secretaries throughout the country, dated 10 January 1939, which told them that the permission to use physical violence against prisoners given in 1937 was still in full force: 'Physical pressure,' the order had said, was correct and 'must without fail be used now against open and un-disarmed enemies of the people, as a completely proper and appropriate method'.

'What shall we say now?' Kaganovich wanted to know.

The Politburo, moreover, had on several occasions passed resolutions – unanimously, of course – on 'anti-Soviet elements' which brought yet more people into the 'first category'. On 31 January 1938, for instance, it approved an order for the execution of a 'further' forty-eight thousand people in twenty-two *oblasts*.[36]

It was only with the support of Saburov, Pervukhin, Bulganin and Kirichenko that Khrushchev managed to obtain the decision to proceed with the work on the report. As to what should be done with it when it was ready, there was no clear idea. Kaganovich proposed it be debated at the Twenty-First Congress (which was scheduled for 1961, but actually took place in 1959), while Molotov suggested the mistakes of the past be gradually 'corrected' without publicity. In the event, Shepilov was told to get on with the report.

The Twentieth Party Congress opened on 14 February 1956 in the Great Kremlin Palace. It proceeded smoothly through the customary reports, approval of the 'Leninist course', applause, standing ovations, ideological oaths and calls to strengthen 'the unity of the Party and people'. Everything had as usual been scripted down to the last detail and the Congress was moving towards a harmonious conclusion, yet no decision had been taken as to what to do with Pospelov's report. Khrushchev's colleagues knew that he had staked everything on it, and was prepared to make it known to the delegates at whatever cost. On several evenings in the course of the Congress he had summoned Pospelov and inserted new material into the report as a result of the background material he had seen.

On 19 February, for instance, his insertions included: 'Enemies of the people need not have been exterminated, they could have been kept in prison or exile'; 'Cite the case of Zinoviev and Kamenev; they betrayed the revolution yet Lenin didn't shoot them'; 'How were confessions extracted? Only one way, by beating, torture, deprivation of consciousness, deprivation of reason, deprivation of human dignity by means of physical violence and intimidation'; 'Smirnov treated Stalin ... yet such people were being arrested ... He [Stalin] said: "Put shackles on Smirnov, put shackles on so-and-so," and so they did'; 'On the Mingrelian case. The Georgian government was accused of wanting to attach flourishing Georgia to the impoverished Turkish state, which was starving, fleeced, illiterate (give figures)'; 'The members of the Politburo looked upon Stalin with different eyes at different times. At first they consciously extolled him because Stalin genuinely was great and capable. He was one of the most powerful Marxists and his logic, strength and will played a positive role in the Party. But then, later ... After the executions there emerged not just intellectual but also physical subjection to this man.'[37] Some of these remarks were included in the report verbatim, others only partially and others not at all.

Khrushchev referred to the case of Zinoviev and Kamenev, and the fact that Lenin had not had them shot. On 22 August 1936, however, Khrushchev himself had told a group of cheering Party activists: 'The bandit ringleaders, Zinoviev, Kamenev, Smirnov, Mrachkovsky, Ter-Baganian and more of their fascist accomplices are in prison ... Not only these blackguards, but Trotsky too should be shot.'[38] And two years after that, as Party boss of Ukraine, he had said: 'We have only just begun the clear-out in Ukraine ... We will carry out a complete rout and finish the job.'[39]

Of course, it would not have been easy for Khrushchev to stand up to Stalin's tyranny, not least because he and his like had lauded the dictator as no one in Russian history had ever been lauded. In three brief election speeches Khrushchev made in 1937, he managed to call Stalin a 'genius', a 'great leader' and a 'great creator' no fewer than fifty-four times. He had called not only for 'more hatred of our class enemies', but also for 'more love of our leader, the great Stalin.'[40]

Nevertheless, while he could never forget the delusions of former years, Khrushchev had the courage to move beyond them, and the strength to exorcize the obsession with terrorist methods. His comrades, however, were not prepared to forgive or forget the fact that he was as implicated in the crimes of the past as they were themselves. Molotov and Kaganovich were particularly persistent. 'What will you say about yourself, Nikita?' they wanted to know. 'After all, we're all involved ... And what are they going to make you tell about what happened? We should be correcting the mistakes without haste, not savouring them.'

Khrushchev replied: 'Some of us didn't know many things because we were part of a regime in which you were told what you were supposed to know and you kept your nose out of everything else ... Some knew what was happening, and some even got their own noses dirty in the events we're speaking about. But while the degree of responsibility for what happened varies among us, I'm prepared as a member of the Central Committee since the Seventeenth Congress [of 1934; here Khrushchev is stressing that he was *not* a member of the Politburo during the worst years of the terror] to bear my share of responsibility before the Party, even if the Party should see fit to bring to task all those who were in the leadership under Stalin.'[41]

Although this argument weakened his opponents, they nonetheless did everything they could to moderate the presentation of the issue, which they rightly felt to be of terrifying force. Finally, during an interval towards the end of the congress, Khrushchev suggested asking all 1,436 delegates if they wanted to hear the report: 'I'll tell them who on the Presidium is for and who against. Let the delegates decide. Whatever they vote for, that's what we'll do.' The others remained silent. Khrushchev was now ready to take his momentous step towards the rostrum.

On the morning of 25 February, Khrushchev read his sensational report 'on the personality cult and its consequences' to a closed session, with no foreign guests or journalists. No minutes were taken, and at Prime Minister Bulganin's suggestion it had been decided not to open the subject to debate. For more than four hours the delegates listened, astonished. As Khrushchev later recalled: 'It was so quiet in the huge hall you could hear a fly buzzing. You must try to imagine how shocked people were by the revelations of the atrocities to which Party members . . . had been subjected. This was the first that most of them had heard of the tragedy which our Party had undergone – a tragedy stemming from the sickness in Stalin's character which Lenin had warned us against in his Testament and which Stalin himself had confirmed in his confession to Mikoyan and me – "I trust no one, not even myself." '[42]

In his speech – which in Russia remained a secret buried in the archives until 1989, decades after the rest of the world knew every word of it – Khrushchev did his best to elevate Lenin, the Party, the Bolshevik system and the 'masses'. He cited Lenin on collective leadership and on Stalin's insulting behaviour towards Krupskaya, and he lamented the fact that the Party had ignored Lenin's warnings. All the woes of the period came precisely from the fact that Stalin's bullying behaviour had gradually turned into 'mass terror against the Party cadres'.[43] The speech's chief importance, Khrushchev wrote in his memoirs, 'was that it touched off the process of purifying the Party of Stalinism and re-establishing in the Party those Leninist norms of life for which the best sons of our country had struggled.'[44]

The paradox was plain: Khrushchev was repudiating one aspect of the heresy in order to resurrect its basic, Leninist, form. It was Khrushchev at his most typical. But neither he nor his fellows, nor indeed rank-and-file Communists, could then see that Stalinism had been born out of Leninism, of which the fundamental tenet was unbridled class violence.

An example of Khrushchev's crusade to 'resurrect Leninist norms' came soon enough. In his memoirs, he recalls that the Polish Communist leader Boleslaw Bierut died during the Twentieth Congress, and that major and prolonged disturbances had ensued in Poland.[45] Finally, in September 1956 Khrushchev, Molotov, Mikoyan, Bulganin and Marshal Konev flew to Warsaw, uninvited and against the wishes of the Polish leadership. Talks between the two 'fraternal' sides were acrimonious. Khrushchev accused Ochaba, Gomulka and Cyrankiewicz of turning their backs on the USSR and leaning towards the West, of giving Soviet Ambassador Marshal Rokossovsky the cold shoulder, allowing anti-Soviet comment to appear in the press, and declining to accept Soviet advisers in the Polish army.

For their part, the Poles stoutly defended themselves and accused Moscow of Stalinist methods in their relations. The talks had reached a high pitch when, according to notes dictated by Mikoyan on 28 May 1960, 'one of the Polish comrades handed Gomulka a note. Gomulka blenched and, turning to Khrushchev, said: "I've been informed that your units in western Poland are moving tanks towards Warsaw at this moment. I ask you to stop this movement and return them to where they were." Khrushchev and I exchanged glances. Khrushchev said: "All right." And he gave the order to Marshal Konev to stop the movement of our troops and return them to their stations.'[46]

This behaviour was characteristic of Khrushchev: having gone to 'normalize' relations with Russia's Polish allies and to put an end to the disorders, he had backed up the initiative with a demonstration of military force. He did not understand that in order to free the system of Stalinism, he must first repudiate Leninism. The target chosen by him at the Twentieth Congress was essentially a secondary one. It was not an individual dictator who was responsible for the atrocities, but the system and the ideology founded on Leninist principles. It was not apparent in 1956, but time would show that the attack on Stalin would in the end bring insight into Lenin. As for Khrushchev himself, he would die without realizing that in defending Lenin he was preserving Stalin.

Even in the report itself, Khrushchev felt it necessary to stress Stalin's services to the Party and the people, though he did not have the courage to tell the people to their face of Stalin's crimes. He concluded his speech: 'We must look at the question of the personality cult with all seriousness. We cannot take this question beyond the confines of the Party, still less to the press. That's why we are reporting on it in closed session here. We have to keep a sense of proportion, not give ammunition to our enemies, not expose our sores to him.'[47] In fact, the stamp 'Top Secret' would soon be removed and replaced by the more lenient 'Not for publication'. The report was produced in brochure form and distributed to all Party committees for information. But its contents had already long been known in the West, where it created a sensation. The foreign Communist parties, especially in Western Europe, began to search their consciences and to revise many aspects of Marxist-Leninist ideology.

Khrushchev was afraid of publicity, imagining that it was possible to keep the lid on the truth forever, as in the past. Secrets, after all, had been the very lifeblood of Leninism, and Khrushchev regarded himself as a 'true Leninist'. He had ended his speech against Stalin with: 'Long live the victorious banner of our Party, Leninism!' Stalinism had been holed, but remained afloat because Leninism seemed unsinkable.

The Impulsive Reformer

On 18 October 1961, on the second day of the Twenty-Second Party Congress – his third and last as Party leader – Khrushchev followed an interminable reading of the Central Committee report with an equally interminable speech on the Party programme. Tracing his text with his finger to make sure he did not lose his place, and pausing at key moments to elicit applause, he came to a section headed, 'Communism, the Great Aim of the Party and the People', and concluded with the words: 'The cup of Communism is the cup of plenty; it must always be full to the brim. Each of us must pour in our own contribution and each drink from it. We are guided by strictly scientific calculation. And our calculations show that in twenty years' time we shall essentially have built the Communist society.'[48] The published minutes of the meeting state that these remarks were greeted with 'stormy applause'. In fact, the delegates – Communist fundamentalists to a man – were very doubtful about Khrushchev's 'strictly scientific' calculations.

He laid out the Party programme which described Communism in detail, and explained why the classes would disappear along with exploitation, and how everyone would be equal. Yet again, in the tradition of the Leninist Utopia, he declared that 'historical development would lead inevitably to the withering away of the state', and wound up by assuring the delegates that 'the present generation of Soviet people will live under Communism.'

Khrushchev knew that many people opposed his policy, but he sensed that he had right on his side. This sense became stronger after he got rid of his main rivals, Malenkov, Kaganovich and Molotov, in a fierce skirmish at the June 1957 plenum, and was able to implement numerous reforms in the stagnant country. The ossified state and society, mired in bureaucracy and dogmatism, adapted poorly to the cascade of change, yet the country did break free of its former anchorage. The decade of Khrushchev's rule demonstrated his potential as an innovator, a demolition artist, experimenter, opportunist and inventor. It was as if he had suddenly woken up. Initiatives followed one after the other, and at the source of each of them stood the stocky figure of the First Secretary, gesticulating energetically, a veritable fount of ideas and activity. Alexander Alexandrov-Agentov, a functionary who spent much of his life in close proximity to the post-war leaders, described Khrushchev as 'authoritative, hot-tempered, unbridled, crude, and self-confident and prone to flattery in relations with his closest colleagues. At the same time he was impetuous, intolerant, carried away, possessed by a spirit of innovation, but with no serious concept.'[49] For such a man, there were many opportunities to apply himself in the country that was beginning to thaw.

His first task was in agriculture. The harvests of 1949 to 1953 had been catastrophically low, something like eight hundred kilogrammes per hectare, when even in 1914 the yield had been seven hundred. The figures, which were a state secret, show that the total yield of grain declined from 36.4 million tonnes in 1940 to 31.1 million in 1953, while over the same period the state reserves increased from 4.1 million tonnes to 17.8.[50] In order to survive, the people stole grain, and in June 1946 the Central Committee and Finance Ministry issued the strictest prohibition against this. Interior Minister Kruglov reported to Stalin regularly on the progress of this order. In December 1946 and January 1947, for instance, '13,559 and 9,928 people, respectively, were charged with criminal responsibility for the theft of grain.'[51] Stalin was not afraid to starve the country, and he would never 'lower' himself to buy grain from the imperialists.

As early as September 1953, Khrushchev urged a Central Committee plenum that if the countryside was to be revived, it was necessary to bear income, costs and profitability in mind. In February 1958 he launched a number of measures designed to raise efficiency in agriculture. When he was invited to the USA by President Eisenhower, he made sure that time would be set aside for him to take a look at US agriculture. He especially wanted to see Iowa, the nation's 'corn capital'. There he was shown a large corn farm owned by a Mr Roswell Garst. Andrei Gromyko, who accompanied Khrushchev as Foreign Minister, recalled that Khrushchev 'inspected the fields, and asked the owner many questions, as he tried to fathom how the man had made a lot of money out of farming land that did not look very different in its fertility from several regions of our own country'. Among his own people, Khrushchev later admitted that, although he had seen much of interest, 'I still don't see how Garst's experience can be transferred into Soviet conditions.'[52]

This should not have surprised him: the fundamental disparities between the two social-economic systems had created utterly different conditions for production and marketing. The system of collective farming had reduced the cultivator of the land's personal interest in his crop to a minimum, and the simple transfer of practice from elsewhere would have been impossible. His American trip nevertheless persuaded Khrushchev that high production of corn could greatly increase the output of livestock, though the over-zealous application of his policy often led to ludicrous results, with the crop being planted in entirely unsuitable places.

The measures applied by Khrushchev in agriculture led to the growth of grain output, without doubt, but also to a sharp rise in consumption. The shortage became chronic, and the consequent drop in reserves was so drastic that he was finally compelled to purchase large supplies abroad. This desperate step was proof, if proof were needed, that the Soviet system of agriculture was bankrupt. The purchase of grain from abroad continued for more than thirty years, as the country literally ate up its gold reserves, which declined from 13.1 million tonnes in 1954 to 6.3 million in 1963.[53]

Khrushchev's 'maize campaign', which lasted for several years, did not save him, and he had to find other ways of raising livestock production. He ordered the compulsory purchase of cattle from collective farmers, but then winter came, and with it a lack of fodder and shelter. Cattle plague ensued. Someone pointed out that horses were eating up the much-needed fodder, so large numbers of them were duly slaughtered.

Similarly, Khrushchev's idea of *agrogorods*, or farm cities, collapsed. The villages became depopulated, collective farms were enlarged to huge size, vastly beyond human scale, and the individual was lost in these great impersonal rural conurbations.

Khrushchev's endless proposals and new regulations produced very little in the way of positive results. Nor could they, as long as it was not realized that the capacity of the Leninist system for reform was extremely limited. The people became disgruntled, and jokes about 'Nikita' proliferated. His courageous speech at the Twentieth Congress had given the population a taste of freedom, and they wanted more, but he had not wanted to alter the basic form of the system or the economic foundations of the country.

Like Stalin, Khrushchev attributed all his failures to 'poor cadres', personal errors and the heritage of the Stalinist past. And to some extent this was so. Like Stalin, he thought in terms of 'catching up and overtaking'. At the Twenty-Second Congress of 1961 he proclaimed: 'In recent years our country has, as before, significantly overtaken the USA in the pace of production, and has begun outstripping it in terms of absolute growth in many of the most important forms of production ... The completion of the Seven-Year Plan will bring our Motherland to the point where only a little time will be needed in order to overtake the United States in economic terms. Having solved the basic task, the Soviet Union will gain a universally historic victory in peaceful competition with the United States of America.'[54] Khrushchev's ideologized view of the economy and its future was the same as Stalin's, based on striving for 'victory' over imperialism.

The agricultural reforms were accompanied by changes to the administrative system. In February 1957 it was decided to abolish branch ministries and to establish in each republic, region and province territorial economic councils, or *sovnarkhozy*, with a Higher National Economic Council of the USSR to run them. Within four years, Khrushchev decided that this new structure also necessitated the reform of the Party administration, and proposed that provincial and regional councils be divided into industrial and agricultural sections. This change caused enormous and steadily growing discontent among Party officials. As the Deputy Chairman of the Council of

Ministers from 1960 to 1963, Ignati Novikov, recalled: 'The overwhelming majority of ministers and their staffs did not welcome these changes. The majority of factory managers was equally against them. Like several other ministerial officials, I thought that qualified enterprise managers would be wasted and that this would endanger technological progress. Ministers in charge of the defence industries were particularly incensed at having to hand factories over to the economic councils.'[55]

However, Khrushchev was convinced of his own Bolshevik infallibility, and continued to take major decisions without consultation. Those who worked close to him were aware of his susceptibility to flattery. Novikov asserts that in 1960 'a new personality cult began operating, that of Nikita Sergeevich. Unfortunately, the apple does not fall far from the tree.'[56] This was an exaggeration, but there was undoubtedly organized glorification of the third leader.

Khrushchev's 1957 slogan, 'It is the population's moral responsibility to catch up and overtake the United States in the production of meat, butter and milk,' naturally turned out to be a fantasy, and not only because he planned to achieve these aims by 1960. He and his advisers mistakenly decided that by sharply reducing livestock production on the collective farmers' private plots and increasing investment in state and collective cattle-farming, they would reach their goal. The policy was implemented with the backing of the June 1957 plenum, and in August 1958 the Central Committee issued an order 'banning the private ownership of cattle by citizens living in towns and workers' settlements'. This utterly absurd order had serious consequences. There was a sharp reduction in meat and dairy products and a sharp rise of public resentment. It was not until 31 May 1962 that the Central Committee and Council of Ministers passed a regulation raising meat and dairy prices. Instead of overtaking the USA, the Communist regime was registering its own bankruptcy.

Public disgruntlement, meanwhile, began to assume more active forms. From towns and cities all over the Soviet Union the KGB was reporting calls for strikes in protest against the price rises, an unheard-of event in the Soviet Union. Home-made posters appeared and hand-written leaflets were circulated secretly, but widely. The most impressive demonstration against the government's policies took place in Novocherkassk, where in June 1962 the workers at an electric locomotive plant staged a riot. The local Party authorities, naturally, called out the troops and the tanks, but the strike gained the support of workers at other plants.

KGB Chairman V. Semichastny reported to the Central Committee: 'At 9.50 all the slackers (about five thousand people) left the factory zone, slipped past the first line of tanks and are moving towards the town of Novocherkassk. The main column is carrying a portrait of V.I. Lenin and flowers in front.'[57] The security services reported that hooligan and criminal elements were distributing the 'provocative' slogan 'Meat, milk and wage increases'. Khrushchev immediately despatched Presidium member Frol Kozlov to Novocherkassk, where he broadcast to the local population: 'In the speech he gave in Moscow yesterday and that was broadcast on the radio, N.S. Khrushchev explained with great conviction and his customary bluntness why the Party and the government took the decision to raise the price of meat and meat products.' He went on to talk about the need for resources to invest in industry, housing construction and defence. 'Nor must it be forgotten that the imperialists are again threatening us with war.'[58]

Clashes with militia took place outside the offices of the town Party committee. The crowd 'tore down portraits', presumably of members of the Presidium, and a meeting held under the red flag and a portrait of Lenin was described by the KGB as a 'provocation'. The troops fired into the crowd, killing twenty-three people and injuring dozens more, all of them workers and students. Semichastny reported to Khrushchev that burials had been carried out at five cemeteries in the district, and that the security organs had taken steps to discover and arrest the most active participants in the disorders. Forty-nine people were arrested.[59]

The KGB staged a public trial in the town, lasting a week. Five of the 'criminals' were sentenced to be shot, while the rest were gaoled for between ten and fifteen years. The Deputy Chairman of the KGB, P. Ivashutin, reported that the sentences 'met the approval of the workers', who allegedly shouted, 'Give the dogs a dog's death!', 'Serve the vermin right, it'll teach others!', 'It's the right sentence, such people should be shot.'[60] The report was followed by another, from the Deputy Chief of the Central Committee Department of Propaganda and Agitation, Vladimir Stepakov: 'The trial played a great educational and precautionary role ... There was repeated applause from the gallery whenever the court called for harsh sentences.'[61]

This was the Stalinist accompaniment to Khrushchev's reforms. Following the Twentieth Congress people had sensed a certain weakening, and they began to express their thoughts more freely. A spontaneous strike, however, had to be suppressed at any cost. Khrushchev did not understand that semi-liberty was a delusion and a deception. But it was not only he who was trapped in the Leninist dogmas: the striking workers carried Lenin's portrait before them. Stalin, the odious dictator of the system, may have been exposed, but the system itself had been left intact.

Needless to say, the country as a whole knew nothing of the Novocherkassk tragedy for nearly three decades, as they knew nothing of a number of other 'undesirable' occurrences, such as a major radioactive disaster near Chelyabinsk and a catastrophe at the satellite launching centre of Baikonur, to name but two.

Another such event took place on 29 October 1955, when as the result of an unexplained explosion the battleship *Novorossiisk* had sunk in Sevastopol harbour with the loss of 603 lives. Khrushchev was furious, and ordered the Minister of Defence to get to the bottom of the affair. The outcome of the investigation was that the naval commander-in-chief, Admiral of the Fleet of the Soviet Union Nikolai Kuznetsov, who as it happens was undergoing medical treatment at the time of the explosion, was demoted (for the second time in his career) to vice-admiral, and other admirals of the Black Sea Fleet were similarly relieved of their commands.[62] Characteristic of Bolshevik practice, everyone even indirectly involved had to be punished.

In another incident, on 24 October 1960, an experimental rocket exploded on the launchpad, engulfing in flame hundreds of people standing in the vicinity. Among them were Marshal Mitrofan Nedelin, commander-in-chief of missile forces, and several top rocket scientists. Next day, the press reported that Nedelin had been killed in an air crash. The Bolshevik tradition had asserted its influence again: lying was an intrinsic part of the Leninist system.

For all his originality, courage and desire for innovation, Khrushchev was a child of his times, and decades of working under Stalin could not but have an effect. He had the manners of a totalitarian dictator: peremptory, dogmatic, arbitrary, concerned with appearances, and harsh when the need arose. He correctly diagnosed the desperate need for deep reform of the economy, but was prepared to alter only the form of administration and management, barely touching its essential nature. The dictatorial style and previous practice continued, whereby the orders of the leader were not questioned. Khrushchev believed it was his right to demote any official who displeased him for whatever reason, and to do so without consultation. He had correctly judged the mood of the moment, which called for reforms, but he tried to carry them out by the old bureaucratic methods.

He would speak on any subject, at any place. At the drop of a hat he would deliver a lecture on the importance of growing maize, the future of space research, architecture and missiles, art, current international problems – always assertive and didactic, teaching and preaching. He acquired the habit of departing from his text to colour his speech with biting aphorisms and often impenetrable proverbs from Russian folklore. His style was to interrupt a speaker, heckling and throwing up all sorts of questions to put him off his stroke. He could be counted on to produce a surprise at any forum, the famous shoe-banging incident at the United Nations being only the most publicized.

Khrushchev had always been impulsive, as the minutes of a meeting of the Moscow Party Committee in 1950, convened to debate ways of improving the management of agriculture, illustrate. The Moscow Party Secretary, S. Morsin, had given his report, and only two other members showed a desire to speak. Khrushchev admonished the others severely: 'Put your names down to speak. If you don't, we'll nominate speakers. We're not going to let you sit here in silence. If we have to, we'll sit here for a week, but we will hear those who should speak.'

The director of a motor tractor station, one Zolotov, responded. He was concerned about the huge quantity of manure in his region that was infected with brucellosis. 'With the floods at the moment, the disease could be carried right into the Caspian itself . . .'

Khrushchev interrupted: 'That's not the main thing, comrade manager. If there's a danger of transmitting the disease, let's deal with it outside the terms of the discussion. Otherwise we'll get bogged down in brucellosis manure and find ourselves sitting on a heap of it.'

Zolotov objected tactfully, an unheard-of impertinence, and was duly rewarded with a hail of questions and insulting remarks. Finally Khrushchev caught Zolotov out on a triviality, which he enjoyed doing, and closed the discussion triumphantly: 'You came here to talk some nonsense about brucellosis and a pile of manure. Write a report. You want to make a speech? We can also make speeches. We're trained orators.'

Khrushchev certainly was an orator, and an inexhaustible one at that. His speeches and news conferences appeared in the press almost daily. They were not read with much enthusiasm, but he believed he could influence the 'masses' and assist the reforms he wanted to introduce through all this activity. When his enemies ousted him in 1964, they cited the fact that his picture had appeared in the press more than a thousand times in a single year. Conversely, Western observers were quick to note that Khrushchev's press appearances dropped dramatically in the days before his political demise.

One of Khrushchev's priorities was equipping the armed forces with nuclear missiles. He summoned weapons designers and builders and leading scientists to the Kremlin. No expense was spared for experiments and tests and the space programme. He could be proud of what he achieved in the military sphere, declaring at the Twenty-Second Party Congress on 17 October 1961: 'As I've departed from my text, I might as well tell you that the tests of the new hydrogen bomb are also going very well. We shall complete these tests. Apparently at the end of October. Finally, we shall probably explode a hydrogen bomb of [equivalent to] 50 million tonnes of TNT [*applause*]. We said we had a bomb of 100 million tonnes of TNT. And that's true. But we're not going to explode it, because if we exploded it even in the most remote areas, we might blow our own windows out [*stormy applause*].'[63]

Khrushchev did not understand that security was not to be found along the path of a monstrous arms race. He told the Congress with pride that 'the re-arming of the Soviet Army with nuclear missile technology was fully complete. Our armed forces now have weapons powerful enough to enable them to crush any aggressor,' although he qualified this by adding that he hoped it would never be necessary to drop such bombs on any country.[64]

Needless to say, Khrushchev did not mention the cost of the nuclear programme, which was ultimately responsible for the pitifully low standard of living of the average Soviet citizen. Nor was anything said about the accidents at the factories producing nuclear weapons. He was silent, for instance, about the huge explosion that took place on 29 September 1957 at Chelyabinsk Combine No. 817. An investigating commission concluded that the accident had been caused by gross negligence of cooling regulations. The fallout from the explosion polluted a large area, including living quarters for army units, a big camp for prisoners and, among others, the villages of Berdyaniki, Saltykovo, Golikaevo, Kirpichiki, Yugo-Konevo and Bogoryak. The Minister for General Machine Building, Ye. Slavsky, reported: 'All the factories at the complex did not cease production following the explosion.'

Khrushchev and the Presidium did not discuss the event until 19 October, a full twenty days later, when they instructed the Council of Ministers to take the necessary measures. The government in its turn did not debate the issue until 12 November, almost six weeks after the disaster had taken place. Its solution was to order that by 1 March 1958 the inhabitants of four villages should be moved to another district. The sinister bell was tolling for Chernobyl, but no one was allowed to hear it. Factory managers and engineers received gaol sentences, but the Presidium's main concern was to hush up the affair. All the documentation was concealed in 'Special Files' marked 'Top Secret' and tucked away in the Presidential Archives.[65]

The system continued to live by Stalinist norms. Human life remained a matter of statistics, and Khrushchev, despite his courageous challenge of the dictatorial past, did not alter his basic view of the value of individuals, or their rights and liberties. For him, results, the achievement of political and economic goals, were everything, and human beings took second place.

Only this, surely, can explain his approval of a plan by Marshal Zhukov to conduct an experiment by exploding an atomic bomb on 14 September 1954 at the Totsk base in a relatively densely populated district in the Orenburg region. The object was to see whether animals, held in tanks, trenches and dug-outs at various distances from the explosion, would survive an atomic blast; to test the reliability of engineering equipment installed in a specially constructed section of urban development; and to measure the extent of radioactive pollution of the area, and the effect on people driven through the bomb zone in armoured cars an hour after the explosion.

A few days after the test, Zhukov reported that the results were highly satisfactory. The nuclear device was exploded 350 metres above ground. I myself visited Totsk some time later, and the scene of devastation, of molten, swollen ground, collapsed trenches and the shredded remains of large trees, was truly apocalyptic. Whether such tests were necessary is arguable, but to hold them virtually in the centre of Russia was the height of irresponsibility.

Khrushchev devoted much attention to space research, the driving force of which was military. He would entertain the top space scientists at his dacha, and he admired them greatly for carrying the USSR into space and putting the country in the lead in this sphere. No expense was spared. The best engineers and technologists were engaged on this work, and their achievements provided both military and propaganda benefits.

Khrushchev was impatient for the first manned space flight, and constantly telephoned the constructors and organizers of the project. On 11 April 1961 he dictated a note for transmission to the members of the Presidium from Pitsunda on the Black Sea: 'I am told that tomorrow, if all goes well, at 09.07 a manned spacecraft will be launched. It will orbit the Earth for an hour and a half and should then land. We would like everything to go well. [The cosmonaut] will be brought to Moscow the day after tomorrow. The flight was originally planned for the thirteenth but was changed out of superstition. We will meet him at Vnukovo airport with all due ceremony ... This is an epoch-making event ...'

He then dictated his chief ideas for an address from the Central Committee to the population, which included the phrase: 'This achievement is an accomplishment not only for our people, but for the whole of humanity.'[66]

The next day Korolev telephoned Khrushchev and, dropping with fatigue and excitement, shouted: 'The parachute has opened, he's coming down to land. The ship's in good shape!' Khrushchev's son-in-law Alexei Adzhubei recalled that Khrushchev kept asking: 'Is he alive, is he sending signals? Is he alive? Is he alive?' Finally, he heard the news: 'He's alive!'[67]

The reception for the first man in space, Yuri Gagarin, took place in the Kremlin on 14 April. At the end of it a slightly tipsy Khrushchev raised his glass for yet another toast: 'Well, Yurka! All those who are sharpening their claws against us now know. They know that Yurka has been in space, seen everything, knows everything [*applause*]. And if we have to do it again, and if he needs back-up, he can take another comrade with him so he can see more. I propose another toast to Yura, whom we have toasted already! I propose a toast to Comrade Yuri Gagarin, to all the scientists, engineers, workers, collective farmers, our entire people, and to you, dear guests, ambassadors of countries accredited to our government. To your health!'[68]

Khrushchev's rule was marked by a host of major historic events, on all of which the stamp of his personality is to be seen. As well as the first manned space flight, the list includes the Berlin crisis, Suez and the Cuban missile crisis, a range of domestic economic reforms, reconciliation with Tito and the Sino–Soviet rift, the sudden fall from grace of the national hero Marshal Zhukov, the mushrooming of five-storey blocks which provided housing for millions, and the American U-2 spy-plane incident.

On 30 October 1961 Khrushchev reinforced his attack on the Stalin personality cult when, on the day before it ended, the Twenty-Second Party Congress passed a resolution: 'The continued preservation of I.V. Stalin's sarcophagus in the mausoleum is inappropriate, as Stalin's serious infringements of Lenin's tenets, his abuse of power, his mass arrests of honest Soviet people and other actions in the period of the personality cult make it impossible to leave his body in V.I. Lenin's mausoleum.'[69]

At the same time, Khrushchev was making strenuous efforts to ensure that some of Stalin's monstrous acts remained buried deep in the Party's most secret repositories. On 3 March 1959 KGB Chairman A. Shelepin wrote to Khrushchev, suggesting that 'the records and other documents relating to the shooting of 21,857 Polish officers, gendarmes, police, settlers and others in 1940' should be destroyed. 'None of these files,' Shelepin wrote, 'are of any operational interest to Soviet agencies, nor are they of historical value . . . On the contrary, some unforeseen event might lead to the exposure of the operation with all the undesirable consequences for our state. Especially as the official version on the shooting of the Poles in Katyn forest is that it was done by the German Fascist invaders.'[70] Khrushchev chose to leave the documents hidden. In 1987, in the new spirit of *glasnost*, a joint Soviet–Polish commission of historians set out to expose this and other 'skeletons in the cupboard', and in February 1990 the newly free Soviet press published the findings on Katyn. Two months later, on 14 April, Mikhail Gorbachev publicly stated that the Soviet regime had committed the atrocity.[71]

The stamp of Khrushchev's contradictory personality marked everything he touched. In July 1956 he received a delegation of Italian Communists, consisting of Giancarlo Paieta, Celeste Negarvile and Giacomo Pellegrini. Their conversation, or rather Khrushchev's monologue, lasted six and a half hours, and dwelt at length on the decisions of the Twentieth Congress and a host of other issues.

Suddenly, out of the blue, Khrushchev started talking about Jews. 'We have released a large number of Polish Jewish Communists from our prisons and sent them to Poland,' he said. 'These people are behaving disgustingly in Poland and are actively pushing their own people into the leading organs of the Party and state.' They were, he said, 'quite brazen'. He told the Italians that when a successor for Bierut was being decided at the Polish Party plenum, which he himself had attended earlier in the year, and the Poles had wanted Zambrowski, he had told them that, 'although Comrade Zambrowski is a good and capable comrade, in Poland's interests, however, you should choose a Pole.' Otherwise, he concluded, 'the fundamental leading posts will be held by Jews'. The Italians listened to all this in depressed silence.

Khrushchev then turned to the question of elections in the USSR, and why only one candidate was put up for any seat: 'We hold to the opinion,' he said, 'that we should continue to put forward just one candidate. We have no other parties, and to create them would mean making concessions to the bourgeoisie.'[72]

This was Khrushchev. Bold and inconsistent, impulsive and unpredictable, ready for change and reform in any field. Nor could he resist the temptation to 'educate' the creative intelligentsia. In 1957 he held his first meeting with leading figures in the cultural field, followed by two further meetings. The meetings revealed not only his ignorance of cultural matters, but his belief, like that of Stalin, that as Party leader he was the best judge of what artists and writers should be doing. Typical was the draft of a speech written on 8 March 1963, which declared that 'Abstractionism and formalism are a form of bourgeois ideology.'[73]

Khrushchev's attempts to drag the intelligentsia into line cost him the support of many of them, but above all it was the Party functionaries and state bureaucrats who took up arms against him. His name invariably provoked argument, and no one was neutral, although by the end he had very little support among any section of the population. His passion for change and experimentation constantly came up against a wall of silent non-acceptance and dissatisfaction.

Revolutionary Diplomacy

Lenin had spent much of his adult life abroad, but once he became head of the Soviet government he never left the country again. Stalin, who had been to Europe twice before 1917, also left Soviet Russia only twice, on both occasions to meet Western leaders during the war. Khrushchev, however, made many visits to foreign capitals, and he was soon raising the eyebrows of diplomats and journalists with his extravagant and eccentric propaganda remarks. The West was amazed when he chose to travel to New York in September 1959 for the Fourteenth Session of the UN General Assembly on the cruise ship *Baltika*, taking several days on the voyage and accompanied by an entourage of a hundred people, including his wife Nina and his family, and the wife and family of his Foreign Minister Andrei Gromyko. He again surprised the world by spending a further two weeks in the US, holding engagingly entertaining press conferences and spontaneous interviews in a coast-to-coast tour that even took in Hollywood.

Although he invariably justified his attacks on the 'imperialists' as being in defence of peace, in fact Khrushchev's diplomacy was typically Bolshevik, militant and aggressive. There was an example on 16 May 1960 in Paris, at a preliminary meeting of the four powers. At the beginning of that month the Soviet Union had shot down a US U-2 spy-plane over its territory, and it demanded an apology. Despite a public admission by the pilot, Gary Powers, the US had denied responsibility. When President Eisenhower extended his hand to greet Khrushchev in Paris, the Soviet leader declined, declaring indignantly: 'This meeting can begin its work if President Eisenhower will apologize to the Soviet Union for Gary Powers' provocation.' Gromyko, who was present, recalled that Eisenhower replied, 'in a barely audible voice', 'I have no intention of making any such apology, as I have nothing to apologize for.' After sitting in strained silence for a couple of minutes, the world leaders left the hall. De Gaulle tried to save the situation by telling Khrushchev that although Eisenhower had behaved wrongly, he should be forgiven. Khrushchev was adamant, and the meeting did not take place.[74]

Khrushchev then held a press conference, and in response to the yelling and din typical of such occasions, delivered a long and wholly unexpected tirade:

> Gentlemen, please forgive me, but I want to give a reply right away to the group who are doing all the booing here. I have been informed that Chancellor Adenauer has sent agents, who were not beaten by us at Stalingrad, into the Soviet Union to boo at us. But we booed at them and chased them three metres into the ground. So, take a look around you when you boo us. We beat you at Stalingrad, in Ukraine and Belorussia, and we finished you off. If the remnant are going to say boo to us and prepare another invasion, we'll boo them so hard that ... These people understand Russian perfectly well without a translation. They are Hitlerite predators who were on Soviet territory and who managed to take to their heels and escape ... I am the representative of the great Soviet people; the people who made the great October socialist revolution under Lenin's leadership; a people who are successfully building a Communist society and who are going forward towards Communism ... If you boo at me you are only making me bolder in my class struggle ... Gentlemen, I will not hide my satisfaction from you, I enjoy fighting the enemies of the working class. I like to hear the imperialist lackeys raging and unable to do anything ... [75]

It was the 'international' Khrushchev at his best: militant, ignorant, irreconcilable and aggressive. The journalists received the speech with excitement, applause, laughter and a mixture of approval and hostility. Having whipped up his audience, Khrushchev then asked for questions. His answers were couched in crude propaganda terms: 'We've given the imperialists one in the eye ... When the cat licked the cream, my mother took it by the ears, gave it a good shake and then stuck its nose in it. Shouldn't we take the American imperialists by the ears and give them a good shake? ... President Eisenhower suggested we call each other "my friend" ... But something smells not quite right about this "friend", something like thievery ... Your working class is of course in favour of socialism, but they're oppressed and downtrodden ... The Americans, with Powers' aircraft, have taken a look into someone's else's backyard, the imperialists have poked their snouts in, and we gave them one in the snout ... By 1965 not a single worker or employee in the Soviet Union will be paying any taxes.'[76]

Khrushchev could be witty, but his wit was often flat-footed and vulgar. The most widely publicized example of this took place during his next trip to the United States, in September 1960, when he addressed the United Nations General Assembly about a dozen times, his speeches covering some three hundred typewritten pages. At one point, while British Prime Minister Harold Macmillan was speaking, Khrushchev, after heckling and gesticulating, finally removed one of his shoes and began pounding it on his desk. The poker-faced Gromyko, sitting next to him, dutifully forced a smile and thumped his fist in a half-hearted show of solidarity – or prudent good sense. The unflappable Macmillan stole the show by drawling a request for a translation.

At an Independence Day reception at the American Embassy in Moscow on 4 July 1961, Khrushchev, in front of the world's press, started talking about missile technology. The veteran American correspondent Henry Shapiro said that his secret weapon was his fountain-pen, to which Khrushchev responded, 'And my secret weapon is my tongue.' One of the crowd said that brains were the best weapon. Khrushchev picked this up and began to talk excitedly about a recent trip to Alma-Ata in Kazakhstan, where as guest of honour at a dinner he was brought, as was the custom, a sheep's head. It was up to the guest to give pieces of it to the others. 'I cut off an ear and an eye,' he said, 'and gave them to the Kazakhstan leaders. Then I asked: "Here are the brains! Who gets the brains?" No one said anything. Then Academician Lavrentyev, undismayed, said, "Give me the brains." An academician needs brains,' said Khrushchev, 'whereas my job is chairman of the Council of Ministers, so I can manage without any brain.' Shapiro asked, not for the first time, why journalists were not permitted to visit certain sites. Smiling, Khrushchev loudly replied: 'Probably because you're a slanderer, a slanderer and a capitalist agent!'[77]

More serious was Khrushchev's elementary understanding of the world, his blind belief that the system he represented was superior.

His coarse rhetoric and moral cynicism helped the West to mobilize extra force in the Cold War. Statements such as 'we will bury you' and 'the liquidation of the capitalist system is a matter of time', horrified world opinion and handed ammunition to the purveyors of anti-Soviet propaganda. When in the USA he declared that missiles were coming off Soviet conveyor-belts 'like sausages', the average American citizen was shocked. No one played up the idea of a 'Soviet military threat' as zealously as Khrushchev, and this may have contributed to Richard Nixon's election defeat in 1960, as his Democrat opponent John F. Kennedy kept stressing that America was lagging behind the USSR in missile production. In the USSR, by contrast, Khrushchev's utterances were parodied in such jokes as: 'The USA is standing on the edge of an abyss. We are going to overtake the USA.'

Khrushchev's foreign policy derived from the simple principles of the ostensibly defunct Comintern, namely support for the 'socialist camp' and for all countries that might join it. As for developing countries, they should be helped to adopt an anti-imperialist position, and gradually be made aware of their socialist prospects. This approach cost the Soviet Union tens of billions of dollars, with no visible sign of success. Finally, while relations with the capitalist countries were meant to be based on the notion of peaceful co-existence, for the Kremlin this was nothing more than a specific form of class war, a tactical device to gain time. Right up to the era of *perestroika*, Central Committee policy remained 'the inevitable victory of socialism on a worldwide scale'.

This was a theme to which Khrushchev frequently returned in his interviews with Western journalists. For instance, on 18 May 1960 in Paris he declared: 'Our cause is true, our path has been properly laid. We will hold to the course of building Communism and march under the Marxist-Leninist banner, and you will follow us, but at the back of the line. We will not reproach you for this, but will help you and share with you our experience of socialist construction.'[78]

On the famous ocean voyage to New York on the *Baltika*, Khrushchev was accompanied by the leaders of three socialist countries, János Kádár of Hungary, Gheorghe Gheorghiu Dej of Romania and Todor Zhivkov of Bulgaria, and together they polished the ideas he was to utter at the United Nations. He wanted the UN to reflect the tri-polar nature of the world in its own structure, and proposed that the Charter be altered so that instead of one Secretary General there should be one from the socialist camp, one from the capitalist and one from the developing countries.

On 14 September, while still on board ship, and assisted by Podgorny, Mazurov and Foreign Minister Andrei Gromyko, Khrushchev dictated further notes for the speech he was scheduled to give on 23 September:

> Say that forcing the will of the majority on the minority is not permissible . . . Remark more sharply on the one-sidedness of the UN organization's actions . . . Secretary General Mr Hammarsköld fuels the UN with a colonialist policy . . . It's worth considering moving the UN (headquarters) to Switzerland, Australia or the USSR . . . In reply to the US note, we have to act to the contrary: they want to do us harm, while we want to do them good. Smash them in the teeth and then say, excuse me, I didn't mean to do it, but look at it from my point of view, I had to do it because you bared your teeth . . . [79]

The rest of the notes were devoted to his pet theme of the triple secretaryship which, had it been instituted, would have paralysed the work of the organization.

The original text which had been drafted in Moscow was substantially altered during the voyage, much to Gromyko's horror. Mazurov and Podgorny were mostly silent during the preparation of the two-hour-plus speech, and Gromyko's input was only occasional. Given Khrushchev's tendency to improvise, no one could be sure that he would not reshape the speech on the podium itself. And that is precisely what happened. Having heard President Eisenhower the day before his own appearance, he made his remarks on the U-2 incident still tougher.

On the American decision to help the world's starving, Khrushchev maliciously stated: 'We can only welcome this – after all, so much wealth has been stolen by the United States in the countries where people are now starving, that it is only right that even a little of what they stole should be returned to the people to whom it belonged. But the sum of $100 million is very little. If this amount is divided equally among all the starving, it won't be enough for one starving person's breakfast. So, it turns out that there's a lot of noise, but the whole thing's not worth an eaten egg.'[80]

For all his often ill-prepared and ill-thought-out initiatives in foreign policy, Khrushchev was determined to have an impact on world relations. In 1955 he was the first Soviet statesman to visit Yugoslavia. He recalled in his memoirs that the Yugoslav leadership had greeted him on his first visit with cool restraint, and that on a tour of the country organized by his hosts, the crowds were hardly more welcoming: 'Mostly they chanted "Long live Tito, Tito, Tito!"' [81]

The reception on his second trip, in September 1956, was warmer. During their talks, Tito told Khrushchev that the Americans were not happy about their rapprochement, that they must do everything possible to tear Greece away from the Western imperialist powers, and that in the latest edition of his speeches he had deleted all the old anti-Soviet utterances. Then, as it were to compensate him for his ideological concessions, he asked Khrushchev for 250,000 tonnes of wheat.

Khrushchev was satisfied. It seemed he had forced the heretic to confess his sins and return to the fold of Muscovite orthodoxy. At the end of their conversation he told Tito he 'must keep in step with the rest of the company ... Think about it.' He complained that the Yugoslavs were still putting officers on trial who had returned home from the USSR, where they had been forced to spend many years. Tito readily promised, 'We won't put any more on trial.' [82]

However one judges the practical measures Khrushchev took in the Yugoslav conflict, he deserves credit for ultimately normalizing relations between the two countries. He was not one to shy away even from apparently insoluble international problems. The territorial dispute over various islands between the USSR and Japan was such an issue. On 16 October 1956, in the course of a long conversation, Khrushchev gave the Japanese Minister of Agriculture and Forestry, Itiro Kono, to understand that the USSR might alter its traditional position. On the same day, at a meeting of the Presidium, he unexpectedly announced: 'The USSR must agree to hand over the islands of Habomai and Shikotan to Japan, with the proviso that the handover will take place after a peace treaty has been signed by the USSR and Japan, and after the island of Okinawa and other islands belonging to Japan, but now under the control of the USA, have been handed back to Japan.' After a pregnant pause, he added: 'Maybe the USSR will agree to hand over the islands of Habomai and Shikotan to Japan without waiting for the liberation of Okinawa.'[83]

But Khrushchev had misjudged the issue. It was easier to transfer a large peninsula belonging to another republic – Crimea to Ukraine – than to solve the problem of remote small islands. The others on the Presidium dug their heels in. Gromyko, a non-voting member, suggested that the question of the islands be connected to other more difficult and unresolved issues. Khrushchev waved a dismissive hand.

The steps Khrushchev took on Middle East policy were equally bold, and had more far-reaching effects. In deciding to support President Nasser of Egypt, he broke the mould of regional politics, in which the role played by the USSR had been minimal. It was nationalist leaders like Nasser who gave the ideologists in Moscow the opportunity to speak of countries 'with a socialist orientation' and the non-capitalist path of development.

Despite considerable doubts expressed by a large part of the Presidium, in 1955 Khrushchev responded at once to an Egyptian request for a wide range of weapons. His role in the Suez crisis of 1956 was significant, and it was only thanks to Soviet aid that Egypt managed to recover from the heavy defeat inflicted by Israel. Much of the military equipment supplied by the USSR – and Western countries – to Egypt had been captured by the Israelis, and the Egyptian armed forces had to be rebuilt virtually from scratch, this time by the USSR alone. Thousands of Soviet advisers and specialists undertook the task.

Soviet help in the economic sphere was also considerable. Khrushchev's pro-active policy cost the Soviet Union many billions of dollars, but he regarded it as an investment to strengthen Soviet influence in the region at the expense of the West. His revolutionary diplomacy did not always produce the desired result, however. The report presented on 14 October 1964 to the Central Committee plenum that ousted him pointed out that in the ten years he had been in power, the USSR had undertaken some six thousand projects. Beneficiaries included Egypt, Iraq, Indonesia, India and Ethiopia, to name but a few. Projects in Guinea alone included an airport, a cannery and sawmill, a power station, a refrigeration plant, a hospital, a hotel, a polytechnic, geological surveys and various research projects. Yet when Khrushchev's 'friend' Sekou Touré requested the withdrawal of Soviet personnel from Guinea, even the use of the airport they had built at Conakry, as a stopover en route to Cuba, was prohibited to them. In Djakarta the USSR had built a stadium for a hundred thousand spectators, in Rangoon a hotel, an atomic research centre in Ghana, a sports complex in Mali – the list is interminable. All these costly ventures only became a bone of contention when the leadership wanted to get rid of Khrushchev.

Following the Twentieth Congress, international issues began to command a greater share of attention than domestic affairs, and this too was thrown in Khrushchev's face in 1964. He was reminded, with meticulously researched data from the Central Committee apparatus, that, for instance, in the first nine months of 1964 he had spent 150 days on trips abroad. When did he do any work, they wanted to know? He had met Mao Tse-tung several times, de Gaulle, Macmillan, Eisenhower, Nasser and many other world leaders.

Khrushchev's energy was prodigious, and he tried to be involved in everything, giving usually superficial and often misguided opinion on any subject, despite being surrounded on his trips by an army of experts and advisers. He had a very short attention span, and would interrupt speakers so crudely that his advisers could only roll their eyes and throw up their hands – mentally, of course. When he went to the four-power meeting in Paris in May 1960, he took twenty-one advisers, five KGB officers, eight interpreters, five coding clerks, ten stenographers, four radio operators, four drivers, twenty-eight bodyguards, several financial advisers and a number of physicians.[84] He had decided what he was going to say beforehand, however, and had no intention of taking further advice. All he required from his staff were the texts of the speeches he was to make, which he altered at will in the delivery. He was a leader who wanted to do and to decide everything himself, which showed an undoubtedly strong personality. But therein lay the danger of incompetence and major miscalculation.

Khrushchev's decade in power saw repeated failure in various aspects of his foreign policy. He was especially persistent in his attempts to detach Japan from the USA by continually offering them territorial concessions, and in the space of two and half years, from 1962 to 1964, he saw Japanese government delegations, statesmen and diplomats no fewer than six times.[85]

He was even less successful in his relations with China. Since the Stalin era, Khrushchev had been accustomed to regard Moscow not merely as the political heart of the international Communist movement, but as the control centre for co-ordinating the international efforts of the socialist countries. He was used to looking down on other socialist countries, including China, as 'younger brothers'.

Khrushchev met Mao on several occasions, and each occasion was more strained than the last. With Stalin dead, the Chinese were reluctant to recognize the USSR as the unquestioned leader of the socialist camp. Peking took a distinctly dim view of the results of the Twentieth Congress. The monolithic union of the two great powers turned out to have been badly cemented. Each of them had its own national interests, which did not necessarily coincide.

When Khrushchev arrived in Peking on 29 September 1954 for the fifth anniversary of the Chinese People's Republic, it seemed that nothing could mar Sino–Soviet friendship. On leaving the plane, he congratulated 'the Chinese people on the acceptance of their socialist constitution and for choosing that great son and leader of the Chinese people, Comrade Mao Tse-tung, as Chairman. The peace-loving peoples of the world see in the indestructible friendship of the two great nations, the Soviet Union and the Chinese People's Republic, a mighty bulwark for peace, a great and unconquerable force which is exerting a growing influence on the solution of international problems.'[86]

Fifteen years later Khrushchev would write of Mao: 'Politics is a game, and Mao Tse-tung has played politics with Asiatic cunning, following his own rules of cajolery, treachery, savage vengeance, and deceit. He deceived us for a number of years before we saw through his tricks.'[87] In his memoirs, Khrushchev blamed his ambassador to Peking, Pavel Yudin, for the rift between the two countries: 'I might remark with some justification that we were sure to have discord with any country where Yudin was sent as ambassador. Yudin was sent to Yugoslavia, and we had a falling-out with Tito. Yudin went to China, and we had a falling-out with Mao. This was no coincidence.'[88]

Of course, the causes of the rift went far deeper. After Stalin's death Mao was not content to remain a vassal of the Soviet Union, and from that cause others flowed. The speech debunking Stalin at the Twentieth Congress was especially offensive to the Chinese, who were busy exalting Mao on a Stalinesque scale. The Chinese leadership was also offended when the USSR first slowed down and then stopped co-operation in the field of nuclear weapons. Mao may have called the atomic bomb 'a paper tiger', but he wanted to have one of his own, nonetheless. Khrushchev commented on these issues in public and in private, making clear his unease.

In October 1964, just a week before he was ousted, Khrushchev received the Japanese politician Fujiyama. When the conversation turned to China, Khrushchev suddenly lifted the veil on Sino–Soviet relations. 'The Chinese are capable of exploding a hydrogen bomb,' he said. 'At the time of our close fraternal relations Chinese scientists were allowed into very many of our secret projects and saw what we were doing ... We gave them the equipment for producing nuclear fuel.' Mikoyan, who was present, added: 'We built factories for the Chinese and gave them other kinds of help.' Khrushchev continued: 'Anyway, they got a lot from us and know very well what to do.'[89] The USSR had indeed done much to assist China's nuclear programme, and even if they ceased to help after 1958, their contribution produced solid results.

At Mao's invitation, at the end of July 1958 Khrushchev made a visit which the Chinese requested be kept secret, although the fact was made known in a communiqué published after the talks. The first meeting took place on 31 July and lasted many hours. It was attended only by the two leaders and their advisers, Boris Ponomarev and Deng Xiao-ping, plus two Soviet note-takers, Nikolai Fedorenko, a future Soviet Ambassador to the UN, and A. Filev, and presumably their Chinese opposite numbers. The chief area of discussion was military.

There was considerable discussion on the building of a modern fleet. The Chinese had understood from Yudin that it was to be a joint Sino–Soviet fleet, and were opposed to the idea. Khrushchev announced that the USSR would lay stress on building a nuclear submarine fleet, torpedo boats and rocket-firing aircraft. China, meanwhile, would make her ports available to the Soviet Navy when needed. Mao replied: 'In case of war, the Soviet Union may use any part of China, Russian sailors may come into any port in China.'

The subject of Stalin came up several times.

MAO: The criticism of Stalin's mistakes is correct. We only disagree with the lack of a precise limit to the criticism. We consider that out of Stalin's ten fingers, only three were bad.

KHRUSHCHEV: I think there were more.

MAO: That's not right. The basis of his life was merit.

KHRUSHCHEV: Stalin was and is Stalin. What we criticized was the scum, the scab, which formed especially in his old age. But it's another matter when Tito criticizes him. In twenty years' time, schoolchildren will search in their schoolbooks to find out who Tito was, whereas everyone will know the name of Stalin.

MAO: When I came to Moscow, he didn't want to sign a treaty of friendship with us and didn't want to terminate his previous treaty with the Kuomintang. I remember that Fedorenko and Kovalev passed on his advice that we should take a trip round the country. I told them I have to do only three things: eat, sleep and defecate. I hadn't come to Moscow just to wish Stalin a happy birthday. So I said: if you don't want to conclude a treaty of friendship, don't. I'll carry out my three functions.

There was a long discussion on the number of missiles it would take to wipe out this or that country, in the event of war. 'Right now,' Khrushchev said, 'with our intercontinental missiles, we have the Americans by the throat.' They also discussed radio-location stations that the USSR wanted to establish in China. Khrushchev proposed that the Chinese should send their people to the Soviet Union for training. Mao did not agree, and Moscow soon recalled all its many thousands of personnel from China. There was no debate on nuclear affairs as such, except for Khrushchev's significant remark that 'we are continuing to perfect atomic and hydrogen bombs.'

Despite the outward assurances of friendship, relations were even then strained. For instance, Mao declared that 'regarding our next meeting, there could be problems. You work by day, and I sleep by day.' Nevertheless, other meetings took place during the visit.[90]

The two leaders met again on 2 October 1959, again in Peking. Khrushchev was accompanied by Mikhail Suslov and Andrei Gromyko, and Mao was flanked by the entire Chinese leadership. They discussed Taiwan, the Sino–Indian conflict, relations with the USA, American prisoners of war and other matters, but all the time it was felt that the two sides were irreconcilable.

Khrushchev mocked the Chinese version of the conflict with India: 'In our view, five kilometres here or there are not important. I take Lenin as an example. He gave up Kars, Ardagan and Ararat to Turkey.

And to this very day there are people in the Caucasus who are still unhappy at Lenin's measures. But I think he did the right thing.'

He criticized the Chinese for allowing the Dalai Lama to leave Tibet. 'It would have been better,' he said, 'if he'd been put in his coffin.' He concluded: 'The events in Tibet are your fault.'

The Chinese exploded, and accused Khrushchev of kowtowing to the Americans. Mao declared: 'You have stuck two labels on us: the conflict with India is our fault, and the Dalai Lama's departure is our mistake. We, however, have stuck one label on you: time-servers. Accept it.'

Khrushchev replied angrily: 'We don't accept it. We hold a principled Communist position.'

By the end of the meeting the atmosphere was incandescent. 'You want to subject us to yourselves,' Khrushchev snapped, 'but you won't succeed.'

Marshal Chen Yi broke in and declared: 'I am indignant at your statement that the worsening of relations is our fault.'

Khrushchev replied: 'And I am indignant at your statement that we are time-servers. We have to support Nehru and help keep him in power . . .'

As the meeting came to a close, Khrushchev and Chen Yi had another set-to.

KHRUSHCHEV: I only mentioned some of your blunders, I didn't make fundamental political accusations, whereas you have levelled a precisely fundamental political accusation against us. If you think we're time-servers, Comrade Chen Yi, then don't offer me your hand, because I won't shake it.

CHEN YI: Me too. I'm telling you, your anger doesn't scare me.

KHRUSHCHEV: Don't you try spitting down on us from your elevation as a marshal. You haven't got the spit. You won't spit on us. It's all very well: on the one hand you utter the formula, 'The [socialist] camp, headed by the Soviet Union', but then you won't let me say a word.[91]

On this sour note Khrushchev's last meeting with the Chinese leadership ended. On the plane back to Moscow, gazing out of the window, he muttered: 'It's hard to make an agreement with an old boot. He can't forgive us for Stalin.'

Two approaches to 'revolutionary diplomacy' had clashed in Peking, and Khrushchev had shown neither flexibility nor tact. Later, Khrushchev described Mao as a nationalist, 'and at least when I knew him he was bursting with an impatient desire to rule the world.' He added: 'Mao may be a nationalist, but he's no fool ... The slogans of the Chinese are very alluring. You're mistaken if you don't think the seeds of these ideas will find fertile soil in our country.'[92]

Bolshevik radicalism is imprinted on the whole of Khrushchev's foreign policy, even though it is also indisputable that he wanted peace and strove for it in his own way. This did not prevent him from embarking on risky policies, from flexing his muscles and from interfering in the affairs of sovereign states.

Speaking to the General Secretary of the Italian Communist Party, Luigi Longo, on 22 January 1957, he asked rhetorically: 'Did we do the right thing in Hungary? We think we did absolutely the right thing. As for the Soviet people, the crushing of the counter-revolution in Hungary was greeted by them, and especially by the army, with general relief.'[93] He believed it was his right to decide what was good for another nation, and to take measures accordingly. The intervention in Hungary was no exception. Diplomacy, with the threat of force in the background – as in the case of Poland in October 1956 – was a favoured form of argument with the Soviet leaders. Paradoxical and contradictory, Khrushchev was an exemplary exponent of this approach. The initiator of major, unilateral Soviet arms reductions, he could speak of turning out missiles like sausages and of 'burying' the West, and still imagine that his political opponents would become more compliant.

He never spoke of the 'world proletarian revolution', but believed that the victory of socialism on a global scale was possible without war. To the end of his life he remained a Stalinist, if an unconscious one, yet it was he who had delivered a mortal blow against that particular form of totalitarianism. This paradox was constantly apparent in his diplomatic activity. His ideas sometimes perplexed his own diplomats, as well as his adversaries.

In 1955 the heads of government of the USSR, the USA, France and Britain met in Geneva. Khrushchev was accompanied by Bulganin, Molotov and Zhukov. The Soviet delegation shocked the assembled statesmen with their provocative declaration of a desire to enter NATO. Alone with his companions later, Khrushchev was gleeful at the patent discomfiture he had caused the Western powers. His reckless initiatives in diplomacy, however, more than once pushed the world towards the brink of nuclear conflict. Such an occasion was the Cuban missile crisis of 1962.

Operation Anadyr

The public was surprised that Khrushchev did not hasten back to the USSR after his visit to the United Nations in September 1959. He turned the trip into an ideological event. Wherever he was taken in the USA, he lectured and hectored, whether in interviews or press conferences, with businessmen or public figures, accusing America and its 'stooges' of imperialism. He thought he had made a good impression, but in fact the effect was the opposite. For all his peace-loving rhetoric, he only managed to reinforce the West's suspicions.

Within two years, the Americans would see for themselves that their suspicions had been justified. The US administration soon realized that Soviet foreign policy had not changed fundamentally, despite the death and discrediting of Stalin. The incompatibility of the capitalist and socialist camps, or the imperialist and anti-imperialist worlds, as Khrushchev would put it, was transferred to the newly created arena of post-war international politics, the UN and the media, by Khrushchev's openly demonstrative style. Khrushchev's constant refrain of the 'liquidation of the capitalist system as the fundamental issue of social development' by the spread of Marxism-Leninism throughout the world and the support of the developing countries was now backed by the growth of Soviet economic power and its nuclear might.

The revolution in Cuba in 1959 led by the thirty-two-year-old Fidel Castro was not expected by the Soviet leadership, but that small country, so close to the USA, soon became the object of Moscow's intense interest. It liked Castro's anti-American stance, and was especially encouraged by the strategic mistake committed by the US administration: instead of trying to exert its influence on the young regime, it adopted a hostile attitude, then declared an economic blockade, thus pushing Castro into the arms of the Soviet Union. The landing of Cuban dissidents at the Bay of Pigs on 17 April 1961 only assisted this process. The day after the landing, at a meeting of the Presidium, Khrushchev proposed a range of measures giving general assistance to Cuba.[94] He increasingly saw this distant island as an unsinkable aircraft-carrier with the potential to join the socialist camp.

In August 1961 one of Castro's aides, Blas Roca, brought an important letter to Moscow. Khrushchev read the translation and marked a number of significant passages. Havana was proposing to proclaim the socialist character of the Cuban revolution and form a Marxist party, and was asking the Soviet Union to express its solidarity with Cuba 'against attacks and threats of military attack on our country by the United States'. Castro also wanted to discuss 'ways of co-ordinating our sugar production with demand in the socialist camp'.[95]

The more Cuba showed a desire for close relations with the USSR, the more militant the USA became. Soviet intelligence warned of the real possibility of US military intervention, and these reports no doubt played a part in the formulation of an unusually audacious scheme in Khrushchev's mind. Gromyko recalled that on a flight back to Moscow from Bulgaria in 1962, Khrushchev had raised the issue of Cuba: 'The situation forming around Cuba at the moment is dangerous. It is essential that we deploy a certain quantity of our nuclear missiles there for its defence, as an independent state.' After a pause, Gromyko replied: 'I have to say quite frankly that taking our nuclear missiles to Cuba will cause a political explosion in the United States.'[96]

In April 1962, during one of his regular and frequent meetings with Defence Minister Malinovsky about forthcoming tests of a new missile system, Khrushchev interrupted Malinovsky's report on the latest missile site with an unexpected question: 'What about putting one of our hedgehogs down the Americans' trousers?' he asked. 'According to our intelligence we are lagging almost fifteen years behind the Americans in warheads. We cannot reduce that lead even in ten years. But our rockets on America's doorstep would drastically alter the situation and go a long way towards compensating us for the lag in time. What does the Marshal think of that?'

Malinovsky replied that he and the Chief of Staff, Marshal Zakharov, had discussed this very question among themselves on two occasions. But he thought it was more a political than a military question. Khrushchev, not wanting to say more at that time, told Malinovsky to discuss it again in a small circle and to report his findings to the Presidium in a month's time.

The meeting took place on 24 May 1962. No minutes were taken, apart from one page of notes recorded by Colonel-General S. Ivanov, head of the Main Operational Directorate of the General Staff and Secretary of the Defence Council. His notes state: 'the question of assistance to Cuba was discussed ... N.S. Khrushchev gave the report. Comrades Kozlov, Brezhnev, Kosygin, Mikoyan, Voronov and Polyansky spoke, all the other members of the Presidium supported and approved the decision. 1) Full and unanimous approval of enterprise "Anadyr" (subject to receiving F. Castro's agreement); 2) A commission to be sent to Fidel Castro for talks.'

The meeting agreed that it was not only strategically sensible to give Cuba military assistance, but also to establish a powerful bridgehead on America's doorstep from which virtually the whole of US territory would be accessible to Soviet missiles in the event of a conflict.

To ascertain Castro's response to these notions, a delegation consisting of S. Rashidov, Marshal S. Biryuzov and a number of Defence Ministry officials would be sent to Havana. At 11 a.m. next day, the Commission, as it is described in the notes, was in Khrushchev's office to receive instructions, and by the end of the month had arrived in Cuba. After meeting Castro and his brother Raoul on their first day, the Soviet delegation met them again on the next day, this time augmented by Che Guevara, Osualdo Dorticos and Ramiro Valdez. It was a brief meeting, and the Cuban leadership announced that they were willing to receive Soviet missiles in Cuba.

This was reported to the Presidium on 10 June, after the delegation had returned. Khrushchev did not want to shoulder all the responsibility himself, and therefore ensured that it was the decision of the entire Presidium. As at all such meetings, there were no objections. On a single sheet of notes, Ivanov wrote: '10.6.62. A session of the Presidium took place ... After hearing Comrades Rashidov and Biryuzov on the results of their trip, the essentials of the problem were discussed, and then R.Ya. Malinovsky read out a note, to which all voted "in favour".'[97]

Malinovsky's note read: 'To the chairman of the Defence Council,

Comrade N.S. Khrushchev (of special importance; the only copy). In accordance with your instructions, the Ministry of Defence proposes: to put a Soviet forces Group on the island of Cuba consisting of combined arms under the sole command of a group headquarters, subordinate to Commander-in-Chief Soviet forces in Cuba.' Missile forces (a division of five missile regiments) was to form the core, and the timetable, delivery, financing and even clothing were all specified.[98] Khrushchev insisted that the transport of this large number of Soviet forces across the ocean be carried out in absolute secrecy, and checked up on the progress of preparations almost every day. The General Staff had suggested the operation be called 'Anadyr', a settlement in the Arctic region of Magadan, to disguise its real destination. A number of ships were ostentatiously loaded with skis and sheepskins to enhance the effect.

As early as 26 May Malinovsky had confirmed the list of generals and other officers who would be involved in the operation. Only ten people were fully informed of the scale of the forthcoming expedition. Khrushchev was elated. He had not felt like this since his days as a member of the Military Council at Stalingrad and Kursk during the war. Then, however, he had been carrying out Stalin's will, whereas now it was he who was generating the ideas and exercising the decisive will needed to bring off this vast enterprise, which required huge resources and a great concentration of forces. He was involved at every phase and concerned with every detail, and saw Malinovsky two or three times a week. On 4 June, an advance reconnaissance group of 161 men was sent to Cuba to form the backbone of the future headquarters staff. At the last minute, Khrushchev replaced Pavel Dankevich as Group Commander-in-Chief with General Issa Pliev, whom he knew well and who incidentally had been in charge of Northern Caucasus Military District at the time of the events in Novocherkassk. The reconnaissance group were ordered to carry out their work 'in the strictest secrecy'. They would be 'transported by plane as Soviet agricultural experts, in the guise of engineers and technologists in irrigation and land improvement'.

Khrushchev confirmed the composition of the Group: 51st Rocket Division (consisting of five regiments with R-14 and R-12 installations), 10th and 11th Anti-Aircraft Missile Divisions, a fighter-aircraft regiment, two guided-missile regiments, a helicopter regiment, four motorized-rifle regiments, a coastal-missile regiment, a mine and torpedo regiment, and various rear and other units. It had also been intended to send a squadron of submarines and a squadron of surface naval ships, but in the course of the operation this decision was altered. Overall, the plan was to land more than fifty thousand Soviet servicemen on Cuba. Shipments began in the middle of July from a number of Soviet ports. Cargoes of tractors and other agricultural machinery were loaded, and more than eighty merchant ships were involved in the operation.

The ships' manifests stated that their cargoes were to be delivered to ports in Africa and Latin America. At fixed points on the ocean and in the presence of specially selected personnel, ships' masters were to open sealed packets which revealed their true destination. They were to pass through any straits only in darkness, and the crews were to be kept in their stuffy quarters almost throughout the voyage, and only allowed to take a breather on deck at night. Nuclear warheads for all types of missile would be carried on the *Indigirka*, *Lena* and *Alexandrovsk*. Sixty strategic R-12 and R-14 missiles, with their ancillary parts, were to be delivered, and indeed forty-two of them arrived in Cuba before the US imposed its blockade.

Khrushchev kept his eye on the operation from wherever he happened to be. On 5 October he called Colonel-General Ivanov on his special line from Tashkent to ask how the transport was going. Ivanov replied: 'The *Indigirka* arrived on 4 October. There has been no buzzing by aircraft. Twenty-two [ships] have yet to leave. Twenty are at sea. The transport *Alexandrovsk* is loaded and ready to go. I request permission for her to depart.' 'The transport *Alexandrovsk* may leave. Where are the *Lena* and IL-28?' 'At sea.' 'All clear. Thank you. I wish you luck.'

Khrushchev's deputy while he was out of Moscow was Frol Kozlov. On 5 October Malinovsky reported to him: 'In accordance with the plan for the enterprise "Anadyr", as ratified by the Presidium of the Central Committee of the CPSU, the second batch of special ammunition is ready for shipment. There are sixty-eight units of special ammunition, namely: twenty-four warheads for R-14 missiles, and forty-four warheads for FKR missiles have been loaded on the *Alexandrovsk* at Severomorsk. Three automatic 37mm guns with 1200 shells each have been fitted on the *Alexandrovsk* for self-defence. The captain has been given permission to open fire only in the event of a blatant attempt to seize the vessel or to sink her.'[99]

Khrushchev had approved an instruction to install two 23mm coaxial anti-aircraft guns on each vessel for self-protection, and 'in the event of an open threat of seizure of our ship, the captain and chief of marines must take steps for the organized abandonment of the ship by the crew in all available lifesaving resources and [then] to sink the ship.'[100]

The attention of Soviet intelligence had long been concentrated on Cuba. On 23 June 1961, before the idea of putting missiles on the island had matured in Khrushchev's mind, the Soviet military intelligence resident in Havana reported that a terrorist action, called 'Condor', had been organized against Castro and his brother by the Cubans Nelson Gutierrez and Marcelino Balida, aided by a Puerto Rican known as 'Negrete'. The action was tentatively planned to take place on 26 July. Knowing that Castro wore an armoured vest, the plan was to shoot him in the head.[101] Khrushchev reported all this to the next meeting of the Presidium on 24 June 1961, and it was agreed that the Soviet Ambassador in Havana should warn Castro at once.[102]

Malinovsky's reports on Operation Anadyr covered not just the logistics, but also the operational and strategic issues. General Pliev had been told that the 'tasks of Soviet forces in Cuba are to prevent the enemy from landing on Cuban territory, whether by sea or air, and to turn the island into an impregnable fortress. Missile forces, who constitute the basis of defence for the Soviet Union and Cuba, must be ready on a signal from Moscow to launch nuclear-missile strikes on important targets in the United States. Missile-carrying submarines must be ready on a signal from Moscow to launch nuclear-missile strikes on important coastal targets in the USA.' Marshal Zakharov suggested that Pliev be given discretion to use tactical nuclear weapons even without Moscow's permission. Malinovsky objected, however, and Pliev was given no such discretion.

The situation, then, was that Khrushchev was fully prepared to carry out nuclear strikes against the United States. He must have known that this would unleash a nuclear war. What did he expect to gain from it? The US, after all, had at least fifteen times more nuclear warheads than the USSR.

We should perhaps not judge him by today's standards. Since 1917 the Soviet leadership thought in Comintern categories, such as 'the inevitable demise of capitalism' and 'the historical correctness of Communism'. Khrushchev genuinely believed that the Soviet Union was the most democratic system, that it was axiomatic that it would overtake the USA and that the precise date for the completion of the Communist society was so sure that it could be put into the Party programme. Even his proposals on disarmament were utterly unrealistic. At the Fifteenth Session of the United Nations General Assembly in September 1960 he proposed that all nuclear arsenals and other weapons of mass destruction be destroyed within four years: this was plainly an ideologically inspired move, and not based on rational calculation. A rejection from the West was anticipated, so that the Soviet propaganda machine could yet again 'unmask aggressive imperialistic circles'.

Marshal Zakharov reported on 25 September that everything was going according to plan. To date, 114 ships had sailed for Cuba, some of them twice, ninety-four had arrived and thirty-five remained to go. Embarkation schedules had been tightened and would be fulfilled by 20 October, with disembarkation in Cuba completed by 3–5 November. In view of the fact, the report continued, that a fleet of surface naval ships would attract the attention of the whole world, which would not be in the interests of the Soviet Union, it was suggested that such a fleet should not be sent to Cuba for the time being. On the other hand, Zakharov continued, not less than sixty-nine submarines carrying eighty-eight torpedoes, including four nuclear warheads, would be despatched. A nuclear-torpedo submarine would escort the transport *Alexandrovsk*, staying immediately underneath the ship during the most sensitive stretches of the crossing in order to maintain secrecy. The despatch of submarines and the Baltic and Black Sea Fleets, however, was postponed on the day of this report. The changes were noted and approved by Khrushchev.[103]

The greater part of Soviet forces on Cuba were in place when photographs taken by an American U-2 spy-plane of the western and central areas of Cuba yielded sensational information. The experts decided, having analysed the pictures, that medium-range Soviet missiles had been installed in Cuba. A report was sent at once to President Kennedy. For several days American security chiefs assessed the information and tried to formulate an effective response. Moscow was not aware until 22 October that Khrushchev's secret plan had been discovered, by which time forty-two nuclear missiles were in Cuba.

Kennedy's radio and TV speech of 22 October shocked the American public: 'in the course of the last week indisputable evidence has established the fact that at present on that imprisoned island a number of launchpads for offensive missiles are being built.'

For the first time the Americans felt the chill of fear. Separated from the rest of the world by great oceans and surrounded by friendly, weak neighbours, they had not until then had a real sense of the nuclear danger. Bomb-shelters and deep cellars were built, and canned and dry goods stocked for the worst. The press added fuel to the fire by pointing out which towns and cities were within range of missiles from Cuba. The resultant hysteria helped to push the administration into taking decisive measures.

On 24 October Kennedy imposed a naval blockade, euphemistically called 'quarantine', on Cuba. The same day, Moscow replied with a statement to the effect that if the USA unleashed a nuclear war, the USSR 'would carry out the most powerful retaliatory strike'. Khrushchev rejected Kennedy's charges and accused the USA of preparing to launch a dangerous undertaking. Soviet diplomats in Washington continued to reassure everyone that there were no offensive weapons in Cuba. A war of nerves began.

The Pentagon seriously considered launching an air strike against the missile sites. Had this gone ahead, it is possible that Moscow, not being fully aware of the intended scale of such bombing, might have approved retaliation. Twenty or 25 per cent of Soviet missiles could have found their targets, and in the first – and no doubt last – assault, ten or twelve nuclear devices would fall on American cities.

The leaders of the two most powerful countries were prepared to take the most awesome actions. Khrushchev did not leave his office for several days. The armed forces of both states were put on full battle-readiness. The irrevocable could occur at any moment. Kennedy remained cool, and at 1.25 a.m. on 25 October he sent a letter to the Soviet Embassy addressed to Khrushchev. It was transmitted at once to Moscow:

Respected Mr Chairman,

I have received your letter of 24 October and much regret that it seems you still do not understand what has motivated us in this affair [i.e. the blockade]. Our government received totally clear assurances from your government and its representatives, both publicly and through unofficial channels, that no offensive weapons were being sent to Cuba. If you will look again at the statement published by TASS in September, you will see how clear that assurance was. All these public assurances were false and your forces have recently begun establishing a complex of missile bases in Cuba. I hope your government will undertake the necessary measures to restore the pre-existing position.

Yours sincerely, John F. Kennedy.[104]

Khrushchev at once summoned a meeting of the Presidium. The members sat in silence as the outwardly calm First Secretary began by reading an urgent communication from Soviet intelligence in Washington, stating that 'the President has apparently taken the decision to invade Cuba today or tomorrow night.'[105]

The Presidium remained silent. Khrushchev then read Kennedy's letter and, surveying the long table, asked: 'What shall we do?'

It was agreed not to give way to American pressure, and to give a tough reply. By the small hours of 26 October, Khrushchev's reply was ready. It ran to eight pages and consisted of Khrushchev's own dictated thoughts. He was still naïvely trying to educate the US President ideologically. Some of his assertions are simply astonishing:

Respected Mr President,

I have received your letter of 25 October. From your letter I sense that you have some understanding of the existing situation and a sense of responsibility. I appreciate that . . . I think you will understand me correctly if you are really concerned about the benefits of peace. Everyone needs peace: both the capitalists, if they have not lost their senses, and more so the Communists who are people who are able to value not only their own lives but, more than that, the lives of other peoples. We Communists are against any wars between states and we have defended the cause of peace since we came into the world.

So much for the moral argument. As for the military aspect of the conflict:

Your arguments about there being offensive weapons in Cuba are completely groundless. You, Mr President, are a military man and should understand that it is hardly possible to launch an offensive, even if one has a vast quantity of missiles of all ranges and force on one's territory . . . To make an offensive with such missiles, even nuclear missiles of 100 megatonnes, is impossible, because it is only people, troops, who can make an offensive . . . You surely do not think that Cuba can advance on the United States or that even we together with Cuba can advance against you from Cuban territory? You surely do not think that? How can it be? We do not understand this.

Amazingly, not a single member of the Presidium, no marshal or general, pointed out that Khrushchev's letter would make him an object of ridicule. The Bolshevik tradition was still in force: no one could contradict the leader. If Khrushchev decided that nuclear weapons were not offensive weapons, so be it. As for what he told the US President, he could say that black was white: 'I assure you that the ships that are on their way to Cuba are carrying the most innocent, peaceful cargoes.'

Khrushchev then gave himself a way out of the impasse by declaring that, if the USA would state that it would not send its troops to Cuba, 'the need for our military experts on Cuba would fall away'. Perhaps as a face-saving gesture, or out of sheer bravado, he closed the letter by rejecting Kennedy's measures as aggressive, and adding: 'If you have done this as the first step towards launching a war, well, all right, evidently there is nothing else we can do but to accept your challenge.'[106] He communicated through diplomatic channels that the USSR would remove the missiles if the US promised not to invade Cuba, and a face-saving formula was found that enabled Khrushchev to depict a humiliating retreat as an unqualified victory.

After Khrushchev's letter had been sent, Malinovsky received a cipher from Pliev – code-named 'Pavlov' – stating that an attack by US strategic air forces was expected 'on the night of 26 or at dawn on 27 October'. Pliev reported: 'The decision has been taken that in the event of attacks on our locations by American aircraft we shall use all available means of anti-aircraft defence.' Malinovsky – signing himself 'Director' – wrote on the report: 'Send to Comrade N.S. Khrushchev. I suggest Pavlov's decision be ratified.' The report was delivered to Khrushchev at once, but it seems he did not approve it until six days later, on 27 October. A few hours after that, another memo from Malinovsky arrived on his desk, reporting that at 18.20

Moscow time on that day a U-2 reconnaissance plane had been shot down by two 507 anti-aircraft missiles over the Chukotka Peninsula in the far eastern part of the USSR.

The Americans were close to hysteria. Generals were demanding an immediate strike against Soviet missile installations. That Saturday was fateful for the whole world. If Kennedy's nerve had failed him and a strike had been carried out, the greatest catastrophe in human history would have taken place. But through his brother Robert, the President contacted Soviet Ambassador Dobrynin and told him that if the missiles were removed from Cuba, there would be no invasion.

The Presidium spent the entire night of 28 October in Khrushchev's office. The leader, having made up his mind to withdraw, read cable after cable from Soviet intelligence, from which it emerged that to delay would be tantamount to war, since the Americans were bound to launch a strike. Again, a collective letter was composed there and then. It was not well done, as none of the Party leaders ever wrote their own reports or speeches, and knew only how to put together directives.

The country was sleeping, completely unaware that its leaders had brought it to the very brink of disaster and were now feverishly trying to drag it back from the edge. There was no time to encode the letter to Kennedy, and it was already being sent by radio in clear text while the final pages were still being corrected at the long table.

The vital passage of the disjointed message read:

> In order to complete the liquidation as soon as possible of the dangerous conflict for the cause of peace, to give reassurance to all peoples thirsting for peace, to pacify the people of America who, I am sure, also want peace, as do the peoples of the Soviet Union, the Soviet government, in addition to orders given earlier for the cessation of further work on the construction sites for the deployment of weapons, has issued a new order for the dismantling of the weapons which you call offensive, for them to be packed up and sent back to the Soviet Union.

The letter was full of pathetic propaganda, such as: 'Our people are contented with the fruits of their peaceful toil. They have achieved huge successes since the October revolution, created the greatest material, spiritual and cultural treasures.'[107] Even as the seconds were ticking away, ideological rhetoric had to have its place.

The Kremlin had retreated. Years later, Khrushchev would tell himself that he had scored 'a great victory ... we had been able to extract from Kennedy a promise that neither America nor any of her allies would invade Cuba.'[108] For the more hard-headed Gromyko, the gain for the Soviets had been a promise from the Americans to remove their rockets from Turkey.[109]

There followed Castro's anger at having been sidelined and not even informed in advance of the Soviet climbdown; detailed discussions on the withdrawal of Soviet forces; the dismantling and destruction of the launchpads; and the humiliating inspection by the US of ships carrying the missiles back to the USSR.

General Ivanov was receiving a stream of cables which no one even dreamed of showing Khrushchev. For instance, from the master of the motor-ship *Volgoles*:

At 08.00 on 9 November, American destroyer No. 878 was following in our wake. It approached to within thirty metres of our port side, lay a parallel course and suggested we remove the tarpaulins from the missiles on the port side of our forward deck. The tarpaulins were removed completely at their request, after which the destroyer asked us to partly remove the tarpaulins from five missiles on the after-deck. At 08.25 the destroyer crossed to the starboard side, looked at the partially exposed missile-heads on the starboard side of the after-deck, then asked us to take the tarpaulin completely off a missile on the starboard side of the forward deck, which we did. The missile markings on the hermetic covers had been preliminarily sealed on the missiles on the forward deck, the missile stabilizers had been concealed by personnel [standing in front of them] during visual inspection and photographing from the destroyer. Throughout all this, an American plane, LR 143176, circled low over the ship. The visual inspection was finished at 09.25, the destroyer raised the 'Thank you' flag and called over the loudhailer in Russian: 'I wish you a safe return to your Motherland.' The destroyer then lay a course in our wake and accompanied us until we altered course away from Cuban shores. The crew of the motor-ship *Volgoles*, both during the culmination of the Cuban crisis and throughout the voyage, was engaged on carrying out ship's duties, looking after the ship and upholding the honour of the Soviet sailor.[110]

In the end, both Khrushchev and Kennedy had shown common sense and agreed to avoid the worst. Those two weeks of October 1962 have gone down in history as one of the climaxes of the confrontation between two different worlds. Perhaps the crisis enhanced the world's awareness of the fragility of life in the nuclear age and the priority of human values over ideological myths.

In October 1964, however, when Khrushchev was removed as First Secretary, the report given at the Central Committee plenum on his activities stated: 'In one of his speeches, Comrade Khrushchev declared that if the USA touched Cuba we would launch a strike against it. He insisted that our missiles be sent to Cuba. This provoked the most serious crisis, bringing the world to the brink of nuclear war; the organizer of this most dangerous venture himself was greatly alarmed. Having no other way out, we were forced to accept all the demands and conditions dictated by the USA, right down to the humiliating inspection of our ships by the Americans.'

Of course, the order to send missiles to Cuba had been signed by every member of the Presidium, but it was Khrushchev's idea and his authority, and therefore his 'comrades-in-arms' thought it only proper that he should be the one to drink the cup of shame.

Following the Cuban crisis, there was growing, if muted, discontent with Khrushchev among the rest of the Presidium, in top military circles and among orthodox Communists. Jokes circulated about his ignorance, the new slums he had built – dubbed *khrushchoby*, a pun on the word for slums, *trushchoby* – his great maize campaign, his promise to overtake America, the three medals of Hero of Soviet Labour he had awarded himself, his hydroponics programme, his humiliating withdrawal from Cuba, and much, much more. It is normal for a leader to be feared or cursed or criticized, but when he is laughed at and made the butt of jokes, his time is up. After the sinister giants Lenin and Stalin, it seems that in the end Khrushchev was somehow too lightweight a figure for the public, an insufficiently standard leader. As a reformer he was not understood, while many were simply not willing to forgive him for exposing the personality cult.

For two more years after Cuba, Khrushchev tried to speed up the rate of reform, but the engine failed to start. He knew that change in society was needed, but he tried to effect it using old Bolshevik methods, though his comrades saw his acts as a dramatic departure from Marxism-Leninism. He was completely isolated, even though he dwelt within a huge crowd of 'Leninists'.

The Defeat of the Reformer

With the exceptions of Khrushchev and Gorbachev, all seven leaders of the USSR remained in office until death carried them off – Lenin, helpless and reduced to a virtually infantile state; Stalin, his mind clouded; Brezhnev, who came to resemble a stuffed dummy; Andropov, wired up for months on end to an artificial kidney; Chernenko, who lost the capacity to put two words together coherently. Not one of them was prepared to vacate the seat of power voluntarily.

Khrushchev was the first exception, ousted by a Party conspiracy, forced into retirement, but not exiled, shot or flung into gaol – a tribute to his own condemnation of such methods in 1956. Although in October 1964 his colleagues stabbed him in the back, at least outwardly they made a show of democratic decorum.

The first attempt to get rid of him had taken place in 1957. The old Stalinists in the Presidium had watched in growing alarm and fury as Khrushchev took hold. Above all, they could not forgive his attack on Stalin. They had all been advanced by the Stalinist system and, to a greater or lesser extent, implicated in the bloody purges, and they had also become used to the regime as it was.

In the summer of 1957 Molotov, Malenkov and Kaganovich held secret meetings with Voroshilov, Bulganin, Pervukhin and Saburov to discuss ways of removing Khrushchev from power. When the routine Presidium meeting opened on 18 June, Molotov and then Malenkov interrupted normal business by tabling a motion to remove Khrushchev as First Secretary. They accused him of ignoring the Presidium, of economic illiteracy and a tendency to commit impulsive and ill-planned acts.

A fierce argument ensued, with insults and recriminations flung back and forth. Khrushchev was supported by Kirilenko, Mikoyan, Suslov and the non-voting members. Molotov eventually succeeded in getting a vote taken, with the result that his motion was passed by seven to four. Khrushchev then announced: 'I do not accept this decision. I was appointed by a Central Committee plenum and only a plenum can remove me. Let us convene a plenum.' Molotov objected: 'We were also appointed by a plenum, but we have the right to take decisions about changes in the leadership in the name of the plenum.'

The session went on the next day. Molotov now proposed that the post of First Secretary itself be abolished. After all, he argued, between March and August 1953 there had been neither a General Secretary nor a First Secretary. The arguments continued through 19, 20 and 21 June. During all this time no minutes were taken.

Meanwhile, the Chairman of the KGB, General A. Serov, who was close to Khrushchev and a hardly less sinister figure than Beria himself, Frol Kozlov, the First Secretary of the Leningrad Regional Party Committee, and several other people in Moscow had informed the Party periphery about what was happening. Senior Party members soon converged on Moscow. At the behest of Molotov and Malenkov, Bulganin, who was chairing the Presidium, met a group of Central Committee members whom Serov had brought to the Kremlin, and tried to convince them that 'the issue has been settled and there is no need to detain you.'

However, Zhukov and Serov, who together represented the basis of real power, demanded that the matter should be debated and settled by a plenary session of the Central Committee, as Khrushchev wanted. The conspirators felt compelled to accept, and at midday on 22 June an extraordinary plenum of the Central Committee opened. Uniquely, it lasted a whole week, from 22 to 29 June, and was attended by 121 members of the Central Committee, ninety-four non-voting members and fifty-one members of the Revising Commission. Of the more than two hundred participants who asked to speak, no fewer than sixty did so, most of them in support of Khrushchev, as they perceived that the resolution tabled by Molotov and his group would mean the restoration of the old order, a return to police rule.

The plenum opened with a sharp exchange between Khrushchev and Molotov on the rules of the meeting. Eventually, Suslov was given the floor. For one of the chief guardians of the purity of Marxism-Leninism, his was a rather disjointed statement, but it served to provide the key the plenum needed to proceed. Suslov laid great stress on the anti-Party activities of Molotov, Kaganovich and Malenkov, while praising Khrushchev for 'the vast, intensive, original work' he had done as First Secretary.[111]

The plenum demanded an explanation from Molotov and the other 'factionalists'. The sessions resembled an oriental bazaar, with speakers being constantly interrupted, hooting and heckling coming from all sides, questions being hurled and murderous judgements heaped on the 'anti-Party group'. The minutes show that Malenkov was interrupted 117 times, Kaganovich 112, and Molotov – the only veteran of 1917 left in the leadership – 244 times. Only Molotov remained true to his conservative, pro-Stalinist position, while the others gradually caved in, retreated, repented and confessed to the sin of factionalism.

It was especially difficult for the opposition to answer the sort of question put to them by Zhukov, who asked why Molotov was silent about certain facts: 'Between 27 February 1937 and 12 November 1938 the NKVD received approval from Stalin, Molotov and Kaganovich for the Military Collegium and Supreme Court to sentence to death by shooting 38,697 people. On one day, 12 November 1938, Stalin and Molotov sanctioned the execution of 3,167 people. On 21 November 1938 the NKVD received approval from Stalin and Molotov to shoot 229 people, including twenty-three members and candidate members of the Central Committee, twenty-two members of the Party Control Commission, twelve regional Party secretaries, twenty-one People's Commissars, 136 commissariat officials, fifteen military personnel . . .'[112]

All too aware of his own past, Khrushchev tried to keep his head down when the purges were being discussed, though he did make occasional remarks. To one of these Malenkov jibed: 'Of course, you are utterly pure, Comrade Khrushchev!' The hall rang with abuse when the opposition tried to speak: 'Horrors . . . Executioners . . . Lies . . . Don't try to blame it all on the deceased [Stalin] . . . Don't pretend . . . What a repulsive speech . . . Shame!'

The opposition found it difficult to conceal their sympathy for Stalin and Stalinism, and for the old days, when they had held the lives of millions in their hands and were not responsible for the consequences. Occasionally, they let slip something that typified them better than any forced confessions or atonement. Kaganovich declared: 'In October 1955, four months before the [Twentieth] Congress, Khrushchev introduced a proposal on Stalin. Five months before the Congress Khrushchev himself spoke of Lenin and Stalin as the great leaders who had secured our victory. Just five months before the Congress! We spoke of the teaching of Marx-Engels-Lenin-Stalin, we said that Stalin was the great continuer of Lenin's cause. All of a sudden there's a question over Stalin. Not everyone can accept it that easily. Some take it one way, others a different way. I took it very painfully. I loved Stalin and there was something to love, he was a great Marxist.'[113]

Khrushchev could say nothing in reply to this tirade, except to mutter quietly: 'That's not a true statement.'

What Kaganovich's speech made clear, even if implicitly, was that the opposition was not fighting Khrushchev because of his campaigns, or his reform of industrial management, or constant reorganization; it was fighting to restore, at least partially, the old Stalinist order of things.

The long plenum ended with the condemnation of the Stalinist orthodoxy, and the expulsion from the Presidium of Molotov, Malenkov and Kaganovich, as well as Shepilov, who had gone over to them in the confrontation. Five non-voting members were rewarded for their support by promotion to full membership. The 'anti-Party group' remained formally in the Party and were given new jobs in the provinces, but not for long. Khrushchev was not one to forgive and forget, and gradually they were all put out to grass on their pensions.

Deputy Prime Minister Novikov recalled an incident in 1960, when Khrushchev was leaving for Paris and the Presidium had accompanied him to the airport. Gathered in the government lounge at Vnukovo, they heard Khrushchev briefly describe what he intended saying to the French leaders. This seemed like the new style, with the Party leader actually consulting his colleagues. When he had finished, he asked for comments, apparently confident of support. And indeed everyone began voicing their approval and praising his ideas.

Central Committee Secretary A. Aristov, however, stroked his cheek and, as if speaking his thoughts aloud, said: 'You might perhaps think about saying something, you know, a bit more interesting?'

Khrushchev puffed himself up, grew red in the face and angrily asked: 'Well, what, what, what?'

Aristov had nothing to say, except to mumble, 'Perhaps, perhaps . . .'

When Khrushchev got back from France, as he came down the aircraft steps he looked for Aristov and shouted out: 'Well, Aristov, did I behave well there?'

As one, the members of the Presidium who had come to greet him called back: 'Of course, Nikita Sergeevich, everything was fine.' Aristov also loudly welcomed the boss back, but a month later he was relieved of his post and later sent as ambassador to Poland.[114]

The number of men in Khrushchev's entourage who were becoming disillusioned and disgruntled with him was growing. They included Brezhnev, Podgorny, Ignatov, Suslov, Ustinov, Semichastny and Shelepin, while other senior figures barely disguised their discontent. They naturally blamed Khrushchev for a series of economic failures, as they did not understand that a shift away from the bureaucratic, totalitarian system was only possible if deep changes were made. No one then had any doubts about the 'socialist path of development'. Probably Khrushchev himself did not realize that the Communist monolith was not susceptible to reform. Even so, he had done the virtually impossible: as a fledgling from Stalin's nest, he had undergone a visible change in himself and in a fundamental way also changed society. However much his successor, Brezhnev, may have sympathized with aspects of Stalinism, he could not bring himself to restore it: the obstacles placed in the way by Khrushchev proved insurmountable. This was the one great historical service performed by the otherwise failed reformer.

In early October 1964 Khrushchev went to Pitsunda for two weeks' holiday. He did not follow the normal routine of Party leaders and do nothing, but continued to work as usual, receiving officials, ministers and foreign guests, and closely following the progress of a three-man Soviet space flight. He was as full of energy and new ideas as ever. With him was Anastas Mikoyan, probably his closest associate.

Khrushchev's son-in-law, the journalist Alexei Adzhubei, has written that Khrushchev 'knew that a particular senior comrade, who was travelling around the regions, was saying outright that Khrushchev must be removed. As he was leaving for Pitsunda, the First Secretary had told Podgorny, who was accompanying him: "Find out from Ignatov what he's chattering about. What are all these intrigues? When I get back we'll have to get to the bottom of it." It was not in his nature to take seriously the conversations of Ignatov, the Chairman of the Presidium of the Supreme Soviet, still less to believe that Ignatov had initiated them himself.'[115]

A new Party conspiracy had formed. With Khrushchev in Pitsunda, members of the Presidium were in Brezhnev's office discussing the details. They agreed that, above all, they must act in strict unison; there must be no 'separate opinions'. They only just managed to persuade Brezhnev to telephone Pitsunda and ask Khrushchev to come to a meeting of the Presidium, ostensibly to discuss issues which could not be settled without him. Several times Brezhnev picked up the receiver and then hung up without making the call. The others egged him on. His heart was not in it; he knew that he was becoming the ringleader, and that the plot was extremely improper. How would it all turn out?

Eventually Khrushchev was contacted. Suslov spoke first, and then Khrushchev heard the shaky voice of Brezhnev. He snapped: 'What's all the rush? I'll get back and we'll sort things out.' Then he added on reflection: 'Okay, I'll think about it.'

Next morning, 13 October, he was back in Moscow. At the airport he was met only by V. Semichastny, the Chairman of the KGB, and the head of security, Chekalov.

'Where are the others?'

'Nikita Sergeevich,' Semichastny replied, 'they're in the Kremlin.'

Khrushchev realized at once that the Presidium had launched a new attack on him. What he did not know was that, while he was in the air on his way back to Moscow the day before, Brezhnev had chaired a meeting of all the members and candidate members of the Presidium, together with a large number of Central Committee secretaries. The agenda had been brief, covering no more than a page and a half: to discuss certain questions on the new Five-Year Plan with N.S. Khrushchev's participation; to depute Brezhnev, Kosygin, Suslov and Podgorny to talk to Khrushchev and transmit the agenda to him in Pitsunda. The meeting had also decided to recall from the provinces a note Khrushchev had circulated on 18 July 1964 'with its confused regulations on "the management of agriculture in the context of changing over to intensification" ',[116] and which had proposed introducing even more cumbersome management agencies than already existed.

Khrushchev went straight from the airport to the meeting. No minutes were taken. It had been agreed by the plotters that each and every member of the Presidium would say his piece. Great emphasis was laid on the way Khrushchev had ignored the collective leadership and ruled by himself, on his unpredictability and numerous mistakes. Much of what was said was true. As previously agreed, every speech unequivocally called for Khrushchev's removal. Mikoyan, who was the sole member present to speak in his favour, proposed that he be asked to step down as First Secretary, but retain the post of head of government. There was an outburst of opposition to this suggestion.

Khrushchev at first interrupted every speaker and tried to halt the direction in which the discussion was going. But he was shocked by the stone wall of hostility that faced him. To begin with he thought that, as in 1957, he would manage the situation. He tried to protest, he objected and counter-attacked, but his voice sounded muffled in the icy silence. The whole scene had been pre-ordained.

But the drama was not over. Khrushchev refused to resign, and the meeting ended without result. He got into his car in silence and left for his dacha. Semichastny had made prior arrangements to change Khrushchev's security team entirely, and had instructed his agencies to obey no orders or instructions from Khrushchev without first obtaining the Presidium's approval. Although he still retained the formal title of First Secretary, in reality the levers of power had been taken from his grasp. He was isolated and broken, betrayed by those who had once fawned on him most enthusiastically – Brezhnev, Suslov, Podgorny, followed by the rest of them.

Next morning, when he arrived for the continuation of the session, Khrushchev was faced with a letter of resignation already prepared by the Central Committee organization, in which he asked to be relieved of his posts as First Secretary, as a member of the Presidium and as Chairman of the Council of Ministers 'for reasons of health'. The document also had him 'promise the Central Committee to devote the rest of my life and strength to work for the good of the Party, the Soviet people, and the construction of Communism'.[117] He signed it at once. Brezhnev and the others could not hide their elation.

Another resolution was passed unanimously – Khrushchev did not vote – which stated that he had 'begun to operate out of control of the Central Committee, and ceased to take account of the opinion of members of the Presidium. In view of the emerging negative qualities in his work, his advanced age and worsening health, Comrade Khrushchev is not able to correct the mistakes he has made or the un-Party-like methods he has employed in his work,' and therefore it had been agreed 'to satisfy Comrade Khrushchev's request to be relieved of his responsibilities'.[118]

Khrushchev sat with his head in his hands. He then got up and left in silence. No one accompanied him. His Party career was suddenly over. For almost two decades his name would barely be mentioned.

Opening the Central Committee plenum next day, 14 October, Brezhnev declared: 'the situation in the Presidium had become abnormal, and the fault for this lay above all with Comrade Khrushchev, who had embarked on a path that transgressed the Leninist principles of collective leadership of the life of the Party and the country, highlighting his own personality cult.'[119]

The main report was given by Suslov, the Party's official inquisitor. Chief eulogist of the status quo, a schemer and an orthodox Marxist, he had steadily risen in the Central Committee to become its most feared member. His speech was a full-scale demolition job:

> Khrushchev systematically engaged in intrigues and did everything he could to cause disagreement between the members of the Presidium [cries of 'Disgraceful!']. But such intrigue cannot continue for long. And in the end all the members of the Presidium realized that Comrade Khrushchev was playing an unworthy game ... Stubbornly, for a year Comrade Khrushchev regrettably tried to disband the Timiryazev Academy on the sole grounds that the majority of its scientists did not share his views on a number of questions of the agricultural system [cries of 'Shame!']. We should add, for the sake of accuracy, that Comrade Khrushchev did not raise the question of disbanding the academy, but he did propose examining the question of moving it out of Moscow to some agricultural region or other.

Suslov took the opportunity to target Khrushchev's son-in-law Alexei Adzhubei, declaring that 'the Presidium has also had to take steps to render harmless the free and easy and irresponsible gossip of this cabaret performer.' His announcement that Adzhubei had been removed as editor of *Izvestiya* was greeted with applause.[120]

Brezhnev was duly appointed First Secretary to the ritual standing ovation, while Khrushchev paced up and down in the state dacha that had once been inhabited by Molotov, until Mikoyan arrived to tell him what had transpired at the meeting. 'They asked me to tell you that this dacha and the apartment in town are yours for life.' Brezhnev had personally written a memo giving Khrushchev an annual pension of five hundred roubles, and permission to continue to have access to the Kremlin restaurant, the 4th Directorate Clinic and his dacha, and offering him a Moscow apartment and a car. There was no need for Brezhnev to write down the fact that Khrushchev's every step would henceforth be watched by the special services, who would report regularly on when he left the dacha or visited the village, drove to Moscow (a rare occurrence), and who came to see him.

Having listened gloomily to Mikoyan's report, Khrushchev snapped, 'I'm willing to live wherever they tell me to.'[121] In 1965 he would be moved to another villa at Petrovo-Dalnee on the River Istra.

The disgraced leader took his forced retirement badly. He sat for long periods on a seat in the woods or wandered up and down the paths around the villa. His restless nature made him eager to find an outlet for his energy, and he began growing tomatoes, took up photography, tried using hydroponics, drove occasionally to Moscow to see a play or exhibition. He also began reading a great deal, and late in life discovered the delights of Tolstoy, Leskov and Turgenev.

As his wife Nina recalled, one day in August 1966 he suddenly announced over breakfast that he was going to write his memoirs. It is possible that one of the reasons for this decision was that he had been reading the large number of memoirs then being published by military men, politicians and cultural figures – it was the season of reminiscences. The sluice-gates of memory had been opened by the Twentieth Congress, and although the propaganda department of the Central Committee scrutinized everything, making sure there was no criticism of Stalin, or mention of the purges and much, much else, many people who felt they had something to say were not deterred. Yet in the memoirs of dozens of people he had personally known well, Khrushchev could find almost no mention of himself. It was as if the Party censor had ordained that he must evaporate from history, disappear from his contemporaries' view, hide from the world forever behind the fence of his dacha. He would not accept that.

And so he sat down to write his memoirs, though 'write' is not quite the precise term. As he had been accustomed to do during his working life, he would dictate what he had to say. A tape-recorder was obtained, and he would talk into it in a low voice either outside the house or in the kitchen. His wife started transcribing the tapes, but then his son Sergei took over and gave them to a professional typist of his acquaintance.

It is obvious from his behaviour that Khrushchev assumed the dacha was bugged, and also that he was aware that he had embarked on an activity that would get him into hot water were it discovered. Did he intend submitting the finished manuscript to a Soviet publisher? Was it to be kept in a drawer for posterity? Did he envisage a time when it would be publishable in Russia?

The fact that Khrushchev was writing his memoirs was soon made known to the Politburo (the old name was restored in 1966), and he was summoned for a 'chat' with Brezhnev. This turned out to be a painful experience, but Khrushchev refused to stop. The matter was discussed again by the Politburo. The minutes of a March 1970 meeting record that Kapitonov and Andropov were to talk to Khrushchev 'in accordance with the exchange of opinions at the Politburo meeting'.[122]

The meeting took place, and on 25 March Andropov reported in a special note to the Central Committee that 'the memoirs contain detailed information consisting of exclusively Party and state secrets . . . even a partial leak of such information could cause our country serious damage . . . Khrushchev is using his son, Sergei Khrushchev, to get the tapes transcribed and edited. We do not know where the tapes are being processed and, all things considered, it is being carefully concealed by N.S. Khrushchev and his son . . . Meetings Sergei Khrushchev has had with foreigners are a matter of concern.'

It is not clear from the report whether the KGB had obtained a copy of the tapes or the transcripts, or had merely been informed of the nature of their contents.

Andropov went on to say that warnings given to Khrushchev by the Central Committee 'have not had the desired effect', and he proposed that 'secret operational surveillance' of Khrushchev and his son be established 'in order to obtain more accurate facts . . . and to forestall any undesirable consequences'.[123]

The meeting had been hard on Khrushchev, and shortly after it he had a heart attack. The Politburo, meanwhile, was not reassured. On Suslov's orders, Khrushchev was again summoned 'for a chat' on 10 November 1970, this time at the Party Control Commission. The minutes of this meeting are extensive and detailed. The chairman,

Arvid Pelshe, launched straight into the attack by declaring that a book entitled *Khrushchev Remembers* was about to be published in America, and he wanted to know how this had come about. Did Khrushchev understand that he bore full responsibility?

The former leader was confused. He genuinely did not know how his manuscripts had got to the West. He could not think it was Sergei's doing, but perhaps it was? There had also been a copy-editor and a typist, both possible channels. He announced: 'I have never given any memoirs to anyone, and never would allow it to happen. As for the fact that I dictated [my memoirs], I regard it as the right of every citizen and Party member. I remember precisely what I dictated. There's too much to publish in the given time.'

Khrushchev was given a long grilling. He was threatened and warned of possible consequences, and told of the harm he was doing to the USSR. Finally, he exploded: 'Please, arrest me, shoot me. I'm fed up with life. When people ask me, I tell them I'm not happy to be alive. Today the radio reported the death of de Gaulle. I envy him. I was an honest man, I was devoted. From the moment the Party was born I was doing Party work.'

It was a long, jumbled, painful conversation. In the course of it Khrushchev referred to the late Ignatov as a 'little idiot'; he asked for the death penalty; expressed his indignation that monuments were being put up to commemorate some old Bolsheviks of the 1930s, whom he called enemies of the people; he declared that 'it wasn't the Americans who started the war in Korea, but Kim Il-sung,' and so on. After this emotional outburst, he reiterated that 'everything I dictated is the truth. I made nothing up, there is nothing forced, on the contrary, there is moderation. I thought I would be invited to write. After all, they published Zhukov's memoirs ... I can't read what Zhukov has written about Stalin. Zhukov is an honest man, a military man, but he's a madcap.'

The members of the Control Commission constantly interrupted him, confusing him with questions and repeated threats about his special responsibility. At the end of the interview, Khrushchev was forced to sign a prepared statement:

According to press reports in the United States of America and some other capitalist countries, the so-called memoirs of N.S. Khrushchev are now ready for publication. They are a fabrication and I am indignant. I have never given any memoirs or materials of a memoir nature to anyone, neither to *Time* nor any other foreign publication. Nor have I given such materials to any Soviet publishing houses, either. I therefore declare that all this is a fabrication. The venal bourgeois press has repeatedly been found guilty of such lies.

The distraught old man then appended a scrawled and uneven signature.[124]

When Khrushchev left the meeting he was clutching his heart, and indeed the result of this 'chat' was another heart attack. He stopped dictating. When he felt better, he heard on a Voice of America broadcast that his book had been published. How it had got to the West he purported not to understand.

In fact, the pressure being exerted by his former comrades-in-arms led Khrushchev to make an agreement with an American publisher by which he and his son Sergei would entrust some of the tapes and transcripts, on condition that they would not be published until he gave the go-ahead. Khrushchev then suffered his second heart attack, and Sergei, who had come under mounting KGB pressure to hand over the materials, felt the time was ripe for the book's publication in the West. It began appearing in serial form, under the title *Khrushchev Remembers*.[125]

The book, which is some six hundred pages long, had been through the hands of many editors and copy-editors, who were concerned to ensure that the end product had a clear political line. Its weakness is perhaps the lack of documentation, but it would have been unusual for someone in Khrushchev's position to be allowed to keep even harmless official papers in his private possession after leaving office. The chapter titles and commentaries were also evidently not produced by the author. Nonetheless, *Khrushchev Remembers* reveals Khrushchev's character as a bold and impulsive politician, and as both an orthodox Marxist and a heretic, and it is among the best works on the period.

Even if Khrushchev had had access to his official papers, there are many he would have wanted to shield from the light of day. For instance, at the Twentieth Congress he made a point of blaming Stalin for the catastrophe at Kharkov in May 1942, yet on 17 May 1942 he had reported to Stalin that 'the offensive on Kharkov is going well', that huge quantities of booty had been captured, 'three hundred built-up areas liberated, four hundred [enemy] tanks destroyed, and 147 aircraft shot down'.[126] The report contained no mention of halting the offensive which had so far cost the Red Army 240,000 men.

Other documents which are not referred to in *Khrushchev Remembers* include his report to Stalin of 21 November 1943 on the situation in recently liberated Kiev. Here he reported the mass murder of Soviet citizens by the Nazis in a ravine at Babi Yar, though he made no mention of the fact that they were Jews.[127] On 16 February 1946, as First Secretary of the Ukrainian Communist Party, he requested Stalin's permission to retain garrisons of Soviet troops in Western Ukraine 'in order to finish off for good the Ukrainian nationalists and bandit groups'.[128] On 17 January 1948, still in Ukraine, he complained to Stalin that 'many collective farmers don't want to join in socially useful labour, but they engage in thievery, produce moonshine and work only their own plots. In 1946, 86,676 collective farmers did not perform one single unit of labour [for the collective].' The solution he proposed was that 'a law should be passed giving the right for the general [village] meeting to sentence the most dangerous anti-social and criminal elements to deportation out of the republic.'[129] Whether Stalin thought that the millions who had already been deported were enough, or that the local Party and punitive agencies could be relied on to 're-educate' the Ukrainian peasants, he did not approve Khrushchev's proposal.

The Politburo's zeal in pursuing him over his memoirs hastened Khrushchev's demise. He sank into himself, gave up photography, abandoned his tomatoes, and read much less. He would sit for hours in the sun, immersed in sad reminiscence. He could see that his successors had practically given up the reforms and were turning the country into a state with placid, tried and tested bureaucratic forms of government. A slow restoration of the past was taking place, if without its bloody excesses. And meanwhile, he was melting away in obscurity. Since he had descended from the Kremlin heights, no senior official ever came to him for advice, and the only contact he had with the leadership was over his memoirs.

In September 1971 Khrushchev was visiting his daughter when he felt unwell. He returned to his dacha, but his family took him to the hospital almost at once, where on the next day, 11 September, he died peacefully.

On 13 September *Pravda* printed his name again for the first time in seven years, in a brief report drained of colour by the Party apparatus: 'The Central committee of the CPSU and the Council of Ministers of the USSR announce with regret that at the age of seventy-eight on 11 September 1971 after a long illness the former First Secretary of the Central Committee of the CPSU and pensioner, Nikita Sergeevich Khrushchev, died.' And nothing more.

4

The Fourth Leader: Leonid Brezhnev

On 16 October 1964, Soviet radio announced the appointment of
Leonid Brezhnev as the new leader. It had taken a coup to get rid of
Khrushchev, but Brezhnev was by nature a mild, indecisive man. He
would not allow the press to demolish his predecessor, as he was being
urged to do by local Party meetings. Above all, he wanted peace and
quiet, serenity and an absence of conflict. Taking part in the removal
of Khrushchev was perhaps the most 'heroic' deed of his life. According to Yu. Aksyutin, when at the beginning of October the plotters
got wind that Khrushchev knew something was up, Brezhnev collapsed
with fear. When he had recovered sufficiently he telephoned his friend
Nikolai Yegorychev, who came round right away.

He was greeted by a white-faced Brezhnev, who hissed in a stage
whisper: 'Kolya, we're finished. Khrushchev knows everything.'

'So what?' Yegorychev replied. 'We've done nothing illegal. Preparing for a Central Committee plenum doesn't contravene the Statute.'

'You don't know him. He'll have the lot of us shot!'

'But there's nothing in our behaviour that is un-Party-like. These
are different times, not Stalinist.'[1]

After Khrushchev had unexpectedly given in without a struggle, it
took Brezhnev some time to absorb it all. He telephoned the leaders
of the 'fraternal countries', thanked his comrades and organized a
feast for his close friends. When he was sure that Khrushchev was
quietly out to grass at his dacha, he personally responded to the former
leader's requests for certain favours, scrawling out a list:

1. Pension 5,000 (500 in new money)
2. Kremlin dining-room

3. 4th Main Directorate Clinic
4. Dacha at Petrovo-Dalnee (Istra)
5. A town apartment of his choice
6. A car

He gave oral instructions that the car should not be a new one, and when Khrushchev asked for his previous supplement for dietary food in the restaurant to be kept at a hundred roubles, Brezhnev would only allow him seventy.[2]

It had not been clear to the leadership that by appointing Brezhnev they were promoting an anti-reformist line. This first emerged in Brezhnev's attitude to Stalin and Stalinism. He knew that a frank return to the old regime was out of the question – not that he was politically capable of bringing it about, anyway – but he was not against preserving or bringing back some elements of it.

The (ungrammatical) notes Brezhnev made during Khrushchev's speech at the Twentieth Congress are indicative of this: 'The report is unbalanced. It's a wrong definition and incorrect approach showing the consequences of the cult of personality – and therefore the material has been selected to show how the cult of personality came about and its harm – yet everything about Stalin that used to be preached and talked about was positive.'[3] Brezhnev's sympathy for the old order obviously outweighed his concern for a more 'balanced' approach to Stalin.

An opportunity eventually arose for him to show his feelings more clearly. On 17 December 1969, a few days before the ninetieth anniversary of Stalin's birth, by which time Brezhnev had made himself General Secretary, a session of the Politburo took place. One question was on the agenda: should *Pravda* publish a laudatory article on Stalin that had been written for the occasion? Of the twenty-two members of the Politburo, only two, Podgorny and Kirilenko, came out against publication. This was unexpected, as neither of them was noted for holding reformist views. Podgorny was alarmed at the thought that they would 'have to say who died and how many died at [Stalin's] hands. This article will bring nothing but harm.' As for Kirilenko, he thought 'there is no party in Europe that would applaud such an article.' The rest were in favour, many of them categorically.

Suslov declared that 'the country is waiting for just such an article.'

Mazurov even suggested that a bust be placed on Stalin's grave, and this was done in due course. Shelepin, Andropov, Solomentsev, Kapitonov, Kunaev and Shcherbitsky were decisively for publication. There was even some debate about giving Volgograd back its previous name of Stalingrad. It was said that Stalin had 'some positive sides, which no one could contest', and that one could not 'ignore the construction of socialism under Stalin'.

When Brezhnev came to sum up the debate, true to his philosophy of life he tried to view the subject from his favourite angle: would the article promote the preservation of peace and quiet in the land, or not? 'Frankly,' he declared, 'at first I took a negative position ... I based myself on the fact that everything is quiet at present, everyone has calmed down, there's nothing to get people worked up as there once was. But, then, talking to regional Party secretaries, and having thought more about it, and then hearing your speeches, I think that after all there really would be more good in publishing the article. After all, no one would contest or has contested his revolutionary services. We should give them the article without fanfare.'[4]

The process of reversing the de-Stalinization had begun, although it would remain far from complete. The cult of personality, the arrests and illegalities of the Stalinist period were put under a Party taboo, as the country was led from the reformist era of Khrushchev to the conservative era of Brezhnev, which also embraced the rule of Andropov and Chernenko.

Of the seven leaders, Brezhnev's personality was the least complex. He was a man of one dimension, with the psychology of a middle-ranking Party functionary, vain, wary and conventional. He was afraid of sharp turns, terrified of reform, but was capable of twisting the Party line in whatever direction the hierarchy desired.

Exceptionally among the seven leaders, apart from Lenin, Brezhnev left behind a large quantity of his working and personal papers, dating from 1944. For most of that time, his notebooks, exercise books, desk diaries and odd bits of paper consisted of a hotchpotch of scrawled, illiterate jottings, many of them incomprehensible. They became more systematic in his last fifteen years, but were still for the most part of scant significance, often recording little more than his weight, how long he had spent in the swimming pool, whom he had telephoned, what he'd had for dinner, what medal he had just been given, his medical regimen, his bag at hunting, and so on. Yet the decrees and resolutions Brezhnev wrote on Party and state papers were precise, unambiguous and to the point (unlike those of Mikhail Gorbachev, for example). However paradoxical it may seem, Brezhnev, for all his intellectual mediocrity, was very much of a piece. He was able to please everyone, unaware perhaps that whoever tries to please everyone will end up pleasing no one.

Some time in the late 1970s, after a routine conversation with me, General A. Yepishev, my boss in the Political Directorate, suddenly got up, opened his safe and removed a thick file labelled 'Personal Dossier of Lieutenant-General Brezhnev'. Without saying a word – he knew that all officials of his rank were bugged – he leafed through the papers in the file, then pointed to a line in a questionnaire where the word 'Russian' had been entered. He turned to a similar page further on, where in answer to the same question the word 'Ukrainian' had been entered. He looked at me significantly, as if asking: 'So, who is he?' Naturally, I was not in a position to answer.

Going through Brezhnev's Party dossier now, I note that during the war, Brezhnev entered 'Ukrainian' as his nationality in a Party registration document. When he was promoted to major-general he was still describing himself as a Ukrainian, and the same appears in dozens of other documents. In the internal passport, or identity paper, issued to him in Zaporozhie on 11 June 1947, his nationality is again given as 'Ukrainian'.[5] Once he had entered the top echelons of the CPSU, however, on all the forms he completed, and in all his biographies, he is described as 'Russian'.

The USSR, like the Russian empire before it, was a huge ethnic melting-pot in which dozens of nationalities blended. As in Lenin's case, there would be no point in dwelling on Brezhnev's national origin if he himself had not altered it in this mysterious way. What led him to change himself from a Ukrainian to a Russian? Perhaps it was a matter of no importance to him? On the other hand, like Khrushchev, Brezhnev made no secret of the fact that Ukraine meant a lot to him, and he was drawn back there, even after becoming established in Moscow. He wrote to Malenkov in May 1953:

> In connection with the reorganization of the Main Political Directorate of the Armed Forces, I should like to ask a big favour of you, Georgy

Maximilianovich. For almost thirty years of my working life I have been involved in working in the national economy. [And] since 1936 in soviet and Party work. I love my work, for me it is a second life. Now that I am approaching fifty, and my health has been damaged by two serious illnesses (a myocardial infarct and endoteritis of the legs), it is hard for me to change the character of my work or learn a new speciality. I would ask you, Georgy Maximilianovich, to send me to work in the Ukrainian Party organization. If there have been any inadequacies or errors in my work, I ask you to forgive me.

Malenkov noted, 'Khrushchev has seen this.'[6]

Brezhnev was not sent to Ukraine, but instead became deputy chief of the Main Political Directorate. Khrushchev must have thought that he would be more useful doing a job in Moscow. Brezhnev would never admit publicly that Khrushchev had appointed him Second Secretary of the Kazakhstan Communist Party in February 1954, arranged his promotion to First Secretary, and then in 1956 brought him back to Moscow as a candidate member of the Presidium, where he became a close comrade-in-arms of his boss.

Under Brezhnev, terms like 'class approach', 'intransigence towards imperialism' and 'the inevitable triumph of Communism' became current once again. Once again the army, the KGB and the military-industrial complex could breathe freely. Again those whose thinking could be described as 'un-Soviet' were hunted down, and the conservative spirit returned to dominate all the most important spheres of life. Having given his complete verbal support to Khrushchev's reformism, Brezhnev turned out to be his very antithesis.

The Way Up

Until 1938 the young Brezhnev was something of a rolling stone, constantly changing his place of work and residence. Apparently he did not find himself until he landed a job in the Party. As the meticulous Party clerks recorded in his dossier, in 1921 he started work at a Kursk oil mill, then in 1923 he became a trainee metalworker in Kamensk. In 1927 he completed a course on land administration at Kursk Technical School, in 1927–28 he was in Sverdlovsk as deputy to the Party's Regional Land Administrator, and in 1929–30 he was

Deputy Chairman of the Sverdlovsk Regional Executive Committee. He spent a year at the Kalinin Agricultural Machinery Institute in Moscow in 1930–31, when he moved to Dneprodzerzhinsk in Ukraine to become Chairman of the Union Committee at the Arsenichev Institute, then Secretary of its Party Committee. From 1933 to 1935 he was head of a metallurgical technical school, then he completed a correspondence course in metallurgy at Kamensk. In 1935 he worked as a shift-boss in a power plant, also taking a course at Chita Tank School in Eastern Siberia and becoming Political Commissar of 14th Mechanized Corps in the Far East. In 1936–37 he was back in Ukraine as head of the Dneprodzerzhinsk Metallurgical Technical School, and in 1937 was made deputy head of the town soviet. In 1938 he became manager of the trade department of the Dnepropetrovsk Regional Party Committee of the Ukrainian Communist Party.[7] He had finally made it into a 'proper' Party job, and, as he put it, his 'second life' began. It was the height of the purges, when the Party's ranks were being decimated at every level.

Such were those terrible times: while some were being swept into the camps, others were catapulted into their empty seats. Brezhnev was among the fortunate. Indeed, he led a charmed life. He reached Regional Party Committee level thanks to the patronage of his boss in the town committee, K. Grushevoi; he had survived a Party check-up in 1934 and was never arrested, nor did he ever come under suspicion. He came through the war without a scratch, was picked out by Stalin in 1952 and entered the Presidium, and although he was removed from it in a short-lived 'housekeeping' clean-up after Stalin died, he remained ensconced among the faceless functionaries of the senior hierarchy, and was reinstated to the Presidium four years later. Life also favoured the elegant, handsome man with the thick eyebrows because he was possessed of a benevolent character: he was obliging, ready to compromise, sociable and not spiteful.

By the eve of the war he was a member of the Party élite on the national republic level, promoted by Grushevoi to run the propaganda section in Dnepropetrovsk and then made secretary in charge of defence production. It seemed that he was set for a typical Party career which might, if he was lucky, lead to the Central Committee of the Ukrainian Communist Party, and even a job in Kiev. He did not dream that he might reach Moscow. The war changed everything.

Brezhnev began as Deputy Chief of the Political Directorate of the Southern Front. His part in the war is described in his own forty-eight-page pamphlet *Malaya Zemlya*, which despite its size was always described as a 'book', and which was actually written by Arkady Sakhnin, commissioned by Konstantin Chernenko, Leonid Zamyatin and Vitali Ignatenko. It begins with the words: 'I did not keep diaries during the war.'[8] In fact, at the end of the war Brezhnev had written what might be called diaries. In a notebook headed '1944' there are many diary-like entries, such as: 'The deputy chief of 2nd Air Division should be pulled up before the Party for looting and expelled from the Party'; 'Talked with Comrade Mekhlis who agreed to withdraw Communists from the blocking units.'[9]

Brezhnev was not only a reluctant writer, he also found reading a chore. Gromyko recalls a time when they were together in a sanatorium outside Moscow: 'I recommended a book on the life of Leonardo da Vinci and even brought it to him. But a week later he gave it back and said, "I haven't read the book. Actually, I've got out of the habit of reading altogether." '[10] When he received notes, reports or cables from abroad, he generally got someone else – often his assistant Galina Doroshina – to read them aloud to him, while he reclined in an armchair and listened, or dozed.

Brezhnev spent most of the war as head of 18th Army's political section. He gained no particular distinction. There is, it is true, an episode in *Malaya Zemlya* when he personally manned a machine-gun and fired at the attacking Germans: 'Only one thought possessed my being: to stop them.'[11] There were, unfortunately, no eye-witnesses to this heroic feat.

At the end of the war, having been promoted to major-general and collected four decorations, Brezhnev was appointed chief of the Political Directorate of the 4th Ukrainian Front, which was soon after turned into Pre-Carpathian Military District.

A matter of special pride was his having taken part in the great Victory Parade on Red Square on 24 June 1945. Much later, as General Secretary, in his delegate's questionnaire at a Moscow Military District conference, he wrote in answer to the question what military training he had had, 'at the front'. For the rest of his life, his favourite reminiscences were of the war. To his credit, Brezhnev did not forget his comrades of those days, and helped many of them.

After the war, Brezhnev's fortunes rose rapidly: in August 1946 he became First Secretary of the Zaporozhie Regional Party Committee (Obkom), and in November 1947 First Secretary of the Dnepropetrovsk Obkom. These posts were nominally elected, but in reality were appointments of the higher Party organs and plenums, which 'unanimously approved' nominations from above. Both these promotions emanated from Khrushchev.

In these years the Soviet Union was making titanic efforts to recover from the effects of the war, and the situation was exacerbated by the confrontation between the Communist and capitalist worlds that emerged at the same time. The regime felt alone again. The army was still vast, and patriotic feeling did not subside with the end of the war. By means of dictatorial methods, harsh orders from the centre and the constant vigilance of the security organs, the people were made to do the impossible. Brezhnev was a middle-ranking Party functionary whose job was to carry out the Kremlin's will.

Eye-witness testimony suggests that Brezhnev got his way not by harsh and peremptory rule and threats, but by goodwill and patience. He did not particularly interfere in the work of his subordinates, and instead relied on practice tested by time. We speak of 'late Brezhnev' as lazy and vain and something of a magnate in style; the 'early Brezhnev', on the other hand, was sincere and able in his handling of people.

In July 1950 he was suddenly called to the Central Committee building on Staraya Square in Moscow, where he was informed that Secretary Khrushchev was recommending him as First Secretary of the Moldavian Party. The economic potential of the Moldavian Republic was probably three or four times less than the region of Dnepropetrovsk, but the top Party leader in any republic significantly outweighed a regional Party Secretary. Without hesitation, Brezhnev accepted the job, especially when he was told that 'Comrade Stalin knows about Comrade Khrushchev's proposal and approves it.'

The Moldavian Soviet Republic came into being in 1940, when the Soviet Union recovered territory it had lost in 1918. In sending Brezhnev to Moldavia, the leadership – in particular Malenkov and Khrushchev – gave him clearly to understand that his task was to bring about collectivization as quickly as possible, and to eradicate the influence of the Romanian middle class. Brezhnev nodded and made some notes, but mentally he was already on the Dniester, and wondering which of his team to take with him from Dnepropetrovsk. It had become commonplace that when a provincial boss was transferred to another location, he would take his favourite assistants with him. In Brezhnev's case the practice was especially marked. When I was working in the Political Directorate I saw a report – later removed from his personal dossier – by Brezhnev's Regimental Political Commissar, Verkhorubov, dated 1942, which stated that he 'avoids dirty work. Comrade Brezhnev's military knowledge is extremely poor. He deals with many questions like an economic planner, not a political worker. He is not even-handed in his dealings with people, and tends to have favourites.'

During his early years in Moldavia, Brezhnev tackled agriculture and industry with energy, not forgetting ideology. In the autumn of 1950, mindful of the Central Committee's orders, he told a meeting of District Party Secretaries: 'The further organizational and economic strengthening of the collective farms requires still greater determined struggle against the remnants of the kulaks and bourgeois nationalists by improving the work of our [security] organs. We must arouse still greater hatred among the toilers for the people's worst enemies, the kulaks and bourgeois nationalists.'[12]

As for everyone else, so for Brezhnev the sole authority was Stalin. Speaking in December 1950 at a meeting of women's Party sections, he declared: 'Comrade Stalin is recommending the enlargement of collective farms. The collective farmers know that, as long as Comrade Stalin is recommending it, it must be important and useful.'[13]

In a speech to the Third Congress of the Moldavian Party, Brezhnev laid special emphasis on ideological affairs. Mocking the dogmatism of some functionaries, he gave an example of the editor of the district newspaper, one Novak, who was asked to explain the meaning of Lenin's masterpiece *What is to be Done?* 'And this is what Novak told his readers: "Lenin had read Chernyshevsky's book *What is to be Done?* and wrote his own book *What is to be Done?* But it is not Chernyshevsky's *What is to be Done?*, it is a different, Leninist *What is to be Done?* Its importance is as a fundamental, organizing, leading [book]. Other books by Lenin are also leading, but this one is especially leading."'[14]

Brezhnev's own definitions of high-quality work were hardly more sophisticated than those of the unfortunate Comrade Novak. He told his audience: 'Comrade Stalin says: here is a piece of wood, we remove the bark, then we make it into a board, thin it down and paint it with lacquer. Look at the number of operations we've done! But to make sure a living person can lead and not make mistakes far more work is needed. Especially in the kind of work we do.'[15]

This was the level of 'ideological' education given to Party executives. They learned to think in dogmatic, mechanical categories, predigested from 'leading' sources, such as the works of Lenin and the 'founding fathers', and dished out by local and regional leaders of the Stalinist mould, such as Brezhnev and thousands like him.

A major milestone in Brezhnev's life and career was the Nineteenth Party Congress of October 1952, the first to take place for thirteen years and the last one attended by Stalin. Brezhnev was told that he would be making a speech as First Secretary of the Moldavian Party, and on 5 October he sent in a draft that had been worked on long and hard by the Kishinev propaganda department. It was duly re-edited and polished up at Staraya Square, and returned to the author.

Brezhnev's speech, which he gave on the fourth day, was much like all the others: it contained a eulogy of Stalin, an account of local achievements, then more panegyrics of Stalin. But it seems that Stalin noticed Brezhnev. At the organizational plenum of the Central Committee, when proposing names for the Presidium, Stalin unexpectedly mentioned his name as someone he would like to recommend as a Secretary of the Central Committee and candidate for membership of the Presidium. Brezhnev was shaken. To enter the Central Committee of the CPSU, the 'headquarters of the Leninist-Stalinist Party', was far more than he could ever have expected.

However, five months later Stalin was dead, and his old comrades-in-arms reduced the size of the Presidium by more than half. Brezhnev had barely had time to find his feet in Moscow when events took this unpleasant turn. But, as we know, Brezhnev was lucky. He spent another year and a half in the Political Directorate, but made sure that the Central Committee did not forget his existence. He made no secret of his wish to return to a job in the Party organization of one of the republics. As First Secretary in Moldavia he had had a taste of the very real power and privileges enjoyed by such people. In the top job in the provinces, one did not have to jump to Moscow's every instruction, supply a plan for the harvest and all the other things the centre ordered. When Brezhnev became General Secretary, and the boot, so to speak, was on the other foot, he would continue the old Stalinist tradition of racking up quotas. His papers contain a typical example from 1973: 'On 12 August I spoke on the phone to Bonda-renko from Rostov. He said 270 million puds [4.4 million tonnes]. After our conversation he promised to stretch to 300 million. I spoke to Masherov. He said 60 million. He'll give 70 million puds.'[16]

The power of the First Secretary of a region or republic was almost absolute. As long as he submitted his plan, showed himself willing to respond to new initiatives from Moscow, and could present a report that made his territory look like a success, his life would be untroubled.

As it happens, I worked for a time in the same office at the Main Political Directorate which was Lieutenant-General Brezhnev's in 1953–54. His adjutant, Lieutenant-Colonel Sergei Mezentsev, was still working there. He told me, in a quiet voice, that his old boss had been bored to distraction by the work. After the morning mail had been brought in he would frown and growl: 'Again lessons, meetings, puttees . . . What a bore!' According to Mezentsev, Brezhnev spent a lot of time on the special internal phone talking to his friends on the Central Committee, asking them to put in a word for him 'up above' about getting him into 'a proper job'.

The head of the service, Colonel-General Zheltov, told me in the 1980s that his report on Brezhnev to the Central Committee all those years ago had mentioned among his subordinate's shortcomings a lack of initiative and effort. That particular document vanished from Brezhnev's dossier, but he never forgot the slight, and several efforts to promote Zheltov to army general sank without trace in the labyrin-thine corridors of the Central Committee.

Brezhnev waited. Zheltov, even though he did not like his lazy deputy, went easy on him. He was after all a Central Committee Secretary, and might suddenly be called to higher things again. As indeed he was. In January 1954 he was summoned to the Kremlin, where he was seen first by Malenkov and then by Khrushchev. They offered him the job of Second Secretary of the Party Central Commit-tee in Kazakhstan. 'You will be in charge,' Khrushchev told him, 'of state affairs for the further development of the virgin lands.' Brezhnev accepted without demur, even though his agreement was not asked for.

The mass cultivation of virgin land, a special interest of Khrushchev's, was at its height when the new boss arrived in Alma-Ata. The Presidium was expecting 10–15 million hectares of new land to have been cultivated within two years, and believed that this would solve the country's grain problem. The idea, according to a pamphlet signed by Brezhnev but written for him by Alexander Murzin, was to plough an area greater than the size of England.[17]

Brezhnev remained in Kazakhstan for only two years before being brought back to Moscow by Khrushchev. Indeed, virtually every one of his promotions, starting after the war and continuing until 1960, when he became Chairman of the Presidium of the Supreme Soviet (i.e. formal head of state), a post he would relinquish in 1964 to concentrate on his work in the Central Committee, was initiated by Khrushchev, who saw a loyal supporter in his protégé. In February 1956 Brezhnev was promoted to candidate membership of the Presidium and made a Central Committee Secretary. He was now firmly ensconced in the Party's 'staff headquarters', and would remain so until his dying day.

Even at this time, many politicians and economic managers, on meeting Brezhnev, would wonder how a man of such mediocre abilities and limited outlook could have reached such heights. Suave and handsome he may have been, but he had very little education. His papers are spattered with spelling mistakes. If he departed from his text, his speeches became simply wretched. It is almost impossible to find an interesting, let alone original, idea anywhere in his writings.

Yet Brezhnev kept rising higher and higher through the hierarchy. The fact is that in politics, the promotion of an obvious mediocrity may result from the need of opposing sides to exploit his weaknesses. He may be seen as transitional (as Brezhnev was at the beginning), and useful to bridge a gap between stronger personalities, in other words as a puppet. Indeed, at the end of his life, when he was being officially lauded while countless jokes about him were circulating, Brezhnev appeared very much like a puppet, twisted around the fingers of more influential members of the Politburo like Ustinov, Chernenko, Grishin, Tikhonov and Gromyko, much as they wished.

The higher Brezhnev climbed towards the summit of power, the more plainly it seemed to be slipping from his grasp. And the reason it did not was that his closest associates, Andropov, the head of the

KGB, and Chernenko, Brezhnev's chief of staff, also had it in their grip. The totalitarian system showed that it could function even without a personal dictator.

From Stability to Stagnation

Brezhnev must have realized that his intellectual mediocrity would be compensated for by the system, that the Party apparatus, which was vast, experienced and influential, would take on itself many of the functions that were the responsibility of the highest officials. Whatever the question, the relevant section of the Central Committee would prepare the appropriate documentation, draft a resolution, submit analytical arguments, texts of speeches to be made, and guidance. Party functionaries played an enormous role, as the preparation of decisions invariably took place in a department of the Central Committee. An idea originating from elsewhere would always meet with suspicion and be allowed to go further only after the strictest scrutiny by the 'experts'.

In effect, all the General Secretaries after Stalin were voluntary prisoners of the almighty apparatus. Not even Gorbachev could free himself of its tenacious grip. It was during Brezhnev's rule that the machine approached its apogee, although it only reached it when Chernenko, the supreme personification of the Party clerk, got his hands on the wheel. The power of the apparatus made puppets of the General Secretaries, with the result that the country approached the future at a slower and slower rate.

When the Politburo discussed an issue, the final act was always planned down to the last detail, roles were allocated and the scenario carefully scripted. On several occasions it was my job to write the speeches for a succession of Defence Ministers – Grechko, Ustinov and Sokolov – who were members of the Politburo. As a rule there would be no dissent from the prepared decree, which they would all have been informed of beforehand. Even the General Secretary, who might not agree with a certain point in the decree, would usually toe the line. On 27 December 1973, when the work of the Politburo and Secretariat was being debated at the Politburo, Brezhnev declared: 'I sign some decrees, for instance, even though I do not agree with

Lenin in Moscow, 1918.

Above right: Lenin at the Military-Revolutionary Committee, discussing the seizure of power, October 1917.

Right: In conversation with H.G. Wells, 1920.

Below: At the funeral of Lenin's brother-in-law, Mark Yelizarov, 1919. His sister Anna stands beside the grave.

Left: Stalin – 'The Lenin of today'.

Right: Khrushchev, wearing a peasant shirt, harangues a meeting in the countryside in the 1950s.

Far right: Khrushchev shows off the fruits of his maize campaign at the Enbekesh Pioneer Camp in Kazakhstan, 1961.

Below right: Fidel Castro enjoys the Georgian horn of plenty with his host, Khrushchev, in Abkhazia, 1963.

Below: Left to right: Mikoyan, Khrushchev, Stalin, Malenkov, Beria and Molotov on their way to a sports meeting in Moscow, 1945.

Below: Brezhnev before decrepitude.

Right: Brezhnev receiving the Order of Victory in 1976. Prime Minister Kosygin applauds.

Bottom: Flanked by his senescent comrades-in-arms, Brezhnev celebrates his birthday in 1978. Chernenko (centre) and Gorbachev (second from right) in line for succession.

Above right: Yuri Andropov.

Right: Andropov with his local host, Gorbachev, in Pyatigorsk, Stavropol region, 1974.

Below: Chernenko in his border guards uniform, 1930.

Right: Chernenko returning from rest and recuperation, 1984.

Bottom: The straw man meets the Iron Lady: Chernenko and Margaret Thatcher, 1984.

Chernenko's first, and last, appearance on the Mausoleum as General Secretary, 1984.

Stavropol Party Chief Gorbachev greets Prime Minister Kosygin, 1972.

Gorbachev relaxing with US President George Bush at Novo-Ogarevo, 1991.

The last General Secretary in reflective mood.

them. True, there have been very few of them. I do it because the majority of the Politburo voted in favour.'[18]

Whether at congresses, plenums, regional or district committees, everyone supported the Central Committee's 'general line'. Criticism and dissenting opinions were heard only on personal or economic issues. It was normal in the Brezhnev period to deal with Party or state problems in a quietly pacifying way, avoiding 'sudden movements' or upsetting the smooth passage of Party and social life. To a great extent, this occurred because many issues were dealt with only verbally, or by declaration. The decrepit members of Brezhnev's Politburo valued stability above all, an unchanging course and bland decisions. At the meeting of 27 December 1973, Brezhnev remarked, as an achievement of enormous importance: 'You and I, comrades, work in agreement, in the spirit of Lenin's precepts ... In our Party we have complete unity, there are no opposition groupings and it is easier for us to decide all issues.' He then lamented: 'the comradely collective of the Politburo has to do an enormous amount of work. Often, quite naturally, we get tired, we overload ourselves, but, comrades, it's all for the good of our country, all for the sake of serving our great Leninist Party, our people. Sometimes one just has to throw off the feeling of fatigue in order to deal with this or that problem.'[19]

In his speeches Brezhnev was inclined to stress that the country was stable, peaceful and in good condition. He visited the Central Committee Secretariat only rarely, and restricted his governing role to the Politburo. On one of his rare appearances at a session of the Secretariat, on 20 November 1972, he announced: 'In general, I am happy to say that everything is going all right, everyone is on the job working hard and fruitfully, in general and overall all tasks are being dealt with in time and correctly, and both routine and problematical issues are being resolved.'[20]

This remark, which tended to lull everyone into a state of acceptance and to dull the edge of any desire for real change, was typical of the Brezhnev period. Stability is undoubtedly a virtue, in economic and social life no less than in international relations, but the level and quality of the conditions on which that stability exists are equally important as indicators of progress. In the Soviet Union those indicators were far from showing a satisfactory state of affairs.

There were other factors which predetermined the condition of stability, above all the 'centrism' that emerged after the overthrow of Khrushchev, whose reforms had been rejected along with him, even if they were still mentioned as a formality. For instance, on 29 September 1965, a year after Khrushchev's removal, Brezhnev told a Central Committee plenum: 'In order to exploit all the possibilities of the socialist system of production, it is proposed that we adopt economic methods in directing the economy.' There was talk of material interest, raising labour efficiency and self-financing. But it was just talk. The old system of managing by means of directives and regulations from the Central Committee continued.

Despite the frank sympathy that many Politburo members felt for Stalinism, it was impossible to bring about a return to it. Khrushchev's revelations at the Twentieth Congress had forever cured a large part of society of nostalgia for the past, and whether the leadership liked it or not, something like a new path, between Khrushchev's reformism and the Stalinist dictatorship, was being laid. This centrism tried to preserve some of the momentum of the post-Stalin era, while making sure that no significant changes took place. And, just as continuing talk of reforms remained little more than talk, so the occasional, mild criticism of the notorious cult of personality was never permitted to explore the origins of the Stalinist form of socialism.

The period from the Soviet invasion of Czechoslovakia in 1968 to the intervention in Afghanistan in 1979 was the most peaceful time in Soviet history. Although this period came to be called a decade of 'stagnation', the importance of stability in those years should not be underestimated. The question to ask is, at what historic cost was this relative tranquillity bought?

One factor which reflected the condition of stability was the Soviet achievement of military and strategic parity with the United States. The long pursuit of the USA in the build-up of nuclear weapons and the development of rockets to deliver them culminated in the 1970s in an unstable military balance. The achievement of this military parity, however, cost the USSR so much that it threatened to degrade the already low general standard of living. The arms race strained the very sinews of the command economy, and brought closer the approaching crisis of the entire system.

Simultaneously, the two sides came to realize that any attempt to resolve their irreconcilable differences by nuclear means was tantamount to the destruction of the planet. In the USSR, as in the USA, the idea gained ground that political détente required military détente.

The peace programme approved by the Twenty-Fourth Party Congress in 1971 was not purely a propaganda exercise. In Washington in June 1973 Brezhnev and President Nixon signed a historic document aimed at preventing nuclear war between the two countries, and perhaps it was this that enabled Brezhnev to announce on US television: 'We are proud of having created a new society, a most stable and steadily developing society.'[21]

Brezhnev's personality also played a part in achieving military parity. In Khrushchev's time, the Politburo had given Brezhnev the job of keeping an eye on the military-industrial complex. His notes for 1958, chaotic and illegible though they are, include such items as: 'Establishing new design bureaux', 'Chalimei rockets (guided missiles)', 'Ustinov's tasks' (Ustinov was Defence Minister), 'New ships to be built', 'Flying targets'. The names of hundreds of defence specialists with whom he worked appear in his diaries. These entries are mixed up with such notes as, 'Zavidovo, elk,' 'Called NS [Khrushchev]. Ate together at 1,' 'Left at 4 to hunt with Yura,' 'Talked to NS about hunting.'[22]

In effect, society continued to be stable thanks to the momentum of the Khrushchev period, while the energy for the country's barely perceptible forward movement came from yet more campaigns, directives and resolutions of 'historic plenums'. At a Central Committee plenum on 27 November 1978, Brezhnev stressed some of the features for which his period of rule had become best known: 'Three years of the tenth Five-Year Plan are behind us. They were good years. A lot was done. A lot was altered for the better ... A number of material surpluses were created with effort. Some forms of resources are still in short supply ... The position on capital construction is improving slowly ... The position that has arisen in transport is not easy, especially on the railways ... The loss of grain, potatoes, vegetables and fruit is still significant.' He went on in this vein, enumerating all the sectors of the national economy. As for the reasons, again his assertions were muffled by his desire to present an emollient picture: 'The central economic agencies, ministries and departments are gradually effecting the shift of the entire economy onto the rails of intensive development. They have not managed to achieve the necessary improvement in the quality indicators of the work, nor the acceleration of scientific and technological progress.'[23]

It had long been clear that the Communist ship of state was becalmed, its sails sagging. Party rule in the centre and the periphery was characterized by the outward appearance of activity concealing internal passivity. Public apathy grew. Corruption flourished at every level, the higher, the worse. Deceit, lies and mendacious information became the rule. Brezhnev's entourage consisted of a court, with numerous favourites, intrigues and machinations, to which he, being a mild soul, tended to turn a blind eye, even when his own relations were involved in unseemly operations. His friends and intimates started to exert a major influence on the organizational side of Party life. His tendency to create favourites, noted at the beginning of the war by his chief in the Political Directorate, acquired grotesque proportions.

It also became clear to everyone that Brezhnev had no political will, no broad economic views, and no clear idea of real possibilities. Because the central structures were in a state of decay, something like a feudal system came into being in the local Party Committees in the republics and provinces. The First Secretary or Regional Party Secretary acquired virtually unlimited power in his own bailiwick, and this corrupted him, exacerbating the social pessimism, hypocrisy and mental dualism. People were saying one thing, but thinking and doing another.

Mental dualism had, of course, existed for a long time within Soviet society. Indeed, Brezhnev himself was not immune from it, as some of his desk diary entries for late 1959 show: 'A good meeting [with Khrushchev] at Luzhniki ... N.S.'s speech was very good.'[24] As it emerged later, in fact Brezhnev was harbouring extremely malevolent feelings towards Khrushchev. It seems he made these and other remarks in his desk diary in the certain expectation that his enthusiastic loyalty would be reported to Khrushchev. As we now know, monitoring telephone conversations between members of the Politburo and digging around in their personal papers were standard practices right up to 1990.

It might well have been dissatisfaction with the lack of change and the continuing extremely low standard of living that prompted an attempt on the life of the General Secretary in January 1969. A team of astronauts who had been orbiting the earth were being welcomed in Moscow. With them in the motorcade heading for the Kremlin was Brezhnev. At the Borovitsky Gate, Second Lieutenant Viktor Ivanovich Ilyin fired a revolver at the leading car, killing the driver. Brezhnev was in another car, and was unharmed.

It was decided that it would not be expedient to put Ilyin on trial, as the political repercussions might be undesirable. Two months later, although he had until then been regarded as perfectly sane, Ilyin was diagnosed as suffering from schizophrenia and condemned to spend the next eighteen years in a special psychiatric clinic in Kazan, and a further two years in Leningrad. He was released in 1990 as cured.

It seems that Brezhnev did not ascribe great significance to this event. Unlike Stalin, he did not suffer from persecution mania. Nevertheless, the 9th Main Directorate of the KGB, which was responsible for looking after Politburo members, tripled its efforts.

In the growing climate of bureaucratization and corruption, Brezhnev's most faithful supporters were to be found among the military. Marshal of the Soviet Union Dmitri Ustinov was a classic example. I attended many meetings at the Ministry of Defence under his chairmanship, and it was his invariable custom to open the proceedings with a panegyric on the General Secretary: 'I have just been talking with our dear and beloved Leonid Ilyich. He sends you all his greetings and wishes us great success.' No doubt he expected these words to find their way back to Brezhnev.

Flattery, toadying and protectionism were the norm under Brezhnev. His 'stable and peaceful society' harboured trends which would lead to the stagnation and ultimately the disintegration of the totalitarian state. It was not Gorbachev who originated *perestroika*. The sources of inevitable if indefinable change were woven into the very fabric of the socialist society. The Brezhnev era in effect created a bridgehead for the social and political convulsions that would lead to the dismemberment of the USSR.

Under Brezhnev's leadership the country exhausted the possibilities of the command economy, bureaucratic control was parodied by cries of 'Glory to the CPSU!', and the 'values' of Communism were eroded. Society was fast approaching the limits of 'socialist development'. Stagnation and the decay of the political foundations of 'developed

socialism' were evident in many trends. Above all, the forced repudi-
ation of the old repressive methods showed that the Party leadership
had no other effective means at its disposal to influence economic
growth, social stability or spiritual development. Yet the vast machine
of compulsion remained in place. Even if it could not be used as fully
as it had been in the 1930s and 1940s, the threat was still there. But
it no longer had the desired effect in the economy. Rates of growth
in many spheres of industry were zero. Agriculture was in a state of
terminal sickness. The Politburo regularly allocated hundreds of
tonnes of gold to buy food from the West for the vast country. More
and more goods were in short supply, causing still more corruption
and economic criminality.

The country was floundering, but Brezhnev and his Politburo
seemed not to want to notice. On 3 January 1980 Chernenko told his
colleagues that in the forty-seven sessions they had held during the
preceding year, they had examined 450 questions and passed more
than four thousand decrees. They had dealt with fourteen Party organizational issues, forty-six on ideology, 227 on defence, 159 on industry,
transport and capital construction, 1,845 on foreign policy and foreign
trade, eleven on economic planning, 330 on personnel, 927 on state
awards, and so on.

He stressed the fact that 'Central Committee plenums last year were
conducted in a spirit of complete unanimity,' prompting Andropov to
remark, 'That is an entirely proper conclusion. The plenums really
did proceed in complete unanimity,' and Pelshe to add, 'And their
decisions were also adopted unanimously.' And when Chernenko mentioned that fifty-one sessions of the Central Committee Secretariat
had taken place and that they had passed 1,327 regulations, Suslov
and Andropov together piped up, 'Like the Politburo, the Secretariat
also conducted its business in complete unanimity.'[25]

The country might be engaged in a war in Afghanistan, détente
might be a dead letter, and industry and agriculture might be on their
knees, while local Party barons got fatter and more powerful, but
the Politburo was unruffled. The Leninist tradition of 'maintaining
complete unanimity' was more important than economic statistics,
and so the lethargy continued.

The stagnation was particularly marked by inordinate efforts in the
military sphere. The achievement of strategic parity with the USA

was regarded as an event of historic importance, but less was said of the fact that American economic power was twice that of the Soviet Union, or that America was not making a special effort to increase its military capability. Washington assessed the position correctly: to win a duel, one does not need a dozen pistols, as long as one pistol is absolutely reliable. The USA exhausted the Soviet Union with the arms race which the Soviet leadership entered mindlessly. They ostensibly reached the target of strategic parity, but the cost determined the ultimate fate of the system.

In an open letter to Brezhnev in 1980, the Nobel Peace Prize-winner and nuclear physicist Andrei Sakharov wrote: 'The ruinous super-militarization of the country is getting worse (it is especially destructive in conditions of economic difficulty), vitally important reforms in the consumer economy and social spheres are not coming into being.'[26] Brezhnev did not even read the letter, but sent it on to Andropov, leaving it to the special services to deal with this awkward customer, who had already been exiled to Gorki (now Nizhni Novgorod). Like the rest of the Politburo, Brezhnev was deaf to such warnings.

Brezhnev had dealt with defence matters for some time even before becoming General Secretary, and he unwittingly came to believe that the military-industrial complex was a mirror-image of the country's economy as a whole. He could not grasp the significance of the fact that defence took the lion's share, and this led to a deepening of the economic crisis, the stagnation of the entire economy and, ultimately, the dramatic changes after 1985.

Against this background, outstanding scientific and technological advances were achieved in the military field. The KGB also became much stronger. Not only did it keep the spiritual and political life of the country under tight control, it also carried out Party policy abroad. For instance, in the summer of 1969 there was an explosion at Al-Aqsa mosque in Jerusalem, provoking great anger not only throughout the Muslim world, but also in Delhi. Andropov wrote to the Central Committee: 'The KGB residency in India has the opportunity to organize a protest demonstration of up to 20,000 Muslims in front of the US embassy in India. The cost of the demonstration would be 5,000 rupees and would be covered in the 1969–1971 budget allocated by the Central Committee for special tasks in India. I request consideration.' Brezhnev wrote 'Agreed' on the document.[27] The Politburo was not only the superior organ of the Party, it also governed the KGB, a state body.

It was also during the Brezhnev period that the dissident social movement gained momentum. Intellectual and moral protest against police persecution of unorthodox thinking and freedom of expression were symptomatic of the deepening decay of the Communist system. Sinyavsky, Daniel, Bukovsky, Rostropovich, Solzhenitsyn, Sakharov and Grigorenko were among the brave few who published books and articles, made speeches and led protests which highlighted the humanitarian, legal and social decline of the Leninist regime. They were put in prison, incarcerated in psychiatric hospitals, sent into internal exile or deported abroad.

For decades the people had been forced to stay silent. The period of the 'thaw' following the death of Stalin and the Twentieth Congress had proved short-lived. In accordance with well-established Leninist practice, the Central Committee combated un-Communist ideas wherever they arose, working through the security organs. The KGB regularly sent its proposals and reports to Party headquarters. On 15 November 1976, for instance, Andropov sent a note on 'The hostile activity of the so-called "group for facilitating the Helsinki accords with the USSR".' The note stated that this organization was attempting with Western help to create the appearance of an 'internal opposition'. Of ten names cited by Andropov as members of the group, the nationality of seven was given as Jewish, with two Ukrainians and a Russian, making it apparent that the venture could be discredited by depicting it as both anti-Soviet and anti-Russian, and by appealing to the latent anti-Semitic sentiments of the country and the Party leadership.[28]

The leadership approved the measures proposed by the KGB 'to compromise and curtail the hostile activity of the participants in the group', and circulated appropriate instructions to Party committees and Soviet overseas agencies. On 19 May 1977, Brezhnev signed a twenty-page document entitled 'Instructions to Soviet Ambassadors in Connection with the Stir in the West over the Question of Human Rights', calling for them to make clear that 'the anti-Soviet campaign under the false mask of defending human rights' was pursuing the goal of 'distracting the popular masses of the capitalist countries from the serious difficulties being faced by bourgeois society. It should be stated that the revolution, carried out sixty years ago in Russia, was carried out precisely in order to guarantee in reality the basic rights and liberties of the individual, and that only in the USSR have human rights and liberties been realized in the fullest sense and with the greatest consistency.'[29]

Czechoslovakia, Afghanistan

The outwardly serene years of Brezhnev's rule were interrupted by two violent international events, one at the beginning and one at the end of his leadership. The first was the crushing of the 'Prague Spring' in 1968, and the second the armed intervention in Afghanistan in 1979. In addition, in August 1980 the Politburo set measures in motion to 'give military assistance' to Poland.

Although by virtue of his position Brezhnev was at the very heart of events, he himself did not initiate these actions, but rather carried out the will of the hawks in the Politburo and the almighty KGB. He may have looked like the undisputed ruler of the great empire, but he was in reality more like the chief puppet of the totalitarian system, a role he carried out to perfection.

Against a background of a number of internal and external factors, the atmosphere in Czechoslovakia began to undergo a marked change in 1967. People started talking about the consequences of Stalinism for the country and its future, and the press and television began airing ideas about the need for democracy and political pluralism, and for relations with the USSR to be on an equal footing. Czechoslovak Communist leaders came forward with demands for democratic reform. To their great misfortune, the 'Prague Spring' coincided with the upsurge of conservative trends in the USSR. Khrushchev's departure had meant more than a change of leader: it led to a major alteration in the direction of Communist orthodoxy.

As usual, the Soviet leaders based their judgement of events at home and abroad mainly on information fed to them by the KGB. The Central Committee was receiving constant reports from Prague via the Lubyanka about 'the activation of revisionist forces' in Czechoslovakia, the 'counter-revolutionary tendencies' of Czech Communist leaders Dubček, Černik, Pelikan, Šik, Smrkovsky and others, 'the

Czech Party's loss of control over the mass media', 'US and NATO interference', and so on. This was perhaps the only way the Soviet special services could interpret such unfamiliar ideas as liberalization and democratization, the appeal to human values, the demand for liberty and condemnation of the repression of the past. The Chekist spectacles worn by Soviet leaders since the time of Lenin had replaced the need for normal analysis of events and required instead a Comintern approach in assessing any political or ideological phenomenon.

As Zdenek Mlinarž, one of the leaders of the 'Prague Spring', has written: 'Dubček was not thinking of a split with Moscow.' He was bound to Moscow by too many links, Mlinarž went on, not only because he spent his childhood and youth in the USSR, but also because he genuinely believed in socialist ideals, though he wanted to remove from them the scab of Stalinism. He naïvely believed that one could make Communism democratic. His personal honesty and decency guaranteed him enormous authority in Czechoslovakia: 'In the period of the "Prague Spring", the people saw in Dubček a symbol of the great ideals of democratic socialism.'[30] In Moscow's eyes, however, Dubček was an opportunist, a revisionist putting his dark counter-revolutionary plans into effect.

When Dubček became the Czech Party leader in January 1968, Moscow applied the well-tried policy of combining its own pressure with that of its satellites. Brezhnev's diaries and notes contain numerous entries such as: 'Phoned Kádár [the Hungarian Party chief] to say he should talk again with Dubček', 'Zhivkov [Bulgaria] promised to put pressure on the Prague leadership', 'Gomulka [Poland] and Ulbricht [East Germany] are both concerned by the course of events in Czechoslovakia and will exert appropriate influence on Dubček and his friends.'

The Czechoslovak people's desire for liberty, independence and democracy was seen in the Kremlin as 'counter-revolution', 'opportunism' and 'an attempt to go over to the capitalist camp'. The 'Programme of the Czechoslovak Communist Party' and 'Two Thousand Words', which laid out the ideas of democratic socialism, were condemned by Moscow as counter-revolutionary platforms. Every step taken by Prague, every word uttered by Dubček or Smrkovsky was interpreted as yet another act of treachery to the socialist cause. At times the reaction from Brezhnev, Suslov, Shelest and other Soviet leaders was simply hysterical.

Although much that was said and done by Dubček and his colleagues made them attractive to the Czech intelligentsia and public opinion in the West, at no time did they repudiate socialism. They could not, however, ignore the widespread indignation at facts that were coming to light in the media about the treatment of well-known Czech figures in the past, including the mystery surrounding the death of the great post-war pre-Communist leader Jan Masaryk, which was being investigated by Czech television, with the finger pointing at the Soviet secret service.

The work of the Politburo throughout the first half of 1968 was dominated by events in Czechoslovakia, and it appears that the Soviet leaders thought of almost nothing else. The Politburo agreed that Brezhnev should be in constant telephone contact with Prague, and on 14 February, for example, just after having shot several wild boar while on a hunting trip, he called Dubček on his special car-phone.

Apart from personal pressure, the Soviet leadership raised the 'Czech question' at a session of the Political Consultative Committee of the Warsaw Pact, then at a meeting of East European leaders, and also in bilateral talks between the Politburo and the Czech Presidium on the border at Čierna-nad Tisou at the end of July 1968.

In June Brezhnev approved Warsaw Pact troop-training exercises, deploying sixteen thousand men, including Soviet units drawn from Hungary and Poland. His notebooks show that he was contemplating a military solution to the 'Czech problem' as early as April. Called 'Operation Tumour', it spoke of the need for Soviet Defence Minister Marshal A. Grechko to go to Prague, for Brezhnev himself to talk to Dubček again, and for the Soviet leaders to reconvene with the Czech leaders.

The escalation of events emerges from the Politburo minutes of 5 March:

BREZHNEV: Our reliance on Dubček has not been justified.
ANDROPOV: The situation is serious. It is reminiscent of the Hungarian events.

On 21 March Brezhnev spoke of the forthcoming meeting in Dresden, and on 25 March he reported its results: 'The disintegration of socialism is taking place in the CzSSR. They are talking of the need for freedom from the USSR.'

On 6 May the Politburo discussed the results of Brezhnev's meeting with Dubček. The Soviet leader gave his opinion: 'The party is headless.'

The Czech question was discussed again on 16 May, and on 23 May Marshal Grechko gave a gloomy report on his trip to Prague. Brezhnev summed up: 'The army has disintegrated. Liberalization and democratization are in essence counter-revolution.'

On 27 May Prime Minister Kosygin reported on his meetings with the Czech leadership in Prague. Brezhnev responded by asking Grechko: 'How is the preparation for the training exercise going?' Grechko replied: 'Forty responsible personnel are already in Prague. We're getting ready.'

On 6 June Brezhnev read out KGB ciphers, and measures that should be taken to put more pressure on the Czech leadership were discussed.

On 13 June Brezhnev reported on his conversation with Kádár, who was about to take a high-level delegation to Prague.

On 2 July Brezhnev announced that Dubček and Černik had finally gone over to revisionism. The Politburo debated whether Soviet troops in Czechoslovakia for the training exercise should be withdrawn. Grechko proposed that a strong force be placed on the border and held in full readiness.

The Politburo met again next day, 3 July, to discuss the 'counter-revolutionary essence of [the document] Two Thousand Words'. Brezhnev reported a conversation with Kádár, and instructions were issued on the use of mobile army radio stations for broadcasting into Czechoslovakia. Further meetings were held on 9, 19, 22, 26 and 27 July, 16, 21 and 27 August, and on each occasion one item was discussed: the situation in Czechoslovakia and the measures to be taken 'to curtail the counter-revolution'. Detailed unrecorded discussion took place on the preparation of massive armed intervention. Yet, strangely, there was no discussion of what the Warsaw Pact troops would actually do on entering the country. Was it thought that tanks would make the population think differently? Some members of the Poliburo thought that if there really was going to be 'armed international assistance', it would be better if the USSR were 'asked' to supply it. This idea was accepted, and within a couple of days 'reliable' people in Prague had been informed.

Some time in mid-July, a confidential letter addressed to Brezhnev came via KGB channels from Antonin Kapek, a candidate member of the Czechoslovak Presidium. It said, among other things: 'A group of leading party members in the Central Committee, consisting of Smrkovsky, Kriegel, Špaček, Šimon, Cisarž and Slavik, have seized all means of mass communication and are conducting anti-Soviet and anti-socialist activity.' The letter concluded: 'I appeal to you, Comrade Brezhnev, with a call and a request for fraternal assistance to our party and our people to repel the forces which . . . are creating a serious danger for the very future of socialism in the Czechoslovak Socialist Republic.'

Brezhnev read the letter to the Politburo and the general view was that, while it was serious, it was inadequate as a pretext for military intervention. A few days later, via the same channels, another letter arrived for Brezhnev, this time signed by five senior Czech figures and expressed in more decisive and compelling terms. Brezhnev gathered the members of the Politburo in his Kremlin office and read it to them, punctuating the reading with such remarks as: 'They've got themselves into this mess and now we have to get them out of it . . . What lousy Marxists . . .'

This important document, which remained locked up in the Party archives until 1992, spoke of the possibility of a 'counter-revolutionary revolt':

> In these difficult circumstances we ask you, Soviet Communists and leading representatives of the CPSU and the USSR, to give us your active support and assistance by all the means at your disposal. Only with your assistance can the CzSSR be torn away from the danger of counter-revolution. We recognize that for the CPSU and USSR this last step in defence of socialism in the CzSSR would not be easy . . . In view of the difficulty and danger of developing circumstances in our country, we request maximum secrecy for our statement and for that reason we are addressing it directly to you in person and in Russian.[31]

Brezhnev was seeing Grechko almost every day. It was agreed that when the troops were moved in the entire Czech leadership should be arrested and brought to Moscow. 'They'll talk differently once they're here. If they don't understand, we'll dictate what they're to do,' Brezhnev warned ominously.

'The army will paralyse the counter-revolution and prevent the "departure" of Czechoslovakia to the West,' Grechko replied cautiously, 'but the main role must be played by the politicians. It would be dangerous for us to appear as occupiers. They must "summon" us. And those who have made the counter-revolution must themselves correct the situation subsequently.'

Brezhnev, as always, agreed. Zero hour was approaching. On Suslov's orders, a hysterical campaign was launched in the Soviet press and on television, depicting the small country of Czechoslovakia as a deadly threat to the gigantic USSR. In a sense, this was true: the monolithic 'socialist commonwealth', which was to fall apart a quarter of a century later, might well have done so much earlier.

From the military point of view, Moscow carried out the operation smoothly. The landing force, tank columns, seizure of bridges, communication points and airfields, were all managed at lightning speed. There was no armed resistance. Czechs lined up in their thousands along the route and glowered or shouted at the 'allied' armoured columns. President Svoboda, seeing the futility of armed resistance, called on the people to exercise wisdom and restraint. The Soviet soldiers stopped their tanks and armoured vehicles on city squares, not sure of what to do next. The 'counter-revolutionaries' were not armed. All they had were posters and placards showing their discontent. Western 'advisers' were nowhere to be seen.

Brezhnev did not leave his office for several days, taking three or four hours a day to sleep soundly in a rest room. Contrary to the KGB's predictions, the Czechs did not come out in their masses to support the invasion of Soviet troops. The whole population stood behind Dubček.

Zdenek Mlinarž recalled: 'At some time after 4 a.m. on 21 August a black Volga from the Soviet embassy drew up at the Central Committee building, which was soon surrounded by armoured vehicles and tanks. Troops jumped out in their claret-coloured berets and striped vests, and carrying automatics . . . The doors of Dubček's office were thrown open and about a dozen machine-gunners rushed in and surrounded us, pointing their guns at the back of our necks. They were followed into the room by two officers. One of them was a colonel. Someone, I think it may have been Dubček, said something and the colonel roared: "No talking! Keep quiet! Don't talk in Czech!"[32]

The obstinate First Secretary and several other members of the Czech leadership were ordered out of their offices. To their confused and uncomprehending questions, they received the reply: 'This is being done in the interests of your safety.'

They were taken in closed vehicles to an airfield, where they were unceremoniously thrown into Soviet transport planes. Dubček, Špaček, Cisarž, Kriegel, Černik, Smrkovsky and others were now the prisoners of their almighty 'ally'. Dubček was a source of special irritation to his captors, who regarded him as a traitor. At his personal meetings with Brezhnev he had been affectionately called 'Sasha', but now, when he was thrown into the plane, he was struck in the back with a rifle butt and fell, banging his head.

The Soviet troops in Prague found themselves totally isolated. The few Czech quislings were afraid to raise their voices. Brezhnev was extremely anxious. According to Moscow's plan, 'healthy forces' were supposed to replace all the counter-revolutionaries in the Party leadership at once, form a new government, condemn the 'crimes' of the revisionists and try to effect a rapid return to Leninist-Stalinist socialism. But there was no sign of any support for the invaders.

The lights burned through the night in the Central Committee building in Moscow. The leadership had lost its head. President Svoboda arrived and demanded the release of Dubček and the others, otherwise, he said, he would have no choice but to kill himself in protest.

Sitting on a sofa next to the old general, whose war record he respected, Brezhnev kept repeating: 'Calm down, Ludwig Ivanovich. Everything will be all right ... It'll be all right ... All Dubček and Černik have to do to make it so, is just to condemn the counter-revolution.'

Finally, after endless consultation in Moscow and Prague, the KGB and Central Committee decided to start talks 'between delegations of the CPSU and CPCz'. Dubček and his comrades, in shock from the invasion, their capture and harsh treatment, were forced to agree. They were also persuaded by General Svoboda that they had no choice. They decided to compose an agreement in which they would seek compromise solutions. It consists of fifty closely-typed pages, and was signed on 28 August 1968.

The two sides sat opposite each other at a long table. The atmosphere was strained, and the talks difficult. Brezhnev and Dubček did all the talking, except that Černik opened for the Czech side, as Dubček was feeling unwell.

ČERNIK: Our country is now in a position in which it has not been since the war. We assess the position as critical and fraught with heavy bloodshed ... Allied forces of friendly countries have entered Czechoslovak territory without our knowledge. The Presidium did not ask for such assistance ... The actions of the governments of socialist countries, associated with the presence and withdrawal of allied forces from Czechoslovak territory, are of decisive importance.

DUBČEK: Throwing in the troops has dealt a strong blow to the thoughts and ideas of our party ... We regard the throwing in of troops as a mistake, a premature act that has brought and will bring great harm, not only to our party but to the entire Communist movement. The entry of five allied [i.e. Warsaw Pact] armies will create a source of tension within the party, within the country and outside it ... Bringing in troops has touched the soul of the Czechoslovak people and I do not know how we are going to get out of this difficult position.

BREZHNEV: What Comrade Černik has said here, and especially what Comrade Dubček has said, throws us far, far back. We were certainly not thinking about sending in troops when we were invited to the meeting in Dresden. [In fact, preparations for armed intervention were already under way.] You recall that we told you then that, if things were hard for you in the material sense, then our Party and our people are such that we can help our Czechoslovak brothers even to our own detriment. We have 13.5 million Communists and 240 million citizens, we can slice off 100 grammes of bread and cut down so much on meat, and no one will even notice it. You say you do not have a counter-revolution, but that there are anti-socialist elements. Do you call that honey? Are anti-socialist elements sugar to the working class?

The style of your work is quite impossible. Such a style can only help anti-socialist, counter-revolutionary forces to develop and become bold ... In Dresden we didn't advise you at all to put anyone in prison. But we did say that to relieve unsuitable people from their posts was the right of your party Central Committee. About Pelikan.

He's in charge of a television service that is bringing disgrace on the CPCz with his help. What is he doing in such a job?

Then we came to Sofia. There each of us in turn spoke with you personally. [Brezhnev addressed Dubček in the familiar form of *ty*.] Remember, I was sitting on a small divan and I said: 'Sasha, look around you, what is going on behind your back? We don't understand why the propaganda media are still not in your hands.' If I'm lying, call me a liar in front of everyone here.

DUBČEK: No, it was as you said.

BREZHNEV: I want to say something else about your carelessness, Alexander Stepanovich. Your style of working is based on personal authority. And that is very wrong ... You remember, I once sent you a letter of a personal kind, written by hand. You must still have it.

DUBČEK: I do.

BREZHNEV: I want to say something to all of you sitting here: every one of you who has accepted the development of counter-revolution in your country, who did nothing right up to the entry of the troops, bears personal responsibility. Who else is responsible for what has happened – surely, not us? Or are you going to be brave and say that you made a mistake? It was the most severe political mistake to reconcile yourselves to counter-revolutionary propaganda. If we had not sent in troops, Czechoslovakia would have taken the path of capitalist development. What you have said today is worse than before, because you want to put all the blame for what has happened on us.[33]

Brezhnev spoke for nearly an hour and a half. He said in so many words that Moscow had the right both to judge and be merciful, that it had 'legal' grounds for sending troops into a sovereign state, and that the Czech leadership must bear full responsibility for the situation. He was in effect exercising the self-appointed authority of the CPSU to carry out sentences on its 'younger brothers'.

Mlinarž recalled that the atmosphere at the table was incandescent: 'Brezhnev was genuinely indignant at the fact that Dubček had not merited his trust and had not agreed his every step with the Kremlin beforehand. "I believed you, I defended you against others," he reproached Dubček. "I said that our Sasha was a good comrade, after all. And you have let us all down!" At similar moments, Brezhnev's voice trembled with self-pity; stammering, he spoke with tears in his voice. He looked like an insulted tribal chief who thinks he is patently and uniquely correct, and that his position as head of the tribe rests on unquestioning submission and obedience, and that only his opinion and only his will ultimately count.'

There were hysterics and shouting and cries from the Czechs about 'peaceful co-existence'. Brezhnev swept them aside with: 'War isn't going to start over you. Comrades Tito and Ceausescu will make speeches, Comrade Berlinguer will make a speech. So what? You're counting on the Communist movement of Western Europe, but it hasn't bothered anyone for fifty years!' It was an eloquent admission.

After hours of talk, pressure and threats, the Czechoslovak delegation finally agreed to sign a protocol signalling the end of the democratic reforms in their country.

'Everything was ready by midnight,' Mlinarž recalled. 'The moment for signing had arrived. Suddenly the doors were flung open and into the hall burst a dozen photographers and cameramen. Then and there, as if under orders, the Soviet Politburo stood up and, leaning across the table, tried to embrace the members of the Czechoslovak delegation, who were still sitting down. One thought of the theatre of the absurd.'[34]

Moscow's interpretation of the role of the CPSU and the character of its allies' 'independence' was dubbed in the West 'the Brezhnev Doctrine'. However, Brezhnev was not the author of this concept. He was merely the megaphone. The doctrine itself was Leninist-Stalinist-Cominternist in origin, and the treatment of Czechoslovakia was intended as a warning to other satellites that their sovereignty was secondary to their 'international duty'.

Speaking at the Fifth Congress of the Polish United Workers' Party, i.e. the ruling Communists, in Warsaw on 12 November 1968, Brezhnev declared: 'It is well known that the Soviet Union has done much to really strengthen the sovereignty and independence of the socialist countries . . . It is also known, comrades, that there are general principles of socialist construction, and that a departure from them can lead to a departure from socialism itself . . . And when a threat arises to the cause of socialism in that country, and a threat to the security of the socialist commonwealth as a whole, then it becomes not only a problem for the people concerned, but a general problem and concern of all socialist countries.'[35]

In the 1977 'Brezhnev' Constitution, of which he was inordinately proud, claiming that it would last many decades, he included not only the notorious Article 6 on the CPSU as 'the leading and guiding force of Soviet society', but also the hypocritical Article 29, which read: 'Relations between the USSR and other states are founded on the basis of observing the principles of sovereign equality; mutual rejection of the use of force and the threat of force; inviolability of frontiers; territorial integrity of states; the peaceful settlement of disputes; non-interference in internal affairs; respect for human rights and the basic liberties; equality and the rights of peoples to manage their own affairs . . .'[36]

This was not the 'Brezhnev Doctrine', but the CPSU Doctrine. It expressed the deep continuity of Lenin's and Stalin's views of the nature of relations between the Party and its allies in the Communist brotherhood.

The Soviet leaders were masters at creating international problems – Poland, East Germany, Hungary, Czechoslovakia, China, Afghanistan – but they were less adept at solving them. This is what happened during Brezhnev's rule over Afghanistan, the USSR's southern neighbour, with which it had signed its first treaty of friendship and co-operation in 1921.

I was in Afghanistan several times before and after Soviet troops were sent in. The Kabul 'revolution' of 27 April 1978 was a typical palace coup. One squadron of aircraft, one tank battalion and a few hundred supporters of the Popular Democratic Party of Afghanistan, led by Noor Mohammed Taraki, seized the former royal palace, killing the President, the former dynastic prince Mohammed Daoud.

It has often been asserted that these events were as unexpected for Moscow as they were for Washington. Perhaps the White House was indeed surprised, but Soviet foreign intelligence had certainly informed the KGB and the Central Committee well in advance, although it took no part, beyond 'making recommendations', in the coup itself. Moscow's practised agents did no more than give oral advice and assurances that, in the event of a successful outcome, measures of support and Soviet recognition would follow.

A year later, on 17 June 1979, Brezhnev met US President Jimmy Carter for the signing of a strategic arms limitation treaty. After the official ceremonies and talks were over, and when the two men were alone together with their interpreters, Carter told Brezhnev that the US did not intend to allow armed intervention in Iran and Afghanistan, and was counting on the USSR to adopt the same approach.

Brezhnev was unprepared for this. He was used to reading out documents prepared for him by the Foreign Ministry and his aides, and he could not respond, except to say that Moscow hoped the USA would not facilitate attacks on the new regime in Kabul. It was as if he did not know that the leader of the Afghan 'revolution', Taraki, had declared on 30 April that his aim was 'to build socialism in Afghanistan', though he said at the same time that he intended entering the non-aligned movement.

In April 1979, as a member of a delegation, I visited Kabul and several other towns in Afghanistan, where I met Taraki and Foreign Minister Hafizullah Amin. Taraki gave the impression of being an ideological dreamer who had seen his utopian goal, but had no idea how to reach it. Amin, by contrast, had a clear idea of the 'revolution's' resources, but was less concerned about utopian goals. For him the highest virtue was power.

Noor Mohammed Taraki, gazing somewhere over our heads, quietly asserted that Afghanistan would become a socialist country, but that it would not happen quickly. 'We have practically no educated people,' he said. 'All our hopes rest on the army.' He paused. 'Among the officers we have many enemies and traitors, but the soldiers will follow us. But we have nothing with which to pay them. They are half-starved . . . We will ask the USSR to help. Tell Brezhnev he has now got another reliable ally.'

We met a group of young officers, many of whom had studied in the USSR. Most of them would perish in the slaughter of the civil war. Watching these revolutionary romantics, I was alarmed at the thought that my country was about to burden itself with new shackles, and had no chance of extricating itself with honour from this adventure. I listened in amazement when, after the official talks, the Afghans told General Yepishev that they could raise a rebellion among the Beluchis in Pakistan and thus acquire an outlet to the sea: 'That means you would have access, too. Just help us.'

Yepishev's only comment was: 'Don't talk about that. Your main task at the moment is to secure your regime.'

Their regime turned out to be very weak. By the summer of 1979, differences had erupted between Taraki and Amin. On 29 June the Politburo decided to send Central Committee Secretary Boris Ponomaryov to Kabul to 'stabilize' the situation and to hold talks with the Afghan leaders. The visit was preceded by a note to Brezhnev – formally addressed to the Central Committee – signed by members and candidate members of the Politburo Gromyko, Andropov, Ustinov and Ponomaryov, urging that the situation in Afghanistan could only be 'stabilized' by 'intensifying the struggle against counter-revolution and strengthening people-power'. They proposed increasing the number of Soviet military, 'special' and Party advisers in the country, sending a landing force of battalion size to Bagram airfield, disguised as aviation technicians, a special KGB unit of 125 to 150 men, and a special General Staff Intelligence (GRU) unit of around five hundred men.[37]

In Moscow in September, Taraki told Brezhnev of the danger to his regime being posed by Amin, and asked for Soviet troops to be sent to Afghanistan: 'Without them we cannot defend the Afghan revolution.' In Andropov's presence, Brezhnev told Taraki that they 'would take responsibility for Amin', but urged Taraki to try to 'normalize' relations in the leadership for the sake of the revolution.

While the KGB was trying to deal with Amin, Taraki decided to take matters into his own hands. Brezhnev soon received a report on what was happening in Kabul. Taraki had invited Amin, as his second in command, to his residence for a chat. Amin's supporters warned him that it was a trap, but the Soviet ambassador A. Puzanov, who was at Taraki's house, reassured Amin that he was under no threat. What happened then was related by the Afghan Foreign Minister, Shah Wali, to Gromyko in New York on 27 September 1979: 'When Amin arrived at Taraki's residence and began going up the stairs, with Central Committee member Tarun, his adjutant and security guards, Taraki's adjutant fired at Tarun, who was in front, killing him instantly. Other associates of Taraki then opened fire, seriously wounding Amin's adjutant, but missing Amin himself. It later emerged that Taraki's supporters were on the roof of the house when they opened fire on Amin's group, and that Amin had escaped by sheer luck.

GROMYKO: You think this was deliberately planned with the Soviet Ambassador there and not knowing about it?

SHAH WALI: What happened was that, when the Soviet Ambassador reassured Amin that he was not under any sort of threat, Amin went, but took his security guards with him.[38]

Taraki was arrested, and Amin became General Secretary of the Party, Chairman of the Revolutionary Council, Prime Minister and Defence Minister. On 9 October 1979 Kabul Radio made a brief announcement that Taraki and his wife had died suddenly. In fact, Taraki had been strangled on his prison bunk by Amin's henchmen.

Brezhnev was shocked and indignant. Not three weeks before, he had received Taraki with all due honour in his office, promised him help of all kinds, apart from troops – as yet – and now this treachery! Ambassador Puzanov and General I. Pavlovsky reported from Kabul that the leaders of the 'April revolution' were starting to devour each other.

Amin sent telegram after telegram to Moscow, asking to be received and promising to explain everything. It was Taraki, he wrote, who had started the civil strife. Fearing that his telegrams were not reaching the Kremlin, he handed a confidential letter for Brezhnev to Soviet adviser General V. Zaplatin, in which he swore complete loyalty to Moscow and again asked Brezhnev to see him. The Kremlin, however, had already decided to dispense with Amin and to replace him with a new puppet as 'head of the revolution', Babrak Karmal.

Reports from Soviet special services in Kabul were urging the leadership to send in Soviet troops. The generals who were pushing Brezhnev and Andropov into this policy were planning the physical removal of Amin, and they used a pretext he himself supplied.

The decision was taken by the Politburo on 6 December 1979 to accept a proposal by Andropov and Marshal N. Ogarkov (Chief of General Staff) to send a special General Staff Intelligence unit 'of about five thousand men in uniform, not hiding their membership of the armed forces', to 'defend Amin's residence'. 'As the question of despatching a unit to Kabul has been agreed with the Afghan side,' the proposal went on, 'we suppose it is possible to do so using aircraft of military transport aviation in the first ten days of the year. Comrade D.F. Ustinov is in agreement.'[39]

The decision to send Soviet troops to Afghanistan was taken some time at the end of November 1979. Its initiators were Brezhnev, Suslov, Andropov, Ustinov and Gromyko, it was formulated as a decree on 12 December, and signed on various dates between 12 and 26 December by Brezhnev, Andropov, Ustinov, Chernenko, Suslov, Grishin, Kirilenko, Pelshe, Gromyko, Tikhonov, Ponomaryov and Shcherbitsky.[40]

Soviet troops crossed the Afghan border on 27 December, sending a shock wave around the world. The day before, the special General Staff Intelligence unit, sent 'to protect Amin', had taken his palace by storm. I was in the palace myself a few days later and saw the blown-out windows, shell-pocked walls, smoke-stained ceilings, and dozens of spent cartridges on the floor. Amin, his family and everyone else in the palace – bodyguards, relations, servants – had been killed. During the attack, Amin had desperately tried to make contact with the Soviet embassy. On the expensive parquet there was a large stain, smeared by the boots of the soldiers. It was the blood of the unfortunate dictator who had proved unsatisfactory to his bosses in Moscow.

The attack had been short and savage, and carried out with high professional skill. New heroes were named, and medals were handed out. The Politburo decree of 27 December had asserted that, 'as a result of acts of external aggression and growing interference in Afghanistan's internal affairs, there is a threat to the gains of the April revolution.' The motive of 'international duty' had been used to disguise crude intervention by force in the affairs of a sovereign country. The USSR became directly involved in someone else's civil war and, up to 15 February 1989 when Soviet forces left the country, paid for it with 13,826 Soviet lives and 49,985 Soviet injured.

My job in Kabul was to augment and organize the work of the special propaganda units. At the time I was head of the service known to the Americans as the 'psychological war agency'. These agitation units, generally accompanied by a reinforced platoon, sometimes even a company, travelled throughout the provinces of Afghanistan, especially in the early days after the invasion. I took part in one raid. The men in the villages had run off into the mountains, from where they fired at our vehicles. For hours on end our loudspeakers urged them to support the April revolution and tried to explain why the *shuravi*, the Soviets, had come. Sometimes a couple of dozen old men, women and children would approach the armoured troop-carriers. Gingerly, they would accept a bag of flour from the soldiers, or tea, sugar, sweets and toys, and then return in silence to their stone huts. To them we were conquerors.

Gradually the hostility and emptiness around the Soviet forces in the country grew. Even at that time, many officers were convinced of the futility of their mission. Colonel Yu. Shershnev, who worked in my agency, spoke openly of the harmful effects of Soviet military intervention, and even wrote to the Central Committee. I had a hard time trying to protect him from unpleasant consequences.

A month after the invasion, in January 1980, the Politburo sent Andropov to Kabul for talks with the new Afghan leadership. On 7 February he reported to his colleagues. He thought the removal of Amin had been a positive move, and judged that the situation in the country had improved. Ustinov added the judgement that 'our limited contingent will remain a year or a year and a half in Afghanistan, until full stabilization is achieved.' In summing up, Brezhnev proposed 'increasing the number of troops in Afghanistan'.[41] By the beginning of January the number of troops had already reached fifty thousand.[42] The leadership was on a direct path to political defeat.

By now Brezhnev was a sick man. His entourage, especially Andropov, Ustinov and Chernenko, avoided disturbing him with news of Afghanistan. Even they did not realize what a trap they had led the USSR into. Together with other political, social and economic factors, Afghanistan was one of the causes of the deep crisis the system was entering, from which the inevitable outcome was the break-up of the Union.

Until 1985 the Kremlin leaders believed it was possible to stabilize the situation in Afghanistan. They thought they had only to settle the split in the Popular Democratic Party of Afghanistan between the 'Khalk' and the 'Parcham' factions, activate Soviet military operations, establish organs of authority in the provinces that were loyal to Kabul, and everything would be fine. The Twenty-Sixth Party Congress in February 1981 even passed a resolution stating that our task was the complete stabilization of the situation in Afghanistan. If everything had depended on Party resolutions, the USSR would long ago have been a heaven on earth.

It was at the same congress that Brezhnev, who could barely speak any more, announced why Soviet troops had been sent into the neighbouring country. Even then it sounded like cheap propaganda: 'Imperialism launched the present undeclared war against the Afghan revolution. That created a direct threat and a danger to our southern border. The situation compelled us to provide the armed assistance this friendly country was asking for ... As for the Soviet contingent, we are ready to withdraw it in agreement with the Afghan government. For that to happen, the sending of counter-revolutionary bands into Afghanistan must cease altogether ... Reliable guarantees are required that there will be no new intervention.'[43]

Talk of a threat to the USSR's southern border, of counter-revolutionary bands and some other intervention, simply produced derision in the West and was dismissed as ridiculous.

In the face of almost universal condemnation, the experts in the Central Committee apparatus tried to find ways of saving face, or at least of looking if not respectable then at least tolerable in the eyes of world public opinion. The chiefs of the mass media, the army and Party committees were periodically sent interpretations of questions connected with changes in the Afghan leadership and the sending of Soviet troops into the country. They were told to say that the Afghan leadership 'repeatedly, at least fourteen times, asked us to send Soviet troops'. Karmal, they must say, had returned to the country illegally in the second half of October 1979, soon after the murder of Taraki by Amin, and had headed the underground organizations against Amin. 'On the night of 27/28 December 1979,' the official version must say, 'the underground, that is members of the PDPA, came out, as a result of which the Amin regime was overthrown.' (The General Staff Special Intelligence unit had no idea that it had played the part of 'underground' party members so brilliantly.) Then, the message went on, on 28 December Karmal, having become General Secretary of the Central Committee of the PDPA, Chairman of the Revolutionary Council and Prime Minister of the Democratic Republic of Afghanistan, requested military assistance from the USSR. The fact that the removal of Amin took place when Soviet military contingents were beginning to arrive in Afghanistan 'was no more than a coincidence in time and there is no causal connection. Soviet military units were not involved in the removal of Amin and his stooges.'[44]

There was not a single word of truth in this 'interpretation', but the propaganda and international information departments of the Central

Committee were past masters at fooling the Soviet public, and most people swallowed it. Paradoxically, the true reason for the intervention was uttered by the Politburo itself: 'The Soviet forces in Afghanistan are carrying out their international duty.' For Brezhnev and his comrades, still thinking in Comintern terms, their ideological commitment to the Marxist doctrine of making whole populations happy despite themselves was their justification for crude interference in the affairs of other countries.

Two years before he died, Brezhnev and his decrepit comrades-in-arms almost dragged the USSR into another, possibly even more dangerous, adventure. If Poland had not been gripped by the pincers of Soviet troops in East Germany and the USSR itself in the east, it is virtually certain that the Communist regime in that country would have collapsed long before it did – assuming it had even come into being. In August 1980, Moscow sent Marshal V. Kulikov to Warsaw to prevent the situation created by the hugely popular Solidarity movement from getting further out of control. As a lieutenant-general, I was sent along as Kulikov's adjutant. Our group's mission was to 'explain' to the Polish leadership the Central Committee's 'advice' and 'recommendations'.

Once or twice a week, the Polish Prime Minister General Jaruzelski would come to the Helenów Palace outside Warsaw, where Kulikov, having received his new instructions from Moscow, would conduct the talks. General V. Anoshkin and I sat alongside the Marshal, while Jaruzelski was usually alone. Kulikov's instructions were always the same: Jaruzelski must take tough control of the mass media, discredit the opposition activists and carry out various political manoeuvres. There was already then discussion of a 'tougher response by the authorities in socialist Poland' to the actions of Solidarity.

With a sad face, Jaruzelski would sit and listen to the routine list of Moscow's counsels and then, at the end, declare that the Polish regime had the situation under control, and that direct intervention by the USSR would lead to a catastrophe. He was between the anvil of Poland's problems and the hammer of massive Soviet military force. Against all the odds, he managed to convince the Soviet leadership not to send in troops, even though he had not been told in so many words that this was being considered. Kulikov himself did much to facilitate Jaruzelski's position, and it became clear to me that he was personally against drawing the USSR into yet another dangerous adventure. Nevertheless, Soviet troops in Czechoslovakia, East Germany and the border districts of the USSR were secretly preparing for an operation.

I was very worried, and when I found myself alone with Kulikov I asked him if we were about to commit yet another fatal mistake. He replied in a low voice that this 'mistake' must not be allowed to happen, and then shifted the conversation to a less dangerous topic.

Although he could not know everything, Jaruzelski must have guessed that Afghanistan had not persuaded Moscow of the folly of such operations, and that an even more terrible war was a real possibility. He may have felt that the seriously ill Brezhnev had given Chernenko and other Politburo members the task of reviewing necessary measures with regard to Poland, 'just in case'.

The measures envisaged were outlined in a one-page document composed by the Kremlin 'hawks' Suslov, Gromyko, Andropov, Ustinov and Chernenko, which was handed to Brezhnev on 28 August 1980. Noting that the situation in Poland 'continues to remain tense, with the strike movement having reached state-wide proportions', and assuming Soviet military intervention, the group requested that three tank divisions and a motorized rifle division be put onto full battle-readiness from 1800 hours on 29 August. A hundred thousand reserves would be called up, and fifteen thousand vehicles requisitioned from the agricultural sector.

'In the event of a further worsening of the situation in Poland,' the note continued, 'the divisions on permanent readiness in the Baltic, Belorussian and Pre-Carpathian Military Districts should be brought up to wartime strength, and if the main strength of Polish forces should come out in support of the counter-revolutionary forces, our troops should be further reinforced by five to seven divisions.'[45]

Two or three years later, in a confidential conversation, Marshal Ogarkov told me that he had been extremely anxious. 'Another war, this time in Europe,' he said, 'could have become an insupportable burden for the country.' He hinted that he'd had talks with several Politburo members and cautiously tried to persuade them not to accept this solution to the 'Polish problem'. In any event, after reading the memorandum, Brezhnev grunted: 'We'll wait a while.'

Whether he did not realize the seriousness of the situation or did not want to take on another burden for himself and the country, his caution was providential. The decision as to whether to invade had hung by a thread.

That was the nature of the regime created by Lenin: more depended on the will of the leader, even if he had been minimally endowed by nature with intelligence, or was terminally ill, than on that of the population.

Marshal, Hero, Laureate

It is doubtful whether any country in the world has so many jokes about its leaders as the Soviet Union. Jokes about Lenin and Stalin were heard in public only after the 'wonderful Georgian' was dead, but the other General Secretaries were often the subject of hilarity during their lifetimes. Lacking the opportunity to speak openly about the 'the most equitable Leninist order', or Communist ideology, or the omnipotent secret police, ordinary Soviet citizens in the seclusion of their homes mocked their leaders, who provided ample material for the purpose. Brezhnev was a classic target. In time, he became a symbol of the entire decrepit leadership, that could not even manage the simplest functions.

There was often no need to invent jokes about Brezhnev. As former Administrator of Affairs of the Council of Ministers, Mikhail Smirtyukov, has said, the author of many Brezhnev jokes was Brezhnev himself. He would pull a stunt, one of his entourage would tell his friends, and the joke would be on its way.[46]

At the end of his life, Brezhnev could not utter even a few phrases in public unless they were printed out for him. He had literally become the prisoner of texts prepared by his assistants. This was reflected in many jokes.

Brezhnev is meeting Margaret Thatcher at the airport, and reads from his text: 'Dear and much respected Mrs Indira Gandhi . . .'

'Leonid Ilyich,' an aide whispers, 'it's Margaret Thatcher.'

'Dear and much respected Mrs Indira Gandhi . . .' growls Brezhnev again, straightening his spectacles.

His aide tries again in desperation.

'I know it's Margaret Thatcher,' says Brezhnev, 'but it says here Indira Gandhi!'

Brezhnev is speaking at a Politburo meeting, having just come from yet another funeral: 'Comrade Pelshe deserves to be properly rewarded: he has turned out to be the most gallant gentleman in the Politburo. When Suslov was being buried and they were playing funeral music, only he thought of getting up and asking the widow to dance.'[47]

Of all his 'endearing' qualities, Brezhnev's vanity and propensity to award himself ever more decorations were the most ridiculous.

The government asked the appropriate committee: 'Where is the epicentre of the last earthquake?' Answer: 'Under the clothes-hanger that Brezhnev's parade tunic fell off.'

Vanity is a common vice, but most people find ways of disguising it. Brezhnev was different. His war record was undistinguished, but when he became General Secretary he also became, according to an unwritten law, Supreme Commander of the Soviet Armed Forces. In 1975, as my boss Yepishev told me, he kept raising the issue of his military rank with senior army men: 'People are writing to me and insisting that, as I am the supreme commander, I ought to have a rank consistent with my position . . . A lieutenant-general [a rank he was given after the war] cannot be the supremo. I don't know what to do . . . The pressure of public opinion, especially among the military, is very strong.'

By May 1976 the Ministry of Defence had arranged to have the rank of Marshal of the Soviet Union conferred on Brezhnev. A marshal's uniform, however, needs medals, and they duly appeared, one after the other, as from a magical cornucopia. He received Hero of the Soviet Union stars, the highest state awards, four times: in 1966, 1976, 1978 and 1981. He had already been decorated as a Hero of Socialist Labour under Khrushchev, and the sprinkling of gold and jewelled orders on his chest went on being augmented until the end of his days. He never saw the comical absurdity of it all.

In December 1966 Suslov said to Podgorny: 'Leonid Ilyich will be sixty in a week's time. I suggest we make him a Hero of the Soviet Union. It'll be nice for him.'

Podgorny replied: 'I have no objection. We should ring round the members of the Politburo.'

There and then a Central Committee decree was dictated giving Brezhnev 'the title of Hero of the Soviet Union and decorating him with the Order of Lenin and the Gold Star Medal'.[48] There was a proposal from a certain S. Davidyuk in Kiev that a new and even higher order be created, Hero of Communist Labour, and that Brezhnev should be its first recipient.[49] The Politburo seems to have had the common sense not to report this to the General Secretary, otherwise he most certainly would have agreed. The leaders of the socialist countries vied with each other in pinning their own country's highest orders on Brezhnev's overloaded chest. He probably had more medals than all the other leaders, from Lenin to Gorbachev, put together.

Curiously, Brezhnev sincerely believed that he had genuinely earned his decorations, and in time he also came to believe that he had played a historic role in the war, and that his marshal's rank and Victory Medal were really deserved. He even began to feel a sense of rivalry towards Marshal Zhukov and his memory as the Soviet Union's greatest military commander. His toadying entourage constantly assured him that his works, his decisions and his participation in various events were of an epoch-making nature. It was they who made sure that the first six editions of Zhukov's memoirs contained the barefaced lie that Zhukov, when he was with 18th Army, had wanted 'to consult with the head of the political section of the force, L.I. Brezhnev,' but that this had not happened because the hero of Malaya Zemlya was at the bridgehead.

Books and photographic albums, endless television programmes and the unctuous praise of bootlickers created a climate of adulation for this feeble old man, who was so generous to his cronies. The parading of his colourless personality, his love of medals and any kind of trinket, became practically pathological. He was as thrilled as a child when he was given a statuette of the Golden Mercury, the Lenin Peace Prize, the Joliot Curie Gold Medal for Peace, the Afghan Sun of Victory Order, the Karl Marx Gold Medal, the Lenin Prize for Literature, a new Party card with the number 00000002 – the first having, of course, been issued to the long-dead Lenin – Komsomol card No. 1, or even the first badge marking 'fifty years in the CPSU'.

Brezhnev's vanity became so grotesque that the whole country could barely hide its smirks, and was almost openly laughing at its unfortunate leader. Most of his colleagues would smile politely when he was having yet another medal pinned on his chest, or avert their faces from the cameras. Even they felt ashamed. At one of his first Politburo sessions as General Secretary, Gorbachev, citing a letter from a Communist, declared: 'The people are saying that L.I. Brezhnev's nineteen Gold Stars and K.V. Chernenko's third Gold Star not only undermined their personal authority, but also rebounded on the members of the Politburo. The people are complaining with justification: "Where are the Politburo's eyes? They surely don't think you can decorate General Secretaries anyway you like and as much as you like?"'[50]

Apart from Lenin, and to some extent Stalin, the Party leaders wrote little or nothing, at least while they were in office. The mountains of their papers in the Party archives were created by aides and apparatchiks, and all they themselves wrote was contained in resolutions and decrees, notepads or desk diaries. In this regard, Brezhnev's creativity as a laureate of Soviet literature is unique. His countless bulging volumes of speeches and articles reflect the level of the Party's mastery of bureaucratic technique. It is impossible to find a personal element in any of these speeches.

Moreover, Brezhnev, who loved making speeches and appearing on television or at large gatherings, had a strange way of speaking, which was due to some extent to dental work. In a note to the Soviet Ambassador in Bonn, V. Falin, in October 1974, he wrote: 'Please tell the physicians that I am waiting for them with the hope of success. It's very difficult for me to convey in detail the sensation I experience from wearing the model they left me, though I use it all the time. In general, I'd like it to be lighter – it's particularly uncomfortable where it touches my bridge – the protrusion of my back teeth makes an unpleasant feeling on the tongue. We talked about all this in Moscow, and therefore I wouldn't want to make any more comments.' A postscript added: 'Tomorrow, 23 October, two cargoes addressed to you are going by train with a special courier from the Foreign Ministry; one contains two rifles which I want you to give to the physicians, the second [a wild boar] I'm sending for you personally.'[51]

On 13 April 1978, under 'any other business' at a Politburo meeting, Brezhnev asked his colleagues for their support in continuing to publish his 'memoirs'. 'When I meet leading officials, military men and other comrades,' he said, 'they tell me that these memoirs are useful for the education of the people. If there are no objections from members of the Politburo, I could go on writing them with a small group of comrades.' Naturally, there was a chorus of approval and support for the 'selfless' literary activity of the General Secretary.[52] Immediately a group of writers was recruited and set to work under the direction of Brezhnev's officials.

Brezhnev's 'books' were beautifully produced and published in huge print-runs. But despite the fact that they were put together by professional writers, they are lifeless. They contain nothing of Brezhnev, nothing deeply personal or unknown, certainly nothing reflective, emotional or unexpected. However graphic the descriptions of the war, the post-war reconstruction or the virgin lands campaign, there is nothing of Brezhnev himself in any of it. And however many medals and titles are showered on a mediocrity, he cannot be turned into a genius, or even an outstanding personality. His books were doomed to have a very short life, and today they serve as no more than a memory of the Brezhnev era.

While pointing out Brezhnev's vanity, it is also worth noting that he was highly sentimental, a fact that was often exploited by his numerous hangers-on. He liked people and was very approachable, often helping someone outside his immediate circle who had touched his heart with a sad story or a request. Sometimes, while watching a film or listening to a concert, he would want there and then to give the chief performer a medal or an honorific title, or in some other way show his appreciation. And he often did.

Gorbachev's assistant Anatoly Chernyaev recalls in his memoirs: 'Leonid Ilyich loved watching the TV series *Seventeen Moments of Spring*. He watched it some twenty times. Once, when at the end of an episode they tell [the character] Shtirlits that he's been awarded the title of Hero of the Soviet Union, Brezhnev turned to the others and asked: "Have they given it already? I'd like to have done it myself." Ryabenko, his chief of security, started praising the actor Tikhonov, and others joined in. Brezhnev interrupted: "Well, if that's the case . . ." And a few days later he personally handed a Hero of the Soviet Union Star and Order of Lenin . . . to Tikhonov, fully convinced that he was really Shtirlits.'[53]

In some ways, Brezhnev was a kind of good tsar, a Communist tsar, and if it had not been for Czechoslovakia, Afghanistan and Poland, history's view of him might be very different. Like any good tsar, he liked to make things pleasant for those around him, bestowing gifts and showing lordly concern. As Roy Medvedev has written, Brezhnev had many friends, whom he always remembered with gifts or promotion.[54] The list of those who benefited is very long.

Even when he criticized someone, he did it in a way that never left them feeling offended.[55] He cemented the foundations of his power by exploiting the friendly, benevolent nature of his personal relations – the very antithesis of Stalin's tyranny of fear. He loved long, leisurely meals, big-game hunting, fishing with a group of friends, driving fast in luxury cars, of which he had a collection of no fewer than eighty.

Like the other members of the Politburo, during Khrushchev's rule Brezhnev had worked ten or twelve hours a day, gone on frequent missions, endured long hours at countless meetings, and chaired numerous commissions. As General Secretary, he organized his day quite differently. The Central Committee apparatus did all his work for him, only requiring his signature on the most important papers. He also tried to make life easier for his cronies.

On 28 July 1966, not long after he came to power, at his insistence the Politburo passed a decree according to which Politburo members must take ten weeks' holiday a year. They were also 'to start work at 9 a.m. and finish at 5 p.m., with a compulsory break for lunch'.[56] During his last five or six years, when he had become senile, Brezhnev would turn up at the office for two or three hours, and spend most of the rest of the week at Zavidovo, with its splendid hunting, a hundred miles from Moscow. When it became apparent to everyone, inside the USSR and abroad, that Brezhnev was declining, the Politburo adopted additional measures to protect the precious health of their leader. He was accompanied everywhere by an ambulance equipped with resuscitation equipment and staffed by medical personnel. His places of work were similarly equipped, and from 1978 his summer break alone was increased to ten weeks.[57]

The whole world might be aware that Brezhnev was a sick man, but the Central Committee and the Politburo, and he himself, did everything they could to hide the fact. Speaking to East European Communist leaders in Budapest on 18 March 1975, he spent a long time telling them that he was 'overtired', but not at all ill: 'I would earnestly ask you, comrades, to bear in mind that, although for a while

I really was unwell, we made a firm decision not to talk about it publicly. I need a certain amount of time and a proper regime in order to get over the tiredness. I have nothing else wrong with me. I am grateful to you, comrades, for your concern about my health and I would like to take this opportunity to let you know that I am a fighter and will remain one to the end.'[58] In fact, he was already seriously ill.

The Politburo, the Health Minister Petrovsky and his successor Chazov, and the chiefs of the Kremlin medical service were in effect carrying out an experiment to see how long a fatally sick old man could give the impression of working. I recall an incident at the end of October 1982, two weeks before Brezhnev died, and the last time I saw him alive. It was the annual convention of the Supreme Command Staff of the Army and Navy. On the second day, we were told that the next day's session would take place in the Sverdlov Hall of the Kremlin. At 10 a.m., when I was in my place with all the other marshals and generals, Brezhnev was brought on stage from behind the curtains. He was accompanied by Marshal Ustinov on one side and by a well-built young man on the other holding a glass of tea in one hand and, more firmly, the elbow of the General Secretary with the other. In this way, the trio made their way unhurriedly to the podium.

I cannot now recall what it was Brezhnev struggled for about fifteen minutes to say. As he moved his finger along the line of large print his eyes wandered over the text, skipping lines, so that what his audience heard was gibberish. No one paid attention to what he was saying, however, but rather wondered if he would get through it without collapsing and falling down right there in front of them. Why Ustinov had to organize such a pathetic spectacle I never understood. Everyone felt pity for Brezhnev and shame for their country. When the young man helped him off the stage, the whole hall heaved a sigh of relief.

None of the seven leaders left office voluntarily, even when it was plain that they could no longer do the job. It is true that on more than one occasion among his intimates Brezhnev spoke of getting old, and it being 'time to go out to grass'. But all this really meant was that he wanted to hear more words of praise, to be told again that he was irreplaceable and that 'the people would not understand'.

The General Secretary's Papers

For all his lack of culture and education, Brezhnev left a large quantity of working papers of all kinds. They are interesting for the light they throw on the man who stood at the peak of Soviet power for eighteen years, and they also raise the curtain on some of the secrets, large and small, associated with running a great country. They constitute something of the elusive fabric of Soviet history.

It is doubtful if his vanity motivated Brezhnev to make these notes. It was usual for Party leaders to write down the orders of their superiors in order to carry them out, then years later to write them down again as orders of their own, and then, as General Secretary, to file them as snapshots of their own great lives. Much was intended for posterity: 'To Chernenko: Probably this letter should be put in my *personal archives* with V.A. Golikov's note. Even now I am still doing my correspondence with the people and it's hard to keep everything. Signed L. Brezhnev, 13 June 1976.'[59]

From 1944, long before he was engaged in his 'correspondence with the people', Brezhnev was keeping working notes, the common practice of a non-professional middle-ranking army officer. Unusually, Brezhnev kept all these scraps of paper, and carried them around with him until they ended up in his archives.

Brezhnev's working papers show the close attention he paid to Khrushchev's remarks at meetings and to the instructions Khrushchev issued on everything from arms production to how and when to fatten cattle. Until Khrushchev was removed from office, Brezhnev seems to have recorded every time he saw his boss, where he was taking his holiday, what he'd said on the telephone, what papers to prepare for his arrival, and so on.

In October 1957 he was sent by Khrushchev to talk to a Party group of the Soviet forces in East Germany about the removal of Marshal Zhukov from his post as Defence Minister. His papers contain notes for his speech: 'The facts testify to Comrade Zhukov's tendency towards unlimited power. Recently Comrade Zhukov suggested replacing the Chairman of the Committee of State Security [KGB] and Minister of the Interior with military personnel. What lay behind this proposal? Was it not so that the top posts in these organs should be headed by his own people, officers owing him personal loyalty? Is this not a desire to establish his own control over the KGB and MVD?'[60] It had not been so long ago that Brezhnev, Khrushchev and even Stalin (to some extent) had been afraid of the great war leader whom he could now so readily disparage on his boss's orders.

As Khrushchev's favourite, Brezhnev was given a lot of work to do, though he also found plenty of time for his beloved hunting: 'Went with Khrushchev to Zavidovo'; 'Was at Zavidovo'; 'Spoke with N.S. about hunting'; 'Left at 4 p.m. to hunt with Yura'; 'Shot three wild boar at Zavidovo'; 'Zavidovo – elk'. Hunting was an odd sport for someone of Brezhnev's background. Perhaps it gave him a sense of connection with an aristocratic tradition of the distant past. Nicholas I, summing up the first year of his reign, had noted: 'Altogether I shot 3 bison, 28 deer, 3 goats, 8 wild boar, and 3 foxes = 45.'[61]

In time hunting became Brezhnev's chief form of relaxation, perhaps even his main occupation. In the last two or three years of his life, he could no longer hold the rifle steady – he had a collection of over a hundred beautifully made, expensive weapons. Several times at Zavidovo he bruised his forehead and nose because he could not control the recoil. His former security chief, General Vladimir Medvedev, has written that while Brezhnev directed and commanded operations, he had huntsmen who did the actual shooting for him. He was engaged in this sporting activity twenty-four hours before he died.[62] He loved it so much that he made the chief huntsman at Zavidovo a general, and over a brief period bestowed on him all three degrees of a newly created order, 'For Service to the Motherland'. The hunter's assistants were also showered with medals.

Brezhnev liked to give his hunting trophies to friends and 'useful' individuals. As well as the entire wild boar he sent to the Soviet ambassador in Bonn, he had his last bag from Zavidovo sent by plane to 'doctor Jakob from Bon' and 'doctor Ozinga from Diusendorf' [sic].[63]

Curiously, Brezhnev's notes cease for a time in the middle of 1964. He went on working, speaking and recording Khrushchev's instructions on separate sheets of paper, but there are no notes of any other activity. As we know, Khrushchev's removal was being carefully planned at this time, and Brezhnev was therefore being extra cautious. He wrote down nothing about his meetings with other 'comrades', made no mention of telephone calls, or even of hunting. Only when Khrushchev was safely out of the way, from the second half of October 1964, did the notes start again. They refer to speeches on Khrushchev's behaviour by Polyansky and Suslov, and the response of local Party Committees to his removal, and they mention a phone call from Ignatov, who asked if he should speak at the next plenum, as he believed 'it is not all over, and so on'. 'I don't share that view,' Brezhnev noted.[64]

This last entry is important. As we now know, some members of the leadership in 1964, including Ignatov, wanted to go further than getting rid of Khrushchev alone. They were motivated by the old habit of removing anyone who had been closely associated with the disgraced victim, and were suggesting a small purge of the leadership in the centre and the provinces. For all his conformity to the Party tradition, Brezhnev had no desire to follow that path, if only because he himself had been his predecessor's favourite. Instead, Party managers were told to pursue a policy proposed by Suslov: to talk at their plenums in general terms about the harm done by 'voluntarism and subjectivism' and to do their best to erase Khrushchev from the public memory. The policy failed, even though a taboo on Khrushchev's name survived for almost two decades.

Memory, however, does not depend on rules laid down by the Politburo. The majority of those who helped get rid of Khrushchev are completely unknown to most people living in Russia today. Nobody issued orders that they should be forgotten, yet their names have been swallowed up, while that of Khrushchev remains part of the discourse of recent history.

Soon after Brezhnev came to power, some of his close associates, notably S. Trapeznikov, who became head of the Politburo's science sector and, despite his primitivism, an academician, and one of his assistants, V. Golikov, urged the new leader to re-examine the decisions of the Twentieth and Twenty-Second Party Congresses which had condemned the personality cult. Among Brezhnev's papers is the decision of the Twentieth Congress with somebody's underlining – it is not clear whose – and the (rejected) draft of his speech in Tbilisi which shows a clear Stalinist tinge. Other members of his entourage who held Stalinist views at the time were Chernenko and Tikhonov.

Academician Georgy Arbatov has written in his *From the Recent Past* that these people, 'along with the most conservative members of the Presidium and Central Committee Secretariat, were soon able to cobble together something like a general political platform' which sought to overturn the decisions of the Twentieth and Twenty-Second Congresses and to bring about 'the complete rehabilitation of Stalin'.[65]

Brezhnev was sympathetic to Stalin, but was afraid to put him back on his pedestal. He hesitated, however, chiefly because a radical review of attitudes to Stalin's role in Soviet history would arouse intellectual ferment, protest and a storm of emotions. And that was something he wished to avoid. In the end, he compromised. Stalin would no longer be criticized in the press, but would barely be mentioned in terms of his 'service to the people' either. Brezhnev had no stomach for reviewing the decisions of the anti-Stalinist congresses. Times had changed, he felt, and open rehabilitation of the tyrant would evoke a huge wave of anti-Soviet feeling abroad, not to mention what it might lead to at home. Given his weakness as a theoretician, he decided to occupy a middle position between half-condemning Stalin and half-rehabilitating him.

Up to 1968 Brezhnev kept his records haphazardly and irregularly, often omitting the date. It is as if they were purely for his own record. For instance, the entries for 1968 include: 'Establishment of an Academy of Literature and Art ... Who's going to write my speech in Czechoslovakia? ... Decorations: Give Grechko the Order of Lenin, make Voroshilov and Budenny heroes. Yepishev gets a Lenin, Timoshenko, Yeremenko, Bagramyan and Moskalenko get october revolution orders. Give all the marshals a service chaika [limousine] ... Legislation – deport beyond the country's borders ... Khrushchev and his "memoirs" ... On access for any riff-raff to military archives and their use for improper purposes – toughen up.'[66]

The notes for 1973–74, written with a fountain-pen or ballpoint and kept in a red binder, and those he kept irregularly until his death, are of greater importance for the historical record:

1 September. Conversation with Andropov, Yu.V. The incident in the Mausoleum [presumably one of several attempts on Lenin's mummy by visitors].

8 September. Sakharov – should I receive him or not. I'll consult the CC [Central Committee] again. Aid to India – give 200–250,000.

11 September. Talk to Alexei Nikolaevich [Kosygin] again about receiving Sakharov. We ought to think about deeper and more serious co-operation with the [Federal German Republic], to France's annoyance.

8 October. Talks with Tanaka and the people accompanying him. He talks about the 'peace treaty' and the islands. He says, the people are talking about it!!!

21 October. If there's a civil war in Chile, we should assist (with everything and weapons). Shouldn't we ourselves break off dip[lomatic] relations with this fascist regime together with the soc[ialist] countries it would unite us.[67]

Before talks with foreign statesmen Brezhnev would be supplied by the apparatchiks with prepared questions and answers and comments. Among the notes for a meeting with Henry Kissinger is the scrawled prompt: 'Middle East also a difficult issue where our views are not edintical [sic] doesn't mean we are not at one with you on positions of peace.'[68] Certainly Brezhnev's views were not 'edintical' with those of Kissinger, and he pursued his foreign policy persistently, in a straightforward, inflexible way. In the end, however, he came to see the destructive logic of the late twentieth century: whoever used nuclear missiles first would perish second. The irony of history was that you could turn your enemy into ash, but not be the victor.

Politically, Brezhnev thought in terms of black or white, good or bad. His notes on the meeting of Communist Party leaders of 10–23 November 1960 are characteristic: 'Comrade Violdi (Argentina) praised Khrushchev, Comrade Zhivkov (on Khrushchev's services), Comrade Nuri (Iraq) good speech, Comrade Lonoyan (Cyprus) good, Comrade Saoue (Lebanon) good, Comrade Wensen (Switzerland), good sp[eech], Comrade . . . . . . (Uruguay) good, Comrade . . . . . . (Denmark) good, Comrade . . . . . . (Mexico) all right, Brazil (Pres) OK, but boring, Gomulka spoke beautifully for more than two hours, Morocco (gave it to the Chinese and especially Hoxha) . . .'[69] Brezhnev managed to forget or garble some of the names, as he did when he wrote or spoke the names of Soviet statesmen. His unintelligent responses are what one might have expected of a provincial Communist during the civil war who found himself at a Comintern congress.

The Brezhnev period was a time of struggle against dissidents, civil rights activists and fighters for the rights of the individual. Most of the population to a great extent believed the false official propaganda against these people, especially against Andrei Sakharov and the writer Alexander Solzhenitsyn.

Free thinking and intellectual protest, however, became widespread in those years, and although Brezhnev himself became less and less interested in state affairs, he was always interested in what Andropov and his agencies were up to. He learnt on one such occasion that the security service had 'curtailed such anti-Soviet bodies as a workers' commission for studying the use of psychiatry for political purposes, a Helsinki monitoring group, a committee for defending the rights of believers, a religious-philosophical seminar, and free trade unions. 1,512 authors and distributors of anti-Soviet and slanderous materials have been identified.' The report concluded with the ritual incantation: 'The leadership, the Board and the Party Committee of the KGB, in the name of all its workers, organs and troops, assures the Leninist Central Committee of the CPSU, the Politburo of the Central Committee, and Comrade Brezhnev personally, that the Chekists will remain steadfastly loyal to the Party cause, the great cause of Communism.'[70]

Brezhnev personally approved the expulsion from the Soviet Union of such figures as Solzhenitsyn, Valeri Chalidze, Vladimir Maximov, Victor Krasin, Pavel Litvinov, Alexander Yesenin-Volpin and a host of other dissidents. When he heard that publications in Paris had revealed that there were political prisoners in the USSR, he asked the KGB to let him know the facts. On 29 December 1975 Andropov duly replied with a lengthy memorandum which revealed that, for anti-Soviet agitation and propaganda, 1,583 people were sentenced between 1967 and 1975, and that in the period 1958–66 3,448 people were in prison and camp for the same offences. 'Anti-Soviet agitation and propaganda' were defined by Andropov as 'especially dangerous state crimes'.[71] The regime was of course correct in seeing independent political thought as a danger. The events of the late 1980s demonstrated that truth and unfettered information were weapons against which the Leninist system was no match.

Brezhnev's notes reveal that he was directly involved in the exchange of Vladimir Bukovsky for the Chilean Communist leader Louis Corvalan, the deportation of Solzhenitsyn, the exile of Sakharov to Gorky and many other cases. When on 26 December 1979 Andropov and

Roman Rudenko, the Chief Prosecutor, submitted the KGB's proposals to the Politburo regarding Sakharov, Brezhnev gave his assent. They reported that 'between 1972 and 1979 Sakharov visited foreign embassies in Moscow eighty times, had more than six hundred meetings with other foreigners, conducted more than 150 so-called press conferences, and that Western radio stations had broadcast about 1,200 anti-Soviet transmissions based on his material.' In order to avoid the 'political cost' of a trial, on 3 January 1980 the Politburo agreed to strip Sakharov of all his titles and 'as a preventive measure, deport him from Moscow to a region of the country that is closed to foreigners'.[72]

Unusually for a leading statesman, Brezhnev did not like reading, and therefore he did not read. The diaries of Nicholas II have often been cited for the triviality of his observations, yet they also show that virtually every day of his adult life he read *something*. On 5 April 1907, to take a typical example, he wrote: 'Carried out the inspection, broke the ice, read, played billiards.'[73] How does Brezhnev's diary entry for the same day seven decades later compare?

'Spoke to Comrade Chernenko. Kosygin left at 5 to meet Palme. Later I let Kosygin know through his receptionist that I won't be able to see Palme at all. Mikh. Yevstigneevich sent a blue shirt with buttons all the way down, but it's not wool.'[74] Other entries demonstrate the pathetically low intellectual level of the highest Soviet state official and fourth leader of the Communist Party.

10 May 1976. Bestowed a big marshal's star. Spoke to Comrade A.N. Kopenkin – he talked with the voice of an officer, I heard the voice of a general, now I'm glad I hear the voice of a marshal.

16 May 1976. Went nowhere – rang no one, likewise no one me – haircut, shaved and washed hair in the morning. Walked a bit during the day, then watched Central Army lose to Spartak (the lads played well).

30 May. Zavidovo with Chernenko, K.U. 8 kills.

26 June. Talked with Coms. Chernenko, K.U. Rusakov about Poland. Measured for and received suits. Evening with Muza Vladimirovna and Valentina Alexandrovna.

25 July. As usual no one around in morning Breakfast, shave, swim Today snoozed in rocker on bank. Today T. Nikolaevna went on cleaning teeth – and Muza examined the prosthesis Talked with Comrade Chernenko, K.U. – he's still not well, everything possible is being done.

31 July. Swam 1 hour in pool 30 minutes. Shave – chewed the fat with Podgorny. Gifts for Husak G.N. presented at 11 a.m. Andropov about Kosygin Podgorny played dominoes then I told him about Kosygin.

7 August. 19th day of holiday. Swam in sea 1.30 – massage pool 30 minutes Washed head – with children's soap.

17 August. 29th day of holiday Ask when Kosygin turned over on the boat Chazov Ye.I., – conscious good conversation reacted calmly that he'll have to undergo treatment in mid-October. Galya [his daughter] and Yuri Mikhailovich [Churbanov, his son-in-law] flew back to Moscow. Suslov, M.A. is flying to Sochi today.

21 August. Flew to Astrakhan with N.V. Podgorny. Spent evening hunting (evening) Killed 34 geese.

23 August. Morning – divided up the beluga [caviare] – and sturgeon preparation of caviare Flight to Simferopol – they couldn't accept [so] we landed at naval aerodrome at Saki Met Blatov and Victoria Arrived at the house for dinner ate borshch.

10 March 1977. Went to work was at CC till 2.10 Chazov orthopedist was here in morning. Received and long talk with Chernenko Called in on Kirilenko – it was 'announced' he'd gone to work.

14 March. Galochka's birthday Talked with Gorodovikov asked him to tell Comrade Chernenko K.U. what he needs as he's asked me for heaps of favours it was hard for me to understand – he wants to come to Moscow tomorrow to go round the Ministries. Received Com. Ponomaryov and Chernenko on question of Constitution.

18 March. Exercise. Then talked to Chernenko then with Coms. Gromyko A.A. Andropov Ustinov – read material on Vance's visit. Called Pavlov G.S. on cost (yes) of 28,800. Read various materials with Galya Doroshina [i.e. she read them to him]. Went to the circus.

13 April. Morning – usual domestic arrangements They took blood from a vein Talk with Daoud from 11 a.m. Question of one to one meeting fell away Rest – good – (lunch). Work with Doroshina.

22 April. 86.400 [kilos – he had started weighing himself regularly] 5 p.m. session on his [Lenin's] birthday Talked with Grishin Gromyko – Chernenko Doroshina.

23–24 April. days off.

3 May. Chat with Ryabenko Conversation about teleph with Storozhev . . . usual question Talk with Chernenko K.U. on PB agenda Tailors – I gave them the grey suit – and the leath. jacket. Took a walk. Yu.A. Andropov phoned – he came we talked Worked with Doroshina.

16 June. 86.00 10 a.m. Supreme Soviet session. Appointment of Com. Brezhnev as chairman of the Presidium of the Supreme Soviet (a lot of congratulations).

2 August. 85.800 naked Breakfast. – Shave – swam Strolled on the jetty. Drew at dominoes. Lunch. Doroshina – Blatov Inform Chaushestko [Ceausescu] – reception with me at 6 p.m.

27 October. Spent at Pburo also on Rashidov 2nd Hero for success in work (cotton) and sixtieth birthday Received Kirilenko – he's on commission to examine anonymous letter on Bodyul criticizes him for complexes – he got his doctorate and so on He's not a creminal [sic] ... M.A. Suslov on Academy of Sciences Alexandrov A.P. wants Loginov An.Alex. to be vice-president.

21 November. Was at N.V. Lopatkin's in morning half-regime Received Com. Ligachev Yegor Kuzmich – Tomsk on improving children's material situation Received D.F. Ustinov Questions on 60th anniversary of Army. Moskalenko – give him 2nd hero star Make Yepishev hero Karaglanov title of hero of soc[ialist] labour and other awards and decorations.[75]

Brezhnev made no notes showing that he had given any thought to the new Constitution, the passing of new laws, the national economy, the dangers of the Cold War, the nuclear arms race, culture or books he had read. For some reason he felt it important to keep a record of the amount of money the Central Committee finance department had given him for a trip to Brussels, how much he had paid for a set of gold and diamond ornaments, how much he'd given his assistant Tsukanov to pay into his, Brezhnev's, deposit account, and similar domestic details. Yet he neglected to mention in 1977 that he had had himself made formal head of state, a post he had already held from 1960 to 1964, but which had now acquired a status in international relations closer to that of foreign Presidents.

Brezhnev might have been a perfectly adequate, possibly even a good, factory manager, office head or middle-ranking economic administrator. Fate, however, carried him to the top of the tree and kept him there for almost two decades. Only Stalin, of all the seven leaders, was in power longer.

The Party élite found in Brezhnev the most suitable instrument for their purposes. Lenin, respected by his colleagues but fatally ill, could not leave his post because he was needed as a symbol. There could be no talk of removing Stalin. Khrushchev, to his credit, created an atmosphere in which a more flexible model could emerge as an 'authoritarian' bridge from bloody totalitarianism to something else.

Brezhnev was put in place by a *nomenklatura* that was afraid of the new, but was unable to turn the clock back. He suited everyone, and hence suited none, neither his comrades, his 'loyal followers', nor his allies. Under Brezhnev Communism was talked about from habit, though no one believed in it any longer. Without a great idea that will uplift the nation, the ship of state lies becalmed. Spiritual erosion joins forces with economic stagnation.

The Harbinger of Collapse

On 2 November 1977 a ceremonial session of the Central Committee, Supreme Soviet of the USSR and Supreme Soviet of the RSFSR took place in the Kremlin Palace of Congresses in commemoration of the sixtieth anniversary of October 1917. Brezhnev had told his speech-writers a week or two earlier that he didn't want to speak for more than fifty minutes. He had come to dislike reading long texts.

The speech, which had been gone over several times by the Politburo, was entirely devoted to the future, and was called 'The Great October and the Progress of Mankind'. 'This epoch', Brezhnev proclaimed to orchestrated applause, 'is the epoch of the transition to socialism and Communism . . . and by this path, the whole of mankind is destined to go.'[76]

Brezhnev still retained his Comintern-inspired views on the future of Communism. At 'his' Twenty-Third and Twenty-Fourth Party Congresses he expressed a belief in the ultimate triumph of Lenin's cause. He told the Twenty-Fourth Congress that the world system of socialism was 'the prototype of the future world commonwealth of free peoples', and that 'the complete triumph of the socialist cause throughout the world is inevitable!'[77]

Forecasting the collapse of capitalism and the triumph of Communism, Brezhnev overlooked the fact that without the capitalists, the USSR could not survive. Some two months before his prophetic speech in the Kremlin, on 30 August 1977, he had approved a report marked, 'Of special importance' and 'Special file', signed by the country's top economic and financial managers. Had he given even a hint of what was in that report, his Kremlin speech would have crumbled into dust. Since Lenin's days, the Bolsheviks had been past masters at double book-keeping, one for themselves and another for the 'broad toiling masses'. Kosygin and the other authors of the report had written:

'On 18 June 1977 the CC and the Council of Ministers took the decision to purchase abroad 11.5 million tonnes of grain for delivery to the USSR in 1977/78.' Now, they went on, 'an urgent need has arisen to buy abroad for convertible currency an additional 10 million tonnes of grain (wheat, corn, barley) for delivery to the USSR in 1978. The additional purchase of grain will permit the satisfaction of demand in the national economy, although not completely.'

Already accustomed to shortages of national resources, the report's authors were taking into account a number of other factors: it was assumed that there would be poor harvests among the USSR's friends, and that Poland, Czechoslovakia, East Germany and China were also preparing to buy grain from the capitalists. The idea was not so much how to achieve higher yields from Soviet fields, but to stock up with overseas grain, at the cost of hundreds and thousands of tonnes of the country's gold.[78]

Perhaps Brezhnev had this in mind when he declared in his speech that 'our orientation is not only towards current needs, but also towards the future and notably our agrarian policy. We are striving for a fundamental solution to the food problem, to satisfy the country's growing demand.'[79] Declaiming these high-flown phrases, he could not know, nor could the country know, that he was the harbinger of fundamental change. The more he spoke of the 'successes of socialism' and the 'decisive influence of the socialist commonwealth on the development of civilization', the plainer became the approach of total crisis in the system.

Of course, the worsening stagnation was not the fault of the incompetent General Secretary alone. The system itself was cracking up, even if barely perceptibly as yet. It had insufficient inner reserves for its own proper functioning. It had exhausted itself. In the decade between the Prague events of 1968 and the entry into Afghanistan, the Soviet Union appeared to be enjoying a period of calm. Anomalies became the norm: people worked little, yet were given substantial bonuses; scientists, sportsmen, performers and members of delegations were defecting in greater numbers; regional Party Secretaries became more like local barons; the military-industrial complex made greater and greater demands in order to maintain 'parity' with the USA; the people became accustomed to saying one thing while thinking another; Brezhnev proclaimed that 'the future belongs to Communism', while his comrades and assistants sent gold to the USA, Canada, Argentina and elsewhere in exchange for grain, meat and other food products.

The problem of how to clothe and feed the population had hung like a curse over the Communist regime since its inception, and a solution was no nearer under Brezhnev. He convened four Party Congresses as General Secretary, from the Twenty-Third to the Twenty-Sixth, and at all of them, after the ritual description of the historic achievements of socialism, he spoke of chronic shortages. At the Twenty-Third Congress he said: 'The production of certain goods lags behind demand. A wide choice of meat products is not available everywhere in the trade network. The market does not receive sufficient quantities of necessary goods.'[80] At the next congress he spoke briefly about goods in acute short supply,[81] and at the next he admitted that it had not been possible to achieve a rise in the quantity and quality of goods and services.[82] At his last congress, the Twenty-Sixth, reading his speech with great difficulty, he repeated: 'From year to year plans are not being met for the output of many consumer goods, especially fabrics, knitted goods, leather footwear, furniture, television sets. There has been no rise in quality.'[83]

Reasons were given for these failures: poor harvests, bad planning, negligence, the 'subjectivism' of previous leaders, and of course 'the aggressive actions of the imperialists in the USA who have forced us in recent years to divert additional significant resources to strengthening the country's defence capability'.[84] Among the regime's successes, however, the Twenty-Fourth Congress heard that 'in the year 1969–70, Lenin's works and books on Lenin exceeded 76 million copies.'[85]

Two months before he died, Brezhnev returned from a holiday in the Crimea to chair a routine session of the Politburo, something he had been doing less and less owing to his infirmity. The Central Committee apparatus had long been aware that the state was going nowhere, as signs came from all sides indicating total crisis. Brezhnev's aides tried to put at least some critical and constructive ideas into his mouth.

Without taking his eyes off the text in front of him, Brezhnev described his traditional meetings with the leaders of 'fraternal' parties from other socialist countries. 'It's unpleasant, but it's a fact,' he read, 'that several of our ministries are suffering from the chronic disease of not being able to fulfil their goods contracts with the socialist countries.' He sipped from his glass of tea. 'I cannot refrain from saying that there is a marked increase in dissatisfaction with Comecon [the Council of Economic Co-operation] among our friends. We are experiencing it, too. The root of the problem lies in the fact that time has outgrown the forms that were created thirty years ago when the organization was founded ... Our allies are trying to improve the co-ordination of management decisions by resorting to economic levers and stimuli, and are rejecting extreme centralization of leadership.'

This was the truth, which the General Secretary was unused to uttering. But words were one thing; actions were something else.

'Our economy is gigantic,' Brezhnev continued. 'Take any ministry – it's almost the size of an army. The government apparatus has proliferated. And we have far too many miscalculations and all kinds of misunderstandings.' For a solution to these problems, Brezhnev resorted to the Bolsheviks' faithful old hobby-horse: 'Perhaps the key problem for us today is to tighten discipline. Both in the state and among labour ... The tightening of discipline must be done across the board, not by [individual] campaigns. Maybe we should prepare a special decree on this.'[86]

What had seemed like hints of a sober analysis at the start of his speech ended up slipping through the leadership's fingers.

The most penetrating view of the impending crisis was presented by the Chairman of the KGB, Yuri Andropov. The Central Committee archives contain, under 'Special Files', several memoranda from Andropov warning Brezhnev of hard times to come. The General Secretary would append his signature, and they were then sealed into special envelopes which only he had the authority to open. There are no signs of responses to these notes, which start in about 1975. It is possible that Brezhnev had meetings with Andropov, whom he greatly admired, to discuss his ideas, and that written comment was not thought necessary. But that is mere surmise. In any case, Andropov usually accompanied his well-informed warnings with nothing more constructive than suggestions for additional tough administrative and organizational measures.

As one of the cleverest and most perceptive of the Party leaders, and also because of his position, Andropov enjoyed a trusted and confidential relationship with Brezhnev. Possibly only Chernenko, a typical courtier who could anticipate his master's wishes, was closer. On 8 January 1976 Andropov wrote a strictly personal letter of no fewer than eighteen pages to Brezhnev. It began: 'This document, which I wrote myself, is intended for you alone. If you find something in it of value to the cause, I shall be very glad, and if not, then I ask you to consider it as never having happened.'

Despite this intriguing opening, Andropov urged nothing more than a routine strengthening of the role of the Party as the solution to the country's problems. The Party, he wrote, needed to arm itself with tested Leninist principles: Bolshevik Party-mindedness, strict organization and iron discipline. He pondered on how to make the fifteen million Party members work, 'every single one of them', and how to ensure that membership was not used 'as a springboard for rising up the career ladder'. He called for an end to 'irresponsible chatter, carping criticism and dissipation', pointed out the danger which he saw in the work of the West European Communist parties, and detected 'the social democratic taint that V.I. Lenin had fought against so passionately and furiously'.

Several times Andropov referred disparagingly in his letter to Khrushchev, in effect condemning him for transferring professional agrarian specialists and industrialists to Party work, when what was needed was 'political leadership'. He was against 'business managers' or 'businessmen'. In his words, they 'begin any conversation by scratching numbers on paper. How, one asks, does such a leader differ, for instance, from an American manager, for whom business is first of all accounts and money, while people come second. In our conditions, such "business people" are working for themselves.' He concluded by proposing that regional Party secretaries should be moved after several years to a different field, to avoid 'stagnation'.[87]

Such ideas only served to push the already conservatively inclined Brezhnev into a more orthodox, Bolshevik way of thinking. Andropov, and others like him, could see and feel the deepening crisis, but could suggest only outdated and discredited Leninist solutions to prevent it.

By the end of Brezhnev's rule, several of his associates felt that changes were needed. Yet even the intelligent Andropov saw salvation in resuscitating, 'within reasonable limits', the old Bolshevik practices in running the country. He revealed his nostalgia for the old methods by referring to the Party by its original name of Bolshevik. In his view, it was Bolshevism that signified the implacable struggle against 'political opportunism, conciliationism, slackening and woolly thinking'.

The regime managed to delay collapse by systematically squandering and selling off the country's colossal quantities of gas, oil, gold and other natural wealth, but this could not continue forever. Responsible decisions were essential for fundamental change. The Party leadership was, however, totally unwilling to take such decisions. The records of the Politburo contain not a single word of criticism of the General Secretary for his inactivity and incapacity. Each member was concerned about his own well-being, not that of the state or the population.

The reflections of V.I. Boldin, a senior figure in the Central Committee, are worth noting, as they are relatively objective: 'Yes, Brezhnev had his weaknesses, and there were things to surprise one and things to detest. Why, then, was everyone silent, rejoicing and bowing down to him? Where were the leaders whose duty it was to speak the truth about the state of affairs both to their decrepit leader and the Central Committee and the people? Was it not this gang of cowards who held power in the centre and the localities who brought our country to the impasse, and should they not bear the responsibility for what happened to the great power? Only when Brezhnev was dead did every one of them start to revile their idol, trying to show what brave men they had always been. What a lack of principles and poverty of spirit they must have had to remain silent and to hide the truth from the people!'[88]

Boldin was right, but it was not the old men who were to blame, it was an organic flaw in the system. At the peak of the pyramid there was always the image of the first leader, beyond criticism or reproach. Other leaders were debunked after their deaths, but Lenin was as necessary to his successors dead as he had been alive. Even Gorbachev was not above the tradition. At the Party plenum on 21 October 1987, the last General Secretary found an opportunity to tweak Brezhnev: 'I savoured Leonid Ilyich Brezhnev's style of work as it was in the last stages. I know everything, comrades. It was the misfortune of our Party.'[89] He 'knew everything', but waited quite a while before saying anything about it.

In effect, from the middle of the 1970s Brezhnev took no active part in either Party or state activity, yet he still wanted to appear every day on the television screens. The result was that everyone, at home and abroad, could see his slow decline, the effort it cost him even to descend a staircase or lift the heavy volume containing the SALT-2 treaty in Vienna.[90] It had long been common knowledge in Moscow that at the rear of the cavalcade of black limousines accompanying Brezhnev on his increasingly rare visits to the capital would be a resuscitation vehicle. The Central Committee provided him with a highly qualified medical bodyguard that was on duty wherever he happened to be.

Yet Brezhnev still thought of himself as indispensable because of his 'great experience and wisdom'. He did not see that a wise man, with an understanding of the past and a feeling for what is to come, does not regard himself as the centre of existence, but can observe himself objectively. Brezhnev had no such ability. The shuffling gait, disjointed speech, wooden movements and complete inability to understand anything became the object of national pity and the butt of merciless jokes.

In 1982, the year of his death, Brezhnev was still able to make some trips around the country. As he walked under a gantry during a visit to an aircraft factory in Tashkent in March, it collapsed under the weight of the workers standing on it. The people around him tried to ward off the falling girders, but Brezhnev's collarbone was broken. He was in shock, and the strain on his heart and circulation was considerable.

On 28 October, two weeks before his death, Brezhnev was still able with great difficulty to 'make a speech' in the Kremlin in front of the Supreme Command Staff of the Soviet Army. And on the high holiday of the Bolshevik calendar, 7 November, when the October Revolution was commemorated with all due ceremony, Brezhnev got up onto the

Mausoleum and stood throughout the parade and processions. In their warm shoes, woollen underwear and almost identical mink hats, the ancient leaders alongside Brezhnev waved their fur-gloved hands weakly to the 'rejoicing masses' marching by. On that day, the present and three future General Secretaries were standing on the Mausoleum: Brezhnev, Andropov, Chernenko and Gorbachev.

In his last years, one of Brezhnev's eccentricities was his concern about his weight. He would begin the day by weighing himself, and would be unnerved by the slightest increase, as he seemed to think that weight-control was the answer to all ills. He loved walking and swimming, but this exercise did not save his rapidly deteriorating health. He suffered from insomnia and started taking sleeping pills in increasing doses, becoming addicted in due course. As his chief of security, General V. Medvedev, recalled, one of the members of the Politburo once advised Brezhnev to take his medicine with zubrovka, a flavoured vodka. According to Medvedev, it was the zubrovka that became the narcotic. Brezhnev did not drink a great deal of it, but with his failing system it acted as a depressant.[91] He had already suffered heart attacks, strokes and other illnesses. The nurse who took care of him, and of whom he became very fond, only encouraged his abuse of the sleeping pills. As a former smoker, moreover, Brezhnev had a constant craving to smell tobacco smoke, and General Medvedev relates that sometimes in the middle of the night he and his assistants would have to light up and 'fumigate' their sick leader as he lay in bed.

Following the incident in Tashkent, Brezhnev went downhill rapidly. He still made strenuous efforts to appear at parades and ceremonies, but all routine matters he handed over to Chernenko.

The day before he died was passed like most other days. He arrived back from Zavidovo after the 'shoot', and went to bed after supper, though it had been his usual practice first to watch the late evening news. Next morning at about nine, his bodyguards, Medvedev and Sobachenko, went in to wake him up, and found him dead in his bed.

Artificial respiration, the resuscitation team and the advice of Academician Chazov were to no avail. The first member of the Politburo to hear of the event, and also the first to arrive, was of course Andropov. Medvedev recalls that after he had told Andropov what had happened, the KGB chief remained perfectly calm and 'asked no unnecessary or unpleasant questions'.[92] Brezhnev's death was a surprise to no one.

By now the country was practically at a standstill, as stagnation had smothered every sphere of life. At his last Party Congress in 1981, the Twenty-Sixth, Brezhnev had opened his speech with the words: 'Comrades! The new Central Committee appointed by the Congress has just held its first plenum. Allow me to report its results. At its first Central Committee plenum, which passed in an atmosphere of exceptional unity and solidarity, the leading organs of our Party have been elected unanimously. The plenum has unanimously appointed as General Secretary of the Central Committee of the CPSU Comrade L.I. Brezhnev.'[93]

Naturally, everyone jumped up and gave the ritual 'storm of applause'. Brezhnev evidently felt no discomfort at the fact that, despite being utterly impotent, he was still holding the highest post in the land, and had reported it to the delegates himself. The most elementary moral values had become totally debased. Brezhnev and the other senile leaders at his side had become symbols of the decay, decline and erosion of the system.

Eighteen months later he was dead. While many in the country greeted the news with relief, the old men in the Politburo were alarmed. The question on their minds was, who should now take the first place among them? The military-industrial lobby was also concerned, as they had been Brezhnev's favourites. In the country at large, some people dared to wonder if something positive might now start to happen. The nation entered a long period of mourning. It seemed as if the very founder of the system was being buried, not merely its fourth leader.

A special meeting of the Politburo was convened the day Brezhnev died, at which the usual epithets were poured out, debasing further the vocabulary of praise: he had been a 'man of the greatest authority ... enchanting simplicity ... exceptional talent, an outstanding leader'. He had died on the morning of 10 November, but in true Bolshevik custom it was decided to 'darken the picture' by announcing that it had been on the eleventh, at 11 a.m. Mourning would last three days, 12–15 November. Schools were let out on the day of the burial, salvoes were fired, sirens sounded for five minutes and so on.[94]

For a week or two people still talked about Brezhnev, out of sheer habit, and then he somehow disappeared from their lives, without bitterness or sorrow. The Politburo, to be sure, a week after his death discussed a special item on the agenda: 'On immortalizing the memory of L.I. Brezhnev.' They had a draft resolution before them. First to speak was, of course, the new General Secretary. Andropov had been 'elected', on Chernenko's nomination, a matter of ten hours after Brezhnev's death:

ANDROPOV: I have some doubt about renaming the town of Zaporozhie [in Ukraine] as Brezhnev. Why? First, because it would be desirable to give the name of Brezhnev to a town in the [Russian Federative Republic]. Secondly, from the historical point of view Zaporozhie is not particularly suitable. It is associated with the Zaporozhian Sech [Cossack Host], with Cossack unrest and so on. Maybe it would be better to give the name Brezhnev to the town of Naberezhnye Chelny. Nor do I think we should name the cosmodrome after Leonid Ilyich. We shouldn't link the name of Leonid Ilyich with rockets, and the cosmodrome means rockets. It seems to me the best thing would be to name Star City in the Shchelkovsk district of Moscow region after Leonid Ilyich.

TIKHONOV: I support Comrade Andropov's suggestions, and I also think it would be right to give the name of Leonid Ilyich, for instance, to the Nurek Hydro-Electric Station [in Tadzhikistan]. Perhaps we could also give the name of Brezhnev to the Raspad coalmine in Kemerovo Oblast?

ANDROPOV: There was a big accident at the Raspad recently, a lot of people died. Perhaps we shouldn't include it in this.

TIKHONOV: Fine. Maybe we could give Leonid Ilyich's name to the icebreaker *Arktika*.

ANDROPOV: I'm for that.

TIKHONOV: What about giving Leonid Ilyich's name to the Oskol metalworks . . . And as for renaming squares, we should include the city of Kiev.

USTINOV: We could also give Brezhnev's name to an ocean-going passenger ship, but wait a while on a rivercraft.

A resolution was passed, and it was decided to raise the question of further renaming again at a later date.[95] This never happened.

Brezhnev's image was not only as the harbinger of the collapse of the system, but also as a symbol of the decline of Bolshevik power, towards which the people had long become indifferent. The regime no longer inspired fear or respect. If Lenin and Stalin, and to some extent even Khrushchev, were able to 'enliven' the moribund ideology of Communism, it was quite beyond Brezhnev, or for that matter anyone else. The most 'untroubled' period of Soviet history had come to an end. The country was on the threshold of dramatic change.

5

The Fifth Leader: Yuri Andropov

When Brezhnev died, there was a widespread feeling in the country that now change must come. The rest of the leadership, however, had other ideas. This was especially true of those who felt they had a claim to succeed to the supreme position, particularly Yuri Andropov and Konstantin Chernenko, of whom the former took precedence, as he had the support of the army in the person of Marshal Ustinov, who was also a friend, and of course of the almighty KGB, of which he had been the Chairman for fifteen years. He now became head of Brezhnev's funeral commission, which virtually indicated primacy in the leadership and the likelihood of succession.

The Politburo met in the afternoon of 10 November 1982, before the country had been officially informed of Brezhnev's death – although the rest of the world knew. Twenty-one members, candidates (non-voting members) and secretaries attended, and Andropov chaired the meeting. The entire procedure for the handover of supreme power took less than an hour.

Andropov remained calm, knowing that the helm of the Party (and state) was already in his hands. After asking the Politburo to 'stand in memory of dear Leonid Ilyich', he read out a short speech:

All people of goodwill have learnt of the death of Leonid Ilyich with deep sorrow. We, his close friends who worked with him in the Polit-buro, saw the great charm he possessed, the great force that bound us together in the Politburo, the great authority, love and respect that he enjoyed among all Communists, among the Soviet people and the peoples of the world. He enchanted everyone with his simplicity, his transparency, his unique talent as the leader of a great Party and country. He was indeed an outstanding leader, a wonderful friend, counsellor, comrade.

Andropov was playing a part. His speech was a ritual dictated by the unwritten rules of Party etiquette. As head of the KGB, he had formed a special unit to monitor public opinion, and to keep an eye and ear on the movements and utterances of the members of the Politburo. He knew better than most that in recent years Brezhnev's authority had fallen to the lowest point, that for practical purposes he had long ago left the affairs of office to others, that he had been capable of little more than his hunting trips to Zavidovo. Senile and confused, Brezhnev had for years been the butt of jokes and kitchen gossip for millions of Soviet citizens.

At the beginning of 1992 I stayed for ten days at Barvikha, the former nursing-home 'reserve' of the Central Committee. An elderly female member of staff told me in a hushed voice that whenever she had finished one of her minor tasks in the grand rooms specially built for Politburo members, if she had seen or talked with any of them she had to report it to a particular official at the sanatorium. He would want to know exactly what had been said and about whom, and what attitudes had been shown towards other leaders. The same procedure was followed everywhere: everything about the lives of Politburo members was known to the KGB.

Andropov also knew that Brezhnev had lost prestige not only because of the state of his health and his innate mediocrity, but also thanks to his, Andropov's, help. As Chairman of the KGB, a non-voting member of the Politburo since 1967 and from early 1972 a full member, Andropov had gone to great lengths to compromise Brezhnev's friends and relatives, as well as his own former deputy, S. Tsvigun, who was a protégé of Brezhnev. A. Kirilenko, a close associate of Brezhnev, Interior Minister N. Shchelokov, a favourite of the late leader, and even Brezhnev's daughter Galina had all been targets. It was Andropov who proposed that Brezhnev's authority should be raised by showing more of him on television. The daily exhibition on screen of the helpless and confused Party leader of course had the opposite effect, and Brezhnev steadily faded before the eyes of the population and the world.

In Brezhnev's last months, the foreign news digests prepared for

Andropov's eyes alone had been asking how much longer Brezhnev could last, and who would take over. They were quoting dissidents and repeating the jokes that were circulating about the moribund leader: Chernenko reports to Brezhnev: 'The General Secretary is very ill, and the people are saying that, to reassure the population, a dummy is riding around in his car.' Brezhnev retorts angrily: 'What nonsense! It's not true! I'm alive, and it's me in the dummy's seat!'[1]

Now, at the Politburo meeting only ten hours after Brezhnev's death, and in behind-the-scenes, one-to-one conversations, Andropov knew that he had elbowed his chief rival Chernenko aside. Throughout history, he knew, favourites were unloved, except by their master. The other members of the Politburo had not taken kindly to Brezhnev's blatant affection for Chernenko, a courtier with nothing to recommend him but zeal, flattery and loyalty to his patron. Andropov's position was crucially strengthened by the support of Marshal Ustinov. Prompted by Andropov, Ustinov approached Chernenko and suggested that Chernenko should nominate Andropov as the next General Secretary. Chernenko knew that Ustinov would not have made this proposal unless other important members of the Politburo had already been squared, and even though he knew his friend Tikhonov was prepared to nominate him, he agreed. To have refused would have meant complete defeat.

The succession meeting continued. In an even, calm voice, Andropov read his prepared speech:

> The course laid down by the Party at its recent congresses is the Leninist course. It was along this course that the Politburo, under the leadership of Leonid Ilyich, led our Party and the entire Soviet people in a straight line towards Communism. Of course, our enemies will do everything to destroy our unity and our faith in the future, to disrupt our ranks and our steadfastness. They will draw conclusions from the fact of Leonid Ilyich's death. None of us can replace Leonid Ilyich Brezhnev as General Secretary. We can successfully decide the issues which the Party must decide only collectively.
>
> On our agenda today we have the question of the General Secretaryship of the Central Committee of the CPSU. As for proposals, I would ask you, Comrades, to express yourselves.

Only Chernenko 'expressed himself', while emphasizing the fact that 'Leonid Ilyich had accorded enormous importance to collective leadership'; the Party and country could not be governed 'except by adhering to this founding principle'. He went on: 'I propose that Comrade Andropov be appointed General Secretary and that one of us be instructed to make this recommendation at a Central Committee plenum.'

The resolution was passed by general acclamation, and Ustinov proposed that Chernenko be asked to put it formally to the Central Committee. This too was greeted with unanimous approval, and Andropov, omitting to ask for further nominations or opinion, thanked his comrades for their 'high confidence' and ended business.[2]

A great country should have great plans and ideals. The USSR had had no real plans for years, and its ideals had faded long ago. Andropov, however, made a desperate, brief attempt to breathe new life into the ossified policies. At first it seemed he might succeed, backed as he was by the enormously experienced KGB, successor of Lenin's brainchild the Cheka. But the system had exhausted its historic resources, and the old methods for resolving economic, political, social and spiritual problems were no longer applicable. Authoritarian ways could only be effective in preserving the system for a while. What the country needed were big, radical solutions, and Andropov, an old orthodox Communist, was not up to it, even had he had more time.

To overcome the crisis facing the country, he resorted to 'Lenin's ideas' on discipline, order and organization. It was a course that appealed to many bureaucrats and Party leaders, as well as to ordinary citizens, and it was a course that soon proved ineffective.

Fifteen Years as KGB Chief

As early as the beginning of the century, Lenin, pondering the notion of liberty, knew that his version of an 'earthly paradise' could be accomplished only by force and the might of a dictatorial regime. The driving force of the social movement that was created in Lenin's wake was not the 'pre-eminence of the socialist order', or 'friendship of the peoples', or the 'growing role of the CPSU', but coercion. The weapon that wielded this force was the Party and its special services, which in Andropov's day was called the Committee of State Security, or KGB.

Lenin loved his Cheka, because he understood that the regime he had created could not survive without the systematic use of state terror. The chiefs of the 'punitive organs' were immeasurably more important than all the chairmen, people's commissars and ministers put together, for they personified the regime's capacity to survive. Andropov also understood this. Officially, for twenty-five years, since 1957, he had held high positions in the Central Committee and KGB.

A Marxist idealist, Andropov had a profound belief in the virtually messianic role of the KGB and the inexhaustible vitality of Leninism. On the 106th anniversary of Lenin's birth on 22 April 1976, for instance, he could say with complete conviction: 'Only socialism can guarantee genuine people's power . . . All this is the enormous achievement of Soviet society, the enormous successes in the development of socialist democracy. Everything that has been achieved here has long put socialism far ahead of the most democratic bourgeois states.'[3]

Those in high places were largely unknown quantities to the general public, yet people somehow had the idea that Andropov was a 'liberal Chekist' who knew English and German, was a jazz fan and even loved abstract art. Practically no one knew that he had written a little poetry. The intelligent-looking man in glasses, always in a snow-white shirt and dark suit, was outwardly quite unlike the early Chekists in their leather tunics with Mausers at their belts. A good family man, Andropov did not attend university, but was self-taught and extremely well read. Everyone who met him found him educated, modest and reserved in his manner.

He was born in 1914 in Stavropol in the Northern Caucasus. His father died when he was two years old, and his mother when he was seventeen. At the age of fourteen, after seven years of school, the young Andropov worked for two years as assistant to a film projectionist at the railwaymen's club in Mozdok, then as a telegraph worker and later as a sailor on a riverboat. In 1932 he entered Rybinsk Water Economy Technical School. In his application he wrote: 'I request a hostel room and a grant, as I have no means for my continued existence.'[4]

After completing his studies he worked for a while as a sailor, river-pilot and first mate on a rivercraft. He was good at his job, and socially active. His personal dossier contains such trivial information as the fact that he 'distributed tickets for Osoaviakhim [the Society for Assisting the Defence and Aero-Chemical Construction of the USSR]' and that 'he did this work well.' Also that he took an active part in the Komsomol cell at Mozdok, helped in a campaign to eliminate illiteracy and wrote for the newspaper *Signal*.[5] He then entered Petrozavodsk University, but did not stay long. Later, he completed the Higher Party School.

Andropov made a good impression wherever he went and was, inevitably, spotted by the Party's talent scouts, ever watchful for gifted young people. In due course he became an organizer for the river-wharf Komsomol, and in 1937–38 Secretary and then First Secretary of the Yaroslavl Regional Komsomol Committee. In 1944 he was made First Komsomol Secretary in Karelia, which put him in line for a fully-fledged Party job. In 1951 he became a Central Committee Inspector, with a four-year break during which he was engaged in diplomatic work. From 1961 he was a member of the Central Committee, and from the following year a Central Committee Secretary with responsibility for KGB affairs.

Andropov's posting as Ambassador to Hungary between 1954 and 1957 made a deep impression on him and on his attitudes towards Moscow's satellites. As an orthodox Marxist, he interpreted the events of 1956, which shocked him profoundly, as 'the hand of imperialism', and he remained a firm advocate of tough measures.

Khrushchev recalled that after a debate on the Hungarian situation in the Presidium: 'We asked Marshal Konev, who was the commander of Warsaw Pact troops, "How much time would it take if we instructed you to restore order in Hungary and to crush the counter-revolutionary forces?"

'He thought for a moment and replied, "Three days, no longer."

'"Then start getting ready. You'll hear from us when it's time to begin."'[6]

Andropov's role was to prepare politically for the suppression. As Ambassador his function was extremely important: acting as a Chekist, he helped decapitate the revolution. The Hungarian Prime Minister Imre Nagy and the Defence Minister Pal Máléter were both arrested with Andropov's assistance. It was Andropov who persuaded János Kádár to adopt a clear pro-Soviet position and to head a government formed by Moscow. And he maintained constant contact with the Soviet generals in charge of the operation.

Andropov knew Imre Nagy well, and when Nagy announced that Hungary would leave the Warsaw Pact, he urged Moscow to hasten its decision to send in troops. He also advised on how to extricate Nagy from the Yugoslav Embassy, where he had taken refuge. The 'guarantees' given for the Hungarian leader's safety turned out to be worthless, of course, and Nagy was shot six months later. How Andropov felt about the fate of this one-time friend is unknown. What is known is that they had shared an interest in poetry and had talked about Nagy's favourite, the Hungarian national poet Sandor Petöfi. Andropov must have wondered how Nagy, who had at one time worked for the NKVD, could have turned 'traitor'.

Memoirs written by the Hungarian Party chief Mátyás Rákosi, who was ousted by the uprising and went back to Russia, were seized by the KGB when he died, as it was feared they might reach the West. In fact the manuscript, which is held in the former Party archives, takes a wholly pro-Soviet position, and Andropov was happy to find no adverse comment on his role as Ambassador.

In general, Andropov's career was typical of most of the Soviet leaders of his generation. Having been co-opted as a youth into the nomenklatura, he was not left to languish in the lower and middle ranks, but made his way quickly to the top. Of all seven Soviet leaders, however, he was the first to move from the KGB to the highest Party position. This transition was no accident: the nearer the system came to the edge of the abyss, the stronger and more widespread the influence of the KGB. It is important to note, however, that policy had shifted from the physical terror of the time of Lenin and Stalin, to the spiritual and ideological control of society. As head of the KGB for fifteen years, Andropov had come to the conclusion that the widespread use of concentration camps had had its day. It had discredited the Party and the USSR in the eyes of the world, and, more important, it had been ineffectual. Nor could it be claimed that the perfection of the terror machine was compatible with the assertion that socialism was 'far more democratic than the most democratic states'.

When Khrushchev dealt his blow against the punitive organs at the Twentieth Congress, he forced them to seek other means of controlling and containing society. Andropov proved himself able to carry out a certain degree of 'liberalization' of the KGB, shifting its main effort from the isolation and incarceration of unreliable elements to the monitoring of individual and public opinion. Of course, people were still arrested and exiled, imprisoned or deported abroad for their convictions. But the centre of gravity moved to so-called 'preventive work'. In this regard Andropov achieved much: he engaged academic research in the study of trends and attitudes, he strengthened security in Party circles and drew attention to the need to 'purify' Marxism-Leninism. Under him, the KGB emerged as the guardian of ideas, and most of the speeches he made were on ideology in one form or another.

His articles bore such titles as 'Leninism Lights Our Way', 'Proletarian Internationalism: The Communists' Battle Banner', 'Friendship of the Soviet Peoples: The Inexhaustible Source of Our Victories', 'Leninism: The Science and Art of Revolutionary Creativity', 'Ideological Sabotage: The Poisonous Weapon of Imperialism', 'Leninism: The Inexhaustible Source of the Masses' Revolutionary Energy and Creativity'. One would seek in vain for unorthodox content in any of these writings, still less any personal touch. Even in what might be called his 'testamentary' article, 'The Teaching of Karl Marx and Problems of Socialist Construction in the USSR', published in *Kommunist* in the spring of 1983, one finds only the old, traditional themes about the inexhaustibility and creative character of Marxism, and the need to raise discipline, order and organization.

Andropov believed that the only way to preserve the stagnant system was by maintaining and strengthening control of thought, public opinion and the people's mood. 'The strict measurement and strict observance of this principle' was of great importance to him.[7]

No sooner had he taken up his new post as head of the KGB in 1967 than he asked to see the files for some old cases. These included 'Case-log No. 8355' on 'Ramsay', the code name for Richard Sorge, whom he regarded as one of the best Soviet agents. During the spy-mania of the 1930s, the NKVD labelled Sorge a 'German-Japanese spy', and would have arrested him after his recall had he not decided to stay in Tokyo, where the Japanese eventually hanged him anyway. Stalin wrote such an insulting comment on one of Sorge's most important reports that none of his further despatches was ever shown to him. Under Andropov's rule at the KGB, Sorge was not merely rehabilitated, but a postage stamp was issued with his face on it.

Andropov was familiar with the system of permanent surveillance of 'dangerous individuals', both in the USSR and abroad. An example was Alexander Kerensky, Prime Minister of the Provisional Government in 1917 and known to the Soviet secret service as 'The Clown'. His file was only closed in 1963, 'on account of his advanced age and the unlikelihood of results'.

The files also showed that the rules introduced by Stalin to ensure the smooth operation of the terror of the 1930s were still observed to the letter as late as 1950. For instance, when Kuznetsov, Voznesensky, Popkov and other leading figures in Leningrad were sentenced on 30 September 1950, and shot a few hours later, no appeal had been permitted and the event was reported at once, as required by the government decree of 1 December 1934.[8]

Andropov spent a long time leafing through the thick volume of the Politburo Commission on Judicial Affairs, chaired by Kalinin, that had ratified the Supreme Court sentences. It contained interminable lists of Trotskyist, Japanese, Polish, British, Romanian, Estonian, Latvian and French 'spies'.[9] The file on thirteen leading figures of the Jewish Anti-Fascist Committee may have interested the new Chairman, as a number of commentators in the West had asserted that his wife was Jewish. The case had been mounted by Stalin and his henchmen in order to inflame anti-Semitic feeling in the country at large – partly to create scapegoats to deflect attention from the pitifully low standard of living, partly to sustain anti-foreign hysteria in the Cold War. Among the 'damning evidence' in the file was a photograph showing the Chairman of the Committee, the actor Solomon Mikhoels, and the poet Itsik Fefer in the smiling company of Albert Einstein. It had been taken at Einstein's Princeton house when a Soviet Jewish delegation visited the USA during the war to raise funds for the Soviet war effort.[10] One Colonel Vorobyov had carefully noted in the file that the thirteen 'Jewish nationalists' were shot on the night of 12 August 1952.[11]

Andropov also saw a host of material showing that the physical foundations of Communism had been constructed by the labour of millions of camp inmates. When the Central Committee issued Stalin's directive to establish the Norilsk metal-mining complex, for instance, the order was simply given to 'organize a special camp'.[12]

It is hard to know what Andropov felt as he read through these dreadful papers. He had already spent many years in the middle levels of power, and knew a great deal, but it was only when he became head of the KGB that he saw the scale of the Stalinist state terror, which had been so thoroughly concealed by the Party leadership. What he thought of his sinister agency's history may be deduced from his speeches, in which he followed the spirit of the Twentieth Congress by condemning the 'illegal repressions', but consistently defended the KGB's right to monitor the whole of society.

As for foreign intelligence and counter-intelligence, under Andropov they were guarded ever more jealously, despite a number of failures caused mostly by sensational defections. Thanks to the skills of its practitioners, foreign intelligence delivered confidential information of the highest quality. In his first annual report to Brezhnev, Andropov wrote that in the course of 1967 the service had succeeded in 'recruiting 218 foreigners, of whom sixty-four have operational opportunities in our work against the USA'. In the same period the KGB had managed to obtain the ciphers of several capitalist countries, and to send the Central Committee and Defence Ministry more than nine thousand intelligence items, including designs of foreign technology.[13]

Andropov's last major report as Chairman, for the year of Brezhnev's death, was a much less informative document, though even there he was able to note that the KGB had managed to obtain all the technical information requested by the military-industrial complex and the Ministry of Defence.[14] It was probably during Andropov's tenure at the KGB that the Soviet secret service achieved its greatest successes abroad.

It is clear now that Andropov knew far more than the General Secretary about many things. Among the closely guarded secrets known to him were: the location of the secret protocols to the Molotov–Ribbentrop Pact of 1939; the Soviet leadership's decision to exterminate Polish officers and other Polish citizens at Katyn; where Hitler's bones were buried; what had happened to the White Russian anti-Soviet activists Generals Miller and Kutepov, who were kidnapped in Paris in the 1930s; details of the plan to assassinate Tito; the location of the remains of Lin Piao, whose plane had crashed in Mongolia as he attempted to flee from China to the USSR; the extent of Soviet gold reserves; the real attitudes of the Soviet people to Brezhnev; how many informers there were in the country; the names of Western social and political figures who were working for the USSR. And he knew far better and in greater depth than any of his colleagues the true state of the country.

Possessed of a powerful analytical mind, Andropov led an ascetic, closed life. He knew his personnel well and had great authority in the agency, as well as in top Party circles. He was somewhat feared, but respected. He rarely made public appearances, apart from the obligatory official meetings, and was regarded in general as an enigmatic figure. He left far fewer documents, especially personal ones, than his predecessors. Most of them are still in KGB archives under the seal 'of special importance'. He made many of his jottings in very small notebooks and scratch-pads or on bits of paper, which he no doubt carried in his pocket. And, in true Chekist tradition, what he committed to paper was minimal in the extreme. The exception was his thoroughness in recording the names of people he received and the length of time they were with him. The number of people he saw is not great, but he seems to have seen them on a regular basis. For instance, the yellowish velvet-bound diary for 1982 – his last year as Chairman of the KGB – shows that he received all the senior officers of the special services, and that he did so often. He also met such senior officials in the Party and government administration as Gorbachev, Grishin, Pelshe and others, as well as leading figures from the fields of mass communication and culture. He had worked with many of these people in the Central Committee apparatus, including Georgy Shakhnazarov, Arkady Volsky, Alexander Bovin and Georgy Arbatov.

Andropov was a strictly desk-bound leader with an analytical bent. He rarely left the capital to visit the provinces, and hardly ever appeared on television or met the press. He was in many ways a classic Chekist of the Leninist school. Those who knew him saw in him the manner of an old-fashioned intellectual. He never shouted, like Khrushchev, never cursed, like Gorbachev, did not talk about himself, like Brezhnev. He looked people straight in the eye, unlike Chernenko, and his quiet voice made everyone listen intently to what he was saying. His manner of speaking was terse and to the point. It was clear that he did not favour empty phrases or vagueness. He made it a condition for giving an interview to R. Augstein of *Der Spiegel* in 1983 that his photograph should not appear on the cover of the magazine. Gazing myopically at his interlocutors, Augstein wrote,

Andropov unhurriedly, but precisely, formulated phrases that could be printed with no further editing. But everything he said was already well known; he revealed nothing new or sensational.

In an eleven-page report to Brezhnev on KGB activity in March 1981, in which, as always, he referred to his men as 'Chekists', Andropov wrote:

> In carrying out the instructions of the Central Committee, in good time [the KGB] executed the necessary measures to ensure state security during the run-up to the Twenty-Sixth Party Congress; satisfactory results were obtained in a number of important sectors of intelligence work to gain information of a political, economic, scientific-technological, military character; the Committee attached exceptional importance to the meetings and talks Comrade L.I. Brezhnev had with the leaders of France, the Federal German Republic, India and other foreign countries; facts were acquired systematically about the hostile plans and the anti-Soviet activities of the secret services of the USA and other foreign states, and foreign centres of ideological sabotage; the Committee has sent the Instance [General Secretary], the ministries and departments more than eight thousand items of information, including more than five hundred analytical reports. About six thousand items were sent to the Central Committee and Council of Ministers of the USSR; [the Committee] succeeded in dealing with several major tasks in scientific-technological intelligence. Documentary materials have been acquired, as well as US and other leading capitalist countries' plans for important problems of economics, science and technology ... On military-industrial questions about fourteen thousand items and two thousand types of design have been obtained; the work of strengthening illegal intelligence has continued. The Committee carried out a large number of special missions and instructions of the Politburo and Central Committee Secretariat; ninety-six attempts to recruit Soviet citizens who were likely to betray the Motherland were intercepted; we failed to prevent the non-return to the USSR of twenty tourists and delegation-members, and fifteen ocean-going seamen and fishermen; a perceptible blow was struck at the structure of leadership and the illegal printing base of Baptist-sectarians ... six illegal presses and printing locations and more than thirty staging posts have been discovered and destroyed; 1,512 authors and distributors of anonymous anti-Soviet and slanderous documents have been identified; 15,557 Soviet citizens have been cautioned, 433 arrested for hostile activity ... [15]

The report omitted to point out that the KGB had carried out the transfer of large sums of money in foreign currency to 'fraternal parties' through its own channels. The Central Committee had established a special 'International Fund for Aid to Left Workers' Organizations' which supplemented the money Moscow gave its foreign supporters. In 1971 the Party deposited US$14 million in the fund, in 1972 the same amount, and from 1973 to 1977 US$15 million each year, and various other large sums almost until the end of détente. The usual form of the Central Committee's instructions was: 'Order the management of Gosbank (Comrade M.N. Sveshnikov) to issue $14,000,000 to Comrade B.N. Ponomaryov for special purposes.'[16]

Apart from the Romanians, who condemned the Soviet invasion of Czechoslovakia in 1968, and thereafter pursued a more or less independent foreign policy, all the Communist parties of the Warsaw Pact contributed on average half a million dollars a year to the fund. The Italian, French and American parties received the largest sums, along with a few others. After receiving an order, the KGB would organize the transfer to the 'fraternal parties' through bank accounts in numerous capital cities. Communist Party leaders who were banned in their own countries usually lived in Moscow on a full pension approved by the Central Committee. These matters were dealt with by the Central Committee's International Department and by the KGB itself.

It was Andropov's idea to hold regular meetings with top officials from the security services of other socialist countries on the struggle against 'imperialist ideological sabotage'. These meetings were held in Moscow, Havana, Budapest, Sofia and elsewhere,[17] and were as much an opportunity for Moscow to give direction to 'fraternal organs' as to co-ordinate activities and exchange experience.

While maintaining the traditional burden of 'Chekist' work, under Andropov the KGB devoted a great deal of time and effort to political, ideological, military-industrial and 'preventive' issues. Having repudiated mass repression, it nevertheless was becoming more than ever a state within a state. Even the Central Committee did not have complete control over the KGB: apart from the General Secretary, the head of the Administrative Department and two or three members of the Politburo, no one had the right to poke their nose into the KGB's affairs.

Thanks to Andropov, the KGB greatly increased the activities of the intelligence and counter-intelligence services abroad, with the emphasis on military-industrial information. Its chief domestic task was dealing with the dissident movement, or more accurately, anyone who expressed a dissident thought. It was Andropov who approved the numerous trials of such human rights activists as Peter Grigorenko, Natalya Gorbanevskaya, Andrei Amalrik, Alexander Ginzburg, Vladimir Bukovsky, Anatoly Shcharansky, Zviad Gamsakhurdia, Vyacheslav Chornovil and others. He had learnt his 'Hungarian lesson', and knew that those events had begun with 'the toleration of trouble-makers'. On 5 December 1979, the Day of the Constitution, fifty human rights activists, including Andrei Sakharov, gathered at the Pushkin monument in Moscow to protest against the Soviet Union's record on human rights. At 6 p.m. they removed their hats and observed a minute's silence in memory of the victims of Bolshevik repression. Next morning, a report on the incident, giving all the names and signed by Andropov, lay on the desks of the General Secretary and Politburo members.[18]

The old Leninist policy of deporting dissidents abroad was revived by Andropov. In 1981, for instance, fourteen people were deprived of their Soviet citizenship and expelled. When the Politburo debated the subject of Alexander Solzhenitsyn on 7 January 1974, Andropov declared: 'Comrades, I have been raising the question of Solzhenitsyn since 1965. He has now reached a new stage in his hostile activity. He is attacking Lenin, the October Revolution, the Soviet system. His book *The Gulag Archipelago* is not a work of creative literature, it is a political document. This is dangerous. We have in the country hundreds of thousands of Vlasovites, Ounites and other hostile elements. [Vlasov was a Soviet general who, as a prisoner of war, defected to the Nazis; the OUN was the Union of Ukrainian Nationalists.] Therefore, all the measures I have proposed to the Central Committee about Solzhenitsyn should be implemented, that is, he should be deported from the country.'[19]

The other speakers all supported Andropov, of course. *Pravda* and other newspapers began a propaganda campaign along these lines, while the majority of duped Soviet citizens believed the lies that were peddled about Solzhenitsyn, Sakharov and other truth-tellers.

Andropov had a prodigious capacity for work. He read a vast

amount, and was deeply interested in the most varied of his agency's activities. For instance, in 1976, when the exchange of Luis Corvalan, the Chilean Communist leader, for the Soviet dissident Vladimir Bukovsky was being arranged, he took personal charge of the operation. In 1980, before the Olympic Games opened in Moscow, he showered the Central Committee with warnings about 'impending ideological sabotage', 'possible terrorist acts' and 'exceptional activity by Western secret services'.

Some Western observers, and not a few Russians, have called Andropov a 'liberal Chekist'. Undoubtedly, he was distinguished from his predecessors as leader by his breadth of mind, his analytical ability and his personal modesty. Yet he was to the marrow of his bones a Chekist of the Lenin school. He adapted quickly to the new circumstances, saw the approaching crisis sooner than many, and understood that the main threat to the system came not only from economic stagnation, but also from a rise in the rebellious state of mind of a growing number of people.

For all his intellectual ability, Andropov could propose nothing to save either society or the Party, beyond the orthodox framework of Leninist doctrine. Even had he lived longer, with his habits and outlook he could have changed nothing in a fundamental way. The collapse of the system could not be averted by administrative means, and he was not capable of proposing deep reforms. He would not live to see the reformation of the USSR. The Chekist, police view of the world was an ephemeral basis for the radical changes that were coming.

Fifteen Months as Party Leader

Andropov was sixty-eight when he became General Secretary. He had spent the first half of his adult life in Party organizations, and the second in the security organs. True to unwritten Bolshevik tradition, he assured his comrades in the Politburo that movement along the 'Leninist path' would continue as before. On the other hand, he had to prove himself by undertaking some new initiative or adopting a new concept. Stalin concentrated on acquiring the monopoly on Lenin's heritage, making himself impregnable. Khrushchev chose to stress agriculture and the gradual reinforcement of anti-Stalinist positions.

Brezhnev directed the Party's attention to a rebirth of the 'Leninist norms' and finding ways to maintain stability.

Each successive leader, while swearing allegiance to Leninism, had in some sense disavowed his predecessor. While usually not speaking of it openly, each General Secretary created his own policy, his manner of governing and his own line. Andropov, too, felt he must do something new and original that would give the people hope, especially as the population was so tired of Brezhnev's 'stability' and wanted the new leader to do something tangible in their interest. Everyone knew he had been the chief of the KGB, but no one knew what sort of person he was. His portrait might be hanging in every club and public place, but that told the people nothing. He had to do something to declare himself.

He began by reorganizing the work of the Politburo and reallocating it among its members. One week after he came to power, an item appeared on the agenda: 'Questions of organizing the work of the Politburo and the Central Committee Secretariat'. Andropov opened the debate by discussing his own work (referring to himself in the third person, a habit that harked back to the early years of Bolshevism): 'I would regard it as essential that Andropov should deal with such questions as organizing the work of the Politburo, the country's defence, fundamental issues of the CPSU's domestic and foreign policy and foreign trade, and deployment of the leading cadres of Party and state.'[20]

He then unequivocally indicated that his deputy was to be none other than Brezhnev's favourite Konstantin Chernenko. He had not done this earlier, but Chernenko had his friends and supporters, and not to have done so now would have looked too much like an anti-Brezhnev declaration. But he then proceeded to overburden Chernenko with tasks he could not possibly shoulder. Either this was a ploy to knock him out of the picture, or he believed no one else in the Politburo was capable of bearing such an impossible load.

In any event, Andropov announced: 'In the light of changed circumstances, Comrade K.U. Chernenko should, in my opinion, handle the issues I used to handle, plus KGB and MVD [Interior Ministry] matters, plus all the work of the Administrative Department in general, plus the Party organs department, the general department and the letters department. Comrade Chernenko's attention should be concentrated on questions of ideology in the work of the Central Committee: the propaganda, cultural, scientific and higher educational departments. He should also handle Central Committee Secretariat matters.'[21] In effect, this meant that Chernenko did all the work of the Central Committee, apart from the areas Andropov had appropriated for himself. Two ill old men now held the main levers of influence over the most varied spheres of Party and national life. They had divided between them the lion's share of responsibilities, while avoiding direct control of the economy.

As General Secretary, at first Andropov sat in his office until late at night, holding meetings with numerous officials, conferring frequently with Chernenko, and calling for endless information and files. It seems clear now that he was seeking a way to restore the health of society, looking for miracle cures and ways to resuscitate the decaying system, to reassure the population, breathe new life into the Party and launch the final 'ascent' to the Communist heights.

He tried not to see that this was an impossible task. He had no choice. He had to stem the crisis before it erupted. As an integral part of the Party mechanism created by Lenin and Stalin, he was incapable of seeing the need for widespread and radical reform, or for a review of certain basic assumptions of Marxism-Leninism, or for mobilizing the human resources of the population for the genuine democratization of society. Class dogma held Andropov firmly within the framework of the Leninist way of thinking and acting.

Following the November 1982 Plenum which appointed him General Secretary, Andropov held a series of meetings at the Central Committee in which he harped on a single idea: any improvement in the health of society and the state was possible only on the basis of the wholesale strengthening of discipline. This was not a new idea. Since Lenin's time, the Party had done little other than pass resolutions and issue tougher and tougher demands on the Soviet population, whether at work, in their behaviour or their loyalty. In Stalin's day, people were put in prison for being absent from work, and prohibited from changing their jobs. Farm-labouring hours were set by the state, and there was incessant ideological control. While this police regime was somewhat slackened in later years, the Party organs were always poised for the chance to 'tighten the screw', intensify surveillance, and 'introduce order' at work and in everyday life.

In order to gauge the response of ordinary people to the Central Committee's edicts, literally *millions* of undercover agents were recruited among workers, farmers, soldiers, intellectuals, priests, cultural figures and clerks. For decades the country had been wrapped in a web of informers, 'observers' and secret agents, known colloquially as *stukachi* and *seksoty*, 'knockers' and secret assistants. Paid small but regular sums, these people, who went in constant fear of exposure, informed the 'organs' of any 'suspicious' utterances they may have heard or acts they may have seen.

The Politburo examined this issue periodically. On 20 December 1960, for instance, KGB Chairman Alexander Shelepin reported that 'groups of unofficial informers' were being formed 'to assist in surveillance on an unpaid basis'.[22] Widespread surveillance continued right up to the end of the 1980s.

Andropov wanted to try to mobilize the spiritual, moral and physical forces of the country to carry out the Party's programmes, but as a good Bolshevik, he persisted in the belief that society could not be allowed to develop its own initiatives. Instead, he stuck to the tried and tested – and useless – methods pursued by his immediate predecessor.

He knew from the Party and KGB reports that flowed into his office that the majority of the people would support his policy of 'introducing order'. In one sense, order is an important feature of any healthy society, but the Soviet people had become used over the years to having their entire lives harshly regimented. This bureaucratic, administrative programming had gradually made them unresponsive, obedient, cowed and willing to support any new 'initiative' emanating from the authorities. And Andropov, because he was orthodox and could not stray beyond the prescribed framework, could think of nothing better than yet again saddling up the worn-out nag of Bolshevik discipline.

A speech he made at a meeting of Central Committee Secretaries on 18 January 1983 was typical: 'At the top of our agenda at the moment is the question of strengthening labour and production discipline, and the methods and style of our work . . . As is known, Muscovites have already spoken up in favour of strengthening labour and production discipline, and on introducing much-needed order into production and in the city as a whole. Their initiative has been approved by the Central Committee.'[23]

In his ninety-minute speech, Andropov repeated again and again the phrase 'it is necessary to strengthen production and labour discipline', to the point where his audience became uncomfortable. He punctuated his emphasis on this 'new' panacea with incantations about the need to ensure that 'discipline must be conscious', for which purpose it was necessary to develop 'all forms of mass political work' by mobilizing 'the press, and Party, Soviet and trade union organizations'.

The speech went beyond recognizing the stagnant condition of the economy and society, and was a call for a change in leadership style. Andropov repeated the well-worn clichés of Party-speak in demanding 'concrete information' and a 'concentration of attention on the most important issues', fewer meetings and more 'grassroots work with people'. These banalities had been common parlance since Lenin's day. Behind their expediency, rationality and businesslike character lay the leadership's inability to fathom the underlying causes of the permanent crisis in which Soviet history had been lived.

To an objection by Pelshe that the Central Committee organization 'sometimes handles problems that should be dealt with by the ministries and departments', Andropov retorted: 'Our job is to sort out the less important issues from the more important and leave it to the ministries and departments to handle the trivial issues.' He could not have made it plainer that the Politburo and Central Committee would continue to operate as a super-government, running the national economy and governing society by directive, while the nominal government would be left to handle 'trivial issues'. His remarks drew grunts of 'Quite right,' 'Agreed.'

In their brief speeches the Secretaries supported the 'Andropov line' on tightening discipline. Gorbachev agreed that one of the most important questions was 'strengthening labour and production discipline'. He spoke of 'raising the role of the labour collective', 'brigade contracts', 'strengthening the checks on [work] completion', and similar familiar themes. However, he also stressed an idea that was floating around at the time, that Andropov had 'given rise to very good hopes for change'. Following this meeting, Party organizations everywhere began debating measures to strengthen all manner of discipline: office, technological, military. It was as if Andropov had discovered the elixir that would revive society. Tired of their grey and colourless lives, people seized even this weak ray of light as a sign that things were going to improve. They wanted to believe that life could get better.

A couple of weeks after the meeting, Andropov suddenly appeared at the Ordzhonikidze machine-tool plant in Moscow. He went at once to the workshops, cast a managerial eye over the production process, and chatted with workers and engineers. He did not promise a better life soon, but he did stress that order and discipline would be toughened up and that output would be more and better. The workers listened in silence as the tall, pale-faced man talked to them like a foreman about order, discipline, absenteeism – the all-too familiar slogans of Soviet industrial life. They were more interested in wages, housing, local transport, empty shops and endless queues.

Andropov still had the strength to begin his campaign against slackness, disorder and inefficiency, and also to strike several telling blows against the fat-cat Secretaries of republics and regions, as well as senior officials in the ministries, where corruption, nepotism and embezzlement were rife. The courts were full of cases of people who were more interested in criminal gain than 'production and labour discipline'. Several prominent individuals were even shot for 'theft on an especially large scale'. The manager of the most important food shop in Moscow made front-page news when he was charged with criminal malpractice. The public reaction was largely approving, as if to demonstrate that the people longed for the old times, when 'antisocial' acts were vigorously dealt with by the courts.

Andropov's demand for order was not aimed only at ordinary citizens. He showed that he also intended to deal decisively with leading figures in the system. The first major victim of the 'new course' was the Minister of the Interior, N. Shchelokov, one of Brezhnev's old cronies. A little over a month after taking office, Andropov removed Shchelokov and instituted judicial proceedings against him for corruption. Andropov's death delayed proceedings, but soon after Chernenko came to power Shchelokov decided not to wait for the outcome of a trial, but went home and killed himself.

It is hard to tell how far Andropov would have gone in toughening up the system. He might have preserved it for a while, but it is obvious that his old Bolshevik methods would have cured nothing. He was plainly looking backwards for a solution, rather than forwards. Nevertheless, among the older generation he inspired some hope and a good deal of respect. They saw that he was prepared to remove a corrupt and powerful minister, that he did not pin medals on himself, and that he was dealing seriously with bribery and laziness. Reports from the provinces spoke of 'general approval for the course of introducing order and strengthening discipline'.

Andropov glanced swiftly at these reports. He would have expected nothing else – instructions from the centre invariably received the 'approval' of the people. Visitors arriving at Leningrad Airport in the mid-1980s, for instance, were greeted by a huge banner above the terminal building which proclaaimed, 'We approve the foreign policy of the CPSU'. Who 'we' were and what other choice 'we' might have made were not real questions.

For as long as his health permitted, Andropov dedicated himself to tightening things up. He was less preoccupied with foreign policy than his predecessors, and concentrated instead on rooting out corruption. Chairing the Politburo and countless other meetings, he tried to keep his comrades' attention focused on the single idea he had expressed when taking office. On 1 July 1983 he held a meeting in his office with a group of senior officials, including Mikhail Gorbachev, Grigory Romanov, Konstantin Chernenko, Vladimir Dolgikh and Nikolai Ryzhkov, to discuss 'the restoration of order in the country', but the talk shifted to a wider range of topics, such as the mountain of paperwork facing Politburo members, the poor quality of Soviet automobiles, and the poor performance of gas sales abroad.

Andropov kept drawing the discussion back to his main theme: how were the decisions of the November Plenum on discipline being implemented? Dolgikh announced, 'We have sent draft instructions on labour discipline to the Politburo. It is a good document.' Andropov replied irritably: 'But there are still a lot of people loafing about doing nothing, still a lot of absentees.'[24]

Half a year had passed since the line on discipline had been adopted, and yet only now had a draft decree been prepared for the Party leadership. Everyone felt, though no one would say, that the deep-seated malaise of the system would not be cured by rounding up unemployed young people or deporting spongers from the capital. Discussions on discipline and order were well and good, but they would have no perceptible effect on the economic situation as a whole.

Andropov's efforts seem today as doomed as the labours of Sisyphus. Perhaps the stone could have been rolled to the top of the hill, but what was the point? And why prolong the agony of a system that had no future? Andropov believed in a mirage, an illusory goal. Socialist competition, threatening orders from the Central Committee and administrative sanctions were no substitute for personal self-interest and the objective laws of economics. The system was standing still. The national reservoir of enthusiasm, on which the Bolsheviks had relied for decades, had run out. No amount of 'historic decisions' by Party plenums could overcome the apathy and indifference of millions. More and more people came to realize this.

Andropov might have been helped by international difficulties, by 'imperialist intrigues'. To some extent, the shooting down on 1 September 1983 of a South Korean civilian aircraft carrying 269 passengers by Soviet fighter aircraft was used with this in mind. The Politburo did everything possible to use the tragic incident to paper over the cracks in the system by referring to 'the imperialist threat' and the need to 'strengthen the socialist commonwealth' in the face of America's militaristic forces. But it was precisely this incident that highlighted the single-mindedness and inflexibility of Soviet foreign policy, and that became the unfortunate symbol of Andropov's decline.

The General Secretary and the Politburo

All four previous General Secretaries had been younger than Andropov when they came to power. Lenin had been forty-seven, Stalin forty-two, Khrushchev and Brezhnev fifty-nine. Andropov, despite the fact that he was younger than a good many of his comrades in the leadership, was in his late sixties. He had little time to sit and ponder his position.

But it was not only time he lacked: his range of options was also strictly limited. He could imitate the 'historic decisions' of the past, parade the 'superiority of socialism', delude himself and the millions of people he governed with 'the inexhaustibility of the Leninist heritage'. But he could do nothing to bring about basic change. As a convinced conservative, he could not undertake any reform that might place the 'socialist conquests' at risk. He could not imagine introducing a free-market economy, or officially encourage liberalism, let alone dissidence. He may have been highly intelligent, but he was also bound by the orthodoxy of his convictions, the rules of the 'Party game' and the demands of the system. Shortly before coming to power he had said: 'There are many in the West who desperately want there to be an organized opposition in the USSR, even an artificial one. The Soviet people will never allow this, and they are capable of shielding themselves from renegades and their Western defenders.'

The system had nothing to offer but Bolshevik arguments: missiles, tanks, intellectual control, Party directives and the secret service. The counter-arguments were, however, stronger: the country's economic bankruptcy, the people's complete lack of freedom, a deadening bureaucracy, dogmatism, and the absence of any acceptable Soviet solutions to the impasse. As General Secretary and head of state Andropov retained full control of the KGB, and the record shows that his most frequent visitors were his KGB deputies and senior officials.

Unlike Brezhnev, Andropov thought a good deal about ways of increasing the Party's influence on economic and social issues, and of improving the quality of that influence, while at the same time reducing the extent of the leadership's involvement in the economy. Speaking to Central Committee Secretaries on 7 December 1982, he made an extraordinary remark: 'It is important to ask whether a symbiosis of senior officials in the Central Committee apparatus with ministers and other officials is not taking place. Unfortunately, our officials, including deputy heads of department, are not always aware of this shortcoming. If the Central Committee does not take timely action against this intolerable phenomenon, the fire will spread to the Central Committee as a whole.'[25]

He was less concerned about the fallibility of government by directive than about the possible identification of everyday economic and other failures with the Central Committee. Despite some attempts to alter the position, the Politburo continued working as it always had, as a super-government. It was the only way Soviet society and the state could function.

To illustrate this point, on 18 November 1982, a week after Andropov took power, the Politburo discussed thirteen issues and voted, by name, on no fewer than *seventy-eight* resolutions. Among the matters dealt with were: the outcome of talks with delegations in Moscow for Brezhnev's funeral; the forthcoming meetings of the Warsaw Pact Control Commission; congratulations to the new President of Turkey;

the dissident Anatoly Shcharansky; a draft decree making Andropov a member of the Supreme Soviet. The Politburo also addressed economic issues, such as the 1983 budget, production of nuclear material and war supplies for the Seventh Five-Year Plan, the production of harvesting machines at the Ukhtomsky plant, and many others, from major issues to the award of medals to pig-breeders. Thus it was under Andropov, as it had been before him and would be after he had gone.

It is obvious that the Politburo had neither the personnel nor the time, still less the professional expertise, to deal with such matters properly. It gave the force of law to draft decisions that had been prepared for it by the Central Committee apparatus, which in turn used the advice and counsel of specialists. Andropov regarded this situation as abnormal: even if the Politburo were able to look at a thousand issues, thousands more would remain untouched. Supercentralization was a trap in which one organ, and not a very competent one at that, decided everything, burdening the system with bureaucratic shackles and making it cumbersome, sluggish and inefficient.

Since Lenin's day, the Bolsheviks had prescribed everything for the hushed populace: what to do, whom to support, how to live, whom to respect, whom to hate. Since its inception, the Leninist Politburo had created a unique model of the Party super-government. Just as it had for the previous sixty years, in Andropov's time the Politburo determined such matters as whether or not to send troops into Hungary, Czechoslovakia and Afghanistan, as well as trivial issues which the most minor functionary could have settled. For instance, with Andropov in the chair, the Politburo confirmed the feeding norms for animals on the establishment of MVD organs,[26] examined the servicing of light automobiles, pistons in tank diesel engines, the award of a foreign decoration to a minister, and much else.[27]

From the outset, the Politburo had sat on Thursdays. Non-members who had been ordered to attend for a particular question would crowd into the ante-room. The conveyor belt worked non-stop, as one decision followed another. Discussion was a rare event. The most important matters were not minuted, but were marked 'top secret' and destined for one of the 'Special Files'. When debate did take place, it was not about economic or social problems, but political issues, appearing on the agenda as 'Any other business'.

Among the issues secreted in Special Files during Andropov's tenure were, for example: restriction of access to new weapons designs for representatives of the Romanian army; delivery of special property [weapons] to Nicaragua;[28] counter-intelligence security in the MVD, its organs and internal troops;[29] individuals who pose a special danger to the state in wartime conditions;[30] the CPSU budget for 1983;[31] the sale of gold.[32]

The minutes sometimes include a brief note, such as 'KGB', 'MO [Ministry of Defence]', 'International Department of Central Committee', and the decisions on these matters would have been placed at once in the Special Files. They covered such issues as Soviet intelligence and counter-intelligence, the development and testing of new weapons, the funding of foreign Communist Parties and the remuneration of Politburo members.

It is noticeable that under Andropov the Politburo dealt with KGB issues far more often than in the past. The role of the KGB in society was growing apace at this time. Andropov had barely assumed office when, on 10 December 1983, he agreed to discuss 'at the highest level' the question of 'using Soviet citizens of Jewish nationality for active participation in counter-Zionist propaganda'. An explanatory note added that 'people of Jewish nationality, with rare exceptions, hold back from making public judgement of Zionism.' It was, naturally, decided that an appropriate 'group' should be formed under the aegis of the KGB.[33]

Other KGB issues that came to the Politburo included: supplementing the list of the main items constituting state secrets;[34] measures for strengthening radio defences [i.e. jamming] against anti-Soviet radio broadcasts;[35] delivery of special property [mostly weapons] to certain Communist Parties and foreign organizations.[36]

As General Secretary, Andropov remained closely involved in a number of extremely controversial spheres of KGB activity. It is no secret that the Soviet secret service maintained covert links with terrorist organizations, some of which received arms from the USSR. Many terrorists received ideological and special training in the Soviet Union, and some were given asylum. The super-government tried to control everything, its approval or disapproval being required for the most varied and often unlikely issues. Andropov spoke to the Polish Prime Minister General Jaruzelski by telephone on 13 April 1983. The Politburo duly noted in its minutes that it had 'approved a conversation between General Secretary Comrade Andropov and First Secretary of the Central Committee of the PORP [Polish United Workers Party] W. Jaruzelski'.[37]

When the General Secretary invited his colleagues from the socialist countries to come to the USSR for a vacation, the Politburo's approval was required. Following tradition, in 1983 Andropov invited almost all the Communist leaders, from Castro to Ceausescu, not forgetting his old friend János Kádár, to whom he wrote personally: 'On behalf of my colleagues on the Politburo and myself, I am delighted to invite yourself and Maria Timofeyevna to spend your holidays in the Soviet Union this year at any time that suits you. If you are able to take up this invitation, you will have the opportunity to holiday in any part of the country and visit any republic and cities that interest you.'[38]

Since the far-off days of October 1956, Andropov had retained the friendliest of relations with Kádár. They talked on the phone and met often. Andropov even chose the presents for Kádár and his wife – an expensive custom-built Tula hunting rifle and shawls from Orenburg – when they came to Moscow, something he did for no other guests.[39] Kádár and Hungary had been a turning-point for Andropov. Since then he had become extremely, even pathologically, sensitive to anything that smacked of 'counter-revolution', 'bourgeois nationalism' or 'imperialist sabotage'. Kádár was a living reminder of those days.

Andropov's instructions to 'introduce order and strengthen discipline' were greeted with approval by most Soviet people, though they produced extremely modest results, to say the least. The society and the system were sick, and they would not be cured by the regular setting of an alarm clock or by employing a ubiquitous army of controllers. Even if Andropov realized this, he took no basic steps in the economic or political spheres. His activities were directed towards removing corrupt officials. He missed the mark.

There are no perfect social-political systems. All suffer from corruption and bureaucracy to some degree, but experience suggests that these defects are best dealt with not by making tougher laws, but by guaranteeing the liberties and rights of the citizen, by openness in the media, public accountability, a minimum of secrecy and the improvement of living conditions. By taking up the old Bolshevik methodology, Andropov was doomed to defeat.

He was, however, courageous enough to take on a number of ministers and regional leaders and to remove them from their posts. What he attempted was in some cases regarded in Party circles as simply blasphemous. For instance, following Lenin's hundredth anniversary in 1970 there was a new boom in erecting monuments to the 'deathless' leader. Statues were put up not only in all the republican and regional centres, but in every town, factory, university and army unit, and more and more new projects for 'immortalizing the leader' were submitted.

Andropov told a small group of colleagues that it was time to stop this ruinously expensive concern for external show. In April 1983, as the sixtieth anniversary of Lenin's death approached, and with it a new spasm of monumental activity, the Politburo adopted a remarkable decision. It bore a neutral heading: 'The elimination of excessive expenditure of state and public funds on the building of commemorative structures'. The document was blunt, however, in its wording: 'In 1983–85 the construction and the continuation of construction already begun of commemorative museums, monuments, obelisks, except for bronze busts ordered by the Presidium of the Supreme Soviet of the USSR and inexpensive memorials to the fallen in the Patriotic War, is prohibited.'[40]

Andropov was trying to put a stop to the ideological mindlessness, but he was ill, and had only to be admitted to hospital for his position to be weakened. The Leninists in the Politburo ignored their own decree of April 1983. At the beginning of December 1983 a proposal by Grishin was supported by Chernenko, Tikhonov, Gorbachev, Gromyko, Romanov and others, 'To erect a monument to Lenin at October Square in Moscow',[41] even though there were dozens of similar ones in the capital already. But it was so much easier to build monuments than to provide the basic necessities of life for the population. For years long queues at the shops for practically everything had been one of the more picturesque sights in Moscow and other Soviet cities.

Neither an economist nor an industrial manager, Andropov approached the question of reforms of any kind in industry and agriculture with great caution. He would not, for instance, agree to the Central Committee's plan to broaden the rights of enterprises, giving them greater economic independence and responsibility, and urged that they must 'first try it out at a few plants and factories'.[42] At the same time, he was quick to agree with the idea of Central Committee economists that the brigade, or team, approach to organizing labour should be developed.[43] He understood perfectly well that if the Soviet economy was to rise from its low level of efficiency, changes must be made in order to involve the workers' personal interest in the production process, but he continued to act with caution. Perhaps he also knew that the socialist economy, based as it was on the harsh ideological rejection of private property and the free market, was not capable of basic reform. Instead, he sought to make partial improvements and innovation, while trying to 'introduce order' in production.

He was no less cautious in politics. It was already difficult to ignore the criticism – even from 'friends' – of the extremely undemocratic nature of Soviet elections, and it was becoming harder to explain it away by saying that the USSR needed only one party, the CPSU, to express the interests of the entire people, and therefore only one candidate was required on each ballot. In October 1983 the Politburo was taken by surprise when Andropov presented a memorandum suggesting that they consider the possibility of broadening certain 'democratic procedures' in the forthcoming elections to the Supreme Soviet. The degree of 'broadening' he had in mind, however, was extremely cautious and limited. What he was advising was that 'the choice of candidate should not be determined by profession'.

For many years the practice had existed of putting up candidates for the Supreme Soviet according to their jobs. Politburo members and Central Committee Secretaries could be candidates, as could ministers, secretaries of republican and regional Party Committees, managers of large plants and factories, military district commanders, the secretaries of the unions of writers, composers and artists. For cosmetic purposes, the Supreme Soviet was diluted by a certain number of workers, collective farmers, physicians, teachers, and so on. Every last trivial detail in the process was worked out and scripted before the 'elections' took place. In reality, the composition of the Supreme Soviet had been determined long before by the Central Committee apparatus.

Andropov's suggestion was that the choice should go beyond the usual Party categories to include 'interesting' and 'distinguished' people, 'bearers of the Party line among the people'. He also proposed that the persecuted nations – the Ethnic Germans, Crimean Tatars,

Ingushes and others – be represented in this purely ceremonial body.[44] These 'innovations' did not of course affect the foundations of the disgraceful electoral system, but they nevertheless indicated that the leadership had started to think of ways to give more respectability to the Soviet institutions of power.

Such was Andropov: cautious, circumspect and vigilant in economic, social, political and ideological issues, orthodox in his thinking. Some of his measures were no more than bureaucratic imitations of movement, however frequently he repeated the slogan 'the future belongs to socialism.'

In one respect Andropov was not hesitant, and that was in his native sphere, the KGB, which continued to gain his support for virtually all of its proposals. Even when he was in hospital in November 1983, for instance, he gave his consent for the Politburo to discuss 'measures to uncover sabotage by centres of Ukrainian nationalists abroad'. The Politburo decreed a full programme of ways to combat the so-called 'Anti-Bolshevik Bloc of Nations', proposing, among other things, that efforts be made 'to sow discord among the nationalists'.[45]

Espionage, counter-intelligence and police affairs continued to be one of the Politburo's favourite diversions. It spent hours discussing proposals by Gromyko and Chebrikov on toughening up the issue of Soviet visas to US citizens; on how to catch more American diplomats for parking and traffic violations; and how to reduce the importance of protocol regulations at the US Embassy in Moscow.[46]

Andropov never missed an opportunity to use ideological weapons against his chief adversary, 'American imperialism'. At times this was done in a clumsy, primitive way, but occasionally he acted with surprising elegance. Early in 1983, while going through the usual pile of papers on his desk, he made a note on one of them: 'We should start thinking right away about the year 2000.' His aides and speech-writers and the propaganda department all seized on the idea, which had a certain universal ring to it and might therefore be exploited to yield considerable ideological dividends. Long hours and much effort were devoted to a document which finally emerged as a resolution for the Politburo to consider: 'An initiative of the Soviet state in connection with the forthcoming entry of mankind into the third millennium'. A special commission was formed, headed by Chernenko and including Gorbachev, Aliyev and others. It was agreed that a proposal be put to the United Nations to accept Moscow's draft declaration, entitled 'Peace, progress and the well-being of mankind (a programme for the international community of nations for 1985–2000)'.

The document, promoted as a 'manifesto for the twenty-first century', was offered as a basis for strengthening the struggle against the threat of nuclear war, environmental damage, poverty, famine and disease. The idea was that the Soviet Union, as a socialist country that could anticipate the future, would show the nations of the earth the path to tomorrow's world.

Naturally, this ambitious plan was not acceptable to the world community. Who would take any notice of the admonitions of a state that was embroiled in a dirty war in Afghanistan, supported international terrorism, subjected dissidents to psychiatric drug treatment, and was incapable of honestly admitting the facts of the shooting down of a passenger aircraft over the Sea of Japan?

Symbol of the Andropov Era

Three months after becoming General Secretary, Andropov had to undergo dialysis for kidney failure. His activity and physical mobility as leader were now severely restricted by his rapidly deteriorating health.

If in domestic politics Andropov chose the strategy of 'introducing order' to overcome the crisis, in foreign policy no similar universal option was available. A host of external problems faced him. When he arrived at his office in the Kremlin every morning he was greeted by a pile of cipher telegrams and reports on the hopeless situation in Afghanistan, the continuing tension in Poland, the deep uncertainty of relations with China and Japan, the dangerous deterioration of the situation in the Middle East, Ethiopia and South Africa. Relations with Western Europe were not good, but over everything loomed relations with the United States and the continuing nuclear missile drama. By the end of Brezhnev's rule, at colossal cost and harm to its economy in general, the USSR had achieved nuclear parity with the USA. The competition, into which every Soviet leader had entered without hesitation, had sapped the Communist system. The sick leader of the sick country had not only accepted every new challenge from the USA and NATO, but had provoked them into dangerous actions.

General Secretaries in the USSR had far more power than a US President or other Western leaders. The US President is, for instance, limited by his finite term in office, by the Constitution, by Congress and by the pressure of public opinion. In contrast, General Secretaries were absolute rulers, able to remain in power for an unlimited time, usually until they died, while the one-party Supreme Soviet – the system's excuse for a parliament – obediently rubber-stamped whatever decisions the Politburo chose to hand down.

What is remarkable about Andropov is that he continued to conduct policy while he was seriously ill, kept alive by an artificial kidney, yet still in possession of a clear mind and strong will. He knew what he wanted, although he did not always know how best to achieve it.

He paid special attention to the permanent Commissions set up by the Politburo. Those on China and Poland – which Andropov had headed himself before becoming General Secretary – and Afghanistan met most frequently. In August 1983 he proposed the setting up of a permanent Commission on the Middle East and advised Ustinov, Gromyko and the other members of this Commission that while they should continue providing effective military aid to Syria and other friendly Arab regimes, they 'should not allow us to become directly involved in the conflict in the region'.[47]

Despite his cautious approach, Andropov held to firmly confrontational positions towards the USA and Israel, and would not countenance even the thought that the best policy would be to normalize relations with both the Jewish state and the Arab countries. Instead he approved the continuing supply of billions of dollars' worth of aid to Syria, Iraq, Libya, South Yemen, the PLO, Cuba and North Korea. Thousands of tanks and armoured troop-carriers, hundreds of fighter aircraft and anti-aircraft missiles, artillery systems and other equipment were delivered, making those countries among the most militarized in the world.

No country ever had as many Russian-speaking advisers as Syria. I spent time there on a number of occasions, and found many Soviet advisers and specialists in the two dozen garrisons of the country's disproportionately large army. It was the main Arab force opposing Israel. Everyone lived in a state of half-war, half-peace. The Soviet Union and its ideology were not wanted by anyone there, but its tanks, guns and technicians were highly valued. While maintaining the Soviet Union's powerful military hold in the region, Andropov nevertheless did everything to avoid a new armed conflict.

Soviet relations with China were a major preoccupation for Andropov. After armed clashes on Damansky Island in the Far East in 1969, the Soviet Union moved large numbers of troops to Transbaikal and Siberia, and deployed several formations in Mongolia, with the agreement of the government in Ulan-Bator. The two mightiest powers in Asia, with the longest land border in the world, and both possessing nuclear weapons, were watching each other suspiciously. Moscow could not get it out of its mind that the US was gaining most from this silent confrontation.

On several occasions Andropov personally gave instructions to the diplomats who were conducting desultory talks with China in Moscow and Peking. He knew that the Soviet Union was incapable of bearing the burden of an armed conflict with China while also groaning under the weight of the unbelievably costly nuclear race and the space race with the USA, the endless war in Afghanistan, and the ferment in Eastern Europe, where its main land forces were posted. He told his China Commission that ways must be found to regulate relations with their huge neighbour, but the differences were so deep that virtually no positive results were obtainable. The Central Committee's experts came up with proposals to sign a non-aggression treaty, as well as measures to increase military trust, but these were invariably met by 'three conditions' from the Chinese side: the USSR must get out of Afghanistan, it must 'force' Vietnam to liberate Cambodia, and it must withdraw its forces from Mongolia. The Kremlin could accept none of these conditions.

Enmeshed in traps set by itself in the global confrontation with the US and NATO, and burdened by obligations to its 'friends' throughout the world, the Soviet Union continued to undermine its already inefficient economy. As long as it was possible to keep the system on the track of militarization, the USSR had been able to achieve at least one thing: it was feared. Andropov knew that throughout the world this was his main trump card; he knew that the successive cycles of Cold War frosts and détente thaws in relations between the two camps had meant mutual fear and an inability to overcome fixed prejudices. The USA was hampered by having to be the world leader, while the

Soviet Union was constrained by its allegiance to class concepts and Leninist dogma.

As soon as Andropov became General Secretary, the Political Literature Publishing House rushed out his *Selected Speeches and Articles*. In 'Leninism – The Science and Art of Revolutionary Creativity', the phrase 'Our policy is class policy in its principles and in its aims'[48] appears prominently. Since its creation the class approach had condemned the USSR to confrontation and struggle, and it was undoubtedly at least partly responsible for its ultimate disintegration.

Like its adversary, the Soviet Union wanted to achieve unilateral advantage. By deploying its SS-20 medium-range missiles in the westernmost Warsaw Pact territory, it could threaten the whole of Western Europe. Astronomical amounts of money were spent on reaching this goal. It was obvious that the Americans would soon come up with a response, and they did so by deploying their Pershing-2 guided missiles in Europe. Moscow made every effort to prevent this from happening. In 1983 Andropov devoted practically all of his limited time to this issue. Wholesale efforts were made to mobilize world opinion against the American move, and the socialist and Communist Parties of Western Europe were exploited to this end. Andropov called an extraordinary meeting of fraternal Communist Party Secretaries just to discuss the missile question.[49]

It was all in vain. The build-up of Soviet missiles in Eastern Europe was matched by a build-up of US missiles in Western Europe. American missiles could reach important population centres in the USSR in seven minutes, while it would take a Soviet missile thirty minutes to reach the USA. The short-sighted Soviet strategists had handed the Americans a knife with which to cut the Soviet throat. Added to which, they had further undermined their own economy. In the Soviet Union, the leadership never took the blame, whether for the fatal mistakes of 1939–41, the Stalinist terror, the intervention in Hungary and Czechoslovakia, becoming involved in the Afghan civil war, or the impasse over the missiles.

In interviews with the Soviet and foreign press, Andropov claimed it was the USA that was blocking the talks on medium-range missiles. In October 1983, when the Italian Communist leader Enrico Berlinguer proposed in a confidential letter that Andropov should make a move towards unilateral reduction of medium-range missiles in order to prevent US missiles being deployed in Europe, the General Secretary replied: 'But where is the guarantee that it will restrain the Americans from deploying rockets in Europe? There are no such guarantees.'[50] He would not countenance the possibility of even a partial concession. In a statement on 25 November 1983 he reasserted that the USSR would 'take responsive measures' to the deployment of US missiles in Europe.

In his short time in power, Andropov was unable to return the country even to the brief spell of 'détente' of the Brezhnev period. The class mentality dictated that the struggle for parity must go on, and that no concessions or compromises could be made if there was any chance of achieving supremacy. In October 1983, when the Soviet delegation was preparing to go to a preliminary meeting in Helsinki on measures to strengthen trust, security and disarmament in Europe, the Politburo – with Andropov's blessing – issued an instruction that the delegation must support the idea of the mutual non-use of force, but 'must not agree to disclose the military activity of states'.[51] Just as the Soviet leadership had been terrified in 1955 by President Eisenhower's proposal to exchange military information and make aerial photography of each other's installations possible by an 'open skies' policy, so, years later, while appearing to agree on certain measures of trust, the Soviet Union did not want to go as far as joint inspections.

Meanwhile the country was sinking deeper and deeper into economic ruin. Seventy per cent of the state budget was being spent on military needs, although this figure was of course never disclosed. The reliance on force rather than reason, on geopolitical interests rather than human values, brought the world and the rival sides to the brink of nuclear catastrophe.

Andropov chaired his last Politburo meeting on 1 September 1983. As always, the meeting dealt with a wide range of issues, from the production of chassis for self-propelled vehicles and colour television sets to methods for raising labour productivity, demographic research, aid to Afghanistan, and the choice of a speaker for the sixty-sixth anniversary of the October Revolution.[52]

Just before the meeting, Ustinov approached Andropov and told him: 'A plane's been shot down. It turned out not to be American but South Korean, and a civil aircraft, at that. We'll find out more and report in greater detail.'

Andropov, who clearly had other sources of information, replied: 'Fine. But I was told there'd been a spy plane above Kamchatka. I'm flying to the Crimea later today after the meeting. I must have a rest and get some treatment. As for the plane, you sort it out.'

The incident of the South Korean Boeing did not at first seem especially important. The USSR had shot down dozens of US planes that had violated its airspace in the Far East, over the Baltic, the Barents Sea, Armenia and Sverdlovsk. Not a few Soviet planes had similarly disappeared without trace at all latitudes. Nothing was ever said in public about the missing Soviet aircraft, following the old Bolshevik rule that the less the people know, the easier it is to govern them.

No one in the Kremlin could have anticipated the wave of indignation and condemnation from around the world at the shooting down of the South Korean jumbo jet over the Sea of Japan, in which all 269 passengers and crew were killed. The story, as far as it can be known, has been recounted many times, and does not require recapitulation here. What is of more immediate interest is the reaction of Andropov and his comrades.

Early on the morning of 1 September, while he was still at home in the outskirts of Moscow, the General Secretary was told that a US warplane had been shot down over the southern half of Sakhalin. He knew the rule that when a foreign plane was detected in Soviet airspace, a visual or radio signal must be sent ordering it to land immediately on Soviet territory. If the pilot ignored the signal, the nearest border command post could give the order to destroy the plane. On 8 September 1958, for instance, when a US C-130 with thirteen crew members penetrated Soviet airspace over Armenia, the Soviet border guard acted in precisely this way. The fighter pilots gave preliminary signals and then launched a rocket attack, bringing down the huge aircraft, which crashed and burned for several hours. Only five charred corpses were handed over to the Americans. At first, the shooting-down was denied: 'It came down by itself.' This was virtually the required response. In conversation with Mao Tse-tung on 2 October 1959, Khrushchev declared: 'We have shot down more than one American plane, but we always say they came down by themselves.'

It is difficult to exonerate the US authorities that sent spy planes into Soviet airspace. No doubt the absolute secrecy of the Soviet regime, its stubborn refusal to allow joint inspections, and fears about the Kremlin's unknown plans all combined to prompt the CIA and other secret US bodies to take this course, but it contravened international law.

To the first US and Japanese enquiries about the missing Boeing 747, Moscow replied that it knew nothing about the aircraft's fate. Then, when it had become clear to everyone that the plane had been shot down, the 'Khrushchev line' was used: 'It came down by itself.' However, all the conversations between the Soviet fighter pilots and their ground control had been monitored and recorded by US electronic surveillance, and no one was duped by Moscow's clumsy attempts to cloud the issue. Moscow was unable to give a satisfactory answer to the simple question of how it was possible to mistake a huge civil aircraft for any sort of warplane. Reports were coming in from Soviet embassies of representations, pickets, demonstrations and widespread anger. Even 'friends' of the USSR were deeply embarrassed and unable to do anything to mollify public opinion.

Andropov, in the Crimea, was kept informed by the Ministry of Defence, the KGB and the Foreign Ministry. But most of all he was in touch with Chernenko, whom he had put in charge of the Politburo in his absence.[53] He told Chernenko to discuss the issue at the Politburo, and to work out a 'line' that conceded nothing, that was not defensive, and that took account of the possible sanctions against the USSR. As soon as he had put down the receiver, Chernenko arranged for an extraordinary meeting of the Politburo to take place the next day, 2 September. He then consulted Ustinov, Chebrikov and Gromyko about the immediate measures to be taken to meet Andropov's orders.

By the time the Politburo met, *Pravda* had published its first announcement of the incident: 'On the night of 31 August/1 September an aircraft of unknown origin entered Soviet airspace over the Kamchatka peninsula, and then violated Soviet airspace again over the island of Sakhalin ... Soviet border patrol fighter-aircraft took off and attempted to assist the offending aircraft to the nearest airfield. The offending aircraft, however, did not respond to warning signals from the Soviet fighters and continued its flight above the Sea of Japan.'[54] No mention was made of the plane being shot down or that there were casualties. The report was vague and indefinite in the extreme.

The Politburo addressed the issue in terms of the violation of Soviet airspace. It learnt that the Boeing had been shot down by two rockets, fired by a pilot called Osipovich, who claimed he had been unable to distinguish a passenger aircraft from a military spy-plane.[55]

Chernenko opened the discussion by announcing: 'measures taken yesterday, in connection with the incident of the South Korean aircraft, have already been discussed by members of the Politburo. You have received more detailed information, and Yuri Vladimirovich [Andropov] has expressed the wish that we should discuss this difficult matter in the Politburo ... We have to discuss our position in the wild orgy of American propaganda.'

It was an unwritten rule on difficult issues that every member of the Politburo should express a view, in order to demonstrate unity. The speeches reveal a shocking lack of remorse – or even the expression of remorse – for the 269 victims of the crash. It was absolutely clear that the plane was a civil aircraft carrying innocent men, women and children. If the Politburo had shown any regret for what had happened, and had given a factual account of the event, the world reaction would have been different. That was impossible, however.

GROMYKO: Reagan immediately made a speech on the incident with the South Korean aircraft. As before, his speech was of a crude anti-Soviet character and included a call for 'the entire world community to unite' against the Soviet Union ... The Security Council has not met yet, but it will, and it will discuss the most hostile resolutions against us. Obviously, we'll have to use the right of veto on this ... We must be clear about this and above all we must say firmly that we acted lawfully ...

USTINOV: I can assure the Politburo that our pilots acted in complete conformity with the demands of their military duty, and everything in this memorandum is the honest truth. Our actions were absolutely correct, insofar as the American-built South Korean aircraft penetrated our territory up to five hundred kilometres. It is extremely difficult to distinguish this aircraft by its shape from a reconnaissance aircraft. Soviet military pilots are prohibited from firing on passenger aircraft. But in this case their actions were completely justified ... The question is, what's the best way to report our opening fire?

GROMYKO: We can't deny that our plane opened fire.

CHEBRIKOV: The Americans admit that the plane was fired on over our Soviet territory and that it crashed into the ocean in our waters. In fact, it happened in neutral waters. We have ships and an aircraft there at this moment . . . We have collected a number of items. The depth there is about eighty to a hundred metres.

GROMYKO: That means they can find the plane's 'black box', and we can, too.

TIKHONOV: Clearly, sooner or later they'll come across the remains of the plane.

DOLGIKH: But if they do, they'll have evidence of the fact that the plane was shot down.

GORBACHEV: Have they established that there was a live shot?

CHEBRIKOV: No, they haven't. But I want to re-emphasize that our actions were entirely legitimate.

TIKHONOV: If we were acting correctly, legally, then we have to say straight out that we shot this plane down.

GROMYKO: We have to say that shots were fired. We should say that openly to prevent our adversary from accusing us of deception.

GRISHIN: First of all, I'd like to say that we should declare openly that the plane was shot down . . . and at the same time it's essential to speak out fiercely against any kind of anti-Soviet provocation.

GORBACHEV: First of all, I want to say that I'm convinced that our actions were lawful . . . We have to show precisely in our statements that this was a crude violation of international conventions. We mustn't remain silent at this moment, we must take up an offensive position. We must support the existing version, and develop it further . . .

It is a matter of regret that Gorbachev spoke of a 'version' of events, even though what had happened was perfectly plain. Like the others, he was concerned only about finding a way to extricate the leadership from an unseemly affair, and to shift the blame onto the other side. Nor did he utter a word of regret for the victims.

ROMANOV: I agree with everything that has been said . . .

OGARKOV: It's quite possible that this was a deliberate provocation . . . The Ministry of Defence has all the recordings of the conversations that took place in the air that day. They show that we can adhere completely to the version that has been reported in our newspapers.

ZIMYANIN: First of all, we have to rebuff Reagan's reckless statement. It was crude and unbridled.

(President Reagan had said that the 'brutal' Soviet action indicated a stark contrast between Soviet words and deeds. 'What can we think of a regime,' he asked, 'that so broadly trumpets its vision of peace and global disarmament and yet so callously and quickly commits a terrorist act to sacrifice the lives of innocent human beings?')

DOLGIKH: I support the view that we have to adopt an offensive line in resolving this matter.

KORNIENKO: We have enough evidence to express the view that this was a deliberate provocation by the CIA . . . But we shouldn't withdraw from the fact that shots were fired. After all, imperialist propaganda can even now broadcast the recordings of our pilots' conversations.

SOLOMENTSEV: We should adopt an offensive position, but perhaps it's possible we could also say that we commiserate with the families of those who perished as a result of this deliberate provocation.

This was the first time anyone thought to mention the victims and that, possibly, an expression of regret was in order.

KUZNETSOV: I support the proposals made here. I also think this was a well-planned anti-Soviet action.

VOROTNIKOV: I would like to support everything said here by the comrades . . .

KAPITONOV: There is no doubt that the actions of our pilots were correct. Now, in refuting the attacks of imperialist propaganda, we have to act firmly and with circumspection. We should, of course, acknowledge opening fire, but we must stress that there was no fault in this.

GROMYKO: [We must] confidentially inform the leaders of the fraternal socialist countries and some other states. As for the Americans, we must give them a firm, official reply . . . It would be expedient for the TASS statement to say that we regret the casualties.

CHERNENKO: I'm delighted that we are all of the same view, the same position. We must take the offensive, not defend ourselves . . . I will inform Yuri Vladimirovich Andropov of today's discussion at once.[56]

The wheezing and unprepossessing Chernenko was making the most of his time as the General Secretary's deputy. A resolution along the lines of the discussion was adopted. Stammering and shuffling his papers with trembling hands, Chernenko said: 'Yuri Vladimirovich told me on the phone that we mustn't retreat and that we must react decisively.' He read out the Politburo's statement on the incident, which contained not a word of regret for the fatalities:

> 1. The measures taken in connection with the violation of Soviet airspace by the South Korean aircraft on 31 August are approved. It proceeds from this that the violation was a deliberate provocation by imperialist forces ... capable of distracting from the USSR's peaceful initiatives.
>
> 2. Central Committee departments are instructed to ensure an offensive line in our propaganda ... [57]

The Andropov Politburo acted in the spirit of the Stalinist principle of turning defeat into victory and victory into a triumph. But it did not work.

The Soviet mass media went on pumping out the 'version' approved by the Politburo on 2 September, while a surge of indignation swept the USA, Europe, Japan and South Korea. People in the non-socialist world asked why the Soviets were lying again, and why they were unwilling to admit the fact that they had destroyed a civil aircraft. They could not understand why Andropov, Gromyko or anyone else in the Soviet leadership had not expressed commiseration for the families of the dead passengers.

Only a week after the event, on 7 September, did a statement by the Soviet government admit that the plane had been shot down. It was stated that it had violated Soviet airspace for intelligence purposes. Andropov telephoned from the Crimea and recommended that Gromyko put off a planned trip to New York and Havana to avoid 'running up against a provocation'.

The way this incident was dealt with throws light on the mentality of the Soviet leadership. Andropov himself was silent on the issue for more than a month. When he did refer to it, his judgement was even more harsh than that of his comrades. The plane's 'black box' had been found and brought to the surface. It was decided to say nothing of this, either to the world's press or to Seoul, and Soviet ships were kept in the area for another two weeks to give the impression that the fruitless search was still going on.

The official version required that everything possible be kept secret, and so it was, until 1992 when the new democratic regime opened the archives. In August 1993 the Russian government released the report of the commission it had set up to investigate the affair. The commission found that the shooting down had been the result of a chain of errors and coincidences, and had not been premeditated. The first cause was the aircraft's deviation from its proper course; the second was the local Soviet conviction that it had deliberately penetrated Soviet airspace. The commission found that the Soviet defence forces had acted correctly by firing when the aircraft failed to respond to warnings. Even the old regime's sworn enemies, the new Russian government, concluded that the Soviet action had conformed to international convention. The deviousness of the Politburo, and its inveterate need for secrecy and self-justification, were unnecessary.

The tragic case of the South Korean Boeing became a pathetic symbol of Andropov's rule. Whatever hopes had been raised at its beginning were now dashed. It was obvious that the country could not expect economic prosperity, or the convergence of politics with morality, or a spiritual uplift. The Boeing was symbolic of the failure to purge the system of its Bolshevik ways, ways that were based on class cruelty, confrontation and the cultivation of the lie.

Andropov's fifteen months in office were not rich in memorable events in the foreign policy sphere. SS-20s and Pershing–2 missiles were deployed, the savage war in Afghanistan continued, the conflict in the Middle East worsened, Poland was subdued but not broken, China did not respond positively to 'peaceful proposals' from the USSR, the chilly rhetoric with Washington and NATO continued, and it seemed the winds of the Cold War might prevail again on all continents.

Leadership from Hospital

It was known to everyone in the Politburo that Andropov was seriously ill when he took power. At the insistence of Chernenko – who was hardly less infirm – on 24 March 1983 the Politburo discussed an item headed: 'The working arrangements for members and candidate members of the Politburo and Central Committee Secretaries'.

Chernenko presented the proposal himself: 'Our previous last decision on this was to limit the working day to nine to five, and to give comrades over the age of sixty-five longer holidays and a day a week to work at home.' But, he went on, these decisions were not being observed.

Andropov supported Chernenko: 'It's possible to look at the age structure of the Politburo in all kinds of ways. We have here a concentration of our Party's political experience, and therefore a hasty and ill-thought-out change of people may not always be for the good of the cause ... With an overstrained regime, we might lose more than we gain. We must give every member of the Politburo the possibility of working at home one day a week. Relaxation should take place on one's days off.'

This practical question for the old men of the Politburo was subject to lively debate. Before anyone else could speak, Pelshe declared: 'The main thing is that you yourself, Yuri Vladimirovich, should observe the regime strictly; you must take care of yourself and look after yourself.'[22] It was agreed that members participate in fewer 'evening engagements' (i.e. receptions), and that meetings with ambassadors and delegations should only take place during working days, while medical checks should be stepped up. The old men were keen to increase special care for themselves.

Of the fifteen months that Andropov was in power, half of his time was spent in hospital, where it was hoped that treatment would enable him to return to his previous enormous working capacity, or at least effect a partial cure.

During his winter holiday in February 1983 – all Politburo members had a winter and a summer holiday – Andropov's health suffered a sharp decline. He had had kidney trouble all his life, and now it seemed his kidneys had given up altogether. Consultations with Soviet and foreign specialists confirmed the need for dialysis, or treatment on an artificial kidney. Andropov's personal file shows that in 1965 and 1966 he had 'micro-vascular myocardial infarctions; chronic suprarenal disease; attacks of hypertension, pneumonia, chronic colitis, arthritis, arrhythmia, shingles and other disorders'.[59] It is not hard to imagine his state of mind when confronted with this new misfortune.

Given so many serious medical conditions, it is amazing that Andropov was able to work as much and as hard as he did. He evidently realized that he would not be able to go on for very long. As Roy Medvedev writes: 'He hoped to live another six or seven years, but had to take account of the fact that he might depart this earth much sooner.'[60]

By the summer of 1983 Andropov's health was giving rise to serious concern. He found it hard to move. Painful sores appeared on his body, and signs of general debility increased. Yevgeny Chazov, the Health Minister and Chief of the 4th Main Administration, which included the Kremlin clinic, recalled that Professor A. Rubin, a noted American specialist, was invited to Moscow. Rubin carried out a thorough examination and concurred with the treatment the Soviet physicians had been giving. His diagnosis was generally encouraging and reassuring.[61] Andropov's son Igor recalled that, despite his illness, his father had not imagined that 'fate had allotted him only a year and three months. Also, the doctors were not painting a hopeless picture.'[62]

On his now irregular appearances at work, Andropov could manage to climb the few steps to the lift only with great difficulty. He was greatly embarrassed when his bodyguards or others helped him, and did not want people to know about his deteriorating condition. When he was installed as head of state, he did not walk to the rostrum to make the customary short speech of thanks, as he was afraid his failing strength would let him down before the eyes of the whole country. He simply stood up, thanked everyone and uttered a few suitable remarks.

Brezhnev, who had become senile before his time, had been incapable of functioning in his last years. Now Andropov was terminally ill, and soon it would be Chernenko's turn. Yet there appears to have been no doubt among the leadership that these people could rule the country. Although since Stalin's death it was no longer done to refer to the leader as *vozhd*, thus endowing him with a supra-governmental aura, in fact attitudes had changed little since Lenin's time. Even in the conspiracy against Khrushchev, the plotters' knees trembled until the last minute. The sanctification of the highest person in the land was an old Bolshevik tradition.

When they saw how rapidly he was failing, Andropov's comrades, especially in the KGB, did their best to make his life easier. On

11 May 1983 Chebrikov, the Chairman of the KGB, wrote to the Politburo: 'At the Party-political events on Red Square, the walk from the Kremlin to the Lenin Mausoleum includes a staircase in Senate Tower. The difference in level between the pavement in the Kremlin and the Lenin Mausoleum is more than 3.5 metres. It is thought appropriate to replace the existing staircase in Senate Tower with an escalator. We request consideration of this.'[63] On 28 July 1983 the Politburo agreed.[64]

Andropov was not the only one who found the staircase beyond him and resorted to the 'Lenin' escalator. Practically the entire Politburo, some of whose members were a good deal older and no less decrepit than Andropov, must have wondered why it had taken them so long to think of this wonderful device. Standing on the Mausoleum, especially at the November celebrations, tested their physical endurance to the limit, if not beyond.

On 1 September 1983, having chaired the Politburo for three hours, Andropov went on holiday. His private plane did not take him to Kislovodsk in the North Caucasus as usual, but to Simferopol in the Crimea, from where he was taken by limousine to one of the many luxurious villas reserved for the leadership. With him went not only the customary vacation staff he required for work, but an entire medical facility. He spoke to Chernenko by telephone almost every day, as well as to Ustinov and Gromyko. He was sent the most important papers, and it seemed that he had found a balance between his enormous responsibilities and his failing health.

Following the exhausting medical procedures of the morning, and after a telephone conversation with Chernenko, Andropov liked most of all to sit on a shady veranda overlooking the sea. Often, after one of these periods of contemplation, he would instruct his assistants to prepare an analytical memorandum for the Politburo, or obtain certain statistics for him, or find a particular work of political or sociological literature on an issue that happened to interest him.

We shall of course never know what went through Andropov's mind as he lay on the hospital bed attached to an intravenous drip, or during his short walks in the park. Perhaps he thought about the improbability of his plans for reviving a society that had drifted for so long under Brezhnev. Perhaps he lamented the fact that the Dnepropetrovsk 'mafia' of his predecessor was taking so long to disappear.

Or that his illness had prevented him from accepting a single invitation to make a state visit to a foreign country, one of the most effective instruments of a country's domestic and foreign policies.

As Chairman of the KGB, Andropov had met a few officials from non-socialist countries, and he had made trips to China, Afghanistan and Poland, virtually in secret. Now, as head of state, he was meeting the leaders of many other countries.

In December 1982 he met Nicolae Ceausescu. Diplomatically concealing his dislike for the Romanian President, who was blackmailing the Kremlin with the threat of leaving the Warsaw Pact, Andropov asked directly: 'What will you gain if you leave the defensive alliance?'

'We'll lose nothing,' Ceausescu replied in Russian, without waiting for the translation.[65]

He had also met Samora Machel of Mozambique, another dead weight on the ailing Soviet economy. Andropov had no idea what to do about such 'allies'.

One drama that he could not have put out of his mind was that of Afghanistan. Only now could he appreciate the catastrophic scale of the decision taken so long ago by a Politburo that had taken its cue from Suslov, Ustinov, Brezhnev, Gromyko and himself, as Chairman of the KGB.

Not only had he met all the new Afghan leaders, in Kabul and Moscow, but he had been closely informed about the plot to carry out the palace coup that would later be called 'the April revolution', and had taken part in planning the murder of Hafizullah Amin. The subject of Afghanistan litters his notebooks: 'Vakil's airdrop and his reception at the safe apartment'; 'liaison with General Gul-Ag'; 'Amin's palace "bodyguards"'; and preparations for the operation, which was preceded by the sending in of Soviet troops.

One of Andropov's last meetings with foreign leaders was with the German Chancellor Helmut Kohl and his Foreign Minister Hans-Dietrich Genscher. It was hard for him to rise and greet his guests, but he managed to conceal his pain. No headway was made over the missile question, of course, but the West Germans impressed Andropov with their seriousness and respectful candour. With Washington's knowledge, Kohl sounded Andropov out about meeting the American leadership. It would be a good opportunity, he said, to discuss the problem of the 'Euromissiles'.

The reply was delivered in a calm voice, as if the question had already been settled: 'We're not going to take part in any fancy-dress parade. If the USA doesn't want to respond to our initiatives in a positive way, what's the point of meeting?' He made it plain that the West should be in no doubt: Pershings in Europe would mean the USSR would take corresponding measures.[66] Andropov did, however, accept Kohl's invitation to visit Bonn, though it is impossible to be sure whether this was out of diplomatic courtesy or a real expectation that his health would improve.

After the German visit, Andropov saw very few foreigners. In October 1983 a letter arrived from Enrico Berlinguer requesting a meeting in Moscow, to which Andropov replied that, while he was willing, it would not be possible in the near future, but that the question should be raised again at a later date.[67] In fact, he had no desire to meet the ideologues of Euro-Communism. His attitude to them was similar to Lenin's towards the European social democrats, and he feared their effect on the minds of the Western working class no less than that of the bourgeoisie.

Sick as he was, Andropov remained as ill-disposed to the 'ideological games of the class enemy' as ever. When he was told that the Canadian Prime Minister Pierre Trudeau had written asking for leniency to be shown towards the Jewish dissident Anatoly Shcharansky, he said: 'Reply to the Canadian: "We have no need to prove our humanity, Mr Prime Minister. It is part of the very nature of our society."'[68]

Those words would serve as a suitable epigraph for a book about Andropov: he genuinely believed in the 'democracy' of the Soviet political system.

Even when he was bedridden in the clinic at Kuntsevo, outside Moscow, Andropov wanted to be shown important papers, on which he would write comments and instructions for the Central Committee apparatus. In February 1983 he approved a proposal from Chebrikov to close the Mausoleum while maintenance work was being carried out on Lenin's mummy.[69] It evidently seemed perfectly right to him that the custody and preservation of these Bolshevik relics should be in the hands of the KGB.

He also initiated 'the activation of work with foreign correspondents in the USSR', of whom, he declared, there were 341. 'We can and we must influence the sort of information they are sending out to their own countries.'[70] Gromyko, Chebrikov and Zamyatin were appointed at once to run this operation.

Sometimes he made rather unexpected decisions. For instance, the Russian Orthodox Church, which Lenin and Stalin had practically wiped out, had for years been asking for the return of several churches that had been used as warehouses, clubs, museums and garages by the Bolsheviks. After receiving yet another letter from the church hierarchy, Andropov mused, 'I think we should give them back the Danilov Monastery.' This was, as usual, interpreted as an order, and soon the Politburo approved a decree to 'transfer' (n.b. not to 'give back') the monastery 'for the use of the Moscow Patriarchate'.[71] Ironically, the Danilov Monastery had been the burial site for the NKVD's victims in the 1930s, thrown into mass graves marked only by numbers.

Such acts gained Andropov a reputation among the intelligentsia and foreign journalists as an 'enlightened conservative', or 'liberal Chekist'. No one could speak of him as a reformer, however. In a number of his speeches and actions, he made it clear that, while he was in favour of 'a thought-out perfecting' of the management of the national economy, he saw no need for political reform. For, he felt, in the basic features of developed socialism 'the world recognizes the Leninist dreams being bodied forth in living reality.'[72] In his opinion, there was nothing in Leninist politics that needed altering, merely 'perfecting'. As Nietzsche said, fear of change is 'a narrow door through which delusion fights its way to truth'.

Shortly before he was due to leave the Crimea, Andropov's health severely deteriorated. According to Academician Chazov, who had treated him for several years, as well as Brezhnev before him, the immediate cause was a short walk in the park. The lightly dressed General Secretary had become tired, and had taken a breather on a granite bench in the shade; his body became thoroughly chilled, and he soon began shivering uncontrollably. 'When our well-known surgeon, V.D. Fedorov, and I examined Andropov in the early morning,' Chazov recalled, 'we found widespread inflammation, requiring surgical intervention ... The operation was successful, but his organism was so drained of strength that the post-operative wound would not heal ... His condition gradually worsened, his weakness increased, he again stopped trying to walk, but still the wound would not heal

... Andropov began to realize that he was not going to get any better.'[73]

Chazov was right, but Andropov did not ask the Politburo to be relieved of his colossal burden of responsibility. That would not have been in the Bolshevik tradition. When he could no longer go to work in the Kremlin or attend Politburo meetings, he adopted an original way of governing: he would suggest ideas to his assistants and speech-writers, who would then prepare analytical 'notes' for the Politburo. These missives would then be discussed, decisions would be based on them for inclusion in the work of the Central Committee, and some of them would be circulated to the entire Party.

The impression was created that the General Secretary was on the job and running the gigantic machine of state and Party. In fact, not even the members of the Politburo knew very much about their leader's real condition. The only ones who saw him on a regular basis were Ustinov, Chebrikov, Chernenko and Gromyko. Even in the top echelons the word was, 'the General Secretary is getting better, he'll be giving a report at the next Plenum, and when the October anniversary comes round, he'll definitely be there.'

It had been a custom of Andropov's when he was Chairman of the KGB to send memoranda, often handwritten, for discussion by his colleagues in the Politburo. The habit continued from the clinic at Kuntsevo, where an entire area had been sectioned off for him to work and be treated in. In August 1983, when he was still appearing for work in the Kremlin, the Politburo was discussing his sharp note about 'Euro-missiles' and the need to stimulate a more active anti-missile campaign in Europe. On his recommendation, a timetable was adopted for a programme of action against America's military plans.[74]

A few days later a new note arrived at the Politburo, this time on the missile situation in the East. Andropov proposed that an effort be made to bring China into the anti-missile campaign. It might, he said, be a good way to improve Sino–Soviet relations.[75] Again a programme of action was adopted for anti-American, anti-militarist activities.

Andropov had barely arrived in the Crimea in September when he approved another memorandum for the Politburo, prepared for him by his aides, on a long-term plan for land improvement.[76] Having spent most of his life in Chekist work of one kind or another, he had little understanding of the subtleties of industrial and agricultural production, and relied on his aides and experts to formulate proposals for him. At almost the same time, he signed a memorandum on the position in the Middle East and on the need for a more cautious policy, to ensure that the USSR did not become directly involved.[77] His mind ranged from the international to the domestic and back to the international.

When the Politburo discussed Andropov's suggestion that a cautious attempt might be made to alter in some slight way the procedure in the forthcoming elections to the Supreme Soviet, Chernenko and Gorbachev were especially interested. For Chernenko, who was chairing the session and who was a functionary to his fingertips, the main issue was that fifteen thousand people had come to the Central Committee with complaints, while twenty thousand had complained to the Presidium of the Supreme Soviet. That meant that the officials in the provinces were not doing their job, otherwise the complaints would have been dealt with properly there. Yet another commission was formed, headed by Gorbachev, to work on Andropov's proposals.

Gorbachev supported Andropov's belief in the need to alter the rule of electing candidates according to their profession, and to do something to breathe life into the work of the soviets.[78] On the surface, it appeared that Andropov's colleagues 'conscientiously, wholeheartedly and completely' approved his ideas, but in fact they were hypocritically passing them down the painfully familiar bureaucratic ladder, through new plans, new commissions, new meetings, and new incantations about the need for 'deepening, improving, perfecting' the work. As usual, everything became bogged down in bureaucratic tangle and inertia.

On the evening of 6 November, the sixty-sixth anniversary of the Leninist revolution, foreign correspondents were telling their stations back home that, regardless of Zamyatin's recent announcement from the Central Committee about Andropov's 'slight cold', he had not been seen at any of the most important ceremonies. And indeed, despite all the medical procedures, consultations and special drugs, and the attention of more and more specialists, Andropov's condition was not improving.

Yet, soon after the celebrations, the General Secretary sent another memorandum to the Politburo on 'an experiment to broaden the independence and responsibility of enterprises'.[79] From his hospital bed he was sending note after note to the Politburo and the Central Committee apparatus, trying somehow by an effort of mind and will to focus those bureaucratically ossified bodies to take some decision on the real problems of the state and society. It is impossible not to give him credit for his courage. Critically ill, he was still trying to summon up a fresh breeze to move the ship from its deathly calm. The ship, however, was so vast that a few cautious, administrative puffs of wind were unable to make it stir. With his remaining strength Andropov was trying to improve things in the country, while leaving the fundamentals untouched.

For the last two months of his life Andropov did not get out of bed, except when he was lifted onto a couch while his sheets were changed. He was physically finished, but his mind remained completely clear, and he still read a great deal. His wife was also ill, and every day he asked to be put through to her on the phone. He even wrote poetry to her.

At the end of November 1983 his aides, in collaboration with the Foreign Ministry and Ministry of Defence, wrote one of the last major reports for Andropov's signature, a statement on the consequences of the deployment of American missiles in Europe and corresponding measures by the USSR. It was tough and uncompromising, as befitted one of the last representatives of the class era.

Andropov was still calling for documents, books and cipher telegrams, even though he could no longer hold them in his hands. He was quietly petering out, like a candle, no longer aware of the bustle around him. Meanwhile, his colleagues went on reading his memoranda, determining who was to be appointed to this or that job, who should get what decorations, and putting their seal of approval on the usual range of decrees, unaware that life outside depended less and less on their decisions. While Andropov was moving inexorably towards the end, the Soviet people still believed he was working as before.

The press announced that on 9 December 1983 an extraordinary meeting of the Central Committee Secretaries of the socialist countries had taken place. It was devoted to international and ideological issues. The meeting discussed Andropov's notes of 28 September and 24 November on measures to resist and respond to the deployment of US missiles in Europe. The Soviet hosts told their guests that

Andropov was 'slightly unwell', but was still actively heading the work of the Central Committee. The guests were also told – in the polite form of a recommendation – to intensify their efforts in the anti-war movement and to step up their participation in opposing 'America's provocative actions.' They should use the extraordinary session of the World Peace Council that was due to take place in January 1984, the International Conference for a Non-Nuclear Europe, the Brussels meeting of the European Council of Security and Co-operation in April 1984, the Fourteenth Congress of the International Union of Students in the same month, the Fourth Congress of World Doctors for the Prevention of Thermonuclear War in Helsinki in May, and similar forums.[80]

On 22 December, six weeks before he died, the text of Andropov's speech for the forthcoming Party Plenum was approved by the Polit-buro. It was addressed to members of the Party: 'Dear Comrades, for temporary reasons, to my great regret I am unable to take part in the Plenum . . . I have thought a great deal about our plans and have been preparing to speak.' He went on to say that 'certain measures for the improvement of our economy, and the strengthening of state, labour and planning discipline, have begun to take effect . . . This is only the beginning and we must not lose the pace we have built up and the generally positive effect on things.' He frequently referred to Lenin on 'the competition and self-motivation of the masses', 'the application of Leninist principles in one's work', the need to 'raise efficiency of labour', and similar worn-out clichés.[81] It was perhaps the most ortho-dox speech he had written as General Secretary.

Although he was at death's door, every day following the morning's painful medical procedures Andropov would scan papers, if no longer the hundreds of earlier days, still dozens of them. His fifteen months in office were dogged throughout by the missile problem. When he was told that the US intended deploying nine Pershing-2s in West Germany on 1 January 1984, and that sixteen guided missiles had been put on battle-alert in the United Kingdom, he produced the rapid response he had promised. By 25 December thirty launchpads were installed in East Germany and Czechoslovakia for two increased-range missile units.[82] He could be satisfied: the West could see that the Soviet leadership was capable of backing its words with deeds.

When Chernenko visited Andropov in hospital in the middle of

January, the man he saw had changed beyond recognition. It was plain from the look on the General Secretary's face that the end was near. Hardly in much better condition himself, Chernenko wheezed the news that the new building for Central Committee plenums had been completed in the Kremlin. The decrepit messenger, whom a caprice of fate had made the crown prince, suggested that three hundred of the people involved in the work should be awarded medals, while several dozen more should receive state prizes, and A. Bogomolov of the Central Committee's General Department, who had supervised the project, should be given the Lenin Prize.[83] With a barely detectable nod of the head, Andropov indicated his assent.

The American Embassy was asking for permission for their Ambassador to fly from Moscow to Stockholm by special plane. In the previous year the Americans had terminated Soviet special flights to New York, so Chernenko thought there was no reason to agree.[84] A letter had arrived from the International Labour Organization asking for an explanation of why peasants in the USSR had no right to leave their collective farms. The Politburo had approved a reply which stated that the Collective Farm Statute allowed peasants to enter or leave a collective farm on the basis of a personal declaration. In 1982, 450,000 people had left collective farms, while 617,000 had joined them.[85] Continuing to leaf through his pile of papers, Chernenko asked Andropov to sign letters to Trudeau, Castro and the Mongolian President Tsedenbal, and a letter of congratulation to Ceausescu on the occasion of his birthday on 26 January.[86]

As chief Party functionary, Chernenko was always especially concerned to ensure that the hierarchy was well provided for with all the goods and services appropriate, in his mind, to their high status. Now, taking advantage of Andropov's weakness, he sought his approval for a joint Central Committee and Council of Ministers decree 'on the remuneration of First Secretaries of territorial committees, regional Party Secretaries and Chairmen of territorial and regional Soviet Executive Committees'. This set very high pensions, retained special medical facilities, cars, dachas and so on.[87] Andropov had begun his period of rule by trying to stamp out elitism and special favours, but now he had no more strength to resist Chernenko. He closed his eyes wearily as a sign of assent.

The last memorandum from Andropov was discussed by the Politburo two weeks before he died. In it, he summed up the work of the leadership for 1983, commenting in particular on its 'greater collectivity, and improved control of the execution of its decisions'. He suggested that the Politburo be relieved of dealing with minor issues which could be handled by the Secretariat and Central Committee departments. Once upon a time, Lenin had also advised relieving the leadership of the 'vermicelli' of trivial affairs. As usual, Andropov added, the selection of personnel needed improvement.[88]

At some time in late January, Ustinov, who was especially close to him, visited Andropov. After discussing defence affairs in general, Ustinov turned to the war in Afghanistan, where he still believed that 40th Army would succeed in achieving stabilization. He then produced a long, long list of servicemen who had been recommended for decoration. Andropov peered at the names, taking note of the large number with 'posthumous' next to them. The undeclared war had been going on for three long years, and all there seemed to be to show for it were tin coffins and posthumous awards. Whether Andropov felt remorse or regret we shall never know.

Throughout his last days Andropov still worked, even if this meant little more than signing papers or giving his assent to his aides' proposals. One of the last letters sent in his name was to President Reagan following the US deployment of missiles in Europe. Dated 28 January 1984, it was in an extremely harsh tone, and offered no expression of hope that relations would improve in the near future. 'We shall be frank, Mr President,' he wrote. 'To pretend that nothing has happened will not work. Tension has risen dangerously.'[89] The letter was reread to him before he signed it.

A letter to K. Miamoto, the chairman of the Communist Party of Japan, dated 8 February 1984, twenty-four hours before Andropov died, and bearing a facsimile of his signature, he could neither read nor hear, let alone sign. He had in fact lost consciousness earlier, but the cynical Party machine gave no hint that he was in a coma. His letter to Miamoto went off to Tokyo without his knowledge.

On the day of Andropov's death, 9 February, the Politburo was in session as usual. They discussed the spring sowing, socialist competition, the work of the Party Control Commission, the use of space for peaceful purposes, additional aid to Afghanistan, Soviet–Libyan relations, and many other issues.[90]

The Politburo knew that Andropov was dying, but for them it was 'business as usual'. A visit by Aliyev to Damascus was postponed: the members were already thinking about their chief task after Andropov's death, namely the selection of a new General Secretary, and for the time being all trips were cancelled.

Among Andropov's papers is the sketch of a poem:

> We are fleeting in this world, beneath the moon.
> Life is an instant. Non-being is forever.
> The Earth spins in the universe,
> Men live and vanish . . .

6

The Sixth Leader:
Konstantin Chernenko

Up until the Twentieth Congress in 1956, the Soviet people saw the future through a lens focused by official ideology: the promised Communist utopia, threatened by a host of enemies – the 'capitalist encirclement'. This simplistic view of the world served to underline Soviet 'perfection, truth and historical rightness'. The illusory future gave direction to the Lenin-Stalinist present. It did not seem like a challenge, only a goal – a high goal, but not a remote one. After all, both Lenin and later Khrushchev had given precise timetables for the arrival of the earthly paradise.

Following the Twentieth Congress new touches appeared in the Bolshevik outlook. Against a background of the 'unexpectedly' exposed evil-doings of Stalin, the 'good' Lenin appeared even more of a genius, an absolutely infallible prophet. Naturally, it was stressed that Stalin's villainy was completely unconnected with the system or with Leninist ideology. Nor did the revealed anomalies have any bearing on the goal.

The time came, however, when more and more people began to see that the Bolshevik 'truths' were in fact expressions of a big lie within a whole system of lies. It was on this basis that within the barbed-wired system created by the first two leaders, the crisis deepened and the cracks in the monolith widened. Khrushchev, distracted by his struggle against the 'cult of personality', thought the cracks were temporary. Brezhnev did not even notice them. Andropov, although he knew they were there, was unable to cement them over. The sixth leader, Chernenko, was not in a position to see them or comprehend what they meant, still less to do anything about them.

Yet, despite the paradox and despite himself, it was he who was the precursor of change.

The sixth leader of the Party and state, while leaving no visible mark on Soviet history, nevertheless became the sign of its fate. With his rise to power, even closet Stalinists, orthodox Leninists and adherents of class dogma saw at last that the system had come to the end of its trajectory. It had shown itself incapable even of choosing an acceptable leader. It could not sink lower. Many people now began to anticipate the coming changes.

The new General Secretary, however, was not one of them. The future was not issuing any challenge to him, for he was entirely a man of the past. All of his energy, application, modest intellect and limited imagination had been expended in the making of his career as a bureaucrat. By the time he managed – against all logic and probability – finally to clamber to the topmost pinnacle of power, he had no strength left in him, either physical or spiritual. He was the consummate symbol of a system that had forfeited its future.

Chernenko painstakingly, at times practically crawling, dragged himself up the hierarchical ladder of the Leninist Party. Finally, at the age of seventy-two, he eased himself painfully into the seat of General Secretary. He was the oldest of all the occupants of that post, secretive, cautious, intellectually mediocre, mumbling and indistinct in his speech. His rise to power came at the end of the long push Brezhnev had given him back in their days in Moldavia.

Chernenko had been ready to take over when Brezhnev died, but the implicit alliance between the KGB and the military had prevented him from doing so. Following Andropov's death, however, Ustinov saw Chernenko as preferable to either Grigory Romanov, a former Leningrad Party boss with support in the military-industrial complex, or Viktor Grishin, whose background was as head of the trade unions, while the present KGB chief, Chebrikov, was still not sufficiently influential. Thus, there was no alliance of 'power ministers' to oppose Chernenko.

Also acting in his favour was the fact that since September 1983 he had chaired the Politburo meetings in Andropov's enforced absence: for nearly half a year, Chernenko had held the reins of power in his hands. The other members of the Politburo had become accustomed to their meetings being opened by him, the agenda being fixed by him, who should be given what senior position, all being determined by this unprepossessing little old man. According to custom, the most likely successor to an outgoing leader was given the job of organizing his funeral, and indeed everyone who spoke was for Chernenko.

The Politburo met at 11 a.m. on 10 February 1984, the day following Andropov's death. Several of the members had had private discussions in the preceding days, notably Chernenko and Tikhonov, who were old friends. Twenty men sat at the long table, including full and non-voting members and Central Committee Secretaries. Chernenko rose from the Chairman's seat and said: 'Comrades, we met yesterday to discuss the main organizational issues concerning the funeral of Yu.V. Andropov. We must now decide another matter which we did not decide yesterday.'

He then demonstratively walked to the seat which he had normally occupied when Andropov was in the chair. Knowing that the outcome was already fixed, he chose to add this 'democratic' touch to his little game. There followed the traditional scenario, written by none, but understood by all: the decisive role was played by whoever spoke up first to nominate the candidate. The Chairman knew precisely on whom to call first, at which point the 'law of unity' would come into play and everyone would start speaking in support, heaping praise on the proposed candidate. Anyone who suggested another name would be nothing less than a heretic.

Nineteen stony faces were turned towards Chernenko. He spoke.

CHERNENKO: We have to resolve one issue today, and that is the question of the General Secretary of the Central Committee of the CPSU. What proposals are there? I would like the comrades to express themselves.

Chairman of the Council of Ministers Tikhonov already had his hand up.

TIKHONOV: Comrades, we are all suffering in these sad moments . . . Yuri Vladimirovich was not in the post of General Secretary for very long. But we all know that he did a great deal of creative work . . . Our Party has at its disposal a large number of well trained cadres. I believe that in the Politburo there are also worthy comrades. I therefore propose a resolution recommending to the next Central Committee Plenum that it appoint as General Secretary Comrade

Konstantin Ustinovich Chernenko. I think that we are all united on the fact that Konstantin Ustinovich Chernenko is a worthy candidate for the post of General Secretary of the Party Central Committee ... Comrade K.U. Chernenko has been dealing with the work of the Politburo and Central Committee Secretariat for a long time. He helped Yuri Vladimirovich Andropov, deputizing for him during his illness and holidays ...

GROMYKO: I support N.A. Tikhonov's proposal to recommend Konstantin Ustinovich Chernenko to the Central Committee Plenum as General Secretary ... We must think ahead, bearing in mind that the Party Central Committee and all our organizations are facing very big tasks ...

Quite how far ahead anyone could think with a sick old man like Chernenko in the chair, Gromyko did not make clear.

USTINOV: ... Chernenko was as it were second man in the Central Committee during Leonid Ilyich [Brezhnev]'s absences, and more recently when Yuri Vladimirovich was absent. He conducted meetings of the Politburo and the Secretariat and gained a great deal of experience in doing so.

GRISHIN: We have continuity in the transfer of leading posts in our Party, and that is very good. Konstantin Ustinovich worked with L.I. Brezhnev, frequently deputizing for him, and recently he has worked with Yuri Vladimirovich Andropov and also deputized for him ...

GORBACHEV: Circumstances demand that our Party, and above all its leading organs, the Politburo and Secretariat, should be united as never before ... The Politburo and Secretariat sessions that [Chernenko] has conducted recently have been held in a spirit of unity, a spirit of taking account of all the comrades' opinions ... The unanimity in what we say today about the candidate for General Secretary, in unanimously naming Konstantin Ustinovich as candidate, testifies to the fact that we in the Politburo really are in complete unity in this regard.

Almost everyone spoke. Chebrikov commented on Chernenko's 'exceptional contributions to the strengthening of the KGB', and all the members indicated that there was only one candidate, and it was time to take a decision.

Chernenko closed the discussion: 'Everyone [not quite!] has

expressed himself and nominated a candidate for the post of General Secretary, demonstrating the unanimous opinion that my candidacy should be recommended . . .'

There followed the usual speech of thanks and assurances that the new leader would observe the need for 'collective leadership and unity'.[1]

It is amazing to think that everyone at that table was perfectly aware that the man to whom they had just given the leadership had nothing to recommend him, beyond the diligence of a Party functionary, exceptional obsequiousness before previous General Secretaries and a good knowledge of the rules of bureaucracy. Chernenko was a total mediocrity, hardly educated, without any of the vision needed by a leader of Party and state. But the lack of democratic tradition in the leadership, and the pressure of Bolshevik stereotypes like 'unity', lack of openness and the monopoly of power, predetermined the Politburo's homogeneity and lack of variation in thinking.

At Andropov's funeral, Chernenko was barely able to read his short graveside speech, and those present strained to catch the meaning of what he was trying to say. He swallowed his words, kept coughing, and stopped repeatedly to wipe his lips and forehead. He could only just raise his hand in farewell to his predecessor's coffin. He ascended to the Mausoleum by way of the newly installed escalator, and descended with the help of two bodyguards. Dr David Owen, leader of Britain's Social Democratic Party, was present, and correctly, as it turned out, concluded that Chernenko was suffering from emphysema.

Anatoly Chernyayev, who was to become an aide to Gorbachev, has described the appointment of Chernenko at the Plenum of 13 February 1984:

> Sverdlov Hall was already nearly full . . . The provincial élite were all there. And it was all the usual thing: people kissing each other and shouting greetings across the rows of seats, chattering about the snow and the harvest prospects and generally feeling themselves to be masters of their fate. In all the cacophony I didn't hear the name of Andropov mentioned once, nor anything said about his death.
>
> At twenty minutes to eleven the hall hushed. The waiting began. With each minute the tension rose and the atmosphere felt charged with electricity . . . The tension reached a climax. All eyes turned towards the door . . . Who would come through it first? At precisely

eleven, Chernenko's head appeared in the doorway. He was followed by Tikhonov, Gromyko, Ustinov, Gorbachev and the rest. The delegates' reaction was silence.[2]

Alexander Alexandrov-Agentov, an assistant to several General Secretaries, including Chernenko, later wrote: 'I have often asked myself how it really was that in the highest position of this enormous state there could have appeared this physically, and in many other respects, weak man, who had insufficient knowledge, no experience of real government work, or knowledge of economics. Could those who chose him, or indeed he himself, not see how far things had gone?'[3]

The question was apt. Among many deep-seated historical and social reasons, it should be noted that seventy years of Bolshevism had fundamentally altered the people and their leaders. The rift between politics and morality had become so wide that none of Chernenko's comrades-in-arms felt, then or later, any prick of conscience. Excuses that 'there was no choice, it was tradition, Party custom, a question of unity,' now sound naïve and false.

The long years of rule by the Leninists had distorted morality to conform to the main criterion of the first leader: everything was moral that served the cause of Communism. Everyone, including Chernenko himself, lacked the courage to say that he was not up to the job. No one wanted the chief clerk of the Party to become its General Secretary, but no one objected or openly proposed an alternative. Nor could they have. The system created by Lenin and perfected by Stalin was still working.

Chernenko's appointment was no accident. It was the product of bureaucratic omnipotence and Bolshevik degeneration. Chernenko was not capable of leading the country or the Party into the future. His rise to power symbolized the deepening of the crisis in society, the total lack of positive ideas in the Party, and the inevitability of the convulsions to come.

The Emblem of Stagnation

Chernenko's period as General Secretary lasted thirteen months, a time of lacklustre stagnation in which society was apathetic, politically indifferent, waiting for something to happen and, at times, voicing rebellious thoughts.

Outwardly almost nothing changed. Medals were still handed out to the 'victors' of socialist competition, long queues waited outside half-empty shops, Party cells were still holding interminable, crowded meetings, the suburban trains were still bringing in passengers hoping to be able to buy something, the militia still stopped the traffic to allow through the long black limousines – or 'member-mobiles', as they were known – that were taking the 'untouchables' to their country villas after a long, hard day at the office. The incomprehensible war in Afghanistan was still going on. The pliable and garrulous Karmal was replaced by Mohammed Najibullah, a protégé of the KGB, but still the USSR was bringing home its soldiers in tin coffins every day.

In the 'socialist world' the mood was also one of waiting. In Poland, the Solidarity movement continued its opposition in muffled form; those brave enough to try to scale the Berlin Wall were still being shot; not only in the USSR, but also in Czechoslovakia, Hungary and Bulgaria the 'dissidents' were demanding freedom and human rights more loudly; Soviet planes were ferrying Cuban troops to Angola and Ethiopia to save bankrupt Marxist regimes; North Korea, while distancing itself increasingly from Moscow, was still demanding new weapons and military supplies; China was just waiting, with her 'three demands' still on the table, and rejecting every offer to improve relations; the USSR wanted to remain in Vietnam, but the Vietnamese only wanted its technical support, not its political advice; in the Middle East and Africa, where regimes 'with a socialist orientation' had arisen with Soviet help, their arsenals were still growing, along with the number of Soviet advisers, while their economies sank further into chaos.

In Washington and the NATO capitals it had become clear that the USSR had cracked under the weight of the arms race and the crisis in the command economy, and there was no inclination to make any compromises with what President Reagan called the 'evil empire'.

While some had been prepared to invite Andropov to the West for meetings, very few such invitations were issued to Chernenko, who was universally seen as an extremely temporary figure.

Nothing changed in the 'Communist and labour movement' either. The Kremlin still issued 'recommendations' on how to step up the fight against US missile plans, Euro-Communism and ideological sabotage. Everything went on as before. Foreign Party leaders still came to Moscow for rest, for instructions or, most of all, for money. More than two thousand senior officials from the 'fraternal Communist Parties' visited Moscow in the course of that year. The International Department of the Central Committee, with almost twenty sub-departments, estimated the best ways to divide up its multi-million-dollar budget. As in Lenin's day, the money was dished out in dollars, pounds and francs, except that now there was more experience and better ways of keeping things under wraps. The KGB was responsible for transmitting the funds, and there was not a single slip-up in delivery.

The least perceptive visitor to the Kremlin could not miss the fact that the sixth leader was finding it hard to absorb documents, that he answered questions in monosyllables and on an extremely elementary level. A Paris newspaper wrote in March 1984: 'Chernenko's most notable feature is the absence of anything notable.'[4]

In contrast to Andropov, Chernenko made no serious attempt to change anything. He found it hard enough to walk, let alone to think. He was accustomed to working from a checklist of decisions, decrees and orders. At his first meeting of the Politburo as General Secretary, he stressed the fact that 'the decisions of the February Plenum have received the support of the Party, the country, the socialist countries and the Communist movement.' He repeated Andropov's line on bringing only important matters to the Politburo, on the need to improve the management of agriculture and industry, on monitoring the implementation of decrees, increasing discipline, reducing the flood of paper, and so on.[5]

He then went on to redistribute responsibilities among the members. He took for himself the traditional jobs of a General Secretary: organization of the Politburo's agenda, defence and security, the main questions of domestic and foreign policy, appointment of top Party and state posts, the external propaganda department, and his favourite, the General Department and Administration of Central Committee Affairs, in effect a general 'housekeeping' department for the Central Committee. He acknowledged that 'it is clear that the span of issues I have to deal with is significantly broader.'

Mikhail Gorbachev had become a full member of the Politburo in 1980, brought in by Andropov as an energetic and comparatively young Secretary to handle agriculture and, as Andropov's health declined, a widening range of other fields. Although he had insufficient support to contest the leadership against Chernenko, his responsibilities made it plain that Gorbachev was by now the second man in the Politburo, and Chernenko confirmed this by giving him the work of the Central Committee Secretariat and all agricultural matters. Tikhonov suddenly declared: 'I have some doubts about the proposed distribution of responsibilities of Central Committee Secretaries. It seems that M.S. Gorbachev, who will be managing the work of the Secretariat, will also simultaneously be handling all matters related to the development of agriculture. I have nothing against Mikhail Sergeevich, but will this not mean some distortion?'

Tikhonov had noticed that Chernenko had strengthened the position of the youngest man in the Politburo. Chernenko made reassuring noises, but at the end of the session he also gave Gorbachev the job of chairing the commission on Poland.[6]

Politically, Chernenko was extremely conservative. He had been heard on several occasions, in small gatherings, to speak warmly of Stalin and of the time 'when a Party directive was law'. He could not, however, go further than Brezhnev in half-rehabilitating Stalin. He had neither the strength, the time nor the intelligence to do so. One thing he did manage to rush through, though, was the 'Molotov issue'.

Molotov had been Stalin's number two, his co-signatory on countless death sentences, commissioned personally by him to carry out various tasks in the bloody purges.[7] Molotov had been pushed out of power by Khrushchev in 1957, and was now living on a meagre pension in the Moscow suburb of Zhukovka. People who spoke to him in those days testify that he was not at all repentant.

Molotov sent a letter to every Party Congress asking to be rehabilitated and reinstated in the Party, and he had been rejected each time. Even Brezhnev could not bring himself to restore the old Bolshevik's respectability. Now he wrote to Chernenko, who requested the files of this phenomenal survivor from the archives. The agenda of the next Politburo meeting included an item on Molotov's reinstatement to the Party. There were no objections, and Chernenko personally conveyed the good news to Molotov.

It was soon clear to everyone that Chernenko had no intention of introducing any important changes, and that any he did make were likely to be in the direction of the somnolent ways of the Brezhnev era. On 5 April 1984 he gave his consent to the demands of numerous orthodox Leninists to reverse Andropov's ban on the building of monuments, and issued a decree 'to continue building monuments to Lenin in the following centres of population'. The list of towns to be so honoured stretched to two pages.[8]

To judge by his published speeches and writings, Chernenko could almost be regarded as more of a Leninist than his colleagues. Dull, repetitive and hagiographic, the titles alone suggest their author's limited range: 'The Leading Role of V.I. Lenin and the Party in Formulating the Foundation Documents of State Construction'; 'Some Questions of Leninist Style in Party Work'; 'The Twenty-Fifth Party Congress on the Further Development of Leninist Style in Party Work'; 'For a Leninist Style in Party Work'; 'The Growth of the Leading Role of the CPSU in Conditions of Developed Socialism and the Leninist Style of Work'.[9] Chernenko was himself part of that 'style'; he was its embodiment, and the personification of its decline.

Although the articles signed by the Party leaders, like the speeches they recited, were written by others, the leaders nevertheless believed what was written in their name. One of Chernenko's utterly empty articles asserts: 'Our enemies are spreading monstrous lies and absurdities which attempt to present socialism as a society where the initiative, rights and liberties of the people are trampled. In not one capitalist country can one even speak of any sort of participation by the workers in running the affairs of society. Whereas in the Soviet land, people's power lies at the very basis of the political system of socialism.'[10]

It can hardly have occurred to Chernenko that throughout Soviet history none of the leaders, including himself, had been elected by the people. The blatant lie in the article, however, was but a drop in the ocean of lies on which Leninism was based. 'The worker is the real boss of the socialist enterprise', 'socialist democracy is the highest type', and 'Marxism-Leninism is the only true teaching' – the mouthing of these and similar lies helped to consolidate the totalitarian state.

Even people who were honest and decent in themselves became victims of the mendacity. Certainly a majority of the Soviet population believed for decades in the 'historical superiority of socialism, the saving role of the dictatorship of the proletariat, the total lack of rights and liberties for workers in the capitalist countries, the inevitability of the collapse of capitalism and the triumph of Communist ideals throughout the planet'. A morality which contemplated only collective interests turns the individual into a statistical unit, something subsidiary and secondary. Only that which conformed to Marxist-Leninist assumptions, Party decrees and class interests could be regarded as the truth.

As the USSR invaded Hungary, Czechoslovakia and Afghanistan, its propaganda declared that it was fulfilling its international duty; while proclaiming the advantages of the planned economy, for decades it purchased grain from countries which really enjoyed those advantages; while concealing in the archives the secret protocols of the Molotov–Ribbentrop Pact, or evidence of the murder of thousands of Poles, Soviet leaders stated that such documents did not exist.

As the Polish thinker Leszek Kolakowski has written, in totalitarian societies the lie fulfils a special function: 'Versions are released for the people from above and can be altered the very next day. There is no reliable criterion of truth apart from what is the declared truth at any moment. Thus, the lie in fact becomes the truth, or at any rate the distinction between truth and lies, in the ordinary sense of these words, disappears. This is the great triumph of socialism in the sphere of knowledge: to the extent that it succeeds in demolishing the notion of truth, it cannot be accused of lying.'[11]

When the rehabilitation of victims of the terror began in 1955, the leadership was worried about the consequences if the public came to know how many people had been shot. It was therefore decided that the KGB and the State Prosecutor's office should publish 'Instruction No. 108ss on Camps', which stipulated that in the information given to families, for those who had been shot on non-judicial orders the date of death should be given as roughly ten years from the time of their arrest, and the cause should be fictitious. This was just one more example of the regime's impulse to lie.

By the time Chernenko came to power, the social crisis had reached such proportions that lies were no longer able to conceal the cracks in the economy, or the truth about the standard of living or human rights. The myths which supported so many Leninist assumptions were being destroyed. People were tired of lies and promises of a bright future in the next, more distant Five-Year Plan. If they had imagined that Andropov might be the man to make something happen, there was no such hope of Chernenko. Many sensed the approach of stagnation, and society was fraught with apathy, passivity, distrust and disillusionment.

Chernenko would get his assistants to contact the First Secretary of this or that republic, and several regional Party secretaries in sequence, and from a prepared list of questions he would ask:

1. How is the implementation of the last Plenum's decisions going?
2. How about the sowing campaign?
3. You are seriously behind in your delivery of meat. What are you thinking of doing about it?

Having no idea of the true economic situation, he tried at first to 'whip up' the Party committees and to issue advice. The Secretaries gave him servile reports on the position in their patch, but they would also ask for equipment, money and rapid solutions to particular issues, whereupon Chernenko would quickly terminate the conversation, telling them to 'write to the appropriate Central Committee department.' After two or three attempts at this telephonic substitute for actually going to see for himself, Chernenko opted for a quiet life and dropped the practice.

As the former chief editor of *Pravda*, an orthodox Communist to the end of his days, wrote after the collapse of the CPSU: 'Chernenko was utterly detached from earthly affairs.' He had little idea of 'economics, to say nothing of science, technology or culture'.[12] At seventy-two, the old man ought to have been amusing himself with his grandchildren and writing his memoirs, not trying to run a country.

In accordance with established rules, Chernenko regularly reminded the Central Committee Secretaries of the need to 'reward the workers' on the occasion of anniversaries, the completion of a building project or the production of annual figures. It is noteworthy that, even in the depths of the long stagnation, Secretaries did not lose the habit of

finding more and more 'successes in socialist construction'. The Politburo naturally encouraged these efforts. Thus, on 1 March 1984 Chernenko approved a Politburo order 'On the distribution of decorations
and medals as a reward for workers in agriculture on the results of
work in 1983'. It was agreed that 8,500 orders should go to workers
in the Russian Republic, 3,500 to Ukraine, 1,150 to Belorussia, and
that 'all their sisters should be given earrings'.[13] The passion for medals
had been inherited from Brezhnev. Chernenko managed to make
himself a Hero of Socialist Labour three times in his brief period in
office.

In his infrequent speeches, or at Politburo meetings, Chernenko
rarely mentioned Andropov, and totally ignored the memory of Brezhnev, to whom he owed his rapid rise. Brezhnev had loved servility,
flattery and enthusiasm, and Chernenko possessed all these qualities
in abundance. As chief of the Central Committee's General Department, he was in effect head of Brezhnev's personal office. He was
able gradually to win the General Secretary's complete trust, was
accepted by his family as one of them, and carried out many of Leonid
Ilyich's personal domestic errands. And he was well rewarded. At the
Plenum following the Twenty-Fifth Congress in March 1976, which
Chernenko had organized to perfection, Brezhnev proposed – and it
was naturally agreed – that he be made a Central Committee Secretary
and given the title of Hero of Socialist Labour. Chernenko had arrived
at the top, his dream had come true.

Without Brezhnev it would have been impossible for the clerk of
the Central Committee to become its leader. Chernenko's entire Party
career had been passed in second-rank positions. He spent the war
entirely in the rear, studying to become a Party organizer. He had
no education to speak of. He did acquire a diploma from the Kishinev
Teachers' Training Institute, but he was after all in charge of propaganda, not only at the Institute itself, but on the republic's Party
Central Committee. He was a virtual unknown to the population
when he became General Secretary.

Chernenko's rise to power is the most glaring example in Soviet
history of someone reaching the top with nothing more than his
personal closeness to the leader to recommend him. Not only did
society play no part in the selection of its leaders, but the Party itself
was excluded from the process in which the top echelon appointed

themselves from among a small clan of functionaries. When the leader died, the people could do nothing but sit by the radio and wait to hear who was named as the 'outstanding Leninist' to succeed him.

The degeneration of the system was reflected in the deepening economic crisis, the anachronistic political system, the cynical control of spiritual life, and in the nature of the top people themselves. The public could see no hope in such leaders. The head of the Party and state, and commander-in-chief of one of the most powerful armed forces on earth, was a busy little bureaucrat with a dull mind, the career of a clerk and no ideas or plans for getting the country out of the crisis. People began asking each other how long the spectacle of 'triumphant funerals' would go on. Chernenko's red seal on the most important papers of the Central Committee and the Politburo was an emblem of stagnation.

Clerk to the Party

At some time in March 1984, shortly after Chernenko became General Secretary, he circulated an instruction to all Party committees and political organs. It gave a physical description of the documents to be submitted to the Central Committee, giving the exact width of margins, the maximum number of lines per page, and the maximum length as five pages.

This occurred before I was removed from the Army's Political Department, and I well remember the way my fellow officers read the document, signed to show they had read it, and then left, all in silence. They realized that the new General Secretary was a functionary to the marrow of his bones. The country might be facing a sea of problems, but the Party must be told how wide to make the margins on its routine documents.

That was merely the tip of the iceberg. As Georgy Shakhnazarov, a member of Gorbachev's 'brains trust', has written: 'Under Chernenko a directive was issued according to which the only people permitted to work in the Central Committee apparatus were Communists who had first served as Secretaries in district, city or higher Party committees ... The staffing of the apparatus was based entirely on the bureaucratic élite, access to the apparatus was restricted solely to functionaries.'[14] Engineers, diplomats, financial and other experts were all excluded by Chernenko's rules. He had become General Secretary while remaining a clerk in his soul, knowing everything about the way documents originated, the location of the Party seal and the facsimiles of Politburo members' signatures, how to change the profile of a body with a single document, what to report to a head of section and what to his deputy, and so on and so on.

Konstantin Ustinovich Chernenko was born on 11 September 1911 into a poor peasant family in the village of Bolshaya Tes, in the Novoselovo District of Krasnoyarsk Region. Before his call-up for military service he completed three years in a school for peasant children. There for the first time he heard what Lenin had said at the Third Komsomol Congress, the names of the members of the Politburo, the meaning of the class struggle against the kulaks and the dictatorship of the proletariat, the inevitability of world revolution, and he acquired a little schooling. His basic elementary education, plus the 'political consciousness' of a Komsomol propagandist, were duly noted, and in 1929 he was made head of the propaganda and agitation section of the Novoselovo Komsomol District Committee. There he acquired experience of ideological work among the masses.

He next did two years' military service with the border troops, during which time he entered the Party and was appointed Secretary of the Party organization for the 49th Border Unit, stationed in the Taldy-Kurgan region of Kazakhstan. This insignificant fact would probably have remained unknown had Chernenko finished his career as Head of Chancery in the Secretariat of the Supreme Soviet. But, having against all logic become head of the Party and state, his biography had to include at least some fragment of heroism, and since he had not served in the war, his spell in the Border Guards had to do. Stalin had ended the war as Generalissimo, while Khrushchev and Brezhnev became two-star generals. As for Andropov, who did not serve at the front, painstaking research resulted in the discovery that he had 'formed partisan units in Karelia'.

Everything was possible in the Party biography of a Soviet leader. Thus, it was 'found' that in Kazakhstan Chernenko had undergone 'baptism by fire'. One N. Fetisov was writing a book on the new General Secretary's service on the pickets of Khorgos and Narynkol.

It was entitled *Six Heroic Days*, and the author needed a detailed account of his subject's role in combating local nationalist partisan groups of little significance, and also of his life as a border soldier. He wrote to Chernenko for material, adding: 'An interesting entertainment for the soldiers at Narynkol was watching their pet goat, dog and cat play together. Do you remember that?'[15] It is not known if Chernenko replied, but it is a safe guess that had he survived even another three months, a book like Brezhnev's *Malaya Zemlya* could well have appeared, and Chernenko would have been made a Hero of the Soviet Union. In fact, 'The Song of the Border Troops' was published with a dedication to Chernenko during his tenure, although I do not recall ever hearing it on television or radio. This may have been due to the appalling quality of its lyrics, of which the following is just one execrable verse:

> Clouds were gathering over the frontier, darkening.
> The road into the land of the Pamirs was blocked.
> We were led into battle by Konstantin Ustinovich Chernenko.
> The Party organizer was always in the thick of it.[16]

This did not offer much scope for myth-making, and further research was carried out into the General Secretary's life. One of the researchers dug up a front newspaper for 29 September 1942 called *Into Battle for the Motherland*. It contained a brief report by a Red Army man signing himself I. Kazakov, which reads:

> In connection with the twenty-fifth anniversary of the Great October Revolution, our front was visited by a delegation of workers from the Krasnoyarsk region. The delegation was headed by the Agitation and Propaganda Secretary of the Krasnoyarsk Regional Party Committee, Comrade K.U. Chernenko. The workers, collective farmers and intelligentsia of Krasnoyarsk Region had sent a letter to the troops on our front in which they described the heroic work they are doing in the rear, in factories, collective farms and state farms. The delegation brought fifty-nine wagonloads of various gifts for the troops. Among the gifts were meat and sweet products, butter, tobacco, honey, vodka, warm clothes and so on. The delegates are joining their units in the coming days.[17]

This remarkable event in the life of Chernenko was reported in various newspapers forty years later, though they overlooked the fact that the General Secretary had spent 1943 to 1945 at the Higher Party Organizers' School in Moscow. He did not ask to be sent to the front, but his war record earned him a single medal for outstanding work. There was one other attempt to create a legend. Soon after Chernenko came to power, a package arrived at the Central Committee. It contained the manuscript of a play entitled *A Man Presents Himself, a Man is Renowned*. The hero was, of course, Chernenko, who allegedly displayed his exceptional qualities as a leader while he was still in Siberia.[18] Unlike 'The Song of the Border Troops', the play lauded his activity in Party committees, but like the song, it was so bad that it was thought unfit for mass consumption.

Chernenko next spent three years in Penza as Secretary for Ideology. Then for eight decisive years, from 1948 to 1956, he was in charge of propaganda and agitation in Moldavia. In the summer of 1950 he met Brezhnev, who was the new First Secretary. They took a liking to each other at once, and formed a friendship that was to last throughout their lives.

The most formative time for Chernenko was the period, beginning in 1961, he spent in the Central Committee, where he worked for twenty-five years. For nearly eighteen years from 1965 he was in charge of the General Department. In 1976 he was made a Central Committee Secretary, in 1977 a candidate and finally in 1978 a full member of the Politburo.

The General Department of the Central Committee became more important, more influential and more elitist under Chernenko. Among the more than twenty departments, the General Department had always been the main chancery of the Party, the initiator, custodian and interpreter of its documents and its secrets. The department consisted of six sectors and about 150 staff in all. Sectors in other departments bore names such as the Sector for Ukraine and Moldavia, the Sector for Newspapers, Philosophical Sciences, Drama Theatres, Atomic Energy, State Security, USA and Canada, the Sector for Economics, and so on. The sectors of the General Department were simply given numbers.

In accordance with an old Party tradition, the General Department held all the Party's main secrets and the closed archives of the Politburo. At a meeting Chernenko held with the sector heads of his department in June 1976 he told the assembled group, reading from his usual prepared text, that they 'must introduce or refresh their memory of existing rules which have of late simply been broken for some reason ... and that is not permissible in our work, in the work of the general departments.' Then, citing Brezhnev, he said something which exposed the underlying essence of the General Department's work: 'We must never forget that the general departments are the successors of the special departments and special sectors of the Party committees. Remembering that, you must bear in mind that it is only the names of the departments that have changed, while the essence of special tasks and special methods of working have not changed. On the contrary, these special features in our approach to dealing with problems in the work of the general departments have become more necessary, of greater scale and complexity.'[19]

The General (read Special) Department monitored all the information coming into and leaving 'Headquarters', as the Central Committee apparatus liked to call itself. It scrupulously observed the passage of documents and the use made of them, in order, in Chernenko's words, to be able 'to answer enquiries from Central Committee Secretaries, members of the Politburo and those comrades to whom it is appropriate to give such information'.[20] In other words, it managed the entire documentary side of the Central Committee's governing functions, and it maintained a strict embargo on the material, ensuring that only 'the appropriate comrades' gained access to it. As Chernenko added at the 1976 meeting: 'One of the most important needs that distinguishes the special departments is the secrecy of the work ... I have already said that secrecy can only be assured not by widening, but by narrowing the number of people who work on one or another secret document ... to achieve 100 per cent exclusion of all possible loopholes permitting the leak of information.'[21]

On the question of securing 'the seals and facsimile [signatures] of Central Committee Secretaries', Chernenko was most specific, giving instructions that they 'must be kept in special safes. Safes must have two locks. The keys for each lock must be held by different people.' Several pages of instructions indicated how 'especially important documents' should be kept, 'whose permission should be obtained before opening a package', how to handle microfilms and how to keep 'a strict check on all copying and other machines'.[22] It is hard to imagine that within a short time this nitpicker would become head of the Party and state.

It would be a mistake, however, to lose sight of the fact that Chernenko's primary concern was political. 'I must draw comrades' attention once again to the question of voting,' he went on. 'No one, and never without special instructions, should ever give information about who voted and how.' (Many Politburo and Secretariat issues were determined by 'postal' vote on special forms.) 'Voting papers and other documents concerning Central Committee Secretaries, Politburo members and candidate members are absolutely secret.'[23] He ended by reminding his staff that 'we represent above all the entire apparatus of the Politburo and Central Committee Secretariat ... That in itself means that we, the workers of the general departments, are the people who are closest to them and most trusted by them.'[24]

Chernenko cherished the Bolshevik tradition of secrecy surrounding the Party 'HQ'. When he was summoned by Brezhnev to come to Moscow to work in the Central Committee in 1956, he signed the customary 'official secrets act', which read:

> I, the undersigned, Konstantin Ustinovich Chernenko, while working in the apparatus or after dismissal from it, hereby undertake to keep strictly secret all information and facts about my work, and not to make them public in any way or to share them with anyone. I understand that for any breach of this undertaking I am answerable under the Supreme Court Presidium Order of 9 June 1947. I also undertake to report to the Central Committee Board of Affairs all changes in the data given by me in my most recent questionnaire, and, in particular, on relatives and friends who have contact with foreigners and who have travelled abroad.[25]

Because of Chernenko's close personal relations with Brezhnev, the General Department soon became Leonid Ilyich's personal chancery, and with his support throughout the Party machine the role of the general departments grew sharply. Brezhnev himself recognized this when on 19 May 1976, speaking at the Fifth All-Union Convention of General Department Heads, he said: 'There used not to be departments, but sectors of two or three people. Now we have departments, and what departments they are! How they have grown! That's very good!'[26]

The growth of the bureaucratic machine was seen by the Party as a measure of progress, development and improvement. The internal life of the Central Committee had always been secret, as was that of the other Party centres. Like a separate caste within society, hundreds of thousands of Party members lived by different rules and enjoyed special privileges denied to their fellow citizens. These people included secretaries, inspectors, instructors, health workers and hospital staff, academics, restaurant managers, tailors, librarians, archivists, museum curators, workshop managers, and a host of others who both supplied and received special services. Chernenko was the ideal expression of this large, mixed group's interests, and he frequently put forward proposals to improve its financial, medical, housing and other provisions.

Two months before Brezhnev died, Chernenko requested a resolution for the Politburo on 'the creation of a base for the organization of holidays for Party workers' in Moscow and the localities.[27] This was a clear move to increase the importance of the General Department in the provinces, and it was followed by regular meetings of general department officials in the regions. In July 1978, now promoted to candidate membership of the Politburo, Chernenko held one of these meetings in his home territory of Krasnoyarsk. Officials from twenty-one regions of Siberia and the Far East gathered in the beautiful city on the Yenisei River to hear Chernenko, who had deigned to put in a personal appearance, announce that 330 people had attended the district meetings of general departments.[28] He might as well have announced that Siberia had produced an extra million tonnes of steel or grain, to judge by the excitement generated.

Meetings such as those of the general departments were far from unique: they were also being held by the Party Organization Department, the Propaganda Department, science, culture, heavy industry and energy, machine-building, agriculture and food processing, chemical engineering, defence industry and every other Central Committee department and its dependants. The vast bureaucratic machine slowly and remorselessly moved its paper pistons, churning out ever new plans, appeals, resolutions, orders and reports. Bureaucracy, and its way of thinking, dominated the public mind.

The bureaucratic system, cemented in dogma, presented itself as genuine democracy, and the perfection of the machinery of government. As Chernenko wrote: 'The highest Leninist school of leadership and administration of the construction of Communism are the CPSU congresses, the Central Committee plenums, and the activities of the Secretariat and Politburo.'[29] People brought up in this milieu were daily saying one thing and doing another, seeing one thing in slogans and another in reality, and they became used to this way of thinking.

Chernenko worked hard, and he loved his work, the constant shuffle of paper and the glow of the computer screens. He worked practically every day, including Sundays. His wife, daughter and son rarely saw him at home. By virtue of his job, Chernenko knew an enormous amount, but he never departed from his prepared text to surprise an audience with a personal observation or flight of fancy. He was the implacable mandarin, the dedicated custodian of the machine. He became a giant in his profession, but remained a dwarf in his soul.

Chernenko was not just a bureaucrat. The General Department was really the 'Special Department'. In his office he had equipment that enabled him to eavesdrop on conversations between the highest officials in the Central Committee building on Staraya Square, including those on the fifth floor, who included the General Secretary himself, the 'grand inquisitor' Suslov, and other top brass. Chernenko knew more about every facet of Central Committee activity than anyone. Whenever the transfer of an official arose, therefore, Brezhnev would first confer with him, and he was evidently amazed by Chernenko's detailed knowledge of the personal and often intimate lives of leading Party figures.

At the end of Brezhnev's rule Chernenko was handing out dispositions of all kinds in the General Secretary's name. He raised the bureaucratic machine to the highest level. Under his supervision the apparatus was computerized, and the information fed into the system was monitored. On his initiative an underground canal for pneumatic post was installed between the Kremlin, where the Politburo met, and Staraya Square, where the Central Committee organization was located, enabling the transfer of documents in seconds. Brezhnev awarded him a State Prize for this innovation.

Ironically, it was none other than Chernenko who, on becoming General Secretary, complained that the 'flood of correspondence and the flow of paper' in the Party and the country as a whole were 'literally overwhelming the central organs. Is this normal? Without doubt, we have to bring some order into this.'[30]

Bringing order into this, as into many other areas, was easier said than done. The command economy, which worked well enough in extreme times such as war and the terror, was by now barely functioning. The country was over-consuming its natural resources while exporting to the West. In the course of 1984, under Chernenko, the government purchased 46 million tonnes of grain and grain products, about 500,000 tonnes of meat and meat products, more than a million tonnes of animal and vegetable oil and other food products, to the value of eight billion roubles.

The deputy head of the Central Committee's Economic Department, B. Gostev, reported to the Politburo that almost 60 per cent of resources, in the form of convertible currency, had gone on the import of foodstuffs, ferrous metals, chemicals and consumer goods, while the USSR exported only oil, gas, timber and some other raw materials. This report was virtually a condemnation of socialist economic inefficiency.

And what was purchased abroad was used extremely badly. As at 1 January 1985, 506 sets of equipment purchased abroad had not been put into use because of their condition, and half of their guarantees had already expired. A majority of enterprises that had been created on the basis of imported equipment were unable to reach their projected potential for many years, and for a variety of reasons. For instance, the Bratsk timber industry, which produced viscose cellulose, could not get its valuable imported equipment into production for ten years.

The leadership, however, knowing the poor quality of Soviet-made equipment, went on buying more and more new imports. In 1983 Gosplan received 725 demands for imported equipment, and in 1984 the number grew to 924. Many of these imports lay unused, sometimes for years. Yet proposals from the Economic Department on 22 June 1985 were no more than a gentle reminder to officials that on 23 December 1983 the Central Committee had urged them to do their best to justify purchases from abroad.[31]

Evidence of such glaring abuses arrived on Chernenko's desk with lamentable regularity. Since he was unversed in such matters, he usually gave them a quick glance and passed them to someone else to prepare a resolution for him. He believed that a resolution issued by the General Secretary was enough to change the situation and to achieve improvement in any area. His bureaucratic mind was unable to comprehend the inefficacy of extra-economic mechanisms and the failure implicit in trying to run a vast complex on the principles of a command economy. And even when he was able to grasp the nature of a problem, he was unable to think of how to deal with it. He therefore followed his instinct, and went on doing what had been done before.

Chernenko completely failed to appreciate the harm being done by the system. Gostev had pointed out that hundreds of tonnes of gold had been spent on importing 46 million tonnes of grain into a country that had vast agricultural resources. His memorandum indicated nothing less than a catastrophe, yet it was not even discussed by the Politburo, which nevertheless found time to debate what gifts to present to the North Koreans on a forthcoming visit. It was agreed to give Kim Il-sung a gilded sabre, a porcelain vase and a hamper of Soviet wines and vodka, and the rest of the delegation hunting rifles, quartz watches and hampers.[32] Such was the order of priorities.

Chernenko felt infinitely more comfortable with formal, often trivial, issues than when discussing social, economic or financial problems. On such occasions he would not take part, but would merely present texts prepared for him by his assistants. I blush to admit that I wrote several speeches for Ustinov as a Politburo member when I was in the Main Political Administration of the Army and Navy. In my embarrassment, I wondered what sort of people were ruling us.

Chernenko would come to life only during long and boring meetings when the Politburo members were delivering prepared speeches on ideology. For instance, when Central Committee appeals on some public holiday or other were under discussion, Chernenko would add his own touches to the text, altering slogans that had left the people's hearts and minds untouched for years. He believed that Marxist-Leninist ideology would breathe new life into the stagnant society.

Brezhnev's Favourite

Soviet history inherited much from the tsarist empire: messianism, absence of democratic tradition, dominance of autocratic thought, reliance on military might and lack of respect for human liberty. But political favouritism, which was deeply entrenched in the Romanov past, was less in evidence under the Soviets. The main Bolshevik leaders feared favourites, preferring solitary rule and keeping their 'comrades-in-arms' and rivals at arm's length.

The great exception was Brezhnev. The rest of the leadership knew that he had a favourite, and so did most of the country. It was, of course, Chernenko. They met in June 1950 in Kishinev, where Chernenko had been chief of propaganda and agitation for two years, when Brezhnev arrived as the new First Secretary, in effect the Soviet governor of Moldavia. Their relationship was not perhaps one of friendship so much as of a benevolent patron and his servile subordinate. But after leaving Moldavia for the dizzy heights of Moscow politics, Brezhnev remembered Chernenko, his stooping figure and disjointed speech, the fact that he never contradicted him, was punctual and punctilious, always ready with a needed item of information, apt with his suggestions, able to produce the text of a speech or an article for the republic's newspaper when required. Nor was it easy for Brezhnev to forget the loyal servant who regularly sent letters and telegrams of congratulation on holidays and birthdays, or when another award was announced.

Soon after arriving in Moscow in 1956, Brezhnev organized Chernenko's transfer, an outcome Chernenko had devoutly desired. That same year, the propagandist from the periphery became a sector head in the Central Committee's Propaganda Department. The job was not a big one, but it could be a stepping-stone to higher things, for instance the post of a Regional First Secretary or a Deputy Minister. Chernenko was not, however, looking for somewhere to jump to. Nearby, albeit many rungs higher up the hierarchy, was his benefactor. Cautiously, but persistently, Chernenko reminded Brezhnev of his presence. Several times he asked for permission to see Leonid Ilyich, and when they met they reminisced about the good old days in sunny Kishinev. To the sentimental Brezhnev, the dull Chernenko represented something of a fellow-countryman, or old comrade.

When Brezhnev became Chairman of the Presidium of the Supreme Soviet, i.e. the formal head of state, in 1960, he soon managed to winkle Chernenko out of the Central Committee apparatus and make him his chief of staff. Now they met almost every day, and Brezhnev again felt the benefit of his aide's scrupulous attention to detail. As for Chernenko, he was in his element. With his minimal education he could never be a serious ideologist, and as a propagandist he had never advanced a single original idea. He was simply a very good executive. He often performed personal services for Brezhnev, which brought them still closer together. But patronage has no place in friendship, and their relationship remained one of boss and subordinate.

While he was working in the Supreme Soviet, Chernenko gradually acquired considerable knowledge of the inner workings of a state body, moved by the Party engine. He had frequent dealings with senior officials of the Council of Ministers, Gosplan, the cultural bodies, the KGB and Defence Ministry, as well as functionaries from the provinces. As a result, he became an experienced old hand who never embarrassed or angered his boss. Gradually, Brezhnev came to feel he could not do without him.

Brezhnev loved to be flattered and pampered, and Chernenko was more than happy to oblige. He frequently urged the General Secretary, who had never over-burdened himself with work, to take things easy and not to do too much. Brezhnev also loved gossip, and Chernenko was always in a position to offer the latest titbit. He knew when birthdays and other anniversaries were coming up, and would remind Brezhnev to make sure that an appropriate award or title was given. This enhanced Brezhnev's own reputation for kindness and generosity towards those whose loyalty was valuable, but it also gained credit for Chernenko as a valuable right hand.

By the beginning of 1965 Chernenko was promoted to run the General Department, where he would remain throughout Brezhnev's period of rule. Even after becoming a Central Committee Secretary in 1976, a candidate member of the Politburo in 1977 and a full member in 1978, he retained his position at the General Department. Indeed, even when he became General Secretary himself in February 1984, he could not bring himself to let go of his beloved General Department.

Brezhnev's closest relations in the Politburo were with Andropov, Ustinov and Gromyko, but these were really because of their positions in the Party and state. His relationship with Chernenko, especially after he had been elevated to Central Committee Secretary at the

Plenum following the Twenty-Fifth Congress, entered a new and more confidential stage. Chernenko now scrutinized Brezhnev's voluminous personal correspondence, prepared his draft resolutions, screened and prepared material for presentation to the Politburo, and monitored nominations for top jobs. Brezhnev was by this time troubled by ill health, and was all too pleased to offload the boring paperwork onto the willing Chernenko. At first Chernenko would tender advice tentatively, but later, during the last three or four years of Brezhnev's life, particularly after he became a member of the Politburo, he was handling major decisions in Brezhnev's name.

Brezhnev saw more of Chernenko than he did of any other person in the leadership. They met every day, often several times in a day. In Brezhnev's notebooks, Chernenko's name appears more often than all the others put together. Chernenko's image, meanwhile, was growing as a result. Other leaders began to be wary of him, flattering him and asking for his advice, while despising him as a decrepit wreck who had managed to worm his way into Brezhnev's confidence. It was common for Brezhnev, in the company of other leaders, to address Chernenko familiarly as 'Kostya', or if he was absent to say, 'Tell Konstantin,' or 'I'll talk to Kostya.' The others would remain silent, as they saw the position of the favourite being steadily consolidated.

On 19 May 1976, soon after becoming a Secretary of the Central Committee, Chernenko organized an All-Union meeting of heads of general departments. He entered the hall together with Brezhnev. Everyone jumped up and gave a long ovation. Brezhnev did not normally attend meetings of economic specialists, agronomists or chemists, and his presence greatly enhanced Chernenko's prestige. For Brezhnev, the occasion was chiefly another 'fix', as he could not survive long without the life-giving applause, expressions of love and admiration. In his short speech he mentioned the fact that the Central Committee was receiving about 1,800 letters a day from the public – though he refrained from pointing out that most of them were complaints about the lack of housing, abuse by local officials and similar afflictions – and praised the general departments for handling this work.

He then announced: 'Two important events are taking place in the country at the moment which people are talking about: the erection of a statue of me as Hero of the Soviet Union and one of me as Hero of Socialist Labour in my birthplace, and my promotion to the rank of Marshal of the Soviet Union.'[33] Brezhnev must have lost all sense of decency by talking in this way about himself, but he knew his tone would be picked up by others. Sure enough, Chernenko immediately stood up and declared: 'I thought you would be wearing your marshal's uniform. As you aren't, I'll show everyone here the portrait of you in marshal's full-dress uniform.' A full-length painting of Brezhnev in a blaze of gold epaulettes and countless decorations rose from behind the chairman's table to a roar of applause.

Chernenko continued: 'Today is a great occasion for us . . . We are delighted to congratulate you on your title of Marshal . . . Your speech has given us second wind . . . We start every day thinking about your orders and demands . . . Your speech is an inspiration to us . . . Thank you for making me a Secretary of the Central Committee and for the title of Hero of Socialist Labour.'[34] He had done his job: Brezhnev was happy, the delegates were happy, and he had the pleasure of knowing that his own standing was higher in everyone's eyes.

Whenever possible, Chernenko praised Brezhnev, which the General Secretary would immediately hear about. Even in his dullest articles he would mention his name a dozen times, whether or not it was relevant.[35] Brezhnev reciprocated with genuine affection, lavish awards, rapid promotion and total trust. When he was absent from the Politburo, he appointed Chernenko to deputize for him. The other members saw this as an anomaly, but they observed the unwritten rule that commanded obedience to the will of the General Secretary.

The archives contain numerous personal messages from Brezhnev to his favourite. On the eve of the Supreme Soviet meeting that reappointed Brezhnev head of state in June 1977 – the first General Secretary to hold the post – Chernenko wrote to his boss that he had checked all the necessary documents for the meeting, and that everything was in order but, unfortunately, the doctors were insisting he spend the next few days in bed, and he was therefore very sorry, but he would not be at the historic occasion of Leonid Ilyich's elevation.

Brezhnev dictated his reply on 14 June:

Dear Kostya,

I got your note. Thanks. I'm sorry you're ill. I want to tell you that anyone can get ill. It is important, especially on this occasion, to stick firmly to the regime Comrade Chazov and the doctors prescribe. You write that 'it's nothing, it'll go in a couple of days and I'll be back at work.' Don't be offended, but I had to laugh. I thought to myself, that's an agile one: his temperature is almost 40, he gets up, probably to go to the toilet, and when he comes out his temperature's fallen to 36.5. It's not normal, Kostya. Things are going fine, thanks very much. Everything's been organized. And therefore I wish you good health from the bottom of my heart, and when you're well again, we'll see (we'll go to Zavidovo).

With feelings of deep regard, L. Brezhnev.[36]

After the Supreme Soviet had performed its ritual act and made Brezhnev the new President, he wrote to Chernenko with an account of the occasion. The typist added punctuation, which Brezhnev usually left out:

Dear Kostya,

It was with deep emotion that I read your congratulations ... Your words ... could not but touch my heart and move me. Your letter showed once more just how strong our friendship and relationship are.

The Supreme Soviet session went well, I would even say superbly well. There were endless ovations. Mikhail Andreyevich Suslov's speech especially was greeted by a storm of applause. I made my speech of thanks after him and I promised, like a soldier, to justify the confidence of our dear Motherland and our great Party, and to do everything to strengthen peace on earth and develop good co-operation between the peoples. The delegates received my speech very warmly.

Consider that you were there with us. Everything else is going normally. Don't worry. Well, I'll say again: don't rush, as there's absolutely no need. You've prepared everything for the immediate future. I embrace you and kiss you and wish you a speedy recovery.[37]

The form of address and the nature of the message, while they are eloquent testimony to Brezhnev's vanity, as well as his human warmth, give a clear indication of the relationship that had developed between the two men.

For a long time Chernenko was not taken seriously in top Party echelons. He was regarded as an ordinary functionary, more zealous and punctilious than most, perhaps, and nothing but a strict conformist to the orthodox line. He was always silent, and even when he was a member of the Politburo he did not speak on economic, budgetary, technological or military issues. But he was among the first to voice support of Brezhnev, while the ailing General Secretary was still able to make suggestions of his own.

It has been said that Brezhnev was grooming Chernenko to succeed him. This seems unlikely. Brezhnev was well aware that the man he had raised to a great height was a bureaucrat, but he could allow Chernenko to deputize for him at the Politburo because he was so sure of his favourite's loyalty, his predictability and his ability to carry out Brezhnev's line. As for his grooming a successor, there are several indications that Brezhnev had no intention of resigning, and in any case he made no secret of the fact that he greatly valued the intelligence and experience of Andropov.

Roy Medvedev has written of an incident recalled by Alexander Bovin, the former Central Committee official and editor of *Izvestiya*. Bovin was visiting his former boss, Andropov, when the telephone rang: 'It was Brezhnev. He wanted to know who was running the Politburo at the moment. Andropov replied that Chernenko was chairing it. "Then why did we make you a Secretary of the Central Committee?" Brezhnev asked. "You should be chairing these sessions now." Andropov turned to Bovin, his pupil and friend, and made a vague sign, indicating his obvious satisfaction.'[38]

Clearly, after rising so quickly to the highest rungs of the ladder, Chernenko must have had thoughts of doing the top job himself. It is amazing to think of him, a sick old man among other sick old men, wanting still more power than he already had. Having failed to seize the General Secretary's seat on Brezhnev's death, he did his best to hold on to his position as the number two, while nursing his hopes to become number one in due course. And when the last step up became a reality, he did not take account of his poor health and refuse to stand, or withdraw his candidacy. He was not thinking of the country, nor even of the Party. He was thinking only of himself.

Not everyone has the insight in such a situation to see that an honest refusal can raise one infinitely higher than any post. Politicians, and especially Bolshevik politicians, are not such people. Lenin made no serious move towards resigning in the two years before his death when his mind and body were badly impaired. At the Nineteenth Party Congress Stalin cunningly hinted at resigning, but only in order to see how the members of the Politburo would react. The ability to assess one's own capacities honestly for the sake of others is a sign of nobility and wisdom. Chernenko had neither.

After Brezhnev died, hardly anyone ever spoke of him again, in the press, on radio and television, or even in the inner circle of the Politburo. No one needed him now, nor did they need his memory. Chernenko, who owed his entire career to Brezhnev, was no exception. Alexander Alexandrov-Agentov, who was Chernenko's adviser on international affairs, has written that the new General Secretary, while not trying to hide his hostility towards Andropov after his death, remained a Brezhnevite. He complained irritably about Andropov's working methods to a small group of aides, and added: 'We're going to work à la Brezhnev, as we did when Leonid Ilyich was alive.'

This was the last time Chernenko would praise Brezhnev – not because of his lack of moral decency so much as Bolshevik tradition. Whichever leader was in power, he was praised to the skies by his future successor. Once he was dead, his only value was as a scapegoat for the regime's 'errors', while the new leader stepped up to receive the praise. The process acted like a one-way valve, transferring the system's defects to the dead leader.

Brezhnev enjoyed inviting important visitors to hunt at Zavidovo. They included Tito, Kekkonen, Kissinger and Raoul Castro, as well as his closest friends in the leadership. Chernenko was a frequent visitor, though he did not like hunting, but he could not turn down the invitations.

'Everyone understood that an invitation to hunt with Brezhnev was a sign of his special trust,' Brezhnev's chief of personal security, Vladimir Medvedev, has written. 'Whether sick or decrepit, they could not decline the favour, nor expose their own incapacity. "Call Kostya, we'll go out there tomorrow," he told me, giving me the time of departure. I phoned Chernenko. His wife came to the phone. "Vladimir Timofeevich," she said, "Konstantin Ustinovich is very unwell. Please tell Leonid Ilyich." Chernenko took the phone. "Yes, Volodya. I'm not feeling great." I replied, "Okay, I'll tell him the doctor is coming to see you and you can't . . ." "No, no." And he dragged himself out of bed, coughing and wheezing with bronchial asthma, and went on the trip. It was cold and damp, sitting out at the watchtower. Every time, Konstantin Ustinovich would catch cold and have to go to bed with a temperature when he got home.'[39] For Chernenko, it was more important to accommodate his patron than to look after his own health.

When he finally reached the top position, Chernenko was a physical wreck. He could do little beyond savouring his glory, and when he departed the scene he left practically no trace behind him. Like his patron, he was soon forgotten, apart from the jokes.

Thirteen Months

As General Secretary, Chernenko no longer stayed at work until all hours, but the quantity of paper that flowed across his desk was immeasurably greater than that of any of his predecessors. He was deluded by the belief that by initialling a high-level document and passing it on to the appropriate department, he was making things happen and improving the situation. But instructions to 'look into', 'study', 'discuss' or 'prepare for Secretariat to examine' achieved nothing. If the Politburo did not take a decision, nothing happened.

Chernenko himself was beyond doing anything more than glancing superficially at the flood of paper. Like Brezhnev in his later years, he entrusted much, even the solving of major problems, to a small group of people in the leadership, including Ustinov, Gromyko, Tikhonov and Grishin.[40] By the early 1980s, a directive from a ministry or Gosplan meant nothing if it was not backed by an order of the Politburo. Everyone tried to bring their most intractable issues to the top body, whether it was the building of a new jetty, a request for additional credits, the delivery of 'special property' to Nicaragua or the tour of a ballet company to London. The Politburo was able to handle hundreds of such matters every month, but not thousands.

Much of Soviet life, whether in the Party or the country at large, depended on what issues the Politburo dealt with, and the final decision of what to put on its agenda lay with the General Secretary, assisted by aides of every kind, as well as by certain Politburo members. Chernenko was spending more and more time with his physicians, but he began to show an unexpected interest in foreign policy issues. He had been abroad only twice, once to Helsinki in 1975, when Brezhnev attended a meeting on European security and co-operation, and again in 1979 when he accompanied Brezhnev to Vienna to disarmament talks. Of course, Chernenko was not needed at these meetings, but he enjoyed the trips, with their glamorous receptions and high-level discussions, and he retained a desire for more of the same.

When he came to power, invitations began arriving from foreign governments, including the US administration. In March 1984, to an enquiring letter from President Reagan, Chernenko signed a reply which confirmed that the new Soviet leader accorded 'great importance to our correspondence', and that he had no intention of 'making any reproaches'. In an obvious hint that the Americans should make a concession over the deployment of their missiles in Europe, he concluded that 'as long as no encouraging signs of an improvement in relations are visible', it would not be logical to expect anything positive or new to occur.[41] The letter had been composed by the Foreign Ministry and the International Department of the Central Committee, and Chernenko did no more than append his sclerotic signature, agreeing that it would be best to freeze Soviet–US relations in their present state. The aim was to damage Reagan in an election year.

In the case of an invitation from Chancellor Kohl, however, Chernenko told the German Foreign Minister, Hans-Dietrich Genscher, that 'it will be necessary a little later on, no doubt, to consider a definite date in the light of all the circumstances and prevailing conditions.' The Germans were well aware that 'prevailing conditions' referred to the General Secretary's declining health.

Chernenko tried to compensate for his enforced lack of mobility by receiving important foreign visitors at a very high rate. Among the first was the British Prime Minister, Margaret Thatcher, and her Foreign Secretary, Geoffrey Howe. Just as Brezhnev had been furnished by his aides with prompt-notes written in very large letters, so now Chernenko had the text of his 'conversation' ready for his British guests. No sooner had he greeted them than he stuck his nose into his crib and, wheezing and choking out the words, read what he saw there. Mrs Thatcher coolly watched the performance, no doubt wondering how such a pathetically sick old man could have been placed at the head of such a mighty country. With the interpreter barely able to cope with the endless clichés pumped out by Soviet diplomacy, Chernenko staggered on: 'We are supporters of active and serious political dialogue, and we need no persuasion of its expediency.

But dialogue must be conducted as between equals, and not from "a position of strength". And it must be aimed at achieving concrete, mutually acceptable – precisely mutually acceptable – agreements.'[42]

He had said nothing, and when he had satisfied himself that there was nothing more for him to read out, he looked up to meet Mrs Thatcher's gaze. She needed no prompting, and she spoke without notes. Identifying three groups of problems in Anglo–Soviet relations, she laid out a number of possible ways to set about finding solutions. Chernenko remained silent, and looked to Gromyko for help. There was an awkward pause, which Gromyko tried to fill by talking about the forthcoming visit to London of his deputy, G. Kornienko.

Chernenko finally decided he must say something off his own bat, without the benefit of an official text: 'Our short conversation might become significant if our relations improve.' Then he suddenly added: 'Let us be friends in every respect. We have plenty of reserves, contacts and opportunities for real, friendly relations between our peoples and governments.'[43] The interpreter choked.

Chernenko was talking to Margaret Thatcher about friendship as if he were talking to Zhivkov or Honecker. The British Prime Minister showed no emotion. A shadow passed across Gromyko's face. He fidgeted to indicate that the meeting was over. There was no knowing what Chernenko might mumble, once he got started.

Nearly ten years later, in 1993, at the British Embassy in Moscow, I had an hour-long private conversation with Mrs Thatcher. The comparison between her keen intellect and the closed, dogmatic mind of Chernenko still arouses embarrassment. The degradation of the system was expressed in the degradation of its leaders.

Chernenko's meetings with foreign leaders in the spring of 1984 continued with Finnish President Koivisto, Italian Foreign Minister Andreotti, West German Foreign Minister Genscher, and the Secretary General of the Greek Communist Party Florakis. In the summer he received the leaders of the socialist countries, Zhivkov, Kádár, Husak, Rodrigos, Ceausescu, Li Xiannian and Honecker. A month later, in August, Honecker made another visit, this time in secret at his request, in order to discuss inter-German relations and to increase bilateral economic co-operation.[44] On each occasion, the Politburo minutes immutably record: 'The results of the General Secretary's conversation with so-and-so are approved.'

What was there to approve? In his conversation with Genscher on 22 May, Chernenko read his prepared speech for fifteen minutes, then heard what Genscher had to say, and immediately made it clear that he wished to terminate the meeting: 'Taking your talks with A.A. Gromyko and our conversation as a whole, there has been a substantial exchange of opinions. It would now most likely be useful for both sides to reflect on what has been said.'[45] Genscher's attempts to draw Chernenko out came to nothing, as he had nothing to say beyond what was in his script.

In the short time he was General Secretary, Chernenko managed to see a surprising number of foreign statesmen. With none of them did he raise any important issue or achieve a breakthrough in any sphere, or introduce anything resembling 'a Soviet initiative'. He would read his three- or four-page text, listen to the reply, utter a few appropriate words of thanks, again glancing at his notes, and then give his guest a limp handshake in farewell. These were 'talks' without talk.

But, having spent most of his life behind the scenes, Chernenko was hungry for public recognition. He loved to see himself on television, and would ask to be given accounts of what was being said in the press and elsewhere of his performance on the 'world stage'. Finding something positive was no easy task, but the press at home and in the socialist countries could be relied on to oblige. The only topic of interest Chernenko aroused in the West was, when would the next General Secretary emerge?

As before, the Politburo continued to give aid to its foreign allies and supporters. For instance, it agreed to a request from President Mengistu for six new military schools to be established in Ethiopia in order to deal with the 'problem of Eritrea'.[46] Having been a member of a Soviet delegation giving 'political aid' to Ethiopia, I had met Mengistu on many occasions, and knew him to be a bloodthirsty thug. Often I asked myself what sort of 'allies' we had found for ourselves, and what that made us.

For several weeks in Moscow I had the job of 'training' the new political 'commissar' for the Ethiopian army. He was a leader of the 'revolution' and a member of the Provisional Military Administrative Council, as the government was known, called Asrat Destu. He talked a lot about Mengistu's desire to build socialism in his impoverished country, and to 'consolidate democracy' there. When I asked him why people were still being shot in Addis Ababa and elsewhere in Ethiopia, he replied: 'We are doing what Lenin did. You cannot build socialism without the red terror. We have too many enemies.' Chernenko received Mengistu at the end of March 1984, and gave support to the dictator's policy of defending the 'revolution' by force.

Generals and other officers of the Soviet Army's Political Section such as myself taught Destu in a succession of one-to-one lectures on how to use political methods to raise the Ethiopian Army's battle-readiness, and how to strengthen its moral and psychological stability. We had done the same thing with personnel of other armies from the so-called developing countries. A couple of weeks after Destu went home to Addis Ababa I read a cipher telegram from Soviet advisers in Ethiopia who reported that during a meeting of the 'Revolutionary Council', a shoot-out had taken place in the council chamber. 'Our' commissar Asrat Destu and several other officers had been killed.

As deputy head of the Army's Board of Special Propaganda – i.e. psychological warfare – I met the leaders of all of the socialist countries and many others from the Third World. It was during this time that I became convinced that Soviet policy was going up a blind alley. The countries we were trying to put on the rails of 'socialist orientation' were being armed to the teeth while becoming increasingly impoverished, with no hope whatsoever of a solution.

That, however, was not what the Politburo thought. Free aid, in the form of grain, oil and weapons, was being rushed, for instance, to Nicaragua at a cost of hundreds of millions of dollars,[47] as it was to other 'revolutionary' countries. Chernenko approved the orders for this and similar shipments with never a question. He was simply the functionary whose signature was required before supplies were tipped into the black hole of the old Comintern policy.

As before, Moscow tried to guide the international politics of the Communist movement. On 11–12 July 1984, Chernenko convened a meeting of all Communist Party chiefs.[48] Prominent among the issues debated was how to throw a bigger spanner into the works of America's missile plans, and how to use European and world organizations to advance Moscow's line.

The visit by Kim Il-sung aroused Chernenko's curiosity, rather than his interest. In the previous winter the North Korean leader had announced that he would like to take up a long-standing invitation from the USSR. Moscow was keen to comply. Relations with North Korea had for long been of a special kind. When Chernenko was shown the plan of the visit, he unexpectedly asked the sixth sector of the General Department to produce the files on the Korean War. There he discovered that it was Kim who had, on 19 January 1950, first raised the question with Moscow of undertaking a 'military reunification' of North and South Korea. Kim had said that he himself 'could not begin an offensive' because he was 'a good Communist, a disciplined man for whom Comrade Stalin's orders were law'.[49] Stalin had reflected for a couple of weeks and then given his approval, and in exchange for advisers, weapons and military hardware – supplied in abundance – requested several tonnes of gold, silver and several dozen tonnes of rare mineral concentrates.

Kim Il-sung arrived in Moscow on 23 May 1984 by special train. He was met by Tikhonov, Gromyko and Ustinov, and was given the full red-carpet treatment, a guard of honour, a state dinner and a residence. The talks were conducted in the Catherine Hall of the Kremlin. Chernenko read the customary text, written in large letters and short phrases. He had been told that Kim would stress the 'militarization' of South Korea and demand more and more weapons, and he had to sit for nearly an hour listening to the 'great leader' saying what he had been expected to say. He promised to supply everything Kim Il-sung had asked for: aircraft, radio communications and border-defence equipment.

I visited North Korea in August 1985 as a member of Marshal V. Petrov's delegation. All our talks with the Korean leadership revolved around the single issue of arms. Kim Il-sung, a rotund, short man who was always depicted in propaganda portraits as a giant among a people of pygmies, referred several times to the promises Chernenko and Ustinov had made to modernize the North Korean Army. Speaking of the danger from the US and South Korea, he stressed that 'if they attack us, a mighty partisan movement will rise up in the south.' In which case, he went on, he would want to send in units of special forces. The USSR, he said, should therefore build a helicopter factory in North Korea so that he could construct five hundred helicopters for the purpose. He also wanted new aircraft, anti-aircraft missiles and radio equipment.

It was as if they had learnt nothing from the experience of 1950–53. The appalling poverty of the country, its high degree of regimentation and the fanatical faith shown by the people in their leader convinced me that North Korea had come closest to the model of barracks Communism. They still revered Stalin, as no one in the USSR did, and seemed happy that they still had an earthly god.

Chernenko hardly travelled anywhere even within the Soviet Union. It was difficult for him, and he lacked the old Bolshevik gift of being able to 'mix with the masses'. He therefore kept his hands on the wheel at the Politburo. Not until 19 July 1984, when he was away on holiday, was his chairman's seat taken for the first time by Gorbachev, who would probably have been its occupant had Chernenko not had powerful allies who saw in him the guarantor of a quiet life. By the middle of August Chernenko was back in the driver's seat, wary, no doubt, of suffering the same fate as Khrushchev.

Some serious issues were touched on by Chernenko as General Secretary, but only touched on. One of them was nuclear energy. Experts reported to the Politburo that the country's nuclear power capacity had risen 4.5 times since 1976, and had reached 20 million kilowatts. An additional twenty nuclear power stations were being built, with a capacity of 85 million kilowatts. The Politburo's particular attention was drawn by the experts to serious shortcomings in building plans, especially with regard to the dangers of radioactivity and fire. These warnings were ignored.

Breaking off periodically to take a puff from an inhaler he kept in his pocket, Chernenko read out a prepared text that contained terms he could barely pronounce, let alone understand. He dwelt on the fact that 'it takes ten thousand people to build a nuclear power station in the USSR, and two to three times fewer abroad.' Without raising his eyes, he condemned the practice of 'shock-work', poor management, and a lack of order in the nuclear industry. Such criticisms were routine. As for the dangers in building practices, since they had not been spelt out for him he said nothing. The resolution approved by the Politburo ordered ministers 'to deal with serious shortcomings in the manufacture of equipment, in monitoring, in the reliability and increase of technological resources, and in the storage and regeneration of nuclear fuel'.[50] This was a routine resolution, and it produced a routine reaction. The leadership had not registered, either intellectually or emotionally, the dangers inherent in the nuclear industry.

Despite his failing health, Chernenko still wanted to appear in public, and even to make speeches. In the summer of 1984 I heard him speak in the Great Hall of the Kremlin at an All-Army Conference of Komsomol Workers. Following the speeches and reports from the Army's young political officers, Chernenko struggled to the podium. It was completely impossible to understand what he said in his fifteen-minute speech. He would stop every two or three minutes, wipe his forehead and take a puff from his inhaler. The audience sat in silence, their heads bowed.

When it was over we were invited into the St George's Hall to be photographed with the General Secretary. It took him twenty minutes to cover the hundred metres or so, stopping frequently to catch his breath. All the while, those accompanying him kept up some kind of conversation in order to give the impression that he had stopped to talk, and not from exhaustion. From time to time he would give a weak, agonized smile, turning his head to the right and left with difficulty, as if he was unsure where he was being taken, what was going on and what all these people in army uniform were saying to him.

Chernenko risked one last public appearance, in October 1984. He convened an All-Union meeting of public inspectors, of whom, as he revealed, there were no fewer than ten million in the country. Lenin's idea of universal control had reached its monstrous apogee. Everything and everyone was being inspected, monitored and checked, and yet the standard of living was falling lower and lower, living proof that Lenin's dictum, 'Accounting and control – that's our *main* economic task,'[51] was an absurdity.

Chernenko told the delegates: 'Each and every Soviet person must think of himself as an inspector, and he must think and act in accordance with that high civic calling.'[52] He was expressing the essential feature of the system, simply continuing a tradition established by the Bolsheviks – and he was nothing if not an imitator of what his predecessors had done. Like them, in the latter stage of his 'rule' he would bombard his colleagues with notes prepared for him by his aides. The Central Committee and Politburo would ultimately approve a decree relating to one of his notes, and the appropriate department – usually the source of the decree – would be charged with its implementation. The impression was created that the vast system was being efficiently administered. Plans, instructions and programmes were adopted, new banknotes were issued, and meanwhile overall production fell. The economy was stagnating on the edge of a serious crisis.

Chernenko would turn up for work at 9 a.m., if he was not getting medical treatment, take the lift to his office, note the day's timetable, and then settle down to enjoy the large pile of papers waiting for him on his desk. He was only able to get through between fifty and sixty documents a day now. To a request from Chancellor Kohl for clemency to the Nazi war criminal Rudolf Hess, Chernenko replied: 'The question has been reviewed. As hitherto, the Soviet side can see no grounds for releasing Hess.'[53] As he had told a group of war veterans not long before: 'We must not let the West forget that we are the victors.' Another document, from Gromyko, Chebrikov and Alexander Rekunkov, the Chief Procurator, revealed that the dissident scientist Andrei Sakharov had requested permission to go to Italy for medical treatment. The authors of the memorandum reminded the General Secretary that decisions had been taken in 1975, 1976, 1977 and 1979 not to allow Sakharov's wife Yelena Bonner out of the country. If they were threatening to go on hunger strike, so what? Let them be force-fed. Bonner must be warned that if she did not cease her provocative activities, she would be charged under Article 190 of the Criminal Code with defaming the Soviet Union.[54]

Another memorandum reported that Stalin's daughter Svetlana Alliluyeva had arrived in the country with her thirteen-year-old American daughter, Olga Peters. She wanted her Soviet citizenship restored, to find work and do translating. She was ready to speak to the press. She says, 'after everything I've done, I'm not likely to press my demands.'[55] Chernenko turned the document over, thought for a while and then decided it should be discussed by the Politburo. (It was quickly decided to accede to Svetlana's wishes as a great propaganda coup, but she was unhappy in the Soviet Union, and went abroad again in 1986.)

The owners of tsarist loan certificates had brought a suit against the USSR in an American court for $650 million.[56] It was a colossal sum. Of course the case was nonsensical in Chernenko's eyes, but how should the Soviet government respond? Its lawyers should be told to find the appropriate formula for a definite refusal.

There was a proposal from the Department of Foreign Policy Information 'to intensify the exposure of human rights violations in capitalist countries'.[57]

It irked Chernenko terribly when he was unable to go to work through ill health. He worried about the work piling up or not being properly attended to. He also worried about the young and energetic Mikhail Gorbachev, who was a force to be reckoned with in the Politburo, and whom he had burdened with routine tasks to keep him occupied.

On the Eve of Perestroika

If the population had experienced some slight hope of change under Andropov, with Chernenko in charge a feeling of total apathy prevailed. The great majority were now utterly indifferent to him, to the Party, to Marxism-Leninism and to the 'wise policies of the Central Committee'. But there were some who detected distant underground tremors suggesting that the end of stagnation was nigh. Even an orthodox Communist like my then boss, Army General Yepishev, could suddenly say to me in the summer of 1984: 'Things feel sticky, congealed. I don't know what's going to happen, but something must.' I learnt later that he had been with Chernenko the previous evening.

He was perhaps merely expressing the widespread disappointment of the generals, who had thought that Andropov might change things, and had been discouraged by Chernenko's rise to power. They would also have noticed a slackening of authority after Andropov's intention to 'introduce order' had faded. While one might have heard generals speaking among themselves about Brezhnev or Andropov in the past, now they never spoke of Chernenko. He was universally regarded as a nonentity, a spectre of the chancery.

Surprisingly, many of the words attributed to Chernenko during his time as General Secretary (although of course they originated with his aides) foreshadow the ideas advanced by Gorbachev at the beginning of *perestroika*. At the April 1984 Central Committee Plenum, for instance, he told the Party that they 'must make better use of the reserves of the masses' enthusiasm as the foundation of perfecting socialist democracy and the entire political system of society for the future'.[58] The idea of perfecting socialist democracy was one which Gorbachev would use to stir up the Party and society. On Chernenko's lips, it was nothing more than a well-worn Bolshevik slogan, and he never returned to it; but it showed that someone in the backrooms was thinking.

To be sure, Gorbachev also believed, naïvely, that it was enough to renew the Party cadres for everything to start running smoothly. His Plenum on *perestroika* and cadre policy would produce few results, as was to be expected. And Chernenko, at his Plenum in April 1984, seized on the old Leninist theme of cadres. Lenin had argued that one had only to bring more workers and peasants into the 'leading cadres' for the state machine to work properly.

In his 'keynote' speech, Chernenko declared that everything 'depends to a significant extent on the cadres. The cadres really are the gold reserves of the Party and state . . . In the work of the cadres, as nowhere else, a precise and thought-out system is essential. Neither frequent rotation, nor any degree of ossification of staff is permissible in this area.'[59] He followed up the speech with a memorandum to the Politburo entitled 'Some questions of present-day cadre policy', in which one of the ideas expressed may be attributed to him personally. He recommended that personnel be moved not only vertically, but also horizontally. 'It has a refreshing effect,' he wrote, 'as I know for myself.'[60]

For Chernenko, the idea of the 'gold reserves' was nothing more than a cliché, but there were others in his entourage who understood the situation better than he did. In two years' time Gorbachev would make his first, albeit only verbal, onslaught on the *nomenklatura* in the periphery.

Another idea that became a key feature of the early years of Gorbachev's rule was first uttered by Chernenko on 13 February 1984, in his 'coronation speech', when he spoke of 'giving mighty acceleration to the development of the national economy'.[61] He was prompted by his aides to return to this theme only once, in July 1984, and he did so in a note to the Politburo on the 'need to accelerate scientific and technological progress'.[62] It is doubtful that he thought of this formula as anything other than just another slogan, but the idea, when it was popularized in the early stage of *perestroika*, seized the imagination of many people. The first tremors of impending change occurred in 1984, but not because of Chernenko. They were a symptom of the atmosphere which was giving birth to some of the ideas of *perestroika*.

In December 1984 a working conference took place in Moscow on 'The Perfecting of Developed Socialism and the Ideological Work of the Party'. In both Gorbachev's report and Chernenko's speech of welcome the idea of 'perfecting' the system was put forward. As was to be expected on such occasions, Gorbachev cited the General Secretary: 'The theoretical directives and propositions advanced by K.U. Chernenko, concerning the level of maturity achieved by Soviet society, serve as the basis of principle for the Party's strategic line ... As it faces deep changes, the Party is looking to the people.'[63] In time, Gorbachev would substitute *perestroika* for 'perfecting' socialism.

Conversations about 'perfection' may have been taking place at this time precisely because the situation under Chernenko was so blatantly hopeless. Many people, including Gorbachev, were asking themselves how long the current state of affairs could last. The stagnation, which threatened total collapse, prompted some people into action, sometimes in the form of protest and rejection of the status quo. The number of people leaving the country and requesting political asylum abroad grew, especially artists, sportsmen, diplomats and tourists. The amount of anti-Soviet pamphlets, anti-Party graffiti and 'subversive' literature confiscated by customs increased. KGB chief Chebrikov reported that '1,325 writers of 7,537 anonymous documents of an anti-Soviet, nationalistic and politically harmful content, and 628 graffiti had been exposed.' He added that of 1,223 culprits apprehended by the KGB, eighty-nine were Communists.

'In Ukraine,' Chebrikov continued, 'and in the Baltic republics and Transcaucasus seventeen illegal nationalist groups have been rendered harmless. Seventy-five attempts by nationalist elements to commit extremist acts, hostile activity by eleven people who had provoked anti-social acts by groups in Tbilisi, and several agitators trying to arouse emigration sentiments among people of German nationality have been curtailed. Thirteen instigators of hostile incidents in Lithuania, Latvia and Estonia have been charged with criminal offences.'[64]

Long before the bloody events in Alma-Ata, Sumgait, Tbilisi, Baku and Vilnius, worrying signals were being received in Moscow of national unrest in several republics. Chernenko was far out of his depth on this, as on many other issues.

Many people sensed that the country had moved towards an invisible boundary, beyond which the desired changes might be possible. By now few were deluded by the lists of medals and awards being bestowed for 'achievement' in socialist construction. The Politburo approved decorations for the newspaper *Pravda*, the port of Sochi, the cities of Tallin and Archangel, the Meleuzov chemical works, the Union of Writers of the USSR, and so on. The worse the situation in the country became, the more generous were the awards and prizes bestowed by the leadership, not least on itself. The senile rulers had lost control of their own weakness and vanity.

In the middle of September 1984, after a two-month holiday on the Black Sea, Chernenko reappeared in the Kremlin. He showed no sign that the warm southern sun and salt breeze had done him any good. Prompted by his 'comrades-in-arms', he marked the occasion of his return by giving himself the country's highest distinction. On 23 September the Politburo decided to announce on the main television news programme, *Vremya*, and in the press next day, Chernenko's birthday, that 'for outstanding services in Party and state activity on the formulation and implementation of Leninist domestic and foreign policy, the development of the economy and culture, the strengthening of the USSR's defence capability, and his large personal input,' Chernenko had been awarded the Order of Lenin and the Hammer and Sickle Gold Star.[65] He also received his third Hero award.

The absence of morality in the Soviet leadership expressed itself as feigned modesty accompanied by a total lack of discrimination in self-indulgence. In February 1982 the Politburo had approved the award of Lenin and State Prizes to the editors of a two-volume *History of Soviet Foreign Policy, 1917–1980*, and a multi-volume work on the wartime Allied conferences. Among the Lenin Prize-winners was Chernenko, who had made not the least contribution to these publications.

Meanwhile the economy continued to slide. Grain and meat products were purchased abroad in exchange for three hundred tonnes of gold, vast amounts of foreign currency and gas, oil, timber and other raw materials. Unable to find reliable equipment at home, Soviet enterprises were importing increasing quantities from abroad, but through their own inefficiency and lack of infrastructure were either misusing it or leaving it to rot. The manipulated official statistics, on the other hand, indicated an annual industrial growth figure of 4.2 per cent, against a planned 3.8 per cent, while industrial productivity had increased by 3.9 per cent, and real incomes by 3.3 per cent per head of population. But no one believed government figures any more. The shops were empty, and there was a rampant black market and false accounting and fiddling of every kind.

Chernenko was no longer turning up at work every day, and when he did he remained for only two or three hours. Lung disease and heart failure were complicating his chronic hepatitis, and he was dying in front of everyone's eyes. He managed to make it to a large reception in the Kremlin for the celebrations of 7 November 1984, attended by diplomats and top people of the Soviet establishment. His speech was totally incomprehensible. When my wife, who was standing next to me, saw the expression on my face, she asked what was wrong with me. I whispered that I felt shame for all of us and for the country.

When the Politburo was due to meet, Chernenko would summon every ounce of strength to attend. He was unwilling to relinquish the post he had attained in so ridiculous and unexpected a manner. On 3 January 1985 he turned up in such a poor state that his colleagues rushed through fourteen items on the agenda without debate in order to minimize the ordeal. The questions they dealt with were routine: the next session of the Supreme Soviet, directives for Gromyko's meeting with US Secretary of State George Shultz in Geneva, an account of Gorbachev's visit to England, reduction of the retail prices of Zaporozhets and Niva cars, which for the first time ever were in excess supply, and finally a survey of the Politburo's work for 1984.[66]

A month earlier, Chernenko had asked his former deputy, K. Bogolyubov, to prepare an annual summary of his activities as General Secretary for the January meeting, and a document of twenty-eight pages duly emerged. On every page Chernenko was shown to have 'ordered, spoken, argued, written memoranda, held talks...' It was an impressive panegyric to a dying leader, and it was exactly what he wanted to hear: the Politburo had met forty-eight times, and the

Secretariat forty-two times. The Politburo had approved 3,780 decrees, of which 529 were passed at its meetings and 3,231 by postal vote. The Secretariat had passed 5,452 decrees, 980 at meetings and 4,472 by post. The commissions on the Party programme, the fuel and energy industry, the food programme, school reform, Poland, China and Afghanistan, foreign policy propaganda, consumer goods, and still others, had met regularly. Much was made of 'Soviet peace-loving foreign policy' and of Comrade Chernenko's talks with the leaders of the fraternal socialist states, the developing countries and the capitalist powers. The Politburo had continued to strengthen the Party organs by appointing twenty-eight new Secretaries of regional Party Committees and republican Central Committees, and twelve new Union ministers. The Central Committee had received 255,000 items of official correspondence, and more than 600,000 letters. The General Secretary and his colleagues in the Politburo had received more than nine thousand letters.[67]

The report was exhaustive in its bureaucratic detail, but it was lamentably short on analysis of the Politburo's role in trying to over-come the crisis in society, the country's flagging economic activity, the ongoing bureaucratization of state structures, and the effect of the Party's monopoly of power at all levels of the administration. It was proof, if any were needed, of Chernenko's total incapacity to introduce any genuinely reformist ideas whatever. On the other hand, the period of stagnation only served to sharpen expectations of major changes. In a Leninist system, where people like Chernenko could become head of state and Party chief, such changes could only come from above. The population had no choice but to wait and see whether the next leader would rise to meet the challenge and bring in reform.

Anatoly Chernyayev, an official in the International Department of the Central Committee and later one of Gorbachev's aides, wrote about the atmosphere on the eve of Chernenko's departure from the scene:

> Moscow is full of jokes and laughter, and the Western press is full of terrible caricatures and comments about his illness. And everyone's asking, who's next: Gorbachev, Grishin, Gromyko, Romanov . . . One variation – you can expect anything from Russians – even has it that Chernenko's already dead, and that's why they cancelled the Karpov–Kasparov [chess] match in the Hall of Columns in the House of Unions,

as they needed the space 'to say farewell to the body'. Gromyko, Zimyanin and others are being liberally quoted for their praise of the outstanding services, the contribution and qualities of the General Secretary, which, *Express* remarks, will be forgotten before the candles go out at his coffin. Evidently that's why Chernenko has been shown twice on TV, once while voting at an alleged polling station and then when he received his pass as a deputy of the Supreme Soviet of the RSFSR. On that occasion he even tried to say something. A murderous spectacle, and a shameful one.[68]

A clear sign that a break in the regime's conservative tradition was imminent could be observed in the fact that official propaganda started speaking far less of 'achievements', but simply praised the regime and spoke of the blessings that would come at some vague date in the future.

A meeting of the Political Consultative Committee of the Warsaw Pact was scheduled to take place in Sofia in early 1985. At the 9 January meeting of the Politburo, Chernenko called on Marshal Yazov to speak. The Defence Minister said bluntly: 'Konstantin Ustinovich will not be able to head the Soviet delegation. A trip anywhere by the General Secretary is undesirable, and is in any case simply impossible.' It was agreed to inform Sofia that Chernenko was ill and could not attend the talks.[69]

A few years later, Andrei Gromyko, one of the remaining Kremlin elders who had been instrumental in elevating Chernenko, wrote: 'One day in March 1985, Chernenko, whom I had known for twenty years, phoned me: "Andrei Andreevich," he said, "I'm not well. I'm wondering whether I oughtn't to retire? I want your advice."

'"Wouldn't that be rather premature? As I understand it, the doctors are not so pessimistic."

'"You mean I shouldn't make up my mind in a hurry?"

'"Exactly. Don't rush into it. There's no need."

'He seemed pleased with this. "Well, I won't, then." With that the conversation ended.'[70]

While his facsimile signature and seal still graced Politburo minutes and decrees, Chernenko was virtually moribund. Gorbachev chaired the meetings with growing confidence. Decisions were taken to build new underground railways in Chelyabinsk, Omsk and Krasnoyarsk; to increase shoe production; measures were agreed to prevent a split in the Palestinian resistance movement, which was seen as 'an important factor against Israeli aggression'; the issue of handling nuclear waste from other countries was discussed, and so on.[71]

Drawing on his last reserves of strength, Chernenko dragged himself to work for the last time on 7 February 1985. The other members of the Politburo were waiting for him at the long table. He read a short speech: 'We have passed this period of time in a militant manner ... For a time I had to drop out of the ranks, but I tried to read all the papers attentively and to make decisions on all the most important issues. I will say frankly that this period of time has revealed the need once again to inspect our fighting ranks and to show what each comrade can do. I think we must continue to work as we have, without thinking up new forms of some kind ...'

He was prevented from reading further by a coughing fit, but he did manage to wish Romanov a happy birthday.

The Politburo then moved on to discuss two notes submitted by the General Secretary, one on co-ordinating work with the fraternal countries, and the other on the work of the cadres. The draft decrees were ready, and Chernenko had only to sit and listen with pleasure to the praise lavished on the 'timeliness and deep analytical qualities of his notes'.[72]

Chernenko closed the session, struggled to his feet and, in a barely audible voice, said: 'I wish you all, comrades, much success.' It was his farewell. He was afflicted by a whole range of serious diseases. When he was under treatment for lung and heart failure at Kislovodsk, his condition had been exacerbated by pneumonia; he had cirrhosis of the liver and pathological changes in other organs and tissue, and was being treated by a swarm of physicians.

Three or four days before he died, Chernenko was visited by Gorbachev and Ligachev. At the Politburo meeting of 7 March, Gorbachev said they had stayed and talked for about an hour. Chernenko had apparently said that they must preserve what had been achieved in industry and maintain the numbers of livestock. He had agreed that the next Party Congress should take place on 3 December 1985. Practically on his deathbed, he approved the retirement of the chairman of the RSFSR Supreme Soviet, M.A. Yasnov, and settled some issues concerning other senior officials. Gorbachev concluded by saying, 'He's fed up with hospital ... He sends his regards.'

The absence of a rational system of succession entailed grotesque scenes such as that described by Gorbachev. It was as if Lenin's descendants were unwilling to recognize death. Vanity made them cling to power until their last breath. Around Chernenko, meanwhile, the leadership tried to make it look like 'business as usual'. The whole country watched in horror as another old man, Grishin, dragged Chernenko from his hospital bed to the ballot box that had been brought into his hospital room. Chernenko could hardly lift the voting-slip and drop it with a trembling hand into the box.

The last letter with Andropov's facsimile signature had been sent to the Japanese Communist leader Miamoto on 8 February 1984. By an extraordinary coincidence, the last letter bearing Chernenko's facsimile signature was sent on 9 March 1985 to the same Miamoto.

At midday on 10 March Chernenko lost consciousness, and at 7.20 that evening his heart stopped. His long-expected death neither upset nor distressed anyone, except his close family. The members of the Politburo paid their respects one after the other, then left his three children and wife to grieve over him.

The people were weary of big state funerals. As well as Suslov and Ustinov, in three years three General Secretaries had been buried. Chernenko's funeral was a hurried affair, and events also moved quickly. Within twenty-four hours, the country had a new Party leader.

Chernenko left nothing – no sensational working papers, personal notes or reminiscences. When the locksmiths were summoned to open his personal safe, after a short tussle with the combination the steel door was flung open. Apart from a thin file of papers, the entire safe was stuffed with bundles of money.[73] More money was found in the drawers of his writing desk. No one could explain the origin of this large amount of cash and why Chernenko had wanted it. Nor did anyone wish to pursue the matter, bearing in mind that, as General Secretary and before that as head of the General Department, he had controlled the Central Committee's budget and all its expenses.

Next day, the Politburo assembled, minus Shcherbitsky, who had not yet arrived from Kiev. Gorbachev presided in a manner that showed that the days of the gerontocracy and the old system of succession were over. He called first on Academician Chazov, who had led the team of physicians attending Chernenko. He said simply: 'He had been seriously ill. We could see it for ourselves. The doctors tried of course to assist the patient, but the illness was so serious that their treatment could not result in a positive outcome. It is hard to acknowledge that Konstantin Ustinovich is no longer among us.'

Gorbachev then raised the main question, namely, the post of General Secretary.[74] Having nominated him as chairman of the funeral commission, the Politburo had already signalled that the next leader would be its youngest member, Gorbachev.

As if it was obvious, Gorbachev then declared: 'We will bury Chernenko in Red Square.' Three General Secretaries already lay there, alongside Lenin's tomb. At the suggestion of Chebrikov, Chernenko's grave was to be located next to that of Budyonny, the civil war commander of the Red Cavalry. The historic square had been turned into a Bolshevik graveyard.

Chernenko's comrades closed the chapter on him as soon as they could. The country had vague expectations, and even a degree of fear, in case someone like Grishin should succeed and lead the country nowhere. Everyone was tired of stagnation. Who would be the seventh leader? Would it be someone who could, finally, introduce changes for the better?

7

The Seventh Leader:
Mikhail Gorbachev

All of Russia's misfortunes stem from the fact that she was never able to come to terms with liberty. Gorbachev, the seventh leader, tried to do just this.

It is still difficult to write about Gorbachev. First of all, he is our contemporary, his ideas are part of our lives, he is a part of us. To write about him is to write about ourselves. He is among us now, and – like many of us – what he says in his speeches often contradicts what he did when his star was in the ascendant. Moreover, he does not think that his time has passed.

Secondly, of all the leaders, only Lenin has had more written about him. Even Stalin, the greatest tyrant of the century, has attracted less attention in print. In terms of Western publications, Gorbachev reigns supreme. In the Library of Congress in Washington alone, I found more than 250 books on him.

Thirdly, like Lenin, Gorbachev can be considered as a 'frontier' leader: the frontier for Lenin was the line between the defunct old regime and the Soviet regime, and he attained what he was seeking beyond that line, namely power. For Gorbachev the frontier lay between the almost defunct Soviet regime and an unknown future. And he brought about what he emphatically did not want, namely the collapse of the socialist system.

Of the books written about Gorbachev by his close aides, most are by people who have remained loyal to him. Among these are G. Shakhnazarov's balanced and analytical *The Price of Liberty*, and the memoirs of Anatoly Chernyayev, Andrei Grachev and Alexander Alexandrov-Agentov. Gorbachev's chief of security, Vadim Medvedev, has written interestingly on life behind the scenes at the Kremlin. By contrast, a book by Gorbachev's assistant Valeri Boldin, which came out first in America and then in Russia, appears motivated by deep personal animosity towards its subject, and Gorbachev emerges as vain and egocentric, suspicious of everyone and susceptible to flattery from abroad.

Boldin, who quite simply betrayed Gorbachev during the attempted Communist coup of August 1991, also took up arms against Gorbachev's wife Raisa. While most of his attacks amount to little more than gossip, one aspect of his book sounds like a serious charge against the former General Secretary:

> For many years Raisa Maximovna ran not just the domestic set-up, but the entire *perestroika* carnival. She took part in the formulation of policy, where of course this was possible, and the deployment of personnel. But mainly she formed the character of the General Secretary-President, helped him find a course in the stormy sea of political tendencies, in the hope of bringing the ship of state to its intended destination. This can be judged in different ways: both as a wish to divide responsibility, or as interference in the authority of the President, possibly with his consent, but restricting his freedom of action and power.[1]

As Gorbachev's assistant, Boldin knew a great deal of what went on in ruling circles, but even he was a victim of the Soviet mentality, which was accustomed to knowing nothing about the wife of the leader. But Raisa, unlike her predecessors, was deeply involved in public and political activity. Through television, the public in Russia and abroad saw what they took to be evidence of a shift in leadership style, coupled with elements of vanity, played out on the domestic and international scene. In her own book, *I Hope*, Raisa herself has added some touches to the portrait of her husband, as a man rather than as a politician. To that extent, the picture we have of him is quite well rounded.

After Lenin, Gorbachev is the most notable statesman in twentieth-century Russian history. His greatest contribution lies in his having been aware of the profound need for change and his decision to become the first Soviet political figure to try to implement it.

Whatever has been said of him, Gorbachev had no plan or grand strategy. This was only to be expected. He had the Party's official

Leninist 'line', resolutions of the last Congress and the Party programme, and in his place he could not move openly towards dismantling the system. Nor did he have any intention of doing so. Someone
had to make a start, however, and that was Gorbachev. He was the
leader during the transition, the advocate of change as a process of
the 'perfection, improvement, acceleration, and finally the restructuring', or *perestroika*, of the Communist system.

Even after August 1991, Gorbachev did not contemplate the liquidation of the system: he wanted its 'improvement'. How could a
totalitarian society be 'improved'? How was it possible to 'improve'
a monopoly of political power? How could new life be breathed into
a command economy that was all but exhausted? There are no satisfactory answers to these questions, and the seventh leader had none
either.

He wanted to restructure 'everything' without touching the socialist
foundations of state ownership, the Party's 'leading role', and the
regime's Communist goals. It is not hard to see that these goals were
not attainable. To restructure everything, and yet to leave intact the
foundations laid by Lenin, was a logical impossibility. The Communist
system was not reformable. Either it exists, or it does not. This was
something that Gorbachev, who was after all General Secretary of
the Communist Party, either could not or did not want to understand.

Ten years after the beginning of *perestroika*, when the word itself
is fading from memory and the Communists have been consigned to
oblivion, it is clear that Gorbachev will go down in history as the
initiator of one of the greatest reform movements of the century. He
pioneered liberal changes that were begun with no clear aim except
to preserve the Marxist-Leninist foundations of the society and state.
He began a process of democratic reforms over which he soon lost
control. The culmination of *perestroika*, despite his intentions, was the
total disintegration of the Communist system. It was not Gorbachev
who brought this about; but he did nothing to prevent it from happening. The events which he launched developed according to their own
logic and in complete disregard of the command mentality of the men
of the Central Committee.

Finally, the result of Gorbachev's reforms was a fundamental alteration in the character of international relations. The threat of global
nuclear conflict receded greatly, and many universal ideas became a

reality, enabling people to see that there are common values which can be achieved only in concert. Gorbachev can be credited with having done more than anyone else in this century to remove the threat of global war.

A full assessment of his role must wait for some time, at least until the years of *perestroika* have themselves become history. It is, however, possible to say that Gorbachev's rule was the source of epoch-making changes for the good, and was also a catalyst of greatly sharpened conflicts that overshadowed them. Gorbachev was, and indeed remains in the minds of his compatriots, a tragic figure whom some will deify and others hate, some will see as a great reformer, others as a perfidious destroyer.

The Last Leninist

No General Secretary has ever been 'born' as quickly as Mikhail Gorbachev. Konstantin Chernenko died at 7.20 p.m. on 10 March 1985, the Politburo met next day at 2 p.m., and by 6 p.m. an extraordinary Central Committee Plenum had appointed Gorbachev in his place.

In fact, he had been carrying out the duties of the post for several months, reviewing the issues to be put on the Politburo agenda and determining the jobs to be given to the Secretariat and the departments. All the reins of the Party and state were already in his hands. Gromyko, Aliyev, Solomentsev, Chebrikov and Shcherbitsky, indeed virtually everybody, all felt, as he did, that he was the natural successor. 'Consultations' went on all through the night of 10 March in the Kremlin and at Staraya Square. The relatively young but untalented Romanov and the more experienced member of the old guard, Grishin, were potential candidates, but before the Politburo met it was known that the great majority favoured the youngest member, Gorbachev.

Andrei Gromyko, a staunch conservative but a wise politician, had done most to prepare the ground. He believed that only a young man, unfettered by 'complexes', could pump new energy into the Party. For Gorbachev to succeed, Gromyko had to ensure that he spoke first, knowing that no one in the Politburo would dare to break the golden rule by opposing the first candidate named.

As he had done for the last few months, Gorbachev opened the meeting. Having been passed over after Andropov's death in February 1984, when Tikhonov had nominated Chernenko, Gorbachev now had every reason to believe that he had the best claim to the leadership. Once Dr Chazov had given his formal report on the causes of Chernenko's death and left the room, Gorbachev declared: 'We first of all have to decide the question of who is to be General Secretary of the Central Committee. I would ask comrades to express their views on this matter.'

After only a sentence or two of Gromyko's obviously prepared speech, it was clear who would be the next leader: 'I will speak frankly. When one thinks about a candidate for the post of General Secretary, one thinks of course about Mikhail Sergeyevich. That would in my opinion be the absolutely correct choice.' He then listed three qualities that defined Gorbachev: his energy, his Party-mindedness, and his experience. Apparently forgetting that in February 1984 he had supported Tikhonov's nomination of Chernenko by calling on his comrades to look to the future, he went on: 'When one looks into the future – and I will not hide the fact that for many of us that is hard to do – we must have a clear sense of the outlook. And that consists of the fact that we do not have the right to permit any damage to our unity. We do not have the right to allow the world to notice the slightest gap in our relations.'[2]

Everyone around the table knew perfectly well that to offer the least objection to Gromyko's nomination was implicitly forbidden. The deed was done. In turn, each member spoke in favour of Gorbachev, and following accepted ritual, vied with each other to find words with which to laud their new leader's qualities.

Tikhonov, who was no friend of Gorbachev's, stated: 'He is the first Secretary who can understand economics.' This was a strange compliment, since it implied the economic incompetence of all previous leaders.

GRISHIN: We decided this question yesterday when we agreed to make Mikhail Sergeyevich chairman of the funeral commission.

SOLOMENTSEV: Mikhail Sergeyevich is remarkable for his tireless energy and his tendency to become actively involved in events.

KUNAEV: However this debate turns out, the Communists of Kazakhstan will vote for Mikhail Sergeyevich Gorbachev. [Kunaev would soon be out of the Politburo.]

ALIYEV: Mikhail Sergeyevich is straightforward, modest and approachable.

ROMANOV: Mikhail Sergeyevich is very demanding in his work. [Romanov would be an early victim of Gorbachev's purge of the top ranks.]

VOROTNIKOV: I happened to meet a large number of representatives of Russian regional Party organizations today, and they all said they wanted us to select Comrade Gorbachev.

PONOMARYOV: In the last three years we have lost three General Secretaries . . . But our Party is strong because we are going forward, because we are united, because no loss can shake our unity . . .

CHEBRIKOV: The Chekists have told me to nominate Comrade Gorbachev, M.S. for the post of General Secretary . . . And the voice of the Chekists is the voice of the people.

DOLGIKH: He not only has great experience behind him, but a future, too. [Presumably the humour was unintentional.]

KUZNETSOV: He is most accessible and is able to get to the main point of a question quickly.

SHEVARDNADZE: The promotion of Gorbachev is something the whole country and the entire Party are expecting.

DEMICHEV: I am sure we are making an entirely correct choice today . . . [He] has a feeling for the new.

ZIMYANIN: He is notable for constantly adding to his knowledge.

KAPITONOV: He has a sharp, analytical mind.

LIGACHEV: He has great reserves of intellectual and physical strength.

RYZHKOV: We have seen him grow before our eyes as a political figure.

RUSAKOV: He's a man with a capital M.[3]

Whether they meant what they said or not, the portrait of Gorbachev collectively created by his colleagues was a true one, even if they avoided mentioning any negative characteristics. Gorbachev sat, his head slightly bowed, making notes, as the unction flowed. He told his colleagues that he 'took in all their words with enormous emotion and feeling'. Knowing that the entire Central Committee, its members having assembled from all over the Soviet Union, was waiting nearby for the Politburo's decision to be announced, Gorbachev spoke rather disjointedly for less than five minutes. Noticeably, he used the word 'potential' several times: 'Our Party has enormous creative potential'; 'there is potential in collective work'; 'collectivist potential must operate more actively'. He stressed the need for unity and collective leadership, and his readiness to justify the confidence placed in him. One idea that he expressed reflects an essential aspect of Gorbachev's political personality. He declared: 'We must not change our policy. It is a true, correct and genuinely Leninist policy. We have to raise the tempo, move forward, expose shortcomings and overcome them, and see our bright future clearly.'[4]

Thus, at the outset of the new leadership the goal was still to attain the 'bright future' with the help of true Leninist policy. In 1991 Gorbachev still believed in Lenin. Indeed, it was probably his attempt to combine his liberal reforms with Leninism that led to their failure. He was a Leninist because his whole life had made him one. Since his youth he had been held in the Party's close embrace, and it was the Party that formed him into the person who would one day become its General Secretary, the last ruling Leninist.

Mikhail Sergeyevich Gorbachev spent his childhood and youth in the north Caucasian region of Stavropol, in his native village of Privolnoye. He has described his parents as 'peasants, and their parents were also peasants ... My father, Sergei Andreyevich, and my mother, Maria Panteleevna, also worked on the land, first in their own peasant smallholding, and then in a co-operative, and later on a collective farm and machine tractor station.'[5]

He did well at school and at Moscow University, which he entered in 1950. During the vacations he helped his father on the land, and worked on combine-harvesters. At the age of eighteen he received the Order of the Red Labour Banner for 'excellent work'. At school and university he was noted for application and 'political awareness', which was valued above all else at the time. He became a Komsomol leader at school and university, a model Communist youth, as he was to become a model Party member when he joined at the very young age of eighteen.

It may be that the difficult history of his native territory had an influence on the young Gorbachev's outlook. From his father and grandfather he heard what had happened to the Cossacks of the district during the civil war, when their ancient, autonomous social structures were broken down by the Bolsheviks. The collectivization had followed a few years later, with mass arrests and an appalling famine. Then came the German occupation, which he witnessed as an eleven-year-old, and finally the deportation of the north Caucasian peoples to Siberia and Central Asia on Stalin's vicious orders. Both his grandfather and father had been collective farm activists, which would have helped to make him a good Communist.

Gorbachev loved to talk about his family. Once, when the Politburo was discussing the forthcoming seventieth anniversary of the October Revolution, he recalled a conversation with his grandmother, Vasilisa Lukyanovna. He asked her what it had been like when the collective farms were formed. 'She loved me very much, as I was her only grandson. She replied: "The people said: 'What's the devil up to now?'" I asked her what it was like when the collective farms were functioning. "Ah, yes, all night long your granddad gorganized and gorganized [sic], but by the morning the peasants had all cleared off." That's the kind of struggle it was, and all the families were affected. It was a great struggle, a gigantic one.'[6]

In 1953 Gorbachev married Raisa Maximovna, who had been awarded a master's degree for a dissertation on the life of the collective farm peasantry. She became a lecturer, and went on to teach Marxist philosophy for more than twenty years. The young couple left Moscow for Stavropol in 1955, after Gorbachev had been awarded his diploma in law. He now had to make an important choice, and opted not to become a lawyer, but to devote himself instead to work in the Komsomol, an essential training ground for a Party career.

The Party career of the twenty-four-year-old Gorbachev was smooth. He was made head of a department in the Komsomol city committee, then First Secretary, then head of a department at regional level, rising to Second Secretary, and in 1960 to First Komsomol Secretary of the territory. He had mounted all the lower rungs of the ladder rapidly. In 1962 he became head of a department of the Regional Party Committee, an excellent career move at the age of thirty. He had good relations with the First Secretary of the regional Party committee, Fedor Mikhail Kulakov, and with his successor, Yefremov, after Kulakov moved to Moscow to become a member of the Central Committee. Throughout his life, Gorbachev has shown a talent for making friends with his colleagues. His tendency to trust people, however, would backfire badly when he was in the top job.

The First Secretary of a provincial or territorial Party committee (*obkom*) wielded enormous power and influence in his region, and answered only to Moscow and the Kremlin. He was the chief interpreter of the Party statutes and the laws of the land. In his hands he held the cadres, the army enlistment office, and the economic and local government bodies. To the many benefits an *obkom* already enjoyed, in 1987 the retirement package was enhanced by the grant of an apartment in Moscow, maintained at state expense.[7] This benefit was removed in 1990 as part of the onslaught on Party privilege by nascent Soviet democracy.

Gorbachev implemented Party directives expeditiously, which pleased Yefremov, who helped him over his next hurdle when in 1966 he became First Secretary of the Stavropol city Party committee, and then two years later Second Secretary of the territorial committee. This high position signified that he was Yefremov's most likely successor, and indeed when Yefremov moved to Moscow, he recommended Gorbachev for his old job. This was a very important moment for Gorbachev. As a rule, Moscow filled the posts of First and Second Secretary in the provinces with people from the Central Committee apparatus, which it regarded as a nursery for senior staff. It was the usual policy to send a departmental inspector, departmental head or a deputy head to the regions as a First Secretary. This meant that local administrators had been through organizational and ideological training inside the Central Committee apparatus. The Party bureaucracy was in constant need of fresh blood, and officials were often moved sideways from one district to another. Only rarely were locals given the top jobs in their native territory.

Gorbachev, however, had several important factors in his favour. Above all, he had an immaculate record. As City Committee Secretary, he took a second diploma by correspondence, this time in agriculture, which was seen in Moscow as a major plus, as were the recommendations of Kulakov and Yefremov. When Gorbachev was 'recommended' at an open meeting as First Secretary of the Stavropol territorial Party committee, he entered a very high level of the Party hierarchy. In addition to his Party functions, a First Secretary would almost automatically become a Deputy in the Supreme Soviet and a member of the Central Committee at the next Party congress.

Gorbachev, still only thirty-five years old, was perfectly placed for his future career. But everything depended on how much notice Moscow took of him. He had to make sure that all of Moscow's state plans for his enormous agricultural region were implemented. It would also help if he could become personally known to the members of the Politburo. This was not so difficult, as the sick old Party patriarchs often came to Kislovodsk, in his territory, for medical treatment and to take the waters, and Gorbachev developed good relations with Suslov, Kosygin and Andropov. Gorbachev had a firm basis for being an orthodox Leninist. His brilliant Party career had not only raised him as a Leninist, but obliged him to remain one.

Gorbachev's writings and speeches are extensive. Much of them make for rather boring reading, being of an official nature, but there is enough material of a personal kind to help one gain an impression of him as a human being. I do not think he was ever a Leninist fanatic, and there are indeed some fleetingly critical, if indirect, remarks about Lenin. Nevertheless, he always believed in Lenin. Indeed, his entire programme of *perestroika* was a call to 'return to the true Lenin' whom Stalin had 'misrepresented'.

For many years I, like the rest of the Soviet people, also believed in Lenin. After 1985, however, when a fresh breeze came into our lives with Gorbachev, the irreversible erosion of Lenin's image began in my mind. It was not only the mass of hitherto unknown documents in the archives that caused this to happen, but rather the collapse of the Bolshevik experiment itself. Coming to see that Lenin and Leninism had been the source of Russia's misfortunes was akin to a spiritual cleansing. It also created a sense of lasting sadness: for so many years the Bolshevik system had gripped so many people in the dogmatic embrace of Leninism. I began to realize only then why the Mensheviks had not been able to accept Lenin. He had been an enemy of social democracy. He always was and remained a Bolshevik, as did his followers.

Gorbachev's speeches contain no reappraisal of the Leninist heritage.[8] He saw in Lenin the main arguments for his own political correctness. Here lies the source of the incomplete, limited and even ambiguous nature of what was started after 1985 by the great reformer of the twentieth century.

Perhaps Gorbachev could not have acted otherwise, especially at the beginning. At his first Plenum as General Secretary on 23 April 1985, at which the next Party Congress, the Twenty-Seventh, was discussed, he began his report with his basic methodological, philosophical leitmotiv: 'The whole of life and the entire course of history confirms convincingly the great truth of Leninist teaching. It has been and remains for us a guide to action, a source of inspiration, a true compass for fixing the strategy and tactics of our movement forward.'[9]

Gorbachev began his speech by swearing this oath of loyalty to the Leninist course, and ended it with a quotation from Lenin on the need to elaborate 'correct and accurate tactics and strategy for the working class'.[10] The course that Gorbachev ratified was fraught with hazards: Lenin's reliance on the working class was akin to social racism, the one-party monopoly was fundamentally anti-democratic, the command economy contradicted a thousand years of human history, belief in the correctness of only one ideology was tantamount to a secular religion. All these flaws acted like sand in the engine of Gorbachev's locomotive of *perestroika*.

More than two years into the new course, Gorbachev was still wedded to the ideas of Lenin and Leninism. At a meeting of the Politburo on 15 October 1987, the members spent nearly four hours analysing the text of the General Secretary's speech for the forthcoming seventieth anniversary of the October Revolution. In a long reply to remarks by Boris Yeltsin, Gorbachev said: 'There's one problem I want to deal with right away. I regard it as my personal achievement in this speech . . . October embraced everything progressive in our history . . . This is what reveals Lenin's genius and the fact that his comrades-in-arms were of a lower order than he. In this group one can say it: until Lenin's arrival in Petrograd, both Stalin and all the others who were in Russia had adjusted to the idea that everything was just fine now – there would be a legal opposition. And they would be part of it . . . Then Lenin appeared and, without pausing for breath, said: "Long live the socialist revolution!" That was because he had understood the true character of the February revolution . . . It was precisely Lenin who saw the possibility of turning February into October . . . That was perspicacity, and that's what separates genius from you and me.'[11]

It is true that only Lenin saw that power was lying there to be picked up on the streets of the capital in October 1917. The seizure of power was possible because of a rare constellation of circumstances perceived by Lenin. It is what he did with that power that would prove monumentally tragic for Russia.

During the discussion of the seventieth anniversary, Gorbachev interrupted a speech by Shcherbitsky to give an assessment of Lenin on *perestroika*: 'You know, I'd like very much to draw a parallel between history and the present. We didn't mean to do this just artificially, but in reality to build a bridge to Lenin, to connect Lenin's ideas, Lenin's approach to the problems of those years and the issues of our own day. After all, the dialectics applied by Lenin in solving problems is the key to solving present-day problems.'[12] Yet it was obvious that Lenin's prescriptions and goals had been proved not merely flawed, but irrelevant. Gorbachev's faith was not simply a matter of inertia: he believed that Lenin's methods were still viable seventy years on.

Gorbachev was the only General Secretary to make the pilgrimage to the Bolshevik shrine of Shushenskoye in Siberia, where Lenin had been in exile at the end of the nineteenth century. 'The memorial made a powerful impression on me,' he said, describing the trip to his colleagues.[13] Since the centenary of Lenin's birth in 1970, the insane wave of monument-building had been slowly subsiding, yet Gorbachev supported an idea from the Central Committee's Administration Department to create a Lenin museum in Geneva, for which the house he had lived in had to be purchased.[14] The Brezhnev tradition of commemorating the first leader on a massive scale was being upheld by the seventh leader. Under Gorbachev a seventy-volume sixth edition of Lenin's works was planned. The first edition had twenty volumes, and each successive edition had seen an increase of ten volumes.

Despite the failure of Lenin's ideas and methods, Gorbachev seems not to have evolved at all in his attitude to the first leader right up to 1991, when the Party collapsed like a house of cards. Through Gorbachev, the Party repeated the mistake Khrushchev had made in 1956, which was in effect to say, we are knocking Stalin off his pedestal and returning to Lenin, and everything will be all right. Some people knew even then that the problem was not Stalin, but the system, the ideology and the Leninist architecture as a whole.

Gorbachev, too, was now criticizing the situation into which the

Party had led the country, and saying that Lenin's dialectics would provide the solution. This approach, to which Gorbachev, the Party and the Politburo held virtually until the end, undermined many of his ideas for *perestroika*.

In 1988 the Academy of Social Sciences sent Gorbachev a devastating letter on a play by Mikhail Shatrov called *Further, Further, Further*. The letter categorically rejected Shatrov's argument that the October Revolution had been an 'accident', and also criticized his 'detrimental' image of Lenin. Gorbachev suggested that the academics become more actively involved through the press in defence of their hero. He himself held a meeting on 8 January 1988 with leaders of the media, ideological institutes and creative unions, and announced: '[Shatrov] has put twenty-three people all into the same dock, including four White Guard generals, Kerensky, Lenin, Bukharin, Trotsky, Zinoviev and Stalin, and he has them engaging not in what I'd call a discussion. Rather more like a squabble. Moreover, the reviewer has written that everyone is equal before history. So it turns out that Lenin is also being judged; he is repenting before the judgement of history. What has he to repent for?'[15]

For the 120th anniversary of Lenin's birth in 1990, Gorbachev gave a speech entitled 'A Word on Lenin', in which he asserted that to turn away from Lenin was 'to cut the root of society and the state, to lay waste to the minds and hearts of generations'.[16] He described the shameful peace of Brest-Litovsk, in which Lenin handed over half of European Russia to save his regime, as an example of the genius of Lenin's policy of 'sudden turns'. This 'sudden turn' consisted of an undefeated Russia giving a half-collapsed Germany the chance of holding on for a few more months.

Ironically, it was to be an orthodox Leninist who would lead the country straight into de-Leninization. Not that Gorbachev was obsessed by the Leninist catechism: Soviet leaders were not very well schooled in Lenin's works. But the essence of Lenin's views remained close to his heart. When he was liberated from his palace at Foros on the Black Sea in August 1991 by the Russian democrats, at his first meeting with journalists Gorbachev declared that he still believed in the ideals of socialism and was ready to perfect the Communist Party still further. He could not bring himself to say that it was time to destroy the Party. He still thought of restructuring it, when everyone else could see the futility of the task, as long as it clung to Leninist ideology.

Perestroika

In her memoirs, Raisa Gorbachev recalls 10 March 1985, when her husband told her that he was likely to succeed Chernenko, who had died that day. As they walked together, he voiced his thoughts: '"All those years I worked in Stavropol. Now I'm in my seventh year of working in Moscow. Yet it's been impossible to do anything important, large-scale, properly prepared. It's like a brick wall. But life demands [action], and has done so for a long time. No," I heard him say, "we can't go on living like this any more." It was the first time I heard those words. Millions of people are repeating them today and entire legends have been created about them. That night, I think, a new stage began that brought big changes in our lives.'[17]

The idea that 'we cannot go on living like this any more' had, of course, been widespread long before this. Indeed, all the leading dissidents and their brave followers had for years been saying by their words and deeds that it was not possible to live a human life under the Communist regime. Gorbachev could not fail to be aware of the public mood. He did not instigate the people's protest that had long awaited public expression, but he will go down in history for having made it possible.

The belief that 'we can't go on living like this any more' was an echo of the thought that people in Gorbachev's circle had had for some time. But only the leader himself, or perhaps a group belonging to the 'ruling circles', could introduce fundamental change in so conservative a system. Khrushchev, thanks to his personal courage, had managed fatally to undermine the image of his terrible predecessor, while Brezhnev, enjoying equal power, had been able to halt the process of de-Stalinization.

Gorbachev was right when he told his wife that he had achieved nothing of great importance in his work. Indeed, in Stavropol he is remembered for nothing more than what he went on to become. Other regional First Secretaries made their mark at Party Congresses, getting into the national press for a speech, or some initiative or other.

This was not the case with Gorbachev, who was an unknown quantity as far as the public were concerned.

On his arrival in Moscow in 1978, Gorbachev was put in charge of the Central Committee's agricultural production sphere, and then of the ambitiously named USSR Food Programme. As was to be expected, this collapsed spectacularly. Issuing directives was never going to solve the food problem. Throughout Gorbachev's years as the Central Committee Secretary in charge of agriculture, the country saw almost the lowest harvests since the war, and continued to make vast grain purchases abroad. It seems that Gorbachev brought nothing fundamentally new to the Party's agrarian policy. But no one else had been able to clear up the mess produced by the disastrous campaign launched against the peasantry by Stalin and the Communist Party in 1929–33.

At the end of 1979 the Party was preparing for its next plenum, at which, naturally, there would be a review of the state of the national economy. A draft of Brezhnev's speech was circulated to all members of the Politburo for comment and suggestions. Gorbachev's were typical of those made by the rest: 'With his characteristic depth, range and substance, Leonid Ilyich examines a wide range of present-day problems of the economic and social progress of the country. With Leninist adherence to principle, he raises questions of the working style and methods of the Party cadres and state administration, the development of their initiative and raising their responsibility for the work in hand.' That was how everyone wrote, and Gorbachev had to do so too. His requests for agriculture amounted to a suggestion to 'link' these issues with 'the decisions of the July (1978) Plenum'.[18]

Neither Gorbachev nor anyone else was in a position to extricate agriculture from the crisis into which it had been plunged by the Bolsheviks decades earlier. And whatever initiatives were taken were doomed to failure. In January 1989 the Politburo met to debate the questions on agriculture that were to be put before the plenum. As the expert on the subject, Gorbachev spoke a great deal: 'We have come to a decisive stage in the preparation and formulation of the positions and decisions to put to the plenum. *Perestroika* in the villages is being held up by the cadres. The salary of the First Secretary of a rural district committee [*raikom*] is the same as that of the head of a section on a state farm ... Who would want to be a *raikom*?'[19]

If so much had really depended on the salaries of Party function-aries, the Soviet Union would not have been buying grain abroad for decades, but would have been exporting it to the whole world.

It was Gorbachev's bad luck as Agriculture Secretary that he had to grapple with problems that no one was capable of solving. With every good intention, he approved documents, letters and recommen-dations that could change nothing. But he was not making his mark, or to be more precise, he was noticeable among the other members of the Politburo only for being relatively young. To be fair, this was the effect of a system which did not allow anyone other than the General Secretary to shine.

As General Secretary, Gorbachev at first behaved like the leaders he had worked under, or so it seemed. On 15 March 1985, two days after Chernenko's funeral, he held a meeting in his office with a number of Central Committee Secretaries and told them about the conversations he had had with the leaders of foreign delegations who had attended the funeral. At the end of the meeting, he suddenly started talking about what new steps he hoped to take as General Secretary: 'The question has arisen as to whether we should devise a plan of measures to accompany my speech to the March Plenum. I think that devising such plans of measures in general, either now or in the future, is not necessary. The speech has been published, it has been sent to the Party organizations and the comrades in the localities themselves know what has to be done in this regard.'

The group glanced at each other. Hitherto a General Secretary's speech at a plenum was an event. The Party Committees used it to justify the most varied 'measures' in explaining, propagandizing and implementing directives.

Gorbachev went further: 'I was telephoned today by Viktor Vasilie-vich Grishin. He told me there was a plan in Moscow to form a group of Party activists in connection with implementing the decisions of the recent plenum, and the instructions and arguments of the General Secretary. I don't think the "instructions and arguments of the Gen-eral Secretary" should be mentioned in the agendas of our plenums.'

This was something new. The Secretaries scribbled in their note-books, summarizing the unusual 'instructions' of the new General Secretary. He hadn't finished.

'I also had a call today from Zia Nurevich Nuriyev [the Deputy

Prime Minister of the Russian Federation]. He was on his way to the Estonian SSR to present the republic with the Red Banner and he asked my permission to pass on my greetings to the participants at the ceremony. I told him there was no need to give them such greetings, and that in general it was time to stop giving these greetings, which everyone's been sick and tired of for ages.'[20]

The Secretaries were not used to hearing such things. Gorbachev was voluntarily denying himself an important ritual part of what was due to him at the top of the hierarchical pyramid. He knew, however, that such small but meaningful gestures would be noticed at all levels of the Party as a good omen of possible change.

Some of the minutes of the meeting reveal that Gorbachev still had the dust of the provinces on him:

> When I got round to Ceausescu he became evasive ... He ought to have replied quite decisively that we are all united on the question of signing the protocol to continue the Warsaw Pact ... Ceausescu swallowed these words and said nothing ...
>
> President Mitterrand of France looked ill and found it hard to speak ... We told him frankly that the Soviet Union and France had been at the origins of détente ... and that the need for such collaboration has grown even greater.
>
> [West German] Chancellor Kohl was bursting to talk to us ... He is worried by the situation that has arisen in which England and France and Italy are actively bypassing [West Germany] in trying to improve co-operation with the Soviet Union. We had to tell him frankly ...
>
> The conversation with the Japanese Prime Minister, Nakasone, was difficult. He opened by talking about Japan's territorial claims on the Soviet Union. We deflected his demands in the most decisive way and showed the direction in which the Japanese leadership is gradually drifting.
>
> Our longest conversation (nearly two hours) was with US Vice-President Bush and Secretary of State Shultz. Frankly, the American delegation made a pretty ordinary impression on us. They are not a very serious lot ... When I touched on questions that were outside the framework of Bush's text, he became confused.
>
> As for the Pakistani President, Zia ul-Haq, he's a wily politician ... We had to tell him frankly that as we are neighbouring states we ought to behave in a neighbourly manner ... We pointed out to the Pakistani President ... I told Zia ul-Haq frankly ... All in all, we put quite

serious pressure on Zia ul-Haq, and when he left the meeting he was plainly upset.[21]

And so on. Gorbachev was showing the Secretaries how decisive and frank he had been when talking to foreign presidents, although the minutes of those talks indicate that they were rather general and bland.

Gorbachev's readiness to use a cutting, often unprintable, word, was often surprising. His aide Chernyayev recalls in his memoirs an occasion when Gorbachev was reading one of his memoranda and 'cursing like a trooper with foul language'.[22] Judging his partners and rivals – behind their backs, of course – in disparaging terms was very much Gorbachev's style. This was a clear expression of his provincialism and the categorical way of thinking bred in him by the Party. For instance, in 1986 he told the Politburo: 'In Reagan at Reykjavik we were fighting not only with the class enemy, but with one who is extremely primitive, has the looks of a troglodyte and displays mental incapacity.'[23] Such remarks suggest a lack of general culture, provincialism, an excess of 'Party-mindedness' and a Lenin-like intolerance of the 'class enemy'. In time Gorbachev would weed out some of these flaws, but not all of them. In any event, he was concerned with a much bigger task. He felt he must try to 'cure' the Leninist system, and to this end he began using three terms that became the hallmark of his rule: *uskorenie* (acceleration), *glasnost* (openness) and *perestroika* (reconstruction).

Apart from having decided that it was no longer possible to go on living 'like this', when he became General Secretary Gorbachev had no clear idea of what to do. Ideas about improving this, changing that, liberating society from something, came to him gradually, albeit in fairly rapid succession. Much of what he said found fertile soil in the public mind. Almost daily his colleagues were surprised by him. Above all, he was meeting people of all kinds: ministers, ambassadors, writers, *obkoms*, newspaper and magazine editors. Some of them may have thought that he was just getting used to the job, or taking a break from the responsibilities of office, or establishing himself quickly, while others regarded him as a mere populist who would sooner or later reveal himself in his true colours. But he continued in the same way, amazing the Politburo and Central Committee Secretaries with his style of work.

On 4 April 1985, the Politburo discussed the agenda for the forth-coming plenum on 23 April. Gorbachev evidently determined that this plenum should be a watershed, even though the question he set himself appeared to be a strictly internal Party issue: 'The Twenty-Seventh Party Congress and the tasks connected with preparing and holding it.' The Central Committee apparatus had decided everything in advance, as always. The Politburo members were already gathering up their papers and pushing back their chairs when Gorbachev suddenly stopped them: 'I would ask the comrades to wait a few minutes. I would like to exchange opinions with Politburo members on a certain issue. There has been an unexpectedly big response in the country to the idea expressed at the March Plenum about the need to struggle systematically against ostentation, arrogance, eulogies and boot-licking.'

Gorbachev had decided not to delay in striking a cautious but telling blow against his predecessors. There was nothing very new in this – all previous General Secretaries, apart from Stalin, had consolidated their own positions by criticizing and debunking the previous incumbent: 'The darker the night, the brighter the stars,' as the poet Maikov wrote. Nor was the practice a dangerous one. Still, Gorbachev was cautious. He chose as his weapon of attack a letter addressed to the Central Committee by an old Communist in Leningrad, V. Zavyalov.

The members of the Politburo pricked up their ears. It took Gorbachev about ten minutes to read the letter, which included:

> In his time Stalin gave the nod to eulogies. I'm thinking of the selection of honorary chairmen, greetings letters to the Central Committee on the occasion of some event or other or the birthday of important personages, speeches of praise for the General Secretary, reports to him of labour achievements, and so on . . . Ostentation does not serve the cause. Historical experience shows that behind all the pomp and ceremony the leadership loses direction and a sense of proportion. The people think that Brezhnev's nineteen Gold Stars and Chernenko's third Gold Star not only undermined their personal authority, but also backfired on the members of the Politburo. Do they really think that they and the General Secretaries should get all and any awards they feel like giving themselves?[24]

After he had read the indignant letter, Gorbachev told the Politburo it was time to strengthen the authority of the Party without 'overdoing the authority of the leaders', adding that there must be proportion in all things. He had made it plain that he was distancing himself from Chernenko and Brezhnev, regardless of the fact that he had sung his part in the choir of praise during their time in the top office. Less than four months earlier, on 10 December 1984, he had opened a report with a panegyric to his senile chief: 'Taking account of the current situation and with a broad historical perspective, in his greet-ings as a participant in the conference General Secretary Konstantin Ustinovich Chernenko expressed deep and principled propositions on the key issues for perfecting developed socialism, and formulated the main tasks arising on the ideological front from the decisions of the June (1983) Plenum. We must be rigorously guided by these pro-positions and arguments.'[25]

No decisions were taken on the letter from Leningrad, but Gorba-chev summed up: an honorary presidium of Politburo members could still be formed as before, but without the usual mention of the General Secretary in 'letters' to the Central Committee. In general, 'we should try to emulate Leninist modesty, not permit either excessive or any other kind of eulogy.'[26]

Step by step, Gorbachev was trying to free himself from the custom-ary, shameful trappings of Party tradition. And he wanted to free others. He was thinking more and more of the big, important funda-mentals that needed to be addressed if Soviet life was to change for the better. He possibly understood even then that the system he had inherited actually worked quite well in extreme circumstances, such as wars or national crises. It was in normal, everyday conditions that it was sluggish and ineffectual. The question was how to make it more efficient, flexible and attractive. As he said throughout the years of *perestroika*, Gorbachev was not looking for democratic alternatives to the Party monopoly. But his aides, such as Alexandrov, Chernyayev, Frolov and Shakhnazarov, were constantly feeding him with sum-maries, reports, books and translations from the West that included analyses of possible developments in the USSR under the new leader. The general view in 1985 was that the system was susceptible only to cosmetic changes, and that Gorbachev was right for the job, but for no more than that. Milovan Djilas, the Yugoslav ex-Communist heretic, wrote: 'The prevailing conditions in the Soviet Union do not yet permit a leader to act boldly and independently . . . Gorbachev is not a sufficiently decisive and creative personality to undertake radical changes.'[27]

Gorbachev had other ideas. He wanted to make major changes. He knew that the country was fast approaching a crossroads that would present him with a choice of three different paths: radical reform, liberal development, or conservative restoration. All the evidence shows that he decisively rejected the conservative option. It had in effect been taken by his three predecessors, and had brought the country to its present crisis.

Radical reform would mean destroying the 'socialist foundations': resorting to private ownership, a free market, political pluralism and the end of the monopoly of a single ideology. Gorbachev was possibly afraid even to analyse this option. At the Plenum of 23 April 1985, which the entire Party press – albeit out of inertia – starting calling 'historic', absolutely nothing historically new in principle was said. Instead, Gorbachev uttered the same old tired formulas: 'the Leninist tradition', 'the advantages of a new order', 'deepening of socialist democracy', 'the socialist way of life', 'the successes of socialism and Communism', all of which depended on the Party.[28]

The slogan 'uskorenie' (acceleration) was indeed relatively new, but was little more than a propaganda ploy. The 'achievement of social-economic progress' without basic changes in the social and political structures meant nothing more than the old policy underpinned by 'discipline', 'competition' and 'correct Party leadership'. The usual rush for quantity would change nothing in any significant way. Stalin's description was more easily understood: 'The Five-Year Plan in four years'.

There remained the path of liberal development, to which I believe Gorbachev had always been committed. His speeches reveal that he wanted to accommodate both the plan and the market, both state and private enterprise, centralization and decentralization. In effect, liberalization of the system was an attempt to create a model which, put simply, would include the best of socialism and the best of capitalism. The steps Gorbachev took, especially in the first and second stages, demonstrated an intention to preserve a socialist economy that would be essentially mixed. Yugoslavia and China have shown that such an arrangement can produce temporarily positive results, but that it also gives rise to new difficulties that are not susceptible to a quick solution.

Many people today criticize Gorbachev for lacking an effective 'strategy' for *perestroika*, but no one at the time was proposing an alternative path, or putting forward a more effective strategy. We now have a clearer view of Gorbachev's 'mistakes', but he did not have the time to comprehend them. As a reformer, he did not contemplate, he acted. And often he had to act immediately, that very day or minute. One should not forget that it must have been harder for him, as head of the Party and state, to change himself than it is for ordinary mortals. As he once announced to his colleagues: 'A huge restructuring [*perestroika*] is going on, a restructuring of us ourselves. We are not gods.'[29]

Undoubtedly, Gorbachev had his failings, some of them significant, most notably on the national problem. Moreover, he was burdened by the fundamentally flawed system of state structure brought in by Lenin in the early 1920s.

Gorbachev acted *ad hoc*, and he had no one to learn from. His most striking weaknesses were indecisiveness and the half-heartedness of some of the measures he took. Many of his positive efforts remained incomplete as a result. A duality emerged, caused partly by the unclear, mixed nature of the liberal option, but also by the tortuous process of shedding the stereotypes endowed by the Bolshevik mentality. It is important to understand this, in order to grasp the meaning of *perestroika* as a process of *attempts* to introduce changes to the socialist system. Those who were trying to bring this about were still holding on to many of the old ideas. The reappraisal of Stalin is one example.

At the 4 April 1985 meeting of the Politburo, Gorbachev said it was 'no secret that when Khrushchev took his criticism of Stalin's actions to unbelievable limits, it caused only harm, and to some extent we haven't managed yet to pick up all the pieces'.[30] Two years later, in October 1987, the Politburo was debating the draft of the speech Gorbachev was to make on the seventieth anniversary of the October Revolution. The discussion turned to the subject of Stalin, and with varying degrees of qualification, the members were all for a critical assessment. Gorbachev gave his view: 'The draft was no good until the idea arose of separating the 1920s and 1930s after Lenin, and then the big, the huge service Stalin had given emerged ... It was then that Stalin found his place. That was after all the decisive stage: the question of where the country was going was decided.'[31] It is hard to believe that Gorbachev could say this more than thirty years after the Twentieth Congress.

Gorbachev's speech mentioned Stalin three times, and each time the name was greeted by a storm of applause: 'In the attainment of victory a role was played by the enormous political will, the purposefulness and persistence, the ability to organize and discipline people, shown by I.V. Stalin during the war years.'[32] The man who had exterminated the officers corps on the eve of the war, who had contracted a shameful treaty of friendship with Hitler, who had restrained the troops from going onto war alert as Germany's forces were moving in to attack, now turned out to have been the saviour of the country. What about the 26.5 million war dead, many of whom had perished because of Stalin's crimes and mistakes? For a long time Gorbachev retained a dual attitude to Stalin, as a leader who had been a monster, but who had 'defended' socialism.

When Stalin's daughter, Svetlana Alliluyeva, requested permission to leave the country again in 1986 after her impetuous return, it was thought that a chat with her might make her change her mind. Gorbachev, however, refused to see her: 'If I have to meet her, I'll be asked to evaluate Stalin, Stalingrad and so on. I come from one of those families myself. My grandfather's health was ruined. Mother came from the poorest of families and had five children. I got a medal for an essay on "Stalin, our fighting glory, Stalin, the aspiration of our youth!" Maybe it would be more expedient to get Comrade Solomentsev to meet her.'[33]

It took time and effort for Gorbachev to free himself of the Stalinist mythology. If it was so hard for him to change himself, how much harder was it going to be for him to change society. The applause at the mention of Stalin's name showed how painful even the best-informed Soviet citizens were finding their self-emancipation. The published pamphlet of Gorbachev's speech states that Stalin's name was greeted by 'prolonged applause'. That understates the case. Even the editors of the minutes were ashamed to write that the applause had in fact been a stormy ovation, and they downgraded it to 'prolonged'.

In essence, the process of *perestroika* was an attempt to transform a sluggish, dogmatic, bureaucratic, command system in the direction of a sort of liberalism. But it was no part of its architect's scheme to knock away its Communist supports. Its results were therefore limited, although they served as important prerequisites for the democratic changes to come. Gorbachev could not have done more than he did. Nor could anyone else. Perhaps his most important achievement was to widen the avenues of public access to information of all kinds, thus giving people a view of many aspects of political life that had hitherto been closed to them. This was called *glasnost* – openness, publicity, or just telling the truth. The process was begun by Gorbachev, but continued to evolve without regard to his decisions. The system based on the class lie was destroyed from within by *glasnost*.

Gorbachev did not sit on top of a theoretical hill, meditating on the essence, forms and methods of *perestroika*. He had to respond instantly to the demands of everyday life. He had no choice but to do so, especially because from the very outset he was confronted by opposition. As early as February 1986 Gorbachev felt constrained to declare: 'Even after the April (1985) Plenum, a new clan of people has emerged who indulge in phrase-mongering instead of getting things going . . . The time-servers are back.'[34] He was dissatisfied that so many leaders were paying only lip service to the reforms he had launched.

Under Gorbachev the Politburo dealt with precisely the same issues it had dealt with under Brezhnev, Andropov and Chernenko. Typical examples are:

May Day demonstration on 1 May 1985 (4 April 1985)

Preparation and course of spring sowing (11 April 1985)

Technical re-equipping of Gorky automobile factory (6 May 1985)

The rising demand for grain usage (6 May 1985)

Uniforms, food and weapons for the Sandinista army (Nicaragua) (6 May 1985)

Results of meeting with Central Committee Secretaries of the fraternal parties (23 May 1985)

Retail prices of fruit juice and bread-making yeast (1 August 1985)

Plan for the economic and social development of the USSR for 1986 and the Twelfth Five-Year Plan (29 August 1985).

In 1985 the Politburo passed 4,112 decrees, almost four hundred more than in the previous year. The number of joint Central

Committee/Council of Ministers decrees rose from 228 to 241, while the Secretariat passed 5,512.[35] What time was there for the Party leadership to think of a strategy for *perestroika*? And if the Politburo could not restructure itself, how could it change the country? Surely it was obvious that questions of sowing and mowing-machines, grain, yeast and fruit juice, transport and public canteens, could and should have been dealt with by the government?

On 26 June 1986 the Politburo spent a long time discussing the candidates for the leadership of the Union of Writers, to be elected at its forthcoming congress. The candidates were Yuri Bondarev, Sergei Zalygin and Valentin Rasputin:

GORBACHEV: Of course, Markov would be the best choice. What do you think of Comrade Bondarev?

GROMYKO: He's a major writer.

SOLOMENTSEV: He sticks to the correct line.

GORBACHEV: If Comrade Markov doesn't get through, we could go for Zalygin. He's a bit old, not very strong. Better all the same to steer a course for Comrade Bondarev.

He then asked the deputy chairman of the KGB for his opinion.

BOBKOV: If news of our support for Comrade Bondarev gets out, he may not be elected, so it should not be leaked prematurely.

GORBACHEV: Let's agree in the first instance to go for Comrade Markov as President and Comrade Bondarev as Secretary. We must use whatever influence we can to make this happen.[36]

The meeting also discussed whether Politburo permission should be required for a heart transplant operation. The members were against becoming involved, in case the operation went wrong.

These were the kinds of issues being debated by the Politburo a year after the beginning of *perestroika*, and they continued in this vein until 1990. A Politburo without power over everyone and everything would simply not have been the Politburo, and although this ought to have been a central issue for Gorbachev's reforms, no one was prepared to raise it.

The new General Secretary wanted to engage the masses, knowing that any reform of the top echelons of power would produce only cosmetic results. But after seven decades of Bolshevik rule, the masses had lost any sense of independent action, beyond complaining about small abuses or voicing support for orders from above. Gradually, more and more people were coming to see that the Communist system was not reformable. Any radical arguments, however, were at once rebuffed. As Gorbachev wrote in an article of late 1989, 'The Socialist Idea and Revolutionary *Perestroika*': those who think 'that the previous path allegedly completely reversed the choice made in October [1917], are proposing the capitalization of society. We reject that path.'[37]

What did its chief architect understand by '*perestroika*'? '*Perestroika* decisively overcomes stagnant processes and dismantles the braking mechanism, it creates a reliable and effective mechanism for accelerating the social and economic development of society and imparts more dynamism to it.'[38]

Neither in philosophical nor practical terms do the notions of 'braking and accelerating mechanisms' answer the main question: what is the aim of *perestroika*? Gorbachev himself must have sensed this, and at different times he gave different definitions. For instance, in 1989: '*Perestroika* is an entire revolutionary process, brought about by democratic methods, by the people for the people, and in relation to which the Party acts as a political vanguard.'[39]

The outcome, then, was 'for the people'. But what precisely was the outcome to be? The 'revolutionary process' itself? The people had already had that up to their back teeth. Lenin and Stalin had talked so much about the people and the revolution that the mere mention of the words immediately aroused suspicion that a new state of emergency was about to be declared. Revolution and excess went hand in hand.

Neither the Party nor the Politburo and its chairman, the General Secretary, were prepared to state the obvious: that *perestroika* would be genuine only when it was aimed at transforming the totalitarian, bureaucratic society into a democratic society. For the Party this would have been suicidal, and it was not prepared to accept the idea. The Bolsheviks had never repented. Their goal, and their notion of *perestroika*, was, in Gorbachev's words, 'to continue the cause of the [October] Revolution'.[40]

It was extremely hard for Gorbachev to get things moving. The people had had their first taste of liberty, and could no longer remain silent. Sores which had been covered up for decades were suddenly exposed. The old system started coming apart at the seams, but there was no clear idea of what would replace it.

The climate of *perestroika* was extremely contradictory. The whole country was alive with meetings. The Central Committee was issuing decrees, such as that of 8 September 1989, which stated that soap, washing powder, school exercise books, razor blades, toothpaste, electric irons, teapots, shoes and many other items had disappeared from the shops.[41] This was followed by a notice of 'serious shortages of medical supplies for the population',[42] and the customary call for 'leader-Communists to heighten their responsibility for supplying the population with food'.[43] The country was faced with shortages of every kind, with long queues at shops and a thriving black market. Moscow was relatively better off than most cities, but hundreds of thousands of people were streaming into it in the hope of finding something to buy.

The Bolsheviks had always boasted that there was no unemployment in the country – overlooking the fact that the same had been true under serfdom – although in the Central Asian republics, the Transcaucasus and the Northern Caucasus 10.4 per cent of the working population 'were not engaged in the public economy'.[44] The Central Committee apparatus was inundated with letters (485,214 in 1989), overwhelmingly complaints asking for the Central Committee to take action. Complaining was the one outlet left to the Soviet population.

By 1990 it was clear that a turning-point had been reached, not only within the Soviet Union, but also in its relations with the 'fraternal countries'. In May 1989, during a state visit to Peking, Gorbachev had witnessed the huge student demonstrations in Tiananmen Square demanding democratic reform. Similarly, but more irresistibly, the momentum of 'people power' was building up in Eastern Europe. In East Germany in October, Gorbachev in effect made it clear that the Brezhnev Doctrine was dead, that the Soviet Union would no longer intervene in the 'People's Democracies' if their regimes got into difficulties. He told the East German Communists that they were doomed if they did not adopt the sort of reforms the Soviet leadership had introduced. In December the Berlin Wall was torn down, and Germany was reunified. Throughout the socialist world, the call for liberation from Moscow's grip rose to a peak. The Czechoslovaks went far beyond the 'Prague Spring' of 1968, and staged a 'velvet revolution'.

In Poland and Hungary the dissolution of the Warsaw Pact was openly discussed, and it became clear that the event itself was now inevitable. As one Communist regime after another made way for governments led by former dissidents, the satellite empire that Stalin had created on the ruins of post-war Europe collapsed at breathtaking speed.

In the Soviet Union, meanwhile, Party organizations in universities and institutes were disbanding themselves. Thousands were leaving the Party as a protest against the continuing political monopoly and leadership methods. The ideological immunity once enjoyed by Party members was failing fast, as the devaluation of the 'founding values' of Marxism-Leninism gathered pace. Since 1987 heads of academic and research institutes had been left to their own devices, no longer harassed by telephone calls from the Central Committee checking up on their activities. None of the earlier sanctions against a member who did not turn up to a Party meeting – they were being held with declining frequency – or failed to pay his or her dues, were now applied. Perhaps a local branch secretary would telephone with a gentle reminder, but would desist when he received a firm negative. The Party was adrift, and ready to melt away.

The country was also adrift, except that the intellectual ferment was rising. It was becoming difficult to defend Lenin and Leninism or the 'class line' in public. Resistance to reform was mounting. Neither the Politburo nor Gorbachev knew how to stop the effects of *perestroika*. Instead, Gorbachev battled to create a socialist society with a human face. One unexpected and, from the architect's point of view, undesirable effect was to accelerate the process of self-destruction of the totalitarian system. *Perestroika*, which was not fully understood either by its creators or by those who implemented it as a policy, was a transitional but important condition for shifting the country onto a track that would lead to a democratic society.

Meanwhile, Gorbachev continued to deal with dozens of issues as he tried to start the main engine of *perestroika* – 'democratization of society'. Regrettably, he had given the decisive role in this to his 'vanguard', the CPSU, a force that at once disabled the engine and ensured that it could never properly start.

The Gorbachev Paradox

When he used the indignant letter from Leningrad on 4 April 1985 to attack the lack of restraint of his predecessors, Gorbachev knew that he would gain wide support among rank and file Communists, and also that he would find himself the centre of attention from admirers, adversaries, other leaders and the public at large. He did not give himself medals, opposed the practice of referring in agendas to his 'orders', and banned his colleagues from routinely passing on his greetings at every meeting they attended. This was widely noticed and approved.

But, like his predecessors, Gorbachev succumbed to the temptation to see his works in print. Chernenko had managed to have his tedious speeches and articles reissued in the short time he was in office, even to have them published in East Germany. All the members of the Politburo had appeared in print, their books remaining unsold on bookshop shelves gathering dust. I have never met a soul who had bought – or would admit to having bought – a single one of these turgid volumes. Gorbachev must have known this. M. Nenashev, the head of the State Publishing Committee, reported to the Central Committee in the summer of 1986 that several million copies of Brezhnev's 166 books and pamphlets were lying like a dead weight in the shops. Similarly, nobody was buying the works of Andropov, Grishin, Kulakov, Pelshe, Ponomarev, Romanov, Suslov, Tikhonov, Ustinov or Chernenko. 'The bookselling network,' Nenashev said, 'is also holding more than 700,000 portraits of Brezhnev, 130,000 of Andropov, 170,000 of Chernenko. Only books supplied on the blanket orders of public libraries have been sold.'

On 6 August 1986 Gorbachev wrote on Nenashev's report: 'For circulation to Politburo members only.'[45] It seemed like a warning to his colleagues that readers were not interested in their committee-manufactured, faceless works. He seems, however, to have had a different scale of values for himself.

As early as December 1985 Gorbachev's speeches and articles were collected and published in a rushed edition – 420 pages of 'secretarial' text printed on high-quality paper. Since Gorbachev had published practically nothing in the central press, the collection garnered whatever was available, even if it deserved scant attention. The headings alone indicate that this was the kind of 'banquet' book, or vanity edition, that would be presented as a gift: speeches given at a reception in Warsaw on 25 April, at a reception in the Kremlin on 9 May, at a dinner in the Kremlin in honour of Rajiv Gandhi on 21 May, at a lunch for Willi Brandt on 27 May, at a dinner for Bettino Craxi on 29 May, at a dinner for Gustav Husak on 31 May, another for Li Xiannian on 28 June, at the Elysées Palace on 2 October, in the Kremlin at a dinner for Colonel Qaddafi – the list goes on.[46]

Having condemned others for vanity and abusing their privilege, Gorbachev was not slow to immortalize himself. Volumes of his works would follow one after the other, most of them of as little interest to the general reader as they are to the historian, except for the ideas on *perestroika*, the bloodless revolution and the new thinking, which are important to an understanding of the process he began. Soon after Gorbachev became General Secretary, the sixth section of the General Department began printing, collating and binding everything he said or wrote: speeches, directives, articles, reports and memoranda. Thirty-nine volumes in beautiful morocco leather with gold lettering – more than twice as many as Stalin's collected works – were prepared, but in only two copies, whether for publication we do not know, but a literary monument in any event. No other General Secretary was as quick off the mark. Practically everything Gorbachev said in 1985 was published in book form in the same year. His strict imprecations to observe Leninist modesty and not to indulge in bragging and eulogizing seem to have been temporarily forgotten.[47]

Having begun *perestroika* under the slogan of 'renewing' socialism, Gorbachev came six years later to its liquidation, despite his own desire. He had not taken account of the fact that the chief attributes of the Soviet system were inertia, stagnation and conservatism. Once *glasnost* and the comparative democratization of society began to erode these foundations, the system began to fall apart.

Gorbachev could not but understand that socialism in the USSR was doomed, but he lacked the character and the will to accept this. In August 1990, speaking at a military gathering in Odessa Military District, he repeated: 'the object of the reform remains unshakeable: to bring about the socialist idea.'[48] In reality, *perestroika* was not a strategy to improve and renew socialism, but rather, as Mikhail Geller has written, an effort 'to delay the demise of the Soviet system for as long as possible'.[49] This was a historical paradox: an orthodox Communist objectively and despite his own intentions emerging as the grave-digger of the Leninist system.

The painful changes of *perestroika* bore the indelible imprint of Gorbachev's intellect, attitudes and will. When speaking of a leader's image, the hasty proviso was added that the decisive role was always played by 'the popular masses'. Yet the more bureaucratic or totalitarian a system, the more significant the role of the leader. Gorbachev was the seventh leader of a state in which no democratic institutions had ever existed, where people had no real idea of the meaning of human rights, and where liberty was not the chief spiritual value. He became leader at the very beginning of a tortuous road to a new historical condition.

In analysing Gorbachev's actions, achievements and failures, the kind of society of which he was leader should not be forgotten, just as it should be realized that he was not a god, a messiah or a prophet. He intended much more than he accomplished; there was often a gulf between his intention and the eventual outcome. This arose not only from the force of events, but also from a certain dissonance between Gorbachev's mind and his character, his intellect and his will.

Among the mass of papers he had to deal with every day, Gorbachev must have been especially disheartened by the flow of reports from Kabul, forwarded to him by the Ministry of Defence and the KGB. There seemed to be no end in sight to the bloody war in which the Soviet Union had become embroiled. Reports from Gromyko, Sokolov and Chebrikov, despite the obligatory doses of optimism, gave little cause for satisfaction. Recommendations for decorations and medals included long lists of names followed by the depressing legend '(posthumous)'.[50] In the year Gorbachev came to power, the Soviet Union spent 3 billion roubles on the war, in 1986 4 billion, in 1987 more than 5.5 billion.[51] Between December 1979 and February 1989, 546,255 Soviet officers and men served in Afghanistan, of whom 13,826 lost their lives.[52] The country was in a trap from which it could escape only by frankly admitting that the whole idea of an international mission to Afghanistan had been a mistake, and by withdrawing its troops.

The Afghan war had been going on for longer than the Second

World War, and to what end? In what cause had all these men died? As a relatively junior figure in 1979, Gorbachev had not been asked whether troops should be sent into an independent and sovereign foreign country, nor had he taken part in the fateful decision to do so. He had, however, soon been acquainted with the relevant resolution from Politburo minutes, which he had had to sign, thus signifying his official approval.

As early as 1986 he was saying that 'the Afghan knot must be untangled' as soon as possible. The war was to drag on for another four years, however. For all his enormous power, Gorbachev was unwilling to oppose the conservatives, the Defence Minister and the KGB. The paradox was at work: having come to a firm decision, often as a trailblazer in a particular cause, he would drag his feet over implementing his intention. He would hesitate, vacillate, reflect, weigh up the pros and cons, and delay, hoping with his colleagues to extract something good from the hopelessly failed adventure.

Having firmly made up his mind by the beginning of 1986 that the troops must be withdrawn, Gorbachev constantly gave instructions to 'study this question', 'submit proposals', 'prepare for withdrawal'. Even in November 1987, into the third year of *perestroika*, when he met the pro-Soviet Afghan leader Mohammed Najibullah, he said very little, and that only indirectly, about pulling out, despite the fact that the Defence Ministry was at that time working on a plan for withdrawal. Instead, for nearly an hour Gorbachev talked about the way Lenin had acted in a crisis situation, about 'the flexibility of Leninist national policy', the forthcoming presidential election in Afghanistan, and the new assembly, the Loya Djirga, in Kabul.

His advice was simple, not to say simplistic: 'You have had a good party conference. Now you face the task of implementing its decisions firmly and of going forward. As for those in the People's Democratic Party of Afghanistan who do not believe in national reconciliation, these sceptics should be given a good pension or sent abroad.' In the middle of the conversation, he hastily informed his guest: 'In general, Comrade Najib, an exceptionally important and responsible phase is about to begin. Unfortunately, we do not have time now to discuss all the deserving problems, as I have a meeting arranged with Comrade János Kádár.'[53]

On 1 April 1988, prior to Gorbachev's next meeting with Najibullah in Tashkent, the Politburo ratified a plan to withdraw Soviet forces, then numbering 109,000 men. At last Gorbachev was firm: 'The forces will be withdrawn by 15 February 1989. We will begin pulling out on 15 May.' The decision that had matured in his mind when he became General Secretary had taken three years to implement, and it would need another year to complete. Before withdrawal operations began, however, Gorbachev still wanted in effect to justify the original decision to send the troops in. At a Politburo meeting on 18 April, while discussing the practical measures for the withdrawal, he stated in a special letter to the Party: 'We must say that our people have not given their lives in vain.'[54]

On 24 January 1989, the Foreign Minister Eduard Shevardnadze reported on his visit to Kabul and declared: 'In withdrawing from Afghanistan, we must recognize that we are leaving that country in a lamentable state, in the literal sense of the word: its cities and villages have been destroyed, the capital is starving, the economy is virtually paralysed ... Hundreds of thousands of people have perished ...'

Gorbachev replied: 'It is important that this regime and its cadres are not swept away altogether ... We must not appear before the world in our underpants, or even without any ... A defeatist position is not permissible ...'[55]

There were times when Gorbachev had the ability to issue a firm yes or no. In March 1989, when Soviet troops had been withdrawn from Afghanistan, Shevardnadze, yielding to Najibullah's persuasion, suddenly raised the defence of the tottering regime in Kabul as an issue. The question was whether to carry out bombing missions from Soviet territory against mujahedin in the vicinity of Jellalabad. The Defence Ministry, in the person of Marshal Yazov, gave its support to the Foreign Ministry only reluctantly. At this point Gorbachev exploded: 'No other reply to Najibullah, except an absolute refusal to do these bombing raids!' He ordered the appropriate telegram be sent to Kabul at once.[56]

Another feature of Gorbachev's approach was his tendency to engage others enthusiastically in his excitement over an idea that within a year or two he would have forgotten completely. While this reflected a personal trait, it also illustrated the Bolshevik understanding of the leader's role in society.

Once the programme of 'acceleration' was launched, it quickly became clear that increasing the quantity of goods produced had a negative effect on their quality. A functionary advised the General Secretary to toughen up quality control severely by increasing the powers of state inspectors. The idea had immense appeal for Gorbachev. I once attended a large meeting of Central Committee officials at which, with great excitement and conviction, he told us that if we could solve the problem of quality, we would finally make a 'great leap forward'. Quality could, however, only be improved by strengthening the role and number of inspectors. The solution was an old one: another enormous layer of many thousands of 'independent' state inspectors was introduced. A law was passed according to which from 1 January 1987 a large number of enterprises would come under 'state inspection'. In the course of that year, 15 per cent of production failed on grounds of quality. The factory managers were up in arms, and the workers set up a howl: they worked just as everyone else did, they had no choice. Within two years the 'golden key' to the question of quality was quietly lost, and Gorbachev never spoke of it again.

By now he was taken up with a new 'democratic' idea, this time the election of leaders. The time had come 'for necessary changes, for democratization of the process of forming leading cadres in enterprises on the basis of elective principles'.[57] Throughout the country, managers and directors were replaced in a wave of general meetings of 'councils of labour collectives', their jobs being taken over by their deputies, who were men of the same ilk.

Another idea was to combine the job of First Secretaries, whether of region or district, with that of chairman of the Soviet of People's Deputies of the given territory. This hybrid of Party and state power, under the full aegis of the CPSU, was already the *de facto* state of affairs, of course. Putting it on the statute book would mean legitimizing the Party's omnipotence. At the Nineteenth Party Conference in June 1988, Gorbachev gave a long speech in which he dwelt on this idea. He said it was necessary to return to the congresses of soviets of Lenin's day, and voiced other thoughts on the reform of the political system. Much of what he said sounded convincing and sensible.

He was adamant on the necessity to synthesize Party and state posts, and defended the idea with passion. In fact, he was merely prolonging the Party's dying agony, preserving for a brief spell its political monopoly. For longer than anyone else, he defended the idea of the CPSU as the ruling Party,[58] and would therefore not agree to remove Article 6 of the Brezhnev Constitution, which defined the Party as the nucleus of the political system. He regarded the suggestion as 'premature and hasty', and still believed that only the CPSU was capable of implementing the changes he envisaged.

In a strange sense, he was right. There was indeed only one powerful, formally 'social' but in practice state-like force, and that was the CPSU. It had accumulated vast organizational experience, and still exerted strong influence on millions of people. It could not be ignored, but nor should it be strengthened. Only its gradual dismantling and a shift of support to new democratic bodies would create the conditions necessary to change society.

Gorbachev's 'passions' should not be dismissed as mindless experimentation. He was compelled and obliged to seek new devices to introduce reform. Much seemed mistaken and superficially traditional. The failure of his administrative changes among the highest ranks of the Party steadily built up dissatisfaction among rank-and-file Communists, and caused disappointment with the slogans of *perestroika*. A totally new phenomenon for the Soviet Union was the exodus from the Party. In 1988 eighteen thousand members handed in their Party cards, and in the following year the number rose to 136,600, more than half of them workers.[59] Even though these figures represented only a minute proportion of the total of twenty million, the phenomenon of voluntary exit was unprecedented, and demonstrated a dramatic trend.

Gorbachev's personal paradox is expressed not only in the opposition between his intellect and his character, but also in the fact that by trying ineffectually to strengthen the system, he actually facilitated its self-destruction. This was a reflection of the complex interplay of the deep changes taking place in the USSR. These changes, moreover, were not an expression of 'acceleration' of development, nor of a strengthening of the 'economic independence' of enterprises. After three or four years of *perestroika* it was clear that no radical breakthrough in the economy had occurred, and that instead the Brezhnevite stagnation had continued and even worsened, making the USSR a country of universal shortages. Changes were, however, taking place in people's minds, in the gradual exposure of myths about the Party, the 'advantages of the socialist order', and the 'democratism' of the Soviet system.

The spiritual deconstruction, facilitated by the astonishing phenomenon of *glasnost*, began earlier than the material and organizational deconstruction. Some people saw at once that the idea of 'acceleration' was merely a restoration of the Bolshevik call to fulfil the Five-Year Plan in four years, that it would lead to poor-quality production, and that it flew in the face of objective economic laws.

Gorbachev did not jettison the old Bolshevik tactic of postponing the earthly paradise to an ever-receding horizon. The economic measures taken by the Soviet authorities, as the Western economist A. Katsenelenboigen has written, were not merely bad, 'they were simply inadequate to the crisis situation of the economy. One need only recall the housing problem. If not so long ago every Soviet family was promised an apartment by 1980, that promise has now been postponed to the year 2000.'[60] How many other promises of 'jam tomorrow' had the Communist authorities made? Gorbachev was unwilling to break with this principle. If the 'Leninist ideals of socialism become the property of the people', he declared, then we will attain our goals.[61] By the beginning of the 1990s it had become transparently clear that the economic part of Gorbachev's reforms had not worked. It is doubtful whether anyone else would have achieved a different result. As is now obvious, a new machine was required, not the old one somehow patched up.

Democratization of production, satisfaction of the huge consumer demand, and improving quality were impossible in the context of old Bolshevik economic relations. The system Lenin had created had shown that it was not amenable to radical democratic reform. Communism with a democratic face, a free market and political pluralism, is not Communism. The paradox of Gorbachev, in other words, was that he believed it was possible to change that which could not be changed. What was needed was not a restructuring – *perestroika* – but a new structure – *novostroika*.

Having heard Gorbachev's report on restructuring the Party's cadres policy, the Plenum of 28 January 1987 formulated a resolution: 'The ultimate aim of *perestroika* is the renewal of all aspects of the life of our society, imparting to socialism the most contemporary forms of social organization, and the fullest opening up of the creative

potential of the socialist order.'[62] For decades Gorbachev's predecessors had been similarly preoccupied with perfecting, improving and
renewing socialism, and with equal 'success'. Gorbachev stands out
as superior to the rest for doing his best to give socialism a human
face. It was a noble attempt, but hardly within anyone's power to
achieve. In the process of trying, however, he accomplished a major
advance by underwriting *glasnost* as a means of eliminating all the lies.
The Leninist system, regardless of the wishes of its functionaries, was
built on lies, secrecy, control of information and management of public
and private consciousness. As soon as the public began to learn the
truth about the regime and its countless myths, the foundations of
the system began to crack. Truth was a weapon against which the
Leninist system was now powerless to fight.

Gorbachev opened his career as General Secretary by launching a
frontal attack on the defects and running sores of Soviet society, and
he received widespread popular support for doing so. His first campaign was against drunkenness and alcoholism, which had long been
a serious problem. In 1984, no fewer than 9.3 million drunks had
been literally picked up on the streets of the country's towns and
villages. In the same year the annual consumption of pure alcohol per
head of population was 8.3 litres, not counting illicit and domestically
brewed alcohol. In some parts of the country consumption of alcohol
had reached epic proportions: in Kamchatka fourteen litres per head,
and in Sakhalin seventeen litres. Absenteeism, crime and human
degradation had become so widespread that they could be ignored no
longer.

On 4 April 1985 the Politburo discussed the problem. M. Solomentsev, who chaired the commission on this matter, gave his report
and produced his recommendations. Most of them amounted to some
form of prohibition: raising prices and reducing production, increasing
fines, denying prizes or bonuses and passes to rest homes, delaying
the issue of an apartment, prohibiting the sale of alcohol to anyone
under twenty-one years of age, and so on. As always, a new 'public
organization', the All-Union Society 'Sobriety', was created and
staffed with many thousands of workers.

V. Dementsev, First Deputy Minister of Finance, although he was
generally in support of the tone of the debate, noted with caution
that reducing the production and sale of alcohol would reduce income

to the state budget in 1984 by 4 billion roubles, in 1987 by 7.5 billion, in 1988 by 11 billion, in 1989 by 14 billion, and in 1990 by 15–16 billion. What would compensate for such losses, and how would the budget be brought back into balance?

Gorbachev interrupted him brusquely: 'What you've said is nothing new. We all know there's no money to cover it. But you're not proposing anything other than to keep the people drunk. So, try to make your comments more brief; you're not at the Finance Ministry, you're at a meeting of the Politburo.'[63] He was being demonstratively tough, partly to show his new authority, but also because the country was demanding tough action to put a stop to drunkenness.

However, the measures undertaken with such determination were quickly shown not to be working. Enormous queues for drink were everywhere, a thriving black market in vodka came into being, and home-distilling became widespread, using up hundreds of thousands of tonnes of sugar, which then disappeared from the shops, leading to sugar rationing. After three years, Gorbachev admitted defeat. A new instruction of October 1988 spoke of 'exaggerations', 'over-administering', 'inadmissible methods of prohibition', and so on. The ill-thought-out cavalry attack on drunkenness produced no positive results, and in time caused serious harm to the economic, social and even psychological state of the country, to say nothing of Gorbachev's public image.

Gorbachev altered himself in tune with society. The evolution was difficult and contradictory, but it was marked. This was particularly so in the sphere in which the Soviet Union lagged most seriously: that of human rights.

In the summer of 1985, on the eve of the Twelfth World Youth and Student Festival in Moscow, Chebrikov, Fedorchuk and Rekunkov – KGB chief, Interior Minister and Chief Procurator, respectively – requested Gorbachev's permission to take 'preventive measures' against politically unreliable people. They proposed that twenty-five Moscow citizens holding anti-Soviet views 'be arrested by decree for the duration of the festival'. As if without thinking, Gorbachev gave his approval, signing the order on 24 June.[64] The principle of dealing with political undesirables by 'administrative means', i.e. with no trial or due process, had of course been applied by Gorbachev's predecessors, most savagely by Stalin. Such acts throughout the Soviet period derived from the same Bolshevik impulse. Like so many Soviet citizens, Gorbachev would take some time to erase this Bolshevism from his soul.

General Secretaries always cherished the special services, on whom they relied above all. In May 1986 an All-Union convention of senior KGB officers took place in Moscow. Gorbachev made a speech, praising the 'organs' for their effective defence of state security. He was later sent a photograph of himself on the platform, surrounded by the KGB leadership. It was signed by Chebrikov on behalf of 'your loyal and devoted Chekists'.

By the following year, when he received Chebrikov's regular report on 'the enemy's sabotage among the Soviet creative intelligentsia', Gorbachev had become more circumspect. The report included the names of many well known Soviet writers who were allegedly being persistently 'worked on' by imperialist intelligence services. Chebrikov claimed that 'the enemy's secret services' were keeping a close watch on such writers as Anatoly Rybakov, Felix Svetov, Vladimir Soloukhin, Bulat Okudzhava, Faizil Iskander, Boris Mozhaev and Vladimir Kornilov, and he named Alexander Solzhenitsyn, Lev Kopelev, Vladimir Maximov and Vasili Aksyonov, all of them now living abroad, as 'hostile elements'. Gorbachev's response was neutral. On 16 July 1986 he replied: 'Circulate to all members of the Politburo and candidate members, and Central Committee Secretaries. Comrades Ligachev and Yakovlev to discuss this with me.'[65]

We now know that Gorbachev was not in full agreement with the KGB's proposals, and that he intended conducting a more flexible policy towards the creative intelligentsia, in order to win their support for his reforms. In October 1986 Andrei Sakharov wrote to Gorbachev, complaining about the treatment of dissidents and about his own internal exile. He wanted to be allowed to go home to Moscow. In December, Gorbachev took a bold and important decision: he would telephone Sakharov in Gorky and suggest that he return to Moscow to continue his scientific research.

A year earlier, in August 1985, the Politburo had discussed Sakharov's request to allow his wife, Yelena Bonner, to go abroad for medical treatment. Chebrikov declared that 'Bonner exercises 100 per cent influence on Sakharov,' to which Gorbachev responded: 'That's Zionism for you.' Ryzhkov took a more lenient line: 'I am in favour of letting Bonner go abroad. It is the humane thing to do. If she stays there, there'll be a fuss, of course. But then we would have a chance to influence Sakharov ourselves.'[66]

Gorbachev realized that the regime had far more to gain by releasing Sakharov from exile than by keeping him bottled up in a town that was closed to foreigners. When the West heard about the telephone call from the General Secretary to the highest-ranking dissident inside the country, it was seen as an expression of generosity of spirit and humanitarianism, and Gorbachev's rating soared. What was forgotten in the euphoria was the fact that Sakharov had been exiled in the first place as an act of unbridled arbitrary rule, for which Gorbachev had not found it necessary to apologize, and the question of how a single phone call was enough to correct the situation. That one call was a breakthrough in the official attitude to dissidents, but it also demonstrated the absence of the rule of law that still characterized the USSR.

The Supreme Court issued a decree terminating the exile and giving a pardon to Sakharov's wife. The President of the Academy of Science, Guri Marchuk, was asked by Gorbachev to go to Gorky. On 22 December 1986, after returning from seeing Sakharov, Marchuk reported to the Central Committee: 'An important moment in our conversation was the point M.S. Gorbachev had asked me to raise with Sakharov, namely, that he believed in the sincerity of Sakharov's letter. There was a most powerful reaction to this. For a long time Sakharov was silent, he tried to say something but could not.' Besieged by the KGB on all sides, Sakharov could hardly believe that the first Communist in the land was capable of believing his letter. The very possibility struck him dumb.

Marchuk wrote further: 'I have formed the following impression of my two-hour conversation with Sakharov. He is in a state of shock and utter confusion from the telephone conversation with M.S. Gorbachev. He plainly never expected such a turn of events and will take a long time trying to comprehend the new situation. Knowing that his letter to Gorbachev has been believed, he is in a new and very responsible position. He is beginning to realize that in Moscow he faces a struggle above all with his wife and her anti-social circle, and he is simply tired of it all and would like to carry on quietly with his scientific work.'[67]

The Sakharov episode demonstrated not only that Gorbachev was capable of human feeling, but was also proof that he meant it when he said that 'democratism was not just a slogan, but is the essence of *perestroika*.'[68] He wanted the whole of society to trust him, as Sakharov had, and he was right to think that confidence in him would rise outside the country too.

As the person on whom so much depended, it was hard for Gorbachev to free himself of many of the defects he would later condemn. Practically until the failed coup in August 1991 he unequivocally trusted the security services, though they were fundamentally hostile to his reforms. Even as he was speaking of *glasnost*, democracy and human rights, he was reading KGB reports that effectively disavowed his democratic efforts. On 21 March 1988, for instance, Chebrikov reported on 'the work of the security organs in identifying authors of anonymous materials of a hostile character'. He wrote that there had been 'a 9.4 per cent increase in the number of people engaged in this practice, and that 1,312 authors of leaflets and letters, and signatories of petitions of an anti-Soviet character had been identified'. The report gave a breakdown of the number of blue-collar and white-collar workers, students and old-age pensioners thus discovered, the number who had been warned and those arrested and brought to trial on criminal charges.[69]

Behind the scenes of *perestroika*, Cheka life went on. Gorbachev, as General Secretary, was actively involved in running the agency. As before, the backbone of KGB personnel was approved by the Central Committee. Between 1986 and 1990 the Politburo approved KGB posts for a host of experts from the most varied spheres. Many came from the Ministry of Higher and Middle Special Education Institutions, the Ministry of Defence, specialist scientific research institutes and military schools. The Party itself supplied cadres directly to the KGB.

For seven decades the Bolshevik leadership had induced ingrained hypocrisy: they would say one thing, think another and do a third. Therefore any democratic act by the new General Secretary was taken by the majority of the population as an unexpected revelation, a statesmanlike event hinting at salvation. And on the whole Gorbachev did not disappoint these expectations. When USSR Procurator V. Terebilov wrote to the Central Committee in May 1986 proposing that the death penalty be abolished for women and persons aged between eighteen and twenty, Gorbachev noted on the margin of his memorandum: 'We recently agreed to widen the practice of commuting the death penalty to twenty years' loss of liberty. That was right. Comrade Terebilov's note broadens the issue further: should we keep so many criminal charges in the law for which the death penalty is applicable? We'll discuss this in the Politburo.'[70]

Gorbachev understood perfectly that the chief enemy of *perestroika* was the Party. He also knew that nothing could be done without the Party, which itself had begun the cosmetic repair of the system. Yet he did not want 'voluntarily' to annul Article 6 of the Soviet Constitution, which began: 'The leading and guiding force of Soviet society, the nucleus of its political system, its state and public organizations, is the Communist Party of the Soviet Union.'[71] On a number of occasions the Politburo discussed the question of how to preserve this article. The members knew it was not possible, but they still hoped. It is not easy to give up power.

On 20 November 1989 Gorbachev announced: 'We will have to fight for Article 6 of the Constitution ... We have to stick by the argument that there's no great hurry, no emergency.'[72]

A fortnight or so later he again proposed a way to postpone making any decision on this fundamental issue. At the Second Congress of Deputies of the USSR, he suggested: 'The Party congress is coming. There, we shall discuss and bring in a resolution [on Article 6].' He added: 'The Party will not hold on to Article 6, but to real politics and action.'[73] The experienced politician was retreating slowly, clinging to the least foothold in a desperate rearguard action. Such measures suggest that Gorbachev was one of the last Communist 'romantics', a man who believed in the possibility of reconstructing Communism with a human face, of preserving the Leninist system after its 'renewal'.

Another of Gorbachev's paradoxes is that, though a convinced Communist and Leninist, he thought it was possible to introduce democracy into the Leninist system, albeit a Communist kind of democracy. Even when the infamous Article 6 had been removed from the Constitution, Gorbachev did all he could to maintain the influence of the Party in society, and several sessions of the Politburo were devoted to finding ways of doing this in the changed circumstances. A special resolution was adopted on 'certain measures for the lawful guarantee of the Party's viability'. Many state properties were re-designated as Party property, including printing presses, archives, libraries and rest homes, and there was vague mention of the Party's funding activities.[74] This is probably where the mysterious question of the Party funds originated, a problem that the post-Soviet government has so far been unable to solve. The Party was quietly preparing to live in the new 'democratic society', and to this end undoubtedly salted away large sums in Russia and abroad. In 1995, when the democratic parties and groups in Russia had only a handful of publications in their hands, the Communist organizations owned more than a hundred central and provincial newspapers.

In his keynote article 'The Socialist Idea and Revolutionary *Perestroika*', which appeared at the end of 1989, Gorbachev recognized that 'usually even the term "democratic socialism" provoked a negative reaction, being identified with a reformist, opportunistic line in the socialist movement.' But he declared that, with the help of *perestroika*, it would be possible to create 'not just human, but also democratic socialism'.[75] This amounted to an admission that Gorbachev personified reformism and opportunism in the socialist movement, though it took little courage to say so on the threshold of 1990.

The paradox of Gorbachev can be simply expressed: the man who killed Communism was a convinced Communist. Even at the Twenty-Eighth Party Congress in the summer of 1990, under the heading 'Towards a human, democratic socialism', and at which many new and sensible ideas were expressed, a thesis was advanced which at once rendered everything pointless: 'The CPSU is a party of socialist choice and Communist prospects.'[76] They just could not part with the old Leninist baggage. I was a candidate for the programme commission of that Congress, but I was voted out by the orthodox Bolsheviks.

Gorbachev genuinely wanted to bring democracy closer, but not at the price of 'Communist prospects'.

The Lesson of Chernobyl

Many incidents which seemed at first glance to be of a regional character left an indelible mark on the last years of the USSR. One such was the huge accident at the nuclear power station at Chernobyl, near

Kiev. The tragedy, which was caused by incompetent, if not criminal, handling of the advanced technology, became a symbol of the collapse of the Communist system, and revealed the authorities' profound neglect of the interests of the population as a whole. There had been many forewarnings of a disaster such as that which eventually took place at Chernobyl, but the public knew little about them.

The USSR entered the nuclear race when at 7 a.m. on 29 August 1949 the Soviet army exploded its first atomic bomb. On 30 October 1961 the developers of the Soviet hydrogen bomb exploded a device on Novaya Zemlya, an island above the Arctic Circle, equivalent to fifty megatonnes of TNT, and another of thirty megatonnes was exploded 'in honour of the Twenty-Second Party Congress'. Khrushchev was delighted, and immediately gave his assent for a test of 100 megatonnes. The scientists, however, managed to persuade him not to go ahead with this experiment.

On 14 September 1954, at the Totsk testing-ground in the region of Chkalov (later Orenburg) in western Siberia, a troop-training exercise under Marshal Zhukov took place with real nuclear weapons. As the Supreme Soviet Deputy from Orenburg in the 1980s, I visited the village of Totsk several times. My first visit had been much earlier, when as the commanding officer of a tank unit I took part in routine training exercises at the site of the nuclear explosion. The earth had the appearance of worn-out asphalt.

Before the explosion, all the inhabitants of the villages of Yelshanka-2, Orlovka, Ivanovka and Makhovka, in all 1,633 families, were removed from their dwellings. Left behind were forty head of livestock, including cows, horses and camels, and three hundred sheep. From a height of nine thousand metres a TU-4 dropped the bomb, which was timed to explode at 350 metres. A large number of shelters, dug-outs, trenches and houses had been built and filled with the animals. Military equipment was placed all over the site, and after the explosion troops were carried on top of tanks through the epicentre of the blast.[77] Only forty years later would a democratic Russian government consider it necessary to provide some compensation to the victims of that monstrous test.

Three years after the Totsk experiment, in September 1957 in Chelyabinsk region at weapons-grade plutonium plant No. 817, a huge explosion occurred, destroying a tank containing radioactive solution. This minor Chernobyl was kept completely secret from the country and the rest of the world. The site of the newly constructed factory, the army engineers' barracks, a concentration camp and the villages of Berdyaniki, Saltykovo, Golikaevo and others were all subjected to powerful radiation. A very large expanse of land was blanketed by Strontium-90.

On 19 October 1957, the Council of Ministers and Central Committee responded to this calamity by decreeing that 'within a two-week period proposals would be submitted on the resettlement of the inhabitants of the villages of Berdyaniki, Saltykovo, Golikaevo and Kirpichiki before 1 March 1958.' Five months to evacuate a small number of villagers from their devastated homes.[78] The accident had taken place on 29 September 1957, the Presidium, i.e. Politburo, had been informed on 7 October, but did not even discuss the affair until 19 October. Its decree was eloquent: 'The measures taken by the Ministry of Medium Machine-Building on this issue are sufficient.'[79] Apart from evacuation by 1 March 1958, these measures boiled down to the setting up of radiation monitoring-posts, a one-off payment of four hundred roubles to villagers capable of working and of one hundred to those who were not, and the building of some protective huts.

The decree ignored that fact that the fallout had passed through many other populated areas. The absence of publicity deprived the local population of any chance of learning about the real dimensions of the threat, even though, according to plainly doctored figures, the area affected immediately after the explosion alone was twenty thousand square kilometres.

At the end of October 1978 the Minister of Shipbuilding reported to the Central Committee: 'On 20 October 1978 at 23.52 hours, a barge carrying radioactive waste from refitted atomic submarines sank eighteen miles north-west of the island of Kolguev [in the Barents Sea], in water forty-five metres deep ... A special commission has been set up to investigate the unauthorized sinking of the barge.'[80] Such incidents were effectively hushed up by the authorities, and the population knew nothing. Not that there was anything they could have said or done had they been told. In 1986 the situation was very different. It was no longer possible to keep such things quiet, however much the government wished to do so.

A year after taking office, Gorbachev faced a test of the most serious kind. It was perhaps then that he finally realized that *glasnost* was two-edged, and that any attempt to apply the old rules of publicity would be harshly judged. The catastrophe at Chernobyl, like the Afghan war, materially exacerbated the economic and political aspects of the crisis facing the country, as well as the position of the General Secretary.

On 25–27 April 1986 the Ministry of Defence was conducting refresher courses for senior commanding and political officers at the Lvov training ground. Everything was going as usual, with speeches and lectures from the Defence Minister, the Chief of Political Administration, and so on. During a break on 26 April, I was with a group of generals when we were told by the Chief of the General Staff that an accident had occurred at the Chernobyl nuclear power station 130 kilometres north of Kiev. The news was given to us calmly, and none of us paid particular attention. Accidents were not exactly a rarity in our country. Defence Minister Sokolov, however, flew straight to Moscow, and next day a number of participants left the meeting in military aircraft.

At midday on 26 April Deputy Energy Minister A. Makhunin had sent an 'urgent report' to the Central Committee, where it was passed from the General Department to the Atomic Energy Department and, later in the day, finally to the General Secretary. The report read: 'On 26.04.86 at 01.21 hours at the Chernobyl AES [atomic energy power station], following shutdown of the reactor in Block 4 and during removal of parts for repair, an explosion occurred in the upper part of the reactor.' The report mentioned fire damage. 'At 03.30 hours the fire was extinguished. AES personnel are taking steps to cool the active zone of the reactor. In the opinion of the Third Main Administration of the USSR Health Ministry, special measures, including evacuation of the population from the town, are not required.'[81]

By the evening of 26 April the whole world was talking about a major nuclear disaster in the USSR. Moscow was silent. Throughout the next day the foreign news media were reporting the movement of radioactive clouds towards the west, north and south. Explanations were demanded of the Kremlin, but Moscow said nothing.

Finally, on 28 April at 11 a.m. the Politburo met as usual. No major decision could be taken without its assent, whether the issue was a foreign tour by the Bolshoi Theatre, military manoeuvres, building a bridge, or giving out information on a nuclear accident. Candidate member V. Dolgikh gave an inconsistent account of the position at the power station: 'An explosion took place . . . The level of radiation in the area of the reactor is one thousand Roentgens . . . The population is being evacuated, out of twenty-five thousand people in the town five thousand still remain . . . Helicopters have begun dropping red clay and lead . . .'

The discussion between these non-specialists was inevitably of an amateurish nature. They talked about lead, sandbags and the temperature inside the reactor. Finally, Gorbachev asked: 'How should we handle the information?'

DOLGIKH: We have to complete the localization of the source of radiation.

GORBACHEV: We must issue an announcement as soon as possible, we must not delay . . .

LIGACHEV: We should not postpone giving information of what has happened . . .

YAKOVLEV: The quicker we announce it, the better it'll be . . .

Hours passed, the meeting closed, but still nothing came out of Moscow. Finally, late that evening a bland announcement that an accident had taken place and that measures were in hand was broadcast on radio and television.

Meanwhile, the outside world was testing the atmosphere for fallout. Western journalists jammed the switchboards of Soviet official agencies. Ambassadors from numerous countries were becoming involved. Gorbachev was told that hundreds of millions of people around the world were gripped by the drama at Chernobyl, far more than when the South Korean Boeing had been shot down in 1983. On that occasion, a wave of indignation had swept the world, whereas now a surge of alarm was being felt. Realizing that he had anything but a routine problem on his hands, and that a combined approach was needed, Gorbachev summoned physicists, the Defence Minister, nuclear energy experts and KGB officers. He called another Politburo meeting for the next day, 29 April, and came to it armed with advice from the experts. He opened with a terse remark: 'Perhaps we aren't reacting as sharply as the states around us?'

Dolgikh replied with a new report: 'The glow inside the crater has diminished ... Bags are still being dropped by helicopters. 360 personnel plus 160 volunteers are engaged here. But there have been refusals to do this work...'

Gorbachev made a practical proposal which had been prepared for him: 'We must form an operational group from the Politburo, with Ryzhkov as chairman, and Ligachev, Vorotnikov, Chebrikov, Dolgikh, Sokolov and Vlasov.'

He then asked: 'How are we to deal with the population and inter-national public opinion?' After a pause, he continued: 'The more honestly we conduct ourselves, the better. To ensure that a shadow of suspicion should not fall on our equipment, we must say that the power station was undergoing a planned repair...'

As for public opinion, only Yakovlev and Aliyev had a definite idea: the public and foreign journalists must be given full information.

GROMYKO: We should give more information to the fraternal coun-
    tries, and London and Washington should be given particular infor-
    mation. The situation should be explained to Soviet Ambassadors.
LIGACHEV: Maybe we ought not to give a press conference?
GORBACHEV: Most probably the best thing would be to issue a single
    progress report on the handling of the accident.[82]

The meeting finally agreed the text of an announcement in the name of the Council of Ministers, couched in terms that might have been used to announce an ordinary fire at a warehouse:

... the accident occurred in one of the areas of Block 4 and caused the
destruction of part of the reactor housing, damage to the reactor itself
and a degree of leakage of radioactive substances. The three remaining
blocks have been shut down, they are in good order and are being held
in reserve. Two people were killed in the accident.
    Immediate measures have been taken to deal with the breakdown.
At the present time, the radiation situation at the power station and
its vicinity has been stabilized, and medical assistance is being given to
the victims ...

In the text distributed to socialist countries, another sentence was added: 'Levels of pollution exceed the permitted norms by a small amount, but not to an extent that calls for special measures to protect the population.'[83]

The Politburo's Operational Group now began meeting regularly. Everyone was concerned about conditions at the country's other eighteen nuclear power stations. The West was offering specialist technical and medical assistance, but Moscow responded to this with great restraint.

There were almost forty thousand servicemen in the vicinity of Chernobyl. Dykes were built, and a tunnel was dug underneath the reactor. It was decided to erect a tomb over Block 4. Gorbachev remarked: 'We were the first to build an AES, and we're the first to build a coffin for one.'[84]

The question that continued to torment the Politburo had been expressed by Gorbachev again on 5 May: 'What about the outside world?' Giving the reply himself, he said: 'We must give out information calmly and in a balanced way, but without complacency.'

Chernobyl, which became a symbol of the decay of the Soviet system, was also a lesson for Gorbachev, a test of his willingness to engage in genuine *glasnost*. Two weeks after the disaster, Ryzhkov began his Politburo report on the situation: 'The main thing is that the accident is being dealt with directly by the Politburo and General Secretary M.S. Gorbachev, who is in continuous charge of the question.'[85] Greater pressure was being put on subordinates, however confused and discouraged they might be, to find practical solutions and carry out the orders issued by the Politburo and the General Secretary. Gorbachev knew he must remain cool-headed in the whirlwind of world alarm. On 5 May he had told his colleagues: 'Panic is a luxury subordinates can afford, but not the Politburo and the government.'[86]

It seems that it was not long after the explosion at Chernoybyl that Gorbachev came to understand the power of world opinion. It took him a long time to work out a policy of what should and what should not be said, how to save the country's face, and his own, while measuring out information. Although on 28 April he had told the Politburo, 'We must issue an announcement as soon as possible, we must not delay,'[87] he subsequently tried on several occasions to control the content and quantity of information. On 5 May, for instance, he said: 'More general information on Ukraine should be given via local channels. Factological [sic] information should be given via Union channels. Maybe the scale of information for the outside world could be widened. The enemy is asking questions that might allow him to make a general judgement of us and at the same time fling mud at us.'[88] The outside world was still 'the enemy', and still wanted to 'fling mud'.

At about this time, Ryzhkov and Chebrikov sent a note to Gorbachev advising that 'the nature of information on the accident at Chernobyl AES should remain unchanged (especially for the USA, England, Canada and other capitalist countries).'[89] Gorbachev signed the report and evidently agreed with its content. In his book on *perestroika*, however, he would write of Chernobyl: 'The whole truth was told ... It was impermissible to think that we would restrict ourselves to half-measures and try to be smart ... That would have been a cowardly position to take, and one unworthy of a politician.'[90]

Although Gorbachev was exceptional in seeing how deep in the mire of class hatred and irreconcilability Lenin and his successors had engulfed the country, offers of aid from 'capitalist countries' were being viewed with suspicion. Even the questions they were asking were allegedly calculated to be used to fling mud at the Soviet Union. In July 1986, Armand Hammer, the president of Occidental Petroleum, and Professor Gale of the University of California proposed holding an international conference in Los Angeles on the effects of Chernobyl and how to overcome them. Moscow naturally received an invitation. Health Minister S. Burenkov and one of the heads of the Central Committee Department of Science, V. Grigoriev, urged the Politburo not to accept an invitation to a conference that was devoted to a Soviet misfortune.[91]

Even a month after the accident Gorbachev had lingering suspicions of a traditional Bolshevik kind. On 29 May he voiced these at the Politburo: 'Workers are writing that there was sabotage at Chernobyl. That's hardly possible. The explosion took place inside the reactor.'[92] Had the explosion occurred outside the reactor, he implied, he would have been less certain.

Chernobyl exposed much about the system that Gorbachev wanted to reform. Sluggishness and inflexibility, the habit of waiting for orders from above, the lack of accurate accounting and preparedness for emergencies. No precautionary measures were in place in the event of an accident, and there were no protective measures for individuals. 'Civil defence', while impressive in scale, was poorly planned. As might

be expected, the families of the top officials were the first to be evacuated. Yet again the lapses of local leaders were made up for by the
heroism of ordinary people, such as Major L. Telyatnikov and Lieutenants V. Pravik and V. Kibenok, who died from exposure to
radiation.

First responses to Chernobyl were often superficial and uncon-
cerned. The chairman of the state agricultural sector, V. Murakhov-
sky, an old friend of Gorbachev's from Stavropol, reported to the
Politburo on 8 May that experimental data had so far shown that the
loss of agricultural production due to fallout in the vicinity of the
power station was minimal. 'With the appropriate processing, production can be used for consumption or as animal feed. At present,
the high content of radioactive iodine in nearly all the milk in the
Gomel region, in five districts of Kiev region, three districts of Cherni-
gov region and two of Zhitomir, means that milk cannot be used in
the fresh state. It should therefore be reprocessed as butter or cheese.
It has been established during the slaughter of large horned-cattle
and pigs that washing the animals and also removing their lymph
nodes produces meat suitable for consumption.'[93]

It was clear that neither the Health Ministry, Civil Defence, Ministry of Energy and Electrification, nor the local authorities had any
idea of what to do. They were waiting for instructions from the
leadership, and not all of them were willing or able to implement the
practical steps recommended by the scientists. The gigantic nuclear
site virtually lacked any warning system. On 5 May the deputy chairman of the government, Boris Shcherbina, told the Politburo that
'weddings were going on in Chernobyl until the evening of 26 April'.[94]
Only the army and the builders of the sarcophagus responded
adequately to the disaster.

Chernobyl may have jolted Gorbachev closer to his 'new thinking'.
On the other hand, even before it, his attitude to the nuclear problem
had been profoundly realistic. In April 1985 he had ordered that the
North Korean leadership be told that a nuclear reactor being built
with Soviet help must be under the control of the International Atomic
Energy Commission.[95] In July of the same year he had informed
Colonel Qaddafi that he would not agree to the Soviet-built nuclear
research centre in Libya being used for the production of heavy water,
which could lead to Libya's acquiring nuclear weapons.[96] He insisted

that the Libyans place their nuclear research under the control of the International Atomic Energy Commission.

The nuclear, or anti-nuclear, side of Gorbachev's maturing 'new thinking' was always clear. He understood that without fundamental improvements in nuclear security, *perestroika* would accomplish nothing substantive internationally. Without drawing attention to his 'reformist' point of view, in July 1986 Gorbachev announced: 'Global nuclear war can no longer be the continuation of rational politics, as it would bring the end of all life, and therefore of all politics.'[97] For a Leninist, this was undoubtedly an original – and true – argument.

The disaster at Chernobyl appeared to be of a technological, organizational kind, but in fact it highlighted a host of weaknesses in the Soviet Union. The great glowing crater at Block 4 had revealed deep cracks in the state. The symbolism of the event was not fully appreciated. Such insights would only come later. After the Afghan fiasco, which Gorbachev condemned but which dragged on for another four years, Chernobyl was the next bell tolling for the system. There were many such along the thorny path to reform: the failure of efforts to accelerate economic recovery, the attempts to stifle democratic heresies in the Party, the failed hope of saving *perestroika* by moving around Party cadres, and the delayed response to the rise of national consciousness in the republics.

The End of Empire

All the empires in history have fallen apart sooner or later. The chief destroyer of the USSR was also its creator, Lenin, who in 1920 began to abolish the most progressive form of state administration, the provinces, forming in their place the national entities. For as long as the USSR was a unitary state, this innovation had little significance. As soon as the process of democratization and *glasnost* began after 1985, however, a powerful upsurge of national spirit ensued.

It was not universally understood that, in fighting against Communist totalitarianism, the enemy was also the physical expression of its existence, namely the USSR. The socio-political system and the national-state system were closely connected. The weaker the Communist oligarchy became, the weaker the bindings of the USSR.

Whether a confederative 'Union of Soviet Sovereign Republics', as Gorbachev proposed to name a new structure, would have survived is a hypothetical question. All such efforts were destroyed by the coup of August 1991. It was the last push that toppled the state edifice.

When in May 1991 work began at Novo-Ogarevo to prepare a new Union Treaty, it was clear that in the circumstances a new Union was unlikely to be a federation, but rather a confederation. This might have been a positive achievement, a historic compromise. As President Yeltsin's military adviser, I went with him several times to see Gorbachev in the Kremlin in order to discuss the more complex aspects of the treaty, in particular the status of the former autonomous territories. For instance, the Tatar Autonomous Republic was insisting on signing the treaty as a Union republic. Yeltsin, Khasbulatov and myself, representing Russia, and Gorbachev, Shakhnazarov and Lukyanov, representing the Union, were in agreement that it was important to act quickly. On several occasions I witnessed Gorbachev and Yeltsin trying to form a treaty that would preserve the Union, albeit not in strictly unitary form. Both of them have since been accused of causing the break-up of the Union, but in fact they both wanted to save it, if necessary in altered form.[98]

In July 1991 the USSR Supreme Soviet supported the draft treaty on a union of sovereign states, and on 2 August Gorbachev, speaking on television as the Soviet President, announced that the treaty would be signed on 20 August.[99] One other step was needed to safeguard the Union, and that had already been accomplished by the referendum of 17 March 1991, which supported the idea of a renewed USSR. Gorbachev ought to have seen to the immediate signing of the Union Treaty, but instead, having fixed the date as 20 August, he went on holiday. This was a momentous mistake.

His strategic error was that, having declared that democracy was the essence of *perestroika*, he found no common language with the forces of anti-Communism. 'I see no other way than democracy,' he declared even after the coup,[100] but before the drama of 19–21 August he had been keeping the spokesmen of democracy at arm's length, and since then he has cast doubt on their credentials as democrats. Just as the country itself had been corrupted by Communism, so was its democracy.

The draft treaty was attacked from left and right. The democrats argued that it should not be signed for up to a year, during which time elections should be held for a Constituent Assembly that would determine all matters of power, as well as the form of the new Union.[101] This was probably a bad idea. The new Union Treaty ought to have been signed as soon as possible, and then, perhaps, a Constituent Assembly could have been convened on the basis of the 'new' USSR as an objective fact. It is possible that once the treaty had been signed, a Constituent Assembly would not have been needed.

For their part, the conservatives, especially the Chairman of the USSR Supreme Soviet, Anatoly Lukyanov, cast doubt on the text of the treaty when the coup was already under way, and proposed 'additional discussion at a session of the USSR Supreme Soviet, and then, perhaps, at the Congress of People's Deputies'.[102] Had the coup succeeded, which Lukyanov was counting on, it is not difficult to imagine the kind of 'discussion' that would have taken place.

The conservatives were opposed to the very meaning of the treaty, the idea of a Union of sovereign states. The word 'socialist' had been diplomatically dropped after a long battle by the democrats, and even the Supreme Soviet had been compelled to accept this on 12 July. The point was fundamental and historic: the USSR could be preserved, but not as a *socialist* state. But as what? The democrats argued that this was precisely what a Constituent Assembly should decide, but that it should be a democratic state, whatever the outcome.

The summer of 1991 was a turbulent time. At the G7 summit in London in June, Gorbachev had received nothing but patronizing words of encouragement from the powerful Western countries which were watching the Soviet Union as it slid further into economic disarray, and they were still unwilling to commit funds to support the reforms. Yeltsin was elected President of the Russian Federation on a huge wave of popularity. Along with Russia, all the other republics had declared their sovereignty and were preparing to secure the maximum possible rights in the new Treaty of Union that had been elaborated in the Novo-Ogarevo negotiations and that was scheduled for signature on 20 August.

On 18 August, a group of those who wanted to restore hardline Bolshevik rule set up a 'State Committee for the State of Emergency'. It included Vice-President Gennady Yanaev, KGB chief Vladimir Kryuchkov, Prime Minister Valentin Pavlov, Interior Minister Boris

Pugo, Defence Minister Marshal Yazov, the head of the Party's General Department Valeri Boldin, Central Committee Secretary Oleg Baklanov, Politburo member Oleg Shenin, Deputy Defence Minister Valentin Varennikov, the President's own KGB head of security Yuri Plekhanov, Chairman of the Peasants' Union Vasili Starodubtsev, and Alexander Tizyakov, who represented the interests of the military-industrial sector.

A five-man delegation from the Committee, consisting of Baklanov, Shenin, Boldin, Varennikov and Plekhanov, arrived at Gorbachev's new summer palace at Foros that night with a demand that he sign a decree declaring a state of emergency. He did not believe their claim that Yeltsin had already been arrested, but they succeeded in isolating him by cutting the palace's communications and surrounding it with a double line of guards. Gorbachev nevertheless flatly refused to cooperate with what he denounced as a criminal conspiracy, and the delegation returned to Moscow to impart the bad news to their fellow-plotters, who now had serious doubts about the whole idea.

Having crossed the Rubicon, however, they decided there was no turning back. On 19 August they announced that, for reasons of health, Gorbachev was no longer able to carry out his duties as head of state, and that his deputy, Yanaev, was taking over. Tanks were sent to surround the Russian parliament building, known as the White House, where tens of thousands of Muscovites gathered in demonstrative support of the Russian President, Yeltsin, who showed himself to be a master of public relations on an international scale. Live film was transmitted to the world's television screens of Yeltsin standing on a tank, denouncing the Emergency Committee and proclaiming his own control of the army and the KGB. The BBC World Service and other Western TV and radio networks kept the Russian population informed, their own mass media having been placed under strict control.

But the Soviet Army was as disoriented and confused as Soviet society itself, and it was extremely unlikely from the start that any soldier would fire on unarmed citizens in the heart of the capital. Three people died, all as a result of accidents. The Commander-in-Chief of the armed forces, Marshal Yevgeny Shaposhnikov, later revealed that he refused an order to send fighter-bombers to the White House with the presumed object of bombing it.

Without the backing of even the diminished authority of the Soviet President, who was also still the Party General Secretary and Supreme Commander-in-Chief, the army might bark, but it would not bite. It was faced down by Yeltsin, who had the power of the people at his back, and it sensed the lack of resolve among the plotters, whose nominal leader, Yanaev, was said to be in a state of permanent drunkenness.

With reports coming in of huge demonstrations in support of Yeltsin on the streets of the second capital, Leningrad, the coup collapsed. Pugo, the Party Treasurer Nikolai Kruchina and Marshal Akhromeev all committed suicide within a day or two, and there were false reports that others, including Yazov and Marshal Moiseev, had followed suit. The coup leaders were arrested and imprisoned, as was Anatoly Lukyanov, the Chairman of the Supreme Soviet and Gorbachev's closest associate, but now regarded as a co-conspirator. They were accused of high treason, but the trial, which began in 1992 on amended charges, was suspended in confusion, and they were released from custody in 1993.

At the Fifth Congress of People's Deputies on 3 September 1991, Yeltsin announced: 'The revolt disrupted the signing of the Union Treaty, but it was unable to destroy the desire of the republics to build a new Union.' The new Union would be 'a free commonwealth of sovereign states with a common economic area, common armed forces, and strict guarantees of human rights in the territory of the entire country.'[103]

After the coup the disintegration of the USSR began, with Ukraine playing a particular role. The rupture of economic, spiritual and family ties, and the rift in an ancient history, now took place. Gorbachev's worst fears were realized. The Union had self-destructed. It is senseless to look for culprits. Almost everyone who wanted to break with the old, regimented, Bolshevik way of life despite themselves weakened the state structure, the Union, even as they weakened the Communist system. It was the bitter price of liberation.

Strictly speaking, the coup was not unexpected. Many people had spoken and written of the possibility of an army revolt. Transparent hints about 'a firm hand' were made at the Congress of People's Deputies. Generals stood as potential candidates in the presidential elections. Yeltsin, who had no need of extra votes and would have defeated anyone who stood against him, invited Colonel-General Alexander Rutskoi to be his Vice-President as a means of gaining greater leverage with the army. This would turn out to have been a grave error of judgement. Rutskoi was an ambitious, vain man, who had been most economically endowed by nature with intellectual ability, but once he had tasted power, he wanted more. He was, however, instrumental in helping to foil the coup, and at that time was a firm supporter of Yeltsin.

As the situation in the country worsened, Gorbachev, who was not popular with the military, tried somehow to secure their loyalty, but he had never taken a deep interest in military issues. The army was the ultimate argument in any internal quarrel, and had been used as such many times in Russian history. The Communists resorted to the army in August 1991, just as the nationalists and neo-fascists have done since then, and may continue to do until Russian democracy has stronger roots. In 1991, however, the army was not willing to risk the outbreak of civil war.

Gorbachev did not destroy the Communist system, but nothing he did stood in the way of its self-destruction. The system was doomed in any case. Even without Gorbachev it was likely to fall apart within another decade or two. The only field in which the USSR could compete with other countries was in the production of nuclear missiles. The approaching self-destruction of the system, as distinct from the USSR, was determined by a number of factors.

First, the insane arms race, in which, having achieved parity at fantastic cost, the Soviet Union finally overstrained itself. With more than a third of all the country's resources committed to military expenditure, sooner or later the effort would result in collapse.

Second, economic stagnation, which had become a permanent feature, increasingly exposed the economy's extremely low level of efficiency in the post-industrial age.

Third, the bureaucratic ossification of society, accompanied by dogmatic myths residing in the public mind, was turning the individual into a single-dimensional being.

Fourth, the unitary nature of the Union had hitherto managed to contain the pressure of nationalism inside the Bolshevik cauldron, but it was bound to burst sooner or later.

Fifth, the monopoly of a single political power, which had demonstrated its savage efficacy in time of war or other social upheaval, had become a heavy brake on the development of the country.

Sixth, the system, which ruled in the name of the 'collective' and 'society', had deprived the citizen of important rights and liberties. Up to three million Soviet citizens had left the country since its inception, drawn by the lure of freedom.

Seventh, the senseless adventure in Afghanistan dealt a severe blow to the system, as the authorities were unable to justify the losses to an increasingly sceptical and disgruntled population.

Darling of the West

When Gorbachev met George Bush after the August coup, the President was especially interested to know when the conspirators would be put on trial. Andrei Grachev, Gorbachev's press secretary, recalled that his boss brushed the question off with a joke, nodding in the direction of Brent Scowcroft, the US National Security Adviser: 'You should also keep an eye on your generals.'

Bush jokingly replied: 'If Scowcroft wanted my job, I'd let him have it with pleasure.'

'I wouldn't give mine up,' Gorbachev said, with unexpected seriousness. 'Especially at such a difficult time. The country is ready for radical changes, and is even demanding them.'[104]

Gorbachev approached the end of his rule sadly and, typically, surrounded by paradox: however ecstatic the West was about him, at home he was reviled in equal measure. Abroad he was practically deified. He received thousands of letters, congratulatory telegrams and invitations from the West, and innumerable articles and books were published on him. It is unlikely that any politician has ever had so much written about him in his own lifetime. He had clearly caught the world's imagination, symbolizing as he did the departure from the scene of the Bolshevik monster. Television viewers around the world saw a normal, pleasant-looking man who bore no resemblance to his six predecessors. When he spoke – which he did a great deal – people no longer felt the old fear.

It was not just that Gorbachev made a real impact on the hitherto ineffectual disarmament process: people responded to his ready smile, and felt they could trust him. He became an almost mythical personality, invested with far more virtues than he really possessed. It was easy to overlook the fact that he had begun his rule as had all previous General Secretaries, by swearing allegiance to Lenin and uttering barely concealed anathemas on the 'class enemy'.

Gorbachev's adviser on international affairs, Anatoly Chernyayev, has written of him:

> He is a clever, honest, conscientious, passionate man, made the wiser by knowing the rules of the organization game from top to bottom, wanting to improve everything, to perfect everything, to put an end to the absurdity and the disgraceful state of things ... He had a number of ideas on how to 'improve' the way of life. But at that stage they did not extend beyond the existing framework of society. This was the origin of the term *'obnovlenie'* (renewal), which soon emerged (and long remained on his lips). It took years of painful struggle to realize that this society could not be renewed. It was doomed and needed to be completely replaced.[105]

For his first two years in office, the seventh leader was viewed with suspicion by Western journalists and quite a few serious Sovietologists, who wondered how he differed from Brezhnev or Andropov, and whether his outward appearance was deceptive. In an article for the Russian-language magazine *Kontinent*, published in Germany, entitled 'Gorbachev – a Warning', Milovan Djilas wrote: 'Gorbachev will most likely turn out to be a temporary figure. In fact he is more the successor of Andropov than of the passive and immobile Chernenko ... The complexities and difficulties brought about by post-industrial change will compel Gorbachev to devote more attention to foreign policy. None the less, this will not make him ignore the interests of the Soviet empire or abolish the supreme position of the Party bureaucracy.'[106]

Until he became the darling of the West, Gorbachev acted almost in the same way as his predecessors. The last years of Brezhnev's rule, like those of Andropov and Chernenko, had been a time of morbid coagulation within the hierarchy. Practically as soon as he took office, Gorbachev began little by little to take the organization into his own hands. He saw that positive results were not going to come in foreign policy as long as Andrei Gromyko was Foreign Minister. Gromyko was an experienced diplomat, but he was also a conservative of the Stalinist school. However, Gorbachev was indebted to him for nominating him as General Secretary. It would be difficult to put him out to grass on a pension, but nor could he be kept on at the Foreign Ministry. Gorbachev was a wily tactician. At a Politburo meeting at the end of July 1985, he proposed making Gromyko Chairman of the Presidium of the USSR Supreme Soviet, effectively head of state – a post as high as it was decorative, given the omnipotence of the Party and the impotence of the soviets.

Gromyko, approaching his eightieth year, accepted the gift with pleasure. The session continued:

> GORBACHEV: The question now is, who should be Foreign Minister? We won't find a second Gromyko, with his experience and knowledge of world problems. But then Andrei Andreyevich himself didn't start out on his diplomatic career with the experience and knowledge he has now. He was not the same man at the Tehran Conference that he is now. We have plenty of qualified diplomats. Kornienko is capable. Maltsev less so. Chervonenko has done both Party work and diplomatic work. There is also Dobrynin. But still our thoughts have been moving in a different direction. The post requires a major figure, someone from our own group.[107]

He then proposed Eduard Shevardnadze. This caused some surprise, as Shevardnadze, in stark contrast to Gromyko, had no experience whatever of foreign relations, virtually all of his political life having been spent in Georgia. But, as always, everyone agreed with the General Secretary. In this way, Gorbachev was giving notice of major changes to come in foreign policy.

Andropov and Chernenko had been forced by ill-health to be virtual hermits, but without personal contact at the highest level it is hardly possible to conduct international politics. With the Politburo's approval, therefore, in November 1985 Gorbachev met President Reagan in Geneva in what was essentially a reconnaissance encounter.

Much was new to him: the army of journalists, the punctilious diplomatic protocol, the long-range camera lenses scanning every feature of his face. He naïvely believed that he had 'got the better' of Reagan in the talks, and this was reflected in the 'orientation' telegram he sent to Castro, Li Xiannian, Kim Il-sung, and other Communist Third World leaders: 'The talk with Reagan was a real skirmish. [Donald] Regan – Reagan's closest aide – later said that no one had ever talked so frankly and with such force to the President before ... In Geneva we had no intention of letting Reagan get away with just a photo session, which he loves so much.'[108]

From Geneva Gorbachev flew to Prague, where on 21 November he met leaders of the Warsaw Pact countries. Within the familiar circle of the socialist camp, he felt like a conqueror, and spoke about the meeting with Reagan in a tone of triumph. This was understandable, given his background as an unknown Party functionary from the provinces.

At the Politburo after his return, Gorbachev's colleagues naturally approved his report and noted in a resolution: 'The principle and flexibility displayed by Gorbachev, in carrying out our line, have secured advantageous political and propaganda results for the Soviet Union and for the cause of peace ... The willingness we showed for sensible compromises have placed the present American administration on the defensive and landed a serious blow on the ideology and policy of their "crusade".'[109]

Gromyko was no longer Foreign Minister, but the language of diplomatic and political decrees remained the same: enemies, adversaries, offensives, defence, blows and counterblows.

In 1986, a year before Gorbachev's book *Perestroika and New Thinking for Our Country and the Whole World* came out, the Politburo passed a 'top secret' decree on 'measures for strengthening our resistance to the American policy of "neo-globalism"'. The measures proposed were 'to implement plans for the social and economic development of the country', and 'to maintain military power at the proper level'.[110] A year later Gorbachev would make an offer to the world community to 'put moral and ethical norms at the basis of international politics'.[111] The evolution of his views on foreign policy, to judge by the documents, was happening very fast.

Western observers were quick to note Gorbachev's advantages over his predecessors: his lack of constraint, his fluency in speech and, albeit still slight, his emphasis on universal human values. They were, however, put on their guard by his constant references to Lenin and socialism. Despite these tendencies, however, he made a good impression with his openness, goodwill, persuasiveness and readiness to compromise. To be sure, some of those who knew him well were less sure about these positive qualities. In particular, Alexandrov-Agentov was of the opinion that Gorbachev's 'outward openness and benevolent affability was rather a habitual mask behind which there was no truly warm and good attitude towards people. Inside he was always coldly calculating'.[112]

The West studied Gorbachev closely, observing how he dressed, how he spoke, how he handled journalists and behaved in front of the camera. Unlike Andropov and Chernenko, he provided them with plenty of opportunities, as he loved meeting world statesmen, ambassadors and journalists. It was widely noticed that he listened very little and spoke very much. Of course he talked about *perestroika*, the new phase, the progress of the changes, the renewal of socialism, and the fact that he was thinking of returning to Lenin. In 1993 an American publisher was inspired to bring out an encyclopedia of Gorbachevian expressions, there were so many.[113] In the West it was thought that, intentionally or not, Gorbachev's actions were slowing down and weakening the Communist system and making it more accessible to liberal ideas. The idea that a General Secretary, while proclaiming his loyalty to Lenin, was actually bringing about the destruction of Leninism, was breathtaking. So unlikely was this proposition that some analysts believed the Gorbachev phenomenon was nothing but an elaborate plan of the Kremlin, if not of the KGB, to infiltrate a Trojan horse into the West.

Nevertheless, serious Western publications began to speak of Gorbachev in increasingly respectful and ultimately ecstatic tones, and it seems he may have succumbed to the flattery and adulation. He had been propelled from virtual obscurity in the Russian provinces to the centre of the world stage in so few years that it would have been surprising if he had not been affected.

On occasion, Gorbachev himself would refer to his personal role. In February 1986, at the end of a Politburo meeting, he held his colleagues back and said: 'I'd like to give the comrades an important item of recent information. On 12 February this year the White House Chief of Staff, Regan, held a confidential talk with the heads of the newspaper the *Washington Post* on the question of US policy towards the Soviet Union. He said they had regarded the most dangerous

Soviet leader in recent years to be Andropov. But the new Soviet leader, Gorbachev, is even more dangerous.'[114]

It would have been perfectly normal for the Politburo Secretariat to have circulated information such as this to the members, but for Gorbachev to have done so suggests that perhaps the image he had gained abroad had gone to his head.

His book *Perestroika and New Thinking for Our Country and the Whole World* (1987) was striking not so much for the positive message it contained as for the fact that its ideas had been expressed long before by such thinkers as Albert Schweitzer, Bertrand Russell, Andrei Sakharov and many others. Gorbachev was of course entitled to offer his own interpretation, whether or not he was entitled to describe as 'new thinking' ideas which had barely taken root in his own mind. The essence of the idea was, in his own words, a simple one: 'Nuclear war cannot be the means to achieve political, economic, ideological or any other goals whatsoever.'[115] This laudable sentiment was of course included in all the main declarations, resolutions and documents of the United Nations.

Gorbachev's 'new thinking', moreover, cohabited in his mind with more traditional Bolshevik-militaristic motives. On returning from his meeting with Ronald Reagan at Reykjavik, he gave a detailed account to the Politburo in which it was not the peacemaker speaking, but the Bolshevik fighter, the robust ideologue, the political victor:

> After Reykjavik we have scored more points in our favour than we did after Geneva ... But the new situation demands new approaches in our military doctrine, in the structure of our armed forces, their deployment and so on, and in the defence industry. We have to think carefully about what we should do, if there are not going to be any medium-range missiles, what other kinds of weapons should we develop, if there are to be no long-range offensive weapons and so on. We must issue the proper orders for these questions to be analysed. The defence industry must be brought into line with the military doctrine. We cannot allow pacifism to penetrate the armed forces or the arms industry. It is important that we have everything we need to guarantee the inevitability of our retaliatory attack. In this connection, we should not touch the money allocated to defence ... The meeting at Reykjavik showed that, in the representatives of the American administration, we are dealing with people who have no conscience, no morality ... In Reagan at

Reykjavik we were fighting not only with the class enemy, but with one who is extremely primitive, has the looks of a troglodyte and exhibits mental incapacity.[116]

These were the words of a Leninist General Secretary. After 1986 Gorbachev learned to use more diplomatic language.

In a section of Gorbachev's book on 'honest and open foreign policy', he wrote: 'In proclaiming our commitment to an honest and open policy, we have in mind honesty, decency and sincerity, and we are applying these principles in practice. These principles are not new in themselves, they have come down to us from Lenin. What is new is that we are trying to free them of the ambiguities that are so widespread in the world today.' The idea that Lenin's foreign policy was based on 'honesty and sincerity' is laughable, and Gorbachev, especially towards the end of his rule, was anything but a Cominternist in his way of thinking.

He was, however, right to refer to widespread ambiguities; they derived, however, precisely from the class-based, irreconcilable, paranoid approach that had always characterized Soviet foreign policy. And indeed Gorbachev himself was still imbued with this approach, even if he was struggling mentally to find a new way.

Gorbachev was unable, and indeed at first did not even try, to stop the flow of weapons and military hardware to Vietnam, Syria, South Yemen, Ethiopia, Angola, Somalia, Algeria and elsewhere. This aspect of Soviet foreign policy was evidently not subject to the 'new thinking'. Thus, after talks with a Nicaraguan delegation, and despite the fact that the tiny country already owed the USSR $US1.1 billion, the Politburo agreed 'to supply free of charge uniforms, food and medicines to seventy thousand servicemen of the Sandinista army'.[117]

'New thinking' would come later. It is not hard to imagine how difficult it must have been for Gorbachev to shed traditional Comintern attitudes. At the outset of his rule he was himself doubtful about the prospects for fundamental change in Soviet–American relations. In the autumn of 1986, while discussing in the Politburo how to react to the expulsion of fifty-five Soviet diplomats by the Americans, he remarked: 'In general, this confirms what I told the US President at Reykjavik, namely, that normalization of Soviet–American relations is obviously going to be for future generations to do.'[118]

Gorbachev's immense popularity in the outside world owed much to his skill as a negotiator, his talent in public relations and his personal charm. People listened to him and liked what they heard: the Soviet Union was always about to enter the 'next phase' of its transformation into a modern state which would put democracy, peace and human rights at the top of its list of priorities.

The main reasons for his popularity, however, were the visible signs that the huge, sullen country was changing. Moscow's grip on Eastern Europe slackened, Germany was able to move towards reunification, the destruction of an entire class of missiles began, and – unimaginably – it was possible to buy Western newspapers and magazines from kiosks on Moscow's streets. The cloak of secrecy was slowly being lifted, Sakharov was invited back to Moscow, dissidents in foreign exile were allowed to visit their homeland, the press began publishing sensational articles on Stalin, the murders at Katyn, the German invasion and NKVD interrogations of writers. Gorbachev had opened the sluice-gates, and he could not have closed them again, even had he wished to. He enabled the people to gain a sense of themselves as individuals, and he thus accelerated the erosion of the system.

The world was right to credit him with this monumental act of purification. But outside observers also saw that his clumsy attempts to revive the command economy and the collective farms were doomed to failure, crushed as they were by the demands of the military-industrial complex no less than by the irrational nature of the economic system itself.

Between April 1985 and December 1991 Gorbachev received about five hundred official visitors, including heads of state and government, political leaders, public figures and delegations. This was no mechanical conveyor belt of talks and official receptions: Gorbachev was carrying on a fruitful ʹdialogue with the whole world. And he succeeded in convincing the world that he meant what he said. He managed somehow to set aside the resolutions of the Twenty-Seventh and Twenty-Eighth Congresses (of 1986 and 1990 respectively) – described in the USSR, of course, as 'historic' – and his call for 'an all-embracing system of international security'[119] was soon forgotten. The Soviet propaganda machine had been pumping out such slogans for many years, yet they still inspired fear in the world community, though it had not believed a word of them. Now at last they felt they could believe the Communist Gorbachev. However much he may have protested that he was indifferent to his popularity, much of what he did subsequently was motivated by the possible reaction abroad, and among the many world leaders he had come to know personally.

Gorbachev's popularity was at its highest in the period from the end of 1988 to 1990. His address to the UN General Assembly on 7 December 1988 was an unprecedented personal triumph. When he finished speaking, the overcrowded hall erupted in an ovation the like of which experienced observers had never seen. He had been acknowledged as a leader of global importance. The provincialism, the Bolshevik orthodoxy and the intellectual narrowness of the Party functionary had been left behind, and he stood on an equal footing with the great political leaders of the century. The award of the Nobel Peace Prize in December 1990 came as a sign of the world's gratitude for his efforts to bring a reformed Soviet Union into the civilized world.

His pleasure at this well-deserved honour, however, must have been clouded by the almost unanimous negative reaction it caused among his compatriots. To the Soviet people, still trapped in the old, rigid ways of thinking, and resentful of the changes Gorbachev was trying to bring about, it seemed he was being rewarded for bringing their country to ruin, that all he had done was talk, and that the West was encouraging him to go on with his work of destroying the Soviet Union. To the rest of the world, however, the Prize represented global recognition of Gorbachev's desperate, if only partially successful, efforts to improve his country. It was the apogee of his fame abroad.

Anatoly Chernyayev has remarked that the effect on Gorbachev of his ovation at the UN should not be underrated.[120] Chernyayev believes that Gorbachev ought to have used the enormous capital of universal goodwill to free himself altogether of Bolshevik dogmas, and the blinkered view of the 'socialist camp' on disarmament and Afghanistan. But that did not happen.

Despite his global recognition as a leader of world stature, at home Gorbachev remained the little-respected leader of a bankrupt party. He lacked the resolve and the insight to cast off the robe of office of General Secretary, and thus remained linked to the crushing defeat of Leninism. It was his greatest paradox that he reached the pinnacle of world acclaim with the dead weight of Communist ideology still clinging to him. Of course, he was still General Secretary, and therein lay his personal drama: his world-scale talent had to be combined with the narrowness of Communist attachments. Even when his disloyal comrades-in-arms attempted to depose him by means of the August 1991 coup, he still clung to this dualism.

Gorbachev seems never to have forgotten what he said at the Twenty-Seventh Congress in 1986: 'You know, when you read [Lenin] again, and you must read him when you're working on a document like this [i.e. his report to the Congress], you come to the conclusion that you have to begin with him and end with him.'[121] And so it was with Gorbachev. He could have dropped Lenin, in favour of deeper values whose significance he had come to understand. Yet he repeatedly returned to Leninism, making the journey back and forth between universal truth and class lies.

Gorbachev and Yeltsin

On taking office, Gorbachev began a cautious 'purge' of the Central Committee and Politburo. He knew that slow-witted functionaries and senile leaders would block any constructive initiatives, and he believed that renewal of the Party and society was possible only with new people. On the other hand, his Central Committee purge was also motivated by traditional Bolshevik suspicion. In January 1986 the Politburo discussed 'measures for regulating contacts between Soviet officials and foreign citizens'. Before adopting the decree, Gorbachev summed up: 'We have a lot of rebels in this matter, such contacts break the elementary rules. People are not reporting on their contacts, not reporting on the content of their conversations . . . We even had to remove two officials from the Central Committee who had permitted this sort of thing. These are serious matters. We literally have to chuck the chatterers out of the Central Committee organization and foreign policy agencies. We have evidence that the enemy is showing an interest in such people.'[122]

None the less, Gorbchev's main intention in renewing the Central Committee was to strengthen it with energetic, knowledgeable and progressively-minded people. He knew that Boris Yeltsin, a former building engineer who was now the Party chief of Sverdlovsk, one of the most heavily industrialized regions, was a man with a dynamic personality and boundless energy. At the beginning of April 1985 Gorbachev ordered V. Dolgikh to telephone Yeltsin and offer him the job of head of the Construction Department of the Central Committee in Moscow, which was responsible for heavy industry, industrial, transport and agricultural construction, planning, research and architectural affairs, building materials and much else.

Yeltsin did not hesitate: he declined respectfully. Perhaps he thought the job was not big enough; perhaps he preferred to stay in direct contact with the people, meeting them in their factories, on building projects and in canteens. He was at his best when he was out of the office and among people at work. In this respect he was a 'populist'. He had always had a jaundiced view of office work, and this could be observed throughout his subsequent career. All his successes and popularity are associated with his mingling with the crowds, whom he knew how to uplift, inflame and inspire. By contrast, all his failures and defeats are connected with the work of the organization, the apparatus and the actions of the indestructible bureaucracy. In addition to this, he loved the Urals and was not keen to move to Moscow.

The next day, it was the turn of Yegor Ligachev to try. Ligachev was the Politburo member in charge of ideology and Party organization. He too was a provincial, from Novosibirsk, who had quickly risen to the top ranks of the Party after being summoned to Moscow by Andropov. His influence in the Politburo was considerable: when Gorbachev had taken his first holiday as General Secretary, in the summer of 1985, Ligachev chaired the meetings in his absence.[123]

Ligachev was insistent in his conversation with Yeltsin: 'Your refusal won't be accepted by the Politburo. Do you think I was so keen to come to Moscow? Come on, don't be so clever, say you'll come. I'm seeing the General Secretary today. There's nothing to think about. You have to.' Yeltsin reluctantly submitted to the demands of Party discipline, and on 11 April 1985 the Politburo duly approved his appointment.[124] Gorbachev concluded patronizingly: 'We're relying on you. It's not a cushy number. You'll manage.' Yeltsin's move to Moscow would turn out to have momentous effects for Gorbachev and for the country.

At first Yeltsin found it hard to settle in the capital. He found it difficult to adapt to working in the vast Central Committee machine, with its unwritten rules, norms of behaviour and etiquette. As deputy head of the Main Political Administration of the Soviet Army and Navy, I was invited several times to meetings of the Politburo, and I was struck by the sensitivity to rank among the top echelons – a hierarchy complex, one could say. Although everyone addressed everyone else respectfully, by name and patronymic, I sensed an inner imperative of authority and harsh subordination. An insignificant Departmental Inspector, who would prostrate himself before his head of sector, would address an army commander who had been summoned to the Central Committee as arrogantly and peremptorily as if he were the General Secretary's deputy himself.

Yeltsin did not remain a department chief for long, and within two months was made a Central Committee Secretary, a post carrying with it awesome authority. Henceforth his contact with Gorbachev became personal and frequent. They were almost the same age, and both were from the provinces, though Gorbachev, after several years at Staraya Square, was more flexible and calculating than Yeltsin, who was more direct and less complicated.

Since Gorbachev intended pensioning off such veterans as Gromyko, Romanov and Grishin, he needed replacements, and these soon appeared in the form of Alexander Yakovlev, Georgy Razumovsky, Baklanov, Yuri Manayenkov, Ivan Frolov, Valentin Falin, Lev Zaikov and Vadim Medvedev. Gorbachev was frankly fed up with Grishin, the Secretary of the Moscow City Party Committee and a quiet, highly experienced operator who personified the Brezhnev era. A few months after Gorbachev took over, Grishin was given a hint that his days were numbered. He at once sent in his resignation, hoping to negotiate a better retirement package. At the next Politburo meeting, in December 1985, Gorbachev introduced the first item on the agenda: 'Comrade Yeltsin, B.N.' He announced that Grishin was retiring, and that he would be joining an advisory group in the Supreme Soviet, then turned to the question of his replacement. 'We are talking about the Party organization of the capital,' he said. 'We should therefore find someone in the Central Committee with experience of working in a major Party organization, who knows about economics, science and culture. We have a proposal to nominate Comrade B.N. Yeltsin.'

The usual grunts of approval came from around the table. Gorbachev continued: 'In that case, Comrade Yeltsin, you are recommended as First Secretary of the Moscow City Committee of the CPSU. For the time being, he will remain a Central Committee Secretary. We'll decide that issue later. A plenum of the Moscow City Committee could be held tomorrow at 11 a.m.' The minutes show that Grishin wished his successor well, while Yeltsin said very little beyond accepting that the new post was 'super-responsible'.[125]

A new chapter had opened in Yeltsin's life, one that would lead to open conflict with the Party, the Politburo and Gorbachev. But for the time being, he behaved almost like an orthodox Communist. Muscovites remember the way he zealously set about improving the running of the capital. Within two or three months half the district Party Secretaries had been sacked. A large number of top officials in trading agencies, communal and other services were similarly got rid of, and a semblance of order began to appear in the allocation of housing, the repair of schools and roads, and the use of funds allocated for social expenditure. Ordinary citizens would be amazed to meet Yeltsin on a bus, at the vegetable market, queuing for meat or to get into the cinema. He wanted to find out for himself the causes of complaint, and what it was the people wanted. Large crowds would turn up to hear him lecturing at a Party meeting. He managed to answer hundreds of letters and receive large numbers of people in his office, while also dealing with the vast quantity of the huge city's affairs. The people were excited by *perestroika*, but Yeltsin knew that they would only be satisfied by tangible success, and of that there was still little sign.

In Moscow Yeltsin quickly became a favourite topic of conversation, even the object of a new mythology. He was said to be at work at eight in the morning, and still in his office at midnight. On visits to factories he ordered the instant closure of special restaurants for management; he got rid of privileged grocery-distribution; he re-established a more equitable waiting list for apartments; he introduced the practice of selling agricultural produce direct from the farmers; he reduced the black market in goods in short supply; he improved the city's transport system. My long-serving secretary came to work one morning and told me excitedly that Yeltsin had suddenly appeared the day before in her grocery shop. When he saw the empty shelves he went to see the manager 'for a little chat'. Ten minutes later the shop staff began wheeling out trolleys laden with things no one had seen for years: smoked fish, caviar, sausage, and more. 'And the manager was sacked on the spot,' Valentina concluded, a flush of victory on her face. Here was the 'good tsar' the Russians always dreamed of.

The Communist Don Quixote from Sverdlovsk appeared to want to help and support everyone and relieve them of their many ills. The more cynical, or perhaps more experienced, knew that he would come unstuck, that he would not be able to rid Moscow of its inveterate bureaucracy, corruption and muddle. The general public, however, saw clearly that what was needed was precisely a new *perestroika*-minded leader, one who was not like all the rest. Yeltsin's popularity grew among the populace, but hostility and anger were mounting in the Party elite.

News of Yeltsin's populism reached the Central Committee. Officials there heard with astonishment that he had declined a luxury country villa and selected a much more modest one instead. He had not accepted the offer of his own plane to fly to the south on holiday, and he went on living in the fairly ordinary apartment he had been given when he first arrived in Moscow. Gorbachev and his colleagues took notice, but Yeltsin's populism was not a cause for conflict, although there were mutterings from some that he was 'after cheap authority'.

Gorbachev saw no cause to intervene. He had put Yeltsin into the Moscow organization precisely in order to clean up the city, to eliminate scandals, denunciations and conflict. He was, as his Russian biographers Vladimir Solovyov and Yelena Klepikova have written, Gorbachev's 'new broom', and he took his work seriously: 'For the time being these two men were absolutely necessary to each other: Yeltsin needed Gorbachev as a shield, and Gorbachev needed Yeltsin as a sword ... The alliance was temporary because it was tactical.'[126]

Gorbachev underestimated Yeltsin, thinking that he would always be an obedient executive who would strictly follow the path of *perestroika* laid down by himself. For the single-minded new arrival from Sverdlovsk, however, *perestroika* should not be a mere patching up of the old Bolshevik edifice, but a fundamental modernization. To be sure, in the early years of *perestroika* Yeltsin, like most of us, had no doubts about socialism, Leninism or the role of the Party. It was only after his clash with Gorbachev and the leadership at the end of 1987 that he understood the threat to any genuinely democratic innovation posed by the constraints and narrowness of Party orthodoxy. The intellectual entourage that began to form around him at this time brought his 'rebellious' views to rapid maturity. As a member of the Party's top echelons, Yeltsin knew that it was not capable of fundamental reform. The best that could be hoped for was superficial liberalization and the dropping of some of the more odious dogmas.

I first met Yeltsin in 1989, and had many private conversations with him. After I was sacked from the Main Political Administration and, in June 1991, from the Institute of Military History, I became one of his advisers, and I believe him to be one of the most courageous and honest of all Soviet politicians. It is true that there were many who had for a long time seen the incompatibility between the high ideals and the dark practices of Leninism, but there were very few – and most of those had fled abroad – who dared to rebel against its innate defects.

Within a year of becoming the Moscow Party Secretary, Yeltsin began to sense Gorbachev's unspoken jealousy at his growing popularity. He felt dissatisfaction and frustration at the knowledge that in many respects *perestroika* was merely superficial, and would not touch the foundations of the system. In September 1987, two months before the seventieth anniversary of the October Revolution, and after long reflection, Yeltsin wrote to Gorbachev, who was on holiday at Pitsunda on the Black Sea. He wrote of feeling 'superfluous' and 'awkward' in the Politburo. His directness and style of work did not fit that of the supreme body. He ended the letter on a firm note: 'I request that you release me from the job of First Secretary of the Moscow Organization and my responsibilities as a candidate member of the Politburo. I request that you regard this as an official announcement.'

Gorbachev did not reply until a week after his return to Moscow, when he telephoned Yeltsin. 'We'll talk about your letter later,' he said. But still no conversation took place.

A month later, on 15 October, the Politburo met and spent nearly four hours discussing the General Secretary's speech for the seventieth anniversary. What strikes one today, reading the minutes, is the virtual defence of Stalin and Stalinism. Gorbachev even declared that in the 1920s and thirties Stalin had defended 'Lenin's concept of revolution', and that this had been 'his enormous contribution'. One is also struck by the Politburo's deep suspicion of anything of a democratic or innovative nature that did not emanate from the Central Committee itself. It is enough to read these minutes to feel that, for the Party, *perestroika* was a means of survival, a small degree of modernization to make the Party 'contemporary'. This attitude harboured a deep contradiction between what the Party *nomenklatura* – especially its top echelon – wanted and expected from *perestroika*, and what the population was hoping for: on the one hand, the 'renewal' of the Party and the system, on the other, the basis of a new society without Bolsheviks. The debate at the Politburo showed that the contradiction was real, and that it would eventually lead to the collapse of the CPSU.

Yeltsin was the seventh member to speak. He spoke in quite traditional terms, despite the fact that only a month before he had asked Gorbachev to release him. Yeltsin suggested that the General Secretary's speech at the ceremony should not just refer to Lenin, but also to his comrades. Gorbachev, as was his wont, interrupted with a long tirade which contained an obvious message to Yeltsin over his letter of resignation: 'When a personal element enters into the sphere of high politics and top politicians are involved, personal ambition, grudges and an inability to work in the collective and so on and so forth can often transform themselves into a person's political position. So, you see, none of this is simple, the dialectics are subtle.'[127]

Gorbachev was using Yeltsin's suggestion that Lenin's comrades be mentioned in his speech as a device to attack him. When Gorbachev finally stopped talking, Yeltsin sharpened his own tone: 'The theme of *perestroika*, which is developing in the country, is very important, as are questions of the timetable, the time reckoned for a *perestroika* that has begun. The people are waiting for very precise formulations. In general, we here think that *perestroika* is going to take fifteen to twenty years; that is, it's a long-term policy. But we should deal with current and urgent tasks literally in two, three or five years. This should be in the speech.'

Gorbachev, who was to interrupt Yeltsin's brief speech no fewer than six times, replied: 'The issue of timing needs thinking about.'[128]

Yeltsin was expressing his dissatisfaction with the course of *perestroika* by criticizing the absence of a timetable, which, he said, 'disoriented' people by depriving them of a sense of direction.

He continued in the same vein a week later at the plenum of 21 October, where Gorbachev's anniversary speech was debated again. Everything was running smoothly, the delegates voicing support for the Politburo and the General Secretary. Suddenly, Yeltsin raised his hand and made his way uncertainly to the rostrum. His speech was poorly constructed and badly conceived, but two particular points stood out as unusual for this forum: 'What was said at the congress about *perestroika* in two or three years – two years have passed or almost passed, and again another two to three years are being indicated – this disorients people very much, it disorients the Party, disorients the masses, to the extent that we who know the mood of the people can now sense the fluctuating character of their attitude to *perestroika*.'

The delegates listened, hushed. This amounted to criticism of the Party line. Ostensibly Yeltsin's speech was about timetables, but in reality it was about the low level of results and public dissatisfaction with the way *perestroika* was being carried out.

'In the history of the Party,' he continued nervously, 'there have been many defeats due to the fact that Party authority was given to one sole pair of hands, due to the fact that he, that one man, was totally protected from any criticism. I'm very worried, for instance, by the fact that among the Politburo members . . . recently there has been a distinct growth, I'd say, in eulogies from some members of the Politburo about the General Secretary.'

Such criticism of a living General Secretary was unheard of. The delegates froze. Gorbachev looked at Yeltsin with a mixture of surprise and irony. Yeltsin became even more nervous. He had no prepared text to resort to: 'Evidently my work in the Politburo is not going well. For various reasons. Evidently, my experience and other things, maybe also a certain lack of support, especially from Comrade Ligachev, I would stress, have led me to think that I should raise with you the question of releasing me from my post and responsibilities as a candidate member of the Politburo. I have handed in the proper notice, and as for my being First Secretary of the City Party Committee, that will no doubt be decided by a plenum of the City Party Committee.'[129] He remained standing at the podium for a moment, as if he wanted to say something else, but then returned heavily to his seat. The silence was broken by Gorbachev: 'This is something new for us. Is it about a department of the Moscow Party organization?

Or has Comrade Yeltsin raised the question of his leaving the Polit-buro, but remaining First Secretary of the Moscow City Party Com-mittee? There seems to be a desire to fight with the Central Committee. That's how it looks to me, though maybe I'm making it worse than it is.'[130]

As a practised bureaucrat, Gorbachev knew that the rest of the Politburo would start jumping on Yeltsin the heretic. When had a General Secretary been criticized at a plenum before? And Yeltsin had voiced his doubts about *perestroika*. They would see him as scepti-cal and ambitious. Gorbachev was at once supported by a forest of hands; then came the speeches from Ryzhkov, Vorotnikov, Chebrikov, Shevardnadze, Gromyko and others. Yeltsin's speech was condemned as slanderous, rabble-rousing, groundless, capitulatory, capricious and primitive. Addressing Yeltsin in the familiar form, *ty*, Gorbachev went in for the kill: 'Are you so politically illiterate that we have to organize a grammar lesson for you here?' He called Yeltsin's confused but courageous speech a trick to shift the debate away from the main report: 'I personally regard this as disrespectful to the General Secre-tary. Look what he said, that in reality for two years the people have got nothing.'

Twenty-seven members of the Central Committee spoke. Apart from Georgy Arbatov, who made a cautious attempt to defend him, they all condemned Yeltsin. Few of them could have imagined that Yeltsin's moral and political ascendancy began that day. It was from that moment also that a four-year political struggle between Gorba-chev and Yeltsin began.

The dramatic rivalry between the two leaders took place as Soviet society was in transition from totalitarian to democratic form. Gorba-chev was in the limelight during the first five years of the period, and Yeltsin during the second five years. Gorbachev plainly underrated Yeltsin, who was able more rapidly than he to shed the dogmatic shackles of Communism and identify the path of democratization. Gorbachev's strength lay in his ability to influence the course of world opinion. His contribution to reducing the threat of nuclear war was immense. Within the USSR, with the help of Alexander Yakovlev he initiated *glasnost*, which, more than any bombs, terror or orders by the omnipotent Central Committee, undermined Leninist totalitari-anism by revealing the truth about the country and the world outside.

It was perhaps a unique example in history of the truth alone achieving what was beyond the power of a mighty state.

Both Gorbachev and Yeltsin committed serious mistakes in their confrontation. Because each had a different view of the object of *perestroika* and democratization, they had to make important decisions without the benefit of a common denominator in their relations. It was only when the force of nationalism and separatism exploded, and threatened the disintegration of the Union, that the Soviet President and the Russian President made an effort to co-ordinate their efforts. But they were too late. Gorbachev's delay gave time for the opposition in the leadership to organize their coup d'état and bring down the entire edifice of the Union.

Yeltsin's evolution into a national leader began after his confused speech in October 1987. Henceforth Gorbachev would personify a *perestroika* which in the people's minds 'had given them nothing' – a massive misjudgement by them – while Yeltsin would play the part of the remorseless critic, fighter for the interests of ordinary people, and advocate of 'real' *perestroika*.

All of Gorbachev's talk of democratization and *glasnost* in planning, methods of stimulating the socialist market and a new understanding of centralism[131] were in fact attempts to renew, improve and preserve the bankrupt Leninist system. He undoubtedly believed what he was saying, but he was still clinging to the Leninist delusion. Despite his claims of 'new thinking' for 'the whole world', he remained wedded to old thinking for the socialist world. He said on numerous occasions that he could continue to rule for another ten years without changing the system, but that it was not in his character to do so. The impulse for change had begun with Khrushchev and continued with Andropov. By the time Gorbachev came to power the system was in desperate need of change. A return to Stalinism was out of the question, nor would Gorbachev have wished it. Building a bridge to the future was an imperative. Gorbachev attempted this, and deserves credit for doing so. As he himself wrote, it was hard if not impossible for a true Communist 'to change the social system, to return to methods and forms that typify another social order'.[132]

Even had he been able to introduce radical changes in the social order, Gorbachev would not have been permitted to do so. *Perestroika* itself had slipped unnoticed into the stagnation phase, in which slogans about a new revolution, new stages and more socialism meaning more democracy could change nothing without first creating new foundations.

Gorbachev was becoming nervous. His actions at times were impulsive and over-emotional. The thread of reform had slipped from his grasp and the position was becoming worse, not only in the economy, but also in the political and national spheres. He became extremely sensitive to criticism, and could not forgive himself for bringing Yeltsin from Sverdlovsk onto the national stage, where he could display his self-will and exploit his rising popularity. As Solovyov and Klepikova have written: 'The rivalry which arose between Gorbachev and Yeltsin was both personal and political in equal measure. It arose as the revolution begun by Gorbachev began to decline, when he had lost control of the events he himself had brought to life. At that very moment Gorbachev, a completely sane person, acquired a fixed idea: whatever happened, he blamed Yeltsin. Yeltsin became his *bête noire*. Things would soon reach a point where Gorbachev would turn any conversation to Yeltsin. Everything about him irritated Gorbachev, even when his criticism was not aimed at him. Gorbachev was irritated by his popularity, which was growing in direct proportion to the fall in Gorbachev's own, and it seemed that Yeltsin was drawing the people's affection to himself.'[133]

Relations between the two worsened still further after the Nineteenth Party Conference of June 1988, the first such conference since 1941. At first all seemed normal. All the delegates in the Palace of Congresses rose when Gorbachev appeared on the platform and was invited to speak. He talked of political reform, heightening the role of the soviets, the weak performance of the food programme, the fact that not everyone was satisfied with *perestroika*, and again he recalled Lenin.

The delegation of which I was a member had been allocated seats in the balcony. As it happened, Yeltsin was sitting a little in front of me. Without waiting for Gorbachev to finish speaking, he sent a note to the platform stating his wish to speak. Time passed, days passed, and as one new speaker after another was called to the podium, Yeltsin sat in silence. During an interval he said: 'They want to shut me up.'

The conference was moving towards its close, and still Yeltsin had not been asked to speak. Suddenly he left his seat and went to the exit. After a few minutes he emerged in the body of the hall, walked to the front and sat down. It was obvious that he wanted to speak. Gorbachev realized this, and got up and left. Men in grey uniforms approached Yeltsin and asked him to leave too. He was unmoved. Then, after one more speaker, he was given the floor. Again his speech was rather confused, but it was a frank criticism of the Politburo, the General Secretary and the course of *perestroika*. About a third of the delegates greeted the speech warmly, the rest either cautiously or in an openly hostile manner. Afterwards, a manifest spirit of confrontation arose in the great hall between the old Party élite and the new supporters of democracy. Ligachev and a number of other delegates devoted their speeches to an essentially anti-Yeltsin theme.

The gulf between Gorbachev and Yeltsin became deeper and wider. Regrettably, Gorbachev, still not free of the old Bolshevik way of thinking, saw the radical, democratic wing in the Party and society not as opponents, but as enemies. Between 1989 and 1991, when the Politburo discussed almost any topic the terms 'opportunists', 'radicals', 'anti-Communists', 'regionalists' cropped up with dismaying regularity, and the closer the demise of *perestroika* approached, the more was said and the less was done. The long sessions, at which Gorbachev was invariably the most loquacious speaker, testify to the leadership's confusion. Gorbachev did his best to invigorate his colleagues by urging the need for concrete measures and calling on everyone to stay at his post and see the course through. On occasion he was more blunt: 'We mustn't give in and we mustn't panic.'[134]

It seems that Gorbachev saw one of the causes of his mounting difficulties as the activities of the political opposition, which he sometimes called, with a degree of disparagement, 'the democrats'. Attacking the inter-regional group of democratically inclined People's Deputies, which included Andrei Sakharov, Gorbachev told the Politburo: 'We look at them and we see they're like snotty intellectuals, though we also see that they're degenerates and turncoats, yet we are unable to put them in their places. No, this is simply intolerable!' 'I'll tell you frankly,' he continued, '80 per cent of the members in the regional group are normal people. There is a group of political opportunists there who are not the "leaders", so to speak . . . We have to defeat them intellectually. There are also incorrigibles, people like those "leaders".'[135]

Gorbachev spoke of democracy as the axis of *perestroika*, yet he denounced those who advocated and expressed democracy. A special decree was adopted on his initiative by the Politburo on 22 March 1990, according to which it would be 'appropriate . . . to keep to a line on the intellectual and organizational demarcation of the supporters of the "Democratic Platform"'.[136] In other words, there were to be no 'democrats' in the Party.

On occasion Gorbachev's hatred of Yeltsin was expressed quite blatantly. An excessively long meeting of the Politburo on 3 May 1990 was discussing the forthcoming Twenty-Eighth Party Congress and Russian Party Conference, as well as the next Congress of People's Deputies. *Perestroika* was still failing to deliver, and it was plain that Soviet socialism was beyond redemption. For this, it seems, there had to be culprits.

Gorbachev's angry and confused speech amounted to saying that the 'democrats' could put an end to *perestroika* by their opposition: 'Why has Yeltsin seized on the question of the formation of the Russian Communist Party? He does it to play . . . to use it to get to power in Russia. And through Russia to break up the CPSU as well, and the country . . . These are not the aims of socialism, the renewal of socialism. It's all a rabble-rousing disguise. They need power. These people are omnivorous. They're willing even to consume themselves, to close ranks with the most "hardline Marxists and even with dictators . . ." Just as long as they get into power. But they are dangerous. Under certain circumstances they could completely ruin *perestroika*, bury all hope of ennobling and renewing our society.'[137]

Yeltsin was mentioned again in the context of a completely different issue. One of the members had the idea of inviting him to take part in a television debate and tripping him up. A journalist would be engaged to ask him questions about Lithuania, the Kurile Islands, AIDS and other potentially inflammatory subjects. Yeltsin had acquired a reputation for being accident-prone and unstable. In 1991 newspapers carried reports of his appearing late one night at a militia station soaking wet, explaining that he had somehow found himself in the Moscow River. Was he drunk? Had a jealous husband tried to settle a score? The media were naturally interested. Yeltsin claimed to have been thrown in the river by secret agents hoping to provoke a public outcry and industrial unrest, which would provide an excuse for imposing martial law.

Whatever the truth, this was novel behaviour for a politician of Yeltsin's rank. Gorbachev played on this theme when he added: 'Our man has a reputation. He drank half a bucket – that took some doing!' Someone else mentioned that Yeltsin was ill. Gorbachev replied: 'Yes, I'm sure ... We are always motivated by moral considerations, whereas they have no morals whatever ... They're just a bunch of opportunists, simply the dregs of politics.'[138]

From this kind of discussion, it is obvious where the gossip about Yeltsin at that time originated.

Gorbachev rejected Yeltsin both as a political opponent and as an individual. What was the essence of this deep personal hostility? Chernyayev identifies a fatal mistake in Gorbachev's actions: 'Despite his constant refrain that the aim of *perestroika* was to liberate the natural logic of social development, and not to impose yet another scheme, he took on the role of chief constructor himself, as well as the job of clerk of works in building the "new" society. But this became an objective impossibility.'[139]

Gorbachev did not want a *perestroika* that would lead to replacing the old Bolshevik totalitarian order, even in 'improved' form, with a democratic, non-socialist one. Yeltsin, on the other hand, at first indistinctly but with growing definition, wanted just that. After the autumn of 1987, each leader perceived *perestroika* differently: Gorbachev in terms of the socialist renewal, and Yeltsin effectively in a pro-capitalist sense. As a Party pariah in self-imposed isolation, Yeltsin became unrestrained in his public criticism of the General Secretary.

As a rule, Gorbachev was enraged by criticism, especially when it consisted of arguments about his alleged lack of direction, that he was dictating from the 'centre', that he had no strategy for change. When on 16 October 1990 at the Russian Supreme Soviet Yeltsin declared that Russia would not allow itself to be ordered about by the centre, Gorbachev let loose: 'Yeltsin's busting to get the Presidency [of Russia] ... and at such a time as this. He's simply out of his mind. He's setting his people on me ... They need a good smash in the face.'[140]

Gorbachev tried to trip Yeltsin up at every opportunity. When the Russian President made foreign visits, efforts were made to ensure that he was only 'half-received' by senior foreign officials. In early 1991 a visit by Yeltsin to Peking was repeatedly discussed by the Soviet and Chinese governments. Gorbachev did not want it to take place, and Alexander Bessmertnykh, the Foreign Minister since Shevardnadze's resignation in December 1990, submitted a proposal to the Politburo: 'The Chinese comrades should be asked to invite B.N. Yeltsin on behalf of the governments of the three Chinese provinces that border the Soviet Union (in north-eastern China) and that have extensive ties and co-operation with the RSFSR. If someone in the Chinese leadership in Peking wants to meet B.N. Yeltsin after his visit to these three provinces, that's their business. But that would not constitute a visit to China.' Gorbachev gave his approval to the plan.[141]

For Yeltsin the break with his Communist past was anything but simple. It was not the case, as many thought, that he became a 'heretic' as his populism peaked and during his personal confrontation with Gorbachev. I shall never forget the way he took the floor at the last Party Congress [the Twenty-Eighth, in 1990] and announced that he was leaving the Communist Party. It was a short speech, and it stunned the delegates. 'In connection with my appointment [on 25 May 1990] as Chairman of the Supreme Soviet of the RSFSR and my enormous responsibility to the people and to Russia, and considering the shift of society to a multi-party situation, I shall no longer be able to carry out only the decisions of the CPSU . . . Therefore, in accordance with the responsibilities I have in the pre-election period, I am announcing my departure from the CPSU.'[142]

The speech was met by silence at first, and then a rising howl of condemnation and hostility. Yeltsin meanwhile left the hall with a heavy gait, and did not look at anyone. He passed close to where I was sitting, and I could see that his face was grey. He told me a few days later: 'When I announced my exit from the Party, I literally felt something snap in my chest . . . I couldn't sleep all night.' The shedding of a lifetime of spiritual shackles had not been easy.

Relations between Gorbachev and Yeltsin reached such a pitch that the General Secretary could not utter Yeltsin's name without becoming angry. Almost every important foreign visitor would find Gorbachev turning the conversation to Yeltsin, at times in the most abusive terms. Yeltsin was closely followed by the special services, and all his telephone calls were bugged. After the August 1991 coup, investigators found a mountain of files containing transcripts of his telephone conversations in two safes in the office of Gorbachev's assistant Valeri Boldin. 'For several years,' Yeltsin wrote, 'they noted down everything I said, morning, noon and night.'[143]

From the beginning of 1991, however, there were sound reasons for a rapprochement between the two men, or at least between the groups whose interests they expressed. They were pushed towards each other by the growing threat of the break-up of the Soviet Union. The Novo-Ogarevo process, as it became known (after one of the Soviet President's residences), began in April 1991, when Gorbachev initiated talks with nine of the republican heads, including Yeltsin – all fifteen had been invited, but six were not interested in anything less than complete separation from the USSR. On 4 May Yeltsin, who favoured a new Union, declared that the meeting of '9+1' had been 'a great event' which had achieved agreement in principle for a new 'Union of Sovereign States, joining with each other voluntarily'.[144] The Union would be preserved, he said, and that was the main thing.

Yeltsin recalled that the talks at Novo-Ogarevo 'dictated (and allowed) that Gorbachev and I would behave like normal people. We set aside our personal feelings. The price of each word we spoke was too high ... After the talks we would normally go to another room for a friendly supper with Gorbachev's favourite brandy, Jubilee. We would come out of supper warmed up and excited by the circumstances of the meeting, and by the supper.'[145]

The talks were leading towards a powerful Confederation with a common economic area, a common army and a common currency. Both leaders saw in this arrangement a real possibility of preserving what used to be called the USSR.

'Nevertheless,' Yeltsin went on, 'to say that my relations with Gorbachev at that time were simple would be quite wrong. While taking this step towards Russia in the Novo-Ogarevo process, he did everything in his power to prevent my appointment as President of Russia.'[146]

In the event, both men became Presidents. In the previous year, at the Congress of People's Deputies of 27 March 1990, it had been announced that 1,834 of the 2,486 Deputies had voted in favour of Gorbachev as head of state. He was elated, and barely able to contain his excitement.

Yeltsin's approach was on a much broader political base: he submitted himself for election by the entire voting population in June 1991, and became the first man to be elected President of Russia, beating all his rivals in the first round. His popularity rose even higher. Gorbachev offered his reserved congratulations, and expressed the hope of 'collaboration and agreement in the renewal of the multi-national state, which the signing of the new Union Treaty should serve'.

On 2 August 1991 Gorbachev appeared on national television from his palace at Foros and announced that the new treaty would be signed on 20 August. Why not earlier? Why did he stay at Foros, delaying what could have been done sooner? He evidently believed that, despite all the criticism and attacks being aimed at him and Yeltsin alike by the conservatives, nothing would prevent the signing of the new treaty in three weeks' time.

On 19 August the attempted *coup d'état* took place. From my hospital bed in Oxford, where I was to undergo a major operation that very day, I sent a fax to the Speaker of the Parliament,[147] consisting of an appeal to the Russian population during this 'change of epochs'.[148]

Attempts by Varennikov and other members of the so-called 'State Committee for the State of Emergency' to blame Gorbachev and Yeltsin for 'the collapse of the USSR' are not supported by the facts. Gorbachev had finally come to reject the socialist Utopia, but it was too late. The conservatives, or more accurately reactionaries, in the Central Committee and his entourage were incapable of dropping the idea of 'real socialism'. By being indecisive towards his treacherous colleagues, Gorbachev had created the conditions for the bungled coup. The conspiracy, however, was enough to destroy the old Union and prevent the formation of a new one.

The trauma suffered by Gorbachev and his family under house arrest was enormous, and bears no comparison with what had befallen Khrushchev. What happened at Foros was like something out of Russia's pre-Revolutionary history, when tsars were removed by means of palace coups or assassinations. No General Secretary, invested as he was with the panoply of power and authority, had ever been subjected to such indignity, to say nothing of the threat of physical danger. It was Gorbachev's wife Raisa who most clearly suffered from the ordeal.[149]

The coup failed for many reasons, chief of which was the people's widespread desire not to return to the past. Another was the impossible orders the plotters issued, such as that addressed by General Varennikov to the headquarters of the Emergency Committee: 'We all earnestly ask you to take immediate measures to liquidate the adventurer B.N. Yeltsin's group.'[150] Nor was their order to the air force 'to destroy in mid-air the plane carrying the Russian government delegation headed by B.N. Yeltsin back from Kazakhstan on the night of 18 August' obeyed.[151]

Yeltsin was spared, and he in turn saved Gorbachev. It was he who kept the world informed of what was happening at Foros, and on 21 August he sent a delegation to the Crimea to rescue Gorbachev, who was in fact out of danger by then. The coup leaders also flew to Foros in a vain attempt to justify their actions, but were apprehended by guards loyal to Yeltsin and brought back to Moscow under arrest. Gorbachev chose to return to the capital with the 'democrats', thus creating the impression that he had survived thanks to Yeltsin's intervention.

But the alliance between the two men, that had seemed so close, did not come to pass. On his arrival in Moscow, Gorbachev spoke of the need to reform the Party, as if he was unaware that it was the Party itself – or its significant elements – that had brought about his downfall, not to say its own imminent destruction. Yeltsin, meanwhile, pressed home his advantage by seizing the assets of the CPSU and banning the recently formed Russian Communist Party. At the Russian Parliament on 23 August, which was televised, Yeltsin insisted that Gorbachev read out the names of those of his own Ministers – almost all of them – who had supported the coup. This was perhaps the most humiliating moment of Gorbachev's career.

Gorbachev resigned as General Secretary the next day, and called on the Central Committee to disband itself, effectively announcing the demise of the Party. Simultaneously, the Union itself began to fall apart along its ethnic seams, as one republic after another declared itself independent or desirous of becoming so. Most damaging to the chances of the Union's survival, on 1 December a referendum in Ukraine returned an overwhelming vote in favour of complete independence. On 25 December Gorbachev resigned as President in a televised address that also drew a line under the history of the Soviet

Union, and opened the era of independent states which replaced it.

Both Yeltsin and Gorbachev were embodiments of the changes taking place in the country. Gorbachev started his utopian effort to 'renew' socialism by unwittingly opening the sluice-gates that would wash away the ruins of Leninism. Yeltsin, as the first leader ever to be elected by the entire people in Russia's long history, had to try to create a modern, democratic society in the midst of ruin and chaos. It was a task no less difficult than liquidating the Communist system.

Gorbachev as a Historic Figure

Mikhail Gorbachev launched the most fundamental and irreversible changes in Soviet history since Lenin. Many people still see him as a saviour, while just as many regard him as a destroyer, and those who are indifferent are growing in number. If he does not evoke sympathy among his contemporaries, he has certainly earned the gratitude of future generations.

Kerensky, the Russian Prime Minister in post-tsarist 1917, was also underrated, yet in a certain sense what Gorbachev tried to do, perhaps without even realizing it, was to set Russia back on the path that had been started in February 1917 and that was blocked in October by the Bolshevik coup. Like Kerensky, Gorbachev left the scene apparently defeated. But history often awards its laurels many years after the event. Lenin, whom Gorbachev so revered, seemed for seven decades to be the victor, yet the October Revolution was seen by his political enemies, including Kerensky, as the harbinger of inevitable historic defeat. Now, eighty years later, it is clear that they were right.

As a historical figure, Gorbachev does not deserve blame, nor does he need vindication; and if he does not want his historical image to be blurred, he should not attempt to blame or vindicate others. A political figure of his stature should be neither prosecutor nor defendant. Having lived for most of his life as an unknown Party official, he remained so until Chernenko's infirmity compelled the geriatric Politburo to think hard about a younger successor. Gorbachev knew this, and did not force events. His trump card was his age, and he could afford to wait.

Some writers have claimed that he was already voicing embryonic ideas of *perestroika* as early as 10 December 1984, at a conference on 'Perfecting Developed Socialism'. Former Politburo member Vadim Medvedev, who was a close comrade of Gorbachev's, claims that his speech was 'a fundamental pre-*perestroika* document', and that 'it was distinguished for its manifest originality,' and gave a 'realistic and for that period highly critical assessment of the development of the country, and in a generalized political form advanced the need to accelerate social and economic development'. Medvedev further asserts that 'the conference produced a big and profound impression on public opinion. Gorbachev had made himself known as a major political leader, with a deep understanding of economic and political life and international relations.'[152]

I was at that conference, and listened carefully to what was said. Certainly, everyone looked at Gorbachev with heightened interest as the most likely successor of the dying Chernenko. As for his speech, it was entirely in the Central Committee mode of those made under Brezhnev and Andropov. In other words, he was performing a ritual that was expected of him. Most of the ideas he expressed were worn-out Leninist propaganda, the classic Bolshevik catalogue: 'the superiority of socialism', in the form of 'the planned character of our economy, the priority of the social goals of economic development', 'the working class as the leading force in society right up to the complete overcoming of class differences'. He also mentioned 'democratic centralism' and how to 'organize competition', the importance of preserving 'socialist principles of distribution', and dwelt on the idea that 'capitalism has no historic prospects', that what was needed was 'Bolshevik restlessness', and much more in the same vein.[153]

Gorbachev said what we all said, marooned as we were in our would-be Utopia. He uttered his first broad notions of *perestroika* on 8 April 1986 in the industrial city of Togliatti, but continued to uphold the Bolshevik style and methods that had evolved over decades. As late as May 1987, he told his colleagues in the Politburo that they must 'stress that *perestroika* has a socialist character and has nothing in common with bourgeois liberalization'.[154] The 'revolutionariness' of which he loved to speak did not extend beyond the limits of the existing order, although that was to be liberalized, if in a socialist and not bourgeois spirit. He, too, needed time to change, or to begin to change.

However much he did to democratize society – and he did a great deal – Gorbachev retained a soft spot for the special services. He did not abolish political investigation and telephone tapping – even of the members of the Politburo – and he relied to a great extent on the reports and information fed to him by the security organs, who were thus able to influence his decisions to a certain extent.

At a November 1988 meeting of the Politburo, Gorbachev raised the issue of the recently formed 'Memorial' Society. A number of such bodies had sprung up with the aim of finding out the truth about the atrocities and excesses committed in the past by the NKVD and the Party, establishing the number and names of the innocent victims and publishing the names of those who had committed these crimes against humanity. The security services were, of course, telling Gorbachev to quietly extinguish this nationwide movement, and to reduce it to strictly local or regional status.

Gorbachev gave his frank opinion of this kind of de-Stalinization. 'This "Memorial",' he declared, 'is mushrooming. Its latest efforts show that it is trying to get bigger than society.' Later in the debate he said: 'I'd like to link two issues: the [secret NKVD] burial-grounds and "Memorial" . . . we have to somehow de-energize "Memorial", to really give it a local character, and the Party organizations in the localities should take all this business into their own hands . . . What this is about is not "Memorial". It's a cover for something else again.'[155]

Having thought about the problem, he returned to it next day: 'We have to take a political decision that includes a political appraisal of the trials and decisions taken by the *troikas* [three-man NKVD tribunals] without judicial investigation. [We have] to acknowledge that they were illegal. And that's all, comrades . . . If we do this, we will beat off all these "Memorials".'[156] What was being 'beaten off', however, was not 'Memorial', but the desire to restore the country's historical memory and to bring justice to the victims of Bolshevik oppression.

Gorbachev rarely made a major decision without Politburo approval. He also often discussed questions that were neither on the agenda nor included in the final, edited form of the minutes, remaining only in draft form under 'any other business'. As a rule such issues were too trivial to clutter the official record, but on occasion they were of particular importance. In April 1988 Gorbachev raised the question of the Party's attitude to religion in the circumstances of *perestroika*. The minutes show that only he spoke on the subject. 'The Politburo,' he said, 'has recognized my meeting with [Patriarch] Pimen and the Synod [the governing body of the Orthodox Church] as expedient in principle. People say there hasn't been such a meeting in a long time. Something similar took place during the war, in 1943. True, at official occasions when members of the clergy were present, Leonid Ilyich [Brezhnev] made a gesture towards them and later said, "It was a good conversation." The churchmen will raise the issue of opening a seminary in the Tarnopol region. I recall in my time having had a hand in closing a seminary in Stavropol region ... We shouldn't bow and scrape to religion, or cosy up to it. But we have to deal with it as a reality ... We shouldn't adopt an apologetic position of any sort.'[157]

Under 'any other business' Gorbachev informed the Politburo that Malenkov had died: 'Should an official announcement be published?' he wanted to know. Other members remembered that Malenkov had had a hand in the purges of the 1930s, and it was agreed that there was no need for an official announcement. The death of one of its former leaders was an internal Party matter. As for where he should be buried, it was finally agreed that next to his wife's grave in Novo-kuntsevo Cemetery would be 'permissible'.[158]

Decisions on more aid going abroad were being debated in the Politburo under 'any other business'. In January 1986 Gorbachev told the Politburo that he had received a 'worrying telegram' from Aden, where a short, sharp civil war had broken out: 'They want to shoot fifty people. I think we ought to send an appeal, pointing out to them that the main thing is unification.' But Ali Muhammad al-Hasani, leader of the pro-Soviet Socialist Party of South Yemen, went ahead with his plans. He left the room where he had been chairing his Politburo, and his special forces rushed in and gunned down everyone around the table. The army did not support him, however, and he soon had to flee to North Yemen and thence to Ethiopia. In Aden, meanwhile, the mutual slaughter of his supporters and opponents went on.

After a time, Commander-in-Chief Ground Forces General Yev-geni Ivanovsky was despatched to South Yemen. I accompanied him on this 'peacemaking' mission, and the signs of the recent slaughter were awful to observe. Almost a third of the officers who died in the bloody seizure of power had been to Soviet military schools and academies. Now, in our meetings with the new Yemeni leadership, they sang the old tune: 'We need your help – economic and technological help, advisers, places in Soviet universities.'

Sometimes issues were discussed under 'any other business' which show how slowly the Soviet leadership was practising the 'new thinking'. At the end of one of their June 1989 meetings, Gorbachev asked the Politburo members to remain for further discussion:

GORBACHEV: Now to the question of publishing the works of Solzhenitsyn.

MEDVEDEV: *Gulag Archipelago* is [more than two thousand pages] long ... It's difficult and tedious to read.

RYZHKOV: It begins with the time of Lenin. It will be a bombshell.

GORBACHEV: They slipped up by letting him into the archives when he was writing *Ivan Denisovich* ...

CHEBRIKOV: No, they didn't let him into the archives.

MEDVEDEV: He got about three hundred memoirs from various people.

GORBACHEV: The issue is not about Stalin, but the assertion that he was Lenin's faithful pupil. That he continued his cause. And he does it by quoting Lenin's telephone-tapes and letters.

LIGACHEV: How can we allow this sort of thing to be written about Lenin?

GORBACHEV: Anyway, we are faced with *Gulag Archipelago*. I don't think he's ever going to be our unconditional friend and supporter of *perestroika*.

SHAKHNAZAROV: We should let it be published.

GORBACHEV: Vladimir Alexandrovich [Kryuchkov], let those comrades read it who haven't already done so.

SHEVARDNADZE: I'm in favour of publication.

GORBACHEV: It turns out that, as far as Lenin was concerned, the worse, the better. Let the people suffer, let men die in the trenches ... for him there was only the lust for power ... There's a hint about the link with Inessa Armand ... Contempt for the Russian people ...

YAKOVLEV: We have to publish it. Everyone's in favour of publication: the Union of Writers, the magazines ...

GORBACHEV: So, are we the only ones left? I'd better read it myself.[159]

Without having read the book, Gorbachev was ready to condemn it. I was no better. In two publications I condemned Solzhenitsyn without having read his work, relying instead on the 'correctness' of the Central Committee which fed me its regurgitated opinions. I have many times since expressed repentance, knowing that all of us, from the General Secretary down to rank-and-file Communists, were victims of Bolshevik intolerance of everything that contradicted the Soviet religion of Leninism.

As leader, Gorbachev inherited the style and methods of his predecessors, but he deserves credit for letting the public know what the Central Committee was doing, for initiating the publication of a revamped journal, *Izvestiya TsK KPSS* (News of the Central Committee of the CPSU), containing hitherto secret materials, and for making press conferences by members of the leadership routine. His style became more open and democratic, even though a one-sided interpretation of events, cuts and cover-ups were still practised right up to August 1991.

Although he was man more of mind than will, Gorbachev could be very tough when he was sure of widespread public support. When the young West German Matthias Rust landed his light plane right next to the Kremlin in Moscow, having first flown round it twice, Gorbachev was visibly shaken. He regarded the incident as a national disgrace, even if it was seen in the West as little more than a foolish prank, and his response to it raised his popularity in the Soviet Union.

The Politburo meeting was a stormy one. The military top brass had been summoned, and had to endure the sort of criticism they might have expected if they had lost a war.

Gorbachev was venomous and maliciously sarcastic: 'This went on for two and a half hours, while the offending plane was in the zone of 6th Army.' Turning to General Lushev, he asked: 'Was this reported to you?'

LUSHEV: No. I knew about it when the plane landed in Moscow.
GORBACHEV: I suppose the traffic cops told you?

After a two-hour debate, Gorbachev summed up: 'An event has occurred that surpasses everything that has happened before in terms of its political consequences ... We are talking about the people's loss of faith in our army, for whose sake the people have made many sacrifices. And for a long time. A blow has also been struck against the political leadership of the country, against its authority.' He then announced a thirty-minute break, after which he listed the points of a Politburo decree:

1 To accept [Defence Minister] Comrade Sokolov's notice of retirement.
2 To confirm Comrade Yazov as Defence Minister.
3 Commander-in-Chief Border Troops Comrade Koldunov to be relieved of his post.[160]

On the other hand, there were important instances when Gorbachev's role was more ambiguous. Nationalist feeling had mounted steadily throughout the Caucasus in 1988, nowhere more violently than in the conflict between Azerbaijan and Armenia over the disputed enclave of Nagorno-Karabakh. The Georgian nationalists, meanwhile, had their own local adversary in the form of the movement for independence for the ethnic territory of Abkhazia, but they also had the higher goal of Georgian independence from the Soviet Union. Gorbachev called repeatedly for a political, non-violent outcome to all such claims. In April 1989, however, a peaceful demonstration in the Georgian capital of Tbilisi was attacked by Soviet troops using poison gas and sharpened spades. Nineteen demonstrators, mostly young women, were killed, and more than a hundred injured. If the nationalists had needed further justification for their demands, and more fuel for the fire of their campaign, this senselessly cruel act provided it, and an extremist, Zviad Gamsakhurdia, was elected as the head of an anti-Soviet administration, and in due course as President of an independent state of Georgia.

While it is plain that Gorbachev neither ordered nor approved the vicious actions of Soviet forces in Tbilisi, it is also true that he left it to subordinates to settle what he had been warned was a potentially dangerous situation in an unstable region. The Ministries of the Interior and Defence and the local Communist authorities were undoubtedly directly responsible, tactically and politically, for what happened in Tbilisi, and Gorbachev cannot be faulted for seeking to resolve an explosive situation by peaceful means. But as Soviet President and General Secretary, he cannot be excused for failing to exercise his supreme responsibility for public order and security.

In the Baltic states of Estonia, Latvia and Lithuania, which had been annexed by the Soviet Union in the shameful agreement Stalin had made with Hitler, and where the local nationalists could claim to be undoing an illegal act, many people expected independence to come without bloodshed. Despite the fact that in September 1989 Gorbachev had refused to give the Lithuanian Communist Party independence, in order to contest elections with the nationalists on a level playing-field, as the tide of nationalism rose throughout the Union he adopted a liberal position, urging peaceful discussion and political agreement rather than the use of force. By 1991, however, he was boxed in by the hard-liners in his administration – most of the liberals by now having gone, either of their own accord or let go by him. Forceful rhetoric was used in relation to the Baltic states on a number of occasions, and it seemed that Gorbachev was contemplating tough measures to curb the nationalists' aspirations. In January 1991 fourteen people were killed by Soviet troops during a peaceful demonstration in the Lithuanian capital of Vilnius. Gorbachev said he heard about this bloody event only on the morning after. At such dramatic and tragic moments the President was, astonishingly, left in ignorance on the sidelines.

Gorbachev led the Party and the state not only through the Central Committee and government, but also with the help of what his close adviser Vadim Medvedev called 'the Gorbachev team', meaning his advisers, speech-writers, aides and top officials. They included such men as Alexander Yakovlev, justly called the 'brains' of *perestroika*, Ivan Frolov, Georgy Shakhnazarov, Anatoly Chernyayev, Valeri Boldin, Tatiana Zaslavskaya, Anatoly Lukyanov and a couple of dozen more. This was a very able group, and Medvedev had every reason to say at a meeting of the Politburo that 'the Soviet leadership has created a team for Gorbachev the like of which has never been known in the Soviet Union before.'[161]

The question may be asked, if Gorbachev's team was so talented and professional, why could he not attain his goals, and why did some of them betray him so savagely? Much has been written about the team in the memoirs of its members, though they do not dwell on the reasons for Gorbachev's failure. All of them are highly critical of Yeltsin, and all of them except Lukyanov and Boldin, who stabbed him in the back, depict their former boss in a positive and often flattering light.

Georgy Arbatov, one of Gorbachev's best-informed advisers on foreign policy, wrote to him many times on many issues, sometimes giving simple advice such as 'keep your speeches short', 'interrupt someone if he starts to praise you', and 'you should know that Ligachev is a real threat', at other times on major issues, such as 'your main priority on the external arena is to strengthen the socialist common-wealth: remove the tactical nuclear missiles from the Transcaucasus without delay; after the Twenty-Eighth Congress resign as General Secretary,' and so on.

Gorbachev did indeed make a rather half-hearted attempt in April 1991 to resign as General Secretary, whether or not this was prompted by Arbatov's advice. Had he managed to do so, he would have been able to get rid of a lot of organizational and ideological baggage. He would also have distanced himself, as Yeltsin had done, from the hopelessly discredited Party, which now drifted aimlessly, and many of whose more 'astute' members were profiting from the economic near-anarchy that had evolved since 1989. He would have remained President of the Soviet Union, but it is difficult to imagine that this would have stemmed the tide of national independence that had effec-tively reduced his territory to the Kremlin – and soon only part of that, since Yeltsin installed himself there when he became President of Russia in June 1991.

Gorbachev worked at very high pressure, but he always tried to keep the weekends free for his family and the countryside. 'The few hours of relaxation I have,' he said, 'I try to use to the full. My interests are the most varied: reading creative literature, theatre, music, the cinema. My favourite relaxation is walking in the forest.'[162]

A normal working day would start at 9.30 a.m. and end at about 9 p.m., with the intervening time filled with one meeting after another, with telephone calls to and from local and foreign politicians, and receiving foreign visitors.

Although conditions in the country were worsening, and the feeling was circulating that without a 'strong hand' nothing would improve, the idea of 'saving' democracy by force was unbearable for Gorbachev. It soon became clear to him that *perestroika* had unleashed intra-national problems before which the use of force was ineffectual, and harmful to the entire cause of democratization. The old formula, 'friendship of the peoples' in a unitary state, had quickly shown itself to be inadequate in the new climate, but Gorbachev learned the lesson very late.

In his brief but stormy time as leader, Gorbachev tried more than once to resign as General Secretary of the Party. In December 1989 yet another plenum opened in Moscow to discuss the Second Congress of People's Deputies. Many delegates spoke, but it was the speech of the First Secretary of the Kemerovo region, A. Melnikov, that stung Gorbachev most. An uncompromisingly orthodox Communist, Melnikov spoke in favour of including worker-Communists in the Politburo and Central Committee, according to Leninist methodology. Gorbachev lost his temper, and agitatedly proposed that a new Politburo be appointed, and a new General Secretary as well.[163] He was calmed down with difficulty, and no more was said about replacing him.

At the Politburo on 25 April 1991 Gorbachev again raised the question of resigning. With his deputy, Vladimir Ivashko, in the chair, no discussion took place. Instead a resolution was passed: 'With the highest interests of the country, the people and the Party in mind, the proposal put forward by Mikhail Sergeyevich Gorbachev for his resignation as General Secretary is withdrawn from discussion.'[164] He was prevented from leaving the sinking ship, and forced to sit out the collapse of the Leninist system to the bitter end. One of the most obvious signs that this was the case had occurred in March 1990, when the Party held the first free elections ('free' in the sense that members were no longer compelled to vote for approved candidates) for its top posts. Almost half of the First, Second and Regional Secretaries failed to be elected to their previous positions. Indeed, the fact that elections were held at all testified to the Party's fast-declining influence in society.

In his memoirs, Anatoly Lukyanov, who as Chairman of the USSR Supreme Soviet in 1991 had been one of the initiators of the coup, and who had known Gorbachev since their student days together in Moscow, writes that he found 'the phenomenon of Gorbachev's authority' understandable: the policy of concession and compromise, which led to the 'destruction of the Warsaw Pact', suited the West very well. As for Gorbachev's personal characteristics:

His pernicious tendency to resolve everything, even matters of principle, by compromise, improvisation and vacillation, under the influence of circumstances and his personal adviser, became a sort of curse hanging over him ... He had a blithe belief that everything would somehow be all right and was permanently lagging behind events. He was certain that every presidential word would be effective of itself and he lacked the ability to listen to the opinion of others ... He was astonishingly unwilling to defend people from his own team and had a tendency to quickly get rid of anyone who had fulfilled his task and ceased to be useful to him.[165]

When Lukyanov was asked to define the part Gorbachev had played in the history of Russia, he was unequivocal: 'It was the role of Herostratos ... Gorbachev betrayed his Party.'[166]

Alexander Alexandrov-Agentov, who had been an assistant of Gorbachev's and was replaced by Anatoly Chernyayev, echoed some of Lukyanov's thoughts: 'Unfortunately, Gorbachev suffers from a very serious shortcoming in a leader: he is totally unable to listen, or rather unable to listen to his interlocutor, but is wholly absorbed by what he says himself. I left Gorbachev and took my pension because he had no need of advice.'[167] Thus, one of Gorbachev's enemies says he was swayed by his advisers, and another says he would not take advice.

One episode may serve to illustrate the difficult moral choices Gorbachev was confronted with. For many years relations with Poland were marred by unexplained facts concerning the Soviet–Polish War of 1920, the dissolution of the Polish Communist Party in 1938, the 1939 secret agreements between the USSR and Germany, the execution of Polish officers and others at Katyn and elsewhere, the circumstances surrounding the Warsaw Uprising of 1944, and more.

The Soviet government had never had the courage to deal honestly with any of these issues. For instance, Vadim Medvedev, the Central Committee Secretary responsible for relations with the socialist countries, wrote a memorandum to Gorbachev on 13 March 1987 which proposed that, on the subject of the 1920 war, 'two or three articles should be published on the aims of bourgeois-landlord Poland in that war, and on the positions of individual Soviet political, state and military figures.' On the dissolution of the Polish Communist Party, the fact should be acknowledged, but it should be said that 'at the end of the 1950s the repressed Polish Communists were rehabilitated, many of them posthumously.' As for the 'reunification of Western Ukraine and Western Belorussia with the USSR', and the existence of 'some secret protocols to the Soviet–German treaty of 1939', it should be said that 'there are no grounds for reviewing our position'.[168]

In a note on the Soviet–German treaties of 1939, Gorbachev stated: 'If one takes a realistic view, the Non-Aggression Pact between the USSR and Germany of 23 August was inevitable.'[169] He circulated the documents, marked 'top secret', to all members of the Politburo, in effect closing the ranks. The Poles, however, were persistent, and asked again for an opportunity to work with the Soviets in an attempt to unravel the knotty problem of the 'secret protocols'. At a meeting on 5 May 1988, the Politburo discussed the question of the 'secret Soviet–German documents of 1939 as they affect Poland'. Medvedev suggested they adopt a gradual approach. Georgy Smirnov, the Director of the Institute of Marxism-Leninism, admitted that there were no convincing arguments on the Soviet side, and the other members spoke in roughly the same vein:

> GROMYKO: There definitely were originals. And not to recognize this is a big risk. On the level of history it is better to tell the truth. But the truth should be that we have copies but not the originals. The originals might have been destroyed under Stalin or without Stalin.

(Gromyko remained staunchly mendacious to the end of his life. In his memoirs, and in the face of the evidence from German archives, he insisted that the 'secret protocols' did not exist: 'The Soviet chief prosecutor at Nuremberg labelled it a forgery, and correctly so, since no such "protocol" has ever been found, either in the USSR or in any other country – nor could it be.'[170])

> CHEBRIKOV: It's too soon to decide about publishing . . .
> GORBACHEV: I have a proposal. I believe the Politburo can work out a position when it has the official documents in its hands . . . I suggest we limit ourselves to an exchange of opinions . . . We'll continue to work in the archives to locate the documents. If the documents should become available, maybe we'll come back to this issue . . .

The others mumbled their agreement. Three days later, Gorbachev concluded: 'I think the copies should be kept where they're supposed to be.'[171]

In December 1991 I was appointed Chairman of the Russian Supreme Soviet Commission for the transfer of Party and KGB archives to the public domain, in other words for the opening of the archives. In nearly two years we declassified some *seventy-eight million* files and placed them at the disposal of the relevant archives for the benefit of researchers. Acting on the orders of President Yeltsin, towards the end of 1992 three members of the Commission – Professors Rudolf Pikhoya and A. Korotkov and myself – were in the process of opening 'Special files', i.e. materials of the utmost secrecy. In the Soviet period, these files could only be opened with the permission of the General Secretary. The contents of the files were not indicated on the outside, and only a set of numbers indicated some form of identification. As we had no code-book to decipher the numbers, we simply opened one envelope after another to discover what secrets they held.

We had already found many interesting things when we came to another file, big and thick and, like all the rest, secured with a number of wax seals. Inside we found an inventory showing that it contained 'Documents relating to the Soviet–German Talks of 1939–1941'. Below this was written: 'Original texts of the Soviet-German secret agreements concluded in the period 1939–1941'. Here were the originals, in Russian and German: six protocols, the announcement of the Soviet and German governments of 28 September 1939, the exchange of letters between Molotov and Ribbentrop, and two maps of Poland signed by Stalin and Ribbentrop. There was also a note signed by sector chief A. Moshkov and dated 10 July 1987: 'I reported to Comrade V.I. Boldin. He ordered me to keep this to hand in the sector for the time being.'[172] Boldin could only have asked to see a Special File with the permission of the General Secretary. Clearly, Gorbachev had been acquainted with this material long before 5 May 1988.

The documents on the Soviet massacre of Polish officers at Katyn were treated similarly. On 18 April 1989 Boldin opened the Special File, and must have reported its contents to Gorbachev.[173] (As it happens, the papers show that Andropov had read the file on 15 April 1981, and said nothing.) What then are we to make of Gorbachev's comment on 5 May 1988: 'If the documents become available, maybe we'll come back to this issue . . .'?

It is safe to assume that Gorbachev had had the documents in his hands, but in the name of dishonest Bolshevik secret policy, he chose to sacrifice morality, and in a sense also his historical reputation. After having seen the documents, he claimed that they were not 'available'. At the same time he was writing in his book: 'I support open politics, the politics of real things. Such politics cannot have a false bottom.'[174] Gorbachev was fond of reminding the public that he was open, sincere and honest: in his farewell speech to the country on 25 December 1991 he repeated, 'I am speaking honestly and frankly. It is my moral duty.' But politics is a cynical and ruthless business, and Gorbachev's life, for all his virtues, testifies to that sad fact.

For Gorbachev, Communist ideology was a kind of secular religion that had no place for morality, yet it was also the main source of his dramatic departure from the political scene. The *Wall Street Journal* of 27 December 1991 rightly said: 'Gorbachev was the best thing the Communist Party had to offer. He played the central role in a remarkable chapter of world history, but was forced in the end to go, because in the historical play there was no longer any room for a man who still wanted to be a Communist.'[175]

In his dramatic speech on central television on 25 December 1991, when he lay down the office of President of the USSR, Gorbachev expressed what history will surely decide of his turbulent time as the USSR's seventh leader: 'Society now has liberty, it has been emancipated politically and spiritually. And that is the main achievement that we have not fully comprehended because we have not yet learned how to use that liberty.' Speaking in Paris in May 1993, he declared: 'The Gorbachev era has just begun ... Gorbachev began the reform of society and international relations in a framework of new thinking ... We are moving towards a new civilization which will not be a choice between capitalism and socialism, but a synthesis of our own experience.'[176]

I believe that the historic outcome of the unforgettable years of *perestroika* outweigh all of Gorbachev's mistakes and miscalculations. The invaluable fruit of his reformation was the liberty which has given the former Soviet society a chance to attain a prosperous and democratic way of life.

Postscript

Seven leaders in seven decades – pure coincidence, historical accident. The gradual and inevitable weakening of the leaders' power, however, was no accident. Like that of Bolshevism in general, it was failing almost visibly.

The first and second leaders exercised unlimited dictatorial power, though it was Stalin who wielded it in its most extreme form, guided to be sure by Lenin's precepts and his own 'revolutionary conscience'.

Khrushchev, the third leader, made a conscious effort to lessen the role of one-man rule, while remaining faithful to the idea of Bolshevik absolutism, to whose realization he felt personally committed, as is revealed by his 'gift' of the Crimea to Ukraine, his arbitrary changes of regional borders in the Caucasus, and his Cuban adventure. His power as Party leader was no longer dictatorial, but it was still indisputable.

The fourth leader, Brezhnev, although he tried to preserve the system, lacked the qualities needed to do so. The erosion of the Leninist foundations of society and state reached significant depths during his rule. Despite the ostensibly enormous role played by the leader, a great gulf emerged between the regime's officially recognized attributes and the public's real attitudes. The system's internal weakness and decline was sensed by everyone, and people learned to say one thing while doing another. Many Party bosses, like Molière's Tartuffe, were guided by the rule that 'he who sins in private does not sin at all.'

Paradoxically, at the very moment when the Soviet Union achieved military-strategic parity with the USA, and at the peak of its nuclear might, it began to experience growing spiritual uncertainty. It had no proper reply to the West's criticism of its record on human rights; it could not halt the flight of its citizens to the free world; it had no constructive ideas for relieving its chronic economic crisis. Brezhnev was the leader of a state whose military power did not correspond to its spiritual base. As before, it was the infamous 'class approach' that ruled when political, social and ideological issues were judged.

The fifth and sixth leaders, Andropov and Chernenko, could do nothing to reverse or arrest the erosion of Soviet power. Andropov may have been one of the most intelligent of the leaders, and certainly he tried to do something to alter the ominous state of affairs, but he had little chance of success. His efforts to slow the mounting crisis by administrative means had little effect. This was not the fault of his early death: Andropov was a Leninist who thought like a Chekist, and was therefore incapable of bringing about fundamental change for the better. In many important respects, he behaved like his predecessors. Blind belief in the power of the leader's instructions and the omnipotence of the Party organization was itself a sign of the declining power of the regime, which had nothing but routine decrees to offer the population. While the leaders sat in their offices, their power was slowly draining away. This could be seen in the listless way people carried out their orders, in their formal attitudes to Party directives, and in the growth of bureaucratism.

When Gorbachev took over the top position in the Bolshevik regime, despite its outward respectability and the presence of powerful controls, the system was rife with defects that had accumulated for decades; these defects were precisely an expression of the strength of the totalitarian regime. A simple list is enough to indicate the doom hanging over the Leninist model: a monopoly of power in the hands of a single political party; a command system of administration; a profoundly anti-democratic regime; a closed society; total control; an omnipotent leader who was never elected by the people.

Gorbachev was the best of the seven Bolshevik leaders. He managed to do a great deal, but he could have done more had he relinquished his faith in the possibility of saving the Communist system and its reform programme. But even on 23 August 1991, having just been freed from captivity at Foros, he told journalists that he still believed in the ideals of socialism and thought improvement of the CPSU was possible. He had begun his great reformation without knowing where it would end. That was his tragedy.

Against the background of the rest of the world's indisputable progress, the existence of the Communist system in the USSR was an anomaly. Gorbachev came to power at the moment when the weakness of the system reached a critical point. He had only to open the door a crack to cause a flood of revelations about the past, and this sharpened the people's sense of the regime's weakness as an unjust power. Events in Tbilisi, Vilnius and elsewhere demonstrated that the use of force to settle internal disputes could never achieve the desired effect. Incantations at Party meetings could do nothing to 'accelerate' social and economic development, or arrest the disintegration of Soviet society and the growth of nationalism, or divert the people from trying to live their lives in their own ways.

A positive result of the erosion of the Bolshevik regime and the image of its first leaders was the disappearance of the Leninist system. A negative result was the disappearance of the USSR as a unified state. It could have continued to exist, if in an altered form, as a democratic confederation. Gorbachev tried to achieve this, and it may still be a future possibility.

Attempts to revive the dying system were both fruitless and dangerous. Even if the Communists had returned to power in subsequent elections, they had nothing to offer society. Their Leninist arsenal had been completely exposed for what it was.

The story of the seven leaders reflects the history of the Soviet Union itself. The logic of power is almost always immoral, and Bolshevik power especially so. With the exception of Lenin, whom the rest needed as the justification and basis of their actions, as one leader departed, the next would at once begin to denigrate his predecessor. It was a practical approach: all the sins of the present were buried with the past.

Within a couple of years of his death, Stalin was being reviled by his successor as the bloody scourge of the Party; and Khrushchev himself had barely been put out to grass when the arrows of condemnation and indignation came flying after him. A group of old Bolsheviks wrote to Brezhnev, saying: 'What did he leave after him when he was leader of the Party and state? Nothing at all!'[1] They demanded that Khrushchev's pension be cut, that he be given 'an apartment with a communal lavatory', deprived of his automobile and so on. And indeed, the Politburo halved his pension and gave him a less desirable dacha. These were, after all, old Bolsheviks, 'they had seen Lenin'.

Gorbachev was no exception to the rule of casting his predecessors into oblivion. Shortly after he came to power, towns called Brezhnev and Chernenko were renamed, as were streets and ships, a space centre and a mine. The 'love and respect' of the populace had to be focused on the new leader. To his credit, Gorbachev was the only leader to even attempt to abandon this tradition.

Whatever positive achievements were made over the period of Soviet rule resulted from the labour of the people. The preservation of morality, of the eternal values of truth, goodness and beauty, was due to the people, not to the ideological myths of Leninism. Soviet history, full as it is of terrible times, also contains bright passages that were written despite the logic of Bolshevism.

The portraits of the seven leaders who led the people towards their illusory 'bright future' stand like individual signposts along the way, the most visible part of our history. The leaders have gone, but their history is still with us.

Notes

Abbreviations

APRF	Russian Presidential Archives
Arkhiv MB RF	Archives of the Security Ministry of the Russian Federation, i.e. former KGB
GARF	State Archives of the Russian Federation
RTsKhIDNI	Russian Centre for the Preservation and Study of Documents of Recent History
TsAMO	Central Archives of the Ministry of Defence
TsKhSD	Centre for the Preservation of Contemporary Documentation

Introduction
The Path of Leaders

1 Abramovich, R.A., *Martov i mirovoi menshevizm*, New York, 1959, p. 77
2 Stalin, I., *Voprosy leninizma*, 11th edn, Moscow, 1945, p. 123
3 Lenin, *Polnoe sobranie sochinenii [PSS]*, Moscow, vol.23, p. 43
4 APRF, *Stenogramma zasedaniya politbyuro ot 15 oktyabrya*, l.156
5 Bukharin, N., *Ataka. Sbornik teoreticheskikh rabot*, Moscow, 1924, pp. 91–114

The First Leader
Vladimir Lenin

1 Arkhiv MB RF, n-15318, d.21790, t.1, l.281
2 Ibid., d.14265, t.1, l.1
3 RTsKhIDNI, f.2, op. 1, d.6601, l.1
4 Ibid., d.24632, l.1
5 *Pravda*, No.51, 6 March 1920
6 RTsKhIDNI, f.2, op. 1, d.23478, l.11
7 Ibid., d.7310, ll.1-2
8 Lenin, *Polnoe sobranie sochineniyi*, Moscow, 1961-1965, (hereafter *PSS*), vol.38, p. 186
9 See *Vozhd'. Lenin, kotorogo my ne znali*, Saratov, 1992, p. 97
10 Potresov, A.N., *V plenu u illyuzii*, Paris, 1927, p. 99
11 Potresov, A.N., *Posmertnyi sbornik*

proizvedenii, Paris, 1037, pp. 301–3

12 *Pis'ma Lenin k Gor'komu*, Moscow, 1936, p. 43

13 Aldanov, M., *Portrety*, Paris, 1931, reprinted Moscow, 1994, p. 9

14 RTsKhIDNI, f.5, op. 1, d.1315, ll.1-4

15 Ibid., f.2, op. 1, d.8492, ll.1-2

16 Ibid., op. 2, d.1338, ll.1-2

17 Ibid., f.17, op. 3, d.325, ll.2-3

18 Ibid., f.2, op. 1, d.26003, l.1

19 Lenin, *PSS*, vol.52, p. 179

20 Ibid., vol.50, p. 343

21 RTsKhIDNI, f.2, op. 1, d.23822, ll.1-7 et al

22 Ibid., d.27137, l.1

23 Ibid., d.457, ll.1-9

24 *Lenin V.I. i Gorkii, A.M.*, Moscow, 1961, p. 276

25 See Lenin, *PSS*, vol.33, pp. 100, 118

26 Fischer, Louis, *The Life of Lenin*, London, 1964, pp. 489–90

27 *Lenin V.I. i Gorkii, A.M.*, Moscow, 1961, p. 20

28 Lenin, *PSS*, vol.33, pp. 1–18

29 Ibid., pp. 101–2

30 GARF, f.130, op. 1, d.3, ll.31-3

31 Lenin, *PSS*, vol.14, p. 266

32 Ibid., vol.48, l.295

33 Ibid., vol.20, pp, 21, 23, 40, 71

34 Ibid., vol.14, p. 15; vol.12, pp. 303, 320, 522-3

35 Fischer, Louis, *The Life of Lenin*, London, 1964, pp. 490–1

36 *Veche* (reprint), Paris, No.16, 1984, pp. 152–7

37 Rodzyanko, M.F., *Gosudarstvennaya Duma i fevral'skaya revolyutsiya*, Rostov on Don, 1919, pp. 30–1

38 *Monarkhiya pered krusheniem 1914-1917; iz bumag Nikolaya*, Moscow, 1927

39 Chernov, V., *Rozhdenie*

revolyutsionnoi Rossii, Prague, 1934, p. 155

40 *Leninskii sbornik*, vol.2, p. 195

41 Lenin, *PSS*, vol.26, pp. 1, 6

42 *Leninskii sbornik*, vol.2, p. 205

43 Ibid., p. 195

44 Lenin, *PSS*, vol.26, p. 96

45 Ibid., pp. 108–9

46 Ibid., pp. 165–6

47 Shub, D., Bakunin, Nechayev i Lenin, in *Novyi zhurnal*, No.LV, 1958, p. 268

48 Lenin, *PSS*, vol.26, p. 26

49 Agronyants, O., *Chto delat'? - Ili deleninizatsiya nashego obshchestva*, London, 1989, p. 67

50 Lenin, *PSS*, vol.12, pp. 34, 70

51 Ibid., vol.30, pp. 310, 313, 322, 323, 325, 328

52 *Leninskii sbornik*, vol.2, p. 195

53 Ludendorff, E., *Meine Kriegserinnerungen, 1914-1918*, Berlin, 1919, p. 47

54 Zeman, Z.A.B., *Germany and the Russian Revolution, 1915-1918: Documents from the Archives of the German Foreign Ministry*, London, 1958, pp. 130, 133

55 Bernstein, E., 'Ein dunkeles Kapitel', in *Vorwärts*, Berlin, 14 January 1921

56 APRF, f.3, op. 22, d.10, ll.1-4

57 Lenin, *PSS*, vol.32, p. 182

58 Milyukov, P.N., *Vospominaniya (1859-1917)*, vol.2, New York, 1955, pp. 387–9

59 Lenin, *PSS*, vol.32, p. 331

60 Sukhanov, N., *Revolyutsiya 1917 goda*, Rome, 1971, p. 312

61 Trotskii, L., *O Lenine*, Moscow, 1924, pp. 58-9, 61

62 Lenin, *PSS*, vol.35, p. 247

63 Ibid., vol.34, p. 281

64 *Niva*, No.33, 1917

65 Lenin, *PSS*, vol.34, pp. 383–4

66 Lenin, *Sochineniya*, 3rd edn, vol.29, p. 390

67 Reed, J., *Desiat' dnei, kotorye potryasli ves' mir*, 2nd edn, Moscow, 1924, pp. 69–70

68 Pipes, R., *The Russian Revolution, 1899-1919*, London, p. 493

69 GARF, f.325, op. 1, d.11, l.11

70 In *Versty*, No.2, Paris, 1926, p. 181

71 Krupskaya, N., *Vospominaniya o Lenine*, Moscow, 1989, p. 469

72 *Sed'moi s'ezd RKP, Stenograficheskii otchet*, Moscow-Petrograd, 1923, p. 130

73 Ibid., p. 14

74 Ibid., p. 99

75 Ibid., pp. 33, 34, 42, 47

76 Radek, K., *Portrety i pamflety*, Book 1, Moscow, 1933, p. 34

77 Lenin, *PSS*, vol.22, p. 280

78 Ibid., vol.31, pp. 119-21, 533-4

79 Ibid., vol.34, p. 420

80 *Protokoly TsK RSDRP(b), avgust 1917-fevral' 1918*, Moscow, 1958, pp. 171-2

81 See RTsKhIDNI, f.2, op. 1, d.3972, l.1

82 Ibid., d.8196, l.1

83 Ibid., d.11480, l.1

84 Ibid., d.9852, l.1

85 Gippius, Z., *Izbrannaya poeziya*, Paris, 1984, p. 113

86 Zinoviev, G., *Leninizim. Vvedenie k izucheniyu leninizma*, Leningrad, 1925, pp. 370–1

87 Zinoviev, G., *V.I. Lenin. Kratkii biograficheskii ocherk*, Leningrad, 1924, p. 27

88 AFSK RF, Arkhiv no.R-33833, t.41, l.257

89 RTsKhIDNI, f.17, op. 3, d.78, l.5

90 Ibid., f.2, op. 1, d.2442, l.1

91 Ibid.

92 Ibid., l.2

93 *Dekrety sovetskoi vlasti*, vol.8, Moscow, 1977, p. 222

94 RTsKhIDNI, f.2, op. 1, d.9592, l.1

95 Ibid., d.27071, l.1

96 See Lenin, *PSS*, vol.48, pp. 189–90

97 RTsKhIDNI, f.2, op. 1, d.26159, l.1

98 *Dekrety sovetskoi vlasti*, vol.4, Moscow, 1977, pp. 264–5

99 RTsKhIDNI, f.2, op. 1, d.12390, l.1

100 Fischer, L., *The Life of Lenin*, London, 1964, p. 270

101 RTsKhIDNI, f.2, op. 2, d.391, l.1

102 Ibid., d.122, l.1

103 Ibid., d.27069, l.1

104 Ibid., f.5, op. 2, d.1952, ll.24-5

105 Ibid., f.2, op. 2, d.1119, ll.1-2

106 Ibid., f.5, op. 2, d.1952, ll.38-9

107 Ibid., f.2, op. 1, d.24424, l.1

108 Ibid., op. 2, d.794, l.1

109 APRF, f.31, op. 1, d.4, ll.211-14

110 Stepun, F., *Russkaya ideya. V krugu pisatelei i myslitelei russkogo zarubezhiya*, vol.1, Moscow, 1994, p. 290

111 *Leninskii sbornik*, vol.26, Moscow, 1934, p. 47

112 RTsKhIDNI, f.2, op. 2, d.571, l.2

113 AFSK RF, R-1073, d.11184, l.57

114 RTsKhIDNI, f.2, op. 1, d.19320, ll.1-4

115 Ibid., d.8885, ll.14-25

116 Lenin, *PSS*, vol.30, p. 211

117 Ibid., p. 220

118 Ibid., pp. 334–5

119 Ibid., p. 218

120 In *Novyi zhurnal*, No.56, New York, 1960, p. 260

121 Lenin, *PSS*, vol.37, p. 489

122 Ibid., p. 490

123 *Novyi zhurnal*, No.51, New York, 1960, p. 262

124 Lenin, *PSS*, vol.37, p. 511
125 Fischer, L., *The Life of Lenin*, London, 1964, p. 314
126 Ibid., p. 313
127 Trotsky, L., *O Lenine*, Moscow, 1924, p. 87
128 RTsKhIDNI, f.2, op. 1, d.8924, l.1
129 Ibid.
130 Ibid., d.15000, l.1
131 Ibid., d.15041, l.1
132 Ibid., d.15042, l.1
133 Ibid., d.15088, l.1
134 Lenin, *PSS*, 4th edn, vol.33, Moscow, 1951, p. 48
135 *Vozhd'. Lenin, kotorogo my ne znali*, Saratov, 1992, p. 94
136 APRF, f.3, op. 22, d.10, ll.86, 88
137 Kerensky, A., *Izdaleka (1920–21 gg.)*, Paris, 1922, p. 114
138 RTsKhIDNI, f.2, op. 2, d.708, l.1
139 Ibid., d.441, ll.4–8
140 Ibid., f.5, op. 1, d.2761, l.27
141 Vasilieva, O. and Knyshevsky, P., *Krasnye konkistadory*, Moscow, 1994, p. 84
142 Ibid., p. 85
143 RTsKhIDNI, f.2, op. 2, d.202, ll.1–2
144 Ibid., op. 1, d.25671, ll.1–2
145 Ibid., d.27149, ll.1–3
146 Balabanoff, A., *Impressions of Lenin*, Ann Arbor, 1964, pp. 29–30
147 RTsKhIDNI, f.2, op. 2, d.220, l.1
148 APRF, f.3, op. 20, d.53, l.59
149 Ibid., l.55
150 Ibid., l.29
151 Ibid., l.32
152 RTsKhIDNI, f.17, op. 3, d.85, ll.1–2
153 Ibid., f.2, op. 2, dd.13–18, ll.1–3
154 Lenin, *PSS*, vol.41, p. 234
155 RTsKhIDNI, f.2, op. 2, d.612, l.1
156 Ibid., op. 1, d.8885, l.23
157 Ibid., op. 2, d.1178, ll.1–2
158 Potresov, A., *Posmertnyi sbornik proizvedenii*, Paris, 1937, pp. 202, 203
159 *Lyubyashchii tebya V. Ulyanov. Pis'ma Lenina materi*, Moscow, 1967, p. 36
160 Krupskaya, N., *Vospominaniya o Vladimire Ilyiche Lenine*, vol.2, Moscow, 1989, p. 37
161 APRF, f.3, op. 22, d.307, l.173
162 Fischer, L., *The Life of Lenin*, London, 1965, p. 80, citing a conversation between Kollontai and Marcel Body, the First Secretary of the French legation in Norway, published in *Preuves*, Paris, 1952
163 Krupskaya, N., *Vospominaniya o Vladimire Ilyiche Lenine*, vol.2, Moscow, 1989, pp. 157, 217
164 RTsKhIDNI, f.2, op. 1, d.24299, l.1
165 Ibid., f.127, op. 1, d.61
166 Krupskaya, N., *Vospominaniya o Lenine*, 3rd edn, Moscow, 1989, p. 217
167 RTsKhIDNI, f.2, op. 2, d.24299
168 Ibid., op. 1, d.3327
169 Ibid., d.4462, l.2
170 Ibid., f.127, op. 2, d.61, ll.1–14
171 Ibid., ll.7–14
172 *Leninskii sbornik*, vol.37, Moscow, 1970, p. 233
173 Ibid., p. 143
174 RTsKhIDNI, f.127, op. 1, d.14, l.2
175 Fischer, L. *The Life of Lenin*, London, 1965, p. 80
176 Ibid.
177 APRF, f.45, op. 1, d.694, l.2
178 RTsKhIDNI, f.2, op. 2, d.515, l.1
179 Ibid., d.830, l.1
180 Ibid., d.171, l.1
181 Ibid., f.17, op. 3, d.195, l.1

182 Ibid., d.216, l.4

183 Ibid., f.2, op. 2, dd.741, 1165, ll.1-4

184 Ibid., d.991, l.1

185 Ibid., d.1318, ll.1-3

186 Ibid., d.135, l.1

187 Ibid., f.17, op. 3, d.106, l.4

188 APRF, f.3, op. 22, d.307, ll.8-11

189 Ibid., d.308, l.11

190 Ibid., l.59

191 APRF, Special File, Packet 18/2, ll.7-9

192 APRF, f.3, op. 22, d.307, l.141

193 Ibid., d.310, ll.1-2, 6-8

194 Ibid., d.307, l.176

195 RTsKhIDNI, f.2, op. 2, d.2, l.1

196 Lenin, *PSS*, vol.45, pp. 356-62; see Pipes, R., *Russia Under the Bolshevik Regime, 1919-1924*, London, 1994, p. 482 for an account of this episode

197 Lenin, *PSS*, vol.54, p. 329

198 Ibid., p. 330

199 RTsKhIDNI, f.325, op. 1, d.412, l.147; f.5, op. 2, d.34, l.19

200 Ibid., f.558, op. 1, d.2002, l.21

201 Ibid., f.2, op. 1, d.24472, l.1

202 Ibid., op. 2, d.641, l.1

203 Ibid., f.17, op. 3, d.249, l.6

204 Lenin, *PSS*, vol.45, pp. 300-9

205 RTsKhIDNI, f.2, op. 1, d.23478, ll.1-12

206 Ibid., f.3, op. 22, d.9, ll.1-3

207 Ibid., f.2, op. 1, d.25609, ll.10-11

208 Ibid., op. 2, d.1113, ll.1-3

209 Ibid., f.17, op. 3, d.239, l.1; d.234, l.3

210 Ibid., f.2, op. 1, d.12500, l.14

211 Ibid., f.17, op. 3, d.314, l.6

212 Lenin, *PSS*, vol.40, p. 101

213 AMBF, f.114728, *Materialy Kronshadtskogo myatezha*, l.1

214 RGVA (formerly TsGASA), f.33988, op. 2, d.367, l.40

215 RTsKhIDNI, f.2, op. 1, d.12176, l.1

216 Ibid., d.12500, l.12

217 Ibid., op. 2, d.463, ll.1-2

218 Ibid., op. 1, d.13067

219 Lenin, *PSS*, vol.44, p. 80

220 RTsKhIDNI, f.2, op. 1, d.24327, d.1

221 Lenin, *PSS*, vol.44, p. 79

222 Ibid., vol.35, pp. 200, 201, 204

223 RTsKhIDNI, f.17, op. 3, d.164, l.2

224 Ibid., f.2, op. 1, d.7310, l.1

225 Lenin, *PSS*, vol.44, p. 428

226 RTsKhIDNI, f.2, op. 1, d.23478, l.1-11

227 Ibid., d.12500, ll.10-14

228 Lenin, *PSS*, vol.44, p. 329

229 RTsKhIDNI, f.2, op. 1, d.18195, l.1

230 Ibid., f.17, op. 3, d.147, l.4

231 Ibid., f.2, op. 1, d.17826, l.1

232 Ibid., d.12072, l.1

233 Ibid., d.27071, l.1

234 Ibid., d.24533, l.1

235 Ibid.

236 Ibid., d.976, l.1

237 Ibid., d.18552, l.1

238 Shturman, D., 'Sovetskie vozhdi na yazyke ostroslovov', in *Vremya i my*, No.74, Jersualem, 1983, pp. 141-2

239 APRF, f.3, op. 60, d.25, l.5

240 RTsKhIDNI, f.17, op. 3, d.284, l.9

241 Ibid., d.69, l.2

242 Ibid., d.361, l.15

243 Lenin, *PSS*, vol.44, p. 157

244 Trotskii, L., *Lenin, kak natsional'nyi tip*, 2nd edn, Leningrad, 1924, pp. 6-7

The Second Leader
Joseph Stalin

1 Stalin, I., *O proekte konstitutsii Soyuza SSR*, Central Committee, Moscow, 1937, p. 5
2 Ibid., pp. 16, 17, 23, 24
3 GARF, f.9401, op. 2, d.236, t.III, ll.145–66
4 Ibid., ll.145, 161, 166, 194
5 Stalin, I., *Rech' na predvybornom sobranii 11 dekabrya 1937 g.*, Central Committee, Moscow, 1937, pp. 1–9. The atmosphere described, and the manner of Stalin's delivery, have been authenticated to the translator by Iverach Macdonald of *The Times*, one of the few Western correspondents permitted to attend the meeting
6 Stalin, I., *Rech' na predvybornom sobranii 11 dekabrya 1937 g.*, pp. 7, 12–13
7 APRF, *Stenogramma zasedaniya politbyuro ot 6 fevralya 1988*, l.169
8 Shturman, D., 'Sovetskie vozhdi na yazyke ostroslovov' in *Vremya i my*, No.74, Jerusalem, 1983, p. 130
9 *Izvestiya TsK KPSS*, No.9, 1990, pp. 115–27
10 Lenin, *PSS*, vol.49, pp. 101, 161
11 Ibid., vol.48, p. 162
12 APRF, f.45, op. 1, d.693, ll.100-1
13 Lenin, *PSS*, vol.45, pp. 356–7
14 APRF, f.45, op. 1, d, 25, l.31
15 Aldanov, M., *Sovremenniki*, Paris, 1928, p. 37
16 Lenin, *PSS*, vol.45, p. 346
17 RTsKhIDNI, f.558, op. 1, d.5193, ll.1-3
18 Ibid., d.3112, l.1
19 *Istoriya Vsesoyuznoi kommunistiechskoi partii (bol'shevikov). Kratkii kurs*, Moscow, 1938, pp. 256–7
20 APRF, f.45, op. 1, d.30, l.216
21 Ibid., f.3, op. 24, d.430, l.1.570b
22 Dan, Lydia, 'Bukharin o Staline', in *Novyi Zhurnal*, No.75, 1964, pp. 181–2
23 In *Vremya i my*, No.107, Jerusalem, 1989, p. 255
24 APRF, f.45, op. 1, d.25, l.92
25 Stalin, I., *Voprosy leninizma*, 11th edn., Moscow, 1945, pp. 1–77, 106, 156
26 RTsKhIDNI, f.17, op. 2, d.612, vyp.III, l.9-45
27 Mikoyan, A., *Stalin. K shestidesyatiletiyu so dnya rozhdeniya*, Moscow, 1940, p. 69
28 RTsKhIDNI, f.495, op. 82, d.1, ll.10-100b
29 Stalin, I., *Voprosy leninizma*, 11th edn., Moscow, 1945, pp. 590–1
30 Lenin, *PSS*, vol.35, p. 110
31 Ibid., pp. 311–13
32 Ibid., vol.41, p. 376
33 *Izvestiya TsK KPSS*, No.9, 1990, p. 117
34 Ibid., No.3, 1989, p. 165
35 Stalin, I., *Voprosy leninizma*, 11th edn., Moscow, 1945, p. 491
36 Stalin, I., *Sochineniya*, vol.5, Stanford, 1967, p. 71
37 Stalin, I., *Voprosy leninizma*, 11th edn., Moscow, 1945, p. 121
38 RTsKhIDNI, f.17, op. 2, d.612, vyp.III, l.35
39 Stalin, I., *Sochineniya*, vol.5, p. 66
40 Ibid., vol.13, p. 228
41 Stalin, I., *Voprosy leninizma*, 11th edn., Moscow, 1945, pp. 578–9
42 Ibid., p. 598
43 RTsKhIDNI f.17, op. 125, d.394, l.89; see also *Istochnik*, No.3, 1996, p. 96

44 Barbusse, H., *Stalin*, Moscow, 1936, pp. 351-2

45 Stalin, I., *O proekte Konstitutsii Soyuza SSR*, Central Committee, Moscow, 1937, pp. 5-40

46 Stalin, I, *Sochineniya*, vol.13, p. 104

47 Stalin, I., *Beseda s angliiskim pisatelem G.G. Uellsom*, Central Committee, Moscow, 1935, p. 3

48 Stalin, I, *O proekte Konstitutsii Soyuza SSR*, Central Committee, Moscow, 1937, p. 34

49 Stalin, I., *Voprosy leninizma*, 11th edn, Moscow, 1945, pp. 229-32

50 *Izvestiya TsK KPSS*, No.3, 1990, pp. 150-62

51 APRF, f.45, op. 1, d.412, l.21

52 Arkhiv OGPU, No.471, t.III, pp. 18-31

53 RTsKhIDNI, f.17, op. 2, d.575, ll.1-193

54 Ibid., d.612, vyp.III, ll.9-45

55 *Akten zur deutschen auswärtigen Politik 1918-1945*, Bd.VII, Baden-Baden, 1956, p. 131

56 RTsKhIDNI, f.558, op. 1, d.3808, ll.1-12

57 Stalin, I., *O Velikoi Otechestvennoi voine Sovetskogo Soyuza*, Moscow, 1946, p. 11

58 *Perepiska [Stalina] s prezidentami SShA I premier-ministrami Velikobritanii*, Moscow, 1976, t.1, p. 84

59 APRF, f.3, op. 50, d.45, ll.50-2

60 Ibid., l.50

61 TsAMO, f.15, op. 725558, d.36, l.305

62 Ibid., d.35, ll.2-17

63 APRF, f.45, op. 1, d.28, l.107

64 *Izvestiya TsK KPSS*, No.8, 1991, pp. 197-221

65 Ibid., pp. 220-2

66 APRF, f.45, op. 1, d.413, ll.53-5

67 TsAMO, f.3, op. 11556, d.13, ll.210-12

68 Ibid., f.220, op. 242, d.9, ll.112-14

69 Krivosheev, G. (ed.), *Grif sekretnosti snyat* [Statistics on the losses sustained by Soviet forces], Moscow, 1993, p. 140

70 APRF, f.45, op. 1, d.28, l.116

71 *Izvestiya TsK KPSS*, No.4, 1991, p. 210

72 APRF, f.30, op. 1, l.84

73 TsAMO, f.132A, op. 2642, d.41, ll.75-81

74 Volkov, A., *Nezavershennye frontovye nastupatel'nye operatsii*, Moscow, 1992, p. 94

75 Ibid., p. 134

76 TsAMO, f.204, op. 93, d.7, ll.103-274; f.228, op. 720, d.68, ll.12-574; f.229, op. 209, d.32, ll.1-162; f.213, op. 2066, d.5, ll.307-427; f.208, op. 2579, d.22, ll.66-100; f.221, op. 1364, d.210, ll.31-89; f.214, op. 1441, d.48, ll.184-340; et al

77 Ibid., f.132A, op. 2642, d.13, l.7

78 *Bol'shevik*, No.23, 1949, p. 7

79 APRF, f.45, op. 1, d.321, ll.31-4

80 *Pravda*, 14 November 1948

81 Stalin, I., *Sochineniya*, vol.6, pp. 398-9

82 See Stalin, I., *Sochineniya*, vol.1 [14], pp. 116-31

83 *Annali Feltrinelli*, vol.8, Milan, 1968, p. 670

84 RTsKhIDNI, f.17, op. 120, d.297

85 Ibid., d.259, ll.36-7

86 TsGANKh, f.3429, op. 6, d.28, ll.19-21

87 Hoxha, E., *So Stalinym: Vospominaniya*, Tirana, 1957, pp. 33-52

88 APRF, f.45, op. 1, d.25, l.109

89 RTsKhIDNI, f.495, op. 74, d.411, ll.5, 22

90 Cited in *Voprosy istorii KPSS*, No.12, 1988, p. 52. See Joseph Berger's memoirs, *Shipwreck of a Generation* (London, 1971) for an account of the life of a Polish Comintern functionary in Moscow

91 RTsKhIDNI, f.558, op. 1, dd.28-40, ll.1-29

92 Stalin, I., *Rech' na XIX s'ezde partii*, Moscow, 1952, p. 11

93 APRF, f.45, op. 1, d.319, ll.4-7

94 Ibid., ll.11-15, 19, 14

95 Ibid., d.38, ll.105-14

96 Ibid., d.318, l.12

97 Stalin, I., *Rech' na XIX s'ezde partii*, pp. 8-9

98 APRF, f.45, op. 1, d.310, l.93

99 Ibid., d.311, ll.10-14

100 AVP RF (Russian Foreign Policy Archives), f.0144, op. 30, p. 188, d.15, l.31; p. 5, d.2, l.44, et al

101 APRF, f.45, op. 1, d.397, l.109

102 *Istoricheskii arkhiv*, No.2, 1993, p. 27

103 Ibid., p. 20

104 AVP RF, f.0144, op. 30, p. 118, d.10, l.3

105 Dedijer, V., *Iosip Broz Tito*, Belgrade, 1953, p. 451

106 *Istoricheskii Arkhiv*, no.2, 1993, pp. 20, 28

107 Girenko, Yu., *Stalin-Tito*, Moscow, 1991, p. 386

108 APRF, f.45, op. 1, d.319, ll.21-2

109 Ibid., d.325, l.35

110 Ibid., d.322, l.142

111 Ibid., ll.144-5

112 Ibid., d.336, ll.84-9

113 Ibid., d.329, ll.8-17

114 Mao Tse-tung, *Izbrannye proizvedeniya*, vol.3, Moscow, 1953, p. 189

115 APRF, f.45, op. 1, d.338, l.48

116 Ibid., d.329, ll.86-7

117 Ibid., l.32

118 Ibid., d.303, l.161

119 Stalin, I., *Ekonomicheskie problemy sotsializma v SSSR*, Moscow, 1952, p. 36

120 Stalin, I., *Rech' na XIX s'ezde Partii*, Moscow, 1952, p. 14

121 Girenko, Yu., *Stalin-Tito*, Moscow, 1991, p. 186

122 Stalin, I., *Sochineniya*, vol.12, p. 140

123 In the 1960s, the Hoover Institution, Stanford University, in fact completed the publication of Stalin's works in Russian with three further volumes, thanks to the enterprising efforts of the late Robert McNeal (ed.)

124 *Iosif Vissarionovich Stalin: Kratkaya Biografiya*, Moscow, 1951, pp. 164, 165

125 Stalin, I., *Sochineniya*, vol.2, pp. 333, 340

126 RTsKhIDNI, f.558, op. 1, d.2959, l.19

127 GARF, f.9401, op. 2, d.199

128 APRF, Central Committee and Sovnarkom Order, dated 1 July 1941

129 GARF, f.9401, op. 2, d.134, t.1, ll.1-2

130 APRF, f.45, op. 1, d.26, l.69

131 Ibid., d.27

132 Ibid., d.28, ll.6-7

133 Ibid., d.24, l.32

134 Ibid., d.25, l.95

135 Ibid., d.27, ll.106, 140; d.28, l.41, et al

136 Ibid., d.27, l.107

137 Ibid., d.343, l.141

138 GARF, f.941, op. 1, d.175, t.1, ll.34-235

139 Ibid., op. 2, d.66, t.III, l.34

140 Ibid., d.257, t.III, l.338

141 Lih, L., Naumov, O. and Khlevnikov, O. (eds), *Stalin's Letters to Molotov, 1925-1936*, Yale University Press, New Haven, 1995

142 APRF, f.45, op. 1, d.338, ll.95-6

143 Ibid., d.341, l.114

144 *Perepiska Predsedatelya Soveta Ministrov SSSR s prezidentami SShA i premier-ministrami Velikobritanii*, Moscow, 1976, t.1, pp. 29, 32, 48, 51, 76

145 APRF, f.45, op. 1, d.356, l.26

146 *Perepiska Predsedatelya Soveta Ministrov SSSR s prezidentami SShA in premier-ministrami Velikobritanii*, Moscow, 1976, t.1, p. 145

147 Special File No.9485

148 *Perepiska Predsedatelya Soveta Ministrov SSSR s prezidentami SShA in premier-ministrami Velikobritanii*, Moscow, 1976, t.II, p. 78

149 APRF, f.45, op. 1, d.11, l.60

150 GARF, f.9401, op. 2, d.87, t.IV, ll.124-30

151 Ibid., d.2223, l.237

152 *Perepiska Predsedatelya Soveta Ministrov SSSR s prezidentami SShA in premier-ministrami Velikobritanii*, Moscow, 1976, t.III, p. 304

153 *Berlinskaya (Potsdamskaya) konferentsiya rukovoditelei trekh soyuznykh derzhav - SSSR, SShA i Velikobritanii*, Moscow, 1980, p. 299

154 GARF, f.9401, op. 2, d.235, ll.27-35

155 Ibid., d.199, l.366

156 Ibid., d.269, t.I, ll.141-6

157 Ibid., f.3401, op. 2, d.269, t.I, ll.169-70

158 Ibid., f.9401, op. 2, d.269, t.III, ll.145-267

159 APRF, f.45, op. 1, d.346, ll.24-35

160 Ibid., l.1

161 Ibid., l.7

162 Ibid., l.8

163 Ibid.

164 Ibid., l.80

165 Ibid., l.8

166 Ibid., d.334, l.55

167 Ibid., d.346, l.94

168 Ibid., l.96

169 Ibid., l.109

170 Ibid., ll.145-7

171 *Sovetskaya voennaya entsiklopediya*, vol.4, p. 35

172 Ibid.

173 APRF, f.45, op. 1, d.346, ll.100-3

174 Ibid., d.334, ll.88-9

175 Ibid., d.347, ll.5-8

176 Ibid., ll.14-15

177 Ibid., l.24

178 Ibid., ll.41-5

179 Ibid., d.334, l.97

180 Ibid., ll.110-11

181 Ibid., l.126

182 Ibid., ll.105-6

183 Ibid., l.77

184 Ibid., d.335, ll.117-18

185 Ibid., l.38

186 Ibid., d.347, ll.57-8

187 Ibid., d.329, l.93

188 Ibid., d.348, ll.58, 61

189 Ibid., d.329, ll.54-70

190 *Perepiska Predsedatelya Soveta Ministrov SSSR ... Dokumenty (avgust 1941 - dekabr' 1945 g.)*, Moscow, 1976, p. 223

191 APRF, f.45, op. 1, d.372, ll.109-12, 114-15

192 Mao Tse-tung, *Izbrannye*

proizvedeniya, Moscow, 1963,
p. 453

193 Stalin, I., *Ekonomicheskie problemy
sotsializma v SSSR*, Moscow, 1952,
p. 92

194 *Perepiska Predsedatelya Soveta
Ministrov SSSR . . . Dokumenty
(avgust 1941 - dekabr' 1945 g.)*,
Moscow, 1976, p. 45

195 APRF, f.45, op. 1, d.354, l.107

196 TsAMO, f.3, op. 11556, d.18,
ll.110-11

197 Ibid., ll.1452-4

198 Stalin, I., *Rech' na XIX s'ezde Partii*,
Moscow, 1952, pp. 11–14

199 APRF, f.45, op. 1, d.1550, l.53

200 Ibid., ll.65-6

201 Khrushchev, N., *Khrushchev
vspominaet*, Moscow, 1991, p. 295

202 Ibid., p. 293

203 Ibid., p. 300

204 APRF, f.45, op. 1, d.1486, ll.2-3

205 Ibid., l.1

206 Ibid., l.4

207 Alliluyeva, S., *Dvadtsat' pisem k
drugu*, London, 1967, p. 7

208 APRF, f.45, op. 1, d.1486, l.136

209 Ibid., op. 2, d.196, ll.1-7

210 Ibid., op. 1, d.1486, ll.150-2

211 Ibid., ll.153-6

The Third Leader
Nikita Khrushchev

1 APRF, f.52, op. 1, d.30, ll.6, 8,
14-15, 23

2 Ibid., d.31, ll.3, 4, 5

3 Ibid., d.53, l.17

4 Medvedev, R., *All Stalin's Men*,
trans. Harold Shukman, Oxford,
1983, p. 140, Russian edition *Oni
okruzhali Stalina*, Moscow, 1990,
p. 277

5 APRF, f.3, op. 24, d.435, l.411

6 Burlatsky, F., *Nikita Sergeevich
Khrushchev. Materialy k biografii*,
Moscow, 1989, p. 12

7 *Khrushchev Remembers*, with an
introduction, commentary and
notes by Edward Crankshaw,
translated and edited by Strobe
Talbott, New York, 1970,
pp. 336–7

8 APRF, f.3, op. 24, d.463, l.163

9 Ibid., l.138

10 See *Izvestiya TsK KPSS*, No.1,
Moscow, 1991, pp. 140–8

11 Ibid., pp. 149, 155

12 *Administrativnoe zakonodatel'stvo*,
Moscow, 1936, p. 126

13 APRF, f.52, op. 1, d.103, l.141

14 *Izvestiya TsK KPSS*, No.1, Moscow,
1991, p. 203

15 Ibid., No.2, Moscow, 1991, p. 182

16 Ibid., p. 185

17 Ibid., p. 195

18 APRF, f.3, op. 24, d.463, ll.32-4

19 *Izvestiya*, 24 December 1953

20 APRF, f.3, op. 24, d.463, l.91

21 Vronskaya, J. and Chuguev, V.,
*The Biographical Dictionary of the
Former Soviet Union*, London,
1992, p. 394

22 APRF, f.3, op. 24, d.463, l.172

23 Ibid., d.435, ll.60-70

24 GARF, f.9401, op. 2, d.269, t.1,
ll.141-6

25 Ibid., l.348

26 APRF, f.52, op. 1, d.30, ll.42, 92

27 *Khrushchev Remembers*, New York,
1970, p. 244

28 GARF, f.9401, op. 102, dd.5, 94, 93

29 APRF, f.3, op. 10, d.65, ll.4-5

30 Ibid.

31 TsGA RSFSR, f.385, op. 13,
d.492, ll.1-2

32 GARF, f.7523, op. 57, d.963, ll.1-8

33 Ibid., ll.9-10

34 *Izvestiya TsK KPSS*, No.3, 1989, p. 134

35 Ibid., p. 132

36 APRF, Postanovlenie politbyuro. Protokol No.57, 31 January 1938, ll.11-12

37 APRF, f.52, op. 1, d.134, ll, 33, 34, 38, 43, 45, 48-9

38 Ibid., d.30, l.8

39 Ibid., d.53, ll.7, 17

40 Khrushchev, N., *Rechi na sobraniyakh izbiratel'noy Moskvy*, Moscow, 1937, pp. 3-22

41 *Khrushchev Remembers*, New York, 1970, pp. 348-9

42 Ibid., p. 351

43 *Izvestiya TsK KPSS*, No.3, 1989, pp. 130, 137

44 *Khrushchev Remembers*, New York, 1970, p. 353

45 Ibid., p. 351

46 APRF, Special File No.233, ll.1-10

47 *Izvestiya*, No.3, 1989, p. 165

48 *Materialy XXII s'ezda KPSS*, Moscow, 1961, p. 140

49 Alexandrov-Agentov, A., *Ot Kollontai do Gorbacheva*, Moscow, 1994, p. 117

50 APRF, Special File No.734, p. 2

51 GARF, f.9401, op. 2, d.170, t.III, ll.344-5

52 Gromyko, A., *Pamyatnoe*, vol.1, Moscow, 1990, p. 477

53 APRF, Special File No.734, pp. 2-3

54 *Materialy XXII s'ezda KPSS*, Moscow, 1961, pp. 48, 49-50

55 *Voprosy istorii*, No.1, 1989, p. 108

56 Ibid., p. 115

57 APRF, f.3, op. 58, d.211, ll.92-3

58 Ibid., ll.103-4

59 Ibid., ll.204-6

60 Ibid., ll.268-9

61 Ibid., ll.270-2

62 TsKhSD, f.5, op. 30, d.231, ll.50-94

63 *Materialy XXII s'ezda KPSS*, Moscow, 1961, p. 43

64 Ibid., pp. 43-4

65 APRF, Politburo Minutes, No.P-118/X, pp. 125-30

66 APRF, f.52, op. 1, d.441, ll.2, 5

67 *Nikita Sergeevich Khrushchev. Materialy k biografii*, Moscow, 1989, p. 313

68 APRF, f.52, op. 1, d.441, ll.63-5

69 *Materialy XXII s'ezda KPSS*, Moscow, 1961, p. 449

70 APRF, Special File No.0680, ll.1-2

71 For an authoritative account, see Lebedeva, N., *Katyn: prestuplenie protiv chelovechestva*, Moscow, 1994

72 APRF, f.3, op. 23, d.207, ll.14-41

73 APRF, f.52, op. 1, d.334, ll.20, 22, 42, 43

74 Gromyko, A., *Memories*, London, 1989, p. 171

75 APRF, f.52, op. 1, d.539, ll.186-7

76 Ibid., ll.188-9

77 Ibid., d.468, ll.92-6

78 Ibid., d.539, l.194

79 Ibid., d.446, ll.23-8

80 Ibid., l.53

81 *Khrushchev Remembers*, New York, 1970, pp. 379-80

82 APRF, f.52, op. 1, d.349, ll.7-41

83 Ibid.

84 Ibid., d.539, ll.1-3

85 Ibid., d.597, ll.1-30

86 Ibid., d.498, ll.1-2

87 *Khrushchev Remembers*, New York, 1970, p. 461

88 Ibid., p. 464

89 APRF, f.52, op. 1, d.597, l.145

90 Ibid., d.498, ll.44-7, 151-6

91 Ibid., d.499, ll.1-33

92 *Khrushchev Remembers*, New York, 1970, pp. 474-5

93 APRF, f.52, op. 1, d.588, l.54

94 APRF, f.3, op. 66, d.310, ll.1-2

95 Ibid., op. 65, d.902, ll.80-6

96 Gromyko, A.A., *Pamyatnoe*, Moscow, 1988, p. 480

97 Arkhiv GSh (Archives of the General Staff), f.16, op. 3753, d.6, l.1

98 Ibid., ll.1-7

99 Ibid., ll.1-5

100 Ibid., d.26, l.163

101 APRF.f.3, op. 65, d.902, ll.77-8

102 Ibid., ll.73-5

103 TsAMO, f.16, op. 3657, d.26, l.78

104 APRF, f.3, op. 65, d.905, ll.35-6

105 Ibid., ll.65-6

106 Ibid., ll.9-17

107 Ibid., ll.154-9

108 *Khrushchev Remembers*, New York, 1970, p. 500

109 Gromyko, A., *Memories*, London, 1989, p. 180

110 Arkhiv GSh (Archives of the General Staff), f.16, op. 3753, d.26, ll.16-19

111 APRF, f.2, op. 1, d.259, l.5

112 Ibid., ll.9-10

113 Ibid., d.253, l.20

114 In *Voprosy istorii*, No.2, 1989, pp. 104-5

115 *Nikita Sergeevich Khrushchev, Materialy k biografii*, Moscow, 1989, p. 341

116 APRF, f.2, op. 1, d.749, ll.1-2

117 Ibid., d.753, ll.15-17

118 Ibid., d.749, ll.3-4

119 Ibid., d.752, ll.1-2

120 Ibid., d.753, ll.3-4

121 *Nikita Sergeevich Khrushchev, Materialy k biografii*, Moscow, 1989, p. 285

122 KGB Note to Brezhnev No.745-A, l.1

123 KGB Note to Central Committee, 25 March 1970, No.745-A, 'Of particular importance'

124 APRF, *Stenograficheskaya zapis' besedy s Khrushchevym v KPK 10 Noyabrya 1970 g.*, ll.1-15

125 Tompson, William J., *Khrushchev: A Political Life*, Macmillan/ St Antony's College, Basingstoke and Oxford, 1995, pp. 280-1

126 APRF, f.206, op. 258, d.3, ll.121-2

127 Ibid., f.52, op. 1, d.132, ll.66-70

128 Arkhiv GSh (Archive of General Staff), Vx.N.2697, l.1

129 APRF, f.52, op. 1, d.125, ll.26-31

The Fourth Leader
Leonid Brezhnev

1 Aksyutin, Yu., in *L.I. Brezhnev, Materialy k biografii*, Moscow, 1991, p. 50

2 APRF, f.80, Brezhnev's notes, p. 1

3 Ibid., Brezhnev's notes for 1956, p. 2

4 RTsKhIDNI, Politburo Minutes for 17 December 1969, pp. 1-10

5 APRF, f.80, Personal file No.514 for L.I. Brezhnev, pp. 1-54

6 Ibid., op. 1, d.23, ll.1-2

7 Ibid., Brezhnev personal file, pp. 20-1

8 Brezhnev, L.I., *Malaya Zemlya*, Moscow, 1979, p. 3

9 APRF, f.80, Diary entries for 1944, pp. 51-2

10 Gromyko, A., *Pamyatnoe*, vol.2, Moscow, 1988, p. 525

11 Brezhnev, L.I., *Malaya Zemlya*, Moscow, 1979, p. 43

12 APRF, f.80, op. 1, d.12, l.184

13 Ibid., d.14, l.65

14 Ibid., d.18, l.299

15 Ibid., d.14, l.104

16 Ibid., f.80, Brezhnev's notes for July-August 1973, p. 16

17 Brezhnev, L.I., *Tselina*, Moscow, 1979, p. 10

18 RTsKhIDNI, Politburo Minutes for 27 December 1973, p. 7

19 Ibid., pp. 5-6

20 RTsKhIDNI, Minutes of a Central Committee Secretariat meeting of 20 November 1972, p. 1

21 Brezhnev, L.I., *O vneshnei politike KPSS i sovetskogo gosudarstva*, Moscow, 1973, p. 532

22 APRF, f.80, Brezhnev's notes for 1958-59, pp. 41-8, 1, 2, 24, 27 et al

23 Brezhnev, L.I., *Vystuplenie na plenume TsK KPSS 27 noyabrya 1978*, Moscow, 1978, pp. 3, 7, 8, 9, 11, 14-15

24 APRF, f.80, Brezhnev's notes, pp, 24, 27, 30

25 RTsKhIDNI, Politburo Minutes for 3 January 1980, pp. 1-8

26 Aksyutin, Yu, in *L.I. Brezhnev, Materialy k biografii*, Moscow, 1991, p. 322

27 APRF, KGB notes of 28 August 1969, No.2169A, p. 129

28 RTsKhIDNI, KGB Report of 15 November 1976, No.2577-A, pp. 86-8

29 APRF, Politburo Minutes No.56 for 19 May 1977, pp. 1-13, 1-7

30 Mlinarž, S., *Kholodom veet ot Kremlya*, 2nd edn., New York, 1988, pp. 119-42

31 APRF, Packet No.255, pp. 1-2

32 Mlinarž, S., *Kholodom veet ot Kremlya*, 2nd edn, New York, 1988, p. 209

33 RTsKhIDNI, Politburo Minutes. Talks between CPSU and CPCz delegations, 26 August 1968, pp. 1-39

34 Mlinarž, S., *Kholodom veet ot Kremlya*, 2nd edn, New York, 1988, pp. 280-3

35 Brezhnev, L., *O vneshnei politike KPSS i sovetskogo gosudarstva*, Moscow, 1973, p. 136

36 *Konstitutsiya SSR*, Moscow, 1977, pp. 8, 15

37 APRF, f.3, op. 82, d.138, ll.91-103

38 APRF, Notes of a conversation between A.A. Gromyko and Shah Wali, P-1772, pp. 10-16

39 APRF, f.3, op. 117, d.73, ll.132-3

40 RTsKhIDNI, Politburo Minutes No.176/125 for 12 December 1979, pp. 1-2

41 Ibid., Draft notes of a Politburo session of 7 February 1980, pp. 4-8

42 Ibid., Politburo Minutes No.177 for 1 January 1980

43 *Materialy XXVI s'ezda KPSS*, Moscow, 1981, p. 13

44 APRF, *O edinoi traktovke sobytii v Afganistane* (The single interpretation of events in Afghanistan), No.167 GS for 26 February 1980, pp. 112-14

45 Ibid., Special File No.682, p. 1

46 In *Argumenty i fakty*, No.24, June 1995

47 The Soviet political joke is well described in an article by Dora Shturman in *Vremya i my*, No.74, 1983, Tel Aviv, pp. 128-47

48 APRF, p. 28/34, 17.12.66, l.1

49 Ibid., p. 257, 26.01.74, ll.1-4

50 RTsKhIDNI, Politburo Minutes for 4 April 1985, p. 249

51　Ibid., Politburo Archives, 206-OP, ll.1-2

52　APRF, Politburo Minutes for 13 April 1978, pp. 17-18

53　Chernyaev, A., *Shest' let s Gorbachevym*, Moscow, 1993, pp. 16-17

54　Medvedev, R., *Lichnost' i epokha. Politicheskii portret L.I. Brezhneva*, Moscow, 1991, p. 296

55　Churbanov, Yu., in *L.I. Brezhnev. Materialy k biografii*, Moscow, 1991, p. 363

56　RTsKhIDNI, Politburo Minutes, No.P.12/XVII for 28 July 1966, p. 1

57　Ibid., No.P.111/VI for 6 July 1978, p. 1

58　TsKhSD, Brezhnev's conversation in Budapest, 18 March 1975, p. 20

59　APRF, f.80, op. 1, d.1, l.30

60　Ibid., d.46, l.75

61　TsGAOR, f.601, op. 1, d.248, l.181

62　Medvedev, V., *Chelovek za spinoi*, Moscow, 1994, pp. 78-9

63　APRF, f.80, Diary entry, pp. 1-2

64　Ibid., Brezhnev's notes for 15 October to November 1964, pp. 1-15

65　In *L.I. Brezhnev. Materialy k biografii*, Moscow, 1991, pp. 64-6

66　APRF, f.80, Brezhnev's notes for 1968, pp. 10-26

67　Ibid., Brezhnev's notes for 1973-74, pp. 2-28

68　Ibid., Special File No.206, p. 7

69　Ibid., f.80, Brezhnev's notes on Meeting of Workers' and Communist Parties, pp. 4-10

70　Ibid., Special File No.2526, pp. 2-12

71　TsKhSD, KGB Report No.3213-'A', p. 10

72　RTsKhIDNI, Politburo Minutes No.177 for 3 January 1980, pp. 52-8

73　*Dnevniki imperatora Nikolaya II*, Moscow, 1991, p. 360

74　APRF, f.80, Diary entries for April-May 1977, p. 5

75　Ibid., Brezhnev's notes from various years

76　Brezhnev, L., *Aktual'nye voprosy ideologicheskoi raboty KPSS*, vol.2, Moscow, 1978, p. 387

77　*Materialy XXIV s'ezda KPSS*, Moscow, 1971, pp. 14, 22

78　APRF, Special File No.591, pp. 1-2

79　Brezhnev, L., *Aktual'nye voprosy ideologicheskoi raboty KPSS*, vol.2, Moscow, 1978, p. 395

80　*Materialy XXIII s'ezda KPSS*, Moscow, 1966, p. 59

81　*Materialy XXIV s'ezda KPSS*, Moscow, 1971, p. 53

82　*Materialy XXV s'ezda KPSS*, Moscow, 1976, p. 54

83　*Materialy XXVI s'ezda KPSS*, Moscow, 1981, p. 48

84　*Materialy XXIII s'ezda KPSS*, Moscow, 1966, p. 39

85　*Materialy XXIV s'ezda KPSS*, Moscow, 1971, p. 90

86　RTsKhIDNI, Politburo Minutes for 9 September 1982, pp. 348-50

87　APRF, Special File No.483, pp. 1-18

88　Boldin, V., *Krushenie p'edestala*, Moscow, 1995, pp. 41-2

89　Cited in *Izvestiya Ts KPSS*, No.2, 1988, pp. 282-6

90　Solovyov, V. and Klepikova, Ye., in *Vremya i my*, No.44, 1979, p. 137

91　Medvedev, V., *Chelovek za spinoi*, Moscow, 1994, pp. 146-59

92 Ibid., pp. 177–9
93 *Materialy XXVI s'ezda KPSS*, Moscow, 1981, p. 216
94 RTsKhIDNI, Politburo Minutes for 10 November 1982, pp. 1–5
95 Ibid., Politburo Minutes for 18 November 1982, pp. 464–5

The Fifth Leader
Yuri Andropov

1 *Vremya i my*, No.102, 1988, p. 206
2 RTsKhIDNI, Politburo Minutes, 10 November 1982, pp. 1–3
3 Andropov, Yu., *Izbrannye rechi i stat'i*, 2nd edn., Moscow, 1983, p. 126
4 APRF, f.82, op. 1, d.69, l.8
5 Ibid., d.61, ll.2, 3, 4
6 *Khrushchev Remembers*, New York, 1970, pp. 418–19
7 *Materialy Plenuma TsK KPSS, 14 iyulya 1983*, Moscow, 1983, p. 12
8 *Svod zakonov SSSR*, No.64, 1934, p. 459
9 APRF, Commission Minutes No.6, 21 July 1939
10 See Redlich, S., *War, Holocaust and Stalinism: A Documented History of the Jewish Anti-Fascist Committee in the USSR*, London, 1995, for a reproduction of this photograph
11 Arkhiv KGB, d.2354, ll.227-39
12 RTsKhIDNI, f.85, op. 29, d.349, l.4
13 KGB USSR Report No.1025-'A', 6 May 1968, pp. 1–14
14 KGB USSR Report No.877-'A'/ob, 31 March 1981, pp. 1–11
15 APRF, Special File No.344, pp. 2–12
16 Ibid., Special File Nos.664, 1220, 1520 et al
17 Ibid., f.82, op. 1, d.17, l.71
18 Ibid., KGB Report No.55396, pp. 1–2
19 RTsKhIDNI, Politburo Minutes, 7 January 1974, pp. 19–32
20 APRF, f.82, op. 1, d.2, l.7
21 Ibid., l.8
22 RTsKhIDNI, KGB Report to Central Committee No.3313-'Sh', 20 December 1960, p. 1
23 APRF, Unedited minutes of meeting of Central Committee Secretaries, 18 January 1983, pp. 1–25
24 APRF, f.82, op. 1, d.2, l.63
25 Ibid., l.16
26 Ibid., f.3, op. 73, d.1137, l.198
27 Ibid., d.1113, ll.1-257
28 Ibid., d.1137, l.237
29 Ibid., d.1133, l.65
30 Ibid., d.1131, l.311
31 Ibid., d.1113, l.254
32 Ibid., d.1114, l.226
33 Ibid., d.1113, l.252
34 Ibid., d.1131, l.294
35 Ibid., d.1122, l.7
36 Ibid., ll.51, 58
37 Ibid., d.1133, l.150
38 Ibid., d.1139, l.95
39 Ibid., f.82, op. 1, d.17, ll.1-2
40 Ibid., f.3, op. 73, d.1133, ll.198-9
41 Ibid., d.1170, l.7
42 Ibid., d.1165, l.3
43 Ibid., ll.3-5
44 Ibid., d.1162, ll.10-16
45 Ibid., d.1165, ll.109-10
46 Ibid., d.1148, l.119
47 Ibid., d.1154, ll.11-12
48 Andropov, Yu., *Izbrannye rechi i stat'i*, 2nd edn, Moscow 1983, p. 131
49 APRF, f.3, op. 73, d.1169, ll.214-15

50 Ibid., d.1164, l.47

51 Ibid., d.1161, l.18

52 Ibid., d.1154, ll.2-9

53 Ibid., f.82, op. 1, d.69, l.50

54 *Pravda*, 1 September 1983

55 *Izvestiya*, 25 January 1991

56 RTsKhIDNI, f.3, op. 73, d.1152, ll.2-3; Politburo Minutes of 2 September 1983, pp. 1-9

57 APRF, f.82, op. 1, d.70, l.3

58 RTsKhIDNI, Politburo Minutes for 24 March 1983, pp. 19-21

59 APRF, f.82, op. 1, d.94, ll.1-10

60 Medvedev, R., *Gensek iz Lubyanki*, Moscow, 1993, p. 198

61 Chazov, Ye., *Zdorovie i vlast'*, Moscow, 1991, p. 109

62 In *Komsomolskaya Pravda*, 17 June 1994

63 APRF, f.3, op. 73, d.1138, l.223

64 Ibid., d.1148, l.10

65 Ibid., d.1114, l.154

66 Ibid., d.1147, ll.103-10

67 Ibid., d.1164, l.49

68 Ibid., d.1122, l.160

69 Ibid., f.82, op. 1, d.17, l.1

70 Ibid., f.3, op. 73, d.1116, ll.73-5

71 Ibid., d.1137, l.241

72 Andropov, Yu., *Izbranny rechi i stat'i*, 2nd edn., Moscow, 1983, p. 124

73 Chazov, Ye., *Zdorovie i vlast'*, Moscow, 1991, p. 189

74 APRF, f.3, op. 73, d.1150, ll.11-12

75 Ibid., d.1151, l.5

76 Ibid., d.1152, ll.4-5

77 Ibid., d.1154, ll.11-12

78 Ibid., d.1162, ll.10-16

79 Ibid., d.1165, l.4

80 Ibid., d.1170, ll.265-8

81 Ibid., d.1172, ll.1-25

82 Ibid., d.1175, l.37

83 Ibid., l.117

84 Ibid., l.125

85 Ibid., d.1176, l.51

86 Ibid., l.54

87 Ibid., d.1171, ll.119-20

88 Ibid., ll.5-25

89 Ibid., d.1178, l.91

90 Ibid., d.1179, ll.1-7

The Sixth Leader
Konstantin Chernenko

1 RTsKhIDNI, Politburo Minutes for 10 February 1984, pp. 119-25

2 Chernyayev, A., *Shest' let s Gorbachevym*, Moscow, 1993, pp. 11-12

3 Alexandrov-Agentov, A., *Ot Kollontai do Gorbacheva*, Moscow, 1994, p. 283

4 *Russkaya mysl'*, 1 March 1984, Paris, p. 4

5 APRF, f.3, op. 7, d.1182, ll.7-20

6 RTsKhIDNI, Politburo Minutes for 23 February 1984, pp. 139-40

7 APRF, f.45, op. 1, d.420, l.250b

8 Ibid., f.3, op. 73, d.1189, l.67

9 Chernenko, K., *Izbrannye rechi i stat'i*, 2nd edn, Moscow, 1984, pp. 667-9

10 In *Voprosy istorii*, No.4, 1980, p. 11

11 In *Russkaya mysl'*, 21 March 1986, Paris, p. 9

12 See Afanasiev, V., *Chetvertaya vlast' i chetyre genseka*, Moscow, 1994, pp. 53-4

13 APRF, f.3, op. 73, dd.1183, l.129

14 Shakhnazarov, G., *Tsena svobody*, Moscow, 1993, pp. 40-1

15 APRF, f.83, op. 1, d.408, ll.9-10

16 Ibid., l.2

17 Ibid., l.1

18 Ibid., ll.1-101

19 TsKhSD, f.5, op. 88, d.1061, ll.6-8

20 Ibid., l.8

21 Ibid., l.9

22 Ibid., ll.10-14

23 Ibid., l.14

24 Ibid., l.15

25 APRF, f.83, op. 1, d.336, l.40

26 Ibid., f.5, op. 88, d.1060, l.115

27 Ibid., f.3, op. 73, d.1233, l.263

28 Ibid., f.5, op. 88, d.1069, l.7

29 Chernenko, K.U., *Izbrannye rechi i stat'i*, 2nd edn, Moscow, 1984, p. 386

30 RTsKhIDNI, Politburo Minutes for 23 February 1984, p. 131

31 APRF, f.3, 'On the use of foreign currency in 1984'. Note from the Economic Department of the Central Committee, 22 June 1985, pp. 1–6

32 Ibid., op. 737, d.1196, l.232

33 TsKhSD, f.5, op. 88, d.1060, ll.110-14

34 Ibid., d.1061, ll.114-15

35 Chernenko, K., *Izbrannye rechi i stat'i*, 2nd edn., Moscow, 1984, pp. 368–94

36 APRF, f.83, op. 1, d.233, l.1

37 Ibid., l.2

38 Medvedev, R., *Gensek iz Lubyanki*, Moscow, 1993, p. 110

39 Medvedev, V., *Chelovek za spinoi*, Moscow, 1994, pp. 74–5

40 Alexandrov-Agentov, A., *Ot Kollontai do Gorbacheva*, Moscow, 1994, p. 285

41 APRF, f.3, op. 73, d.1186, ll.75-81

42 Ibid., f.83, op. 1, d.143, l.10

43 APRF, f.83, op. 1, d.143, l.6

44 Ibid., f.3, op. 73, d.1207, l.2

45 Ibid., f.83, op. 1, d.193, ll.38-50

46 Ibid., f.3, op. 73, d.1188, ll.8-9

47 Ibid., d.1190, ll.87-9

48 Ibid., d.1203, l.63

49 Ibid., f.45, op. 1, d.346, l.66

50 Ibid., f.3, op. 73, d.1200, ll.2-20

51 Lenin, *PSS*, vol.35, p. 199

52 Chernenko, K., *Vysokii grazhdanskii dolg kontrolera*, Moscow, 1984, p. 6

53 APRF, f.3, op. 73, d.1187, l.259

54 Ibid., d.1193, ll.81-3

55 Ibid., d.1219, ll.253-5

56 Ibid., d.1220, l.171

57 Ibid., d.1196, l.3

58 *Materialy Plenuma Tsentral'nogo Komiteta KPSS, 10 April 1984*, Moscow, 1984, p. 6

59 Ibid., p. 20

60 APRF, f.3, op. 73, d.1277, ll.3-12

61 *Materialy vneocherednogo Plenuma Tsentral'nogo Komiteta KPSS, 13 fevralya 1984*, Moscow, 1984, p. 9

62 APRF, f.3, op. 73, d.1205, ll.2-3

63 Gorbachev, M., *Zhivoe tvorchestvo naroda*, Moscow, 1985, p. 7

64 APRF, Report on the work of the KGB for 1983, No.408-4 (OV), pp. 55–66

65 Ibid., f.3, op. 73, d.120, l.123

66 Ibid., d.1226, ll.1-7

67 Ibid., ll.131-58

68 Chernyayev, A., *Shest' let s Gorbachevym*, Moscow, 1993, p. 27

69 RTsKhIDNI, Politburo Minutes for 9 January 1985, pp. 21–3

70 Gromyko, A., *Memories*, ed. and trans. Harold Shukman, London, 1989, pp. 339–40

71 APRF, f.3, op. 73, d.1234, ll.3, 4, 173, 213

72 RTsKhIDNI, Politburo Minutes for 7 February 1985, pp. 53–70

73 See Chernyayev, A., *Shest' let s Gorbachevym*, Moscow, 1993, p. 34

74 RTsKhIDNI, Politburo Minutes for 11 March 1985, p. 126

The Seventh Leader
Mikhail Gorbachev

1 Boldin, V., *Krushenie p'edestala*, Moscow, 1995, p. 125
2 APRF, Politburo Minutes for 11 March 1985, p. 127
3 Ibid., pp. 126–36
4 Ibid., p. 137
5 *Izvestiya TsK KPSS*, No.5, Moscow, 1989, p. 58
6 APRF, Politburo Minutes for 15 October 1987, pp. 164–5
7 TsKhSD, Instruction of Secretariat of Central Committee, CPSU, No.1193s, p. 1
8 Lecturing at Oxford University in October 1996, Gorbachev declared that proletarian (i.e. Party) dictatorship had been Lenin's personal choice, and not just a product of extreme conditions. He also stated that at the end of his life Lenin warned his comrades of the dangers inherent in this policy. Lenin is thus condemned, but also implicitly exonerated (HS).
9 Gorbachev, M., *Izbrannye rechi i stat'i*, Moscow, 1985, p. 9
10 Lenin, V., *PSS*, vol.44, pp. 99–100
11 APRF, Politburo Minutes for 15 October 1987, pp. 141–2
12 APRF, Politburo Minutes for 15 October 1987, p. 155
13 APRF, Politburo Minutes for 22 September 1988, p. 293
14 APRF, f.3, op. 104, d.4, l.7
15 *Demokratizatsiya - sut' perestroiki. Sut' sotsializma*, Moscow, 1988, p. 49
16 In *Pravda*, 21 April 1990
17 Gorbacheva, R., *Ya nadeyus'*, Moscow, 1991, p. 13
18 APRF, f.84, Gorbachev's Notes to the Politburo for 20 November 1979, pp. 1–2
19 Ibid., Politburo Minutes for 24 January 1989, pp. 108–11
20 Ibid., f.3, Minutes of Meeting with Central Committee Secretaries of 15 March 1985, pp. 1–12
21 Ibid., Minutes of Meeting with Central Committee Secretaries of 15 March 1985, pp. 3–7
22 Chernyayev, A., *Shest' let s Gorbachevym*, Moscow, 1993, p. 319
23 APRF, Politburo Minutes for 14 October 1986, p. 2
24 Ibid., Politburo Minutes for 4 April 1985, pp, 200, 248-51
25 Gorbachev, M., *Zhivoe tvorchestvo naroda*, Moscow, 1985, p. 5
26 APRF, Politburo Minutes for 4 April 1985, p. 251
27 In *Kontinent*, No.46, Munich, 1985, p. 216
28 Gorbachev, M., *Izbrannye rechi i stat'i*, Moscow, 1985, pp. 9–33
29 APRF, Politburo Minutes for 6 February 1986, p. 185
30 Ibid., Politburo Minutes for 4 April 1985
31 Ibid., Politburo Minutes for 15 October 1987, p. 136
32 Gorbachev, M., *Oktyabr' i perestroika: revolyutsiya prodolzhaetsya*, p. 26
33 APRF, Politburo Minutes for 20 March 1986, p. 41
34 Ibid., Politburo Minutes for 6 February 1986, p. 185
35 Ibid., f.3, op. 109, d.163, l.3
36 Ibid., Politburo Minutes for 26 June 1986, pp. 32–5
37 In *Kommunist*, No.18, 1989, p. 4
38 Gorbachev, M., *Perestroika i novoye*

myshlenie dlya nashei strany i vsego mira, Moscow, 1987, p. 20

39 In *Komunist*, No.18, Moscow, 1989, p. 11

40 Gorbachev, M., *Oktyabr' i perestroika: revolyutsiya prodolzhaetsya*, p. 41

41 *Izvestiya TsK KPSS*, No.10, Moscow, 1989, pp. 16–17

42 Ibid., No.12, Moscow, 1989, pp. 7–10

43 Ibid., No.1, Moscow, 1990, pp. 11–13

44 Ibid., No.5, Moscow, 1989, pp. 29–35

45 APRF, Special File No.644, pp. 1–4

46 Gorbachev, M., *Izbrannye rechi i stat'i*, Moscow, 1985, pp. 1–422

47 APRF, Politburo Minutes for 4 April 1985, p. 251

48 *Pravda*, 19 August 1990

49 Geller, M., *Sed'moi sekretar'*, London, 1991, p. 414

50 APRF, f.3, op. 73, d.1241, ll.118-20

51 Ibid., Special File No.92, January 1988, p. 1

52 Ibid., f.3, USSR Ministry of Defence Memorandum No.04311, pp. 1–4

53 Ibid., Notes of Meeting between M.S. Gorbachev and Najibullah, attached to Politburo Minutes No.92, P.II, pp. 1–15

54 Ibid., Politburo Minutes for 18 April 1988, p. 16

55 Ibid., Politburo Minutes for 24 January 1989, pp. 232–4

56 Chernyayev, A., *Shest' let s Gorbachevym*, Moscow, 1993, pp. 272–3

57 *Materialy plenuma TsK KPSS, 27-28 yanvarya 1987*, Moscow, 1987, p. 29

58 Ibid., p. 70

59 *Izvestiya TsK KPSS*, No.3, Moscow, 1990, p. 124

60 *Vremya i my*, No.99, Tel Aviv, 1987, p. 123

61 Gorbachev, M., *Uspekh perestroiki v rukakh naroda*, Moscow, 1988, p. 22

62 *Materialy plenuma TsK KPSS 27-28 yanvarya 1987*, Moscow, 1987, p. 75

63 APRF, Politburo Minutes for 4 April 1985, p. 212

64 Ibid., f.84, Note No.1107-E, p. 1

65 Ibid., f.3, op. 113, Chebrikov Note No.P1240, pp. 1–5

66 Ibid., Politburo Minutes for 29 August 1985, pp. 22–3

67 Ibid., f.3, op. 113, G. Marchuk's Note to the Central Committee, No.P2362, pp. 1–4

68 *Materialy Plenuma TsK KPSS, 27-28 yanvarya 1987*, Moscow, 1987, p. 28

69 APRF, KGB Report for 21 March 1988, No.458-4, pp. 1–3

70 Ibid., f.84, V. Terebilov's Note to the Central Committee, No.PB-1778, p. 1

71 *Konstitutsiya SSSR*, Moscow, 1977, p. 8

72 APRF, Politburo Minutes for 20 November 1989, p. 409

73 Ibid., Politburo Minutes for 8 December 1989, p. 529

74 TsKhSD, Politburo Minutes No.87 for 28 May 1990, pp. 1–5

75 In *Komunist*, No.18, Moscow, 1989, pp. 16–17

76 *K gumannomu demokraticheskomu sotsializmu. Programmnoe zayavlenie XXVIII s'ezda KPSS*, Moscow, 1990, p. 4

77 TsAMO, f.28, op. 93316ss, ll.55-165

78 TsKhSD, Politburo Minutes for 19 October 1957, No.118, pp. 121–30

79 Ibid., p. 125

80 APRF, Special File No.766, p. 1

81 Ibid., Urgent Report, No.1789-2s, p. 1

82 Ibid., Politburo Minutes for 29 April 1986, pp. 444–9

83 Ibid., f.3, op. 102, d.b/n, ll.1-2

84 Ibid., Politburo Minutes for 15 May 1986, p. 519

85 Ibid., p. 512

86 Ibid., Politburo Minutes for 5 May 1986, p. 465

87 Ibid., Politburo Minutes for 28 April 1986, p. 436

88 Ibid., Politburo Minutes for 5 May 1986, p. 465

89 Ibid., f.84, NR-1097s, l.1

90 Gorbachev, M., *Perestroika i novoye myshlenie*, Moscow, 1987, p. 240

91 TsKhSD, f.89, op. 11, d.51, l.1

92 APRF, Politburo Minutes for 29 May 1986, p. 603

93 TsKhSD, Extract from Politburo Minutes No.11 for 8 May 1986, pp. 1–4

94 APRF, Politburo Minutes for 5 May 1986, p. 458

95 Ibid., Politburo Minutes for 11 April 1985, p. 274

96 Ibid., Politburo Minutes for 25 July 1985, pp. 63–5

97 *Pravda*, 2 July 1986

98 *Izvestiya*, 13 July 1991

99 *Izvestiya*, 3 August 1991

100 Gorbachev, M., *Avgustovskii putch*, Moscow, 1991, p. 63

101 See *Rossiskaya gazeta*, 16 August 1991

102 *Pravda*, 20 August 1991

103 *Izvestiya*, evening edition, 4 September 1991

104 Grachev, A., *Dal'she bez menya: Ukhod prezidenta*, Moscow, 1994, p. 84

105 Chernyayev, A., *Shest' let s Gorbachevym*, Moscow, 1993, p. 32

106 In *Kontinent*, No.46, Munich, 1985, p. 217

107 APRF, Politburo Minutes for 29 June 1985, pp. 2–3

108 Ibid., f.3, op. 73, d.1278, l.192

109 Ibid., d.1276, l.5

110 Ibid., op. 102, d.230, l.174

111 Gorbachev, M., *Perestroika i novoye myshlenie dlya nashei strany i vsego mira*, Moscow, 1987, p. 144

112 Alexandrov-Agentov, A., *Ot Kollontai do Gorbacheva*, Moscow, 1994, p. 190

113 Wieczynski, J. (ed.), *The Gorbachev Encyclopedia*, Los Angeles, 1993

114 APRF, f.3, op. 73, d.1278, l.192

115 Gorbachev, M., *Perestroika i novoye myshlenie dlya nashei strany i vsego mira*, Moscow, 1987, p. 143,

116 APRF, Politburo Minutes for 14 October 1986, pp. 3–4

117 Ibid., Politburo Minutes for 6 May 1986, p. 12

118 Ibid., Politburo Minutes for 22 October 1986, p. 2

119 *Materialy XXVII s'ezda KPSS*, Moscow, 1986, pp. 74–6

120 Chernyayev, A., *Shest' let s Gorbachevym*, Moscow, 1993, pp. 264–5

121 APRF, Politburo Minutes for 6 February 1986, p. 169

122 Ibid., Politburo Minutes for 23 January 1986, p. 104

123 Ibid., f.3, op. 73, d.1254, l.10

124 Ibid., d.1242, l.13

125 Ibid., Politburo Minutes for 23 December 1985, pp. 1–3

126 Solovyov, V. and Klepikova, Ye., *Boris Yeltsin*, Moscow, 1992, p. 44

127 APRF, Politburo Minutes for 15 October 1987, p. 138

128 Ibid., pp. 139–40

129 Ibid., *Materialy plenuma TsK KPSS 21 oktyabrya 1987 g. Vystuplenie B.N. Yeltsina*, Author's copy; see *Izvestiya TsK KPSS*, No.2, 1989, pp. 239–41

130 *Izvestiya TsK KPSS*, No.2, 1989, p. 241

131 Gorbachev, M., *Perestroika i novoye myshlenie dlya nashei strany i vsego mira*, Moscow, 1987, p. 86

132 Ibid., p. 39

133 Solovyov, V. and Klepikova, Ye., *Boris Yeltsin*, Moscow, 1992, p. 57

134 APRF, Politburo Minutes for 20 November 1989, p. 415

135 Ibid., Politburo Minutes for 19 October 1989, p. 522

136 TsKhSD, Extract from Politburo Minutes No.182 for 22 March 1990, p. 1

137 APRF, Politburo Minutes for 3 May 1990, p. 533

138 Ibid., pp. 533, 560

139 Chernyayev, A., *Shest' let s Gorbachevym*, Moscow, 1993, p. 375

140 Ibid., p. 382

141 APRF, Note from Bessmertnykh to M.S. Gorbachev, 6 sector, 72089, p. 1

142 *XXVIII s'ezd kommunisticheskoi partii Sovetskogo Soyuza, 2-13 iyulya 1990 g*, Stenographic report, vol.2, Moscow, 1990, pp. 500–1

143 Yeltsin, B., *Zapiski prezidenta*, Moscow, 1994, p. 56

144 *Kuranty*, Moscow, 7 May 1991

145 Yeltsin, B., *Zapiski prezidenta*, Moscow, 1994, pp. 53–4

146 Ibid., p. 43

147 The fax was sent from St Antony's College by the editor and translator of this book

148 In *Argumenty i fakty*, 24 August 1991

149 See Gorbachev, M., *Avgustovskii putch*, Moscow, 1991

150 Stepankov, V. and Lisov, Ye., *Kremlevskii zagovor*, Moscow, 1992, pp. 149–52

151 Yeltsin, B., *Zapiski prezidenta*, Moscow, 1994, p. 71

152 Medvedev, V., *V komande Gorbacheva: Vzglyad iznutri*, Moscow, 1994, pp. 21–3

153 Gorbachev, M., *Zhivoe tvorchestvo naroda: (materialy konferentsii)*, Moscow, 1985, pp. 3–46

154 APRF, Politburo Minutes for 7-8 May 1987, p. 225

155 Ibid., Politburo Minutes for 27-28 December 1988, pp. 24–246

156 Ibid., Politburo Minutes for 28 December 1988, p. 528

157 Ibid., Politburo Minutes for 18 February 1988, pp. 538–9

158 Ibid., Politburo Minutes for 15 January 1988, p. 320

159 Ibid., Politburo Minutes for 29 June 1989, pp. 200–8

160 Ibid., Politburo Minutes for 30 May 1987, pp. 483–502

161 Ibid., Politburo Minutes for 27-28 December 1988, p. 339

162 *Izvestiya TsK KPSS*, No.5, 1989, p. 60

163 *Izvestiya TsK KPSS*, No.4, 1990, pp. 57–62

164 TsKhSD, Politburo Minutes No.8 for 25 April 1991, pp. 1–2

165 In *Nezavisimaya gazeta*, 17 September 1992

166 In *Ogonek*, No.11, March 1995, p. 11

167 In *Argumenty i fakty*, 20 (657), May 1993

168 APRF, Memorandum to M.S. Gorbachev of 13 March 1987, No.P439, pp. 1–6

169 APRF, f.84, Gorbachev's note on 'The Soviet–German Treaties of 1939', pp. 1–2

170 Gromyko, A., *Memories*, trans. and ed. Harold Shukman, London, 1989, p. 38. In a personal conversation in December 1988 with the editor and translator of this book, Gromyko dismissed the copies of the Russian and German documents, obtained from the German archives and produced for him to see, as forgeries, and resisted my attempts to 'update' his memoirs.

171 APRF, Politburo Minutes for 5 May 1988, pp. 108–22

172 Ibid., Special File No.20-06/197, pp. 1–25

173 Ibid., Special File P-13/144 for 5 March 1940, pp. 1–10

174 Gorbachev, M., *Perestroika i novoye myshlenie dlya nashei strany i vsego mira*, Moscow, 1987, p. 163

175 Cited in *Problemy Vostochnoi Yevropy*, Nos.35-6, New York, 1992, p. 103

176 *Izvestiya*, 25 May 1993

Postscript

1 APRF, f.3, op. 62, d.180., ll.16-17

Index